Anthropology Goes to the Fair

CRITICAL STUDIES IN THE
HISTORY OF ANTHROPOLOGY

Series Editors
Regna Darnell
Stephen O. Murray

Anthropology Goes to the Fair

The 1904 Louisiana Purchase Exposition

UNIVERSITY OF NEBRASKA PRESS · LINCOLN AND LONDON

NANCY J. PAREZO & DON D. FOWLER

Library of Congress
Cataloging-in-Publication Data
Parezo, Nancy J.
Anthropology goes to the fair
: the 1904 Louisiana Purchase Exposition
/ Nancy J. Parezo and Don D. Fowler.
p. cm.
(Critical studies in the history of anthropology)
Includes
bibliographical references
and index.
ISBN 978-0-8032-3759-9 (cloth : alk. paper)
ISBN 978-0-8032-2796-5 (paper : alk. paper)
1. Louisiana Purchase Exposition (1904 : Saint Louis, Mo.)
2. Indians of North America—Exhibitions.
3. Indians in popular culture—History.
4. Indians of North America—Public opinion.
5. Public opinion—United States.
6. Human zoos—United States.
7. United States—Ethnic relations.
8. United States—Race relations.
9. United States—History.
10. McGee, W. J., 1853–1912.
I. Fowler, Don D., 1936– II. Title.
E76.85.P37 2007
305.897007477866—dc22
2006102743

Set in Adobe Garamond by Bob Reitz.
Designed by R. W. Boeche.

Contents

Illustrations

Acknowledgments

Conducting a study as complex as this, in which the data are scattered in libraries and archives across the country, has meant that we have met and relied on countless people over the years as we visited the many institutions listed in the index. We were aided by many curators, archivists, librarians, secretaries, registrars, and students, and we deeply appreciate the time and effort they expended on our behalf. We would especially like to thank those at the Missouri Historical Society, the National Anthropological Archives, the Library of Congress, the University of Chicago Library, the Oklahoma Historical Society, the Omaha Public Library, and the Field Museum of Natural History in Chicago, who spent hours guiding us through their collections, including Jerice Barrios, J. Gail Carmanda, Martha Clevenger, Nina Cummings, Paula Fleming, Jean Gosebrink, Eadie Hedlin, Sara Heitshu, Robert Leopold, Becky Malinsky, Victoria Monks, Steve Nash, Duane Sneddeker, Jeff Todd, and Andrew Walker. Special thanks to Patricia Afable and Mary Ellen Morbeck for providing and verifying information, respectively, on Filipinos and physical anthropology. Our sincere thanks to those individuals who over the past fifteen years helped us locate the rare document, newspaper, and photograph, as well as to photocopy and organize data. Especially we would like to thank former and current students Rebecca Greeling, Aviva Rubin, John Troutman, and Fritz Vandover, who spent many hours of labor. Thanks also to Charles Sternberg for drafting the maps. The National Endowment for the Humanities, the Wenner-Gren Foundation for Anthropological Research, and the Quincentenary Fund of the University of Arizona provided funding for this project.

We would also like to thank our friends and loved ones who provided support for this project, especially our spouses, Richard Ahlstrom and Catherine Fowler, who never complained about our time-warp involvement with 1904 and St. Louis and who listened to our stories about those who went to the fair. Rebecca Allen, Sydel Silverman, Regna Darnell, and David Wilcox read drafts and offered many useful suggestions to improve the manuscript. Karen Brown, copyeditor extraordinaire, saved us from numerous, egregious errors. Our special thanks to her, and to Gary Dunham, Joeth Zucco, and all the others at the University of Nebraska Press who have helped this project come to a completion. To our many colleagues who have listened to us give papers on various subtopics of this book or laughed at some of the outrageous things we found over the last ten years, our gratitude for their tolerance and appreciation for helping us hone our ideas.

Series Editors' Introduction

REGNA DARNELL AND STEPHEN O. MURRAY

The critical history of anthropology, at least as written by practicing anthropologists, habitually employs ethnographic methods. Nancy Parezo and Don Fowler bring to this project their long-established commitments to archaeology, ethnohistory, museum studies, and ethnography as well as the history of anthropology. They, and we as readers, stand as heirs to past traditions whose baggage we have yet to transcend.

Using archival documents and contemporary oral and written commentary, the authors have catalogued exhaustively a single extended occasion for the ritual display of American anthropology and Social Darwinism at the turn of the twentieth century. They have delved into the documents, not just about anthropology at the St. Louis World's Fair, but the fair as a whole. For most, especially the entrepreneurs in charge of the profit-generating capacity of the exhibits, anthropology was a peripheral player in the self-aggrandizement of "the American way." American success in technology and its underlying science was the key to the overall display. The Indian village, school, and crafts posed a sharp contrast. It was a self-referential display, with little international participation or content, given the claim to be a "world's" fair. Yet audiences came, from across the country, particularly from the Midwestern heartland of the United States, to celebrate the century's triumphs, past and yet to come.

The authors have further situated the events of 1904 among those of their predecessors and successors. The 1904 Louisiana Purchase Exposition, in retrospect, was the swan song of American evolutionary progressivism, wherein Manifest Destiny was performed in contrast to primitivism. In 1893, at the better-known Chicago World's Columbian Exposition, voices of nineteenth-century imperialism were counterbalanced by those of the future, of what would become Boasian cultural relativism. St. Louis in 1904 produced nothing comparable to the permanent institutional framework left behind in Chicago's Field Columbian Museum, and WJ McGee was very much a figure of the anthropology of the nineteenth century. McGee was willing to play upon the exoticism of the "living exhibits" of Indians, including the notorious Apache Chief Geronimo, for the grander purposes of public edification. McGee embodied the government and museum mandate of service to non-expert audiences, whereas the discipline of anthropology was already in 1904 moving firmly toward an academic institutional base, toward research carried out by credentialed professionals for whom public education was at best a secondary goal.

The narrative explores the range of characters who participated in the LPE and the inherent conflicts of their constituencies and goals. The intervention of museum and government personnel into the public display of national achievement reflected less concern with scientific rigor than with attracting audiences, loosening their purse strings. Advertising the new science of anthropology and its potential for framing all of human history and nature was at most a bonus. The optimism and hucksterish enthusiasm of McGee failed to attract such an audience in the larger public sphere despite general interest in the exhibits.

This was the last of the world's fairs to attract major attention as a performative encyclopedia of knowledge. The increasingly academic character of anthropology and the other social sciences moved them away from such public display. Books for specialists and articles in academic journals were becoming the primary mode of communication. Political and scientific interpretations of cultural and racial diversity were becoming more discrete, with the Philippines of greater interest to Theodore Roosevelt's expansionism than to the Native American mandate of the government's Bureau of American Ethnology where McGee spent his anthropological career. The Philippine exhibit was far distant from the Indian Village to which the anthropological living exhibits were consigned. McGee's envisioned grand synthesis literally failed to materialize.

The anthropology of only a century ago is vastly anachronistic by contemporary standards. Evolutionary theory, at least of the kind envisioned by Lewis Henry Morgan, Lester Frank Ward, John Wesley Powell, and the follower of those men, WJ McGee, was already well past its prime. The year 1904 also saw Franz Boas's seminal essay in *Science* on the history of anthropology, in which his critique of evolutionary theory was taken as having been concluded and his rivals as having been vanquished—to the point where they are not even mentioned by name, and observations and interpretations by those not accredited with anthropology degrees were obliterated from history by Boas—who also did not have a degree in anthropology.

At the time, the Bureau of American Ethnology's evolutionary synthesis and Boas's emerging historical particularism appeared to coexist, with the outcome for the character of American anthropology still in question. In retrospect, the inevitability of this trajectory is obvious, but the context of the conflict must be recovered by self-conscious historicism. For such a reflexive exercise, the 1904 Louisiana Purchase Exposition provides an ideal vehicle and case study.

"Overlord of the Savage World." Cartoon, *St. Louis Post-Dispatch*, July 14, 1904. WJ McGee Papers, box 32, newspaper scrapbook, Library of Congress.

PROLOGUE

Setting the Stage for St. Louis

The Louisiana Purchase Exposition (LPE) was held in St. Louis, Missouri, from May to December 1904, to commemorate the United States' 1803 purchase of the Louisiana Territory from France for sixty million francs, or roughly three cents an acre, arguably the best land deal in American history. Popularly called the St. Louis World's Fair, the exposition extended over 1,240 acres, the largest in area of any exposition up to that time, or since. The exposition pavilions alone enclosed 128 acres and were filled with wonders.

The organizers wanted to be sure that their fellow Americans understood the historical importance of celebrating the Louisiana Purchase. The federal government, states, and historical societies sent precious iconic heirlooms and reproductions to document American history, patriotism, and nationalism: Daniel Webster's rocking chair, Abraham Lincoln's boyhood cabin, and President Teddy Roosevelt's Western ranch house. New Jersey reconstructed a tavern Washington used during the American Revolution, and Mississippi replicated Jefferson Davis's home, Beauvoir.

The exposition also glorified America's increasing control over the world's natural resources and in particular how business acumen and ingenuity, coupled with scientific and technological know-how, were pushing the United States to the forefront of the industrialized nations. Visitors exclaimed in awe over the symbols of immense accumulated wealth. They gaped at the gigantic electric generators that illuminated buildings and the artificial lagoons. They saw hundreds of the newest technological advances including small electric motors to run factory machines, intended to eliminate the steam engines and belt systems of nineteenth-century factories. There was a Biograph movie showing the giant Westinghouse factory complex in Pittsburgh that covered fourteen hundred acres and employed eleven thousand workers. They saw the first successful "wireless telegraph" that would soon change world communications. Crowds flocked to see the fossil remains of a triceratops in the Government Building, a recreation of a mining camp at the Nevada State pavilion, floral gardens, livestock shows, giant cheeses, and a twenty-foot-tall knight on horseback made of prunes from what is now Silicon Valley.

Visitors listened to thousands of concerts, from the great John Phillips Sousa Band to operettas and the elegant ragtime music of composer Scott Joplin, then living in St. Louis. Everyone played, hummed, or sang the "official" fair song, "Meet Me in St. Louis, Louis," by Broadway songwriter Andrew Sterling. The exposition was designed to impress the world—and it did. Massive in scope, utopian in intent, the LPE made St. Louis the capital of the American Midwest and seemingly America's most progressive city, at least for seven months.

The exposition was a bold, ambitious undertaking for a medium-sized Midwestern city with a long history of corrupt and inefficient government, and it was expensive, costing over fifty million dollars. The leaders of the Louisiana Purchase Exposition Company (LPEC) labeled it the "University of the Future" and an "exposition of processes," not simply things. Under this broad umbrella they had seven major objectives: first, to promote the city of St. Louis and demonstrate its urbanity and economic clout, especially compared to hated Midwestern rival Chicago; second, to make money for stockholders and stimulate regional economic development; third, to demonstrate the superiority of middle-class American democracy, capitalism, and culture; fourth, to celebrate American industrial, commercial, and technological progress; fifth, to directly or indirectly support U.S. foreign policies, especially the nation's recent foray into international imperialism and colonization with the acquisition of Puerto Rico and the Philippine Islands; and sixth, to shape the future using education as a tool for directed, purposeful, progressive change. Finally the entire exposition was designed to celebrate the perceived inevitability of the March of Progress and the unqualified fitness of the white American "race" to lead that march.

To do this they had to entice many, many visitors to come to the fair. There had be something to interest everyone. The LPE, according to its president, David Francis, would be an encyclopedic place providing a summary or compilation of all existing knowledge at the turn of the twentieth century. Colorado College president, William F. Slocum, wrote in *Harper's Weekly* that it would give visitors "new standards, new means of comparison, new insights into the condition of life in the world" and help them discover a sense of purpose in America's rapidly changing society.[1] To aid in this process, the LPE would do something novel. They would host "the world's first assemblage of the world's peoples." Native people, some two thousand to three thousand strong, would be on display to help visitors understand how the other half (indeed, how the other 98 percent) of humanity lived in comparison with their own lives. Its ultimate purpose was to serve as a guide toward a future, albeit vague, utopia. As Francis argued,

> [e]xpositions accentuate the deficiencies of the past, give us a realization of our present advantages, predict the developments of the near future, and equip the arm and the brain alike of the mechanic, the engineer, and the philosopher for future and immediate advances into the realms of the possible. The World's Fair at St. Louis furnishes a magnificent example of what mankind may do when it shall substitute united exertion for contention in one great anthem of harmonious effort.[2]

Brave words at the beginning of a century during which organized "contentions," coupled with starvation and diseases, would kill more humans than had died in all previous wars combined. Similar rhetoric had been evident at every fair since 1851, and there would be more at subsequent fairs during the twentieth century.

A second major feature of the St. Louis fair was the conscious use of nineteenth-century evolutionist anthropological concepts. These undergirded a major theme in exposition rhetoric and interpretive displays to celebrate the assumed racial and cultural superiority of Northern European and American nations and to justify their imperial and colonial ambitions. This book is about how then-current, but now long passé, anthropological theories were used for these purposes, and how "Native peoples" were assembled, cared for, treated, displayed, and interpreted.

World's Fairs and Exposition Anthropology before the Louisiana Purchase Exposition

World's fairs began with London's Great Exhibition of the Works of Industry of All Nations (dubbed the "Crystal Palace" by *Punch* magazine) in 1851. From then until 1915 world's fairs sprang up like mushrooms to celebrate the heyday of European and American industrialism and imperialism. In Europe international exhibitions became grandiose stages on which nations bragged about their industrial, financial, technical, intellectual, social, and scientific "progress," their ability to extract raw materials from their colonies, and their successes in "civilizing" their colonial subjects.[3] The United States began its own bragging process with the 1876 Philadelphia extravaganza and continued through celebrations of the Panama Canal in 1915.

Major expositions came to have standard features, all of which would be seen in St. Louis in elaborated forms. Popular exhibits, events, or practices established at one fair were expected at subsequent fairs, and visitors were disappointed if they were absent. The first feature was the display of industrial machinery, mining technology, trade goods, and agricultural products in gigantic pavilions; the second was "cultural" exhibits, sculpture, painting, music, and other fine arts. The third feature was the establishment of permanent public institutions initially funded by exposition corporation profits and gifts from private donors. The architecturally eclectic Trocadéro complex, which later housed natural history exhibits, was built for the 1878 Paris fair. In the United States, the 1876 Philadelphia fair resulted in Memorial Hall in Philadelphia and the U.S. National Museum in Washington, while the Field Columbian Museum emerged from the Chicago World's Fair of 1893 and the Museum of Man from San Diego's 1915 celebration.[4]

The fourth feature was government funding as direct subsidies or supplemental monies to aid exposition corporations. The process varied from country to country. In the United States, Congress provided loans to the private companies but demanded they be paid back. The United States never accepted total financial responsibility for any exposition but did appropriate money for the construction and operation of government buildings and expeditions to obtain natural history and anthropology collections for exhibits. The largest subsidy for anthropology was for the 1893 Chicago World's Columbian Exposition. The exposition company funded a large, separate anthropology department under the direction of Frederic Ward Putnam and Franz Boas who sent out a number of fledgling anthropologists on collecting expeditions to North, Central, and South America. These materials became part of the Field Columbian Museum. Other governments, most notably Britain, France, Holland, and Belgium, similarly provided large subsidies to underwrite expeditions to amass archaeological and ethnographic collections. These resulted in exhibits that created a prehistoric and historic cultural heritage that supported current nationalist and colonialist ideologies.[5]

At the 1878 Paris exposition, the French added a fifth feature: the public display of new scientific knowledge by emerging disciplines, such as anthropology, and established fields at "international congresses," held as part of the exposition. Numerous scholarly, professional, trade, and benevolent associations and interest groups were invited to hold congresses, drawing many attendees and providing a major venue for airing and debating theoretical, practical, and public policy issues. The 1878 Paris congresses led, for example, to international copyright laws, the international postal union, and international adoption of the Braille system. Congresses were prominently featured at the 1889 Paris fair, including the International Congress of Anthropological and Prehistoric Sciences, and in Chicago in 1893 (Curti 1950; Mason 1894a, 1894b).

The sixth feature of major expositions was extramural entertainment that included "exotic" peoples. Fairs, held for many centuries in nearly all the world's trade centers, were mixtures of commerce, entertainment, and theater with dancers, musicians, actors, circuses, jugglers, food vendors, thieves, prostitutes, hawkers, and con artists. Similar congregations gathered at or near modern expositions and included displayed people, billed as "savages" from Africa or Polynesia, who could be gawked at for a fee. These unofficial, outside-the-gates "public nuisance" sideshows posed major crime-control and public-health problems for fair officials. In Philadelphia a "Shantyville" grew outside the exposition gates with such edifying exhibits as a "gigantic fat woman," talking pigs, fire-proof women, and two "Wild Men of Borneo."[6]

Paris's 1867 world's fair coped with unauthorized entertainment by developing a huge amusement park, installed and operated by the City of Paris, together with international restaurants, arranged around the perimeter of the ovoid-shaped exposition hall. In 1893 Chicago organizers created the Midway Plaisance—a "pleasure area" connecting two sections of the exposition grounds. In the shadow of the great two-hundred-and-fifty-foot-tall Ferris wheel, concessionaires presented dozens of "authentic" peoples from Africa, the Pacific, Arctic, Middle East, and Far East. The most notorious concession was the Streets of Cairo where "Little Egypt" and other women performed belly dances seriatim, ten hours a day, six days a week, ogled by tens of thousands of onlookers. The Streets of Cairo grossed eight hundred and eighty thousand dollars, more than the Ferris wheel, and the exposition company took 20 percent of the gross profits, as it did from all concessions. Subsequent exposition organizers were quick to see how lucrative the strange and exotic could be.

A related phenomenon, beginning in the early 1880s, was the Wild West show. The most famous was "Buffalo Bill" Cody's, which played six hundred and sixty performances in Chicago—outside the exposition gates. These shows employed American Indians, especially Lakotas, who made a much better living as "show Indians" than starving on government rations back on the reservations. Wild West shows rapidly became sanctioned attractions at expositions in the United States and Europe, including St. Louis (Fowler 2000, 205; Moses 1996; Kasson 2000).

The seventh feature was *official* "living exhibits" organized, funded, and managed by the exposition companies. At the 1855 Paris fair, static exhibits from French colonies focused on "primitive" material culture, stressing "cultural differences, especially exoticism." Bringing officially sanctioned, living "exotic" people to expositions came later. There was an attempt to have a federally sponsored exhibit of American Indians in Philadelphia, but Congress balked at the price tag. At the 1883 Amsterdam International Colonial Exposition, the Dutch government underwrote model villages inhabited by "Natives" from its colonies in the Caribbean and Southeast Asia; the price tag was large. Not to be outdone, the French government prominently featured Natives from its far-flung colonial empire at the 1889 Exposition Universelle extravaganza: "On the Esplanade des Invalides *side by side with the latest inventions and with the whole civilized world as spectators* . . . [were] twelve types of African, besides Javanese, Tonkinese, Chinese, Japanese, and other oriental peoples, living in native houses, wearing native costumes, eating native foods, practicing native arts and rites" (Mason 1890, 31; emphasis added). The colonial village also included a Streets of Cairo concession, Angkor Wat models, and replicas of West African mosques. "Human Habitations" was arranged as a "tour" of architectural types, from rock shelters to modern houses. At the 1900 Paris fair, Britain and Belgium erected officially sponsored live and static colonial exhibits, grouped together under the "Moral and Material Work of

Colonialization" stressed the "White Man's Burden" to civilize the rest of the world.[7]

Smaller fairs also saw living Native peoples as essential to their success. In 1889 St. Louis held a modest trade exposition. An enterprising promoter convinced the Indian Service to let him bring San Carlos Apaches "in all their pride and strength" to perform "their weird dances, ceremonies, and incantations" and to demonstrate (it's uncertain just how) "their modes of savage warfare." The Apaches were of great interest, since the U.S. Army had "subdued" them only three years earlier. This seems to be the first officially sanctioned exhibit of Indians in the United States, soon followed by others, including model Indians schools to demonstrate the value of Indian Service assimilationist policies.

The most celebrated gathering of Indians was Omaha's 1898 Trans-Mississippi Exposition, which promoters called the "Last Great Congress of the Red Man." It was designed as an ecumenical assembly of "all" Indian tribes, brought together for the first and last time, apparently to commiserate together before they all "vanished." When fiscal reality set in, the Last Great Congress shrank to about four hundred people from Plains and Southwest tribes. The 1901 Buffalo fair also had a Last Great Congress of the Red Man in 1901, and publicists billed the LPE Wild West show as yet another "Last Great Congress" (Fowler 2000, 205; McCowan 1899; Moses 1996; Rosewater 1897).

Exhibits of "native peoples" included both sideshow attractions presented by individual entrepreneurs and "official" exhibits of subjugated indigenous peoples sponsored and interpreted by their colonialist masters. After 1883, colonial powers officially exhibited subject peoples under the guise of educational endeavors to demonstrate how much better off Natives were under the benevolent care of their imperialist overlords. Private entrepreneurs unofficially exhibited subject people, especially those of color, as ethnic-racial stereotypes to make money. But it was often superficially difficult to distinguish the official from the unofficial, as each played on the other. The underlying difference was that government agencies were consciously promulgating propaganda to justify colonialism and forced acculturation policies. But both the official and the unofficial exhibitions used the same stereotypes—benighted "primitives" who could only be raised to civilization by "enlightened" benevolent white men.

Bridging these supposedly different exhibit categories were anthropologists attempting to legitimize their field of study, broker their specialized knowledge, and prove their status as "scientists." Working at expositions gave them a public forum in which to assert their claims to be experts on, and interpreters of, the physical, linguistic, and cultural similarities and differences of exotic peoples seen in relation to white Americans and northern Europeans. Official exhibits were often arranged or interpreted by anthropologists working closely with colonial administrators. As historian Robert Rydell has noted, anthropologists helped support the economic elite's messages regarding race and social progress and "scientifically" validated and justified overseas imperialist expansion (Rydell 1984, 157). At the same time, participation in expositions was the most public way anthropology—claiming to be a distinctive profession with a unique body of knowledge, methods, subject matter, and interpretive frameworks—could present itself as socially useful and authoritative. Expositions provided them with venues in which to popularize their concepts. The message of its exhibits, both static and living, was: Here are paradigms and concepts through which the "civilized" world may meet, understand, and interpret the "noncivilized" world.

Professionalizing Anthropology

Participation in the exhibition of Native peoples was a part of the campaign that anthropologists had been waging for over two decades to gain public recognition of their professional identity. In the United States, during the 1880s, Lewis Henry Morgan, John Wesley Powell, Frederic Ward Putnam, and their compatriots set out to "organize anthropologic [sic] research in America," as Powell put it in the first annual report of his fledgling Bureau of Ethnology, later the Bureau of American Ethnology (Powell 1881, xxxiii). At the time, anthropology was entirely museum based or was a leisure pursuit of educated amateurs. It can be argued that the first American "professional" anthropologists (individuals paid to do scientific work full time) were members of Powell's "Corps of Ethnologists." Over the next two decades, new museums with anthropology departments were founded in Chicago and Philadelphia (Harvard's Peabody Museum was already in existence), and an anthropology department was established by Putnam at the American Museum of Natural History. Franz Boas developed graduate programs at Clark University (1888) and Columbia (1896), Putnam at Harvard (1890) and the University of California (1901). By 1900, courses labeled "anthropology" were being taught in over thirty American universities and colleges. When the American Anthropological Association (AAA) was established in 1901, two hundred individuals joined.

Many AAA members were also members of Section H of the American Association for the Advancement of Science. In 1900, Section H established a standing committee on university-level anthropological teaching to develop textbooks and curricula and to formulate arguments to convince university administrators to establish departments. Committee members took their case to professional meetings and academic assemblies. Calling the field "the crown and completion of the sciences," Frank Russell, one of the first professionally trained anthropologists and a leader of the initiative, argued for majors in anthropology as the foundation for more specialized courses of study. Anthropology's "very comprehensiveness is a virtue; for thereby it is rendered suitable to serve as a framework for all other knowledge, lacking which the student but too often builds a series of mental watertight compartments that give no unity or harmony to the intellectual edifice" (Russell 1902, 2). It was great rhetoric and became the basis for the message that WJ McGee, the first president of the AAA, carried with him to St. Louis when he became head of the LPE Anthropology Department. Anthropology could pull a fair together into a seamless intellectual whole. The world would see anthropology's critical value for understanding a changing world.

The living exhibits, official and unofficial, at expositions became sites of social interaction. There Euro-Americans and Europeans met Native peoples and interacted with them in face-to-face encounters. These engagements were based on curiosity about the exotic and foreign, safe adventure through what has come to be called the "touristic gaze." Indeed these intercultural meetings had "the interest of strangeness" (McGee 1904a, 4). The "living exhibits" at fairs were exciting, disturbing, compelling, and educational for visitors and for Native demonstrators and performers alike, and anthropology could control their meanings.

This book is the story of how anthropology achieved a pseudocentrality of place in the exposition world in 1904. The LPE organizers were aware that exotic peoples were major draws and therefore money-makers. But they did not want "merely" an exotic sideshow. They wanted their exotic peoples to be interpreted in a modern "scientific" manner and their exposition to be "a vast museum of anthropology and ethnology, of man and his works." So they brought in an anthropologist, a reputed scientific expert in exotic peoples, WJ McGee.[8]

The anthropology that McGee and most (but not all) of his fellow anthropologists brought to the exposition centered in concepts of unilineal evolution developed since the 1860s in Europe and the United States. The concepts contained an essentialist set of assumed universal cultural, physical, and "racial" processes. These processes had *inevitably* produced the superior white Europeans and Euro-Americans who had created the great industrial and imperial nations and who "properly" should (or thought they should) dominate the world. This was the anthropology that the LPE organizers wanted—and got. It was holistic, inclusive, and encompassing. Everything had a place— agriculture, art, ideas, technology, and even people. By illuminating the processes that had produced the past and the present, they could be used to predict the future and legitimate the rapid societal and technological changes and advances that exposition exhibitors predicted. This kind of evolution implied that the new was natural, inevitable, and beneficial to all.

Anthropology also had an added benefit; it was a new science and by definition that meant "better" to men who saw a bright future in the ideas emerging at the beginning of the twentieth century. The dominant paradigm in the American anthropology of 1900 was a product of American society and reflected its values in the way it posed questions, amassed data, and interpreted evidence, particularly the racialist assumptions and Social Darwinist ideologies of the time. It reflected the deeply held and unquestioned beliefs and prejudices of fair organizers that the American way of life was the unquestioned height of civilized development.

Validation was achieved by using the "primitive" as a foil for "enlightened civilization." "Primitive" represented presumed early evolutionary stages of human society. Certain contemporary societies (hunter-gatherers, peasants) became analogs for the past stages through which "advanced" human societies had evolved. This idea—"as they are now, so our ancestors once were"—had been current in the thinking of political economists and social evolutionists since the late 1500s. One aspect of this Primitivism was the long-held premise of the "Vanishing Savage"—that nonliterate cultures were doomed by technological and imperialist expansion.[9] The LPE, like the Omaha and Buffalo expositions, would thus provide the "last chance" to see the "authentic" Native peoples of the world before they "vanished." But unlike Omaha and Buffalo, the LPE would provide hope for the unfortunate "primitives." The exposition would give Natives a chance to understand that Euro-American civilization was the pinnacle of evolutionary development. It was a way of life so superior that they would embrace it once they saw it.

In contrast to the fair's overall evolutionary theme, anthropology as a distinct department was almost an afterthought. It was the first department proposed but the last to be implemented. While the field's ideas proved useful for the exposition's explanatory and taxonomic framework, an anthropology department was not considered absolutely necessary—unlike the departments of manufacturing, electricity, or fine arts.

The LPE organizers recognized that anthropology exhibits were expensive, especially if living peoples were included. Like all expositions, the LPE was a venture intended to be profitable for shareholders, hence the directors wanted to keep expenses to a minimum. There were in fact anthropological exhibits all over the exposition grounds—in government displays, foreign pavilions, business booths, and on the Pike—but other exhibitors or concessionaires paid for them. Getting the LPEC to pay for static and living people exhibits was another matter. A major theme of this book is about that struggle.

About This Book

This book is about how anthropology "came to the fair" in 1904. It has several interwoven stories. There are stories about the men and women, professional and vocational anthropologists, exhibits designers, educators, traders, government officials, hucksters, and entrepreneurs, who used Native peoples and their arts and cultures to both educate and entertain visitors, and to advance their own economic, sociopolitical, and ideological agendas. There is also the story of how concepts of then-current evolutionary anthropology were disseminated and how they both reflected popular culture and influenced public opinion. One story, woven throughout, is about how one anthropologist, WJ McGee, tried to articulate and popularize his vision of anthropology as the Science of Man of the present metamorphosing into the Science of Humanity of the future. The story of exposition anthropology at the LPE is in large part McGee's quest for professional authority and recognition and his use of anthropology's "subject matter" to obtain his objectives.

The second major story focuses on the almost three thousand indigenous peoples who resided (often under miserable conditions) on the exposition grounds while almost continuously performing, or demonstrating, their "traditional" lifeways for thousands of gawking visitors six days a week. This book is the first attempt to systematically discover the names, cultural affiliations, and individual and family stories of these men, women, and children.[10] What has been garnered, however, is woefully incomplete, especially in regard to the observations, reactions, and feelings of the Native participants. We know they all came voluntarily, but we do not know why many came. Some were professional entertainers and had worked at previous expositions. Others had never been outside their homelands and were traveling thousands of miles to an unknown land. We have gleaned some idea of their experiences, some good, some bad. They must have been frightened and elated, bored, awed, and offended, and as interested in the fairgoers, officials, and anthropologists as the latter were in them. They observed and interacted with fairgoers while they went about their daily tasks. There are hints of the tenor of their observations; they were incredulous and appalled at the rude and unthinking behavior of fairgoers, but also made friends with some. Unfortunately their gaze is simply not very accessible in the archival record. We wish that we could have included their oral histories. We wish that there could be people to talk about their memories, but all participants have long since passed away. We leave it to others to discover if the stories told by participants when they returned to their homes were passed on to descendants. Simply locating participants' names and cultural affiliation has proven to be a daunting task involving over ten years of research.[11]

We have based our stories on primary documents held in the archives listed in the endnotes. We have consulted LPEC records, correspondence, exhibit plans, departmental records and reports, scrapbooks, daily programs, and photographs. We have surveyed the many newspaper accounts about the exposition—accounts that conveyed information and shaped public expectations and attitudes about the anthropology displays. All sources tell us much of "what went on" during the fair and reflect something about the social, political, economic, and racialist ideologies of the day.

We begin our tour of the fair with planning efforts, focusing on the LPE's desire for civic bragging rights. Civic leaders wanted to show the rest of the country that "in public spirit and in private enterprise," St. Louis "stands with the first."[12] We then discuss why the Louisiana Purchase Exposition Company organized an anthropology department, since the original goal was to show the development of civilized life in the Louisiana territory, using displays of Indian life in 1800. This would be the "primitive before" picture to contrast with the "civilized after" of American technological and cultural achievements during the nineteenth century.

We then turn to McGee and his vision of anthropology as background for his grandiose exposition plans, his initial attempts to convince fair and government officials to fund them, and the fiscal realities and shifting political winds that required frequent changes in those plans. Major factors forcing changes were the decision by the Indian Service to build a model Indian school and use adult "traditional" Indians as foils and the federal government's desire to bring large numbers of Filipinos to demonstrate how well it was caring for America's new "wards." This is followed by the story of the LPE-sponsored expeditions to convince Native peoples to come to the exposition.

With the LPE ready to open on May 1, we turn to the displays of living peoples whom visitors saw, focusing on the almost three thousand indigenous peoples. Five chapters describe the children and adults associated with the Indian Service's model school and the associated Indian Village, the Philippine Reservation, the LPEC-funded Anthropology Villages, and the "Ten Million Dollar Pike." We look at daily life as these groups lived it, how they coped with fairgoers, earned money, and waded through the mud after torrential rains. It was not easy being a living exhibit in the heat and extraordinary rain of a St. Louis summer and the cold and wet of autumn and early winter.

We next discuss static anthropological exhibits and McGee's attempts to make the exposition a place of original research on Native peoples, including a Special Olympics, a competition designed as part of the third modern Olympic Games. Most projects dealt with anthropometry and psychometry, resulting in what would later charitably be called the "mismeasure of man" (Gould 1977, 1981; Findling and Pelle 1990, 18). We also discuss special events that affected the demonstrators' lives, such as parades and performances, and scientific congresses, arranged to further McGee's professional agenda. We end with the closing and celebration of the fair and a discussion of how the LPE marked a turning point in Americanist anthropology.

Before we begin, a word must be said about derogatory language and cartoons, dubious assumptions, problematic conclusions, incorrect names for peoples, and strange logic sprinkled throughout the book in quotations. We have retained some of the ethnocentric and racist stereotypical language and slang used by organizers, participants, newspaper reporters, and fairgoers. We recognize that this language may cause pain for many descendants of the people who acted as "living exhibits." But to omit or edit it would negate the point of the book. The early 1900s was a time of intense racism in the United States against Indians, blacks, Asians, and Southern Europeans. One of the major points of the book is how some anthropologists at the time fought against these prejudices and how others supported them with their nineteenth-century ideas about human physical and cultural evolution.

From the perspective of the history of Americanist anthropology, the LPE was a turning point. WJ McGee, the director of the LPE Anthropology Department and president of the nascent American Anthropological Association, and Franz Boas, who in 1904 was becoming a major force in anthropology, were close personal friends. At the fair's anthropological congress both gave papers. McGee's paper was filled with the bombast and racialist assumptions of nineteenth-century unilineal anthropology. As things turned out, it was a swan song for an outmoded set of ideas, at least within museum- and university-based anthropology. Boas's paper basically destroyed all the theory underlying McGee's anthropology and laid out the cultural relativism that would permeate Americanist anthropology in the twentieth century. It was McGee's vision of anthropology, in conjunction with that of LPE organizers, that most of the millions of visitors took away with them. And it was a tenacious vision that can unfortunately still be seen today in expositions, in films, and on television.

1. Organizing the
Louisiana Purchase Exposition

Discussions among St. Louis business and political leaders about hosting a national exposition began as early as 1889. Governor David R. Francis led a delegation to Washington DC to seek the exposition to celebrate the four hundredth anniversary of Columbus's "discovery of the New World" for St. Louis. Rival Chicago won and staged its World Columbian Exposition in 1893. Interest waned until early 1896, when St. Louis's Congressman Richard Bartholdt advocated a Louisiana Purchase Exposition to improve the city's sagging economy. Francis again took up the cause along with Pierre Chouteau, third generation scion of a great St. Louis merchant family. On June 7, St. Louis elite met to rally support. Francis declared, "There is one event in the history of this city, second in importance only to the Declaration of Independence . . . and that is the Louisiana Purchase. St. Louis should celebrate its centennial by a great international exposition, second to none ever held in the world."[1] Tentative planning began.

In 1898 Congressman Bartholdt introduced a bill seeking federal recognition for a fair and financial support. A Committee of Fifty began to conceptualize an exposition. A meeting of the governors of the fourteen Louisiana Purchase states and territories was held in January 1899 to solicit their support. A planning committee, with Chouteau as general chair and Francis as chair of the executive committee, began fund-raising; five million dollars was pledged in a single evening and Congress soon matched with it five million in subsidy loans. In 1900 the City of St. Louis passed a bond issue for the fair. On April 29, 1900, the Louisiana Purchase Exposition Company (LPEC) was formally incorporated, with authorized capital of six million dollars and nine million in credit. Francis served without compensation, and ninety-three civic leaders formed a board of directors.

The goal was to erect an exposition more spectacular than Chicago's. Civic pride and status were at stake. Intangibles compensated for the financial risk:

Fig. 1.1. David R. Francis, 1903, LPE president. Photograph by L. Strauss. St. Louis Public Library, image no. LPE01617.

increased commerce for the community and new educational and cultural opportunities. An exposition would allow St. Louis to "gain a cosmopolitan habit that elevates its citizenship and broadens its social life."[2]

Such elevation was badly needed in turn-of-the-century St. Louis. After the Civil War it grew as a major rail center and river port with a wide variety of manufactures, and wholesale, banking, and financial businesses associated with commerce and transportation. By 1900 St. Louis was America's fourth largest city with about 575,000 residents. But there were major social and political ills, including a recent violent and costly transit workers' strike that could undermine a major fair. Political cronyism, bribery, and corruption were endemic, involving both political parties, but principally Republican assemblymen. Democrats ran industrialist Rolla Wells as a reform candidate for mayor. He won, ensuring support for an exposition by improving streets and public services, a critical reform if the LPE was to be a success. The slogan "The New St. Louis" was coined to bring the citizens together in a great cooperative reform effort.

Government, private corporations, and civic groups joined forces to improve the city's transportation infrastructure. A purification system for city water was installed, one hundred miles of roads were built, neighborhoods were cleaned up, playgrounds were built, and a smoke reduction program for steamboats and factories was instituted. St. Louis wanted to present its best face to the world (Findling and Pelle 1996, 180).

Developing an Exposition Focus

With reforms underway, David Francis proceeded to develop the exposition. Francis (fig. 1.1), born in 1850 in Kentucky, was a Washington University graduate, a wealthy grain exporter, banker, and civic leader with a reputation for efficiency, decisiveness, organization, and raising money. He had served as mayor of St. Louis (1885–89), governor of Missouri (1889–93), and secretary of the interior under President Grover Cleveland (1896–97). A prominent Democrat, he had national connections with capitalists and politicians who could ensure that the federal government would approve the LPEC's later financial requests.[3]

By 1902 the LPEC Board had selected Forest Park as the fair site. The 657-acre tract of virgin forest, located away from the crowded downtown area, was surrounded by stately homes and large tracts of agricultural land. The River des Peres, which "had become more of an open sewer than a river," was rerouted, reduced in length, and partially covered.[4] The overall plan (figs. 1.2 and 1.3) centered on Festival Hall, sited on a hilltop. Cascading waterfalls descended to a lagoon, providing a dramatic focal point, celebrated in Scott Joplin's popular ragtime piece "Cascades." The major exhibition buildings fanned out on either side of the cascades (fig. 1.4), and this area was referred to as the Main Picture.

The twenty-four-acre Palace of Agriculture, the horticulture and forestry palaces, foreign pavilions, an athletic field, a stadium, and an aeronautic con-

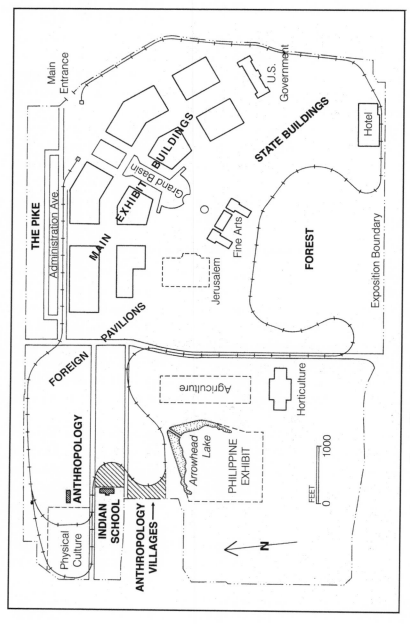

Fig. I.2. Plan map of exposition. Map by Charles Sternberg.

Fig. 1.3. Natives participate in the transportation parade in the Grand Basin. Library of Congress, LC 10901, 3245.

course would be placed to the west, with the Government Pavilion and state pavilions placed to the southeast of the Main Picture. The huge Inside Inn was sited at the southeast corner and the amusement area, the Pike, would extend west for one and a half miles from the main entrance on Lindell Boulevard along Skinker Road.

Organizers also decided on a central theme, the exposition as "University of the Future." Francis told everyone that education would be the keynote of the Universal Exposition. While the LPE would be a place where everyone could learn, for working citizens it would be special. Objects, laboratories, and people would replace textbooks as educational tools so that people "engaged in or interested in [any] activity may come and see, examine, study, and go away advised."[5] Education was conceptualized broadly, but the ultimate goal was to educate men who would use their new knowledge to expand industry and commerce.

The exposition also had to make money. Federal subsidies had to be repaid; the business community wanted its investment to make a great profit. The

Fig. 1.4. Government Building beyond Sunken Garden, with Liberal Arts Building (*left*) and Mines and Metallurgy Building (*right*). Missouri Historical Society, St. Louis, LPE1551, 30990.

LPEC needed to attract large crowds (over one hundred thousand per day) because it was easy to lose revenue with poor attendance. To better understand the problems they faced, the board studied earlier expositions. Some saw earlier fairs as too pedantic. The 1892 Columbian Historical Exposition in Madrid, for example, lost money "because from its very nature it appealed more to the scholar than to the general public, and consequently, so far as popular attendance and financial outcome were concerned was not noteworthy."[6] The Spanish government bore the exposition costs, not a private corporation.

It was clear to LPE organizers that an entertainment area was a requisite. People needed to eat, drink, and relax while studying the exhibits. It was also clear that these were major sources of income, as Chicago's famed Midway had demonstrated. Since 1893 concessionaires had paid 20 to 25 percent of their gross receipts to exposition corporations and had been required to erect their own structures and pay all expenses. Thus St. Louis would have a very large entertainment zone, the Pike. Studies of previous zones indicated that the biggest draws were concessions featuring "exotic" peoples, especially those from other continents. To do this, the organizers decided they needed an anthropology committee (Higginbotham 1898, 482–91; Buel 1904). It was the first departmental committee of the fair.

The First Anthropology Committee

Article 7 of the LPEC's bylaws established a standing committee for a department of anthropology on May 14, 1901. It was charged with overseeing all matters connected with ethnology, archaeology, anthropology, and history: to develop a vision statement, write an implementation plan, submit a budget, and a space allocation request for a pavilion. By focusing on the human exotic, and hiring anthropologists as consultants to help ensure their presence, the exposition directors, as historian Robert Rydell has noted, "turned [a] portrait of the world into an anthropologically validated racial landscape that made the [then recent] acquisition of the Philippine Islands and continued overseas economic expansion seem as much a part of the manifest destiny of the nation as the Louisiana Purchase itself."[7]

It is difficult to gain a picture of the men charged with planning anthropological events because few records remain in the LPEC files. The first mention of anthropology is an archaeological excavation report appended to corporation records from the November 1901 directors' meeting. After construction workers in Forest Park found small Indian mounds, Francis contacted David I. Bushnell Jr., a former St. Louis resident working for the Peabody Museum at Harvard University, and asked him to excavate them before the land was graded. He did so during December 1901 and January 1902. The mounds were about forty-eight feet in diameter and contained human skeletal remains, pottery, and projectile points. Bushnell presented a paper on them at a professional meeting held in St. Louis on December 28, 1903. He speculated that they were Omaha earth lodges or burial sites. The fact that there were Indian sites in Forest Park had no bearing on the fair and the materials recovered were not used in the archaeology exhibits.[8]

Ironically, Bushnell was not appointed to the anthropology committee, nor was his father, a member of the Missouri Historical Society's fair committee. Interestingly, neither was Chouteau. In fact there was no one with any anthro-

Fig. 1.5. Frederick W. Lehmann, 1903, Chair of the Anthropology Committee and International Congress. LPEC publicity photo by L. Strauss. St. Louis Public Library, image no. LPE0167.

pological experience on the committee. Chaired by F. W. Lehmann (fig. 1.5), it included seven members of the business committee.[9]

Since none of these men were anthropologists or had any experience with either museum exhibits or Native peoples, they contacted prominent anthropologists who had participated in the Chicago Exposition (Franz Boas, George Dorsey, Frederic Ward Putnam, and Frederick Starr) and two Smithsonian anthropologists, William Henry Holmes, chief curator of the Department of Anthropology of the National Museum, and WJ McGee, an ethnologist with the Bureau of American Ethnology. All had extensive exposition experience and were respected national figures in turn-of-the-century American anthropology.[10]

Exposition Anthropology and Anthropology's Exposition Experts

Anthropological exhibits seem to have first been shown at the 1867 Paris Exposition. Mexico sent a large-scale temple replica "complete with a row of skulls hanging from the cornice and a cast of the mother of the gods, Coatlicue, standing in the central portal" (Honour 1975, 185; Trennert 1974). The 1876 Philadelphia Fair had three federally funded anthropological exhibits: two from the "Great Geographical Surveys" and one erected by the U.S. National Museum in the Government Building. The National Museum anthropology exhibits, designed largely by Otis T. Mason and Frank Hamilton Cushing, mainly consisted of long rows of glass cases stuffed with artifacts, arranged to demonstrate evolutionary principles. While this was very much in keeping with then-dominant anthropological paradigms (lock-step social evolutionary stages through which all humankind had, or would, pass), the exhibits were widely considered mind-numbing, boring, and confusing. This led George Brown Goode, the Smithsonian's assistant secretary, to rethink exposition and public museum purposes and their exhibits philosophies. He first focused on systems of classification.

The problems of classifying material culture—from machines to vegetables—worried all exposition officials. They needed order so visitors would not be disoriented by a massive jumble; and they needed mutually exclusive groups for purposes of awards. The first systematic attempt was at the 1867 Paris Exposition with ten major groups, each with twenty classes containing dozens of related (in the eyes of the classifiers) types. Goode conceived a more ambitious scheme for the Chicago World's Fair: ten departments with divisions, subdivisions, and groups totaling nearly a thousand categories (Findling and Pelle 1996, 37–38; Goode 1895). The initial St. Louis committees began with this plan.

Goode also considered how objects were displayed. Museums grew out of modern industrial expositions, he argued, and existed to record, for research, and to educate. They contain "materials gathered . . . [to] serve as a basis for scientific thought . . . [which then become] permanent land-marks of the progress of the world in thought, in culture, or in industrial achievement." But these objects needed to be properly displayed to fulfill this education function. To do this required the elimination of duplicate materials and the insertion of "thorough labeling." An efficient display became *a collection of instructive labels, each illustrated by a well-selected specimen.*[11]

Goode's maxim provided clear organizational guidance, but nothing for exhibition form and style. Such guidance began to emerge in 1887 when a young German anthropologist recently arrived in the United States, Franz Boas, published two brief articles in *Science* criticizing Mason's ethnological exhibits in the U.S. National Museum: the mind-stultifying glass cases stuffed with artifacts, arranged to reveal presumed evolutionary sequences. Boas argued such arrangements were specious because the underlying typological assumptions were invalid. Each individual specimen must be understood in its own historical, technological, social, cultural, and environmental contexts, otherwise "we can not understand its meanings . . . for in ethnology all is individuality."[12] Boas's approach was fully compatible with Goode's principles. His arguments pointed directly toward an anthropology based on cultural-environmental contextual analyses as well as new forms of displays based on research. New exhibits incorporating such thinking were tried at world's fairs before being incorporated into museum halls as permanent exhibits.

The key figure in this transition was William H. Holmes, one of the most remarkable individuals in nineteenth- and twentieth-century geology, anthropology, and museology. Holmes began his professional career in 1875 as an artist on the Hayden Survey when Hayden sent him and photographer William Henry Jackson to southwestern Colorado to draw and photograph cliff dwellings. They created a series of plaster-of-Paris models of Southwestern ruins and pueblo villages that were the highlight of the government exhibits at the 1876 Philadelphia Exhibition along with Jackson's photographs. Soon Holmes became a material culture specialist for the Bureau of American Ethnology, noted especially for his study of aboriginal pottery. He became the consummate "museum man"—immersed in material culture studies and what objects can be made to tell (Fernlund 2000; Holmes 1902, 1903a; Meltzer and Dunnell 1992).

In the 1880s and 1890s, Holmes worked closely with Mason, Goode, Walter Hough, and sometimes McGee, creating extensive exhibits for expositions:

New Orleans (1883–84), Louisville (1884), Cincinnati (1888), St. Louis (1889), Madrid (1892), Chicago (1893), Nashville (1897), and Omaha (1898). Over time he combined Goode's minimalist exhibit philosophy with Boas's holistic-contextual orientation and his own sense of visual and artistic presentation. He was also influenced by the work of William T. Hornaday who developed "habitat groups" for natural history displays, and by the life groups exhibited at the 1889 Paris Exposition. As a result, the anthropology exhibits Holmes and his colleagues produced for U.S. expositions were innovative and prec-edent-setting (Mason, 1890, 1894a, 1894b; Wonder, 1990).

By 1890 anthropology exhibit conceptualization was more holistic and var-ied. Hough began producing series tracing the "natural history" of imple-ments such as the lamp and fire-making tools, an idea McGee would use at St. Louis. The exhibits produced by Holmes and Mason for the 1892 Madrid fair, and Holmes, Mason, and Cushing for Chicago, mark transition points in American anthropological exhibits and, indeed, the theoretical orientation of American anthropology. For Chicago, Cushing developed four Southwest-ern life groups (Hopi kitchen, Navajo silversmith, Navajo weavers, and Zuni kiva ceremony,) and Holmes designed Apache, Sioux, and Powhatan family groups. This was the first use of ethnographic life group exhibits in the United States, and they were extremely popular. Seeing life-size figures in "natural" settings carrying out activities to which viewers could relate was very effective. They continued to refine these exhibits at subsequent world's fairs (Fowler 2000, 210; Mason 1892, 1895).

Members of the anthropology committee went to see Holmes's exhibit at the Buffalo Pan-American Exposition—twelve mannequin life groups from Greenland Eskimos to Patagonians. Large groups sat on eight-by-twelve-foot platforms and depicted a family unit, engaged in common food gathering or craft production activities. In addition, there were synthetic series presenting evolutionary histories of various types of material culture or processes (Holmes 1900, 30–33). These became the model for the St. Louis businessmen who thought they could replicate the Buffalo exhibits but make them larger.

In Holmes's eyes the mannequin life groups were ideal for museum displays but for expositions the real thing was better; one could bring the displays to life. "The real family, clothed in its own costumes, engaged in its own occu-pations, and surrounded by its actual belongings, would form the best possible illustration of a people. Future expositions may bring together the living representatives of type tribes, scientifically presented and free from commercial incubus" (Holmes 1902, 201; 1898; 1903b). An undertaking of this nature would require two years' lead time. Holmes and McGee had proposed such a large-scale living exhibit for the Buffalo exposition, but Smithsonian officials had not authorized funds for the ambitious plan.

A "Congress of Races": The Holmes–McGee Plan

Holmes's reputation and ability to see the big picture made him an ideal choice for developing a conceptual framework for the St. Louis Exposition. The anthropology committee, after reviewing the responses from the other anthropologists, asked him to submit a formal exhibition plan. Holmes requested that his friend McGee work with him. Holmes officially submitted his plan in July 1901 and both men traveled to St. Louis in August to meet with the committee. They urged that the anthropology exhibits be about people rather than artifacts, in keeping with the idea of an exposition of processes rather than products.[13] Rather than rely on static dioramas, they described a representative exhibit of the world's primitive peoples (a congress of the world's peoples and races) arranged in assemblages of family groups. One hundred acres of land would be needed for this group, who would erect their own dwellings, conduct games and ceremonies, and make appropriate tools and art. The central portion was to be an island, on which the ruins of a Mayan temple would be reproduced at one end and the great mound of Cahokia (the real mounds were located across the Mississippi River from St. Louis) on the other. Interiors of the structures would be rest areas for visitors. Visitors could also climb to the top of each structure to obtain a panoramic view of the entire anthropology area. In the center of the island would be a workshop where Native artists would demonstrate manufacturing processes. The water around the island would permit the use of various kinds of "primitive" watercraft.

While the island would be a focal point, the main attraction would be people in Native villages. Seventy-five groups would be selected by geographical location, race, and colonial empires, with special prominence given to the American Natives, especially those in the Louisiana Purchase area, and in U.S. protectorates and overseas possessions. It would be a heterogeneous mixture of "primitive" peoples who differed culturally due to climate and environment.

Each group would include four or five families, following their "traditional" lifeways.

While geographical distribution was the primary factor, cultural traits and racial categorizations were also considered important in the selection of specific groups. Exoticism was also important. An Abyssinian tribe lived near the Nile Valley in stockaded huts, used wood and stone tools, and worshiped fetishes. They would be desirable. The nomadic Kabyle would be especially interesting because they used skull trepanning to cure various illness (providing an interesting foil for modern medicine exhibits); the Sarawak head-hunters because they were cannibals; and southeastern Borneans because they supposedly domesticated orangutans as servants. Physical features (size, fine physique, and extensive tattooing) necessitated the inclusion of African Bushmen, Hottentots, Annamese, Andaman Islanders, and Pygmies. Distinctive housing was also critical, reflecting the desire to illustrate environmental adaptation through the display of palm-leaf bowers, yurts, subterranean houses, stockaded huts, hogans, pueblos, and tipis.

Rather than have a separate exhibit building with static exhibits, the plan integrated archaeology with ethnology. The past would be joined with the present to eliminate a false dichotomy and emphasize cultural continuity. Past tribal customs would be shown in connection to each group's ethnographic present. This would implicitly make the primitive groups living memorials of the past of all mankind. Holmes and McGee estimated the "world congress" would cost between one and a half and three million dollars and argued that "the bringing together of living representatives of type tribes, scientifically presented and free from the commercial incubus" was important, but "to secure satisfactory results the work must needs begin not less than two years before the opening of the exposition."[14] They also suggested that the department be called "ethnography."

The anthropology committee agreed that the plan would have great visitor appeal. In fact, it could be the most outstanding feature of the St. Louis Exposition. They unanimously accepted it and sent Francis an outline of the ambitious vision. "It will depart from the plan of all past expositions, and make life and movement its distinguishing and marked characteristic. It will embrace in its scope a comprehensive anthropological exhibition, constituting a congress of races, and exhibiting particularly the barbarous and semi-barbarous peoples

of the world, as nearly as possible in their ordinary and native environments"
(Lehmann 1901).

The committee noted that they did not make a proposal for such an ambitious exhibit lightly nor were they proposing a cheap, chimerical undertaking.
They recommended an allocation of $3 million. "With intelligent direction,
with courage on the part of those who undertake its execution, with ample
financial support, success is assured." The report quoted Holmes and McGee
almost verbatim, "'the proper study of mankind is man,' and the greatest spectacle that can be presented to mankind is man." Popular and scientific interest would be merged in this great exhibit, which, in addition to its intrinsic
worth, would be absolutely unique. "It has been frequently proposed, several
times entered upon, but never yet accomplished."

Lehmann argued further that the proposed exhibit would produce rich
financial returns for the LPEC, making it well worth the expense. It would
serve as an excellent means of publicity, drawing crowds and generating more
gate receipts. He predicted that the anthropology displays would receive more
press coverage than any other part of the fair. Secondly, it would be a quest:

> As the representatives of the Company go out into the barbarous world
> to secure peoples from the various tribes for exhibition here, their move-
> ments, the obstacles they meet, the difficulties they overcome, the dan-
> gers with which they are confronted, the hardships and privations they
> endure, their failures and successes, will all be subjects of legitimate
> news, eagerly sought by newspapers everywhere. (Lehmann 1901)

The scientific expeditions would be exciting, just as Stanley's search for Livingston had made good press copy. Lehmann stressed that the exhibit would
be a spectacle of universal human interest, attractive to the young and old,
native-born Euro-Americans, and foreigners. It would compel the attention of
idle sightseer and the most earnest student. In concluding, he recommended
that the LPEC hire McGee and Holmes to further refine and install the exhibit.
McGee would be in charge of outlining the details and securing ethnic groups.
Holmes would be in charge of the installation. They would call the exhibit
"ethnology" and eliminate "anthropology."

Francis's initial reaction to the grandiose plan is unknown, but he did not immediately turn it down nor ask for revisions. The executive committee looked at

the bottom line and decided it was too expensive; they wanted something more reasonable.[15] Francis wanted more information. He asked Lehmann to talk to other anthropologists to see whether the plan was feasible, to critique its conception, amend it as needed, and comment on the projected costs. These were critical: How much would it really cost to house and feed an aboriginal family for eight months? How much would the gathering expeditions cost?

Lehmann sent out letters to Putnam, Dorsey, and Boas, as well as to others suggested by McGee and Holmes. McGee noted later that all found the plan acceptable intellectually but felt that there were many logistical difficulties. They apparently thought the ambitious plan would be very expensive. One unnamed "leading anthropologist" stated that he estimated that living expenses for each demonstrator would be two dollars per day. There would also be preparatory expenses, travel, outfitting, and wages for the LPEC agents, translators, and enticements for group members. He said that for seventy-five groups the absolute minimum would be one and a half million dollars, but three million was actually realistic (McGee 1905d).

The anthropology committee ultimately relied on Frederic Ward Putnam's assessment of the plan. Putnam sent his departmental report for the 1893 Chicago World Columbian Exposition. He noted that it had taken more than two years to plan the exhibits, locate, transport, and assemble artifacts and peoples, and several months to dismantle the department after the exposition closed. The total cost was just under three hundred thousand dollars. Putnam suggested that the plan would take longer and cost more than anticipated, and that there were innumerable details to be addressed. In conclusion, he recommended it be scaled back or funds significantly increased, and the LPEC sponsor a conference of leading anthropologists to discuss the proposed exhibits. Lehmann took the information, summarized the responses, and asked Francis to approve the original plan for $3 million. Not unexpectedly, there was no response. Francis referred the matter to a new working group (himself, a Mrs. Campbell, and a Mr. Shapleigh), which essentially tabled the decision.

Meanwhile Francis requested his friend, Frederick Skiff (fig. 1.6), director of the Field Museum in Chicago, to think about the matter. Skiff met with Putnam and reviewed the Holmes-McGee plan and decided it would cost more than a million dollars. Putnam next met with Francis and submitted a

Fig. 1.6. Frederick J. V. Skiff, Director of the Field Museum and LPE exhibits. Photograph by L. Strauss, 1904. St. Louis Public Library, image no. LPE 01153.

new plan for an archaeological display with no Native peoples, with himself as director. The centerpiece would be models of Mesoamerican ruins and the complete dismantling of a Mayan temple and its reconstruction in St. Louis. Skiff noted that Putnam insisted the term *anthropology* be used to give greater latitude to the department's operation. He had another reason for making this suggestion. Due to uncertainty over scope and funding that for a department "indicated by the word *ethnology*, the broader term should be selected, so that if it should be determined not to confine the operations . . . to the contemporaneous primitive races of man, there might be presented as a broader, even if upon a less popular scale, man and his works." Skiff took Putnam's advice on this point but not the focus on archeology. Skiff ended his report to Francis by insisting that an international exposition would not be an international exposition if anthropology were omitted and that "the most interesting and popular exhibit, [would be] living, primitive man or man and his works."[16] The board approved the title change but again tabled the report and requested more study.

Skiff Takes Charge of the Division of Exhibits

The LPEC reached no official agreement on the report. It sat with others in Francis's office. The company was in trouble and it was soon clear that it would not make its mid-1903 anticipated opening. The anthropology committee disbanded in frustration. Holmes and McGee received no correspondence about the initiative and there is no further mention of it in their papers. Both had other duties—erecting the Smithsonian and Bureau of American Ethnology exhibits for the 1901 Pan-American Exposition.

The LPEC reorganized in spring 1902 after a period of dormancy and moved its exposition date to 1904. Francis continued as exposition president but several board members had to be replaced as a result of corruption allegations. Frederick Skiff was appointed director of exhibits. The new executive committee reiterated the desire to have an anthropological exhibit but vetoed an expensive ethnological village. They wanted artifacts but no congress of races. Francis now felt that to try to send expeditions was unpractical. Lehmann strenuously objected, so the board tabled the problem yet again. The anthropology committee stagnated. Francis referred the matter to a new group: himself, Lehmann, and Skiff.[17]

Under the new streamlined organization, the LPEC was divided into four executive divisions, with internal departments, without official advisory committees. The Department of Anthropology became Department H, part of the Division of Exhibits under Skiff's direction. Skiff reported directly to Francis. He was very familiar with anthropology and favored the use of a cultural evolutionary paradigm. He was active in developing many exposition classification schemes between 1893 and 1915. He also thought fairs were ideal institutions to advance theories of progress because an exposition was a "social encyclopedia in the most comprehensive and accurate sense." This encyclopedia was valuable because it had full, accurate, and reliable information. If arranged properly, an exposition would give the world "a living picture of the artistic and industrial development at which mankind has arrived" and provide "a new starting point from which all men may direct future exertions." It would contain the best products in industry, art, and science and offer "the achievements of society and trophies of civilization in highly selected, accurately classified, effectively illustrative array." These objects had to be grouped so a visitor could "apply himself directly to [their] examination without having to mentally assemble them, himself, from different parts of the Exposition." And it was here that anthropology was useful, for an exposition's totality was a "record of the social conditions of mankind, registering not only the culture of the world at [the time of the fair], but indicating the particular paths along which different races and peoples may safely proceed, or have begun to advance towards a still higher development."[18]

A New Department of Anthropology

Still no decisions were made. The board was finalizing contracts for the major pavilions and worrying about finding more land. Forest Park only accommodated the Main Picture; there was no room for the Pike, the Philippine Reservation, half of the state pavilions, or an anthropology building. The LPEC leased Washington University's new 110-acre campus and unoccupied buildings, including Cupples Hall, the university stadium, gymnasium, and lecture hall, then land west and north of the park from landowners, bringing the total to over twelve hundred acres.[19]

If Native peoples were to be included, and the idea was still afloat, the department needed more land to build a village near the Philippine Reservation. The land near the university was divided into five narrow strips, owned by different families. Some had readily leased their property, others refused, which led to condemnation proceedings and lengthy court battles, most not settled until December 1902.[20]

Meanwhile, Skiff worked quietly behind the scenes. He asked McGee (but not Holmes) to develop a new plan. Skiff sent it to the executive committee on December 12, 1902. It contained a request to: (a) add two hundred thousand dollars to the Division of Exhibits budget for anthropology; (b) reserve Cupples Hall for exhibits; (c) appoint McGee departmental chief at a salary of five thousand dollars, starting immediately; (d) reserve one hundred thousand dollars for collecting expeditions into remote parts of the world "for the purpose of gathering, transporting, and exhibiting types of living primitive peoples"; (e) include the Indian Service in the department "for the purpose of economy and avoidance of conflict"; and, (f) authorize the distribution of circulars asking for the cooperation of museums and collectors from around the world.[21]

Again the matter was tabled. The trustees took no action except to say that the scope was still too ambitious and expensive. They did not ask Skiff to submit a revised plan that was more fiscally acceptable. But Skiff continued work in the winter and spring. Secretary of the Interior E. A. Hitchcock appointed Indian Service employee Samuel McCowan to organize a model Indian school and obligated forty thousand dollars for its construction and operation. Skiff placed it within the Anthropology Department, with McCowan as assistant director. Since by this time applications to participate in the department were arriving from Mexico, several South American countries, states, universities, and private individuals, Skiff wrote weekly letters asking the board to hire McGee.[22]

In February and March of 1903, the board again tabled the motion. In April, Lehmann informed them he wanted the Department of Anthropology to include history. The board liked the expanded scope but would not approve a budget of one hundred thousand dollars. The company would allocate only sixty thousand dollars for both anthropology and history; the remainder must come from the Indian Service allocation. Again the matter was tabled. What were they waiting for? Apparently it was land. In June of 1903 a final parcel of land was formally leased and the consortium of businessmen who owned it was satisfied with the rental price. The LPE now covered over 1,272 acres, nearly two square miles. There finally was a place for anthropology, at the extreme west end of the grounds (McGee 1905d, 37).

As a result of the delays, it was not until June 1903 that Skiff was authorized to invite McGee to frame yet another departmental plan. The board finally approved McGee's revised plan, and his appointment, on July 14, 1903. Skiff offered him the position the next day. McGee accepted and began officially on

August 31, 1903, the last department head appointed. As he later wrote, the revised plan demanded "a sacrifice in the interests of anthropology . . . [and] he could perhaps save more than any other from the wreck of the original plan."[23] The anthropology displays were now in his hands. It was time to really start planning. McGee had eight months to do a twenty-four-month job.

2. WJ McGee and the Science of Man

William John McGee (fig. 2.1), a practitioner of the new science of anthropology, was also a government bureaucrat, geologist, inventor, agriculturalist, conservationist, policy maker, promoter, and science advocate. He had published more than three hundred articles in several fields by 1903. He liked to do things differently than anyone else. He was known as "no period McGee" because he used "WJ McGee," without the periods following each initial. His over-weaning ambition, desire for personal visibility, and need to popularize and legitimize anthropology as the highest form of enlightened science, has had a lasting effect on how the public viewed Native peoples for years following the LPE and after anthropology had changed its theoretical paradigm.

WJ McGee: Self-Trained Geologist

McGee (1853–1912) was a self-defined Horatio Alger character. His father, James McGee, was an uneducated man of Irish ancestry who worked as a lead miner, and his mother, Martha Anderson, was a teacher from Kentucky. Born in Farley, Iowa, McGee grew up on a small farm, the fourth of nine children. He cultivated a self-made-man image, emphasizing how he overcame adversity and illness in his youth. While his two oldest brothers were able to attend college, he apparently had only five to seven years of irregular rural schooling and tutoring by his mother and oldest brother. McGee liked to claim that he taught himself German, French, Latin, higher mathematics, law, and astronomy, despite limited access to public libraries. He had a remarkable memory and a facility to grasp new knowledge; according to his wife, he read the unabridged Webster's dictionary several times.[1]

McGee learned the rudiments of land surveying from a maternal uncle, worked briefly in a justice court, and dabbled in blacksmithing. In 1874 he invented, patented, and manufactured a number of agricultural implements, building machines in the winter and traveling on foot to sell them during the summer. He recorded archaeological sites and studied local geology as he went, climbing down wells to look for stratigraphic sections.

Fig. 2.1. William J. McGee, 1900, Chair of LPE Department of Anthropology. Photograph by DeLancey Gill. Courtesy of National Anthropological Archives, Smithsonian Institution, negative no. 02861200.

Starting in 1875, McGee spent four years making a geologic and topographic survey in northeastern Iowa. He covered some seventeen thousand square miles, the most extensive area ever surveyed without federal aid. His first published work on glacial geology "was audacious, characterized by a slim foundation of careful, even brilliant observation and a large superstructure of theory. He moved easily from present formations to imaginative reconstruction of earlier processes and structures."[2] These same features were evidenced in McGee's anthropology and were reflected in his activities at the 1904 Exposition.

McGee met John Wesley Powell at the 1878 American Association for the Advancement of Science meeting where he presented his first scientific paper. Powell quickly became the most important individual in McGee's professional life and their careers intertwined. Powell secured a position for him with the Tenth Census (1880) to gather economic geological data and then a position in the U.S. Geological Survey in 1883. He gained a reputation for hard work and administrative acumen and became an advisor to Powell on policy development.[3] By the late 1880s McGee was successful, influential, and self-confident, identified as Powell's protégé. He published scientific treatises on structural and historical geology and water resources, and wrote numerous popular articles on geology, resource conservation, and archaeology in the popular journals. He developed influential political and intellectual contacts, including Lester F. Ward, the founder of American sociology and a proponent of Social Darwinism and unilinear evolution.

In 1888 McGee married Anita Newcomb (1864–1940), the daughter of Simon Newcomb, America's foremost astronomer and a force in Washington's intellectual and social communities, and the wealthy Mary Hassler. The Newcombs saw McGee as an uneducated, unsophisticated bumpkin, lacking the appropriate social ancestry or wealth to fit into elite Washington society. But Anita was strong-willed and saw in McGee a self-made intellectual who had overcome poverty and would achieve notoriety. According to one biographer, she followed "her father's dictum that one decided *first* that a certain person is a desirable mate and falls in love *secondly*."[4] The couple lived in the Newcomb household for fourteen years; Simon Newcomb ignored his son-in-law the entire time. The McGees had a daughter, Klotho, in 1889, a son who died in infancy, and a second son, Eric, in 1902.

Anita was a driving force in McGee's career and helped orchestrate his rise in Washington. She was also a well-known intellectual in her own right. With McGee's encouragement and support she earned an MD from Columbian [George Washington] University's School of Medicine in 1892 and did postgraduate work in gynecology at Johns Hopkins University. She became one of the first women to practice medicine in Virginia and Maryland but soon switched to research and building organizations. She had remarkable skills for working Washington politicians. In 1898 she founded the Army Nursing Corps and trained female nurses to serve in combat areas. She served as acting assistant surgeon general, U.S. Army, during the Spanish-American War. Japan awarded her the Order of the Sacred Crown and two war medals for her efforts during the Russo-Japanese War (1904–5). She was also interested in anthropology and an active member of several professional societies, opening the way for many women in science, medicine, and nursing.[5]

Like his spouse, McGee was extremely active in professional organizations at the national and local levels, using them to move up the ladder of scientific and political structures. By 1903 he had served as the president of the American Anthropological Association (AAA), the Anthropological Society of Washington, and the National Geographic Society, and served as acting president of the American Association for the Advancement of Science and vice president of the Archaeological Institute of America. He was an editor of the *National Geographic Magazine* and for many years chairman of its editorial board. McGee also served as an associate editor of the *American Anthropologist* and editor of the *International Encyclopedia*. He was a founder of the Geological Society of America, the Explorers Club, the Association of American Geographers, the Washington Academy of Sciences, the American Association of Museums, and the Columbia Historical Society.

WJ McGee: Government Anthropologist, 1893–1903

In 1893–94, Powell was forced out as director of the U.S. Geological Survey when his plans for rational settlement and resource use in the West infuriated greedy politicians and mining, timber, and land interests. He retreated to the BAE and brought McGee with him. McGee's official title was ethnologist, on a par with other research scientists, but he soon gave himself the unofficial title of "ethnologist-in-charge," over the objection of Smithsonian officials. As Powell aged and his health declined, McGee took over his administrative duties and unofficially ran the BAE's daily operations. By 1900 he was well-known and respected by many as an able administrator, organizer, and researcher. In an obituary, Frederick Webb Hodge described him as "a man of commanding presence, of remarkable mental vitality, ingenuity, and versatility, and of almost fanatical perseverance. He was the most generous character, sympathetic and helpful, with almost unlimited ambition, and ever ready, whatever the cost, to resent any seeming interference with it." He also vigorously promoted anthropology by "wielding influence less by original contributions than by position" (Hodge 1912, 686; Hinsley 1981, 232).

If McGee was respected for his organizational abilities, colleagues were skeptical about his skills as an ethnological fieldworker or theoretician. His anthropological research was designed to "prove" his and Powell's ideas about the development of human institutions rather than a quest to record or understand distinctive cultures. He strove to find cultures uncontaminated by outside influences, hence "primitive" in the sense of "original," and he yearned for a heroic adventure similar to Powell's on the Colorado River in 1869–72. His actual ethnographic research was almost nonexistent. The best that can be said of it is that he recorded topographic and botanical features well and that his forte was desert ecology, especially soil and water conditions.

His most noteworthy "research" expeditions consisted of three brief trips to the Tohono O'odhams, Pima Bajos, Yaquis, Cocopas, and Seris of Sonora, Mexico, in 1894, 1895, and 1900. On these trips he spent about sixteen hours talking to and observing sixty malnourished Seris who were being incarcerated by Pascual Encinas (a Mexican landowner who had driven the Seris from their homeland and killed about half the population) and interviewing Fernando Kolusio, an old man who had lived for decades with Encinas and no longer knew his native language. On the basis of this highly questionable information about Seri culture, McGee produced a massive three-hundred-page ethnography. It was a work designed to show him as a heroic figure who overcame extraordinary dangers (including those of his own making) in the name of scientific advancement. In the book, McGee used his imaginative powers of generalization and preconceived expectations to portray the Seris as the quintessential "savages" of North America. They became the bottom rung on the human evolutionary ladder, living an "animalistic" existence, which supported Powell's theory.[6]

McGee used his Seri and Tohono O'odham material as an exhibit at the 1895 Atlanta Exposition, and his Cocopa material at the Buffalo Pan-American Exposition in 1901. He also incorporated his Cocopa data into publications, swathing them in unilineal evolutionism. In "The Beginning of Agriculture," "The Beginning of Zooculture," and "The Trend of Human Progress" he outlined a theory of domestication. These papers were important steps in the development of the evolutionary theory that he brought to fruition at the St. Louis Exposition.[7]

Fight for Control of the Bureau of American Ethnology

In his insightful history of Smithsonian anthropology, Curtis Hinsley argues that McGee's driving ambition, dedication, loyalty, independence, bureaucratic skills, and political malleability served him well in his rapid rise in government service. But these personality traits also proved to be his undoing. The end came in 1903, the result of a battle to control anthropology in the BAE and the Smithsonian Institution, in the Washington DC scientific community, and on a national level.

The stage had been set for the drama years earlier in skirmishes for institutional and intellectual control of the new field. Lines were drawn among individuals who wanted to hold center place as intellectual visionaries and power brokers. This included disagreements as to whether professional associations should be exclusive, for experts only, or inclusive, open to all interested parties; McGee favored the latter. He was very active in the Anthropological Society of Washington (ASW), where research and national policy were debated. When the ASW fell into financial disarray in 1898, McGee and Franz Boas personally took over joint ownership of the society's journal, the *American Anthropologist*. They kept it going until they could organize a new professional organization, the American Anthropological Association, and transfer the journal. In March 1902, McGee, along with Stewart Culin, George A. Dorsey, Jesse Walter Fewkes, and Joseph D. McGuire incorporated the AAA. McGee was named president; Boas, Powell, Holmes, and Putnam became vice presidents. McGee's vision of the association and its inclusive and national orientation prevailed. He was at the height of his anthropological prestige and power.

But the ground began to shift later in the year. Powell died on September 23, 1902. McGee assumed he would be named BAE director; he deserved this honor since he was Powell's protégé, still followed his mentor's intellectual lead, had run the agency for years, and could provide continuity for basic research. McGee believed he had the national scientific stature to ensure the appointment, that his candidacy was unassailable. In expectation of a salary increase, he bought a house in late 1901. He also announced plans to transform the BAE into an activist and reform-minded agency that dealt with environmental issues as well as Indian affairs, topics on which he had extremely advanced views. He assumed that he would continue the BAE's independence from Smithsonian control over appropriations, research priorities, and staffing that Powell had enjoyed.[8]

McGee's position was actually far from secure. While he was by all accounts hard working and determined, he was also intemperate, haughty, pompous, and socially insecure. Constantly striving for social and scientific recogni-

Fig. 2.2. William Henry Holmes, ca. 1920, Curator of the Department of Anthropology, United States National Museum. Courtesy of National Anthropological Archives, Smithsonian Institution, negative no. BAE-45-A2.

tion, he took arguments personally, was occasionally arrogant and manipulative, and shouted people down. Over the years he made as many enemies as friends. One of his key personal and professional enemies was Samuel Langley, secretary of the Smithsonian Institution. According to historian Whitney Cross, Langley was a highly educated, orthodox, upper-class Easterner and a respected astronomer, consummate bureaucrat, and administrator, who is remembered best for his experiments in powered flight.[9] He had been Anita Newcomb's suitor whom she rejected in favor of McGee; Langley never married and had few family ties. The authority to appoint Powell's successor rested with him. He had opposed McGee's initial appointment in 1893, feeling he was unqualified and a poor administrator who had tried to undermine his authority; by 1902 he had not changed his mind. Nor had he changed his mind that the BAE, as an agency which provided information on Indians to Congress, should devote its activities to popularizing anthropology and producing useful products, such as an encyclopedia of American Indians, not conducting basic ethnographic or archaeological research. He intended to fold it into the U.S. National Museum's Department of Anthropology to ensure that the type of scientific research demanded by Congress was done. In February 1902, Langley asked Holmes (fig. 2.2) to take over after Powell retired, but Holmes initially declined stating that he would not hurt his friend McGee, Powell's chosen successor.[10]

Langley disapproved of McGee's scholarship, considering him undisciplined, uneducated, and unscientific, and found his theoretical and scientific papers questionable, inappropriate, and politically suspect. In 1894, McGee and sociologist Lester Ward had published papers in the *Smithsonian Annual Report* that offended Langley. McGee's paper, "The Earth, the Home of Man," had been a lecture outlining his ideological beliefs about nature and the environment, his interpretation of what constituted life and how it began, and his holistic vision of human beings as part of the natural world. McGee also included his views on how humans differed in intelligence and sensitivity from other life forms through their control of fire and technology. Adaptation and resource manipulation, he argued, were key principles of evolutionary progress. The paper ended with a call for human stewardship of the world and its natural resources, because McGee envisioned a future in which humans would control bacteria, dam rivers and lakes, and transform minerals into new substances (McGee 1894a, 1894b).

Calling it "atheistic and radical," Langley had the entire annual report recalled and reprinted without the controversial paper.[11] This became an expensive symbol of the independence that the BAE enjoyed and Langley's inability to gain oversight over its activities. McGee became the scapegoat of his resentment. As Powell's health failed, and as he became a target, McGee began to try to shore up his position.

McGee wrote to Langley on September 27, 1902, four days after Powell's death, requesting he be appointed director. Langley did not respond. Instead, on October 10, he asked Holmes to take the post. Holmes discussed the matter with McGee. Langley asked again on October 11 and Holmes, after much persuasion, accepted. Langley officially appointed him chief ethnologist on October 15, 1902, after he made it clear that it was Holmes or an outsider who would run the bureau, not McGee. Holmes, from all accounts, reluctantly took the job only after McGee gave his acquiescence, but retained his position with the U.S. National Museum. McGee was told that he could remain in the BAE as an ethnologist and pursue his scientific investigations but could no longer use the title ethnologist-in-charge.

Langley knew in appointing Holmes that he had made a public enemy of McGee but he seriously miscalculated the extent of the latter's bitterness. McGee immediately began a publicity campaign to oust Holmes. He informed the *Washington Times* that Holmes's appointment had been made behind his back. He or a friend arranged for the *Pittsburgh Press* to announce that he would become head of the bureau, hoping that a *fait accompli* and political pressure would influence Langley; the article called McGee versatile and a good administrator. Carried in other papers, it ended, "It is believed here that those who have the naming of Prof. Powell's successor as the head of the department will make no mistake if Prof. McGee is so named."[12]

Acrimonious public debate over the directorship escalated. McGee mounted a general attack in the scientific community, informing all who would listen that Langley was out to destroy anthropology as an independent science. McGee tried political pressure as well. He wrote to the Speaker of the House, David Henderson, complaining about Langley, accusing him of disloyalty to Powell and of intentionally stifling the BAE's natural growth. Now with Powell gone, "Secretary Langley desires to either abolish the Bureau or reduce it to the grade of a Division of the National Museum."[13] When the letter became public, Langley was furious. McGee's days in the BAE were numbered.

Franz Boas, McGee's friend, wanted the BAE to remain a research institution and not be turned into another Smithsonian exhibition unit. He made matters worse by publishing a letter in *Science* that generated great debate. Boas focused on the U.S. National Museum and its lethargic status under Langley's leadership, his disregard for basic research, underemployment of scientists, and obsession with world's fairs that "make it impossible for the museum to make adequate use of its magnificent collections, and to contribute its share to the advancement of science and education."[14]

Boas, a frequent BAE collaborator, owed much to McGee, who had found ways to pay for his research manuscripts over the years and had financially supported him in 1894 when he was unemployed, after Holmes was given a Field Museum curatorship Boas had badly wanted. Now he began a letter-writing campaign to ensure that Holmes, whom he sarcastically derided as a "museum man," would not be given another professional prize. He felt that Holmes was too pliable and would not fight for the discipline's independence. Only McGee, who valued autonomy, would fight to keep the BAE's purpose solely anthropological research.

McGee's other friends, including Alexander Graham Bell, joined the letter-writing campaign to muster the scientific community's support, but they were not successful. Scholars wrote to Langley and Smithsonian regents complaining about the arm twisting. Geologist J. C. Barnes, vice president of Stanford University, wrote that McGee had only been successful "by a skillful process of leg-pulling." Conversely he found Holmes "pleasant, a gentleman and a good scholar who does not stoop to tricks to gain personal popularity."[15]

After Holmes took over, McGee avoided the BAE offices. He searched for archaeological ruins in Minnesota and Nova Scotia and visited sites in New Mexico. In December 1902 he traveled to Mexico to search for the elusive Seris, but the trip yielded only typhoid fever. For the first third of 1903 McGee was ill, rarely visiting the BAE offices. As a result he refused to work on the *Handbook of North American Indians*, as Langley had directed. Instead he pursued his professional duties and tried to organize an International Commission on Archaeology (Holmes 1907b, xi–xii).

To precipitate a showdown, Langley used a minor scandal to attack McGee and render him politically ineffective. In February 1902, McGee had hired Frank Barnett, formerly an auditor for the Post Office and the Bureau of Labor, as a BAE clerk. On May 9, 1903, Barnett was arrested for embezzlement and forging the signatures of several BAE employees, transferring their paychecks to bogus accounts, and fabricating bills for nonexistent services. He had withheld the paychecks of field researchers, including Matilda Coxe Stevenson, Albert Jenks, Frank Russell, James Mooney, and Jesse Walter Fewkes, used the monies for his own purposes, and then doctored the books.

Responding to congressional pressure, Langley began an internal investigation of BAE accounting practices that eventually went to a federal grand jury.

The committee expanded its inquiries beyond Barnett's embezzlement and accounting irregularities; the resulting 1,021 pages of testimony concentrated on McGee, looking for any administrative irregularities in the preceding ten years. Questionable activities were uncovered: a manuscript paid for but never received and another check forgery. All facets of McGee's professional life came under scrutiny, especially his support of the *American Anthropologist* and Boas, and writing articles for public magazines on government time. The committee concluded that McGee had maintained minimal financial oversight and used funds in ways not approved by Smithsonian administrators. In short, he was a poor administrator who would, if named director, misspend public monies. The investigation consumed the BAE, and Boas labeled it a witch hunt. Misunderstandings, old wounds, and past insults were aired. McGee claimed that his bouts of typhoid fever kept him in bed on the days Barnett committed his forgeries and swore, "My first duty, a self-imposed duty, was to take care of Major Powell to the end of his life. After that I performed administrative and scientific work."[16]

By June, McGee had had enough. Finding the situation intolerable, he asked Holmes for a three-month unpaid leave "to carry forward ethnologic work freely, [and] to relieve the appropriation for ethnological research." Holmes refused; McGee must stay to answer the investigating committee and grand jury's questions. He directed McGee to work in the office and write fieldwork reports, but it is doubtful that he had anything to write. On July 22, McGee requested another unpaid detail, this time to oversee the initial development of the LPEC's Department of Anthropology. He pointed out that this would be an honor for the BAE as well as himself because "the position offered is one of great importance to American anthropology and ethnology."[17]

Under orders from Langley, Holmes refused this request. Assistant Secretary Richard Rathbun told McGee that Langley had instructed Holmes to approve no absences or allow any fieldwork away from the city until the investigation was complete. This meant that every BAE anthropologist was in town and there were not enough desks on which people could work. McGee, considered essential to the investigation, was ordered to stay in town.

McGee felt he had little choice but to resign, when the investigative committee finally adjourned on July 31, 1903. At 4:30 p.m. he handed his resignation to Holmes; he would take the St. Louis position. It was "the sole means left me for engaging in important work."[18] Holmes took McGee's letter to Rathbun who accepted it the following day. His position was abolished; the investigation ceased and the charges were immediately dropped.

Despite his Washington travails, McGee was nationally renowned in 1903. He had been awarded an honorary doctorate (LLD) by Grinnell College, Iowa, in 1901, and thereafter referred to himself as "Dr. McGee." But it was a tenuous grasp at prestige. McGee's personal life also began to fall apart. Anita blamed him for the scandal, which had shamed her, and for not living up to her expectations. They were unofficially separated and never lived together again. After selling the house, she immersed herself in her work; McGee was alone. He left Washington in ill health, tired, distressed about his marriage, and worried about his children, but with plans for a spectacular comeback.[19]

Serving as anthropological director of the Louisiana Purchase Exposition gave McGee an opportunity to salvage his reputation as well as his financial problems. Throughout the turmoil of the investigation, he had informally corresponded with Skiff, Francis, and Lehmann between bouts with typhoid fever, never informing Holmes when he revised their plan. He needed this high-profile job to eliminate the aura of disgrace, far removed from Washington, the Smithsonian, and the scandal.

While McGee used his new position as his public reason for leaving the BAE, few people were fooled by this rationalization. Many knew he had been banished from the nation's capital, his career in anthropology severely compromised. Even in St. Louis, the *St. Louis Globe-Democrat* reported: "It is well known here that there has been much friction in the bureau, and the professor would in all probability have resigned had he nothing else in view . . . the professor felt keenly the slight put upon him by putting another man in charge."[20]

Ever the optimist, McGee saw the LPE as a golden opportunity to move his political agenda forward. The LPEC's desire to make the exposition a university provided an opportunity to demonstrate how important research could be conducted at expositions, not just in "real" universities. This harkened back to his fight for vocational membership in the AAA and reflected the fights that Washington-based anthropologists, none of whom were academically trained, were having with practitioners from Eastern universities. The German university model, focused on graduate and professional training leading to doctorates of philosophy (Ph.D.) or of science (D.Sc.), was gaining ascendancy in

American universities by 1900 (Stocking 1974b). The theoretical stance of the university-based anthropologists, led by Boas, was very different than that held by Powell, McGee, or Holmes. This difference would be reflected in papers given by McGee and Boas at the anthropological congress held during the exposition.

McGee began to plan his exhibits on a grand scale that reflected his conceptualization of the Science of Man. They would clearly demonstrate anthropology's value to society and how social action could be guided. The LPE, the "University of the Future," would permit McGee, as an anthropologist and science advocate, to diffuse his theories to intelligent lay people in a sophisticated manner. They would salvage his reputation within anthropology and the larger world of science.

McGee's Vision of Anthropology and Race

McGee considered himself an abstract theoretician. He valued the Big Picture over disciplinary specialization or the collection and critical analysis of empirical detail. His approach has been charitably described as "a strongly speculative technique, bold in search of unifying hypotheses, but sometimes slender in supporting data." One contemporary said of McGee's work that he was a highly original and occasionally brilliant thinker, but his fieldwork showed "a clear lack of detailed and critical inquiry which is so essential in the formulation of hypotheses and in the rigid testing of them step by step" (Cross 1953, 153; Keyes 1913, 187). This deficiency would be quite apparent in St. Louis.

The early twentieth century has aptly been called by Marvin Harris an age "in which the license to generalize on the basis of fragmentary evidence was claimed by second- and third-rate people." Anthropological theory was dominated by the grandiose stage schemes of Herbert Spencer and Lewis Henry Morgan and their sycophants John Wesley Powell and Lester Ward. McGee selectively added ideas about biological evolution from Darwin, Huxley, and Haeckel, mixing social and biological evolutionary concepts with his own preconceptions about races and their "places" in the world. The result was a "naive stage-scheme replete with jingoistic Spencerian celebrations of America's evolutionary success," a scheme verging on the absurd (Harris 1968, 254).

McGee's version of science would be the central theme for the entire exposition, seen by millions of people and carried away in the form of racial stereotypes. His ideas about biological development, racial vigor, and cultural progress were in accord with many of the biases and prejudices of the exposition organizers and many other white Americans of the day. His vision became, in effect, the fair's underlying organizational scheme. This monistic paradigm with its convoluted terminology did not become part of the established canon of anthropology, nor is McGee's work often discussed in the history of anthropology literature.

McGee wrote in rhetorical flourishes. Like his idol Powell, he was fond of coining new terms, since new ideas warranted them. A century later, McGee's terminology seems strange, his logic faulty, his assumptions prejudiced, and his conclusions overgeneralized. Most of his anthropological peers considered his ideas unique, erroneous, and unusable. Boas, for example, noted at McGee's memorial service, that while his friend searched for meaningful social relationships among isolated facts he did not have the training or the tools to adequately establish them. Later critics have been less kind. According to Marvin Harris, "McGee was an inexhaustible mine of every error of substance and theory that it was possible to commit on the basis of the most vulgar prejudices masquerading as scientific expertise."[21]

To McGee, anthropology was the encompassing Science of Man; its data covered all aspects of humankind in all parts of the globe, because anthropologists saw "mankind as an assemblage of varieties or races, and as social creatures united by language and law and organized in families, communities, societies, commonwealths, and nations" (McGee 1905d, 2, 4–5). He divided anthropology into subfields, each centered on a class of human attributes: (1) andrology studied man as an organism (anthropometry, medicine, anatomy, and physiology); (2) psychology viewed man as an organism dominated by mental power housed in the psyche and seen in body movements and actions (psychometry); (3) demology investigated human activities of man as a producer or creator and the social products of human activities (sociology, art, technology, law, linguistics, and philosophy); and, (4) ethnology considered humanity as an assemblage of races, centered on the identification of humanity's "natural groups," by comparing physical, mental or activity features. When anthropologists investigated past human groups and cultures, they used (1) archaeology, "the science of human relics"; (2) human paleontology, the study of fossils and skeletal remains; (3) paleography, the study of ancient writings; and (4) history.

The ultimate goal of McGee's anthropology was to trace the course of human progress and classify peoples in terms of that progress to illuminate the origin and destiny of man. This endeavor was undertaken to guide future progress. Anthropology was thus a moral undertaking as well as a scientific enterprise, which McGee would visualize through his activities in St. Louis.

This included producing new knowledge. McGee sought to generate definitive anthropological knowledge through comparisons of living peoples who were "living fossils" and analogs for peoples in the evolutionary past. The course of human physical and cultural development could be explicated by the systematic rank ordering of "race-types" in a grand scheme of "human phylogeny" or "androgeny" that generated a scale of relative human physical and cultural "vigor, measured by complexity of blood no less than by extent of knowledge or culture" (McGee 1901a).

This "blood mixing" was thought by some to result in a hybrid vigor, which in turn allowed some "races" to advance up the scale of human physical and sociocultural development. This argument was the central thesis of Josiah Nott and George Gliddon's infamous polygenetic racialist treatise of 1854, *Types of Mankind*, and reflected long-standing ideas in both America and Europe. McGee thought that cultural advancement occurred through mixing, cultural contact, and borrowing. Anthropology's great contribution was its demonstration that a leading factor in human development was progressive acculturation, leading to the unification of knowledge. At first slow, inimical, and effected chiefly through strife and conquest, acculturation in the higher stages is rapid and amicable—schools replace armies, confederations supplant conquest, and Kipling's White Man's Burden becomes the strong man's burden in the political family of nations.[22]

McGee's scheme of human sociocultural development was essentialist. Development was progressive, cumulative, and directional, reaching an apogee in early-twentieth-century white American, middle-class culture. That culture was superior in every way: more intelligent, better adapted, better intentioned, and still developing, headed toward the next stage of mankind's glorious future, driven by purposeful—and inevitable—forces. "Just as patriarchy gives way to hierarchy, and hierarchy to absolute monarchy, so limited monarchy is giving way to democracy or republicanism. . . . So according to the experience of the ages, the best nation is a republican one, and the best citizen is the individual adapted to life under republican conditions" (McGee 1905d, 9). McGee's aim at the LPE was to demonstrate this basic principle so that both white American visitors and Native participants would understand and accept it as the truth.

Demonstrating this required arranging societies sequentially. McGee used an "ethnic" classification in which people were divided into "natural groups," which he called "races," defined chiefly by physical characteristics and correlated with geographical areas of the world: white (Caucasian), red (American Indian), yellow (Mongolian), brown (Malayan), and black (African). He assumed that races were the result of hereditary and environmental influences. But there were anomalies, people who were not yellow or brown, red or black, white or brown (Ainus, Australian "blackfellows," Lapps, Tartars, Patagonians, and Eskimos). These "ethnological puzzles" fascinated McGee and he hoped to bring them to St. Louis.

McGee's races and "ethnological puzzles" were ranked in a "culture-grade" scheme, with each stage expressing characteristic arts, industries, laws, languages, thought patterns, social relations, and philosophies. This was a variation on similar schemes proposed by nineteenth-century developmentalists, such as Lewis Henry Morgan and Powell. Stage 1 was the lowest (that is, closest to animals), and Stage 4, the highest, reflecting advances in "mentality, knowledge, and cerebral capacity, and measurably (with few apparent exceptions) in accordance with general physical development, including strength, endurance, and viability." McGee ranked living tribes, nations, and races on their supposed degree of advancement in activities. Which activities he emphasized in each case reflected his determination to fit individual groups into his predetermined, universal model. In general his placement was color-coded. The darker a specific group, the lower the stage number he assigned to it. Finally McGee produced a cross-cutting Cultural Product Classification matrix with seventy-two cells, many defined by neologisms. He held that his classification was valid for all times and places.[23]

According to McGee's scheme, the highest form of development was the government of the United States, with its rigorous laws and principles formalized in a constitution. McGee called this stage "enlightened civilization." Having achieved this stage, in the new century America would continue to be a nation of strength whose people would achieve a "more and more complete conquest over lower nature" (McGee 1904a, 1894a, 1897b, 1899). This would result in maturation into Stage 5, the Age of Power, the marker of humanity's future, leading the world. It would be seen in St. Louis in the magnificent pavilions. And McGee would provide the context to understand their import.

3. Planning the Anthropology Department and Model Indian School

We will have the world's first assemblage of the world's peoples.
WJ McGee

According to McGee, the purpose of the Department of Anthropology was educational, "to diffuse and incidentally to increase knowledge of Man and his Works" (McGee 1905d, 1). The department would summarize and visualize what was known about humanity, using his evolutionary model as a template to demonstrate human progress. He would organize the exhibits, decide on Native groups, determine physical anthropology experiments, and organize special activities to prove his theories.

McGee wanted to demonstrate that evolutionary anthropology was a useful science that brought order to "the apparent chaos of uncounted thousands of the world's tribes, speaking unreckoned hundreds of tongues and pursuing innumerable vocations." It would show how humanity had passed from the primal to its highest state by displaying Native peoples who would symbolize evolutionary culture grades and race types. But McGee knew there was a risk to this approach. Native peoples were generally stereotyped as exotic oddities that were not quite human. He wanted to combat this attitude while providing the public what they wanted to see. He would develop living exhibits "not so much to gratify untrained curiosity . . . [but] to satisfy the intelligent observer."[1] The anthropology exhibits could *not* degenerate into mere exotic attractions. But would there be enough money?

A Research Plan

McGee claimed that anthropology differed from other LPEC departments because he would include professional research comparable to that done in universities. He intended to combine "the vigorous vitality symbolized by the Universal exposition," with "the virile subject of human progress." Native participants would represent the most striking "Stone Age peoples" not yet studied. The LPE would be the site of in-depth, theoretically cutting-edge inquiry. Evolutionary studies since the 1870s, he believed, had been "the virgin soil whence the richest fruits of each passing decade are gathered." Since anthropology had yet to fulfill its theoretical potential, the LPE would provide "the world's finest opportunity for framing the science and setting it on a firm basis."[2] While McGee agreed to include static museum exhibits, the department's real focus would be the global village of living evolutionary types.

Since he did not have the funds to represent all racial categories, McGee looked for groups Americans had never seen to provide novel interactions. But it was physical type and placement on his evolutionary scale that defined his quest for specific non-American indigenous groups. He sought Australian Aboriginals because they were small, "prognathous, and long-armed and hence strikingly apelike"; the Ainu because the men showed tree-climbing ancestry through "their small stature, their centripetal (or bodyward) movements, their use of the feet as manual adjuncts, and their facility in climbing"; and, the "bony, carnivorous and athletic" Patagonians for their heroic stature (McGee 1904a, 5, 19, 20; 1898b, 161). He planned to use American Indians to illustrate variation, emphasizing height and agility. The Dakotas exemplified tallness, powerful build, and agility, the Pueblos short stature, and the Cocopas an anomaly: extremely tall men and short women.

McGee next considered a group's culture. Natives would serve as analogs for critical moments in the development of humanity (fig. 3.1), emphasized in the static archaeological exhibits: the conquest of fire, the genesis of the knife, and the development of the wheel. He considered Australian Aboriginals critical as they represented people who "lack knife-sense and only use fire ceremoniously." (Both assertions were nonsense, of course.) McGee wanted Seris, because they were uncontaminated "true savages" just entering the Stone Age. He described them in animalistic and exotic terms, in a St. Louis newspaper, as "reputed cannibals, of gigantic stature, and so swift of foot as to capture deer by the hands alone." Because of their isolation in an extremely harsh environment, they were sullen, combative, apathetic, preoccupied with animals and had an inbred "race-sense."[3] McGee wanted indigenous groups to consist of families, who would pursue ordinary activities in appropriate habitations and use materials from their homelands.

Fig. 3.1. "The Missing Link." Repino, a forty-two-year-old Negrito participant from Bataan, in the Philippine Reservation. Photograph by the Gerhard sisters. Library of Congress, Prints and Photographs Division, CPH3627310, LC-USZ62–80323.

Minimally McGee wanted six race-physical types in addition to people from North America: (1) African Pygmies, (2) a tribe of larger Africans, (3) Patagonians, (4) Seris from northern Mexico, (5) Eskimos, and (6) any others who could be convinced, the more exotic, the better. Since it was impossible to include peoples from all continents, McGee was prepared to exclude Australians and Asians. By September he had three categories, based on transportation and maintenance costs: Group A were to be foreign aboriginals obtained and maintained (including wages) using LPEC funds; Group B consisted of American Indians, whose traveling expenses and maintenance would be paid by the

LPEC, but who were expected to produce and sell crafts in lieu of wages; Group C included American Indian celebrities (Geronimo, Chief Joseph, Quanah Parker) and their families, who would pay their own transportation costs but whose subsistence and wages would be provided by the LPEC.[4]

McGee was not particularly worried about American Indian participation because he assumed transportation costs would come from the Department of the Interior's appropriation for the Indian School that Samuel McCowan was organizing. He rationalized that the school would be the culmination of a visitor's journey through the primitive world. While he thought Indians were important components of his cultural scheme, the major selection criteria were houses and artifacts. Cheyennes had tipis, shields, and insignia that reflected their social organization. Basket makers, weavers, potters, carvers, and stone workers were needed so visitors would understand the archaeological exhibits, eliminating the need for extensive label copy. Hopefully, some groups would agree to demonstrate tribal ceremonies, especially those developed before contact. By seeing these activities, "visitors will find an index to the inner life of the Red Race who is passing from the opening epic of American history."[5]

McGee envisioned fairgoers experiencing a journey similar to Gulliver's travels as they strolled through the living villages. By viewing the Tehuelches, people would meet Swift's Brobdingnagians, by interacting with Pygmies, Lilliputians. Like Gulliver, they would return to civilization, appreciating its strengths as they strolled through the industry or electricity buildings. Fairgoers would see that Americans were "perfected men" whose ideas would help humanity rise above evolutionary laws. During their journey, McGee would illustrate "such native lore and legend as those embalmed in Hiawatha" (McGee 1905d, 22). Assuming literate viewers, he used these allusions throughout the exhibits to draw visitors from familiar images to the unfamiliar world of anthropology and its "more informed" representations.

McGee estimated that this scaled-down plan would require at least one hundred and twenty-five thousand dollars (wages for an assistant to oversee the Indian compounds, clerical assistance, installers, and agents to negotiate with foreign Native groups) excluding the static exhibits. He expected funds would come from the LPEC, the federal government, and other as yet unidentified sources. He assumed the LPEC would find additional money as the fair drew nearer and he would gain the cooperation of museums, universities, and other

LPE departments to extend his budget. In July a new anthropology committee unanimously agreed to recommend that the LPEC implement McGee's revised plan as an ethnology exhibit comprised of both foreign Natives and American Indians, provide paths, lavatories, and bathing facilities near the exhibit building and create a lake by draining the lawn area adjacent to the proposed compounds. Finally they recommended McGee be given a "reasonable" part of the twenty-five-thousand-dollar Congressional appropriation to exhibit Indian tribes. On July 14, 1903, the LPEC Executive Committee approved the scaled-down plan, but allocated only fifty thousand dollars for everything.[6]

Since he could not execute his plan for less than one hundred thousand dollars, McGee tried again. He argued that fifty thousand would only cover the travel, administration, and "installation" of the "foreign aliens." His new estimate, $62,167, excluding a twelve-thousand-dollar federal appropriation for American Indians, was still above the approved fifty thousand dollars. Skiff sent the request to the LPEC Board, who decided to let Francis deal with McGee. Francis passed it to his treasurer who decided it was still too high. McGee still had only fifty thousand dollars.

The tenacious McGee was not ready to give up. He made repeated forays to increase his allotment during the fall. One ploy was to state that he would not underwrite Native peoples from the Louisiana Purchase area, which displeased Skiff and Lehmann since they wanted to showcase them. McGee responded to their objections by suggesting he could use more Native Americans to replace a "required" foreign family.[7] He could enlarge the living villages without cost, if they would convince the Indian Service to contribute. He argued that Indians were less interesting educationally and scientifically than foreign indigenous groups. Again the LPEC refused. There was still not enough money for his plans.

McGee next tried public pressure. He gave speeches and news "leaks" designed to generate public expectations to bring pressure on the LPEC to provide additional funds. On October 7, the St. Louis Globe-Democrat reported that the "giant Patagonians" were preparing to leave for St. Louis and that McGee had received an acceptance to his invitation from "Chief Mullato." In fact, McGee had only begun to arrange an expedition to persuade a family to make the journey. McGee also provided names of Indian groups: Apaches, Nez Perces, Washos, Shoshones, Navajos, Mission, Diggers, Crows, Flatheads, Pimas, Chippewas, Cheyennes, Arapahos, Comanches, Wichitas, Osages, Tlingits, and Pawnees.

Each would "live exactly as they would were they at home on their reservation instead of being the center of the greatest exposition every held."[8]

In his attempt to generate interest, McGee stressed the unique and exotic while rewriting history and concocting ethnographic customs. The Hopi "will maintain their ancient tribal customs and their pure Indian maize that filled Columbus with delight when he first made its acquaintance." Much was pure blather and wishful thinking. He even promised that visitors would see a "remnant" European tribe—the Vlacks from Thessaly, descendants of warlike Romans who "in spite of years of oppression," had never mixed with Greeks or Turks. "They live in tents and are followed by flocks of sheep and herds of goats." McGee told reporters he would secure pure Greeks of "classic days" who "have the head and profile of the *Hermes* of Praxiteles, large, blue-gray eyes, golden hair, and are giants in stature." Adventure would be involved in locating these people because they were found only on remote Aegean islands.[9] Late in October McGee traveled to New York City and spoke at the Explorer's Club, trying yet another tactic. The *New York Times* reported he was the victim of penny-pinching simpletons. "The original intention was to have the whole exposition grouped around anthropology in a manner which would make it the greatest exhibition of its kind ever attempted. But the appropriation was cut enormously and the space allotment reduced by 20 per cent, so that Mr. McGee is now at work 'trying to save something out of the wreck,' as he expressed the case."[10] LPEC officials were not happy with such statements, but McGee continued. It seems that he had not learned diplomacy from his previous experiences.

In fact, little deterred McGee. When the American Association for the Advancement of Science held its meetings in St. Louis, McGee asked members to contact their congressmen and senators to bring political pressure on the Department of the Interior to increase his exposition budget. Apparently no one took him up on his request (Pepper 1904). The Indian Service seemed like his only hope, but they were proceeding on their own.

The Indian School and Samuel McCowan

The Indian Service had presented exhibits at earlier expositions. The model Indian School at Chicago had originally included an Indian encampment designed as a foil to the Indians portrayed in the classrooms. But the encampment had been moved away from the school, so the contrastive effect was muted.

Fig. 3.2. Samuel M. McCowan, Superintendent of the Indian School. LPEC publicity photograph originally published in *History of the Louisiana Purchase Exposition*, ed. Mark Bennitt (St. Louis: Universal Exposition Publishing, 1905), 673. Courtesy of the Research Division of the Oklahoma Historical Society, image no. 20425.04.093.

What visitors saw were students who represented "the accomplishments in the arts of civilization and the methods adopted in the management of Indian schools." Tens of thousands passed through the Indian School weekly but most commented only on the stunning Navajo blankets, Pueblo pottery, and Hopi baskets exhibited therein. It was decided that not enough attention had been given to the educational program. St. Louis would be better.[11]

In 1902 Congress appropriated forty thousand dollars for an Indian school and exhibits dealing with the Louisiana Purchase. Interior Secretary E. A. Hitchcock and Indian Service Commissioner W. A. Jones rejected the LPEC's request to recreate Omaha's Congress of Indians as a "detriment to the individual Indians who take part in them." They decided to construct a model Indian School where students would contrast with traditional Indians who would be self-supporting, producing authentic and commercially viable art. The exhibit would highlight federal efforts to solve the "Indian problem." Older Indians would be "self-evident problems," the school children would be the "solution." The Indian Service's appropriation would construct the school building and pay for the expenses of Indian students, selected traditional demonstrators, and Indian Service personnel. Management was given to Samuel M. McCowan (fig. 3.2), superintendent of the Industrial and Agricultural School at Chilocco, Oklahoma. McCowan was at work on preliminary plans long before McGee approached him.[12]

McCowan was born in 1863 in Elmwood, Illinois, and attended Grinnell College and Northern Indiana Normal College. He taught school, worked as a newspaper reporter, and read law in Indiana. He joined the Indian Service in 1889 as superintendent of the Rosebud Reservation day school, later serving at Fort Mohave, Albuquerque, and Phoenix before moving to Chilocco in 1902. He believed in the inevitability of assimilation. Disliking traditional life styles, he felt that superstition and the downgrading of women dominated historic Indian cultures. He was one of the Indian Service's highest-ranking educators with previous exposition experience. While Phoenix Indian School superintendent in 1898, he had administered the Indian encampment at the Omaha Exposition. He brought Arizona Indians, mostly older school children, to demonstrate Native arts, as well as the Phoenix Indian School Band. His goal at both Omaha and St. Louis was to contrast "undeveloped" with "educated" Indians.[13]

McCowan began planning the Indian School in late 1902, asking agency personnel to identify model students, collect typical art, provide photographs of student activities, and find appropriate traditional artists.[14] Unbeknownst to him, McGee was contacting Indian Service officials, working his Washington network. McGee hoped to influence which Indian groups the Indian Service approved, requesting those who fit his evolutionary matrix, which meant few

Fig. 3.3. George A. Dorsey, Curator of Anthropology, Field Columbian Museum, with Colojo, Tehuelche participant. Photograph by Charles Carpenter, June 1904. © The Field Museum, negative no. CSA13257.

from the Louisiana Purchase area. There was little overlap with McCowan's initial recommendations of people with artistic skills who would interest visitors: Sioux pipestone carvers, Navajo weavers, and Washo basket makers. To circumvent McCowan, McGee tried to have anthropologist George Dorsey (fig. 3.3) placed in charge of all Indian demonstrators.

Skiff and Commissioner Jones negotiated. The Department of the Interior contribution was increased to sixty-five thousand dollars. McCowan, as official Indian Service representative, would be in charge of *all* American Indian exhibitors, with the title of assistant chief of the Anthropology Department. He and Jones would have final choice of Indian groups who would demonstrate in the Indian School. The honorary designation meant that while McCowan's salary would not come from LPEC funds, he would nominally report to McGee but it was clear that McGee should leave him alone. The loss of control was acceptable to McGee only because it extended his budget and ensured that more foreign groups could be included. McCowan still wanted to keep the Indian School separate, but Jones convinced him to work with McGee. Interior Secretary Hitchcock instructed McCowan to find American Indian demonstrators that were acceptable to McGee, secure permission from agency personnel for their travel, and see to their proper care in St. Louis.[15]

Even though McCowan was leery of McGee—and he remained so throughout their association—the two men worked fairly well together. The first thing they did was decide on exhibit locations, a difficult undertaking since most exhibit sites had been allocated and no department was willing to relinquish space. They needed two buildings and a large outdoor area for the indigenous people's village. McCowan and McGee walked the grounds and chose a tract of land between the Horticultural Pavilion and the intramural railroad for the Indian School with campgrounds extending southward to Arrowhead Lake, a total of almost thirteen acres. Their plan was approved on October 3.

Fiscal, Climatic, and Political Realities: Reducing the Scope of Anthropology

McGee kept dreaming that his grandiose scheme would be miraculously resurrected, and he periodically approached Skiff to approve pieces that taken together would ultimately bring his original design to fruition. He was never successful in this ruse. Anthropology's final allocation was sixty thousand dollars, only 2 percent of his original fiscal projection. Similar divergence in desired and actual allocations occurred in every LPEC department and it was common for departments to be realigned and even eliminated as separate entities due to fiscal constraints. Chouteau, for example, estimated that creating a department of history would cost two hundred and fifty thousand dollars but the LPEC allocated only fifteen thousand. Chouteau claimed that an underfunded history department was not viable, whereupon Skiff made it part of the Department of Anthropology, increasing Anthropology's budget by fifteen thousand dollars. McGee unexpectedly had control of history, much to Chouteau's annoyance, and more work. He eliminated most static ethnology exhibits to accommodate the history section's extensive needs. As a result the largest displays were those of the Missouri Historical Society.

McGee initially convinced other departments to assume some expenses but this proved problematic. Construction of the Indian Village required extensive grading. In early October the executive committee agreed to grade the tract, build a small lake, and provide pathways, water, and toilet facilities for participants, paid by the LPEC general construction funds. Unfortunately no authorization was given to begin construction. After unexpected rains in April, the LPEC reallocated the funds to cover cost overruns for Main Picture pavilions, without telling McGee. Construction problems, especially the lack of grading and sanitation facilities, made participants miserable (McGee 1905d, 40).

Building the Infrastructure: Leaky Roofs and Flooded Buildings

The Anthropology Department had an exhibit hall, although they could not yet use it, but an Indian School had to be built. The building itself was government property, an extension of the government pavilion, which meant that McCowan did not have a free hand in its design and construction, requiring him to make a great number of alterations. The building's basic design was approved in September 1903 and exterior construction completed in mid-January 1904. Then major headaches began in earnest. Due to flooding from the grading fiasco and reworking of the water mains and sewer system, toilets had to be moved downhill. The roof leaked in over fifty places and caused the interior plaster to fall off in large clumps. The architect and building contractor refused to fix the problems, claiming they were not responsible for the cheap materials supplied by the government contractor. The Indian Service eventually filed a lawsuit and refused to pay their final invoice. Minimal street grading and the lack of sewers caused the Indian School building to flood. McCowan wrote to LPEC staff and asked that surplus dirt be sent to form a terraced front lawn. The LPEC charged the grading and sewer hookups to McCowan's account despite previous agreements.[16]

The building had cost seventeen thousand dollars, well over budget. Housing and feeding students and demonstrators was going to be very costly. The government's low-cost procurement procedures created additional problems; McCowan was still soliciting bids on opening day. Expenses mounted so rapidly that McCowan was forced to have students, demonstrators, and personnel bring their own bedding in order to save the nineteen hundred dollars set aside for blankets. He used student labor to complete the building, landscape the grounds, and install the exhibits. McCowan reasoned that carpentry work, electrical wiring, and plumbing were appropriate for advanced pupils. Since pupils would not be paid, this tactic would save a good deal of money and allow the building to be completed.[17]

There was a problem with this strategy. Using Indian students meant less work for unionized laborers and there was an agreement between the LPEC and the St. Louis Building Trades Council forbidding nonunion labor. McCowan asked fair officials and local labor unions for permission to use students to complete the Indian School. The labor union agreed as long as McCowan paid students a fair wage. McCowan paid the young men the going rate for construction workers (minus their room and board) but insisted "they must work all day, every day, to get any money."[18]

McCowan saved money with this plan and was able to complete the building, but not without problems resulting from St. Louis's miserable winter weather. Work scheduled to start in February was delayed until March. A dozen Chilocco and Haskell Institute students laid floors, built room partitions, installed plumbing and electrical wiring, and built sewing tables, classroom equipment, and special glass cases for the Department of the Interior's exhibit. Meanwhile, boarding schools sent decorations: the sewing class at Grand Junction, Colorado, made curtains and Oneida students embroidered tablecloths. Some promised help failed to materialize. Haskell's superintendent informed McCowan they could not build the central staircase as promised because measles had hit the school.[19]

McCowan was strapped for money and decided to scale back the undertaking. He suggested McGee decrease the number of "old" Indians, but McGee refused. In fact, McGee tried to stretch his appropriation by surreptitiously raiding McCowan's budget. He visited several reservations and promised the agents they could bring a contingent to the fair and McCowan would pay for their expenses. These tactics, as well as McGee's insistence on grandiose plans, caused McCowan constant headaches. An additional forty thousand dollars would be needed to make a credible showing, given McGee's extensive promises. McGee and McCowan lobbied the Department of the Interior for additional funds. By early 1904 McCowan was tired and increasingly frustrated with McGee.

An Indian Trading Post

One unique feature of the Department of Anthropology turned out to save money for McGee and McCowan. J. W. Benham, owner of Benham Indian Trading Companies, asked McCowan for an exclusive commission to sell Indian-made goods in the Indian School. Aggressive and innovative, Benham wrote Jones requesting a salaried position as assistant official Indian agent or post trader, which would give him special standing and an advantage over other traders planning LPE concessions. He wanted to sell art supplies directly to Indian artists, as well as any other items Natives might desire, and thought a government affiliation would be good for business and provide credibility. In return, Benham offered to find materials McCowan might need gratis.[20]

Jones wrote McCowan that he considered it a bad idea to award an exclusive contract since it smacked of favoritism and suggested Benham have a concession in the small industries building. Benham and McCowan mounted a campaign with both Jones and the LPEC to permit a frontier sutlery (trading post) adjacent to the school to provide supplies for Indian participants. It took several proposals, but finally the idea of a retail establishment where Indians could spend their leisure time met with success, especially since McCowan argued it would maintain discipline by keeping Indians from wandering around the fair. Benham was given an honorary appointment as reservation trader and chief clerk; his wife would be appointed as a bookkeeper and his brother a clerk.

Benham came to St. Louis at the end of January 1904 to meet with the chair of the LPEC concessions committee, to eliminate potential competition, and rent a warehouse. Although contrary to LPEC rules, Benham was awarded a special concession, and his business was officially designated as a commissary storehouse to meet the Indian Service's needs to provision Indian participants. McCowan anticipated that at least three hundred and fifty people would be fed daily, a major undertaking requiring planning and coordination. But there was money to be made in feeding Native demonstrators.[21] To stave off counterclaims by other Indian traders, like the Wetherill brothers who had to be content with booths in the manufacturing building, McCowan rationalized that Benham was a special Indian Service assistant for the duration of the exposition.

McCowan had another idea to lower food expenses. In exchange for free advertising placards placed on counters and walls, companies gave him free food for the students and staff. The Hygienic Food Company of Battle Creek, Michigan, supplied boxes of corn and maple flakes as well as recipes on how their products could be used. Several companies contributed food for use in class demonstrations. Food remained a major expense. Everyday McCowan purchased 1,200 gallons of canned or fresh milk, 1,239 loaves of bread, and large quantities of fruit and vegetables.[22]

Finding Indians for the School

McCowan continued to request help from boarding school and reservation staff throughout the winter and spring, searching for students, Indian Service personnel, exhibits, and decorative art without using his appropriation. Unfortunately Commissioner Jones and Estelle Reel decided to erect a second exhibit in the Government Building, apparently without consulting McCowan. It was placed under the direction of a Miss Cook, assisted by anthropologist Alice Fletcher. Cook sent out a request at the same time as McCowan. Confusion reigned. Each received replies from perplexed school officials stating that items were being prepared; Cook or McCowan would respond that they were not sure what they were talking about. McCowan responded to the myriad requests by asking agents to make credible exhibits on anything and ship them to St. Louis, where he and Cook would divide them up. He instructed them simply to tell him the scope and subject matter and keep him informed of progress. This laissez-faire approach meant that no one had any idea of exhibit content until a week before the opening.

Even more important than the art and educational displays was securing students, teachers, and support personnel. McCowan seems to have had several people in mind, especially those with whom he had worked previously and his friends. There were many positions to fill—teachers, escorts, matrons—and McCowan particularly wanted Indians employed in boarding schools as living proof of how successful the Indian Service educational programs were. It was a lengthy process. First he had to convince staff to come, ask them to use their vacation time or convince the Indian Service agent or superintendent to agree to their temporary reassignment, and then obtain Washington's permission.[23]

Requests for adult demonstrators, students, and Wild West show performers were also mired in bureaucratic red tape. Often McCowan went directly to the top rather than follow established channels, asking Assistant Commissioner A. G. Tanner to detail individuals to Chilocco or St. Louis. This was important for his featured student performers and adult demonstrators: musicians, singers, speakers, orators, athletes, and celebrities. McCowan's search for soloists also involved extensive negotiations with parents, working through school and agency personnel. Tohono O'odham soprano Katherine Valenzuela had recently graduated from the Phoenix Indian School. She was an accomplished singer, and McCowan wanted her to give daily concerts as part of the musical and literary programs. As he explained to Commissioner Jones, "It is the purpose to show the Indian, his abilities and capabilities, in as broad a way as possible. Katherine being full blood and talented will be an attractive representative of the educated Indian." McCowan had to obtain her parents' permission—an agreement required for all students. Valenzuela's father was not sanguine; he did not want his daughter to travel unescorted. After more negotiations, it was agreed that Katherine could go to St. Louis if escorted by Addie E. Beaver, a Native teacher.[24]

Indian musicians took extra negotiation because they had to agree to come to Chilocco in February 1904 and remain after the fair's close for a six-month concert tour McCowan had arranged with the Chicago Lyceum Bureau. McCowan obtained permission to offer wages to key musicians. Many were eager to come, viewing it as an adventure and way to earn a living; several were from families that had participated in earlier expositions. Most had one major stipulation. Trumpeter Harry Wilson (Klamath) wrote in response to McCowan's invitation, that he would come, but, "On no account will I go if you expect me to enter school as a pupil for any length of time."[25] McCowan agreed, as he did to concert pianist Gertrude Brewer's demands. She would transfer to Chilocco in exchange for a salary for three months of rehearsal and a full year's employment following the exposition. McCowan would transfer the money to her agency for distribution to her family.

Groups as well as individuals were desired. McCowan asked J. B. Alexander, superintendent at Sacaton, Arizona, to bring a kindergarten class, along with their older siblings and one or two of the parents who could demonstrate pottery and basketry. He especially wanted baseball players so he could make a Chilocco-based team into a contender for the championship games scheduled throughout the fair. He offered to arrange for a special railroad car to transport everyone from Arizona to St. Louis. They came.

McCowan asked friends to locate interesting adult demonstrators. He wanted men and women with small babies who possessed some artistic talent, were interesting to visitors, endowed mentally, physically, and spiritually, were industrious, peaceful, looked Indian, hopefully had worked at a previous fair, and were not "abnormal in any sense." They must be the best with no "drunkards or worthless specimens." They should be able to construct "a native shack in realistic fashion," so should bring raw materials. Indians should bring cooking utensils, baskets, water jars, bedding and clothes, but nothing new, and a large supply of everything necessary to make their crafts. "I expect them to make a great deal of money for themselves from the sale of their manufactured articles."[26] McCowan sent over two thousand letters requesting families who were quiet, reliable, and diligent.

Some agents responded but most did not, and those who did were often negative, citing a lack of financial resources to assemble a delegation or the presence of epidemic disease. In other cases negative replies reflected agents' preconceptions about the people with whom they worked and assessments of how much they had changed during the reservation era. John H. Seger, superintendent of the Colony Indian Training School, found the whole idea counterproductive. "As my work and experience among these Indians for thirty years has been with a view of getting them to forget their old ways and pursuits, and as I have been so far successful . . . I feel that it would now take some time and expense to get them back to where they would make a credible showing in any pursuit peculiar to Indians." A few even said that their groups were professional horse thieves and murderers, lazy, had no artistic skills, or spent all their time smoking and gambling. They assumed that McCowan would not want them.[27]

Other contacts also asserted that the Indians under their jurisdictions were too acculturated and no longer knew the old ways. McCowan asked O. A. Mitscher, the Osage agent, for two full-blood families who could demonstrate crafts and shoot bows and arrows. Mitscher responded that the Osages no longer practiced traditional crafts with the exception of beadwork and had no archers but, "If you want an exhibit of great big fat juicy Indians in their native costumes doing nothing I can supply you with as many as you may want."[28] After repeated requests, Mitscher located a family who agreed to come, provided they could use their oil revenue money to live in a hotel, and remain in their encampment only during demonstration hours. McCowan agreed even though there were no archers.

Some of McCowan's friends suggested specific individuals rather than groups. McCowan turned down men who had a reputation for combativeness although athletic stars merited special consideration even if they had perceived character defects. Sam Morris, a nationally known pitcher who played professional baseball in Seattle, had "a love of whiskey and you will have to discipline him strictly." McCowan initially declined but later offered Morris a salary of seventy-five dollars per month. "If he does good work our team will be a success and we may make money enough to justify paying him what he asks, $100 per month."[29] The team never materialized so McCowan relied on the Fort Shaw women's basketball team who had already agreed to come.

McCowan had better luck with school staff than reservation agents, but most had stipulations, mainly that they wanted to accompany the adult artists and that they and the Indians come for only two months. Many Natives were reluctant because they felt it would be a financial drain, since there were to be no salaries, and would interfere with their agricultural schedules. There was enough enthusiastic support, however, to make the plan feasible. Hugh M. Nobel at White Eagle, Oklahoma, found more Ponca families than could be accommodated. Other superintendents and agents wrote to McCowan or McGee without prompting, asking that their Indians be designated an official delegation. To some they offered transportation vouchers. To others McCowan wrote: "If any old Indians desire to visit the exposition they are cordially invited to do so at their own expense, and in this case, suitable camping facilities will be provided free of charge. The Indians, however, will be expected to pay their own transportation and provide their own subsistence at the fair."[30]

Who Else Will Come to the Fair?

The decision to have McCowan serve as assistant in charge of Native peoples sometimes hindered McGee's attempts to negotiate with potential demonstrators, as it did with all the Mission Indians; at other times it produced unanticipated opportunities. In July 1903 McCowan suggested that Seminoles could demonstrate under the direction of Reverend Henry Gibbs, a well-known linguist, who felt the Seminoles would be a great attraction; they could make canoes, palmetto-thatched shacks, marketable baskets, and beaded belts and were physical giants who "dress so peculiar." Since the government had "no hold over them" it was difficult to get them away from the Everglades because they "expected travel to be some scheme on the part of the government to kidnap them and send them out to the Indian Territory."[31] But Gibbs thought financial inducement might convince them. While intrigued because the group filled a hole in his taxonomy, McGee was not willing to pay them. Neither was McCowan. They did not come.

Old Indian Service enmities also surfaced. Controversy erupted in February when Col. Richard Henry Pratt, Carlisle Indian School superintendent, complained about Indian participation that emphasized traditional lifeways and the fact that he had not been given the prestigious post of organizer. At every opportunity Pratt publicly berated McCowan and Jones for trying to perpetuate the past, claiming they were too much under the influence of his enemies—the ethnologists. In a February 12, 1904, article in *The Red Man* Pratt criticized McGee and Dorsey "who in all they do persuade the Indian to remain in and exaggerate his old Indian life." While McCowan took the remarks in stride, McGee was incensed. He wrote Pratt and demanded a retraction. If Pratt did not, McGee said, he would be compelled to state publicly that Pratt was "a pusillanimous slanderer."[32] Pratt did not retract, but McGee never made good on his threat.

After much argument, McGee and McCowan agreed that all American Indians would participate only as extensions of the Indian School, to ensure they would "conform to their customary habits and observances in every particular." Culturally appropriate ceremonies would be performed, "not in a spectacular way (as they would on the Pike) but at the times and seasons fixed by immemorial custom." They turned down hundreds of offers from lawyers, explorers, bankers, government agents, and businessmen who offered to bring potential demonstrators to the exposition, including some very fanciful schemes. One of the more ambitious plans came from N. F. Shabert of Lawton, Oklahoma, who desired to bring a delegation at his own expense and then charge admission. He thought that Geronimo, Quanah Parker, Jack Peacus (an army scout), and a couple of "squaws" would make a compelling exhibit. McCowan declined.[33]

McCowan received numerous requests from individuals, including some Indians, to rent "booth space" to show how they were helping American Indians assimilate or to highlight the achievements of "progressive" Indians. Cora V. Eddleman, the Cherokee proprietor of *Twin Territories Magazine*, requested a booth, to be manned by an educated Indian girl who would explain her magazine. McCowan turned her down but suggested she obtain space in the Oklahoma Territorial Building, which she did.[34] Others suggested demonstrators from areas McCowan had excluded, such as the North Carolina Cherokees. He generally turned down solicitations unless the promoter offered to pay all expenses, which none did. He also declined individuals who required being paid, including Native artists and performers who had attended other expositions, but offered food and a camping space.

McCowan and McGee turned down all requests for employment, with the exception of favors to prominent men. Frederick Starr asked McGee to hire his student C. E. Hulbert, who served as McGee's assistant throughout the fair and helped supervise the Cocopa encampment. McGee also hired Rosa Bourassa upon McCowan's recommendation. Bourassa was a Chippewa who had worked in several boarding schools, most recently in Phoenix as McCowan's assistant. McGee was quite happy with her efficiency as well as the newspapers' admiration of her beauty.[35] The pair received applications for employment with increasing frequency as opening day approached. Indian Service employees, bored with their current assignments in remote areas, wanted to be detailed. McCowan responded favorably to those he considered good agents. He was not entirely guileless in these requests. He extended his appropriation by paying transportation, room, and board in return for free labor. McCowan was so successful in this scheme that he ran into trouble when all the personnel from one school agreed, leaving no one to look after the children. Jones and Tanner told him to stop contacting people.

All the unsolicited requests McGee accepted led to one goal: to bring as many types of Native peoples as possible in order to prove the correctness of his evolutionary theory. McCowan accepted those who enhanced the Indian School and illustrated the progress that government policies had made. In both cases, the bottom line ultimately determined who came to St. Louis. Both men spent more and more of their time trying to locate additional funds as expenses mounted.

Cutting Back Yet Again

McGee had obtained a "new" anthropology budget of seventy-five thousand dollars in January 1904. In order to ensure that living groups, especially those far away, could come, he quietly moved funds around internally. To allocate twenty-five hundred dollars each for the Ainus from Japan and Cocopas from Mexico, he reduced the history section to one thousand dollars and archaeology and anthropometry to five hundred dollars each. McGee hid expenditures through creative bookkeeping and charged travel expenses for participants to McCowan's budget. He charged his own travel to Skiff's main exhibit account. Neither gentleman was pleased when they began to receive his unexpected bills.[36]

McGee still hoped to raise money through creative alliances with Washington colleagues. There were federal authorizations for anthropological endeavors besides the Department of the Interior. The Smithsonian Institution exhibits and the Philippine Village came out of other allocations. McGee tried unsuccessfully to contact Albert Jenks, the head of the Philippine ethnological section. He also tried to convince Holmes to join forces and produce a "combined" archaeological exhibit using the meager two-thousand-dollar Smithsonian allotment, arguing he could then bring in more Native peoples to enact their original plan. Holmes was incredulous, considering McGee "his own worst enemy . . . disloyal and harmful . . . a permanent sore head and is revengeful and wholly unprincipled." Langley would not even consider the matter. Neither responded, and Holmes refused to go to St. Louis to work on the Smithsonian exhibit because he might run into McGee.[37]

McGee was more successful in another federal arena. The government gave the Alaska Territory a special appropriation to make an exhibit, emphasizing Native peoples and their products. Governor Brady asked McGee to serve as a consultant. McGee saw it as a golden opportunity to have peoples from the Northwest Coast and Arctic represented without cost to his department. It was to be one of the successes of the exposition.

By February, even though McGee had pared down his exhibit drastically and was cutting corners, it was evident that there would be insufficient funds. McCowan likewise had fiscal troubles as building expenses rose. McCowan informed McGee that unless the LPEC gave them an additional allotment, he had operating funds for only four months. There was no way they could stay open for eight. After discussing their options they decided to change the opening day. Every department was supposed to be ready on May 1. Using construction problems as their public excuse, McCowan and McGee decided to open on June 1. Delaying gave them an extra month, necessary since they had begun so late, and allowed them to save one month of living expenses for adult and student demonstrators. Even with this change they were not sure they could keep the exhibits open past October. They did not relay this assessment to Skiff, Francis, Jones, or any of the parties who had would come or who had contracted to have exhibits in the anthropology building. McGee began to downplay the scope of the department in new press announcements while simultaneously generating excitement about the expeditions that had been sent far afield to gather together the peoples of the earth.

4. Assembling the "Races of Mankind"

McGee was disappointed that the grandiose plan he had been publicizing would not be implemented and felt that the LPEC's obstinacy caused him logistical problems as well as damaged his reputation. He had begun his public relations campaign without LPEC Board approval and without a budget, causing Skiff and Francis to keep a tight reign on his activities. McGee later fantasized that "before the [d]epartment was vitalized the voluntary participation of all the world's races and most of the nations was assured" (McGee 1905d, 18). Neither his correspondence nor department records provide any indication that any indigenous family had agreed to participate by January 1904. But McGee had contacted explorers, anthropologists, and government officials asking for help in securing ethnic participants even before he had been hired. He now planned to send seven expeditions to Japan (Ainus), Argentina (Tehuelches), Belgian Congo (Batwa Pygmies), Canada (Kwakiutls and Nootkas), Mexico (Seris), Oklahoma, and the American Southwest.

There was little time left to select people, to ensure the display would be about "man both as creature and as worker."[1] This required immediate expeditions and possibly protracted negotiations with skeptical indigenous peoples. McGee felt that informing the public about the missions as they proceeded would also help the Department of Exploitation (the official title for the publicity department!) advertise the fair. And it did, for they had all the elements of great adventures: danger, war, disease, wild animals, strange lands, wilderness, and recalcitrant, exotic Natives, including "cannibals."

McGee was initially concerned there was not enough time for the longer trips and that natural disaster, transport, or diplomatic difficulties would derail endeavors. He had begun to hire agents for his "ethnology corps" as soon as he was appointed. He chose men based on his "old-boy" network, but rarely anyone with a direct connection to the Smithsonian Institution or the Washington intellectual community.

An LPEC agent needed diplomatic skills to convince people to journey to a strange land without monetary compensation, except for what they could produce by the sale of their art. "My mode of procedure," McGee wrote the Japanese ambassador,

> is to approach aborigines, and, after gaining their confidence, to offer the opportunity of attending this great assemblage of peoples without cost to themselves and with the assurance of ample food and clothing during their absence from their homes. They are also assured of safe return within a stated period, and of receiving either presents or compensation of such character and extent as they and their commissioners may deem appropriate.[2]

On the national level, McGee had to convince officials that attending the exposition would be good for the demonstrators, providing them an opportunity to see their future. The LPE was a rare opportunity for mutual observation and study that would increase sympathy between peoples and races, provide "more advanced" peoples a means of understanding the developmental stages through which their ancestors passed, and allow the "lower peoples" to see possibilities and opportunities for advancement. It was an argument that worked with most officials and a few potential demonstrators. McGee's agents convinced dozens of men, women, and children to travel thousands of miles to a strange land, while the U.S. government's agents convinced (and in a few cases, coerced) hundreds of Filipinos to make the same journey. Hundreds more American Indians made the same decision.

Expedition One: The Pygmies, "Aboriginals of the Dark Continent"

The first agent McGee selected was the Reverend Samuel Phillips Verner, president of Stillman Institute, Tuscaloosa, Alabama, assigned to bring a party of Batwa Pygmies from Central Africa. Verner was a complex man, a naturalist, entrepreneur, and minister who wanted to find the evolutionary missing link. He liked being an explorer and promoted himself as an adventurer who could brave the darkest recesses of the Belgian Congo, interact with headhunters and cannibals, and live to tell of his exploits. Verner had served in the Upper Kasi Valley, Belgian Congo, as an "industrial and evangelical" missionary for the Presbyterian Foreign Missionary Board in the 1890s. He was also experienced in bringing Africans to the United States as part of his missionary endeavors; he had induced two Batwa men (John Kondola and Kassongo, who died accidentally in 1903) to travel to Alabama. Because of these experiences, McGee felt Verner would be an excellent agent. Verner assured McGee that he knew a Native potentate, Ndombe, numerous Pygmies, and officials in Belgium, including King Leopold III. He offered to mount the expedition for only one thousand dollars and an honorarium of five hundred dollars.[3]

Verner was commissioned on October 21, 1903, although not approved by the LPEC Board until much later. McGee increased his budget to five thousand dollars and charged him to secure the voluntary services of fifteen to eighteen Pygmies. But both really wanted something more elaborate. Verner claimed he could convince a Pygmy patriarch, his wife, adult men and women, an unmarried young woman, infants, a priestess or priest, an elderly medicine doctor, and "one fine type of the Red Africans, preferably Ndombe of the Bikenge." Verner promised to bring back the most important type, the Tueki, a mythical group Verner believed were the missing evolutionary link between humans and great apes. To find them would be the scientific discovery of the century. Verner claimed he was the only white man to have ever heard of them. He was sure he could locate twelve Pygmies (six Batwa and six Tueki), and one to six Red Africans, including Ndombe himself. Like other agents, Verner agreed to assume responsibility for the health, comfort, and safety of the travelers until they returned to Africa.[4]

Verner and Kondola (who was paid by Verner) traveled to Africa via Washington DC, New York, and London in December 1903. The newspapers proclaimed the trip to be extremely dangerous. Their first stop was Belgium where Verner presented letters of introduction and requests of assistance from U.S. Secretary of State Hay and McGee to the king of Belgium and received letters of support and introduction to colonial officials. He also obtained seven hundred and fifty dollars' worth of trade goods; one large bag of salt was intended for the Tueki who were said to trade it for meat. Verner and Kondola arrived in Africa in mid-January 1904 and obtained passage on a steamer up the Congo River. They then traveled some distance by train, but soon met delays—missed boats, tribal warfare, and colonial obstruction. After contracting malaria, Verner wrote it was going to take more time and money than he had anticipated. Since the Tueki "refused to be found," he concentrated on the Batwa and jubilantly wrote in March, "The first Pygmy has been secured! He was held captive having been taken prisoner at a remote point in the great

Kasia forest. Although still two hundred miles from our final destination, I thought it well to secure him at once, even if we get all we wish from Ndombe. His name is Ota Benga."[5]

Ota Benga was a member of a "wild cannibal tribe," the Baschileles. Verner "redeemed" (i.e., purchased) him for a pound of salt and cloth, and set him free. He reported that the young man "chose voluntarily to come to America" rather than face reenslavement. He was "so far from his own town that it could not be reached, and the road to it was full of hostile savages."[6] His village had been wiped out by raiders. Verner's expedition took on the aura of a rescue mission with Verner playing the role of heroic savior. It was a tale that was soon embellished.

Verner sought to enlist others who had "pure blood." He met with Ndombe, the paramount chieftain of the tribes near Wissman Falls on the Kasai River. Verner described him as a "man of great stature, of a copper color, without any white blood." He persuaded Ndombe to send his son, Lumbangu (or Lumbango), and Latuna, his chief counselor's son, as his companions (Verner 1904b, 76).

McGee supplied reporters with updates on Verner's progress, building anticipation. From March to May there was no word, which led the *St. Louis Post-Dispatch* to speculate: "Exposition Envoy Pygmies' Victim? Fair Officials Have Not Heard for Two Months from Explorer Sent to African Wilds. Perilous Undertaking of Anthropological Department Approved by Belgium Colonial Government." The article stated that McGee was worried about Verner, who was visiting the Congo Free State to secure "members of a savage tribe of pygmies discovered by Henry M. Stanley and thus far hostile to every attempt made at visiting their villages. . . . In his last letter, Mr. Verner said that he had been discouraged by missionaries familiar with the hazards of his mission, who feared for his life . . . [McGee] fears Mr. Verner's party was ambushed before it reached a pygmy village."[7]

While the exposition publicity machine churned out sensational copy, Verner continued his travels but where he went is unclear. The Pygmies are a large and complex group of related peoples with many subdivisions. Verner and McGee considered them a "race" separate from other Africans. Verner pursued the Batwas because Stanley had mentioned them and eventually convinced four men to attend the exposition, Shamba, Malengu, Bomushubba, and Lumo. Verner also tried to convince several women but "being exceedingly timid, and the men not being willing to let them run the risks of what seemed a terrible undertaking to them all," they were not persuaded. Verner and Kondola eventually convinced nine people to make the ten-thousand-mile trip—the five Pygmies and three Bakubas (Lumbango, Latuna, and Kalamma). Only one group, the Batwas, were technically pygmies, that is, people of unusually short stature. The others were average-sized Africans. McGee called those men who did come, "self-selected volunteers in a desperate venture."[8]

The group was ready to leave in May. They brought parrots and monkeys, as well as materials to build houses. Verner secured items for living in the exhibit compound (sleeping mats, hampers, baskets, fire-making equipment, and eating utensils), hunting equipment for demonstrations, and hundreds of pounds of artifacts Verner hoped to sell for a profit to finance his next expedition. Each man brought clothing, weapons, pipes, and ornaments.[9]

It was a long and arduous journey by horse, train, riverboat, and steamship. First they sailed down the Congo River to the coast and from there to Havana, for Verner thought England would be too cold and damp. This southern route was expensive, however; the freight costs were triple what had been budgeted. When the party reached New Orleans at the end of June, two months late, Verner collapsed and was taken to a hospital. Kondola put the contingent on a train and headed to St. Louis. After Verner recovered, he joined them and helped build their encampment.

Expedition Two: The Tehuelches, "Patagonian Giants"

The second agent McGee approached was Professor J. B. Hatcher, of the Carnegie Museum in Pittsburgh. A noted geologist, Hatcher had made several expeditions to southern Argentina and Chile. He was preparing an Antarctic paleontological expedition and McGee asked him to secure Patagonian participants on his way home. The time schedule was not appropriate, however, and Hatcher declined. A friend suggested Señor Vicente Cane of Buenos Aires who accepted the commission to negotiate with Chief Guechico of the Tehuelches, whom McGee labeled "Patagonian Giants." Cane reported that the Patagonians agreed to come only if they were given horses to ride. According to one account, Cane agreed to provide white horses. On March 25, Cane wrote from Lisbon that the two-hundred-pound advance was almost gone but that the Indians were well. He would use his own funds for food.[10]

There is little information about the trip, but McGee described it as arduous. "Chief Guechico's rancheria lay over two hundred miles from transportation lines and the stalwart tribes being of a most stubborn and intractable disposition, Señor Cane's task was one of extreme difficulty; yet he performed it with signal success, leading the party to Rio Gallegos and accompanying them thence via Lisbon, Liverpool, and New York to Saint Louis."[11] Cane remained at the fair as a special agent, assisted by an interpreter, Juan Wohlers. In recognition of his services, Cane received an honorarium of four thousand dollars, from which he paid the interpreter's salary and the expenses for the party.

Expedition Three: The Seris and Cocopas

Fixated on the "primitive" Seris, McGee hoped to bring a group to St. Louis. In November 1903 he learned that a band had been imprisoned for "depredations" in western Sonora and hoped to free them in exchange for their participation. McGee sent Edwin C. Cushman Jr. to Mexico. Cushman had solicited a position in July 1903 while working for Senator Eugene Hale (Maine) who requested, as a personal favor, that McGee hire him. In exchange Hale agreed to help McGee establish an international commission of anthropological and geographical sciences.

Luckily, Cushman actually had credentials for the position. In 1897 he had been a member of Richard Wetherill's trips into Grand Gulch, Utah, whose archaeological finds led to the definition of the Basket Maker era of Ancestral Puebloan culture. In 1898–99, he traveled among the Navajo and Hopi and worked for the Indian Service relocating Southern Utes to a new reservation. The explorer mentality and ability to work with Indians was exactly what McGee wanted in a special agent. He hired Cushman on November 15 at one hundred dollars per month to escort Seris to the exposition.[12]

McGee's information hinted that Seris were "in the employ of the Government" near Hermosillo, which meant they had forcibly been placed in work camps run by Sonoran landowners. McGee hoped these men could locate a Seri family. Cushman met with official after official, and landowner after landowner, but was unable to find any Seris. They had escaped and were well hidden, as they had been on McGee's trips. Ramon Corral, Mexico's minister of the interior, wrote to McGee that these Seris "who were prisoners have been given their freedom. In order to obtain others, we would have to make a [military] campaign which would be very costly."[13]

McGee actually thought seriously about a military expedition before deciding it was simply too expensive. Instead he sent Cushman back to Mexico to revisit officials and landowners but no Seris were found. Admitting defeat, McGee instructed Cushman to visit the Cocopas. If he could not exhibit Seris as examples of extreme primitiveness, he would use the Cocopas as proxies.

The Cocopas, who lived on the lower Colorado River in communities in Sonora, Baja California, and Arizona Territory, had been placed under the loose jurisdiction of both the U.S. and Mexican governments in the mid-nineteenth century when treaties bisected their traditional lands. In 1904 the U.S. government considered all Cocopas to be "Mexicans" although the Mat Skrui and Hwanyak bands had lived in the Arizona Territory prior to the 1853 Gadsden Purchase. McGee labeled them "foreign aborigines," rather than Indian wards of the United States, so that he, and not McCowan, could look after their personal needs.[14]

McGee wanted a Sonoran contingent, since he considered them less assimilated than those living in Arizona. If this was not possible he suggested Cushman contact Chief Pablo Colorado, whom McGee had met and considered a sophisticated individual. He sent a Chinese silk handkerchief with a note addressed to the "Head Man of all the Cocopa Indians," inviting him "to visit the World's Fair next summer and see with your own eyes the greatest productions of all nations."[15] He argued this was a once-in-a-lifetime opportunity for a man who had never been away from home.

Cushman began negotiating with Colorado and other men in mid-January 1904. McGee wanted them to remain in St. Louis for at least three months with their families, demonstrate crafts, and perform appropriate activities. While Cushman did not offer wages for their time and effort, he offered transportation and food and distributed small gifts of money and tobacco.

Cocopa leaders were not enthusiastic. Colorado dictated a letter to McGee expressing ambivalence about traveling such a long distance and staying so long. Three other headmen argued that the fair would interfere with their planting and harvest schedules. By leaving their fields unattended, they would not be able to survive the next winter. Were there plans to compensate them or to purchase necessary winter supplies? Also it was not appropriate to bring women, since they would not be treated courteously. Several young men thought that they might go alone. Cushman responded that McGee was firmly committed to bringing women, so only families could go, and "that we were doing them a great favor in bringing them at all." The Cocopas made no comment and Cushman was not sure he had or could convince anyone.[16]

Negotiations continued for weeks, with the Cocopas still skeptical. Only after "a hard fight," did Cushman feel confident that fifteen to twenty individuals would come with Captain Tom Moore, the leader of "a typical group," who had consented in early March. He was now hopeful that a new negotiating strategy would be successful with Pablo Colorado. "Captain Pablo says that his place is with his people, and that he cannot leave them, but I think he is trying to see if he can't work me for some money. He is a foxy old fellow."[17]

A week later Colorado agreed, provided there was remuneration for traveling and living expenses. Cushman wanted to pay Annie Flynn twenty-five dollars a month to serve as translator and promoter. The educated Flynn impressed Cushman with her good reputation in the community. She agreed to travel to St. Louis provided she could live in a hotel room. McGee was not at first convinced this was appropriate since Flynn was a woman, but eventually agreed.

The Cocopas were ready by April 1. Two wagonloads of housing materials, tattooing equipment, grasses for baskets, and cooking utensils were packed. But when they arrived at the Yuma train station there were no tickets. After numerous telegrams McCowan sent word on April 13 that everything would be arranged eventually, so Cushman sent everyone home in frustration.

When St. Louis newspapers announced that the fair's "antique Indian tribe" would begin their journey the following Monday, the Cocopas again sat at the Yuma railway station. What was the problem? In essence, a fight between McGee and McCowan. McGee had to make the arrangements. There was an agreement that the railroad would provide half-price "limited first class" tickets per McCowan's arrangement for all Native Americans. But McCowan said the Cocopas were Mexicans and there was no arrangement for them. McGee would have to pay full price. There was another delay; railroad authorities had not arranged for a separate car as requested. McGee had not sent the funds. There was also a new disagreement over the number of Cocopa who would go. McGee and the railroad settled on twelve, but according to Cushman,

Fig. 4.1. Frederick Starr, Professor, University of Chicago, 1909. Photographer unknown. Library of Congress, Prints and Photographs Division, LC-DIG-ggbain, LC01258u.

nineteen people now waited for the train. Eventually Cushman and twenty-two Cocopa left Yuma on April 27, 1904. They took their own food since Cushman had only enough money left for coffee. The freight left separately the next day and somehow arrived before they did.[18]

Expedition Four: The Ainus

The second foreign expedition proposed, but the last to be undertaken, was to Japan. McGee wanted Ainus to represent the aboriginals of the Japanese Empire and to demonstrate crafts that illustrated "some of the most significant stages in industrial development known to students." It was imperative, he maintained, that civilization learn about them because they were rapidly being transformed through their contact with the Japanese. Like American Indians experiencing Euro-American colonialism, it was questionable whether the Ainus would survive culturally (McGee 1904a, 5; 1904b; 1905d, 96).

McGee asked Frederick Starr (fig. 4.1), a self-trained anthropology professor at the University of Chicago, to conduct this expedition. Starr (1858–1933) had a reputation among his contemporaries for outlandish theories, but students, and those who attended his lectures on the Chautauqua circuit, thought him immensely entertaining and provocative. He had strong moral convictions and expressed them often; he spoke against U.S. imperialism in Cuba and the Philippines in 1898. He believed in the natural superiority of Anglo-Saxons but railed against racial assimilationist policies as violations of sovereignty. Like McGee he had personal idiosyncrasies (he refused to wear an overcoat or use a telephone) and unlimited ambition and confidence. He was also a perennial fairgoer, contributing personal displays to exhibits in Nashville, Madrid, New Orleans, Chicago, and Buffalo. He had many loyal supporters, equally numerous detractors, seemingly boundless energy, and loved the limelight.[19]

As a staunch evolutionist who thought anthropology the pinnacle of scientific development, he complemented McGee, and like McGee he did little work that ultimately advanced anthropological theory and practice. His publications were essentially travelogues, superficial field notes of physical and cultural descriptions of the "racial types" he encountered during quick trips. Starr was interested in the "origin, position, structure, appearance, movement, varieties, achievement, and progress" of mankind—basically the agenda of nineteenth-century ethnology. He wanted to meet the Ainus to test an idea advanced by some German scholars that there was an ancient Ainu-Caucasoid connection. According to Yoshinobu Kotani, "this idea was attractive to Europeans because it posited the continuing existence of an early European hunting-and-gathering people and because of the romantic notion of a 'Caucasoid' ethnic group surrounded by a sea of Mongolians." Starr and McGee saw the LPE as an excellent opportunity to "solve" this "problem."[20]

Starr and McGee began to make arrangements in September 1903, knowing that the trip would be difficult. After contacting the Japanese minister to the United States, Kogoro Takahira, McGee wrote encouragingly to Starr, "unless diplomatic difficulties threaten, or the war cloud bursts, we shall probably be able to send the project through." Starr assured McGee that he was ready to go even if war erupted between Japan and Russia. He wrote to missionaries and scholars for suggestions on which villages to visit and asked the Japanese

Ministry of Commerce for travel assistance for the Ainus and shipping house materials.[21]

But the extensive diplomatic negotiations, Starr's teaching schedule, Mc-Gee's recurrent illnesses and mismanagement, and lack of LPEC Executive Committee approval, delayed the journey to the point where it seemed impossible. Starr withdrew and McGee quickly traveled to Chicago to convince him that the funds were being transferred as they spoke. Starr was skeptical and refused to go until he heard from his bank. After more delays David Francis signed his contract, the Japanese ambassador gave his formal approval, and on January 20, 1904, four hours after his bank reported the funds had been received, Starr and his assistant, Manuel Gonzales, a young Mexican photographer, left for Japan. His honorarium was one thousand dollars and his travel budget twenty-five hundred dollars. It was slim but Starr thought he could convince the Japanese to help.[22]

The two men immediately encountered problems—a train wreck meant they arrived in Vancouver only three hours before their boat sailed. They reached Yokohama on February 9, the day before Japan declared war on Russia and spent two frustrating weeks asking for financial and transport assistance from government officials and scholars at the Tokyo Imperial University. The war had priority. According to Starr, "Hokkaido was reached only by hiring a vessel and hoisting the American flag" (Starr 1904a, 2).

Once on Hokkaido, travel to the Ainu villages was by rail and private vessel through an unexpected blizzard. Starr met with no success, so he sought out the Reverend John Batchelor, an Anglican missionary who had conducted extensive linguistic research among the Ainus. Batchelor agreed to help Starr but only after many hours of discussion about the project's value and feasibility and after the provincial governor and local officials approved it. This was a necessary step since the Ainus were government wards. The Japanese government was attempting to transform them into agriculturalists using policies similar to those designed to "modernize" American Indians.

Starr found his first participant in Batchelor's clinic and rest home. Yazo (Ozara Jukataro), a twenty-three-year-old man, worked as Batchelor's assistant and was considered progressive and prosperous because he owned a small farm and several horses. Yazo also had a wife, Shirake, whom Starr considered "a pretty and attractive young girl of eighteen, timid and modest." Starr reasoned they were already familiar with Europeans and would be useful guides for other participants. While Yazo and Shirake returned to their village to make arrangements for the care of their property, Batchelor guided Starr through a bleak landscape to villages in the Shiraoi region. Here Starr purchased 240 artifacts and two thatched houses, meticulously documenting each transaction, noting the object's name, village, and prices paid. Starr considered the trip ethnographic fieldwork for *The Ainu Group at the Saint Louis Exposition*, a booklet designed for fair visitors.[23]

In the book, Starr relates in excruciating detail how he located and convinced potential participants. When told that they would be gone nine months everyone refused, because a long journey would be disastrous economically and might result in death. All the older people decided they were too frail. Starr insisted that participants be "racially and culturally pure," phenotypically "Caucasoid," and that the older men appear with beards and the women lip tattoos. Starr and Batchelor eventually persuaded two families: a young married couple (Kutoroge Himaruma, Shutratek, and baby Kikur) and a patriarchal, gray-haired farmer Sangyea Hiramura, his finely tattooed wife, Santukno, and their six-year-old daughter Kehttle. Starr also hired a translator, Yoichiro Inagaki, an Episcopal Trinity Divinity School student, who spoke English and some Ainu. He conversed with the Ainus in Japanese and agreed to serve as the group's caretaker for a salary of thirty-five yen ($17.50) per month (Starr 1904a, 68).

Each individual was given a negotiated contract that was formally signed with appropriate ceremony. Starr agreed to pay each couple one month's salary in advance, obtain passports from the police, provide transport from Sapporo to St. Louis, their return trip, food, and a salary of thirty-five yen per month per person. Each family agreed to remain until December 1904, erect a house, and "live, dress, and act in a way true to Ainu life." They also agreed to produce bark cloth, rush mats, and carved wooden objects, and cook their own food. They could sell art and keep the proceeds but could not tell other participants that they were being paid. The Ainus struck a good bargain. Half of the wages were given to Batchelor in advance to be kept in an account for their return.[24]

The group departed for the Japanese mainland after another series of diplomatic and logistical delays. There was much weeping when they left, as the travelers "were looked upon as dead men never again to be seen." As they were leaving, Bete Goro, a servant in Batchelor's household, announced that he wanted to go. At first Starr thought he was too assimilated since he wore Europeanized clothing over his embroidered leggings. "Instead of whittling *inao*, he knits stockings! Highly commendable, but no qualification for figuring in an Ainu group at an Exposition." Starr reconsidered because Goro was so anxious to go and decided "his influence would do much to cheer the somewhat morose Yazo and the timid Shirake." Starr refused to take Goro's pregnant wife.[25]

The journey began with delays due to troop movements and inclement weather. In Tokyo, Starr purchased new clothing for everyone and spent another week dealing with government officials. Finally paying the appropriate bribes, they went to Yokohama where everyone was examined by two physicians and fumigated before certificates of embarkation were issued. The certificates stated that all the Ainu would work as Starr's servants in America.[26]

The *Empress of Japan* sailed for Vancouver on March 18. Short of funds, Gonzales and Inagaki traveled in European steerage while the Ainus traveled second class. Starr was upset about this and insisted later that they be given better accommodations when the group returned home. On board ship the Ainus entertained passengers by singing and playing musical instruments while Starr gave lectures and interviewed the adults.

When land was sighted on March 29, "Sangyea and Kutoroge ceremoniously seated themselves facing the shore and in silence rubbed their hands, waved them and stroked their beards, in thanksgiving and worship." The Ainus' first days in North America were filled with events, mainly convincing Canadian immigration officials to let them continue their journey. "Inspected by one physician in Victoria, by another in Vancouver, and by a third in the office of the United States Immigration Bureau on the Vancouver dock, [the Ainus] must have wondered what it all meant. We are sure we did." Starr remembered later, "Of all foolish pretenses at science these inspections deserve the premium."[27]

While officialdom decided whether to allow them to proceed, the Ainus saw the Vancouver sights—a stuffed elk, a dog show in Stanley Park, the zoo—and attended receptions and lectures. Everywhere they attracted crowds. In Seattle they did the same since McGee had failed to make the necessary train arrangements or wire a promised five hundred dollars. They saw Seattle's totem poles and stores and rode the inclined cable cars. Starr eventually got everyone through customs by claiming the Ainus were his personal servants, who would be working at his home in Chicago and not as demonstrators at the exposition (Starr 1904a, 100–101).

The train ride to St. Louis was uneventful except for encounters with drunken men who "were usually bubbling over with good will and were only troublesome in their well-meant advances of kindliness," and the crowds gathered at every station. "The Ainu were amazed to see American Indians among the crowds and at Fort Sheridan, Wyoming, black soldiers." Kutoroge Himaruma personally examined many of these strange people.[28]

They arrived in St. Louis on April 6. A great coach took them to the Indian School where McGee met them. He immediately wrote Starr a personal check from his own account to cover the extra expenses and delivered personal congratulations. "Your expedition was a model one in every way; no less in its financial aspect than in the unexpected and almost unprecedented conformity with schedule and in its general success." Starr left for Chicago the same evening. Saying good-bye, Kutoroge gave him a wooden tray with carved decoration. "All followed us to the door and stood upon the topmost step; tears filled their eyes and all were sobbing; they rubbed their hands and the old men stroked their beards. When almost out of sight we turned and saw them all standing as before, weeping and waving their hands."[29]

Expedition Five: The Pawnees, Osages, Wichitas, and Arapahos

McGee had initially counted on McCowan and the Indian Service to find Indian demonstrators to cut costs. But there were problems with this approach since McCowan did not want men who would perform ceremonies or dance competitively as in a Wild West show. McGee wanted men who would perform elaborate rituals and build old-style houses as well as produce art. They never agreed on these points and had many arguments. McGee also felt McCowan's reliance on Indian Service personnel was unnecessarily tedious and bureaucratic. A more direct approach was needed (Trennert 1987b, 215).

McGee called upon his friend George Amos Dorsey, curator of anthropology at the Field Columbian Museum, who had offered his services when McGee was first hired. "Should you contemplate an exhibition of groups of living

Indians," Dorsey had written, "I should be delighted to have the opportunity of looking after the construction of a Wichita grass lodge, an Osage mat lodge, and a Pawnee or Mandan earth lodge."[30] McGee quickly agreed, offering him an honorarium of three hundred dollars. It was a logical choice. Since Skiff was involved in the exposition, Dorsey considered helping McGee to be part of his museum duties. Skiff concurred, as long as it did not interfere with his regular curatorial work.

Dorsey has been described as ambitious, forceful, driven, intelligent, and flamboyant. He had received one of the first Ph.D.s in American anthropology from Harvard University and worked for Frederic Ward Putnam during the 1893 Chicago World's Fair, collecting South American osteological and archaeological materials. In 1895 he became assistant curator at the Field Columbian Museum, where Skiff was the director. Dorsey concentrated on the rapid accumulation of North American artifacts, a willing participant in the museum scramble for "traditional" materials. He traveled constantly, making numerous, rapid ethnological expeditions to the Plains, Southwest, California, and Northwest Coast between 1895 and 1903. In addition he worked as a special consultant for the Fred Harvey Company and was writing a book and arranging their famous Indian Room in Albuquerque when McGee asked for help.[31]

Dorsey was a sophisticated administrator who put together a remarkable collaborative team for the Field Museum. He sent out field agents (Henry Voth, Stephen Simms, J. W. Hudson, and Charles Newcombe) on extensive expeditions to collect information and artifacts. It was Dorsey's network of collaborators that McGee relied on to locate Indians demonstrators, especially people who could build old-style earth lodges or willow and prairie-grass homes. The ideal group consisted of an elder, who would act as master builder and group leader, accompanied by younger people who would help with the actual construction. Dorsey traveled to Oklahoma in February 1904 and "got the machinery in motion for a representative exhibit." He hired James Murie, a Pawnee scholar, to help him find timbers for the lodges. Murie (1862–1921), also known as Young Eagle (Ri-tahkachiari'), was a noted intellectual who wrote many ethnographic works on the Pawnees and Arikaras. Born in Grand Island, Nebraska, to a Skiri Pawnee mother and a Scots father, Murie attended Genoa Boarding School and the Hampton Normal and Agricultural Institute.

At age twenty he returned to Oklahoma to serve as an assistant teacher, disciplinarian, and drill master at the Pawnee Agency Boarding School. During the 1880s to 1890s he worked as a store clerk, bookkeeper, teacher, and Indian Service interpreter, census taker, and bank clerk. Murie's anthropological career began by collaborating with Alice Fletcher on Pawnee rituals. In 1902 he and Dorsey collected Arikara texts and artifacts. Now called upon to act as cultural broker and interpreter, the Field Museum paid for his time in St. Louis.[32]

Murie and Dorsey visited Pawnee and Wichita communities and found men and women who knew old building techniques and were willing to go to St. Louis. They also made arrangements to have beds, pillows, and lean backs constructed in a proper manner. Dorsey paid for these services from Field Museum funds because McGee claimed he could not. Growing wary of McGee, Dorsey stipulated that the houses and artifacts would go to the Field Museum at the end of the fair. Dorsey also used the trip to collect for both the Harvey Company and the Carnegie Museum.[33]

Technically Dorsey worked for McGee only during April and May as a special agent to negotiate with Pawnee, Arapaho, Osage, and Wichita families, escort them to the fair, and help them erect habitations. McGee and Dorsey wanted all traditional house types occupied by groups living within the Louisiana Territory, especially earth- and grass-lodges. Dorsey and Murie convinced at least twenty-four Arapahos, twenty-seven Pawnees, and twenty-five Wichitas to come and live in family groups. (They were later joined by others not recruited by Dorsey.) Dorsey left as soon as the houses were completed, a situation that had negative ramifications. McGee wanted him to stay and take care of all the Indians, but Dorsey could not afford to do so. In June he wrote a colleague that he had used funds from the Field Museum accounts as well as his own bank account to underwrite his trips. He was more than five hundred dollars in debt and it seemed "apparent the LPEC is not going to be in a hurry about repaying."[34]

Expedition Six: The Kwakiutls and Nootkas of Vancouver

McGee needed a matrilineal group to illustrate Lewis Henry Morgan's clan house. He hoped to obtain an Iroquois long house, like the one built at the Pan-American Exposition in 1901, but decided they "no longer exist in aboriginal perfection." It would be dishonest to use one. The most traditional examples were Kwakiutl clan houses decorated with elaborate totems that illustrated social organization facilitating the maintenance of law during the barbaric stage. Visitors would also be intrigued by the Kwakiutl because they had unusually light skin, elongated head shape, and symbolic cannibalistic scars on their faces.[35]

McGee asked Dorsey to find an agent for the Kwakiutl and Nootka expedition. He suggested Dr. Charles F. Newcombe who had already been asked by William H. Holmes to obtain Haida totem poles for the Smithsonian exhibit and by John Huckel of the Fred Harvey Company to acquire objects for their display and sales room in the New Mexico Building. Dorsey asked Newcombe to collect objects, a house, and demonstrators for McGee. Charles Newcombe (1851–1924) was a wealthy medical doctor originally from Scotland who immigrated to Oregon in 1884. A passionate field naturalist, he collected flora, arrowheads, and stone tools along the Columbia River. Moving to Victoria, British Columbia, in 1889 he became a collaborator of the Provincial Museum and was soon asking the Nootkas and Haidas to sell artifacts. He began his career as an ethnographic collector in 1897 with commissions from a German museum, the Canadian Geological Survey, the provincial government, and the American Museum of Natural History. In 1901 Newcombe began a three-year contract with the Field Museum to collect objects, assisted by Kweeka Kwakiutl leader Charles Nowell, a member of a high-status family of the Kueha tribe living in Fort Rupert. Born in 1870, Nowell had attended the Anglican school at Alert Bay and spoke English well. Around 1895 he had married the daughter of Lagius, chief of the Nimkish. He had a wide circle of relatives through his inherited and acquired statuses.[36]

In mid-March 1904, McGee hired Newcombe to secure the services of a "Klaokwaht" (Kwakiutl or Kwakwaka'wakw) and obtain a clan house ("tribal temple"), totem poles, and house panels. Dorsey, however, instructed Newcombe to obtain a Makah long house, because he thought they were more interesting and traditional, and the services of a famous Haida carver. The Field Museum would provide funds for the house, totem pole, and representative artifacts; the LPEC would pay for transportation.[37] Newcombe began but encountered months of frustration, failing to locate either a Makah or Kwakiutl house. He and Nowell found individuals willing to go to St. Louis, but McGee always refused to meet their terms. Without wages, Newcombe found there was very little interest in Makah, Haida, Nootka, or Kwakiutl settlements.

Nowell agreed to go to St. Louis only if his friend and clan brother, Bob Harris (Xa'Niyus), a religious specialist and dancer from Denatkot, could accompany him. Their wives and children decided not to go and Dorsey agreed, without telling McGee. During the next two months Newcombe and Nowell undertook an eight-day tour of Puget Sound and Neah Bay, two trips to Clayoquot, two to Alert Bay, a canoe trip from Fort Rupert to Hardy Bay, an eleven-mile hike to Koskimo Sound, a trip to Klickitat, and one up the Columbia and Yakima rivers, this last without success. Finally, Dorsey informed McGee that Newcombe had completed negotiations for a fully equipped Makah long house and ten performers, but would need eight hundred dollars now. Due to cumbersome accounting procedures and another debilitating bout of typhoid, McGee could not obtain the funds quickly enough and negotiations collapsed. Newcombe felt the Makah's hesitancy and distrust of whites surfaced when the promised money failed to materialize.

Next Newcombe tried to persuade a "longheaded" Koskimo woman but again negotiations collapsed because of concerns similar to those expressed by the Cocopas. Disheartened, he spent many wearisome hours in Fort Rupert where there were artists who had accompanied Kwakiutl scholar George Hunt to the 1893 Chicago Exposition and had been paid twenty dollars a month to compensate for their lost fishing time in addition to what they earned from their performances. People thought they should be paid the same. Salaries would make the difference; Dorsey asked again but McGee remained adamant.[38]

After other negotiations fell through, Nowell convinced two Nootka families from Clayoquot to go with the promise of sufficient commissions from the Field Museum. They agreed to perform under the direction of "Dr. Atlieu," a noted shaman and literate man who had been German anthropologist Karl van den Steinem's consultant in 1902. Like Cocopa leaders, Atlieu did not undertake the trip lightly. "I depend on you [Newcombe] to have the same mind toward us as we have to you. There are those of the tribe who think it is too great an undertaking for me for they have never been far away from home. But I have no fear. I also want to see the place where we are going and meet the great chiefs who will be there."[39] His wife, Annie, a mat maker; Jasper Turner, a carver, dancer, and singer; Jack Curley, a carver and singer, and his wife, Ellen; as well as Mrs. Emma George, a well-known basket maker from Gold River, accompanied him.

Two days before they were scheduled to leave, Nowell and Newcombe bought a fifty-three-by-forty-two-foot Nootka house with nine bundles of mats for one hundred dollars and Atlieu's great sea-going canoe for another hundred dollars.[40] The Nootka families, Nowell, Harris, and Newcombe left Vancouver; the house and totem poles went COD care of the Fred Harvey Company. The people arrived after an uneventful train trip that included a brief stop in Chicago. The freight, unfortunately, sat at the railroad station unclaimed.

Expedition Seven: Failed Trips to the American Southwest

No fair was complete without Pueblo Indians, and McCowan had arranged for San Juan and Acoma families, spending a great deal of effort to ensure that expert potters would be in attendance. Much to McGee's regret, he did not seriously consider building a pueblo, which would have taken months just to make the adobe bricks. Army tents would serve as their home in St. Louis. Despite this reasonable assessment, McGee wanted Zunis to erect a reproduction of their pueblo, while Dorsey argued that Hopis were necessary to build a replica of a mesa-top village for comparative purposes. McGee hoped that both groups would perform their "impressive fiducial ceremonies, including the snake dance" to trump Tobin's Pike concession that claimed to be authentic. McCowan, needless to say, did not want a snake dance anywhere near the Indian School but had no objections to more Puebloans coming, provided he did not have to pay for their travel. In all his budget iterations, McGee included Zunis and Hopis with cost estimates of ten thousand dollars. McGee repeatedly asked McCowan to pay for the Zunis but he always countered, "I heartily endorse the proposition provided no part of the expense comes out of my funds."[41]

To secure Zunis, McGee hired Matilda Coxe Stevenson, even though she had testified against him in the 1903 investigation. Although she disliked McGee intensely, she agreed to help him to supplement her income. Stevenson, a BAE ethnologist, was one of the first female American anthropologists. She was already at Zuni in early 1904 preparing a manuscript on weaving and clothing. In addition, Holmes had assigned her the task of researching Zuni pottery designs and ritual symbolism for the Smithsonian exhibits, which she did. Stevenson was successful in arranging for a Zuni group to travel to St. Louis, but they never went. Again the problems were the lack of salaries and McGee's failure to send transportation vouchers. Luckily for Stevenson, she had not spent her own money to acquire building materials.[42]

The Hopis received an invitation to attend through the initial canvassing of Indian Service personnel. McCowan asked trader Thomas V. Keam to serve as his agent and suggested a group from Third Mesa who had worked for the Fred Harvey Company as demonstrators. He also wanted Hopi children and requested they come with their parents, the same arrangement he made with the Pimas. An outbreak of scarlet fever and diphtheria at Keams Canyon, however, placed the entire reservation in quarantine. In addition, there was Charles V. Burton, the Hopi agent, who opposed anything that perpetuated Hopi religious ceremonies and refused to allow anyone performing a ritual to leave the reservation. He did not want any Hopis to go to St. Louis, especially given the explosive political situation on Third Mesa, but if someone did, he did not want Keam involved. On April 13 he wrote McCowan that

> Mr. Keam was my bitterest foe and to have him take a company of Indians to perform that which I believe to be a great detriment to them and against which I have contended since coming here would not be consistent at all. I am aware that the Moquis [Hopi] do not belong to me and if the Department insists that they go ... I hope that some other person besides Keam comes for them. However the Moquis would not and should not come without specific remuneration.[43]

McCowan eliminated Keam and requested that someone else help, but no one came forward, fearing Burton's displeasure and retribution. It was soon obvious that McGee and Dorsey would have to intervene. Dorsey asked missionary Henry Voth to find sixty Hopi demonstrators. He was unable to take on the assignment but informed trader P. Staufer of the request. Staufer contacted McGee offering his services as an agent but no answer has been found in McGee's or McCowan's papers.[44]

It is doubtful any Hopis went to St. Louis, even though some scholars have accepted Tobin's hype (see chapter 9) and McGee's unwavering hopes as evidence of their presence. McGee in his final report mentions the Hopis, along with the San Juans and Acomas, but other documentary sources do not support this contention. McGee never gave up his quest to secure groups he referred to as the "short relatives of the Aztecs." He contacted friends in the Southwest even after the exposition opened, begging them to bring Hopis. McCowan told him repeatedly they were overspending their Indian budget, but that he would put aside part of their contingency fund for the Hopis in case they could still come. It was never used.[45]

McGee tried to secure the services of a Papago (Tohono O'odham) family, "the desert folk par excellence of North America" (McGee 1905d, 109). He thought they would contrast with the Cocopas, showing how their dark skin and luxurious hair was well adapted for the high heat and aridity of the American Southwest. Without consulting McCowan, McGee wrote to Indian Service agents in Tucson. They were unable to convince a family to travel to St. Louis, and McGee had to settle for the Pima-Maricopa families from the Gila River Reservation, whom McCowan had already persuaded to represent the desert dwellers.

Seeking Celebrities and Special Artists

By March 1904 McGee was urgently asking his friends to find individuals to fill the holes in his exhibition scheme. Boas discovered that nine Eskimo men, three women, and one child who usually performed at Coney Island were free for the summer and they would come if McGee could pay their expenses and a salary equivalent to what they earned in New York City. McGee had obligated all his funds and was already over budget. He would have to rely on Eskimos already slated for two Pike exhibits, although he would have rather had them under his own care in the Anthropology Department.[46] McGee began to reconceptualize his undertaking to include any non–American Indians in any part of the fair.

McCowan was not pleased that he had to spend so much time fitting Indians into McGee's model. Nevertheless, he continued to ask agents to search their reservations. Arrangements were made and unmade. It was unclear who was actually coming until after May 1.

Dorsey regularly suggested Indian artists. In March 1904 he wrote McGee about Pomo artists William and Mary Benson, from Yukia Reservation, California, who were working for the Fred Harvey Company in Albuquerque. Mary Benson was a superb basket weaver, while William was an outstanding shell and stone bead maker, pipe manufacturer, flint knapper, and feather worker. They were accustomed to working with researchers (having consulted with Dr. John H. Hudson for five years on a Pomo ethnography), spoke English, were accomplished demonstrators, and were "amply able to take care of themselves under any circumstances."[47] Dorsey had Hudson broker an offer and informed McGee of their terms: (1) transportation from Albuquerque to St. Louis and from St. Louis to their home in California, (2) food en route, and (3) room and board during their stay in St. Louis. They also insisted that they be allowed to sell their artwork and retain *all* monies accruing from sales. They would not agree to come if the department, Indian School, or LPEC retained 25 percent of each sale.

McGee agreed, requesting that they leave Albuquerque around April 20. Dorsey continued the negotiations, arranging for Hudson to obtain enough raw materials from California and to send William his tools. He advised the Bensons to make a full range of shell and stone money, wooden pipes, chipped stone tools, mortars and pestles, fire drills, and, of course, fine basketry. He predicted that they would be very busy.[48] The Bensons arrived on May 1 without incident and began demonstrating their arts even before the opening of the department and the Indian School. They became the first Native celebrities of the fair.

The department and the Indian School needed celebrities, especially Indian warriors, to attract visitors. McGee began promising their attendance as soon as he was hired, and from late 1903 until well after the fair was underway the LPEC publicity department stated in innumerable newspaper articles that "Chief Joseph of the Nez Perce, probably the ablest living Indian, will come from Idaho. The Comanche chief, Quanah [Parker], will come from the Indian territory, and also famous old Geronimo, who led the United States troops a wild goose chase for so long on the Arizona frontier."[49] Securing these previously dreaded warriors, who were now safe to observe, proved to be a daunting task.

The problem was to approach each individual, negotiate a contract, and convince government officials (including McCowan). Indian celebrities were initially expected to bear their own transportation costs because McCowan refused to use his school funds. McGee agreed to cover transportation as well as per diem expenses while in St. Louis, reasoning that celebrities would profit substantially from their status, as eager tourists clamored to buy souvenirs made by their hands and samples of their signatures on photographs. Quanah Parker originally agreed to these terms, feeling it would give him an excellent political forum, and was greatly anticipated. He never came, for in February one of his daughters became critically ill. Parker placed family obligations over his desire for adventure. One of his daughters, Esther, was a student in the Indian School, however, and relatives of Parker's came to demonstrate instead.[50]

McGee was disappointed that Parker was not coming. His hopes then turned to Chief Joseph, the "Napoleon of Indians," who while elderly would be interesting because he was a brave man and greatly respected. Chief Joseph never demonstrated at the exposition, but it was not for want of trying on McCowan's part. He staged an extensive letter-writing campaign from December 1903 to September 1904 to locate and entice the Nez Perce leader. There is no evidence Chief Joseph came to St. Louis (except possibly as a tourist for one or two days after a diplomatic mission to Washington DC) even though McGee and Cummins's Wild West show manager said daily that his arrival was imminent. Chief Joseph died in September 1904 of a sudden heart attack and was interred on the Colville Reservation. Ironically, one obituary said he had recently been to St. Louis "where he was paid every attention while inspecting the World's Fair."[51]

Hope now rested with Geronimo, who was to illustrate "a native type and an aboriginal personage of interest to passing throngs of visitors." Publicity was extensive and included such nonsense as that "he has between eighty-five and one hundred white scalps to the credit of his savagery and also a vest made of the hair of the whites whom he has killed" and that "[l]ong years of captivity have broken his spirit and he is docile because he has met his masters."[52] Persuading Geronimo was a delicate affair for he was an excellent negotiator who knew his worth, having attended expositions in Omaha and Buffalo.

Securing Geronimo's participation fell to McCowan, much to his displeasure. He began by writing the secretary of war, since Geronimo was still technically a prisoner of war. Receiving no reply he asked A. G. Tanner (assistant commissioner of the Indian Service) to approach senior officials. The request slowly worked its way through channels, coming to rest on the desk of Lt. Gen. H. M. Young, Army chief of staff. Young contacted Capt. Farrand Sayre, who was in charge of Fort Sill prisoners. Only on April 18 was official permission given for Geronimo and his relatives to travel to St. Louis, accompanied by Sayre. McCowan spent much of May negotiating their travel.[53]

While progress was being made with the federal bureaucracy, private entrepreneurs approached McGee or McCowan asking permission to promote and display for profit the famous gentleman, apparently without discussing their proposals with Geronimo. Most were quite fanciful. Several leaked news of their impending accomplishment to the press, requiring McGee to spend many hours dispelling the rumors.

When McCowan finally approached Geronimo, the Apache elder declined. "When I was first asked to attend the St. Louis World's Fair I did not wish to go," he later remembered. "When I was told that I would receive good attention and protection, and that the president of the United States said that it would be all right, I consented."[54] This was an oversimplification. Geronimo forced McCowan to negotiate and negotiate and negotiate. To McCowan, the fact that he had to bargain at all only confirmed his preconception of Geronimo as difficult and stubborn.

But Geronimo was in a good position to negotiate. There was a demand for his services and the use of his name. Even his old enemy, John Clum, noted: "The name and general character of Geronimo had become so well known throughout the country that he was regarded as a *most valuable asset as an attraction at prominent public affairs*."[55] Geronimo also understood about fairs and the monetary value of his presence. At Buffalo he had been paid a salary of forty-five dollars per month and allowed to select the people who accompanied him. Now Cummins, the promoter of the Wild West show at St. Louis, was offering him one hundred dollars per month. Fearing he would lose his only celebrity, McGee agreed to pay Geronimo one hundred dollars per month, as well as all profits from the sale of his signature. Geronimo was also allowed to select Chiricahua Apaches to accompany him, much to Sayre's consternation. They would not live in summer wickiups but army tents, and would not perform rituals nor wear loincloths. Geronimo left Fort Sill, Oklahoma, on April 24, with Captain Sayre and an interpreter, G. M. Wratten.

The Exhibits Come Together

Students and Indian School personnel also began to arrive as McCowan put the finishing touches on the Indian School. On April 25 he ordered two dozen slop jars, two dozen syrup pitchers, and two dozen washbowls and pitchers. The band arrived from Chilocco to march in the opening day parade, along with a group of girls under the supervision of Emma McCowan. On May 2, fifteen students left Helena, Montana, and the Laguna demonstrators and students from the Albuquerque Indian School boarded a train in Albuquerque. More students came the next week and the Indian School basement became crowded since the bedrooms on the second floor were not finished. Superintendent H. Peairs sent more than ten thousand pounds of harness-making and wagon-making equipment from Haskell Institute. Exhibits from schools arrived daily and were installed. Although not officially opened, the Indian School and the Department of Anthropology drew crowds who watched the young men install stoves and lay parquet floors. Geronimo, the Acomas, Ainus, Tehuelches, Cocopas, and the Bensons sold their wares on the front porch as their encampments were being completed.[56]

Lack of funds continued to be a problem and McGee rethought the department's scope yet again, figuring out what he could cut since every expedition had gone over budget as had expenses for preparing the encampments. He started to talk publicly about who would *not* be in St. Louis, blaming omissions on money, and constructed ways to rationalize substituted groups. For example, he now stated that the lack of Australian Aboriginals was mitigated by the presence of Negritos in the Philippine Exhibit.

McGee still tried to encourage other anthropologists to independently bring the Native peoples with whom they worked or conduct original research at the exposition, but at their own expense. He presented his new requests at scientific societies, historical societies, and universities and wrote an article, "Opportunities in Anthropology at the World's Fair," published in *Science* (McGee 1904f, 253–55). He addressed more than twenty-five civic groups in six weeks but only the Davenport Academy of Sciences took him up on his offer of exhibit space.

Even after the fair opened, McGee tried to enlist State Department acquaintances to persuade foreign governments to send Native people. He asked

Dr. J. H. McCormick to talk to Panama's consul about sending Kunas to live near the Philippine Reservation to complement their exhibits of natural resources. He hoped that McCormick could convince the Panama government to reallocate an appropriation of twenty-five to fifty thousand dollars out of their first canal payment from the U.S. government for the undertaking. Although McCormick broached the subject, Panama declined.[57]

While the anthropology exhibit was less representative than originally planned, there was still much to see, according to McGee. The department now included: (1) a limited representation of the world's least-known ethnic and cultural types, that is, races or sub-races defined physically and societies defined on a technological (or mental) basis; (2) appliances used in laboratory research assessing mankind's physical and mental characters; (3) evidence of the steps and general course of human progress, including prehistoric and proto-historic relics and historical records in static exhibits; and (4) a representation of "actual human development from barbarism toward enlightenment as accelerated by association and training"—the Indian School (McGee 1905d, 18–19).

McGee insisted that these exhibits were educational, not simply curiosities designed to attract visitors. But he now claimed that selected concessions on the Pike—such as those with Eskimos (short, round people adapted to cold climates) and peoples in state and foreign pavilions—reflected his paradigm. He drew the line at the clever frauds on the Pike, such as the blacks from New Jersey posing as men from East Africa. This strategy carried professional danger, for including any Pike concession could undermine his professional authority through the taint of hucksterism and commercialism. He constantly had to assure numerous parties that the Department of Anthropology would easily be distinguished from the Pike. He told Skiff that all his exhibits were "designed for the instruction and edification of visitors . . . None [were] made for any commercial object, either direct or indirect."[58] This was a problematic claim since all the Indian demonstrators were required to produce and sell art. To keep the exhibits authentic, pure, and untainted by commerce required that expenses for the entire enterprise be borne through exposition appropriations, which was not going to happen.

Another feature of McGee's plans, producing new knowledge, was slowly curtailed. McGee had wanted the Anthropology Department to be the locus of "original research by scientific students attracted by the exhibits and by the

World's Congresses" (McGee 1905d, 20). But with the limited number of ethnic-racial groups, the fair no longer could be used for the global comparisons McGee felt anthropology needed to advance theoretically. No ethnologist pursued ethnographic research; only anthropometry and psychometry research was undertaken in two laboratories in the Cupples Hall basement. To McGee these laboratories provided the central rationale for the living exhibits and he was disappointed when other scientists did not feel the same. Still there would be one innovative feature, an ethnographic field school taught by Starr.

If McGee's theories of human diversity and human development formed the departmental foundation, it was the display of living peoples that gave it substance. As June 1 approached, McGee prompted reporters about the people who were coming, emphasizing how they fit into his scheme as physical and cultural types. Tables 1.1 and 1.2, in appendix 1, summarize his final groupings and the physical features that he felt distinguished the ethnic groups. Today these physical, cultural, or "artificial" features sound ludicrous. The Cocopas really did not illustrate "the consistent maintenance of physical types in a single primitive folk," with extreme conservatism, agriculture, and wasteful mortuary customs that symbolized irrational thinking, nor did the Mbutis demonstrate how "the industrial arts of the Little People have been affected by contact and barter with iron-making peoples ever since the Iron Age" (McGee 1905d, 22). But the press liked that McGee had selected Native people because they were exotic, quaint, unusual, and had strange customs. Appendix 2 lists the people who came.

Racial and physical types were supplemented by the "constant stream of visitors from every quarter of the globe." To McGee, visitors were part of anthropology's grand research experiment and critical components of the fair's racial messages. Taking such a broad view integrated all the exposition under a common umbrella of cultural and technological evolution (McGee 1904a, 4–5; 1905d, 21, 23, 26). On opening day, June 1, everything was as ready as it was ever going to be. McGee rationalized that the LPE's general layout recognized anthropology's centrality, even if the department was placed marginally at the far end of the fairgrounds. Visitors had to want to look for the rare and little-known, dark-skinned Native peoples, but it would be worth the effort.

5. Presenting Worthy Indians

Well, I declare!
One-half of the world really doesn't know how the other half lives.
Visitor remark, June 16, 1904.

Almost five hundred individuals from twenty-nine societies were official members of the LPEC's Native encampments, commonly called the Anthropology Villages (for foreign Natives) and Indian Village. In 1913 LPE president David Francis reminisced about the "almost sensational" outdoor reservations he had seen and how they had been construed within the LPE's theme of humanity's rise to civilization, clearly attuned to McGee's arguments of racial development and how groups should be labeled. McGee's introductory labels told visitors how to interpret the people they saw. Each group illustrated "steps in the development of intelligent Man, [and] is at once an object-lesson in the ill-written history of the human past and an object for beneficent example and effort for Man has no higher duty than that of mending the way of human progress." And this was timely. The Indian Village had remnants of once-powerful tribes brought together for one final stand before the onslaught of civilization. What people would see was how Indians lived, before "the white man's civilization forced him to seek the land of the setting sun."[1]

Everything had to be authentic so visitors could appreciate progress. Contamination by Euro-American culture or indications of assimilation would negate the display and call anthropology into question; it would be like the Pike. McGee insisted that Native peoples wear traditional clothes regardless of the weather, build old-style houses, make culturally appropriate art, and perform bona fide songs and dances. Babies must be carried in cradles, not prams. McGee spent hours ensuring that Natives did not borrow from each other or use the manufactured goods and clothing they acquired while in St. Louis. Since participants wanted souvenirs just much as visitors, it was a futile effort. The best McGee could do was request authenticity from 9:00 to 11:00 a.m. and 2:00 to 4:00 p.m., when groups were officially demonstrating.

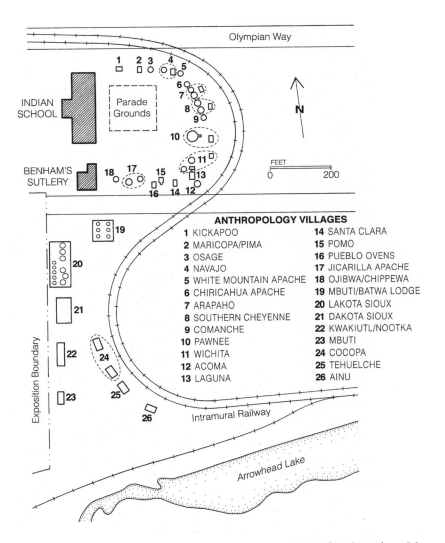

Olympian Way

INDIAN SCHOOL

Parade Grounds

N

BENHAM'S SUTLERY

FEET
0   200

Exposition Boundary

Intramural Railway

Arrowhead Lake

ANTHROPOLOGY VILLAGES

1 KICKAPOO
2 MARICOPA/PIMA
3 OSAGE
4 NAVAJO
5 WHITE MOUNTAIN APACHE
6 CHIRICAHUA APACHE
7 ARAPAHO
8 SOUTHERN CHEYENNE
9 COMANCHE
10 PAWNEE
11 WICHITA
12 ACOMA
13 LAGUNA

14 SANTA CLARA
15 POMO
16 PUEBLO OVENS
17 JICARILLA APACHE
18 OJIBWA/CHIPPEWA
19 MBUTI/BATWA LODGE
20 LAKOTA SIOUX
21 DAKOTA SIOUX
22 KWAKIUTL/NOOTKA
23 MBUTI
24 COCOPA
25 TEHUELCHE
26 AINU

Fig. 5.1 Ground plan of the ethnological exhibits, Department of Anthropology. Map by Charles Sternberg.

Fig. 5.2. Men building roof of the Pawnee earth lodge, the largest Native structure on the fairgrounds. Photograph by Charles Carpenter, May 1904. © The Field Museum, negative no. CSA15648.

But McGee wanted Natives to learn, to see for themselves the inevitability of cultural progress, and in his opinion, there was still a wide gulf to traverse. Fairgoers would teach Natives about American culture and, through their interactions, everyone would become more enlightened and tolerant. McGee hoped that his ethnology section would be a moral example eradicating prejudicial preconceptions. Anthropology would "show each half of the world how the other half lives and thereby promote not only knowledge but also peace and good will among nations" (McGee 1905d, 17). It was great, if essentially empty, rhetoric.

The Layout of the Anthropology Villages and Indian Village

The "Indian Reservation" (see fig. 5.1) was located on a tract west of the intramural railway on the Washington University campus. It was sited on sloping land between Indian School and Arrowhead Lake, across from the Philippine

Reservation. While McGee saw the Anthropology Villages and the Indian Village as distinct units, visitors experienced them as one. Assigned space depended on placement in McGee's evolutionary paradigm, mediated by the size of each group. The model Indian School, with its "transformed boys and girls," was on top of a small hill; the Ainu and Patagonian encampments were at its base, the Cocopas near the Patagonians, the Kwakiutls next to the Mbutis. Indian groups were interspersed, reflecting the supposed evolution of housing styles. As visitors walked up the hill, they successively saw Jicarilla Apache tipis, a Kickapoo bark house, Acoma "adobe houses" (actually tents), Wichita grass huts, a Pawnee "commodious [but] smoky" earth lodge (fig. 5.2), a large Arapaho wattled stockade with painted tipis, a Cheyenne dance ground, and Navajo hogans. Visitors walked into camps where Pima-Maricopas worked under brush ramadas, Chippewas told stories in front of birch-bark dwellings, and Kwakiutls and Nootkas danced in a clan house. Near the top they saw an Osage village representing the Five Civilized Tribes.[2]

At each stop visitors were supposed to see examples of harmonious and simple living, that is, Native people who had agreed to perform daily activities—such as cooking food, dancing, singing, or producing tools—which theoretically reflected the nature of their work, habits, and personalities. In addition, visitors would see them in parades, competing against one another in games and sporting events, and performing "exotic" ceremonies, songs, dances, and rituals. In addition to sales of their art, participants earned money from posing for photographs, tips in exchange for their performances, or from devising innovative ways to extract nickels, dimes, and quarters from visitors (McGee 1905d, 40).

Managing the settling-in period was a major undertaking. Dorsey helped McGee when the Indians first arrived but soon left, leaving McGee to search for a permanent manager. By June 1 there were roughly two hundred Indians assembled; by December more than four hundred had officially participated, and there were others who came for short periods but were never recorded in the official registers, as well as Native tourists. Indians invited themselves and arrived unannounced all the time. Foster Thunderhawk, a Rosebud Sioux compositor and printer, wrote in mid-August stating, "There is some Indians wanting to go and asking me to take them along and if you let me know how many you want all together I will get them as soon as possible. Give me information about the transportation." When he next wrote, Thunderhawk said he was a bit confused that McGee had not been in touch. When McGee wrote they had enough Lakota, Thunderhawk offered to bring Yellow Chief's group in October. McGee finally replied they did not have funds for such an undertaking. They came anyway and McCowan supplied rations.[3]

Representatives eventually came from many American Indian societies. While there is no definitive list of participants, cultural affiliations listed for those coming with official Indian Service approval included: Acoma, Arapaho, Cheyenne, Chippewa/Ojibwa, Chiricahua Apache, Comanche, Crow, Jicarilla Apache, Kickapoo, Kiowa, Laguna, Maricopa, Muskwaki (Sauk and Fox), Navajo, Nez Perce, Osage, Pawnee, Pima, Pomo, San Carlos Apache, Santa Clara or San Juan, "Sioux" (both Lakota and Dakota), and Wichita. (The Nootkas, Cocopas, and Kwakiutls were "foreigners," not Indians.) Others were involved in state and commercial exhibits, but McGee took credit for their appearance in his exhibit catalogues. Sometimes Indians in Cummins's Wild West Show were included in these lists, sometimes not. Appendix 2 summarizes our best—but still incomplete—attempt to identify Indian and other participants.[4]

All participants were instructed to bring bedding, cooking utensils, and their dogs but to leave their horses at home. They also were asked to bring clothing, regalia items emblematic of their culture, and materials for their houses and demonstrations and items to sell. This made the transportation costs for the department quite high; expenses to transport the Wichitas, Arapahos, and Pawnees, and their long tipi poles, reached five hundred dollars. More than forty-two hundred dollars was spent on transportation during May and June.[5]

To McGee these freight costs were worth it, for he hoped the distinctive house styles would dispel the idea that all Indians lived in tipis. In tours for dignitaries he described the tipi as a modern invention, developed by Siouan groups less than a hundred years earlier as they moved onto the Plains. He asked visitors to notice cultural and individual stylistic diversity. Then he switched to types, especially those no longer being made. He told them that for elders the fair was a site to teach younger people about traditional cultural ways and celebrate their knowledge.

Most American Indian participants did not stay for the entire exposition. They came, built their houses, demonstrated for a few weeks or months, and left when they no longer found the fair enticing or profitable. Each group was instructed to follow their regular daily activities, although this was easier for some than others. While frequently encouraged by McGee to perform rituals, each group decided communally which sacred rites or secular dances they could appropriately perform, which stories they would tell, and when they would open their homes to the highly inquisitive visitors. Participants interpreted their roles in their own way.

The First Arrivals: The Arapahos, Pawnees, and Wichitas from Oklahoma

The Pawnees, Wichitas, and Arapahos were the first to arrive. Under Murie's direction, they participated in the LPE's opening ceremonies and soon began to build their houses. The Pawnees were led by Roaming Chief (or Roan Chief), whom McGee said was the most majestic individual at the fair. He stood six feet, eight inches and was "splendidly proportioned, weighing some two hundred and seventy-five pounds." With him were five families, several adult men who were prominent healers, an adult woman, and interpreter Cleveland Warden. They built an old-style, eight-sided earth lodge for which McGee gave them $120. It was by all accounts the most imposing, solid, and coolest Native structure at the fair; a long covered, east-facing entrance helped control the interior temperature. Visitors watched with great interest. When on May 31 the *Daily Official Program* announced that the women were ready to begin pounding sod, hundreds of people observed the procedure.[6]

The Pawnees also built a summer arbor and constructed a sweat lodge for purification ceremonies and cleansing purposes, the latter necessary since the sanitation facilities were unfinished. Most visitors compared it to a fashionable bath but a few referred to it disparagingly ("a rude imitation of the Turkish bath"), because it was a temporary structure, a willow tipi covered with blankets. A more apt comparison would have been a Swedish sauna.[7] A few visitors questioned the authenticity of the earth lodge, ignoring housing changes stemming from Indian Service policy: "I have lived fifty years among the Indians," one man wrote in the Indian School guest book, "and I know that no Indian ever built or ever lived in a house like that Pawnee mud lodge. It's a fake."[8] Negative comparisons with European building styles were common and unfortunately some derogatory images were due to McGee's and Dorsey's poor analogies when speaking to reporters. Dorsey referred to the Pawnees and Wichitas as "dirt lodgers."

*They were like the prairie dogs, the ground hogs, the gophers and bad-
gers. They burrowed their homes in the earth, and raised over them a
framework of willows, covered this over with tough prairie grass, and
then put on the main roof of sod. . . . The lodge was a good shelter
from storms. It was a storehouse in which the meat of the hunters was
safe from the wolves and the coyotes which ran over the plains. It was
a safe retreat from the enemies of the tribe, for the roof was firm and
thick and a single warrior could guard the door against any number
of foe.*[9]

Apparently the Pawnees did not make crafts for sale; no individuals are
recorded in artisan lists. There are also no records that they participated in
staged performances. Most received money by posing for photographs, and
one man, Frank Moore, engaged in athletic competitions and gave orations
in the Indian School. On one occasion he spoke on "The Value of Trade to a
Reservation Indian."

Conversely, the Wichitas produced cradles, sinew-backed bows, and moccasins for sale and were noted for their symbolic games and ability to paint
and bead buckskin. Well-known leader Towakani Jim headed a contingent of
seven families, six adult men, and a boy who was an expert in making miniature bows and arrows.[10] For McGee the Wichitas' main activity was to build
a grass house and live in it. As he told escort John Buntin, "They must bring
everything with them that is possible to make a realistic home environment.
Everything that is of interest to visiting whites on the reservation should be
included in this exhibit." Buntin paid Towakani Jim and his family a small
stipend to collect eight hundred pounds of poles and bark and over twenty-
five hundred pounds of prairie grass, and McGee paid the group forty dollars to build it. They erected a winter grass lodge. The willow sapling frame
and rafters were tied together with willow bark and covered with prairie-grass
thatch and rice grass. Ventilation was quite good, according to one visitor.[11]
The Wichita also erected a summer house and two tipis.

The press wrote little about the Wichitas even though they performed in
parades and did a brisk business selling moccasins. Their main attraction was
a baby girl born to Josephine and Burgess Hunt, aptly named Louisiana Francis. By June 9 the baby was growing vigorously and one visitor remarked, "I

admire the Indian way of taking care of babies. If I have any grandchildren to take care of, I shall buy Indian cradles for them." Not all reporters agreed: "In almost any place but the Indian colony the arrival of the baby would be the cause of long celebration, but not so the Wichitas. The child was wrapped in a gorgeous Indian blanket and left upon the bed, while the mother occupied herself with other duties." The father, another wrote, was "disappointed and openly expressed regret that the child was a girl." How the writers gained this insight must be left to the imagination.[12]

It required all of Dorsey's negotiating skills to convince older Arapaho men to travel to St. Louis. He telegraphed McCowan on April 19 that he had finally arranged for four lodges and that he would escort them and the Chiricahua Apaches from Fort Sill, Oklahoma. Plans altered daily and the Arapaho eventually traveled in three groups at different times. The first group was headed by Chief Black Coyote (Watonga), who "astonished [McCowan] by presenting his visiting card and exhibiting a bank book" when they were first introduced. The first families were joined several weeks later by four married couples and their children and four single men. Soon other married couples arrived. Cleveland Warden, aged thirty-eight, served as interpreter. Educated at Carlisle Indian School (1890–1897) he was proficient in reading and writing English. After working various jobs in Oklahoma, he collaborated with James Mooney on his study of Kiowa and Arapaho shields. He began working for Dorsey in 1899 and was paid thereafter as a staff field collector as well as a collector for the Fred Harvey Company. Warden built a tipi for the Field Museum and should have been credited as a coauthor of Dorsey's Arapaho ethnographies.[13]

When all their building materials arrived, the Arapaho erected and painted six tipis and built three summer houses inside circular brush windbreaks (fig. 5.3). McGee noted that while the housing was standard and not worthy of note, the Arapahos were the most colorfully attired American Indians, "a wealth of costumery and trappings of buckskin, fringed, beaded, and decorated with elk teeth such as has seldom been assembled."[14] The Department of Exploitation and the Indian School used Black Coyote in full regalia (shield, headdress, and feathered spear) as the model for traditional Plains Indian culture. White Shirt was also frequently photographed by visitors because of his interesting attire (white shirt, breech clout, cutaway coat, and black trousers) which McGee complained almost daily was inappropriate.

Fig. 5.3. Arapaho family with tipi and brush stockade. The stockade was later used by a Southern Cheyenne family. Library of Congress, Prints and Photographs Division, LC-USZCA-12808.

Several Arapahos produced and sold beaded buckskin objects. One man may have painted hides but records are contradictory. The most newsworthy event of their stay seems to have also revolved around a baby. Nelson Whiteshirt was six weeks old when he arrived with his parents, Earl and Alice Whiteshirt, on May 2. Since both parents spoke excellent English they frequently interacted with admiring visitors. One reporter remarked, "Baby Nelson is voted very 'cute' as he peeps over his mother's shoulders at visitors to the tepees of the Arapahos. . . . He is one of the youngest persons among the strange people at the World's Fair, a rival of Baby Kiku of the Ainus as candidate for the first favor with strangers."[15] McGee and McCowan were right. Babies drew crowds.

The Arapahos were unhappy because of their living conditions and difficulties with McCowan, causing a well-publicized scandal. As McCowan informed his superiors:

When the Indians were first brought to St. Louis, the weather was very bad; rain and mud constantly. This caused some discontent among them, naturally, but the discontent was very slight, taking the form of expressions of disgust with the locality mainly. [The Arapaho] brought here by Dr. Dorsey for the Exposition, and not by myself for the Indian Exhibit, were displeased at first over the ration issued. The cause of this, however, was that they were not allowed to go to the Commissary and help themselves promiscuously but were given rations regularly, the beef daily and other articles weekly. When the issue was first made, the provisions looked small and they were sure they would starve on such an allowance. . . . After a week they were surprised to learn that the ration had been sufficient, and since then there has been absolutely no discontent on account of subsistence from any of our Indians.[16]

But McCowan was wrong. Dorsey wrote McGee that many Arapahos, Wichitas, and Pawnees wanted to leave because visitors were buying little and the noise from the Igorot groups of the Philippine Reservation annoyed them, as it did many other participants. Mr. Peairs, an Indian Service employee, re-layed their complaints about the Igorots' constant drumming and the canine yelps resulting from their "dog-eating" activities. One reason the Pawnee gave for leaving the fair in June was that the Igorots had eaten all their dogs! The rest of the Pawnees and the Wichitas left on July 19, due to the deplorable sanitation conditions, but their houses remained standing until the end of the fair. Even without occupants, the houses were prominent features, symbols of the region's architectural antecedents. The Pawnee's "strange domicile was the very antipode of those great white buildings which were the glory of the fair. As they typified the best of man's structural genius west of the Mississippi River, so did this queer Indian house represent the very beginning of architecture in the Louisiana territory."[17]

The Stars of the Fair: Geronimo and the Apaches

The exposition would have been a failure without Apaches, McGee claimed, with their "war-like habits, fine physiques and skill as horsemen." The first group erected two tipis between the Pomos and Comanches. It is difficult to determine exactly who they were or to establish their culture and band

Fig. 5.4. Chief Geronimo, in 1904, holding arrows and bow he sold as souvenirs. Photograph by H. W. Wyman, 1904. Library of Congress, Prints and Photographs Division, usz62, 10/327.317744.

affiliations. While a problem for present-day researchers, an Apache was an Apache to newsmen and visitors of the period. All that really mattered was that Geronimo (fig. 5.4) was there (McGee 1904c, 17).

The official exhibition catalogue lists Jicarilla Apaches arriving from New Mexico on June 4. It had been questionable whether they would come. H. H. Dawson, the reservation's school superintendent, had arranged for two families reputed to be expert basket makers. Unfortunately an influenza epidemic swept across the reservation and turned the school into a hospital; no one could travel. In late May, however, agent H. Johnson believed he could convince three women, but they refused to come without their husbands. Johnson did not think this a good idea since the men would only sit around. McCowan responded; bring the "husbands as ornaments if they can't do anything else but look pretty." Johnson still had to convince the unenthusiastic men; an Apache group had gone to the Omaha Exposition in 1898 and been treated badly. But on June 1, Dawson telegraphed to expect them in a few days. They were bringing everything but their tipi poles. McCowan quickly secured long poles from the Arapahos. Dilaya Tafoya (aged fifty) led the group; with him came three noted weavers (Darcia, Lena, and Ramona), their husbands, and Christine Pisente, a man aged thirty-nine. The fascinated press wrote that the women were the world's most expert basket makers. But these preconceptions mirrored that of the Indian Service personnel. "The women, of course, did all the work and the men sat around and smoked industriously."[18]

Apaches from the White Mountain Reservation came soon after the Jicarillas. McGee's family register, compiled in May 1904, lists two families, but fails to designate their tribal affiliation. From McCowan's correspondence they appear to have been Chiricahua from the White River area of the Fort Apache Reservation. This selection was intentional. McCowan had asked agent Cornelius M. Crouse to bring two moccasin makers, a quirt maker, a bow-and-arrow maker, two basket makers, and a tanner, along with their spouses and children. As an inducement he told Crouse that "there will be one of their old Apache friends from Fort Sill at St. Louis and I will have them camp alongside each other." The Martine family was related to Charles Martine (Bah-dah-go-gilth-ilth) and Kayihtah from Fort Sill. Martine was a noted army scout who had been sent by General Miles to Geronimo's camp in 1886 to arrange a meeting. Another member was Yanozha, who had traveled with Geronimo in 1886. One other White Mountain Apache visited the fair and made quite an impression on reporters. Antonio Apache, who had received a BA from Harvard and had extensive ethnographic experience working for Putnam during the 1893 Chicago fair, asked McGee for a job. While he was not given one, he did lecture in the Indian School.[19]

The Fort Apache group lived with their Fort Sill relatives. Much to McGee's chagrin, they wisely refused to live in canvas-covered wickiups. The older men knew how to make them but declined to demonstrate construction techniques since McGee would not pay them. Instead they lived in comfortable army tents brought from Oklahoma. Geronimo lived in a specially painted tent by himself.[20]

In addition to Geronimo and Martine, the most noted individual was the group's leader, Natchez (Naiche). He had been at the Omaha fair with his wife, Ha-o-zine, and their children. Others included Prado, who often drummed for Geronimo, and Thomas and Elaya, Geronimo's son and daughter. Another daughter Lina (or Lena) joined them in late July, traveling from the Mescalero Apache Reservation, her way paid by the New Mexico Territorial Commission who wanted to take advantage of Geronimo's notoriety. She spent her days in the New Mexico Territorial Building distributing pamphlets promoting resorts, but resided with Geronimo, sometimes appearing in his Indian School booth. Unfortunately she developed trachoma and left on August 24. Thomas left, too, to attend school at Chilocco. The Fort Sill Apaches produced and sold bows and arrows in their encampment but received almost no press coverage for attention was focused on Geronimo.[21]

The author of a popular exposition guidebook, Marshall Everett, informed visitors that they would see "Indians! All kinds of them. The Louisiana Purchase Exposition would not have been physically or educationally complete without them," but they should be sure not to miss Geronimo, "The Red Devil." Publicists inflated the reasons for his celebrity by the extensive use of hyperbole and exaggeration; Geronimo was a man "whose presence made every white settler tremble with fear, as his extreme cruelty was dreaded." Others noted he was now more than seventy years old; this would be visitors' last chance to see a "real" Indian warrior and leader.[22]

There was speculation over how free "the bloodthirsty" Geronimo would be in St. Louis and whether he was still dangerous. According to one reporter, "Long years of captivity have broken his spirit and he is docile because he has met his masters. . . . Geronimo will be practically free at the world's fair, but still a prisoner of war." Most reporters conveniently forgot to mention Anglo or Mexican atrocities perpetrated against the Apaches. None provided Geronimo's account of the historic 1886 events, nor mentioned the years he was a prisoner of war, sometimes placed in chains, and who, unlike combatants under the Geneva Convention, was not released at the end of a war. No mention was made of his current life with his sixth wife, Zi-yah, how he grew hay and cared for cattle, or his constant attempts to convince the U.S. government to fulfill their treaty obligations. What they speculated on was whether he had been tamed by Christianity.[23]

Geronimo arrived on June 6, accompanied by the Fort Sill internment camp's adjutant. He was seventy-five, and knew how to manipulate crowds. He was allowed to come and go as he pleased, actually under less strict regulation than other participants, but did not have complete freedom. An article on a dance competition noted that he was not allowed to participate because "the United States government has forbidden him to wear his regalia on account of the bad effect it has on his emotions." Actually he refused to wear anything but European attire. He would cut off and sell his coat buttons as he walked the fairgrounds, a strategy he had developed in Omaha to satisfy visitors' insatiable desire for celebrity souvenirs. He would then sew on another set. Geronimo especially liked to visit the Pike where, "Every Sunday [Francis] sent for me to go to a Wild West show. I took part in the roping contests before the audience. There were many other Indians there, and strange people of whom I had never heard."[24]

Geronimo worked in the Indian School building, arriving each morning around 9:00 a.m. He sat in his booth flanked by Acoma corn grinders and Laguna potters. He worked industriously producing souvenir bows, arrows, and canes that he sold quickly to eager visitors. He also played his fiddle and sang a variety of Apache songs, which were misinterpreted as war chants. He attended an Indian School band concert or literary program almost every afternoon. One of his most lucrative activities was the sale of his image. "I sold my photographs for twenty-five cents," he recounted later, "and was allowed to keep ten cents of this to myself. I also wrote my name for ten, fifteen, or twenty-five cents, as the case may be, and kept all of that money. I often made as much as two dollars a day, and when I returned [to Oklahoma] I had plenty of money—more than I had ever owned before." As one visitor remembered, "I gave him ten cents to see him sign his name and it was worth it. His smile of satisfaction and his flourish indicate the firm belief on his part that he is performing the greatest service of his life. And he is."[25]

Geronimo was popular with visitors, even those who tried to cut off a lock of hair or taunted him. He was described as quiet and dignified, refusing to comply with requests for war whoops or other stereotyped behaviors visitors expected from him. Some visitors objected because he wore Western-style clothes rather than a loincloth and feathers, would say "God bless you" when they parted company, evidently too "civilized" in his behavior. Others complained that he was a feeble old man, not the Geronimo of their imaginations. To counter disappointment, the LPEC periodically publicized, "The old chief still maintains the erect stature and haughty demeanor which characterized him in his prime."[26]

The press was fascinated with Geronimo, the image, but ambivalent about Goyathlay (his Indian name), the man. Reporters commented on how he acted at concerts (if he applauded at the proper time) and what he wore and ate (his fondness for pie and tea). Some said he was happy as a bird, delighted to see old friends, and especially fond of women. There was an element of mistrust in these accounts, which stood for a mistrust of all Indians and the uncertainty that they could assimilate to Euro-American culture and still remain Indian. "Geronimo Is Feeble and Quite Religious" was the headline in one *St. Louis Globe-Democrat* story, while another reporter concluded that even though Goyathlay "had got religion" he still "excited a romantic interest." Others ignored this dilemma by stating that Geronimo's original reputation was overrated: "The more we watch Geronimo, the more we are convinced that the wild Indian has always been overestimated. Where and when were those lofty and laconic speeches delivered that we read about in books? There must be nothing in those Canonicus, Uncas, and Powhatan stories. Geronimo never perpetrated an epigram." Others decided he was simply an old man, bent and mute, waiting for death.[27]

Geronimo was far more alive, resilient, and proactive than that. Part of his supposed muteness was simply a decision not to talk needlessly, especially to visitors who were rude or made jokes at his expense. It was not his problem that people wanted a romanticized dime-novel warrior. He apparently made no comment to one woman who stood in front of him and was overheard to say, "Why do people wish anything *he* makes?" or to another who claimed loudly that he was not really Geronimo because he was too ugly. A few wanted to see the celebrity but were not quite sure why, confused about heritage and historic events. "Is that Geronimo, the one who was chief of the Modoc War?" But most visitors found him engaging and were impressed by his patriotism. As one visitor wrote to the *New York Times*, "Besides the reviewing officer, straight as an arrow and motionless, stood a figure that would attract attention anywhere. . . . As the Indian band played 'The Star Spangled Banner,' this old warrior, standing in the rays of the setting sun, removed his hat and held it against his left shoulder in silent salute to the flag he so long defied."[28]

What Goyathlay remembered in 1909 was not the visitors but the Pike's attractions: the fighting and swordsmanship of Turkish warriors, a "strange-looking negro" escape artist, barkers, and magicians. He recalled the Six Days of Creation concession vividly. "This was a good show, but it was so strange and unnatural that I was glad to be on the streets again." He was fascinated by the Igorots, "the little brown people who do not wear much clothing." Their nakedness bothered him, as it did many Indians, and he thought that they should not have been allowed to come. "They did not seem to know any better. They had some little brass plates, and they tried to play music with these, but I did not think it was music—it was only a rattle. However, they danced to the noise and seemed to think they were giving a fine show."[29]

Geronimo's final assessment of St. Louis was that he was glad he had gone. In addition to earning a good sum of money, he had seen many interesting things. Like other visitors he took some of the technological wonders home, especially souvenirs from his favorite artist, a glass blower. "We went into one place where they made glassware. I had always thought that these things were made by hand, but they are not. . . . I bought many curious things in there and brought them home with me." He also brought home memories and a new assessment of white Americans, just as McGee and McCowan had hoped. He now found white people "very kind and peaceful. During all the time I was at the fair no one tried to harm me in any way. Had this been among the Mexicans I am sure I should have been compelled to defend myself often. I wish all my people could have attended the fair."[30]

The Southern Plains Groups: Southern Cheyennes and Comanches

Some Southern Cheyenne families came during the summer due to the initiative of their leader Richard Davis, an educated man employed by the Indian Service as an interpreter. The Cheyennes had not been on McCowan's or Mc-

Gee's original lists but were included due to Davis's persuasive abilities and his offer to bring them at his own expense. Davis had wanted to come to the fair for a long time. His father, Bull Bear, had been chief of the Dog Soldiers and a signatory to the 1867 Treaty of Medicine Lodge. Davis first contacted McGee in the fall of 1901, asking to be included in the government's exhibit. He saw fairs as a means to educate whites about Cheyenne culture and as places of economic opportunity. "These Expositions are a benefit to our Indians as it brings them in contact with the latest civilization and they learn more during their stay than they would in fifty years' time on an allotment or reservation where they are confined and do not see much of the world."[31] Going to St. Louis would be visible proof that the Cheyennes were still strong and an act of defiance against an Indian Service agent who did not want them to go.

Davis worte numerous letters to McGee, Dorsey, and McCowan but received different offers from each. Davis had promised several prominent families they could go and was anxious about the arrangements. From McCowan he obtained permission to bring twenty-five tipis (households) and camp on the grounds, as well as receive reduced train fares. McCowan also agreed to purchase the tickets for a sixty-day trip (which Davis would later reimburse) and obtain permission for them to sell their art without having to pay the LPEC concession rates (25 percent of sales). McCowan's only condition was that Davis not bring any alcoholics, only "worthy Indians." McCowan was sure that the Cheyennes would like St. Louis and coming would be a wise investment, especially if they brought their ponies. "Other Indians in Oklahoma are arranging parties for this purpose. There will be doubtless several hundred there from all over the country, and you could have some very good times together." Davis assured McCowan he would bring "worthy Indians as I believe they will learn more about the white man's ways in a short time than if they never went there."[32]

In late April, twelve Cheyennes decided to go although Davis still insisted that more than 150 individuals would eventually come. Davis agreed to serve as interpreter and obtained a small salary from McCowan. They waited until their lease and annuity payments arrived since McCowan had instructed their agent to set aside the necessary funds. When they arrived at the train station, railway officials had no knowledge of the arrangements. Davis complained to McGee about McCowan's lack of follow-up. Soon thereafter he discovered that different arrangements had been made for other groups.

There is a party now in Darlington [Oklahoma] getting up a delega-
tion of Arapahos and some Cheyennes to go to St. Louis. They have
eight or ten families now and represent to [them] that EVERYTHING
will be paid for them and furnish all they need. They are told all they
have to do is to pack up and go. On the other hand you have been
writing to us that the government would not pay for our traveling
expenses. If the government would pay for some, we think we have
as much and perhaps better Cheyenne Indian outfits than what they
*already have picked out.*³³

Davis next wrote that Wolf Robe and his wife had decided not to participate but to join the Wild West show because they were assured of fifty dollars
per month each with all their expenses paid. Davis was upset about the agreement. "I wish the government would stop this side show business. . . . We
prefer going there under your direction for we know it is for the good of the
Indians." McCowan responded by saying, "I know there are Arapahos coming from your country whose transportation is furnished by the government."
We can "not care for the Cheyenne for the reason that we have other Indians
who do the same class of work better than they do. It was your proposition
originally to bring Cheyenne here at their own expense. If your Cheyenne still
want to come that way I shall arrange transportation upon receipt of funds. I
shall also provide camping places. Your Indians will have to keep themselves
while here but they can do that as cheaply as they can at home."³⁴

With a new arrangement brokered by McGee, Davis's group arrived in late
June to demonstrate beadwork and moccasin making. Bushy Head and his
wife and Bull Bear and Red Painted Woman (Davis's parents) were the elders
of the group. The Davis family included several children ranging in age from
Lulu (age fourteen) to baby Henry. Since the Arapahos had left, the Southern
Cheyennes erected winter tipis, tall pole frameworks covered by canvas, and
a light bark-covered summer house in the Arapaho compound. Their grass-
covered summer house had a flat roof supported by four corner poles and
was well-ventilated, ideal for the St. Louis summer and for selling art. The
structures were surrounded by a brush stockade, which kept overly inquisitive visitors at bay (fig. 5.3). The Cheyennes also erected a magnificent decorated buckskin display even though the owners had decided not to bring their
prized painted buffalo hides, fearing they would be stolen or ruined. They also

used the Arapahos' Indian School booth to demonstrate symbolic painting on animal hide. Several were unhappy and left in mid-August. While other adults said they regretted not being able to stay and see more of the fair, McCowan was pleased when the rest left since he would no longer have to pay for their food from his diminishing contingency fund.[35]

McGee's choice to represent the Southern Plains was the Comanches. School superintendent J. W. Haddon escorted an extended family of Oklahoma Comanches who knew the old ways. It was unclear until the last moment whether they would consent to come. The problem, once again, was money. As Haddon informed McCowan on April 13, "The old scamps all demand MONEY before they will talk of going. . . . I can get the young Indians to go by the dozens but the old fellows, the ones you desire, are averse to going and care nothing whatsoever about the show."[36] McCowan responded that he would pay only for Quanah Parker, but that he did want Comanches. In the end, Per-da-sof-py and his family erected one tipi next to the Apache and stayed for two months.

There is little mention of the Comanches in the press or exposition publicity although John Hanson wrote in a photo caption that "[l]ong contact with the pale face has made 'good Indians' of these braves; here civilization and savagery meet."[37] Their patience was evidently often tried, however.

> *The ignorance of Uncle Sam's work in this direction [education] was demonstrated by the very many questions posed to the Indian themselves and their attendants by the visitors that swarmed over the grounds. "How, how!" exclaimed a distinguished old man with a gray beard, addressing Red Eagle, chief of the Comanches, "Do you live over there?" he asked, pointing to a Sioux tepee. Red Eagle was making strides like a West Pointer across the campus to his home. Red Eagle halted for a second, looked amused, and then disgusted. "I speak English," he said in the purest of Anglo-Saxon, and stalked off, leaving the disgruntled stranger staring after him.[38]*

The Civilized Tribes: The Kickapoos and Osages Teach Sovereignty

Participant rosters have not been located for the seven Kickapoos who came to the fair on June 11 from Kansas, escorted by D. H. Roubideux, a boarding-school graduate. The men built a traditional circular house in four days. The twelve-by-fifteen-foot structure, a reproduction of the home of Chief White

Cow, was made of woven elm-bark sheets attached to a light sapling frame-work. There was a single low door, covered with tanned hide, and a square smoke hole with a canvas hood that shifted in the wind. The correspondent for *Scientific American* thought it the most striking of the Native structures.[39] Except for this description of their house, there was almost no publicity about the Kickapoos. They declined to demonstrate in the Indian School and worked in their own compound producing baskets and beadwork. They remained for only a few weeks. While they clearly did not like their living conditions, there are no extant records as to why they left. Their house remained and became a static exhibit, dismantled in December.

McGee and McCowan wanted Osage (Wajaji) representatives because they were the original owners of the St. Louis Exposition lands. The public did not pick up on this point; they were more interested in hair styles and ap-parel quality. Reporters noted that the Osage had tattooed necks to promote longevity, were very tall (rivaling the Tehuelches), and extremely wealthy. Six older couples, five of their grandchildren, and three young men came from Oklahoma and erected a village near the Indian School. Their leader, seventy-five-year-old Governor Ohlo-ho-wallah, was "one of the finest types, about six feet, four inches tall and weighing about three hundred pounds."[40] As pre-dicted, there were no archers in the group but they did build a grass house and several ramadas.

St. Louis was a political forum for the Osages, one where they could ex-press their sovereignty and try to influence government policy. If McGee and McCowan felt Native peoples could learn from visiting the fair, Osage elders felt visitors and government officials could learn from them. It was a truly interactive encounter. One participant, Fred Lookout, later became a promi-nent spiritual leader and served his people as principal chief from 1913 until his death in 1949. Lookout was born in 1865 near Independence, Kansas, the son of Eagle-That-Dreams of the Eagle Clan. In the early 1880s he was sent to Carlisle Boarding School, then returned to Oklahoma to farm. An opponent of the allotment system, he fought to retain mineral rights and saw the LPE as an opportunity to educate visitors about Osage culture and their needs. He often gave speeches critical of allotment and other Indian Service policies dur-ing Indian School recital programs, much to McCowan's annoyance. Other Osage elders also made political speeches. Che-sho-hum-kah (Claremore, the lieutenant governor) wore an 1849 peace medal and brought the sheepskin treaty between the Osages and the federal government dating to 1804, which he showed to visitors to emphasize their sovereignty. Both men and their families took daily strolls through the grounds, dressed in "the gayest of blankets and the most expensive adornments they can buy," and engaged visitors in discussions as part of their educational and diplomatic efforts.[41]

While McGee felt the Osages "materially extended the display" of Native Americans, he wrote nothing else about them, because they were no longer ethnographically interesting to him (i.e., were not pure). Another fair official held that they had given up their old ways with the exception of hairstyles and tattooing. Governor Ohlo-ho-wallah employed white laborers at the fair, a fact commented on repeatedly by the press. Their most noteworthy features, according to reporters, were their progressiveness, wealth from oil royalties, and cultural preservation efforts. "With all their wealth and civilization the Osages still preserve memories of the tribal and ceremonial dances."[42]

A group of Osage tourists camped on the fairgrounds in September. They were considered noteworthy because they purchased so much Indian art and for their spectacular attire. "When twenty-one Osage Indians [came], the [Indian School] aisles were blocked with people eager to get a glimpse of this proud tribe. Their shaved heads and little top-knots of 'crowning glory' attracted a great deal of attention. . . . They were gorgeously attired in gay blankets and the [women wore] silk in the new 'plaid effects.'" They returned to Oklahoma on September 16 along with the demonstrators who were not pleased with the Indian Village and made their displeasure known. As one exposition official judgmentally remarked, "In one respect the Osage lead all other Indians; they were extremely hard to please. They were continually objecting to conditions as they found them. They had lived too well at home."[43]

Weavers Extraordinaire: The Navajos

Several Navajos traveled to St. Louis under the auspices of the Fred Harvey Company, arriving on May 7. It would not have been an exposition without them. McGee invited them because of their noted artistic ability in textiles and silver jewelry and considered them among the most picturesque Natives at the fair. A good deal of negotiation took place with several agents to find the right families. Robert Perry, the Fort Defiance school superintendent, located

Fig. 5.5. Navajo old-style hogan with booth for selling jewelry. Arapaho tipis in background. Photograph by Charles Carpenter. Courtesy of National Anthropological Archives, Smithsonian Institution, negative no. T15462.

some older Indians but none wanted to bring their children. McCowan asked Perry to convince them to do so, which he did; twenty Fort Defiance Navajos in five family groups came with two additional adult men. The eldest was Good Luck, aged forty-eight. They built two traditional earth-covered lodges and a modern style wooden hogan (male and female structures) and erected a tent in a compound situated between the Pima-Maricopas and the Arapahos (fig. 5.5). Visitors thought the wooden hogan commodious but found the older style "small and uncomfortable" in comparison to other tribes' houses. The Navajos consecrated their hogans with a Blessingway ceremony attended by many Native participants (McGee 1905d, 110).[44]

The Navajos had two booths in the Indian School where they worked daily for the entire exposition. In one, Mr. Peshlakai made silver and copper bracelets, spoons, and necklaces while Mr. Begay worked in turquoise and shell. In the second booth, one Navajo woman spun wool, while another wove; four women rotated in these activities. Mrs. Taos stayed in the compound and made fry bread, which was a great hit with the visitors. She spent many hours teaching Euro-American women how to make tortillas and fry bread, essentially setting up a cooking school, for which she was paid. Zah Tso, a student at the Santa Fe Indian School and a good weaver, joined her mother, Mrs. Etcitty Jose, an artist who worked for the Fred Harvey Company, in the Navajo women's booth. Zah Tso made a special rug that was given to Senator Shelby M. Cullom whom McCowan was cultivating to increase support of the Indian Service, amidst much ceremony. Indian art was a diplomatic souvenir.[45]

The Navajo babies attracted tremendous attention. Chee, born on July 13, stayed with his mother (Skyblue Peshlakai) in their encampment for a couple weeks and then went with her to their Indian School booth. A second baby was also swaddled and placed in a cradle next to her mother's loom. Most people liked the visual effect but sometimes visitors were critical: "A colored minister with silk hat of the style of many years ago and black broad cloth coat, was examining the wrapping of a papoose in the building. 'Do you tie it up so it can't use its hands?' he asked. The mother nodded. 'Too bad. You all don't know no better,' he said pityingly." Generally, women were so enamored with the babies and the swaddling techniques that the central hallway was completely blocked. Many wanted to hold the babies. A reporter for the *Newark Call*, like most visitors, tried to get the mothers to show him the babies. Generally these persistent requests were ignored. The reporter declared that this was because company was not good for babies and because the mother "dreads the spell of the white man." This was why "she hangs an American coin on the arched board above the baby's head."[46] A more likely explanation is that the women wanted to weave and not constantly wake their babies.

The Navajo encampment clearly illustrates how fairs served as commercial enterprises for Native peoples as well as for exposition organizers and how they created ambivalent publicity. Most visitors seem to have valued Navajo weaving, but some made comparisons that satirically criticized American white women and their decorating expenses, not exactly the type of cultural exchange McGee had envisioned.[47]

The Navajos watched the visitors as intently as the visitors watched them. Like other participants, they were impressed with the material goods they saw and purchased dozens of items. This troubled McGee whose concepts of cultural and racial purity did not include Natives buying souvenirs or labor-

Fig. 5.6. Mon-e-do-wats, "Mrs. Spirit Seeker," Anishinabe (Chippewa/ Ojibwa), Leech Lake band from White Earth, Minnesota. The oldest Native demonstrator at the exposition, aged ninety-two. Photograph by Charles Carpenter, June 1904. © The Field Museum, negative no. CSA14452.

saving devices. On June 18 the *St. Louis Republic* noted that after visiting the Department of Education's model playground, Skyblue Peshlakai decided to purchase a baby carriage for her son Chee. "She was given to understand that she would be permitted to purchase one, but that she would not be allowed to use it while in St. Louis, for the officials argued that such an innovation would spoil their exhibit."[48] Needless to say, she ignored McGee and was often photographed while strolling the grounds, learning from the other half of the world, as McGee theoretically intended.

Elders from the North: The Ojibwas (Chippewas/Anishinabes)

In early September a large contingent of Ojibwas (Anishinabes, Leech Lake band) from White Earth, Minnesota, arrived after completing their wild rice harvest. According to McGee, they attracted great attention due to their skills in tanning animal skins and doing porcupine quill work. They built a "village" of birch-bark houses and demonstrated how birch-bark canoes were constructed. The official exhibition catalogue told visitors to expect them to be highly productive, engaged in basketry, bead and porcupine quill decoration, tanning, metal working, and the expected production of bows and arrows. It also told them they would meet a queen, Mon-e-do-wats (fig. 5.6), translated as Spirit Seeker, a widow of a famous leader, Spirits Here. The oldest Native participant at ninety-two, she was greatly respected and very influential, although visitors often did not quite understand what that meant. Her dignified authority was recognized by other groups and she mediated intercultural disputes. Mon-e-do-wats worked in the Indian School constructing miniature birch-bark canoes. She never missed a day, interacting cordially with visitors but always refused to be photographed. One of the men stood guard to ensure that her wishes were honored.[49]

Nah-ee-Gance was the Anishinabes' official male leader. An elderly gentleman, he wore two beaded honoring sashes that served as a vest. Another leader was eighty-six-year-old Mahshahkegesyhig, or Lowering Feather, a noted diplomat and peacemaker who had helped end an uprising on the Leach Lake Reservation following a series of offenses by Indian agents. Like Mon-e-do-wats, he was called upon to mediate intertribal and individual disputes, but only when the proper ritual could be followed. The leaders had brought special occasion attire—pipes and insignia of office as well as good shirts and ties—intending to wear them at official occasions, such as parades, concerts, while giving speeches, and mediating. Unfortunately their luggage was lost in transit. Nah-ee-Gance and Mahshahkegesyhig refused to appear in public or receive visitors because to be seen only in daily attire would be humiliating and disrespectful. After three weeks the trunks were found in Boston and retrieved. Subsequently the men posed for photographs, receiving the same fees as Geronimo. The younger women demonstrated bead working or wove rush mats, baskets, and yarn bags; Mrs. Jane Walters made floral designs on a loom set up in front of their house. The press considered her docile, which probably meant she was quiet, patient, and industrious or had decided to ignore their constant queries.

Basket Makers of the Western Desert: The Pimas, Maricopas, and Pomos

Francis was very impressed with the "dark-colored desert peoples . . . notable for their agility and endurance," the Pimas (O'odham) and Maricopas, and the "shorthanded and squat and flat-faced natives of California," the Pomos. McGee felt that the Pimas and Maricopas (Pei-Pei) would interest visitors because of their cultural and physical desert adaptation. But he presented them as something of a conundrum because they were negative evidence; they did not fit neatly into his evolutionary framework. According to McGee, they had done too well given their level of technological advancement! "They so adjusted themselves to a harsh environment as to attain a larger population than the same region sustains today despite the lack of transportation and other facilities of enlightenment." He rationalized this success by claiming they were on the brink of new advancement. Their "principles of hospitality, charity, and mutual helpfulness . . . indicate that civilization is a natural and necessary outcome of desert life (Francis 1913, 524; McGee 1905d, 109).

Two Maricopa families, one Pima family, and three adult Pima women came with the Sacaton kindergarten class in a special rail car. They brought a tremendous amount of baggage at McCowan's request: materials for summer and winter houses, furniture, cooking utensils, bread baskets, water jars, bedding, a flour mill, food supplies, raw materials for six months, exhibits from the Pima Training School and supplies for students. It cost over twelve hundred dollars. They left Phoenix on May 13 and reached St. Louis five days later, traveling slowly so as not to tire the children.[50]

On behalf of his wife, Henry Adams (called Chief Blue Wing by the press) brought completed coiled baskets that he sold for between eighty cents and one dollar. He sold everything in the first two weeks and had to send for more of the watertight baskets. The most famous member was Jim Bluebird (Maricopa), an army Indian scout. "He spends his afternoons relating to visitors thrilling experiences of the past on the frontier during the Apache uprising, and passing his time by smoking hand-made cigarettes."[51] His wife produced pottery that sold well and both were said to be "friendly and of kindly disposition," intelligent, and industrious.

While this industriousness could be seen in their rectangular houses, *kees*, the willow-pole-framed structures with walls of wattled arrowwood twigs barely withstood the violent spring and summer rainstorms and had to be frequently repaired. At the suggestion of their Midwestern neighbors, the roof was coated with earth to provide protection against the wind and hail. Visitors compared the Pima-Maricopa dwellings to those of the Kickapoos, referring to the former as "primitive." McGee told people that the Pima-Maricopa houses represented an early stage in architectural evolution that led to the Puebloan earthen mansions. Most reporters ignored his conjectures and noted how well-adapted they were for the hot St. Louis summer: "It is as cool and comfortable as the most approved style of modern architecture could effect."[52]

Pomo artists William and Mary Benson and their escort, James Allen, met Dorsey at the St. Louis train station, who helped them get settled. Hudson had diligently sent their tools, raw materials, and grass for a house in late April and it was all waiting for them—one of the few instances where transport actually worked as planned. The Bensons built a summer house near the Acomas but used it only as a workshop; they slept in the Indian School in a special apartment. On the table in their booth they had a small glass phial containing Mary's award-winning miniature baskets. The largest were smaller than a pea and the smallest hardly larger than a pin's head. McGee felt their art was the finest seen on the fairgrounds; Dorsey agreed, reporting that Mrs. Benson spent a good deal of time preparing her materials. "The straws used in many of their baskets are as finely drawn as coarse linen thread and the designs are masterpieces of art."[53]

The Bensons were highly respected, considered practical, self-reliant, and prosperous. Mary was described by reporters as straight-featured with neatly dressed hair; "With her black tresses and light-brown complexion set off with a bright red shawl, she is positively pretty." She had a superb command of English, perfect pronunciation, and pleasant disposition, as well as a healthy perspective on the whole proceedings and their carnival nature. She was often seen laughing at the intense interest of visitors who were fascinated by daily activities that aroused no interest at home. One reporter recorded her comments on a crowd watching the Acoma women make tortillas. "It's so absurd! Everyone looking and looking, to see so small a thing. It's only the way they have of making bread."[54]

William Benson was also highly regarded. "You will find Benson intelligent and a fine worker in aboriginal material," Hudson had written McGee; Dorsey concurred. "William does beautiful work in all forms of shell and stone beadwork in the way of wampum, belts, necklaces. He is also fine at feather work, such as head dresses, and equally skillful in the manufacture of pipes, both of wood and stone, wood and bone whistles, bows, arrows. He is also an expert chipper in flint and obsidian." Reporters agreed, although a few worried about his origins and seemed to find comfort in the idea that his successes were probably the result of genetic admixture as they whitewashed nineteenth-century California's genocidal treatment of the Pomo:

> *As to his origin, Benson admits a complete ignorance and regards the matter somewhat as a joke. Evidently, scientists have been busy "locating him." "Some say I'm Spanish," he declares. "Others insist that I'm Mexican, while still others declare that my people, the Lomas [sic], are the last descendants of a race which once were the nobility of America. As far as I know I'm a full-blood Indian."*

More common were assessments that the Bensons represented the highest Indian development on the grounds. "Converse with them, and then consider them in comparison with the others of their race whom you may see, and the whole story of the various stages of Indian life will have been forcibly impressed upon you. . . . It is a long way from a Cocopa to a Mr. Benson."[55]

The trip to St. Louis was a financial success for the Bensons. Mary sold as many baskets as she could produce. William flint knapped endlessly, although it was not his favorite activity. Dorsey had warned him that producing projectile points would be his major activity. They sold everything brought from Ukiah, receiving better prices than they had in Albuquerque. The LPEC awarded them silver and bronze medals for their ethnographic activities. Even with these successes they left for Ukiah, California, in the second week of August, no longer able to stand the sweltering heat of the St. Louis summer.

Pueblo Artists: Acomas, Lagunas, and Santa Claras

New Mexico Territory's famous Pueblo Indians were represented by two families from Santa Clara and four from Acoma. They lived in tents, the Acomas between the Wichitas and the Pomos, and the Santa Claras next to the Jicarilla Apaches. C. J. Crandall, superintendent of the Santa Fe Indian School, informed McGee that since they were not to be paid a salary, they would have to concentrate on making and selling pottery. They would only build outdoor ovens to fire the pottery and bake bread. McGee still wanted to show building techniques so he had the men produce adobe bricks for which he paid five cents a piece. Visitors purchased them as souvenirs.[56]

Most Santa Clara women demonstrated pottery making; one man wove belts and others painted. They took turns in the Indian School booth. Women fired pottery every few days, first warming the green ware in a stick fire before placing it in an oven made of sheet iron placed on stones. "The clay models are put in and covered over with sheet iron, then a hot fire is built around and over it of wood and dried manure and the oven is not opened until the woman in charge decides that the pottery is sufficiently burned."[57] The compound was extremely crowded on firing days by those admiring the artistic abilities of the potters.

Genevieve Cajiti became a celebrity because she could walk to the school with a pot balanced on a fiber head ring. She was called the "Belle of the Pueblos" and visitors came specifically to see her. The following story was recorded about one encounter she had.

> Genevieve Cajiti, with her hair freshly oiled, wearing the dress of her people's weaving, the gay scarf around her shoulders, and the deerskin leggings, left her tent on the Indian plaza for a Sunday afternoon walk. As she passed the village of the African Pygmies, Autobang [Oto Benga], wearing a single garment manufactured by himself from a gummy [sic] sack, followed, pointing and shouting loudly, "Pitti, pitti." He was greatly excited and confided to the interpreter that the

Belle of the Pueblos was by all odds the handsomest woman he has seen since he left Africa. . . . Genevieve did not resent the tribute of Autobang but she edged away with a frightened look, for these Pueblo girls are gentle and pleasant mannered.[58]

The Acoma women also demonstrated the use of "primitive millers, and [their] ability to make tortillas." In fact, they spent most of their time baking and selling piki (or wafer) bread, tortillas, fry bread, and loaves of wheat bread. They demonstrated corn grinding every morning in their Indian School booth, occasionally assisted by the Santa Clara women. Using colored corn brought from home, they ground flour with a mano and metate while their husbands drummed and sang to provide a steady beat, "a sort of encouragement," according to the LPE's official daily program. Piki is made by spreading a thin paste over a very hot griddle with the fingers. Newspaper accounts often commented on this activity and invariably noted that the bread was quite distinctive from ordinary tortillas. Many people sampled the ash-colored bread but liked the fry bread and tortillas better. Visitors focused on the hard work involved in baking. Women felt it was too much work, especially since the men did not help with the grinding. "Well," exclaimed one woman, indignantly, who had been watching three women grind corn, while a man sat nearby beating the drum to encourage them, "if I wouldn't get a divorce if I were those women!" Others felt sorry for the baker. "That poor woman is trying to bake bread. Poor thing, she's burning her hands."[59]

The stereotypes of Indian women as drudges and men as lazy were inadvertently reinforced since there were no explanatory labels to describe the value of men's work. No one bothered to explain either the cultural differences or the importance of corn-grinding songs, for there were no interpretive educators present to correct misconceptions. This was actually a major flaw with all the indigenous exhibits and hindered cross-cultural understanding and reinforced preexisting stereotypes. Visitors and the press (somewhat contradictorily) concluded from their visual inspections that "Madame Pueblo" was a superb housewife who managed her children well, especially the babies, who drew dozens of positive comments. Particularly noted was how well they cleaned the floors and the vigor with which they cooked. Reporters were impressed that "Madame Pueblo" worked so industriously under the intense gaze of the crowds who saw daily activities as an unusual performance.[60] Such reports speak to the preconceptions about Indian domesticity within an evolutionary paradigm. Native groups assumed to be on the lower rungs of the evolutionary ladder were never referred to in such glowing terms.

Powerful Peoples of the Northern Plains: The Dakotas and Lakotas

The Siouan groups had been greatly anticipated for it would not have been an exposition without the "nomads of the northern Plains." Unfortunately it is difficult to discern from extant records who actually came, when they arrived, and their cultural affiliations. There were several groups of Lakotas and Dakotas but LPE officials and the press used the word "Sioux" indiscriminately to refer to peoples belonging to a number of cultures and bands. Some of the individuals listed in appendix 2 may actually have participated in the Wild West show on the Pike, for McGee often included them in his press releases. Those performing in Cummins's Wild West Show were likely Dakotas from the Pine Ridge Reservation; those in the Department of Anthropology Lakotas from the Rosebud Reservation. Visitors seemed not to have cared as long as the men wore long, feathered headdresses. Nor did it matter to McGee, because he was presenting them as examples of a culture-grade. Of course, it mattered greatly to the Dakotas and the Lakotas.

On May 6, thirty-six adult Lakotas arrived from the Rosebud Reservation in South Dakota and remained for several months. Like several other groups, they had decided not to bring their children or babies.[61] Their large camp, containing at least a dozen tipis, was located between the Jicarilla Apaches and the Ojibwas, south of the railway station. Like the Arapahos, the men appeared daily in their finest attire, often with their eagle-feather war bonnets. This delighted visitors who complained when the Native men wore everyday clothing. Not all the men had such magnificent regalia anymore; several had to borrow appropriate headdresses from a reservation trader in Nebraska. Impoverished families in the 1890s had sold family heirlooms to gain needed cash for food.

Several Lakota men were famous and received extensive press coverage. Black Tail Deer was a tribal policeman, Two Charge had participated in the battles of Pine Ridge and Wounded Knee, and Singing Goose was a famous orator. Chief Yellow Hair (aged seventy-one) and his wife Julia (aged seventy) led the group. Yellow Hair had participated in the Battle of the Little Big

Horn, commonly called the Custer Massacre, and was often seen in the Lakota encampment wearing a blanket wrapped around his stately form and a single eagle feather. He went daily to the Indian School and watched the Lakota men produce pipestone pipes, bows, and arrows. He was photographed repeatedly by himself or with Roan Chief, his traditional Pawnee enemy, for which each was paid twenty to twenty-five cents per picture. The captions in LPEC photos suggested that the old enemies were now friends; they had "buried the hatchet."[62]

Like Geronimo, Yellow Hair was not a completely free agent. One gentleman, Dr. H. Kinner, an old army surgeon who spoke Lakota, asked McGee for permission to have him visit his home. "A week ago I was so bold to direct a few lines to you asking, whether old Chief Yellow Hair and perhaps some other Indians could be taken out of the Fair grounds to visit me. Yellow Hair is an old acquaintance of mine since about thirty-five years, has visited me once, and insists now on visiting me again. . . . Under what conditions would such a visit possibly be affected?" It took three requests before McGee could facilitate the visit and Yellow Hair and his family spent the afternoon with the Kinner family.[63]

Many reporters developed fanciful scenarios that involved Yellow Hair, Julia (mistakenly called Mohair), and their grandson, nicknamed Horse Hair, interacting with visitors. While he was treated with dignity, the white visitors were generally the butt of jokes. The following is typical of dozens of stories.

> Yellow Hair, chief of the Rosebud Sioux, sat in front of his tepee playing his favorite game of bask. Mohair, his squaw, sat beside him, wondering if she had painted her face yellow enough. Horse Hair, their papoose, was lolling upon his back by the open door wondering if there are any buffaloes on Mars. A man wearing a Prince Albert coat and a silk hat and accompanied by an exquisitely gowned lady appeared before the tepee and looked the Indian family over.
>
> "Oh dear," said the white lady, "these are tepee Indians, aren't they? I have always been so anxious to see some."
>
> "Gosh," said Mohair to her liege lord, speaking in the tongue of their fathers, "I believe this is a pair of flat dwellers. I've been wondering if we wouldn't see some."

"How chief," said the white man addressing Yellow Hair.

"How," said the chief.

"You are real Indians, aren't you," asked the man. "Your wife does all the work, doesn't she?" asked the lady. "And this is just the way you live at home? And is this your little boy? You would rather live in a tent than in a house I suppose. How do you get the paint out of your hair, Mrs. Lo? Did you ever work any, chief? Does your husband treat you well? How old are you? How old is your wife? And how old is the little boy? Did you ever bathe? How does it feel to be a savage? Did you ever hear of Hiawatha? Did you know Hiawatha when he was alive? Why do you keep so mum? Wouldn't you rather be white? Do you like coons? Do you sleep standing up in there? Did you elope when you were married? Were your fathers enemies? Have you a collection of scalps? Good-by. Sorry you can't speak English. There are some things we would have liked to talk to you about."

They walked on and Yellow Hair said, "Mohair, we are poor benighted heathen, but thank God we keep our mouths shut pretty much all the time."[64]

The Lakotas demonstrated in the Indian School, producing porcupine-quill and beaded buckskin, bow and arrow sets, and catlinite pipes. They also participated in McGee's special events, including competitive war dances, precursors to modern powwows. On July 14, a grand procession went from the steps of the Administration Building to the aerodrome, followed by a large crowd. Here Lakota women opened the performance and "chanted a wild and mournful song." Next Apache, Cheyenne, Kickapoo, Pawnee, Puebloan, Lakota, and Wichita men, dressed in appropriate tribal attire, performed "war dances" accompanied by drumming and singing, while the Ainus, Mbutis, Tehuelches, and "Aryans" watched from the bleachers. The best dancers were awarded prizes.[65]

The Lakotas attracted much attention as a result of these periodic performances and those done daily in their compound. Yellow Hair and Tall Crane also decided to sponsor their own events, including a special welcoming ceremony for the Dakotas in the Wild West show when they arrived. In addition, Yellow Hair, Tall Crane, Belle Little Horse, Afraid of Eagle, One Star, Good Bird, and their wives often sang during the Pike concession's afternoon outdoor concerts. They arranged these events without seeking McGee's or McCowan's approval.

The Lakotas were also proficient at impromptu sports and received ample publicity from the *St. Louis Post-Dispatch*, which was fascinated with "nickel hunts." Nickel hunts were started when a tourist threw a nickel into the air. "The nickel is set up on edge about twenty feet away and the Indian first hitting the coin gets the nickel." A few visitors were not impressed. As reported in the *Indian School Journal*, one man was overheard to say: "The Sioux here do not look very fierce. I guess they have just enough civilization to take all the spirit out of them." Some people preferred the Sioux of their imagination to the Lakotas or Dakotas of reality. The Lakota encampment was one of the most publicized and attracted frequent newspaper coverage, which was often stereotyped and contained remarks about how civilization had changed them or how they now recognized the futility of "their resistance to government assimilationist policies."[66]

Several Lakotas were Episcopalians and attended services every Sunday under the direction of Scott Charges Alone, a Lakota ordained minister who had attended the Rosebud Reservation's Little White Day School. Approximately one hundred people sang hymns in Lakota, for Charges Alone conducted the service in his Native language. These services were held in the Indian School, first in the classroom and later in the auditorium because they attracted so much attention from Euro-American visitors and Indian delegates. The Lakotas invited the Dakotas who worked in the Wild West show and the service was apparently a regular feature in the lives of both groups. A visitor who often attended the service found the Sioux language incomprehensible but enjoyed the hymns. "The Sioux language is musical. There have been translations of such familiar hymns as "Rock of Ages," "Nearer, My God, to Thee," and "Blessed Redeemer," that in the Sioux are greatly increased in musical beauty."[67] In addition to preaching, Charges Alone spent much of his time in St. Louis ministering to the sick and advising visitors who sought him out. He displayed Bishop Hare's official orders to come to St. Louis on the flap of his residence. Since he spoke fluent English he also served as a translator for other participants and was given a nominal salary for his services.

Like other groups, not everyone was happy. Two Charge and three male companions left for the Rosebud Agency on July 1; they found the idle life at the fair monotonous and wanted to fish and hunt. Yellow Hair's group left in early August for the same reason but were replaced by another group who remained until November.[68]

The correspondent for *Scientific American* spent a good deal of time in the Indian Village. After a stroll among the Native tribes surrounding the parade ground, he was "pretty thoroughly saturated with the atmosphere of Indian Native and civilized life." He was "impressed with the fact that the North American Indian, particularly such splendid fellows as the Sioux, are greatly superior to the average savage tribes of the world, at least so far as they are represented at St. Louis." He also noted that children who accompanied the Indians were required to attend the model Indian School. McGee advised visitors to go see these children because they were the evolutionary hope for the race. "Anthropologists have discovered that, in human childhood, whether of race or individual, the hand leads the mind, so that the seat of intelligence is best reached through manual training."[69] The Indian School was placed at the top of the hill so the Indians below could see their future as portrayed by the federal government and accept that they must either assimilate and become civilized or become evolutionary dead ends.

6. The Model Indian School

Indian nature is human nature bound in red.
Plaque over entrance to the Indian School

At the top of the hill, visitors came to the Indian School, "a representation of actual human development from savagery and barbarism toward enlightenment as accelerated by association and training," according to Francis. Its placement on the highest ground in Forest Park was intentional; McGee and McCowan wanted a visual symbol of the federal government's achievements in directed acculturation.[1]

Opening on June 1, the Indian School showcased federal educational policy. Estelle Reel, superintendent of Indian schools, had developed a *Uniform Course of Study* (UCS), with the premise that education focus on practical training rather than college preparation. Indians were considered suited for agriculture, manual labor, rural trades, and domestic service. In addition, religious and spiritual development was taught as a way to ready Indians for life in civilized society. Reel's curriculum also strove to shape character and bodies and to develop poise and discipline through physical exercise: marching, breathing drills, calisthenics, and games. As Tsianina Lomawaima has noted, the curriculum was based on a racist ideology that postulated a causal relationship between racially inherited "physical" traits (skin color) and "cultural" traits (hair length), "mental" traits (intelligence), and "oral" traits (virtue, thrift, and monogamy). "The UCS was a blueprint for total control of Indian people—mental, physical, and moral—in excruciating detail." The model Indian School was designed to show citizens that its curriculum turned Indian children into useful manual laborers and servants.[2]

Like some Americans, McGee was critical of Indian Service programs. He did not think the government should destroy Native cultures and turn Indians into "counterfeit Caucasians." "Excellence in Native industries and arts should be encouraged and improved using modern educational methods to counteract the degeneration stemming from the onslaught of White culture.

An Indian School should educate Indians while preserving aspects of Native cultures, especially their art." McGee hoped the model school would mirror the Palace of Education as a template for change by demonstrating the desirability of progress. By focusing selectively on inventions and methods, Indian artists would make a rapid transition into the modern world. This would be done through "progressive acculturation, or interchange and unification of knowledge." When this was accomplished "the white man's burden of the ballad becomes the strong man's burden in the political family of nations as in the personal family of kindred" (McGee 1905d, 113).[3]

The Indian School illustrated one of McGee's central theoretical assumptions that the course of cultural and mental progress was accelerated by formal education and the exposure of Native peoples to Western values. The validity of this contention was to be seen through direct comparisons. "Blanket Indians," men and women who refused to relinquish their Native customs, attire, and attitudes, would demonstrate their artistry inside the school on one side of the hall, while on the other, children would display their achievements in writing, reading, and manual labor. McGee believed that the desirability of change toward middle-class white ideals, values, and American democratic style was indisputable. So strong were his preconceptions that he assumed all Indians agreed with him. "Here [at the Indian School] parents still clinging to native customs and costumes delighted in the progress and achievements of their children in the arts and industries and even in the language and letters required by modern life" (McGee 1905d, 26).[4] Since McGee never asked Native American participants, elders or children, about their wants, these hopes and conclusions represented wishful thinking. They also reflected his desire to support official government efforts, despite his criticisms, and show that anthropology produced theory that justified policy.

It was McCowan, however, who controlled the Indian School, not McGee, and his message held sway. McCowan still saw it as a distinct enterprise from anthropology, involving professional education. It was irrelevant that the LPE's official program listed it as an ethnography exhibit. He insisted that pupils and government employees were distinct from the "adult Indians living in the old way in the old-time habitations and pursuing the handicrafts of their forefathers." To the ambitious and opinionated McCowan, the Indian School symbolized the wisdom of Indian Service policy. He highlighted Indian Ser-

Fig. 6.1. Visitors entering the Model Indian School exhibit. Photograph by Charles Carpenter, 1904. Courtesy of National Anthropological Archives, Smithsonian Institution, negative no. T15599.

vice accomplishments and tried to ignore any criticism or suggested improvements not of his own devising, while providing an entertaining experience for fairgoers. He also wanted to promote current policy to a nation that was expressing waning interest in Indian matters. By 1904 Indians were no longer threats but "managed savages" living on reservations, out of sight of the great majority of American citizens and many politicians who saw them simply as a drain on the economy. This attitude translated into diminishing federal support, despite treaty obligations. McCowan wanted a show case to help increase federal funding.[5]

The Indian School Building: Setting the Stage

The Indian School was designed as a functional stage set. The basic rectangular building was 40-by-208 feet with a rear auditorium, called the Assembly Hall, used for classes, lectures, recitations, conferences, and concerts (fig. 6.1). On Sundays it also served as a chapel for Reverend Charges Alone's services. On the first floor were classrooms, artisans' booths, and workshops. A large front door opened into an entrance area dominated by a new wagon constructed by the Chemawa Boarding School students and two sales tables where visitors purchased souvenirs, art, plants, and food. On the walls were pieces of student handiwork, designed to impress visitors; beadwork, pencil drawings, and exercises were rotated to ensure variety for repeat visitors.[6]

A wide hallway separated two long sections; one was subdivided into classrooms and workshops, the other into artists' booths. Visitors could watch "primitive" manufacturing techniques, then turn around and watch "new Indians pursuing the up-to-date methods taught by the white man." Acoma acorn grinders and bread bakers sat on the floor of an unadorned booth using a stone slab for a griddle. Across the hall was a decorated modern domestic science laboratory with six electric ovens and hot plates where food for about two hundred people as well as visitors was prepared daily.[7]

Next to the domestic science area were print, wagon-making, blacksmith, carpentry, manual-training, sewing, and harness-making shops, each fully functional with up-to-date equipment. The harness-making room also contained a collection of historic saddles along with traditional tools. The equipment contrast between traditional and modern was self-evident to most visitors and was reinforced by the contrast between the plain and highly decorated and equipped spaces. Examples of the students' work and photographs of typical school activities filled every surface and wall. The politically astute McCowan gave the best displays to schools administered by his friends. His office was full of art loaned by Bronson and Nichols, proprietors of the *Thomas (Oklahoma) Tribune*: exquisite Plains beadwork on the walls, bows, arrows, and quivers in display cases, and a Crow elk-tooth robe frequently described in the newspapers.[8]

A special exhibit of female students' lacework and embroidery decorated the domestic arts classroom, while Chilocco students' paintings adorned the reception hall. One captivating piece was a scale model of an "educated" Indian's eighty-acre allotment showing how the land should be irrigated with grains marked off in neat squares. There was a modern frame house, barn, pasture for cattle, and chicken yard. As a backdrop, students built an "old Indians' home" (a tent and tipi within a wattled fence and a few stalks of corn) perched on a barren, rocky hillside, inhabited by wild animals. After viewing this model visitors were directed to see the school's model farm and Children's Garden.[9]

The second floor contained dormitories for pupils and teachers, described in the *Indian School Journal* as "dainty and plain little rooms," which we can translate as extremely Spartan. Unfortunately, the roof still leaked and the more than two hundred canvas-covered cots were often damp and soggy. Many older boys preferred to sleep outside in tents. Visitors could tour the dormitory rooms for two hours at midday but in general the area was off-limits, although this did not stop many. "Visitors are told over and over again that there are no exhibits upstairs, yet about one in every ten cannot depart in peace without making an attempt to slip past the guard and the printed notices, 'no exhibit upstairs.'" The staff concluded that most visitors could not read.[10]

The basement contained a second kitchen and a dining room where the students and staff ate. There were also storage rooms, the demonstration laundry, toilets, a music practice room, an overflow sleeping area, and special apartments for the McCowans' and staff. A wide front porch had a sign, "U.S. Indian Industrial Exhibit," in raised foot-high tin letters. The school's exterior was bleak until McCowan authorized landscaping at the end of June, a simple pattern of Catalpa plants, weeping mulberry, and two trees on each side of the front steps, flowers lining the walkway, and geraniums on the front porch. A road led to the building from the side—a grading compromise that kept the parade ground, where the older boys practiced military drills, and the basement dry.

Opening Day

The Indian School opened on June 1, 1904, in conjunction with the Anthropology building. McCowan recalled that "from 8:00 o'clock in the morning until 6:00 in the evening the building was crammed full of visitors. . . . It was a good-natured, smiling crowd and the nucleus of their remarks was their surprise and amazement at this demonstration that Uncle Sam is not throwing away money upon the education of his red children." He estimated that ten thousand visitors were present including LPE president Francis, Alice Roosevelt, Mrs. George Catlin, foreign visitors, and a delegation of West Point cadets. McCowan basked in the many positive comments: "You see intelligence stamped on the faces of these pupils"; "I have always thought a good Indian was a dead one. After going through and seeing what has been done, I am fully convinced that I was wrong"; "We will come again and make a thorough study of the work done by the educated Indians with a view of obtaining ideas for use in assisting the poor in Ireland."[11]

The day was marked by special events, musical programs, and athletic competitions, in addition to the regular demonstrations of household activities, art, and industrial work. During a morning concert the Chilocco band played "Indian Maiden," "Festive Overture," selections from Verdi's "Ermani," and the "Star Spangled Banner." An afternoon concert featured "I Love Thee Columbia," "William Tell Overture," "Plantation Songs," and "Grand American Fantasia." McCowan recorded that one visitor thought he was listening to Sousa's band. Native demonstrators also provided musical entertainment. According to the *St. Louis Globe-Democrat*, eight "chiefs" sang the "Montezuma Hymn," Santa Clara men performed a "moon dance," Yellow Bird (Lakota) played his flute, and "Chief Good Water" sang a night song. Groups danced in their magnificent attire. "Each tribe endeavored to outdo the other in the hues of their habiliments. There were blankets, feathers, moccasins, beads and other tribal finery never before seen in St. Louis."[12]

Two Indian athletic events were designed, theoretically, to show Native peoples at play. From 12:00 to 2:00 p.m. field sports were held in the stadium: a bow-stringing contest; intertribal short- and long-distance archery; men's and women's one hundred-yard dashes; a thirty-minute "go-as-you-please" for men; four-man intertribal tug-of-war; javelin hurling; Plains tipi raising; an Arapaho versus Pawnee shinny game; and Tehuelche bolo-throwing from horseback. The second competition, held in the late afternoon in front of the Indian School, was limited to "blanket" Indians and included intertribal contests in archery, a tug-of-war, and javelin hurling. There was also another tipi-raising contest in which the Arapahos placed first and the Lakotas second. These competitions were considered a failure, even though they drew sizable crowds, because the ground was saturated from torrential rains.[13]

Native Artists: Contrasting the New with the Old

To McCowan older Indians constituted a necessary evil he would rather have done without, a "before" picture to contextualize the Indian students' progress. But since they had been at earlier expositions, Native adults were "object lessons" that would speak more eloquently about Indians' past than implements crowded monotonously into exhibit cases. Hopefully they would not distract attention from the Indian students. At best the adults would symbolize the handicap of racial heritage and barbarism. But the Indians actually conveyed a different message. They were the producers of beautiful, handmade, nonmechanized objects for which many Americans longed. The arts

Fig. 6.2. O'odham (Pima) basket weavers Effa Rhodes and Amy Enos, working in their booth in the Indian School. Photographer unknown, 1904. Missouri Historical Society, St. Louis, no. 21639.

and crafts movement in the United States was reaching its early peak in 1904, and a focus on Native artistry was becoming part of Indian Service policy, even though McCowan did not approve. Estelle Reel believed that economic initiatives for Indians, especially women, should be based on traditional arts (Lomawaima 1996, 6). McCowan felt that he followed federal policy by including outstanding artists. Since they lived outside in "primitive" tipis and lodges, the visual message was that these adults had not yet benefited from the government's guiding hand.

The artists' activities were entitled "Industrial Work" and were supposedly identical to reservation working conditions. Demonstrators worked two shifts, from 9:30 to 11:30 a.m. and from 2:00 to 4:00 p.m., during which they interacted with visitors, answered questions, and produced authentic, handcrafted art or food for sale. With the exception of Geronimo, artists rotated regularly to provide variety and maintain visitor interest (fig. 6.2). Sometimes the Navajos occupied three booths, one each for weavers, silversmiths, and Santa Fe Indian School students who wove blankets in a modern style. Once a week Osage and Comanche artists worked in the booths rather than their encampments. Arapaho and Cheyenne artists made flutes one day and bow-and-arrow sets the next. The central hall was crowded all day. Visitors purchased pieces at the main hall sales desks where the makers were given credit and the money distributed at the end of the day. Buyers were assured that prices were lower than those of regular curio dealers and traders selling in the manufacturing building. Prices were kept low on purpose but may have been too low. The owner of the Simmons Fur Company of Seattle, remarked to a clerk, "You people don't get enough for those Indian goods. Your prices are lower than I can buy them for in Alaska."[14]

One extremely popular booth housed two Acoma women selling flat bread. A placard read, "Indian wafer bread made from corn meal. Don't be a chump; try it." The cost was five cents. Some people enjoyed the taste (like a cornmeal pancake); others did not, comparing it to pine shavings. The women sold as much as they could produce. The same was true for the Pueblo potters, who always had more requests than they could fill. Visitors lined up as the pots were removed from the outdoor ovens and staff had to stop them from being snapped up before they cooled.[15]

McCowan later rationalized that the Indian booths were a successful tool to educate the average fairgoer. "As one watches the faces of visitors one can almost see the scales drop from their eyes. Prejudice against the Indian disappears . . . and they exclaim, as they pass along, that the Indian is equal to any other race." For many, the authentic older Indians were the most memorable part of the school, and at least one visitor said, "I do hope the Indians won't become too Americanized and lose their originality."[16] To McCowan, however, the really interesting and valuable part of the school was on the other side of the hall.

The Indian Students and Their Daily Activities

About 150 "successfully developed" students came from Chilocco (Oklahoma), Haskell (Kansas), Genoa (Nebraska), Fort Shaw (Montana), and Sacaton (Arizona) to ensure that as many tribes as possible were represented. Whenever possible, a Native artisan's child had been chosen to show they were "training the youth in the sight of their parents in order that all may rise together toward the plane of self-supporting and self-respecting citizenship."[17] Students were nominated by their teachers, and their parents had to give permission for them to attend. About three-quarters came for the entire fair, the rest for the summer months. A few held paid positions, but most were given no salaries.

Indian Service personnel oversaw students' lives, and their duties mirrored those in the schools: teachers, matrons, clerks, administrators, escorts, general assistants, drill instructors, chaperones, and specialty artisans. Only those in charge of classes stayed for the entire duration; most were from Chilocco. Others came for shorter periods; Nellie Barada, a Carlisle graduate and housekeeper at the Crow Creek Agency hospital, ran the school's kitchen for three months. Unpaid Indian Service personnel supplemented the salaried employees, their expenses covered by McCowan. This included individuals who escorted students and demonstrators to St. Louis and staff from the Indian Services' Washington headquarters. Estelle Reel also requested that teachers she wanted to reward, such as Pearl McArthur of Salkalai, Arizona, temporarily join the Chilocco staff. During the summer, it seemed there was as many Indian Service staff as students eating at the school dinner table.[18]

It was not all holiday fun. Teachers assigned for extended periods worked very hard. They had to install exhibits, ensure that equipment worked, secure raw materials, teach, lecture visitors, answer questions, and supervise students. Teachers and specialist craftsmen directed students in a rigid program that mirrored most activities performed in the boarding schools. This meant that half of the students' time was devoted to "literary" work with an emphasis on grammar, memorization, and performance. As examples of elementary class work, a kindergarten class recited each morning and afternoon in the Assembly Hall, followed by a seventh-grade literary class from Chilocco, who did exercises from the Indian Service grammar, math, rhetoric, penmanship, history, and civics curriculum. Visitors thought they did well. Two young men leaving a schoolroom were overheard to say: "They are good in arithmetic. Yes, and they compose well too. They are smart, you know, very smart." In one popular seventh grade exercise, George Selkirk, a Chippewa student at Chilocco, related currents events he had read in the St. Louis newspaper in "his usual self-possessed and intelligent manner." One visitor wrote in the guest book, "What a remarkably fine vocabulary that boy has! He expresses himself more fluently than the average college student."[19]

The Vocational Training Departments

The literary programs were minimal, however. More time was given to practical education, since it was more interesting than classroom work and drew more visitors. Reflecting Indian Service educational policy, the activities varied by gender. Female students from Chilocco staffed the modern domestic department (laundry, kitchen, and dining room) and gave daily demonstrations in cooking and serving food, marketing, and housekeeping. When the young women had completed their three-year course of study it was expected that they would become teachers, professional cooks, or housekeepers. Students working in the model kitchen and dining room wore long navy blue shirtwaist dresses, white aprons, and crisply ironed white caps (fig. 6.3). They looked just like Fred Harvey Company waitresses and were thought to be just as neat and efficient. They baked bread, pies, tarts, and cakes daily and displayed their products county-fair style. Once a week they made jelly about which one visitor remarked, "If I were younger, some of those tempting jars of preserves would disappear."[20] The *Official Daily Program* announced what the students were baking each day; on June 3 it was doughnuts and crullers, while the next day it was apple pies. Students served visitors tea, coffee, and cocoa in tiny porcelain cups, after demonstrating that they knew how to prepare a table for dinner. The sale of baked goods helped to underwrite the cost of the

Fig. 6.3. Mary Shelby (Cherokee) in domestic-science attire, a student at Chilocco Boarding School, aged eighteen, from Payor Creek, Oklahoma. Photograph by Charles Carpenter, 1904. © The Field Museum, negative no. CSA15210.

school. The students received no wages and tipping was discouraged but did occur; the girls surreptitiously acquired spending money.

Food sales became one of the Indian School's main draws and the young women prepared large quantities of food. Cora Peters, head of the section, remembered that most of their time was spent making pies and doughnuts, which sold quickly. They also baked "a large number of cakes, some to sell, some to put into the showcases in the Agricultural Room. Meats, salads, cookies, and bread are put into the show case and many find their way out in some mysterious manner" (Peters 1904, 85).

At first the tea service was held in the dining room as a sit-down activity but as demand increased, coffee was sold through a window hastily cut into the central hallway. A second window was later added for lemonade and water. Visitors then took their food to the dining table themselves and students picked up the used tableware after they were done. Word had spread quickly. "The doughnuts, pie, and coffee served by the becomingly attired maidens in the Domestic Science department are enough to tempt the appetite of the most fastidious epicure and are pronounced par excellent by all who have had the pleasure of sampling them. No wonder the guests haunt this department more than any other."[21]

Soon the crowds became so large that the students could barely keep up and by mid-June even the musicians were serving coffee. The good smells drew people; "Things smell better in the cooking class than they do downtown." One man, munching a doughnut was recorded as saying, "That's the first thing I've gotten in St. Louis that reminds me of home." The crowds took their toll on the exhibits. The fruit preserves and hand-painted china kept disappearing and had to be replaced. So many bottles on shelves were knocked down and broken the remainder were moved to the front sales desks.

By July the demand for food had grown beyond the means of the department to fulfill it, especially since the young women also had to cook three meals a day for all students and staff. This was a time-consuming activity, as were the preparations and service for McCowan's special dinners for visiting dignitaries. By August McCowan had decided to limit services to tea, coffee, and doughnuts. Cooking the popular fruit pies was limited to twice a week despite visitors' objections. "Oh, I am so disappointed. The dining room looked so nice and the cooking smelled so good. I thought I could just go in and order a good dinner."[22]

The domestic department became an extremely popular coffee shop and staff delighted in the positive comments, especially when they overcame initial skepticism. After drinking coffee one older gentleman turned to his wife and said, "I shall have to send you to Chilocco to learn to make coffee." One skeptical woman asked if the crullers were greasy. "She closed her eyes and bit into it as though the next moment might be her last. Then an expression of exquisite joy came over her benevolent countenance. 'My,' she gasped, 'they are just like mine; they are better than mine.'"[23]

Many female visitors stayed for long periods of time while Cora Peters lectured on how to plan a farm kitchen and cellar, select and care for kitchen utensils, prepare vegetables for the table, can fruit, and cook hot cereals. She handed out copies of her course of study. Female visitors commented on how clean and neat the area looked and how nice the students were. Unfortunately a few harkened back to stereotypical preconceptions of "dirty" Indians, expressing surprise at the students' grooming.[24]

Cleanliness was emphasized by Miss Daugherty's laundry class in their daily demonstrations of washing and ironing. On opening day they laundered shirtwaists and starched shirts. According to McCowan, the laundry was both pleasant and profitable, although one can speculate on his definition of pleasant on a hot summer afternoon. Pupils always had plenty of work for there were many requests from visitors to have their own laundry done. One woman tried repeatedly: "I'd like to have my washing and ironing done at that laundry. Do you suppose they would do it if I should beg right hard?" There were so many requests by May 6 that McCowan decided it was more economical to send out all the school laundry to a private St. Louis firm and have the students concentrate on laundering the clothes of people living on the grounds. Another business was born. At times the money taken in was divided equally among the girls, used for pleasure or to supply some need. Periodically McCowan used the proceeds to pay for educational diversions for the students, such as tickets to see plays. McCowan felt a self-supporting business was educational. "That laundry class shows the whole thing. Work like that means Christianity, civilization, and every other good thing."[25]

Like any country fair, women's work and hobbies were displayed: painting, embroidery, decorated china, and delicate lacework. These pieces were for sale; one embroidered tablecloth with a lace border sold for one hundred dollars. They were part of the domestic arts department, directed by Miss Keck and Miss Taylor of Haskell Institute and Miss Lecta Sutton of Chilocco, which contained sixteen girls from Haskell. Students were classified by grade and ability. "Beginners were taught the simplest stitches, advancing rapidly as they prove themselves capable, making plain garments, designing, dressmaking, ladies tailoring, and millinery." On opening day the third grade had sewing machine practice, the fourth made buttonholes, and the fifth drafted a lined waist from measurements. The *Official Daily Program* announced the girls' projects; on June 4, they made hemstitched aprons and handkerchiefs, while the second week of September was devoted to sewing picturesque Gypsy costumes for a special performance in Festival Hall. At first they made student uniforms, but soon their main occupation was making doll dresses for sale. The seamstresses earned spending money and McCowan used the profits to buy additional cloth.[26]

Visitors were impressed with the artistry, and Indian Service staff recorded many compliments in their guest books. Underlying many was a racial comparison to whites. Were the female students measuring up to whites? Could the race be educated? One visitor thought these women could. "I believe the Indian girls come up to the white girls in their art and fancy work."[27] Others decided that these Indian women were more dedicated than whites.

Chilocco male students demonstrated farming and stock husbandry, as well as made displays of food from the Chilocco farm, a table of balanced rations, a geographic map showing the contrast between "old" and "educated" Indians' homes, and colored seed pictures of Indian warriors. Students from Haskell Institute demonstrated blacksmithing, wagon-making, and wheelwrighting. K. C. Kaufman oversaw four recent graduates who were hired as salaried employees. At first they made wagons, which quickly sold. When this market became saturated they made small souvenirs. In late June the harness-making class, which specialized in items for oxen and horses, erected a special display and people rapidly purchased their wares. McCowan paid students a small commission when they produced objects for concessionaires. Visitors remarked on the skills of both groups: "I am a blacksmith myself and after looking at the hammers and horseshoes they make here, I can say that they are all right." Another man asked a student: "And you have only worked three years and gone to school at the same time? Why, I am a harness maker myself and have seen men who have worked at the business fifteen years who can do no better than you are doing!" The harness makers, under the direction of Jesse MacCallum, produced special orders, including the Indian clubs for the girl's physical education class.[28]

C. F. Fitzgerald directed the Haskell carpentry and manual training class, which produced toys, small shelves, and doll furniture. These sold so quickly that the display cases were generally empty. Visitors also readily purchased large pieces, furniture, and farm machinery, which were worked on at set times while Fitzgerald lectured. Students were often "loaned" out to make repairs all over the fair; they were paid union wages, although McCowan kept part of the money to cover their expenses.

Another important activity was printing the *Indian School Journal*, a monthly magazine published at Chilocco that contained articles by Indian School personnel. Published daily during the LPE in the school's fully equipped printing office, it sold for five cents per issue and was the only newspaper published on the fairgrounds. It chronicled LPE news, especially Indian School activities, as well as information on curriculum, Indian Service personnel, newspaper excerpts, poems, and editorials. During the exposition, it also contained numerous complimentary visitors' comments, amusing things visitors said or wrote in the guest books, and some national news dealing with Indians. McCowan wrote articles, as did students, in a special October issue. The daily papers were republished as weekly brochures and widely distributed.

Fifteen Chilocco men, including some specially transferred to the school, worked in the printing department, under the direction of E. K. Miller and Samuel Townsend, a Pawnee graduate. In addition to the *Indian School Journal* they produced and sold brochures, a World's Fair scrapbook with newspaper articles and magazine clippings about the school, and a popular photograph, "A Bunch of American Beauties," depicting several attractive female students. Proceeds were used to purchase raw materials for several departments. McCowan supplemented his budget by printing brochures and posters for other departments. The fees from jobbing work paid for materials. Again students who had not yet graduated were given spending money rather than salaries. Professionals praised the work. The editor of the Brookhaven, Mississippi, *Leader* said, "These young Indian printers do excellent work. This office is a model in its line." Similarly, a delegate to the printer's convention remarked,

"I don't see where your magazine cuts are inferior to those of the *National Magazine* printed by expert white printers in the Liberal Arts Palace on high-class presses."[29]

The Kindergarten Class

A special kindergarten class came as a compelling example of the boarding school system's success. It was under the direction of Emma Johnson, a Pottawatomie who as a student had demonstrated at the 1893 Chicago Exposition. Johnson was not enthusiastic about the assignment. "From my experiences at the Chicago fair I know that the work in St. Louis will be no picnic." She thought six-year-olds were too young for the trip. But McCowan repeatedly suggested she would have light duties, caring for the class, singing occasional solos, and chaperoning field trips around the exposition.[30] He also agreed to pay her mother's expenses from Shawnee, Oklahoma to help with the scarf drill.

As it turned out, the kindergarten class took all Johnson's time even though she handpicked the students, twelve of the brightest and most attractive Pima and Maricopa children from Sacaton. She trained them for four months, assisted by Miss Randall (a good seamstress and drillmaster) and Addie Beaver (general assistant and piano accompanist). The kindergarten was supposed to illustrate how Indians were taught in beginning levels. The youngest Native group at the exposition, aged five to seven years, could not speak English when they arrived so the lessons demonstrated how the teachers taught English. Visitors primarily responded to their youth, not what they learned: "If you want to see something cute come on in here, where they have the Indian school. They're the *dearest* little things."[31]

McCowan intended for the children to perform only in the morning, since they were so small, and not at all when the weather was hot and oppressively humid. But the class proved to be so popular he added afternoon assignments. Every day from 9:30 to 10:30 a.m. they sang good-morning songs and hymns in a classroom, standing in a circle holding hands. This was followed by Child Talk or language instruction using nursery rhymes, useful phrases, and simple dialogue. From 2:00 to 3:00 p.m. the class performed set activities including Opening Exercises, Gift Period, March or Game, Occupation, and Goodbye.[32]

A visitor wrote in the guest book, "I have found more of use in the kindergarten department in the Indian Exhibit than in all the rest of the Fair." Such messages from educators pleased McCowan as did the fact that the kindergarten class was so popular with the press who were amazed that such young children living in a boarding school had such poise and self-assurance. But July's excessively humid weather was too much for them, and their classes and many outings were discontinued. The children were given a vacation but even this was not enough. Illness struck and Mary Thomas died. The entire class was sent back to Phoenix in August in order to avoid an epidemic.[33]

McCowan was disheartened by Thomas's death, the only one recorded among the students, and saddened to see "one of the most popular of all exhibitions" leave. Others agreed. A woman from Philadelphia stated in the guest book, "I told my husband he could go wherever he pleased, I was coming to the kindergarten. I think it is splendid. I've taken the training and understand what they are accomplishing. They do surprisingly well for children who have to learn the language with all the other work."[34]

Performances, Physical Education Demonstrations, and Parades

Performances, concerts, and special events were a large part of the Indian School's agenda and the students' lives. Miss Crawford organized daily recital and musical programs, assisted by Miss Harrison and Miss Ewing. These programs quickly became fashionable, and drew more press coverage than any other Indian School activity except for the kindergarten class. At first the morning program was held in the chapel, or if the weather was nice, on the east porch. McCowan noted in early June that, "If the chapel were five times as large, people would still be compelled to stand outside."[35] Students periodically gave free recitals in Festival Hall in addition to their daily programs, and also participated in special events. Programs changed weekly, so the students would not be bored, and to highlight different soloists.

Examples of exercises thought to be an essential part of physical-education training for women were major activities. Younger students performed umbrella drills or scarf exercises with Delsarte poses, accompanied by music. Older girls performed calisthenics and intricate barbell, club swinging, scarf, and umbrella drills that required great concentration and practice. These often captured visitors' fancies; "I've been in the grounds a week, and that scarf drill is the prettiest thing I've seen." After watching one performance a public school superintendent reportedly said, "It would be impossible to train white girls in a drill when visitors are present, because they do not concentrate their minds on what they are doing, as the Indians do." Visitors especially liked the exercises in which eight older Chilocco girls, dressed in muslin Plains-style dresses, exercised using bows and blunt arrows as props. One visitor wrote to Mrs. McCowan: "Be kind enough to present my compliments to the young ladies who participated in the 'Bow and Arrow' Drill some time ago. It did them much credit, and is a very beautiful spectacle."[36] During the summer several athletic competitions were added to round out the afternoon programs and provide contrast to the boys' marching drills.

Recitations were as prominent as the drills. Iva Miller recited "The Wind" and Walter Rhodes "Deacon Pettigrew's Unfortunate Prayer" or "Little Orphan Annie." Teachers apparently chose the selections—essays, speeches, and poems that were either patriotic or poignant. A rendition of "Hiawatha" always elicited warm applause. McCowan recalled, "I saw several ladies wiping their eyes when Grace Miller [Shawnee] spoke her piece," wearing a rare Cheyenne elk-tooth dress valued at twelve hundred dollars. Visitors often commented on the poise of the students as they recited—even in the face of disturbances. On September 16, Amy Bagnelle (Siletz) was reciting "In the Oregon Country," when a group of Igorots in Native dress came into the auditorium and stood in front of the stage. When they shook their javelins in an appropriate greeting, Euro-American visitors objected and requested that Bagnelle begin again. "With perfect self-possession Amy looked over the vast sea of faces and when the disturbance had subsided, proceeded with her recitation as if nothing had occurred, while the great audience gave vent to their appreciation by a loud outburst of applause."[37] The Filipinos shook their spears again in appreciation.

Elders were regular participants in these programs. On several occasions, James Murie (Dorsey's Pawnee assistant) gave speeches on a variety of subjects, including trade, democracy, and peace. One, entitled "The Value of Trade to a Reservation Indian," was reported in the newspapers; he repeated the presentation almost weekly. These speeches were juxtaposed with student essays: George Selkirk, (Chippewa) regularly presented "What Uncle Sam Has Done for the Indian" and Frank Fish (Peoria) recited his essay, "America." All these lectures were, of course, in English.[38]

One of the most popular musical ensembles was the Fort Shaw Mandolin Club, young women dressed in their best shirtwaist dresses with hair piled stylishly on their heads, who performed every Wednesday and Friday at 4:00 p.m. For other performances they appeared in Native dresses decorated with elk teeth, quills, and shells, appropriate to their cultural heritages. They also staged dramas (*The Famine* from *Hiawatha Dramatized*), skits, and gave concert pantomimes in which participants held a series of Delsarte poses while one member recited a poem. They were considered very graceful as they moved from each series of poses to the next. The group began their programs with poses to the national anthem, followed by the recitations. According to the *Indian School Journal*, the girls had numerous requests for photographs.[39]

McCowan originally wanted a forty-voice chorus, but by December 1903 had decided the available students were rather weak. He decided to concentrate on solos, duets, and quartets who would sing popular works, that is, what music publishers gave him permission to use without royalty payments. Some songs were so popular they were regularly repeated; Caroline Murie and Helario Sierra ended programs with "Dixie." Gertrude Brewer from Chemawa played the piano to much acclaim: "She has exceptional musical talent and is a sweet, attractive Indian girl."[40]

Special musical evenings highlighted the outstanding vocalists. The September 14 literary and musical program began with a prelude by the Fort Shaw Mandolin Club (club swinging exercises and a "gypsy fantasie") followed by the older girls' quartet (Katherine Valenzuela, Bessie Gayton, Bertha Johnson, and Mary Cadreau) singing "The Lost Chord," charming visitors with their "pure and true tones." These older girls were frequently written up in newspapers and in constant demand by the end of June. They performed several times a week at dedications, receptions, and church services; they did not have free Sunday mornings like the other students. Katherine Valenzuela, the Pima–Tohono O'odham woman who had recently graduated from Sacaton, sang by herself or in duet with Bertha Johnson (Wyandotte). One of their most popular songs was "Till We Meet Again." Much was written about Valenzuela. "She possesses the sweetness, the power to sway the soul"; "I have never heard a voice of such seraphic melody"; "It was simply beautiful." Many felt she should go on the stage professionally.[41]

McCowan considered concert bands evidence of his educational success. They played integral roles in the introduction of Euro-American culture and instilled discipline; they were also a source of school pride.[42] The Indian bands were renowned; according to the exposition's publicity department they were more popular than Sousa's band and gave at least two concerts daily. There were probably five different bands although the information on them is a bit confusing. N. S. Nelson directed the initial forty-piece Chilocco School Band, supplemented by students from other schools. They presented their first concert on May 18 and several more during May and early June on the school's front terrace, but it was evident to McCowan that some reorganization was needed.

McCowan had hoped that Nelson could transform Chilocco's band into a world's fair band of outstanding caliber. By May he was disappointed by the band's sloppiness (in part due to a devastating flu and measles epidemic in March and April) and Nelson's limited musical ability. He noted that several key positions had to be improved, and a few students looked "too white." He promoted assistant director Lem Wiley to head conductor without any trepidation even though Wiley was a political appointment; he had been the House of Representatives' doorkeeper. Born in Carmichael, Pennsylvania, Wiley had moved to Illinois as a youth and served in the Civil War as head of a regimental band. A professional cornetist, he was a veteran of expositions and had organized music for presidential inaugurations. Wiley was also a prominent Republican who had helped elect several congressmen important in Indian Service budget appropriations.[43] McCowan had the best musicians transferred to the second band. Nelson and the rest were sent back to Chilocco.

The reconfigured concert band was called the Government Indian Band or World's Fair Indian Band (fig. 6.4). It numbered thirty to forty men from several boarding schools who auditioned for positions. McCowan interviewed them to ensure they had proven Indian ancestry, were phenotypically "red," able to read music, and had reputations for sobriety, reliability, and diligence. Each had to obtain personal letters of recommendation from an Indian Service employee who vouched for their character and heritage and each had to agree not to run away. All band members stayed for the fair's entire run, although several left briefly for various reasons. While a complete roster has not been located, many were probably Lakota since the Reverend Scott Charges Alone was the band's official interpreter. Most appear to have been eighteen to twenty-five years old and had a good deal of musical experience. Several were quite anxious to secure a position because of reservation unemployment and

Fig. 6.4. Indian School Band with students standing on steps of the Indian School. Lem Wiley, conductor (*center*). Photograph by Charles Carpenter. Courtesy of National Anthropological Archives, Smithsonian Institution, negative no. T15582.

the hope of adventure. McCowan spent a large part of his meager appropriation on the musicians' salaries, their transportation and living expenses, and new uniforms. It was important to him that the band look professional; they dressed in dark gray and green attire decorated with braids on the sleeves and a wide braid on the pants' outside seam.[44]

Wiley held intensive sessions, slowly including more difficult music, while giving two daily concerts on the front terrace. He also formed a smaller brass band. "The result," according to the ever-expansive LPEC publicity department, "is the greatest band of Indian musicians in the world, a band that compares favorably with any of the other famous bands in the interpretation of the music of the masters, and far excels in the weird compositions of its own people." According to one publicity release, "Something of the wild, free nature of this interesting people seems to enter into and become a part of the music whatever the score. They appear to feel the deeper and more elusive harmony of the composer, and their usual reticence finds here an utterance that cannot be questioned or criticized."[45]

As the band improved, its reputation spread. It was in constant demand for special functions and parties. By August, Wiley was accepting invitations to play in surrounding communities to train the men for their upcoming, post-fair Lyceum Bureau tour of the Midwest and West. They received immense acclaim everywhere. "The Indian Band received great applause at Bellville. The crowd pressed around them so closely it was difficult for them to play." Even turning down most requests, it was a grueling schedule. Their "private" rehearsals in the basement practice rooms drew crowds of visiting educators who gave workshops for individual students.[46]

The Haskell Indian Band, under the direction of Dennison Wheelock, was the third band invited and paid by the LPEC. Consisting of thirty professionals and students, they played at the fair twice daily for one week in June. They performed a mixture of classical, popular, and "Native" music, usually Wheelock's "Aboriginal Suite," which included Native dances and war whoops by the band members. Reviewers called it "both pleasing and musical to the ear, and an interesting study of genuine Indian music." It would be more accurate, however, to view it as an interpretation of Indian music. A reviewer declared that "the band is made up of gentlemanly fellows, who show what civilization can do for the Native American."[47] Following its summer engagement, the band toured the eastern United States, playing in Philadelphia, Cleveland, Indianapolis, Chicago, and smaller cities. They returned to the exposition later in the season for another two-week engagement before returning to Haskell on October 1.

Students from Wyandotte Boarding School comprised the fourth band. They stopped in St. Louis after performing at the Republican National Convention in Chicago and gave one concert on Saturday, June 25. A fifth band from Carlisle Indian School also came to St. Louis but not under Indian Services auspices. They were engaged to perform for several weeks in the Pennsylvania state pavilion. McCowan was not happy about having to host all these bands. "One Indian band will be a novelty, but more than that I fear would make the feature common and uninteresting."[48]

Boarding school rituals involving the Chilocco band were also followed. At the end of each day, pupils stood in military formation for a dress parade and the lowering of the American flag. Crowds were often so large that teachers had to stand around the parade area perimeter so students could perform.

The boys wore neat gray uniforms and the girls blue skirts and white blouses, which McCowan considered, "very becoming." A bugler sounded assembly and the roll was called. Next the band burst into a stirring march and the students circled it and then returned to their places. The band then marched to the top of the plaza. As the bugles sounded retreat, the sergeant major gave the command, "Uncover," and the boys removed their hats and held them over their hearts. The flag was slowly lowered as the students sang the "Star Spangled Banner." Finally the band led double columns of boys and girls around the parade ground. "The daily vast crowd is silent and looks on with eyes of admiration at these Indians, whose every attitude and expression bespeaks loyalty and devotion to the flag of their country."[49]

After a ragged start, the dress parade was a good show. McCowan was especially proud because it testified to the school's disciplinary success, a key to assimilation. In his October reflections he reported that it was always a "picture for an artist" when "the pupils of the Indian school [were] in military formation, paying reverence to the flag they have come to call their own." Others were also laudatory: "I watched the two hundred students on their return from a parade on the great plaza with intense admiration—and more, as they trooped around the grounds and building. In dress, behavior, and manners they were precisely like a company of white students in any of our schools."[50]

Daily Life at the Fair: Free Time and Following the Rules

Life at Indian boarding schools between 1880 and 1930 was defined by a rigid curriculum, extreme scheduling of activities, little free time, and a pseudo-military system of discipline. Life at the exposition was no different. The students wore uniforms, had their hair cut to standardized lengths, and were required to speak English. Punishments were heavy for infringement and meant being sent back to Chilocco. The daily routine was kept as close to the Chilocco schedule as possible; drilling, cleaning, and a roll call began the day. Following breakfast there were routine housekeeping chores, gardening, and preparing for visitors. Boys swept the porch and girls washed the dishes after the fairgoers had left for the day. They then had free time before bed and spent it studying, visiting, and writing their parents.

While at the exposition, students had less free time than at Chilocco. Saturday afternoons were not free and on Sunday there was church followed by chaperoned outings to St. Louis. This weekly routine never varied, but the presence of so many visitors must have made it somewhat less monotonous than life in a boarding school. In addition, scheduled activities were punctuated by special activities and lectures. The food may have been a bit better, if McCowan's fiscal accounts can be used as a guide. There was enough to celebrate birthdays with parties and games.

Like agency personnel who were quietly sent back to their former posts for overly boisterous behavior, some students had a bit too much fun in St. Louis. Although McCowan downplayed alcoholism, rowdiness, and truancy in his reports, several young men went AWOL at night to see St. Louis's sights or sample libations on the Pike. A few students were sent home for bad deportment, being obnoxious, rude, or working carelessly. At least three students ran away. Running away was a standard form of protest by boarding school students. Several others were sent home early due to disease—which is why the figures for illness were so low in the official LPEC and Indian Service reports.[51]

McCowan regularly scheduled educational outings because he wanted every student to see the fair systematically and visit all major pavilions. Students went in classes with a chaperone; older girls and boys went separately to visit gender-appropriate exhibits. Sometimes exhibitors invited the students. Professor Shedd, in charge of the Nebraska agricultural exhibit, invited the teachers and students to see moving pictures of farm life one morning before work hours. On other occasions they went to see the Boer War, Tyrolean Alps, Creation and the Hereafter, and Battle Abbey concessions on the Pike. To make these attractions educational, McCowan asked concessionaires to give interpretive lectures. Apparently the young women particularly liked their trips to Japan's exhibits and the large band concerts on Saturday evenings. Often these fun events were turned into exercises for Miss Scott's grammar classes. She made students write theme papers, which they read before the class and audience. Several were printed in the October issue of the *Indian School Journal.*[52]

Not every minute was spent on work or lessons. Students had fun on Pike rides (although McCowan disapproved) and took long walks watching fairgoers. They regularly attended firework displays. Mr. Wilson of the Fort Berthold School, North Dakota, drove twenty-two students around the fairgrounds in an automobile, and they visited the Hagenbeck Zoo and Animal Show by invitation of the management. Like Geronimo, many students' favorite was the

Ferris wheel. Students had many new experiences; they took their first rides in a hot air balloon and on a steamer on the Mississippi River. They ate ice cream cones. One of the older boys had seen so much by August that he asked McCowan for a two-week vacation to return home and tell his people what he had seen. McCowan refused but we assume that the student told his family all about his experiences in December.

The Fort Shaw Blues: "Winner of Every Game They Played"

Athletic contests in which many Indian students participated abounded. Watching demonstrations, practices, and games were favorite pastimes for students. The athletic stars of the Indian School were eleven women from Montana called the Fort Shaw Blues. Their main job was to demonstrate their remarkable basketball skills. Under the direction of Lillie B. Crawford and Ferne Evans, the Blues included: Minnie Burton (Shoshone), Genevieve Butch (Yankton Sioux), Genevieve Healy (Gros Ventre), Belle Johnson, (Blackfoot), Flora Luciro (Chippewa), Joan Minesinger (Snake), Sarah Mitchell (Sioux), Emma Sansaver (Chippewa), Katie Snell (Gros Ventre), Lizzie Wirth (Assiniboine), and Nettie Wirth (Assiniboine). One visitor remarked, "They surely are versatile." This was an understatement.[53]

The girls played two exhibition games per week, beginning the night after they arrived. These games were the only opportunity people had to see women's team sports that broke gender taboos about public athletic displays. Most early games were against the Chilocco team but the scores were one-sided and offered little challenge to the athletes the press described as "streaks of lightning" and players of "surpassing excellence."[54] The team soon received challenges from the Illinois and Missouri girls' state champions. On July 1, they beat the Illinois girls in a game sponsored by the State of Illinois pavilion and on July 3, the St. Louis club. In fact, the Blues defeated every team they played against, two or three games per week, including several men's teams. Schools around St. Louis requested they travel to their communities for competitions. They were accompanied by the school band and proceeds from gate receipts were used for charities.

A big game occurred on July 27. The Blues played the O'Fallon High School team, the best athletes in Southern Illinois. Forty-six students as well as the band went with them, while "[t]he anxious ones who remained at home watched the telephone for news of the game." The game took place on the Bellville County fairgrounds with crowds so dense ropes had to be used to cordon off the playing field. "It was a warmly contested game, and while the Indian girls worked to some disadvantage on very uneven ground and without the back-stops to which they are accustomed, they were the favorites of the crowd, and won an easy victory." A church social supper was held after the game and the two teams had "a jolly time." Two enthusiastic St. Louis basketball girls accompanied the Indian girls' team to Bellville. "Why," they said, "They can't be beaten. They haven't a poor player on the team."[55]

In early August, the Blues won another game during a special athletic meet and were given a silver cup with gold lining. A Missouri authority, Philip Stremmel, then decided there had to be some way to defeat them. He assembled a St. Louis "alumnae team" of young women who had played for the city's Central High during its reign as Missouri and Illinois champions. Stremmel's challenge to Fort Shaw was issued and answered, and the teams prepared for a three-game series to determine the "championship of the World's Fair." The Blues were without the full services of their star player, Emma Sansaver, who had sprained her ankle. Nevertheless they controlled the first game—the final score was 24 to 2. According to the press they were "more active, more accurate and cooler than their opponents." When the teams met again on October 8 in front of the Indian School, the Jefferson Guards had to be called in to control the crowds. The Blues won again by a score of 17 to 6 and were named World's Fair Champions, complete with a gold cup. The undefeated Fort Shaw Blues were engaged for a multi-state tour. They left St. Louis for Vassar Preparatory School in Poughkeepsie, New York, where they demonstrated their musical skills before soundly beating the college's basketball team.[56]

The LPEC singled out the Blues' sports performance as one of the reasons McCowan was awarded a grand prize. The girls, however, were not given team or individual awards by the exposition judges and McCowan actually downplayed their performance. He said of the team, "This class did some excellent work in basketball and in our daily entertainments. They were nice girls and made a good record." They did more than that; as historians Linda Peavy and Ursula Smith note, they were "champions of the world" (McCowan 1904a, 50, 46; Peavy and Smith 2001, 3).

Displaying Government Policy, Not Anthropology

Crowds crammed the corridors of the Indian School until it began to be dismantled after Thanksgiving. McCowan estimated that the average daily attendance was thirty thousand, but often exceeded fifty thousand. This was not bad for a small building sited in a peripheral position. As one visitor commented, "The only mistake Col. McCowan made is that he did not make his building large enough. All the people cannot get in here during working hours." Another thought they should have had "a more central location; somewhere near the large buildings; where the people could have easy access to it."[57] Many people came repeatedly, clearly intrigued.

McCowan recorded comments that lauded the value of Indian education and those that upheld his views on the suitability of Indian Service policies: "I always have been told that the Indians were lazy and worthless, but those boys at the manual training and blacksmithing classes are as good workers as I ever saw." To McCowan such utterances were his reward. Even more gratifying were the positive reactions of LPE officials and influential men, like Congressman McGuire of Oklahoma: "Mr. McCowan, when you asked me for my assistance in getting the appropriation for this exhibit, I simply had no idea as to what it would be like. It has entirely exceeded my expectations. In my opinion, it is the finest exhibit on the grounds."[58]

Not everyone was sanguine about the government-directed changes exhibited in the school. Many visitors thought that the Indians were no longer authentic and that government policy was harmful: "*Real* Indians are scarce"; "Do you know, education spoils the looks of the Indian; he is never a *real* Indian after he goes to school." Others noted that students did not look like Indians portrayed in dime novels. One even held that their skin had been bleached by civilization and that a person could no longer distinguish them from whites. Like all such comments, they tell more about the speakers and their preconceptions, prejudices, and ideas of race than they do about the students.[59]

McCowan considered the Indian School a success that would advance his career and help the Indian Service. It exceeded all previous expositions, for "it embraced the results of the ripened experience of the Indian Office. It illustrated in the most striking way the evolutionary steps of progress—from timid, halting ignorance toward confidence, knowledge and competence.

. . . Hundreds of thousands have seen the Indian problem as it actually exists, and just that many thousands have expressed their confidence in its correct solution." People now understood the "Indian Question" and realized that the Indian's talents were the same as the white man's and that education honed those talents and allowed Indians to successfully cope with life's problems. People "leave the building with their minds freed of the belief that the money spent on the education of the Indian is wasted." The Indian School was a Hall of Revelation.[60]

Typically, McGee was more reserved about the Indian School's success since it denigrated anthropology's main research subjects and their lifestyles. He was still critical of the government's educational programs, but expressed cautious hope that the Indian School had demonstrated improvement for he firmly believed that formal education was the future of all peoples.

> One of the gravest tasks of any progressive nation is that of caring for alien wards, i.e. bearing "the White Man's burden," as told by Kipling. . . . No nation may be proud of the way in which this task has been done in the past; our own failures in this regard form the darkest chapter in our country's history; yet [failures] have guided effort in the Indian office and in the National Legislature to a stage in which observation shows that at last our Indian education is good—not beyond betterment, yet good enough to be a boon to the survivors of our passing race. (McGee 1904a, 6)

McGee and McCowan never agreed on whose view was most critical for the success of the entire Department of Anthropology. This is not unexpected since they had distinct professional and political agendas and disagreed on racial potential, part of an ongoing debate in American culture. While McGee felt the Indian School supplemented the Indian Village and that visitors were more interested in "primitive" Indians, McCowan claimed in a lecture at the Lake Mohonk Conference of Friends of the Indian that "in many respects the Indian School was the leading feature of the Department; the building was well located and sightly, and its habitués and programs proved highly attractive." He now said that over three million visitors had passed through the building making it one of the most crowded on the grounds. All "competent visitors were most favorably impressed with the institution as a model school for our Indian wards—though its officials modestly preferred to describe it as a 'typical Indian School' (McCowan 1904b, 58).

One exposition historian, John Hanson, provided an assessment of the school that mirrored McGee's. The Anthropology Department held the key to both the past and the future of indigenous peoples.

> *The school is designed not merely as a consummation, but as a prophecy; for now that other primitive peoples are passing under the beneficent influence and protection of the Stars and Stripes, it is needful to take stock of past progress as a guide to the future. Over against the Indian on the grounds, just below Arrowhead Lake, stand the Filipino, even as over against the Red Man on the continent, just beyond the Pacific, stands the brown man of the nearer Orient; and it was the aim of the Model Indian School to extend influence across both intervening waters to the benefit of both races. (Hanson 1905, 272–73)*

This international assimilated future was down the hill from the Indian School and Indian Village, just beyond Arrowhead Lake. The Filipino Reservation, with its "brown aboriginals" and America's newest wards was where visitors could see how federal policy was being extended to America's newly colonized peoples. As in the Anthropology Department, visitors would see both exotic "savages" and Native "advancement." And there anthropology's policy message, this time interpreted by Albert Jenks, as well as its interpretations of "race narratives" or "odd people who mark time while the world advances" presented a similar picture, but one more finely articulated by the correlation of culture, race, and now religion with evolutionary potential and readiness to leave behind "backwardness" and assume the mantle of citizenship and self government (McGee 1904g, 5186).

7. The Philippine Reservation

*And then there is the Philippine Exposition
and all those curious peoples whom zealous scientists
have gone in search of to the far corners of the earth
and brought to St. Louis as "Anthropologicals" and labeled
interesting.*

Mrs. Charles Lusk, visitor

The Philippine Reservation's display of diverse peoples and its rich program of activities drew enormous crowds, far more than the Indian School. Francis said at the official dedication on June 18 that ninety-nine out of a hundred fairgoers had visited the reservation in the previous six weeks. The impressive visitor rate was not surprising, considering that the United States' role in the Philippines was a bitterly debated topic in 1904. The Philippine Islands had been under Spanish rule since the sixteenth century. By the end of the nineteenth century a Philippine nationalist movement, led by Emilio Aguinaldo, was well underway and an armed revolt had begun in 1896. When the United States initiated the war against Spain in 1898, ostensibly over issues relating to Cuba and Porto Rico, the Philippines quickly became the principal target of U.S. imperialism. After the Battle of Manila Bay in May 1898, the United States armed Aguinaldo's rebels. They captured Luzon and declared a Philippine Republic.

The Treaty of Paris in December 1898 formally ended hostilities between Spain and the United States but also provided for America to buy the Philippine Islands for twenty million dollars. Aguinaldo and his nationalists expected the United States to recognize their self-proclaimed republican government, but U.S. imperialists had other plans. The Philippines gave the United States a colony extremely rich in natural resources that could be extracted for huge profits. President William McKinley proclaimed a policy of "benevolent assimilation"; the Filipinos were to be civilized by processes similar to those used with American Indians, that is, by forced acculturation. The Islands were proclaimed as an independent territory under U.S. rule. Feeling betrayed, Aguinaldo led a revolt against the United States, which quickly degenerated into costly and bloody guerilla warfare. He was finally captured in 1901, although sporadic "insurrections" continued for some time. Opinion over U.S. rule was deeply divided along political party lines, generally with Democrats arguing for independence and Republicans feeling that independence must wait until the Filipinos were "properly civilized."[1]

To showcase American benevolence and solidify public opinion in favor of expansionism, President Teddy Roosevelt and Congress created a Philippine Commission to introduce Americans to the country's newest possession at the Louisiana Purchase Exposition. Territorial governor William Howard Taft gave it his full support and encouraged Filipino participation because it would have "a very great influence in completing pacification" and help Filipinos "improve their condition." According to LPE publicists, the fair would benefit Filipinos through Americanization. Their long sojourn in St. Louis would put them in such close contact with Americans that they would appreciate and emulate American customs. At the same time, the American public would become familiar with the Philippines' "various and incongruous" tribal populations who differed in race, language, and religion and represented stages of social progress from the lowest types of head-hunting savagery to the best products of Christian civilization. The State and Insular Departments felt that the polyglot assemblage of Igorots, Negritos, Visayans, and Moros—representing heathens, Christians, and Muslims—demonstrated the need for a common language and American schools to erase tribal antagonisms and transform them into a harmonious and vigorous nation. The Philippine Reservation was designed to deliver the same political message as the Department of Anthropology and the Indian School, the evolutionary array of indigenous groups and the advancement of humanity toward twentieth-century American civilization. It was the self-proclaimed success of the government as benevolent guardian of Native peoples in its care.[2]

The Philippine exhibit was a gigantic, expensive undertaking and the LPE's best-funded display (called an "exposition within an exposition"). It cost approximately one and a half million dollars (thirty million in contemporary dollars), housed about twelve hundred and fifty individuals, and displayed over seventy-five thousand objects in almost all exhibition categories.[3] Assembling these materials and people from islands populated by a hundred differ- ent tribes speaking disparate languages and dialects was difficult but necessary since cultural diversity was a central theme of the exhibit, unlike that designed by McGee. In addition to displaying the evolutionary "place" of various Na- tive groups, the exhibits focused on culture history—how different groups had come to the islands, what they were like in 1904, and what their future would be under American benevolent rule. The message was also conveyed that American colonialism was superior to Spanish colonialism. To ensure it would work, there had been a trial exposition in Manila in late 1903. For many participants, the LPE was a two-year undertaking.

Visitors to the forty-seven-acre Philippine Reservation were first given a propaganda lesson. "Those who visit the Philippine exhibit must stop to consider that four hundred years ago the inhabitants were a most primitive people, separated into many small tribes, before they can really appreciate the meaning and the value of the picture set before them." Exhibits proclaimed the moral degeneracy of the Spanish colonial system, which profited only gov- ernors and made no attempt to educate or morally uplift people. Then visitors were told how things were different now, for the Filipinos were "going to a dif- ferent school with most beneficial results. . . . There has been palpable, visible advancement, and the time is coming when the purchase of the Philippine Islands will seem as wise to our descendants as does the Louisiana Purchase seem to us who live today." Paradoxically, this message was countered by the Department of War's display of weapons captured "during the insurrection against U.S. occupation," many of which Native allies had used between 1898 and 1901 against insurgents. This message contained no suggestion of the di- vide-and-conquer tactics, exacerbating traditional ethnically based hostilities, used by the U.S. Army in suppressing the insurgents, nor any indication of the number of people who died during the rebellion.[4]

A Small City on Display

The Philippine Reservation was placed on a wooded, rolling uplands area of Forest Park, just beyond the Palace of Agriculture. A green moss-covered wall with antique Spanish guns mounted on the parapets separated it from the rest of the exposition, physically, visually, and symbolically. Visitors entered the area over the Bridge of Spain and walked into a Walled City, where they immediately encountered the War Department's armament exhibit and a replica of Manila's ramparts. A museum housed ethnographic and historical weapons placed in an evolutionary arrangement, to underscore the Islands' military primitiveness and carry a subliminal message about the futility of continued rebellion. In the center of the walled city's plaza was a tall column honoring Fernando de Magellan, the Spanish explorer who "discovered" the islands, mirroring the statues of Lewis and Clark at the LPE's main entrance.

Departing the Walled City via bamboo bridges, visitors could chose from three theme areas: (1) Indigenous Peoples, (2) Spanish Influence, or (3) the American Present. Manila Plaza in the center of one area was surrounded by five Spanish-style structures, including an Education Building that contained exhibits lauding the American occupation.[5] Other large exhibit buildings devoted to agriculture, forestry, photography, and mining contained some seventy-five thousand artifacts chosen to appeal to American men. As in the main LPE exhibits, Native peoples served as the preindustrial "before." Mountains of raw materials were shown being turned into products of Native manufacture. Native tools were interpreted as useful but unrefined, conveying the message that the Philippines needed American expertise to develop prosperous market economies. Messages for cultural items were the same. The Manila Building, designed to illustrate an urban upper-class dwelling, illustrated how Native art could be transformed to decorate modern homes.

The Ethnology Building was a low, cloistered edifice resembling a convent with a thatched, bamboo-roof tree house in the central courtyard. A family of five Samal Moros from Managayne occupied the house, closed to visitors. The museum's interior displays included "an exhaustive collection of materials made by pagan, Muslim, and Christian peoples of the archipelago," and an evolutionary display of weapons. A third exhibit taxonomically equated material culture with tribal social organization, while a fourth focused on regional cultural diversity by utilizing a new display technique. Each unit told the story of a single culture to help visitors interpret the customs, lifestyles, and material cultures of the real stars of the Philippine Reservation, the more than eleven hundred Natives who were on display. As expected of an ethnological enterprise, the museum emphasized exotic "true savages"—Igorots and Negritos, but the wing devoted to Igorot culture contained a mixed message. Savage cultures were technologically simple, one main label stated, yet "here and there something has impelled this group of savages to develop to a high degree an industrial activity which elsewhere in the Archipelago may yet be in its crudest development." While an Igorot may be essentially naked, another label asserted, "[h]e wears a pocket-hat, with a circular straw crown, which he fastens at the back of his head." The implied message was that Igorots were capable of progressing culturally, unlike the Negritos, who were described as a puzzling race with "extremely low intellect," incapable of learning. They were, however, interesting because they were an evolutionary missing link, one that would eventually become extinct. A label near the door instructed people to go see them in their village, located across the bridge. It might be their one and only chance.[6]

As in the Department of Anthropology, the Native peoples fascinated visitors more than did the objects. Christian Visayans, Islamic Moros, and "pagan" Igorots and Negritos were housed in six encampments collectively called the Reservation, a name that was popularly used for the entire Philippine Exhibit. Other Filipinos served in military and police battalions—the Philippine Scouts and Philippine Constabulary. To McGee, the Filipinos filled in the holes in his evolutionary scheme. There were small and tall races who mirrored the Native peoples on the other side of Arrowhead Lake. McGee told the *New York Times* that the Reservation's central theme was "to all intents and purposes ethnological in character," that is, it showed where people were on the road to civilization. Ironically, one criterion for Filipino self-rule was how well the "civilized" Filipinos took care of indigenous populations and prepared them for assimilation. Like the Indian Service, the Philippine Commission and Insular Department had a lot at stake in St. Louis, and an anthropologist was ready to help convey the message while simultaneously transmitting basic ethnological information.[7]

The Philippine Ethnology Division

Albert Jenks (1869–1953), a biologist turned ethnologist, designed and supervised the Philippine Ethnology Division's static and living displays.[8] Interested in their economic conditions, he had briefly been a BAE researcher before heading the Ethnological Survey (or Bureau of Non-Christian Tribes) of the Philippines Commission. From 1900 to 1903 he conducted ethnological research with the Bontoc Igorots and classified Native peoples for the Philippines' first census, essentially reiterating Spanish social terminology by dividing the population into two supergroups, "civilized" (i.e., Christian) and "wild" (i.e., non-Christian, including the Muslim Moros). Jenks used this same reductionist scheme to organize tribal peoples at the fair.

Jenks began working on the exposition in early 1903. He supervised the selection of non-Christian Natives, including Igorots from the Bontoc, Abra, and Suyoc regions. Several individuals who had worked for him as servants or anthropological consultants came as demonstrators. To locate others, Jenks relied on the help of colonial officials and missionaries. For example, in November 1903, Dr. Saleeby, an American-educated Syrian physician, located a Samal Moro group. It took both men several months and all their diplomatic skills to convince the local sultan to undertake the year-long journey. The sultan's main worry was that his people's contact with Christians would defile them. Jenks agreed that the sultan could control the extent and type of contact with infidels (Afable 1995; M. Jenks 1951, 164; A. Jenks 1905).

In addition to securing artifacts for the various exhibits, Jenks arranged transportation for people, artifacts, and traditional building materials to Manila and from there to St. Louis. The Igorots were the first groups to leave Manila. They sailed on the USS *Shawmist* to Tacoma, Washington, landing in March, and continued by rail in an unheated train, escorted by the Philippine Scouts. Jenks had hoped to accompany them, but had to remain in Manila to take care of paperwork and last-minute details. Seeing the demonstrators off, Maud Jenks wrote, "I found them much more comfortable than I had expected they would be. Antero [the Jenks' Filipino servant who served as interpreter] showed me his own particular place, and I told him goodbye until I would see him in America. Poor things—I hope they won't freeze to death" (M. Jenks 1951, 198).

A second Igorot group left soon thereafter, accompanied by a missionary, and arrived in late April without incident. Other groups encountered problems, including living in close quarters with their traditional enemies. In late February the Bagobo Moros and the Lanao Moros refused to stay in the same building for two days while waiting to board a ship. (One can only imagine what the boat journey was like.) After Filipino newspapers reported the need to separate them in exaggerated hyperbole that emphasized the Natives' exoticness, the Moro became quite notorious. As Mrs. Jenks remembered later,

They are as much a curiosity to people here in Manila, as they will be to Americans in St. Louis. The place is crowded with spectators all day. There have to be several policemen on guard to keep the Manila people out of the building. The Moros dislike them so much there is no telling what they would do if they had a chance. One day one of them attacked a Manila man with a spear—a beautiful illustration of the unity of the Filipino people. (M. Jenks 1951, 198–99)

Members of the Philippine Constabulary accompanied the groups to keep the Moros separated and also supposedly to protect other passengers.

The journey for most individuals was long and arduous. To begin, people from outlying areas had to walk two to three days from their villages just to reach a transportation point for Manila. For this reason, most were young, under thirty-five years of age; there were also more single individuals than in the other groups because Jenks did not insist on family groups. Once the people left Manila, they faced a month-long sea journey and a train ride of as much as a week from the West Coast to St. Louis. Several deaths from pneumonia were attributed to the rigorous journey, especially on the unheated trains. One Igorot man, Pagiyen, was accused of killing a Suyoc man in a brawl in Hong Kong. He was detained there and never heard from again. Others became sick and were quarantined upon arriving in San Francisco. Some people were eventually allowed to continue; others were returned to Manila.

The Filipino Groups

Within the Reservation, the individual villages were located on the shores of Arrowhead Lake, arrayed in an evolutionary sequence designed by biologists Dean Worcester and Robert Bennett Bean. The sequence began with the "lowly and anthropoid-like" Negritos from the forests of Luzon, who had no fixed habitations, and then the more highly developed but still "primitive" head-hunting and spirit-worshiping Igorot groups. Next were the "more intelligent" but fanatical Bagobo and Lanao Moros, "fierce Mohammedan fighters who have caused so much trouble in the Mindanao country." They were separated from the politically neutral Samal Moro, "unexcelled pirates and slave traders, treacherous and unreliable to the last degree," and the "beautiful," cultured and civilized Visayan, the "highest type" of tribal peoples who dressed like Europeans and wove silk. The different groups were distinguished by their attire as well as their physical appearance. Reporters always commented on the general lack of clothing of the Igorots and Negritos and the modesty and colorful attire of the Moros and Visayans. The people themselves were probably comfortable, since a hot humid St. Louis summer was likely not too different from the Philippines. Winter months must have been difficult, and by November photographers depicted "naked" people sporting American-style shirts, overcoats, hats, and shoes, much to McGee's and Jenks's consternation since they both considered such behavior inauthentic. Each village contained typical houses, built of the proper materials brought from the Philippines, as well as boats, canoes, and light and heavy carts. Two Asian water buffalo (*carabao*) were even brought for the Visayan village in the attempt to simulate daily life.[9]

As with other living exhibits, the total number of Filipino Native participants fluctuated during the fair. There were at least 115 Igorots, 110 Moros, 80 Visayans, and 40 Negritos on June 12, the official census day. There were also four Manguins and two midgets (who performed acrobatic acts to appeal to American tastes for exotic curiosities).[10] Some groups came later, a few individuals died, others were born, and several left early. Eighteen Visayans and all of the Bagobo Moros did not arrive until August 15—their ship delayed because of a fire. In August the number rose as one hundred Filipino male students, slated to be educated in the United States, arrived. They served as guides in the Ethnology Building, practiced English, and answered questions about politics, religions, and the peoples of their country. In mid-September they left to attend American universities.

Contrasting with the Native villages, Spanish-Filipino mestizo families occupied replicas of houses used by Spanish officials in Manila in the "American Present" section of the Reservation. These fifty highly educated, elite men and women (attorneys, judges, editors, writers, coffee planters, businessmen, and government officials) traveled at U.S. taxpayers' expense to learn American ways. While the Native peoples were demonstrating and performing, this group toured the United States as foreign envoys with diplomatic status. President Roosevelt received them at the White House, where they argued for self-government. In St. Louis their main duty was to interact with Americans. Called honorary commissioners, they spent their time socializing with St. Louis's elite.

The Philippine Constabulary and Scouts were paramilitary troops and police who had been enlisted by the American military to aid in suppressing the ongoing insurrection in the Islands. The Scouts had 12 American officers and 420 Filipino enlisted men, including a forty-five-piece band. The men had rigorously trained for several months. It was considered an honor to be chosen and many applicants were turned down. "Those men who showed even the slightest signs of poor discipline or being unsuited or unwilling to travel abroad" were discharged. On the exposition grounds they lived in seventy-five canvas tents with wooden floors and electric lights. Both groups' duties were to escort, guard, prevent intergroup strife, police, and help maintain the compounds. They also served as a fire department, general carpenters, and laborers for the entire exposition. The Scouts gave two drill performances daily. As soon as they arrived they began practicing, providing entertainment for large crowds even before the fair officially opened. They were described as "a fine looking body of men [who] have an excellent band." Their roles extended beyond policing and entertaining; they were housed next to the Igorots and Negritos so visitors could see the Philippines' social extremes. They illustrated the "result of American rule," suggesting the possibility of successful cultural advancement under U.S. colonial administration and the readiness for self-rule.[11]

Daily Activities in the Villages and Special Events

The entire Philippine Reservation was officially dedicated on June 18 and all the villages opened at noon. While it cost nothing to enter the Reservation and view the museum displays, there was a twenty-five-cent admission for each village, with extra charges for special events and performances. To draw visitors, the *World's Fair Authentic Guide* enticed people with free "cold filtered drinking water" and lavatories. One could visit the United States' newest Native wards in comfort and safety. LPE officials also stressed that the Filipinos were eager to entertain their American guests. The Igorots apparently loved to perform dances. "As soon as one band of the Igorot community finishes the dance another band takes the ground. The first band squats on the ground and closely observes the movements of its successors." Fascinated visitors stood behind the squatting group.[12]

"Bright-looking and energetic young" Scouts went on dress parade daily at 5:30 p.m. They "carried themselves with an air of military pride and precision and commanded admiration for their soldierly qualities." On August 13, Philippine Day, the sixth anniversary of the American capture of Manila, they conducted a mock battle, like those held in the Wild West show and the Boer War concession. Some also participated in special athletic and dance competitions arranged by McGee. What the press focused on was their marching; "It was an impressive sight—this long line of Filipinos in blue, stretching down the green parade ground at sunset. It shows the real work accomplished in the Philippines—the bringing of law and order and discipline out of insurrection and ignorance—the lesson of good government" (Bennitt 1905, 475).[13]

Others commented on the Scouts' intelligence, fitness, and conduct. Generally their conduct was exemplary but there were negative incidents reported in the newspapers. The LPE police arrested several Scouts for carrying concealed weapons (knives), fistfights, or resisting arrest. A few contracted venereal diseases, indirect evidence of Saturday night extracurricular activities not recorded in final reports to the LPEC Board. There were also a half-dozen cases of drunkenness, but far less than those recorded for the American military or police forces stationed at the LPE. One notorious incident occurred when a Scout overheard a man from the Boer War concession disparage their drill performance and beat him senseless. The Scout was convicted of assault in St. Louis police court, but the mayor remitted the fine due to "extenuating" circumstances. The other major incident occurred when U.S. Army troops and Scouts had a fight in which one soldier was knifed to death and several others injured. No individual was charged, since the Scouts left the scene quickly. However, thereafter they were allowed out only on Sundays between noon and midnight and were otherwise confined to the grounds, like other indigenous peoples (Newell 1904, 5142).[14]

It was hoped that the Scouts would learn the value of American culture while in the United States. One means to accomplish this was formal American-style education. There was a separate school for the Scouts and Constabulary in which a daily one-hour class in conversational English, American history, and geography was given by Army Chaplain J. C. Granville. At first it included only noncommissioned officers, but soon was open to all troops. The curriculum also included visits to LPE exhibits and attendance at special lectures, activities that must have helped break up the monotony of the daily activities (Laurie 1994–95, 52).

Indigenous participants were also expected to learn from their experience. Like the children in the Indian School, Filipino children attended a model American school every morning under the direction of Miss Marie Pilar Zamora, a teacher from the Philippine Normal College. Zamora was Visayan and a Christian missionary. The students included men and women, not just young children. While the adult men were allowed to wear only their loincloths, the women had to don western blouses as well as their traditional hand-woven skirts. Children wore uniforms modeled on Indian Service attire. They sat at American desks and worked on a blackboard hung on bamboo poles in the school's single small classroom or the bamboo-and-palm ramada. Unlike the Indian School, there were no dormitories or workshops. Students came at set times during the day and then returned to their camps. Like the Indian School, the building had a viewing gallery for visitors, and all classes were taught in English. The school opened on July 19 with forty-one students, aged twelve to twenty; the official school census included twenty Visayan, thirteen Igorot, two Moro, and six Negrito students. Zamora lectured daily from 9:30 to 11:00 a.m., until the end of November. The Visayans were taught by themselves because it was assumed they were naturally more advanced, being Christians. The Moros, Igorots, and Negritos attended a beginner's class. (The Negrito children often refused to attend, disliking the school uniforms.) All "non-Christians" were taught English using American patriotic songs and nursery rhymes. The star pupil was Antero, a fifteen-year-old Igorot. Zamora told Jenks that the Igorot children were the most intelligent, reinforcing Jenks's predictions of their assimilative potential.[15] Potential for Americanization was a dominant theme in the school, seen as a sign of readiness for self-rule. Placards stressed how seven hundred American educators were teaching English to three thousand Filipino teachers to produce a lingua franca to facilitate modernization. Wall displays emphasized industrial, agricultural, and nautical trades. The school drew national attention when President Theodore Roosevelt visited at the end of November. Zamora had the Igorot students sing a chorus of "My Country 'Tis of Thee." The president was reported as commenting on how quickly the Igorots had advanced after being exposed to civilization. "It is wonderful. Such advancement and in so short a time!"[16]

School and life in the compounds were kept distinct in the name of ethnographic authenticity. When children were in their villages they wore traditional attire, which assumed the flavor of stage costumes. Children were expected to play traditional games, not baseball. Sometimes American boys and children from the Pike concessions joined them in games of marbles. The Samal Moro children particularly liked American games as well as improvised water sports. Jenks and McGee soon gave up trying to keep the "American contamination" at bay. Like the peoples living in the Anthropology Villages, Filipino people did not blindly follow the anthropologists' agendas.

Native dress was considered important because the Filipinos were among the most photographed people at the LPE. This was not always a welcome event and a placard at each compound's entrance informed fairgoers that photographers took snapshots at their own risk; the LPEC was not responsible for damaged cameras.[17] Due to the number of photographs, however, it appears that the Igorots were not camera shy, but there are no records of how many of the proud Moros, Visayans, or Negritos smashed cameras. Several times the Scouts "rescued" cameras, especially when tourists wanted to take photos for free. The people simply wanted to be paid.

Another common activity was greeting dignitaries who visited the Reservation. Giving welcoming speeches to every trade and professional association became a prominent duty of each group's leader. It was hoped that these visitors would buy lots of souvenirs. And they did, but not quite enough. During November there was "a sacrifice sale of beautiful fiber cloths, mantillas, laces and embroideries" made by Visayan women (Bennitt 1905, 475). The extremely popular Igorot groups had nothing left over; they went home with only American manufactured items.

The Popular But Controversial Igorots

The Igorot village was the first camp to officially open. LPE personnel called three distinct groups of Cordillera people "Igorots," the Bontocs, Suyocs (Cuyocs), and Tinguians. The much-photographed Bontocs performed in the May 1 opening-day festivities and drew large crowds as they built their straw-covered houses during April and May. Truman Hunt and his two assistants—Julio Balinag (interpreter) and Alvin M. Pettit (an American miner married to a Suyoc woman)—supervised the three groups. Hunt also ran a soft drink concession near the village (Afable 1997, 19; 2000).[18]

Delayed by inclement weather, the Igorots' multi-acre village was not officially completed until May 19. It was surrounded by a bamboo stockade

Fig. 7.1. Bontoc Igorot men sitting on their drums, eating dog meat, with visitors watching in background. LPEC photographer. Library of Congress, Prints and Photographs Division, 3245–4975.

topped with human skull trophies brought from the Philippines. Hunt obtained bovine skulls in St. Louis to relieve the monotony of the "Igorrote decorative scheme." In the compound center was a small stone enclosure, a justice court to which offenders were sent. Settling disputes was a common occurrence and each Igorot group followed its own customs.[19]

Within the main enclosure, each group had an area separated by a fence and marked to indicate that they were separate peoples. For example, for the Bontocs the symbol was a row of cattle skulls placed on a shelf in front of their huts and a telephone pole. Chief Antonio insisted that he have a telephone placed in his hut as a sign of his status. In the center of the Bontoc village was a shrine and stone fireplace where morning prayers were said and the site of their infamous dog feasts (more on that below). The compound was the most visited site on the fairgrounds (fig. 7.1), much to the annoyance of other

Fig. 7.2. "As the Lady Managers wanted to have them" — Pierre Chouteau. Bontoc Igorot men dancing in Western attire during the controversy over "nakedness." Photograph by Jessie Tarbox Beals. Missouri Historical Society, St. Louis, no. LPE1304.2, WF 1016.

Filipinos who complained that the Bontocs "hogged the limelight" (Afable 1997, 20).[20]

The Igorots were mountain peoples from northern Luzon, who were considered the Philippines' true pagans. They were greatly anticipated because the Department of Exploitation had made it well-known that they were naked dog eaters, symbolic markers of their "low" evolutionary grade. The Bontocs were publicized as a most primitive and warlike group, headhunters with "copper-colored skin, high cheek bones, flat noses, thick lips and long, straight, black hair" that hung over their shoulders. There were numerous newspaper accounts of their hourly dance performances and physical appearance, but few about their other cultural accomplishments. "The Igorot wears no clothes," wrote Alfred Newell, a popular journalist. This statement is probably the single most common assertion used to describe them, and was often overgeneralized to other Native groups and used as a symbol of general primitiveness. It referred to the fact that the Bontoc men undressed to honor special visitors in official receiving lines, the exact opposite of middle-class American dictates. Many visitors, including the Exposition Board of Lady Managers, complained of the practice (fig. 7.2). It is not recorded what other Native participants thought of the Igorot clothing style.[21]

Bontoc men wore brightly colored G-strings, small loincloths, coats, and small hats, rather than the pants that had been issued to them, while they worked or performed. The lack of attire to cover male genitals, and the gaze of innocent American children and apparently easily offended women, led to extensive discussions during the spring and soon erupted into controversy. According to one historian, "The most ambitious and advanced of the Igorot community are not above fascinations of the dance, nor can they resist the life long habit to appear without clothing."[22]

Discontent about male nakedness finally erupted into threats of boycotts of the Philippine Reservation. Taft feared political ramifications for the Democratic Party (which was staking its reputation on the Philippine question) and perceived a threat in what he interpreted as the press's glorification of nakedness. The popular Igorots looked too uncivilized; visitors would generalize from them to all other Filipinos. He sent directives to Jenks requesting that the Igorots (and the Negritos) be made to wear brightly colored short trunks instead of loincloths.[23] Unlike Jenks, Taft did not care about "authenticity" or teaching Americans about cultural diversity.

Jenks, with McGee's support, argued that loincloths were necessary to ensure scientific validity. Starr got into the controversy by lecturing on clothing, stating there was nothing wrong with Igorot clothing. It was the "innate immodesty of our best citizens which resulted in the demand that the natives at the fair be adorned with trousers. . . . It was not false modesty but immodesty that inspired the attempt to clothe these wards of the nation." It was also perilous in summer, he insisted. "To force them to wear clothing would be cruel—dangerous because they are not used to it and cruel because it is so hot now." While Starr was serious, most reporters poked fun at him, at anthropologists, and the controversy. "Their native attire is good! *Exempla gratia*—a gee string and a broad grin." At the conclusion of the controversy, the *St. Louis*

Post-Dispatch announced, "Igorrotes Not to Wear Breeches." Taft had backed down and visitors would see authentic Native attire for men.[24]

Visitors considered the Suyoc Igorots less picturesque. Boyongasan led the group of seven women, four young boys, and fifteen adult men. The Suyocs were excellent metal workers, and little was written about them besides their artistic abilities and industry. Rather than dance continuously, they demonstrated cooking methods using copper vessels and wove. "Hour after hour [the women] sit in front of their hand looms, [and] weave the gay colored yarn into cloth, ignoring the hundreds of curious American eyes and the frank American tongues." At the end of the exposition, the LPEC awarded Boyongasan a third-class medal. Similarly, the more modestly attired Tinguian Igorots, eighteen individuals from Abra, received little mention by the press or in LPEC accounts. "They show a rude architectural skill in the construction of their bamboo and nipa huts. These have small balconies in front on which the women sit and weave."[25] They gave rice planting and gardening demonstrations and were considered to have a peaceful nature. They spurned the Bontocs' dog-meat-eating rituals and considered themselves a superior people.

All three groups gave hourly dance demonstrations to gong music and artistic demonstrations. Bontoc men did a "realistic pantomime in the use of the shield and spear, advancing, retreating, poising and thrusting." It was several weeks before they permitted visitors to examine their musical instruments. Thereafter, "men visitors were invited to join the dance which they frequently did, borrowing the tom-toms while the owners sat watching and laughing at their attempts to execute the peculiar Igorrote gyrations. . . . If the dancer was successful, he was rewarded by crises of 'good boy, good boy' from the Igorrotes, who found great enjoyment in watching the dance."[26]

There are many references to the Igorots' courtesy, but there were also limits. Leaders often had to keep crowds at bay. In April, one had to stand guard to keep intruders outside the new fence and not interfere with the workmen. "The chief brandished a huge war club and strode up and down in front of the enclosure with all the dignity he could command. Either the club or the dignity was enough and afterwards the visitors kept a respectful distance."[27]

The Igorots were often compared to American Indians, especially in their dance styles. Groups and their cultural distinctions were simplified to facilitate racial comparisons with evolutionary implications, sometimes to Jenks's consternation but usually not McGee's. Like the American Indians, the Igorots had to earn money from the sale of their art and photographs and tips following demonstrations. Commentators noted that understanding the value of money was evidence of their rapid cultural progress since coming to America. "A visitor stopped at a bamboo hut and offered an Igorot child a penny. The little one threw it on the ground. The visitor offered a five-cent piece, and the child accepted it." People also gave them gifts, clothing, hand mirrors, suitcases, and cigars. "When they point to their mouths it is to express willingness to accept the American filler of peace and good will."[28]

Reporters mentioned how incensed the Igorots became when they learned that their enemies, the Visayans, were at the fair. They were especially angry at the Visayans' special treatment, and the fact that Scouts were sent to control them, that is, to keep them from moving at will around the fairgrounds. Fair officials constrained Igorot life by confining them to the Reservation and letting them go to other parts of Forest Park or outside the fairgrounds only in supervised groups with a translator. The Scouts, Constabulary, and Visayans were not so confined. As Christians, they received invitations to visit St. Louis families or go sightseeing. According to historian Clayton Laurie, the Igorots retaliated when they discovered the discriminatory policies "by loudly beating their drums during Scout drill exhibitions, preventing the Scouts from hearing voice commands." Scout leaders threatened to leave "if the Igorots were not disciplined and brought under control." Since the Scouts did not leave, some compromise must have been reached.[29]

As they did with the American Indians, the press created celebrities. The most famous Igorot was Balonglong (Antero), the star pupil of the model school. Antero knew English since he was Jenks's houseboy and ethnographic consultant and served as the Bontocs' interpreter. Mrs. Jenks found him exceptionably bright, a remarkable individual who wanted adventure. "Antero always stands straight and carries himself gracefully, so that he commands respect. He has a way of getting along with the Igorot, and I never saw one of them question his little authoritative way. When he is with the Igorot alone, he is just one of them but when he is with us he is the boss." Antero often gave impromptu vocal concerts of American tunes. He met President Roosevelt and, according to Jenks, had a good time in St. Louis. Jenks took him to Wisconsin to meet his parents at the close of the exposition (M. Jenks 1951, 123, 139, 197).[30]

Anthropologist Patricia Afable found Bontoc descendants who described their ancestors' trip to America as "exhilarating adventures from which people returned with some American goods, money, a bit of American English, and a fairly limited, often amusing view of American life" (Afable 1997, 20–21). Women brought back blouses, skirts, and bloomers, while the men collected coats, trousers, and hats. American material culture, if not ideas, traveled back to the Islands. Evidently the idea that Native peoples would become enamored of American democracy was not born out.

The Bontoc Igorot Dog Feasts

The curious fairgoers came to regard all the Igorot groups as fascinating because the Bontoc ate dog meat. Reporters frequently commented on the "savage" culinary preferences that repelled middle-class Americans. While the people were asked to be as "native" as possible—to perform their daily activities according to a daily routine—eating dogs went over an invisible line of propriety and acceptability for many visitors. It was too exotic, too primitive, too sickening, and too inhumane. For others it came to symbolize the contrast being reinforced in every corner of the exposition. Savage dog feasts clearly illustrated how far Americans had come from humanity's heathen beginnings. A postcard depicting Bontoc men slaughtering a dog was a sought-after souvenir, symbolizing the dichotomy between primitiveness and civilization. Poems reflecting their authors' prejudices and humor were written about it:

> You must see the Igorotte
> From his Filipino bog,
> Dressed in style that we call naughty,
> Being in a mental fog,
> Who asserts in manner haughty
> He shall, must, and will have dog.[31]

The Igorot Dog Feast was originally not intended to be performed several times a week, but was a one-time event to celebrate their safe arrival and dedicate their shrine. As one appalled visitor described the event, "They first bind the dog to a stick. Then its throat is cut while the tribesmen mumble something. It is then skinned and roasted." Missouri governor Hunt was tearfully upset, stating that the feast would not have occurred if he had known about it. He called it

> *a sad spectacle which the United States never witnessed before. I could not bear it; neither could any other of our Caucasian party, and we retired, leaving the little brown boys alone in their bamboo stockade. There they tom-tommed and danced the true savage dance and cut the throats of the six dogs, which had been several days fattening. The crowd of spectators came so near breaking down the frail stockade that we had to call off the dance.[32]*

With this type of newspaper coverage and visitor reaction, the Dog Feast quickly became one of the biggest draws on the Philippine Reservation. One headline read, "Dog Gone—Happy Are Igorrotes. Old Time Feasts in Luzon Repeated, with Canine Steak as Piece de Resistance. Biggest Crowds for a Year." To attract larger crowds, nine stray dogs were rounded up the following Sunday. The Department of Exploitation tried to both deflate and capitalize on the notoriety by describing dogs as the Bontocs' "normal food." Some reporters were sarcastic, finding humor in the controversy while others were matter-of-fact. Historian Virgilio Pilapil has written that the city provided twenty dogs a month so that the Igorots could stage the performance. Paducah, Kentucky, also sent forty strays when reporters speculated that St. Louis had insufficient mutts. People living near the fairgrounds feared for their dogs and tales that missing pets were eaten surfaced quickly and lived on after the exposition. Visitor Dorothy Birk later wrote, "Either the quality or the quantity didn't quite satisfy the dog-eaters, [so] when your pet didn't come back quickly, you could be pretty sure that it had landed in the soup kettle."[33] The Pawnees and Wichitas were said to have departed when their dogs disappeared. They blamed the Filipinos.

Controversies over where the dogs would be obtained and how they would be killed had surfaced before the fair began and continued unabated until December. Jenks, fair officials, and city bureaucrats decided that the dogs used would be strays from the city pound. Members of the St. Louis Humane Society were appalled. As one reporter told readers, "Just when the wild men from Luzon are about to lay hands upon the un-ransomed pack of dogs at the city pound, the Humane Society rushes in, gatherers the dogs to its breast, and forbids another feast." John Finnel found a 1903 city ordinance that forbade eating dogs within the city limits. The Humane Society condemned the "contemplated localization of the Igorotte custom of tying a dog to a stake, beating him to death with clubs, and then baking him in a long pan, with young onions laid on his ribs" (Afable 1995, 16).

While Jenks kept a low profile, McGee publicly condemned the Humane Society, citing cultural relativism: "Those who like dog meat should eat it." This pronouncement did little to stem the controversy and the Igorot compound became known as "Dogtown." A *St. Louis Post-Dispatch* cartoon showed a small black man with abundant hair, earrings, wide lips, large feet, clothed in a white skirt and holding a club, being confronted by a Humane Society member in checkered pants, shoes, and high hat, who shielded a dog. Both stand in front of a meat market where a sloppy butcher, covered in blood, holds a meat cleaver (fig. 7.3). According to one reporter, the Igorots' "barbaric minds can suggest nothing more humane than to tie the poor dog to a stake, hit him in the face four or five times with a gnarled bole of a banyan tree, and then skin him for baking." But what about American slaughter houses?

> *What meat do these citizens feed upon that they have become so humane? How dies the poor little calf in the slaughter houses of St. Louis? We shudder to think how butchers put a rope around the dear little [calf's] neck, pass the rope through a ring on the floor, and pull the poor, bleating little calf down on his knees. Of course, this isn't anything like so horrible as tying a dog to a stake for slaughter; but it isn't nice either.*

But he undermined his argument by claiming the difference between a sledge hammer and a war club is that "one is a savage implement and the other a product of the force of civilization. It would be a great mistake to suppose that they are in any wise analogous from a humanitarian point of view."[34]

As Afable has pointed out, why the LPEC exploited the Dog Feast is puzzling, given the emphasis on authenticity. "It can only be explained by its role in sensationalizing the strange and exotic nature of the people who performed it. . . . Jenks describes dog-eating briefly as something that happens occasionally in the villages he had studied and only for ceremonial purposes" (Afable 1997, 21). The LPE Igorot village became completely identified with the spectacle of dog slaughter, producing a durable and damaging stereotype that lasts to this day.

*IS IT BEEF TRUST, SPEAKING THROUGH
HUMANE SOCIETY, THAT WOULD ROB
IRROGOTE OF HIS CHERISHED DOG MEAT?*

Fig. 7.3. Cartoon by Chopin for the *St. Louis Post-Dispatch*, April 6, 1904. WJ McGee
Papers, box 32, newspaper scrapbook, Library of Congress.

There are no extant records that Jenks, McGee, or any other anthropologist, protested the sensationalizing of the rite. It may have been that publicity,
no matter what its repercussions, was simply too good for gate receipts. It
is unclear how much dog meat the Igorots actually ate. Participants "got so
sick of dog meat, especially because of the high fat content of American dogs,
that they would sometimes bury it at the edge of the festival grounds." One
anthropologist thinks that the Bontocs knew that they were having one over
on the fairgoers, making the spectacle as gory as possible to elicit looks of
horror.[35]

The Samal, Lake Lanao, and Bagobo Moro Encampments

The Samal Moros and Lake Lanao Moros (hereditary enemies) had two encampments on the northern arm of Arrowhead Lake, west of the Bridge of Spain. According to official fair histories, the tribes were "so hostile to each other that an armed guard was at first maintained between the two villages." A sign on the path between their villages read, "Persons photographing the Moros do so at their own peril."[36] There are few extant photographs.

While both groups were said to be descendants of Malayans, proud and aggressive, they were considered the most civilized of the non-Christian demonstrators. According to LPE publicists, the Lake Lanao people were in rebellion against the United States, and government officials hoped they would learn to respect Western authority by visiting the exposition. The hope was in vain. The people seldom left their village and were uninterested in visiting other parts of the LPE. Fair officials considered them unfriendly and exclusive. "It is characteristic of them to manifest aversion to being touched by the hand of a Christian. They avoid the shaking of hands." Photographers complained that they would never smile. When they did appear, they wore tight-fitting, colorful clothes "fashioned of the flimsiest of silk and draped about them without regard to fit." The men produced hammered brass boxes, musical instruments, and knives with inlaid handles. The women wove colorful blankets on backstrap looms. All items were for sale, and sales were apparently brisk.[37]

The thirty-eight Lake Lanao Moros were Muslims from the mountainous interior of Mindanao. Their neatly arranged village of thatched bamboo houses replicated the household of the sultan of Sulu, complete with retainers, sentinels, and bodyguards. There were apparently four headmen or "sultans," two lesser heads of households (*datta*), an ayatollah, thirteen women, and six children. The religious leader, Rajah Muda Sumbayangui, was the highest-ranking man and Sultan Demasanky acted as a servant in his household. Each man flew his private flag in front of his house and had a large placard beside the front door with his name, village in the archipelago, and the number of Moros he ruled. These men refused to perform for the amusement of visitors and as a result fair organizers considered them a disappointment. "The trouble was too many sultans and dattos, too few hombres. . . . These high officials remained secluded, and wholly unwilling to perform in accordance with the

Fig. 7.4. Colony of Samal Moros, from the Island of Mindanao, Philippine Reservation. Photograph by Jessie Tarbox Beals. Missouri Historical Society, St. Louis, no. 20684.

wishes of the showmen. The result was that the gate fees to the Lanao Village were small."[38]

If the Lake Lanao Moros were perceived as imperious, the Samal Moros (fig. 7.4) were seen as intelligent pirates and pearl fishermen, "long the terror of the Philippine coasts, but now friendly and loyal to American authorities." Government officials considered them the most intelligent and advanced of the Mindanao tribes but on account of their "fanatical Islamic faith," difficult to assimilate. Rajah Muda Mand led the Samals although he did not attend the fair; his brother and prime minister, Datto Facundi, served as his representative. Facundi was described as a stately, bronze-hued person of dignity who was very courteous to all visitors, touching his turban as they departed. "Like all the Samal Moros, he has become a staunch ally of the United States."[39] Facundi emphasized his position, status, and authority. His large house had a private porch and young girls beat tonal brass drums to announce his entrances and exits.

The Samal Moro village, the Philippines' Venice, was sited on the lakeshore and contained forty people. Gay red flags fluttered overhead and dugouts and outriggers with different colored sails bobbed on rope moorings. Bamboo and rattan houses with nipa-covered roofs were built over the water on stilts driven into the mud; a bamboo bridge connected each with the lakeshore. The Samals were noted for their superb music and facility with percussion instruments. The women sang and drummed while the men performed a variety of dances, most notably the Moro-Moro, billed as the "frenzied Mohammedan spear dance." On special days, brightly colored lanterns illuminated the village and the men held water carnivals. Unlike the reclusive Lanaos, the Samals marched in parades, dressed in bright silks with colorful sashes.

The visitors enjoyed these sights; gate receipts were high. The most noted Samal activity was diving for coins visitors threw in the lake. The divers were selective; "nothing less than a nickel will tempt these thrifty sea gypsies." Children were successful; "the smaller the Moro the greater the income [for] the Exposition visitor finds it more difficult to resist the expectant eyes of the urchins than of the full grown pearl divers." Children generally earned three dollars to four dollars a day. Most divers were boys, but one small girl, "Little Anise," was quite successful. The Samals had brought a ton of pearl shells, which they used to illustrate pearl fishing. The shells were then polished and sold.[40]

The Samals conducted daily boat races and gave water sport demonstrations. In warm weather children spent most of their time swimming and playing, sliding down wooden plank slides and water shoots constructed to resemble the slides at the Pike's "Shooting the Chutes" concession. "They usually capsized following the descent," according to an observer, "but such result in no way detracted from the new sport."[41]

One reason to bring the Moros was the hope that they would see the superiority of American life and stop rebelling. The Lake Lanaos' standoffishness led one policy commentator to conclude: "The Moros are lending themselves less readily to the ways of the American. It is believed in many quarters that the assimilation of the Igorot men, the headhunters, will not be difficult, but the assimilation of the Moros as a race will be impossible." Another reason for this assessment was that both Samal and Lake Lanao Moros were perceived to be inveterate gamblers. They spent most of their spare time playing Monte, a game of chance they had learned from the Spanish. Apparently several fortunes were won and lost, evidenced by the holes in their house supports which were used as banks. "The larger the number of holes, the stronger the evidence of impecuniousness."[42]

There was one other Moro group but little is recorded about them. The Bagobo Moros were from a remote region on the western coast of Mindanao whom Jenks saw as distinct morally because they wore more clothing than other groups. The press still considered them savages who were slave holders and practiced human sacrifice. Jenks categorized them as primitive and only nominally Muslim, practitioners of a cult rather than a true religion, to keep the preconceived categories intact and neat.[43]

The Bagobos did not arrive until July, but then quickly built a nipa-hut village. The twenty-three men and seven women were regarded with admiration by all visitors because they were handsome, graceful, and picturesquely attired. They wore colorful kemp attire (knee pants and jackets for men and skirts and jackets for women) heavily decorated in geometric patterns with mollusk shell beads. Bulon, a nineteen-year-old with hair down to his hips and a colorful head covering, was often compared to the Sioux. The press commented on the large knife he used in mock combat.[44] Visitors watched for hours as the men produced shell beads and the women sewed them on clothing; they were considered the best bead workers at the exposition. Since the Bagobos did not gamble and tolerated visitors, reporters decided they were primed to accept American cultural leadership, if they would only stop fighting.

The children quickly learned English and enjoyed conversing with visitors. The adults were friendly, laughing readily and heartily, talking with fairgoers and visiting other groups. But reporters regarded them with suspicion. They "are said to be fiercer even than the other Moros, practicing human sacrifices as a cult rather than as a religion." There was, of course, no evidence of such a practice during the exposition.[45]

The Negrito Village

The Negrito village on the Reservation's eastern edge housed about thirty individuals said to be the Philippines' real aboriginal inhabitants and an ethnological puzzle. Their difference was reflected in language, religion, tribal customs, and physical characteristics, especially their bushy hair, short stature, and very black skin. They were a "distinctive race," in the terminology of the day, "true savages" who used "primitive" weapons (e.g. poisoned arrows) and were said to have "primate-like" tree-climbing ability. The press mentioned their shyness and eating habits, which were considered indications of a relative lack of intelligence. An equally important indication of backwardness was how they inappropriately combined Western and traditional garb: "The full dress costume of the Negrito is a dirty cotton rag tied loosely around his loins. The chief of the village wears a plug hat." The fact that they ate roots, grubs, and snails was considered evidence that they were a "missing link." According to William Curtis,

> the Negritos are very interesting. The lowest grade of human creatures under the jurisdiction of the President of the United States, they are more debased in morals, more feeble of intellect than the Digger Indians of California, and the intelligence of the children particularly offers encouragement to those who would lift them out of their degradation.[46]

Most commentators insisted that the Negritos were headed for extinction by 1950 because there were fewer than ten thousand of them. But they also felt that there was hope because they were extremely clever and skillful. Some reporters even contended that they were the Filipino group most ready to adapt to civilized ways. "You may see a dwarfish Negrito woman, sitting in the doorway of her bamboo hut sewing with an American needle, a pair of American scissors at her side." They were entrepreneurial. "They wander about the village shooting sparrows or practicing at marks. [One] little fellow [age 7] . . . can knock a nickel unerringly at twenty-five paces. Without a smile he picks up the coin that he has won by his prowess, and awaits the next chance."[47]

There were approximately thirty-three people, led by El Captain who wore a silk hat, and on special occasions, a shirt, collar, and cravat. All the Negritos were said to be very cordial and amiable, and the children were praised as exceptionally quick learners. "Most of them have learned to say 'Thank you.'" They were also very useful to fair officials. Their skills were put to practical use in June when sparrows infested the exposition gardens; the boys were hired as guards who "rarely missed a bird" (Newell 1904, 5137–38).

The Negritos apparently had an elaborate demonstration and performance schedule. Hourly they presented festival dances, songs, and special reenactments. At 9:00 a.m. they staged a social ritual, a flute duet entitled "Bansai," and a wedding ceremony. At 10:00 a.m. they performed the Huso dance, reenacted a wild boar hunt by driving an animal into a net, and held a mock public assembly to elect a chief. Next the women cooked. In the afternoon,

Fig. 7.5. Stereocard of the Visayan Village on Arrowhead Lake, Philippine Reservation. Photograph by C. H. Graves. Library of Congress, Prints and Photographs Division, CPH3CII774, USZ62-11774.

they executed a Kutagag dance with bolos and spears, lit a fire using bamboo sticks, and smoked bees from the tops of tall trees. Then they planted rice to musical accompaniment, showed how rice was cleaned, and demonstrated hunting techniques. They completed each day with a reenactment of a commemoration for the dead. Every Saturday they made tattoos—the signs by which they showed "their record of lives taken" on their "transparent copper-brown skins."[48] Gate receipts were good.

The Visayan Village

The Visayan village with its ornate bamboo dwellings was located on the southern arm of Arrowhead Lake (fig. 7.5). The Visayans numbered ninety-eight individuals, selected to symbolize Christian Natives. "Visayan" was actually an ethnolinguistic designation used to refer to any Roman Catholics. Those in St. Louis were probably Cebuano cultivators and fisherman from the densely populated mountains in the Bisaya Island group. They were characterized as serene, even-tempered, industrious, and polite people who wore modest, white cotton clothing. They lived in fifteen houses around a theater and a Catholic Church surrounded by a bamboo fence. Scattered around the compound were agricultural implements, carts, and two water buffalos.

One of the village's main attractions was a fifteen-member orchestra that played two concerts a day, specializing in light Spanish airs, interspersed with lively performances by a troupe of singers and dancers. Each performance ended with "The Star Spangled Banner," which the Visayans sang in English, while two small children ran onstage and waved the American and exposition flags. "The performance invariably 'brings down the house' with American enthusiasm." Actors presented a repertoire of skits hourly from 2:00 p.m. until closing. A special attraction was two Visayan midgets, boxer Juan de la Cruz and his sister Mirtina, aged twenty-nine and thirty-one, respectively. They were well-educated residents of Panay and spoke three dialects, Spanish, and some English.[49]

Popular as these productions were, what attracted many visitors was the Visayans' productivity. "The Visayans sit in the open, lower story of their houses carrying on their industries. . . . If an American visitor asks a question the answer is given readily and courteously but the eyes are seldom raised from their work. In the evenings the young fellows bring out the guitars. The girls sing. The Visayan are home people." One reporter was very taken with the women and tried to make their attire understandable to his female readers, describing it as traditional yet modern. On the opening day,

> *Feminine Visayans had on their party dresses and every coiffure was in the latest American style, which has been the Visayan style since Adam—I mean since Eve. . . . Visayan female loveliness is something like the Japanese, petite and winsome, and there are some pretty girls in the Visayan village. . . . The young ladies spoke no English and the visitors spoke no Spanish but not withstanding this trifling drawback, the conversation never flagged on either side. It was greatly pieced out with smiles. The Filipino young women made an unmistakable hit with their American visitors.[50]*

These were the encounters McGee had wanted, where one half of the world met and appreciated the other, turning stereotypes into cultural understanding.

The crowds kept coming to buy and watch the fabrics being produced. The Visayans were experts in weaving, woodcarving, and fiber braiding. Skilled families had been chosen to ensure that all art forms would be demonstrated. The women wove, "sitting on the ground with feet braced, slowly and laboriously turning out the jusi [*sic*] cloth an inch or two at a sitting." Several men and women combed long strands of pineapple fiber, while others produced mats, manila hats, and canes. In addition, a house on stilts was constructed. As with other Native participants, life progressed for the Visayans during the fair. Three babies were born and there was at least one wedding in the Catholic Chapel that was not open to visitors, but was recorded by a fair historian as an exotic event. "In true Visayan custom the bride fainted at just the proper moment at the conclusion of the ceremony, fell into her husband's arms and was carried away to the new home, the guests applauding."[51]

Trying to See That One Last Tribe

The Philippine Reservation attracted millions of visitors curious about the U.S. government's new wards and anxious to see the changes wrought by six years of colonial administration. Gate receipts ranged from three thousand to five thousand dollars daily, an astonishing figure given that people paid twenty-five or fifty cents apiece. The Reservation was successful, described repeatedly as the "most remarkable display of people ever shown at an exposition," much to Jenks's and McGee's satisfaction. More people visited the Filipinos than they did the Pike, the industrial pavilions, or the LPEC Anthropology Department. Many people concluded it showed them "the condition of the savage tribes; the most advanced civilization; what the United States has accomplished during its rule of the archipelago; and the nature of the Philippine problem in all its phases."[52] It was certainly how the colonized half of the world lived, at least as envisioned by evolutionary ethnologists. Jenks had done his job well and McGee was pleased with how it complemented his exhibits.

But not everyone was pleased. There was some disappointment when people finally encountered one "other tribe" from the Philippines, the ethnologists. In mid-May the *St. Louis Republic* ran the following story.

She was fashionably dressed and had gone to the Philippine reserva-
tion to see all the wild and weird people. She met Capt. George S.
Clark, the purchasing agent of the Philippine exposition, and im-
pressed him into service as lexicographer and guide. He, gallant man,
nothing loath, proceeded to tell her all that he knew, and some things
he had not before suspected himself of knowing.

"What different tribes are represented here now?" the woman
asked.

"Oh, there are the Igorrotes, the Moros, the Negritos, and . . ."

"Yes, I have seen all of them and how interesting they are! But, don't
you know, I haven't seen the Ethnologists yet. I have heard so much about
them that I am real eager to see them. Where are they?"

At that moment Albert Ernest Jenks, chief of the ethnological sur-
vey, came into sight.

"There's one now," exclaimed Clark. "That's the chief."

The woman was visibly disappointed, for Prof. Jenks is quite a
good-looking white man, who wears eyeglasses and clothes and is, as
he seems, quite incapable of doing anything very shocking.

"Is he a real Ethnologist?" asked the woman, doubtingly.

"As real as they make 'em," said Capt. Clark.

"He looks tame."

"Yes, but you should see him with his war paint on, beating the
tom-tom."

"Are ethnologists a numerous tribe?"

"I should say so. The woods are full of them."

"How interesting," she answered as she walked away.[53]

Maybe McGee, strolling and lecturing in the Anthropology Villages across
Arrowhead Lake, would have been more to her liking.

8. The Anthropology Villages

Self-selected volunteers in a desperate venture.
Louisiana Purchase Exposition
president David Francis

McGee had gathered Native people from north, south, east, and west into an extensive outdoor exhibit. Francis always referred to them as the anthropology "colonies," emphasizing the political status of the inhabitants. LPEC publicists and McGee emphasized the peoples' strangeness, billing them as exotic extremes—the tallest or shortest race, the ones who lived in the most remote places. Newspapers focused on the novelty and exoticism of cultural differences and presented them with mockery, ridicule, fascination, and incredulity. One reporter wrote of the Tehuelches:

> *While the management is overjoyed at the prospect of another royal visitor to swell the list of crowned heads at the fair, they are somewhat perplexed as to the matter of full dress which his Patagonian majesty may elect to wear at the numerous functions at which he will be asked to assist. Although Patagonia is a cold country, the people of those parts are singularly unconventional about the amount of dress necessary, and full court costume there as a rule is said to consist of a bright smile and a nose ring. However, this rumor may prove untrue.[1]*

Commentators rarely saw the foreign participants as individuals but as stereotypes. Visitors reacted to the Native peoples as cultural-racial types, just as McGee intended.

Red Giants from the Extreme South: The Patagonian Tehuelches

The local press greatly anticipated the Tehuelches' arrival in mid-April. McGee fed reporters ethnographic information and tidbits about their journey. They responded with numerous articles, including a long description of their physical attributes and customs in the *St. Louis Post-Dispatch*'s *Sunday Maga-*

zine. One combined McGee's information with European fantasies, remarking that "[t]he giant has always had a place in legends, and literature. No other member of the human family has so readily lent himself to the imagination of humankind, all the world over. But never until now has the giant had a place at a world's fair." The reporter gave reasons for this: (1) rarity—"there is but one race of giants in the world"; (2) the negotiating ability of LPEC agents—never before had "any white man enjoyed the confidence of these big barbarians to such an extent that he could induce them to leave the wilderness in which they live"; and (3) McGee's insight—"not until Prof. McGee did any fair enjoy the services of a man whose knowledge of the primitive peoples of the world enabled him to know how to go about getting some of the races that had never been seen out of their own countries."[2]

Another reporter wrote, "Professor McGee says that the Giants are up to expectations," considering the Tehuelches the finest physical specimens to be seen at the fair. "Their strong serene and not uncomely faces indicate high mentality. Morally they are beyond unfavorable criticism. They are always gentle and courteous to each other. They are together a splendid type of pastoral people." A fair historian wrote, "their chests are so deep, their bodies so robust and their limbs so large as to place them easily in the lead of the known primitive tribes in physical development." Most were fascinated with their hair. The men's "is thick and they wear it parted in the middle and bobbed even with the lobes of the ears, like the 'Cromwell cuts' now in vogue for little girls." The women's hair was longer than the men's and "hangs in straight strings about the neck."[3]

The Tehuelche contingent consisted of an extended family from the province of Santa Cruz, Argentina (fig. 8.1). There were five adult men, one adult woman (Lorenza), an eight-year-old girl named Giga, and a "yellow mongrel dog that was the mascot and acted as the autocrat of the group" (there were two dogs). Newspaper articles prominently featured the dog, which never left Lorenza's side. The Patagonians referred to themselves as Tzonecas and tried unsuccessfully to get McGee, the press, and visitors to use their proper name, rather than Tehuelches, which means "southerners," a term used by their neighbors. To avoid confusion, McGee preferred to use the term *Patagonians* so visitors would associate them with an exotic and mysterious locale at the southernmost end of South America. He was sure people would want to see

Fig. 8.1. "The Patagonian Giants." Tehuelche family from Patagonia, Argentina, in front of their tent. *From left*: Colojo, Guechico, Casimiro, Bonifacio, Giga, and Lorenzo. Photograph by Charles Carpenter. © The Field Museum, negative no. CSA13262.

them, because the Red Giants were "notable for large stature, robust frame, and great physical strength, as well as for skill as hunters and horsemen." People wondered about the accuracy of these assertions once they saw the Tehuelches. Even Francis concluded, "The men and the matron displayed a massiveness of frame and face and a bigness of body and limb more apparent to the beholder than to the student of statistics."[4]

There was intense press coverage of their activities, including courtesy visits to other tribal participants upon their arrival and an honoring banquet of roasted beef and bread prepared by the Indian School students:

> *No sooner had they finished their repast than they were forced to flee for safety from the camera fiends to the basement of the building. When the first photographer planted his camera under the nose of the Patagonians, Chief Guechico gave a few guttural sounds and grasped*

the machine, to the great terror of the photographer. A few words from Lorenza, his wife, caused Guechico to release his hold on the machine, and obeying Lorenza's command the six stalwart braves, the little girl, and the tiny dog filed through the basement door and bolted it against further intrusion. "We would not care so much," explained one of the younger chiefs, through an interpreter, "but we have been treated badly by the White man. Many have taken our pictures, both in Liverpool and New York, and they always promised us some but we never received them."[5]

Guechico, their seventy-one-year-old leader, severely limited their interaction, and photographs of the group became greatly prized. This did not stop reporters from creating fanciful interpretations of their activities. Soon after arriving, two men developed a bronchial infection. Having never experienced such an illness, they began a "deathwatch," according to one reporter. This involved an all-night vigil with "a blowing of horns and a beating of pans and chanting as is customary when a body is about to die." The next morning Doctor Walbridge, an LPEC physician, determined that everyone had severe colds. After further discussion through an interpreter and assurance that the diseases would subside, the ritual was suspended "with the probability that there was hope for a corpse to come forward soon and make the death watch good." The editor entitled the report "Patagonian Death Watch Was Held in Vain."[6]

The Tehuelches' camp was located near Arrowhead Lake so the men could demonstrate their water craft—large vessels containing fires for warmth and cooking. The public was fascinated by this and their large house, called a *toldo*, made of eighty dressed guanaco skins. Many visitors were not impressed by the people and felt they had been misled by McGee. The six-foot-tall men were simply too short.

Although the specimens at the fair were of fair height, they would not by any means pass for giants in America. How the Patagonian race acquired their reputation for giant stature is difficult to explain, except by the hypothesis that the white races of many centuries ago were smaller of stature than they are today, and when early navigators first saw the Patagonians, they appeared as giants compared to themselves.[7]

Given what is known about average European stature in the sixteenth century, this might have been an accurate assessment.

Uncertainty about the status of the group's leader was also expressed. Chief Guechico was referred to as a king, for the press could not resist labeling any political leader as royalty. To both undermine and ridicule this image and contrast it to American industriousness and cleanliness, reporters referred to him as lazy and one of "the dirtiest people on the globe." "The big Tehuelche chief rolled himself up in his great skin mantle and, sitting down on the tracks of the Intramural Railroad, just outside his quarters, contemplatively puddled his bare feet in the slush in his favorite position of doing nothing."[8]

The press's assessment of the "sullen" Lorenza was always negative, especially in comparison to Native Americans: "[D]espite the fact that she is as tall and muscular as her husband—or possibly because she is—[Lorenza] works only when she so desires, and hunts and fishes at her pleasure." Another disillusioned person did not know how to interpret her since she did not meet his middle-class expectations of womanhood. She "is a study. Yesterday she did not exert herself even so much as to grunt. She smoked her pipe and quite frequently availed herself of a bottle of Kentucky bourbon." The trope of the drunken savage was further invoked as an explanation for the reporter's antipathy. To further the analogy he invoked the stereotypes of belligerent Irish immigrants and Indians. "The Patagonians like whisky quite as well as some members of the Caucasian race, and it has the same effect upon them as is noticed in the North American Indian. . . . When the Patagonian gets his fill of liquor, he is in a fighting mood, and woe unto the photographer who tries to photograph him."[9]

The group's distinctive attire was constantly mentioned. Lorenza wore skirts and hand-woven blankets that hung from her shoulders. The men wore horse-skin boots, guanaco skin mantles with leather or woven hoods, baggy leather trousers designed for life in the saddle, and woven, custom-made shirts. Their rhea feather and guanaco pelt robes were quite magnificent. McGee reported that the Tehuelches brought several of these highly valued robes, hung them on the fence around their compound, and hoped to trade. In Argentina the robes were staples of exchange and the Tehuelches "were much disappointed at the indifference of visitors toward them" McGee (1905d, 100). They were eventually all sold for fifty to one hundred and fifty dollars each.

Typically the Tehuelches' living expenses were not large but added up quickly. After salaries for the interpreter and escorts, food was the major expense, charged to monthly departmental accounts, and included four hundred and fifty pounds of beef and sixty-four loaves of bread. Other purchases were two dozen blankets, a tent fly, a cord of oak wood, and a wall tent, totaling $143.74.[10]

While McGee wanted the Patagonians as representatives of human beings of massive size and exemplars of "primitive maternal organization," visitors wanted to see their much-publicized and exalted horsemanship. They were generally disappointed, as were the Tehuelches, who had agreed to come only if they were given white horses. McGee often complained to LPEC officials that better facilities were needed in the anthropology area to let the Tehuelches truly demonstrate their specialties. It never materialized. Still, the men demonstrated their gaucho style riding whenever they could, which apparently was infrequently. They repeatedly demanded their white horses. By August 12 they had still not been given their own horses and their complaints were bitter enough that the newspapers began seeing it as a scandal. McGee did not particularly want horses in the small encampment because of the logistical problems and lack of money in his rapidly shrinking budget for feed. Without horses the men were melancholy. Cummins, the owner of the Wild West show, offered them horses and asked them to participate in his rodeo contests. They began to attend as often as they could and, despite unfamiliar stock and roping rules, "on unaccustomed saddles as well as horses, and handicapped by Humane Society restrictions," they set records in competitions with experienced American cowboys and Mexican vaqueros. Reporters noted their athletic abilities but always with caveats. "The Patagonians, reported to be the largest people in the world as a race, are big, lumbering and lazy. They are deft in handling a rope, but beyond that have no accomplishments as far as common knowledge goes." The Tehuelches used the money they earned to buy Western-style clothing, which they preferred to wear on the exposition grounds when not performing, much to McGee's chagrin.[11]

The Tehuelches' technological attraction was the bolo, a triple thong loaded with stone weights at the ends, thrown great distances to entangle a quarry. McGee considered the bolo a most effective primitive weapon and a primary reason for their attendance. The Tehuelches gave daily demonstrations and their dexterity, immense power of endurance, and ability to stay in the saddle all day was often noted.[12]

McGee wanted Natives to perform important rituals as evidence of cultural and mental progress. For the Tehuelches, he requested a sacrificial horse feast in which a newly mature gray mare is slain and consumed and innards elaborately consecrated. The group was willing but after much debate, the LPEC Board vetoed the ritual, not wanting another public outcry over food. The Igorot dog feast had generated enough ridiculing publicity. Slaughtering a horse and eating it on the exposition grounds would be too much.[13]

It appears the Tehuelches did not have a particularly good time. They disliked situations in which they were not accorded privacy. They had shared quarters with the Ainus when they first arrived, a situation distasteful to both groups. One newspaper reported that when the Tehuelches' encampment was completed, the Ainus, who never laughed aloud, were vocal in their pleasure. McCowan thought that the Patagonians enjoyed their life in the United States but had reservations.

> *They like the American men, but have not as yet become civilized enough to thoroughly appreciate the American women. They strongly object to unceremonious feminine visits at their homes, where like their American brother they sometimes wish to indulge in negligee garments, and enjoy a quite [sic] game. One too-curious lady, who ignored polite hints, was rather strenuously pushed out of the door; another mourns a ruined garment as the result of an unwelcome visit.*

Seemingly, the Tehuelches were often depressed, homesick, and convinced that they would die and never see their homeland again. As McGee wrote, "They were stoically resigned under the fatalism characteristic of primitive thought, but no other group so gladly shook the dust of the Exposition from their feet when the term of their agreement ended."[14]

Small Savages and Red Africans from West Africa: The Mbuti Pygmies

The Mbuti (Batwa) Pygmies and "Red Africans" (figs. 8.2, 8.3) were located near the Lakotas. McGee called them all Batwa Pygmies, "real aboriginals of the Dark Continent." They were people who had been displaced by others of "normal" height, which he considered an inevitable evolutionary advance.

Fig. 8.2. Batwa Pygmies from the Belgian Congo performing in front of the Manufacturing Building. *Left to right*: Lumbango, Shamba, Limo, Prince Latuna, Malengu, and Ota Benga. Photograph by Jessie Tarbox Beals, 1904. St. Louis Public Library, image no. LPE00125.

This demographic pressure, he argued, would force them to extinction; hence the exposition would be fairgoers' only time to see these "vanishing savages." In the official exhibition catalogue, McGee described the Africans as "notable for imperfect development of language, for skill and courage in the chase, and subservience in the presence of larger men." He also emphasized that little was known about their culture, language, laws, and beliefs. Their physical qualities earned them a low placement on his evolutionary ladder.

> They are prognathous—the lower portion of the face projects and the forehead retreats in a manner allying them with Simians more closely than with advanced humans. The brain-size is small, approaching the Simian standard. The forelimbs are relatively longer, in which character also they approach the Simian standards, and in habitual movements and attitudes many other resemblances to the human pro-

Fig. 8.3. Batwa Pygmies performing a beheading pantomime in their compound. *Left to right*: Shamba, Bomushubba, Malengu, Lumbo, and Ota Benga. Photograph by Frances Benjamin Johnston. Library of Congress, Prints and Photographs Division, LCJ696–40.

> *totype inferred from researches on man and lower animals may be found by the careful observer.*

Visitors would be especially interested in "their diminutive stature" as well as in the fact that they were superior hunters.[15] To McGee, securing real Pygmies was the crowning achievement of his quest to assemble the world's peoples.

But were these people really Pygmies? Extant information is confusing. Of the nine Africans, Verner said five were real Mbuti (Batwa) and the other four "Africans of ordinary type and stature" whom the press referred to as the Pygmies' Red African cousins. Since they all had the same skin color, which approached "red more nearly than does the North American Indian copper skin," height was the distinguishing trait. Small size meant a lower place on the evolutionary ladder. McGee felt three Batetele and Bakuba individuals were full-sized and easily distinguishable from the Batwa but that Bakuba boys were commonly confused with Pygmies. Lumbango (a Bakuba man) was even said to be of heroic stature. Verner stated that of the four "ordinary" Africans, Kalamma was a representative of the Bakubas, who "furnished more slaves to America than any other in Central Africa." The real confusion over identification seemed to center on Ota Benga. He was slightly taller than the other Pygmies, a characteristic common to his society, the Badinga or Chiri-chiri. Verner considered the Chiri-chiris a Pygmy society and McGee and the press decided not to quibble over details. Verner thought Ota Benga was the ideal representative of the small people.

The press agreed, and Ota Benga became a celebrity, receiving almost as much press coverage as Geronimo. He was a twenty-eight-year-old married man with two children whose family had been slaughtered by tax collectors of King Leopold's Force Publique when he had been captured and sold into slavery. Due to language differences, he had no one to talk to and was frequently said to be sad, heartsick, and lonely. While a press favorite, he was also the subject of ridicule. According to biographers Samuel Bradford and Harvey Blume, most reporters could not write about him without resorting to mockery, although they recorded Ota Benga's many activities and willingness to experiment with strange customs.

> *His Royal Highness, Prince Autobang, of the Pygmies, was out early this morning taking exercise on horseback and his strange appearance attracted a great crowd of spectators. Instead of sitting astride the horse, as is customary with equestrians, this dusky prince stood erect and, although the spirited animal he was riding cavorted and gave unmistakable signs of resentment, he rode with all the abandon, ease and grace of the professional circus rider. His fellow pygmies expressed their approval of his daring feat by dancing madly, clapping their hands, and uttering weird shrieks of delight. From a distance he approached his camp with a grand flourish and, leaping lightly to the ground, made a profound obeisance in answer to the prolonged applause which greeted his return.* [16]

A daring man, Ota Benga's pluck led some Americans to label him "a wild man," a savage loose in the city, and to view all the Pygmies as childish people who acted like American school boys: "The Pygmies had a lively scrap yesterday afternoon. After they finally had been separated by two or three men, Autobang sat pouting over the loss of his penny. The other Pygmy poured at his feet the whole day's collection as a peace offering. Autobang scornfully pawed the dust over it with his feet and refused to touch it. However the war is ended and all are friendly again." Ota Benga was a good mimic and entrepreneur, which in another era would have been ample evidence of his extraordinary intelligence and adaptability. "He has learned to hold out his hand to visitors and to say, "Gim nick, show teef." Teeth filed to sharp points in imitation of crocodile's teeth were his most visible feature. Years later Francis claimed that Ota Benga "confessed to feasts of human flesh but a few months before his departure from Africa, while his mouth watered at the sight of some of the plump colored folk among the visitors at the Exposition." The dangerous wild man had been tamed, and Verner was not above claiming credit for the deed. In one article he wrote: "Otabenga is a cannibal, the only genuine African cannibal in America today. He's also the only human chattel. He belongs to the Exposition Company. Step right up. There's no charge except to see his teeth. He has the reputation of being a man eater and has an exhibition of the identical molars and incisors with which it was done. They're worth the five cents he charges for showing them to visitors."[17]

McGee thought the "Red Africans" were interesting because of their "reddish or coppery skin-color, fine physique, intelligence and force." They were members of the Batetela and Bakuba tribes, the ruling class in the Congo, he informed visitors in the official exhibit catalogue, governed by King Ndombe. McGee also noted the unique experience visitors would have when they interacted with real African royalty. As always, he underscored that this was the first time any of the Batetelas had visited North America. To meet them was a once-in-a-lifetime experience (McGee 1905d, 102; 1904c, 16).

The nine Africans were from five different tribes and spoke different languages: Bakuba (Batubat), Batetela, Mbutu (Batwata), Baluba (Balula), and Chiri-chiri (Badinga). They had difficulty communicating with each other until they developed a lingua franca and a pidgin language that they used with other indigenous Native participants as well as amongst themselves. Clever linguists, they quickly learned English phrases, much to the delight of visitors. Lumbango was thought to be particularly intelligent. He "is a bright little fellow, about four feet in height. His big dark eyes sparkle with intelligence as he talks." He also began calling the ladies, "pretty," and "the fair ones invariably blush and turn away in embarrassment when the epithet is applied to them." All the men quickly learned slang, which one man jokingly remarked demonstrated their evolutionary potential: "There can be no doubt, now, that they are ripe for civilization and the higher life."[18]

They constantly talked to the crowds who pressed against the fence of their two compounds. "Their tongues rattle away with seemingly as much irresponsibility as the parrots they brought with them, and their laugh is quite as inane as anything that ever came from Africa," an Indian School employee wrote. "It is safe to say that for the size of their exhibit the African Pygmies excite as much interest as anything in the Exposition. Certainly there is nothing that will furnish more amusement than these queer little black men from across the ocean."[19] McGee was pleased with the crowds.

Unlike most visitors, McCowan was not impressed and wished the group had never come; he thought they were detestable. He made derogatory and racist comments to his friends, voicing his displeasure that the men did not live up to Euro-American fantasies created about them and the fact that they refused to obey rules. He thought the Pygmies were shams, bigger in physical stature than anticipated, and should be renamed "Hogmies" because of their eating habits.[20] He was not alone. The press commented that their activities were rude except in one area—music. While their melodies were "not musical to the American ear," it was authentic.

When the Pygmies donned khaki clothing the press deemed them less authentic; they had lost their "personal charm." Controversy began in the fall when torrential rains wiped out their huts and left the men asking for blankets. When McGee refused to give them ethnographically unsuitable warm clothing, students in the Indian School gave the men their own blankets. Eventually in early November they were each given brown khaki uniforms and the press reacted as McGee has feared, calling into question whether anthropology was staging a hoax. "With the polarized winds of autumn and their assumption of the white man's attire much of the old-time snap and nerve of the vivacious little Africans has disappeared, and they wander about the west end in a disconsolate way, as though longing for the freedom of their gunnysack skirts and the ostrich plumes which constituted their native attire."[21]

The Mbuti also requested suitable housing, and Verner promised to obtain it. But "suitable" to McGee meant something different than it did to the Africans. The men erected a number of huts, although at first they were reluctant because this was considered women's work in their cultures. Since insufficient materials had been brought from Africa, they collected materials in the forest south of the Main Picture. McGee felt these huts were more elaborate then they would have been in Africa and hence not completely accurate. He requested that they be made flimsier, and they were. Then the rains came. The huts were rebuilt with new materials and a central fireplace installed, but not without a good deal of controversy and coercion.

> *The camp became almost a quagmire. The Pygmy folk were glum. To ameliorate the condition wagon planks and cinders were dumped beside the houses. But when Mr. Dorsey asked them to use the cinders inside they stubbornly refused. Thereupon [Verner] came and gathered up his belongings and announced his intention to leave them to their fate at the Universal Exposition. The little black fellows ran after him, caught hold of his clothing and exclaimed, "We be good." They went to work vigorously. When the cinders were spread, they shook hands with Mr. Verner but left one of their number on duty in front of his tent to see that the "good man" did not leave them.*[22]

Overall, the African men fascinated the press who often repeated the saga of Verner's dangerous collecting expedition. Verner added to the mystique by lecturing daily. He discussed what was known about their lifestyle (hunting with javelins and poisoned arrows) and character, which he described as courageous and crafty. He said they were linguistically adept, usually speaking several languages to facilitate their barter economy, but undermined the compliment by saying their languages were simple. Verner consistently listed elements of "civilized" culture they did not practice while reminding visitors how little was known of their exotic religion and social life. He added further to their mystique with fanciful speculations on the origin of the term *pygmy* and their history of European contact. He also described the great explorers who had ventured into west central Africa in the nineteenth century, always ending with his own exploits.[23]

Exposition visitors and other indigenous participants were evidently captivated by the men, who were, in turn, intrigued by them. Except for Kondola, none had ever been out of central Africa. Curious and adventuresome were adjectives often used to describe them. Apparently at first the group was enchanted by the novelty of their surroundings and the strange sights, including the passing crowds. They received many gifts from strangers, some of which, according to Francis were not really welcomed. "Their last two monkeys and some of the parrots succumbed to lighted cigars and other vicious gifts forced on them by too attentive visitors—a fate from which the pygmies themselves were saved only by dint of constant surveillance" (Francis 1913, 527).[24] Other gifts were appreciated. Prince Latuna was given an American hat, which he wore when posing for photographs. Francis gave each man a watch and fob before they left for home.

Their public performances attracted huge crowds, including an estimated 125,000 on July 4. One performance created near panic.

> *The scream of a woman, frightened at the realism of a dance by eight unclad African pygmies at the end of the anthropological performance on the Plaza St. Louis last night, started a panic that brought the chief feature of midsummer carnival day at the Fair to a tumultuous end. Brandishing their spears, bows and arrows and murderous-looking knives, shouting blood-curdling cries and dashing toward the crowd as if to cut their way through the 75,000 people closely packed about the limits of the plaza, the pygmies so terrified a woman that she involuntarily cried out. Another woman equally frightened, screamed and in a moment the crowd breaking through the lines of Jefferson guards, swarmed into the plaza toward the pygmies, who appeared as much frightened as the women had been. The hurried arrival of a detail of soldiers from the First Illinois regiment gave the pygmies, Indians and other members of the anthropological exhibit on the plaza a chance to scurry to their quarters near the Administration building. Order among the crowd was restored.[25]*

Such experiences soured the group's enthusiasm, as did living in such close quarters. McGee noted they often conferred long and hard with Verner to hasten their return to Africa. These requests became more frequent when chill winds arrived. "It required constant vigilance and half-cruel constraint to keep them out of close-fitting clothing (acquired from the small coin showered on them by visitors) which would have interfered with the functions normal to their naked skins and brought serious if not fatal results. They left the grounds gladly" (McGee 1904e).

During the long months in St. Louis the Africans coped with their disappointments, homesickness, and suffering by using humor, a technique that got them through many uncomfortable situations. The men poked fun at the inexplicable behavior they saw. McCowan recounted that they were "blessed with a fine sense of humor. They laugh frequently and heartily, and generally manage to see the funny side of things." They tried to make other performers laugh; standing in a row at the front of the main bandstand they helped John Phillip Sousa direct his band with small batons. They frequently mimicked people giving lectures, pantomiming the orators and breaking into laughter. They often teased visitors. Shamba liked to frighten passing horses. "He gives a peculiar cry, difficult to imitate, and impossible to write, and when the startled animal pricks up his ears and breaks into a run, he emits a yell of supreme pleasure. It is difficult for one who has not seen it to believe that a man forty years of age could indulge in such a past-time, but it is so and the skeptical may find proof of it almost any day by visiting the little black men's camp."[26]

On another occasion they decided to ridicule American clothing. "The pygmies decided among themselves at a secret conference to discard the costumes they have been wearing since their arrival at the World's Fair ground and have adopted a costume more in keeping with their home life. Yesterday morning they made their appearance clad in all sorts of garments, most of which were made of gunny sacks. These they ripped apart and wrapped around their waists and tied with ropes or straps" (McCowan 1904e).[27]

In late August, the men organized an orchestra, directed by Latuna, and gave concerts in their camp. The free concerts were well attended according to fair publicists who evidently missed the point of the satire. "Latuna directs the orchestra with great vim and earnestness. He uses a large board as a baton. The instruments consist of a water bucket, two tin lard cans, a cigar box, two bucket lids and a beer bottle. In addition to the instruments they have added the art of whistling to their accomplishments since arriving at the World's Fair, and vary the program with a whistling chorus." Two Mbutis played their pipes on a regular basis, much to the amusement of the crowd and pleasure of the Africans in the Boer War concession. Equally amusing was their military drill based on the Indian School boys' evening drill. They would march next to the

Indian band in their own formation. "Not once during the entire drill did they interfere with the Indians except to keep them convulsed with laughter."[28]

Fair officials labeled them "very capricious and troublesome." Bennitt rationalized that "their erratic behavior showed the influences of the lower creatures upon their habits of thought. They were more troublesome even than the headstrong Patagonian, and indefinitely worse than the peaceful Ainu." The press also reported strife or "family quarrels" in the African camp, portraying them as extremely volatile, except for Ota Benga who during quarrels "sat in lone dignity under the trading store porch, obviously scornful of the childish proceedings."[29]

Evidently the group's unending impulsiveness led McGee to take action. On September 8 the LPEC reported that

> [t]he Pygmies are now comfortably installed in new glass front houses, and of course, can no longer throw stones [from the cinder floors] at the tourists, though they still retain their pugilistic instincts, one of them getting into a difficulty with Mr. Peairs yesterday and striking him. The Pygmies now make a daily display of their curious spears, knives, musical instruments, etc. on the roof of their dwelling and offer them for sale at the price of 'one dollah.' Theirs is a distinctively one price house, one price for everything. The Pygmies never fail to amuse, and from the stand point of pure comedy, are without doubt the best free show in the grounds. They could secure a concession on The Pike and coin money.[30]

It is doubtful the Africans knew they represented McGee's "subhuman" form, or were judged by some to be the most primitive peoples at the fair. Their satire and antics were uniformly interpreted as evidence of a low position on the evolutionary ladder even though it was keen evidence of their superior intellectual and adaptive skills. Many considered them caged animals rather than human beings, belonging at the bottom of the hill, below the dignified Indians.

At least one visitor decided they had advanced by developing capitalistic tendencies. "We are quite sure they are human now, for they are blessed with an instinctive love of the filthy lucre, and the cannibal has already raised his prices for admission to a view of his teeth. And Prince What's-His-Name sells last week's papers, and refuses to give back your change. Fact is, we would not be a bit surprised to see them erect a wooden fence around their palatial residences, call it the Pygmy Village, and charge ten cents for admission."[31]

Ethnographic Anomalies from the Far East: The Ainus

The "hairy" Ainu were chosen for their small stature, light skin color, abundant hair, luxuriant beards, "bodyward or centripedal movements," and extensive tattooing, as well as their indeterminate racial affinity. Added to these physical features were their agricultural practices, house forms, and elaborate bear-worshiping practices. Stereotypical misinformation was printed repeatedly in newspapers and reports: "The Ainu have no conception of a hell and no laws; They never laugh aloud; The women do all the work; The Ainu never wash, brush or comb the hair; They are the gentlest known race of barbarians; They despise cowardice and they reverence old age; They are a cold-blooded people, without strong emotions; They have flat bones in their arms and legs like the cave men of Europe."[32] The list went on as did the speculation about their origins. Were they Caucasians? Were they related to the Cossacks of Siberia? How did they get to be so hairy?

The press was excited to meet anthropology's great racial mystery. In honor of their arrival a *St. Louis Post-Dispatch* editorial writer wrote a poem, "The Ainus: A World's Fair Idyll," in which he jokingly said he wanted to be an Ainu, described why, and in the process told potential visitors what they would see, which of course, was wrong. Starr thought visitors needed assistance in understanding Ainu life based on the speculative press coverage and wrote *The Ainu Group at the St. Louis Exposition.* The slim volume was an ethnographic account of the people and their culture, based on interviews he conducted during the Pacific crossing. It was completed by July, quickly printed, and sold for seventy-five cents at the Ainu Village. Inagaki, the Ainu's interpreter who looked after daily needs, sold the book for Starr. He also served as fiscal agent for the Ainu artists and kept their monies for them. A Christian, he formed an association with a local church, which arranged for him to board with a St. Louis family. He took the Ainu to services every Sunday morning, including those of Rev. Charges Alone, and held regular Christian services at their encampment, which greatly astonished visitors.[33]

The Ainus had nothing to do for the first few weeks because they did not have their paraphernalia to perform a blessing ceremony needed to commence their new life and work. The Ainus and Starr had gathered enough materials for this ritual as well as to produce two houses, but their freight was lost in transit, side-tracked somewhere between Seattle and Denver. This forced them to reside in the Indian School basement, much to their displeasure.

The ninety-two packages finally arrived (along with some missing Arapaho lodges) on May 17, and the Ainus began house building the next day. Since they were so late, they decided to construct only one house. It had vertical walls covered with rush matting, a center ridgepole, pitched thatched roof, and an open fireplace next to a seat of honor for guests. Mats covered the floor, and wall hangings separated each person's sleeping area; a special window was cut in the eastern wall and a shrine placed in the northeast corner. When the exterior was completed, the Ainus conducted their blessing ceremony to commemorate the placing of prayer sticks on the house's roof and the construction of an exterior fence decorated with religious symbols and bear skulls to ward off evil. Visitors were warned not to touch the fence: "These sticks represent their deities, and the greatest insult that may be offered an Ainu is to knock down or carry away one of these rude fetishes."[34] On May 23, the LPE's *Official Daily Program* announced that they had settled into their "artistic straw hut."

Their departure from the Indian School building was marked by one of their esoteric dances. In the great dining room of the school the nine Ainus celebrated the lengthy ceremony that the people of their rough mountain country use on the occasion of moving from an old habitation.

> *Superintendent McCowan and others long acquainted with Indian life of the American West, watched with interest one of the strangest sights they have ever witnessed, when the North American tribes from all over the reservation came crowding into the room. Grunts of astonishment and gesticulations of surprise came from Sioux, Pawnees, Arapahos, Navajos, Pimas, Apaches, Comanches, Pueblos, Cocopas, Maricopas, Wichitas, Moquis [sic] and representatives of the far distant Patagonians as they watched what was to their eyes an unexplainable dance.*[35]

When the house was completed, Sangea and Yazo Osawa conducted a new fire ceremony. McGee was particularly pleased because this ritual supposedly demonstrated his theory about the development of fire, which was displayed as a static exhibit in Cupples Hall. The spark for the new fire "was struck in imitation of the ancient use of pyrite and flint and the tinder was kindled by indrawn breath through a section of porous vine." Reporters did not comment on this but did mention that the festivities marked the opening of the Ainu home to visitors. The rituals "took the form of an elaborate reception, for which invitations were issued to the chiefs of the Indian encampments. The program included speeches in Ainu by the receiving committee and responses by the visiting Indians." The program lasted four hours. Inagaki translated as four bowls were taken from a chest in the sacred corner and a mustache stick placed in each bowl. The women poured wine in the bowls and the male guests drank, followed by the women. After serving rice cakes, Sangea conducted the blessing ritual. At the end of the speeches, singing, and dancing, Sangea thanked all the visitors for helping to bless the new home. McGee closed the proceedings by welcoming the Ainus and declaring the encampment officially open.[36]

The Ainus worked in front of their house, making traditional arts. They were frequently photographed at work seated on the ground wearing their colorful robes and hats. Shutratek made grass mats on a vertical loom, while Santukno wove bast fabric, prepared food, or ground millet. "Women do the pounding," Starr stated in his lectures, "often two of them worked together, dealing alternate blows, and singing wordless songs to give time to the blows" (Starr 1904a, 39). Both men and women devoted a good deal of time to carving and selling swords, mustache lifters, hunting knives, and replicas of the symbolic arrowheads used in their bear feast. The women also made small baskets and the men rectangular wooden plaques carved with the clothing designs. These souvenirs cost visitors ten to twenty-five cents. The Ainu also cultivated millet, native beans, and corn in a garden near the house.

In September, reporters noted that the Ainu were "attracting more intelligent interest" than any other group. This may partly have been because Starr returned periodically from Chicago and lectured in the Ainu camp. His main lecture series, which he entitled "A Glimpse of the Japanese" to coincide with a class he was teaching in Chicago, portrayed the Ainu as a stranded family of the Aryan race. He began by showing students how to recognize key racial characteristics such as the set of the eyes and then proceeded to discuss architecture and religious customs. The Ainus performed activities as he talked.

The young bride Shirake sang while her older companion ground millet in a mortar. Men sang a war song and modeled the attire worn during bear hunting rituals while Starr described the ceremonies. Following the lecture the audience was invited into the house to inspect the furnishings.[37]

The Ainus were billed as gentle, peaceful "savages," "shy, retiring, ill at ease when approached," and the cleanest and most refined of the Native groups. According to fair publicists, they were "far removed from the typical blood-thirsty savage of childhood's imagination and of much of the juvenile literature of adventure and travel." Other adjectives used to describe them were hospitable, pleasant, kindly, and gracious. The children, Kiku ("Gold") and Kehttle or Kin ("Chrysanthemum"), were charming attractions, by all accounts. Kiku, who "looked more like a Japanese doll than a baby," had a disposition that won visitors' admiration, and it was feared that she would be a spoiled baby before the exposition ended. Her personality caused visitors to marvel. "She was a keen observer and amazingly quick. Apparently she had a longing to become the possessor of everything she saw." Kin and Kiku regularly played in the Department of Education's model playground where they also were regarded as enchanting.[38] McGee felt the Ainus were the most courteous Native peoples at the fair. They seemed to like entertaining and only objected when visitors peeked through their windows. He also believed that of all the participants, the Ainus most faithfully illustrated their Native customs, rituals, and daily living patterns, and had superior aesthetic sensibilities.

Living on the fairgrounds influenced the Ainus. Visitors gave them "small coins and other gifts so often that most of their time seemed to be spent in bowing and gesturing their elaborate thanks." The young men who had been beardless before starting the journey grew beards, partly in response to visitor expectations; people wanted to see the "hairy Ainu." This physical trait was the primary reason casual visitors sought to meet the Ainus. Francis recalled that what fascinated him were their strikingly large heads, full foreheads, horizontal eyes, Caucasian facial features, and head shape. The main attraction for most visitors was their luxuriant, neatly trimmed, wavy hair. McGee even waxed eloquent about the men's beards and their importance in Ainu culture. "Their beards played a constant role in the social and religious ceremonies as sacred appendages recalling the cult of Samson and the oath 'by the beard of the Prophet' in raby." Some reporters disagreed. One held that the men did not seem very hairy but the women did and "even the children have fur down their backs as soft and fine as a cat's."[39]

Using a gendered comparison to comment on American culture, a writer also noted that because the women were bearded, they were accorded a special status unavailable to American women. In addition to the well-advertised hair, the women's tattoos were so foreign to middle-class conceptions of beauty that they fascinated everyone. Mrs. Charles Lusk was harder on the women than the men: "Of all the 'Anthropologicals' none are more curious than the Ainu. They are dark and short, and their manners are exceptionally elegant. In urbanity they are not to be surpassed [but they] are ugly. They are almond-eyed and have high check-bones, and in youth an elaborate and unsightly mustache is tattooed on their lips, which remains to the end of their days, and is by no means the mark of beauty, while they seem to esteem it." Ainu attire seemed to be extensions of their bodies. Their woven bast garments (a Japanese kimono with short sleeves tapering at the end and cinched by a wide band at the waist) were decorated with elaborate embroidered designs. These intricate patterns were mirrored in the symmetrical tattoos on women's arms and wrists.[40]

Ironically, it was in physical performance that the Ainus most disappointed James E. Sullivan, head of the Department of Physical Culture, who organized athletic competitions. In describing their performance in a fifty-six-pound weight throw, Sullivan concluded that "the performance would compel many to believe that they had a great deal to accomplish in the way of developing their bodies." Three Ainus took part; they threw seven feet four inches, five feet, and three feet six inches. "It can probably be said, without fear of contradiction, that never before in the history of sport in the world were such poor performances recorded for weight throwing" (Sullivan 1905a, 257, 263).

John Hanson did not care about athletic competitions. He noted that the Ainus' polite manners, soft expressions, kind bearing, uniform courtesy, and cleanliness disappointed many sightseers because they expected to see wild men, cannibals, or dog-eaters. Visitors compared the Ainus to the Tehuelches since they tended to visit both compounds sequentially. "The Ainu were not as dirty nor nearly as lazy looking as the Patagonians" (Hanson 1905, 393). The Ainus looked almost civilized, many thought. It had to be because of their "Caucasian" heritage.

Traditional Agriculturalists from Sonora, Mexico: The Cocopas

While the press and visitors readily accepted McGee's interpretations of the anomalous and mysterious Ainus, they were decidedly skeptical of his theories about the Cocopas. McGee had selected the Cocopas to illustrate the consistent maintenance of what he called a barbaric physical or ethnic type "in which the stature [of] the two sexes is strikingly different—the males being among the tallest of our aborigines and the females among the shortest of our native women." McGee asserted that the Cocopas' flood-plain agricultural methods had remained unchanged since before contact and therefore they could illustrate "such native lore and legend as those embalmed in Hiawatha." Since they cultivated pre-Columbian corn and beans using traditional methods, they would be of interest to visitors. Unfortunately they did no farming at the fair, although they had brought their agricultural utensils, harvesting baskets, and ample seed, and we can only speculate how McGee planned to flood their fields to visualize his theoretical point or edify visitors. What visitors did like, and came back time and time again to see, was evidence of McGee's assertion that the Cocopas "are our finest archers, and perform significant ceremonies of devotional character, attesting [to] the close interrelation between early man and their natural surroundings." In addition, he portrayed the Cocopas as having some of the "most extravagant mortuary customs, in which the goods of the descendant are distributed to non-relatives while his house and body are burned together, so that the people are perpetually impoverished and prevented from gathering in communities."[41]

McGee believed visitors required his professional skills to interpret the obscure Cocopas. After interviewing him, one reporter disseminated his views as well as his attempts to arouse curiosity through references to timeless authenticity. "These Indians are . . . a tribe of undoubted antiquity, but scientists have never been able to trace their origin. They inhabited the Colorado River valley when Cortez came to America and their mode of life is now the same as it was then." One reporter also added, "Their early extinction seems inevitable; and it would seem probable that they will have the distinction of melting away through voluntary adoption of unfit Caucasian customs without the aid of church or state."[42]

McGee prepared fairgoers for visits with the "timid and home-loving" Cocopas. They would not be as expected, but would challenge stereotypes and preconceptions, demonstrating that not all Indians were the same. Describing his idealized version of Cocopa personality, he wrote:

> *No Cocopa Indians have ever before been induced to leave their homes. They are shy and gentle, and their children are the happiest of all the little "barbarians." They play marbles and other games—their brown eyes flashing with interest—and they shoot arrows at a mark with unerring accuracy. . . . If a visitor to their encampment set up a coin for a mark, every Cocopa boy turns as quickly as a flash; there is a whiz of arrows, and the coin goes spinning into the air. (McGee 1904f, 5187)*

St. Louisians knew much about the Cocopas because McGee continuously talked about "his people" whenever he spoke to civic groups. Like McGee, reporters made up customs to enhance their special status. The Cocopas were labeled foreign Natives, not American Indians, so as not to be under the authority of the Indian Service. They were under McGee's personal charge, assisted by Cushman and Hulbert, who also assisted the Kwakiutls and Nootkas who were also considered foreigners. Their upkeep was a major departmental expense. By the end of June, McGee had spent $2,236 of his $2,500 allotment for the group. Needing more money he transferred funds from the archaeology exhibits and building maintenance, a decision that provoked numerous visitor and exhibitor complaints. To McGee, however, providing for the Cocopas was always his first priority.[43]

The delegation arrived in time to participate in the exposition opening ceremonies. How large the group was is unclear. One photograph shows McGee and Cushman with twenty-one individuals (seven adult men, five adult women, two adolescent males, four boys, a girl, and two babies) (fig. 8.4). McGee's various reports list twenty-two to twenty-four people. Men named Chizi, John Roy, and Coldwater were also listed in the "Special Olympics" roster. It is likely all were members of the Hwanyak band from Somerton, Arizona.

Unlike the other Indians in the Native encampments, as foreigners they were not required to build their own houses or compelled to do any work. Whether this was true or not, McGee had one tule-and-brush house erected for them before they arrived. The Cocopas built another tule house next to the

Fig. 8.4. William J. McGee (*center*) and Edward J. Cushman (*third from right*) standing with the Cocopas in their compound. Tom Moore and Pablo Colorado flank McGee. Photograph by the Official Photographic Company, 1904. Missouri Historical Society, St. Louis, negative no. LPE1265, OWFN 4580.

Kwakiutl and Tehuelche camps. Each was a square room in which the women and children spent most of their time. Two large storage baskets designed to hold grain were placed on the roofs while smaller square, lidded baskets and shouldered jars were placed on the ground. Straw was strewn as a floor inside and in front of the structures. Tables and benches were placed under a ramada and served as a place to display crafts for sale. A single row fence of 2-by-4-inch boards was erected around the 100-by-120-foot compound to prevent the crowds from overrunning the area.[44]

Press reaction was generally favorable. Some reporters even noted that the Cocopas were superior to other Indians because they were self-supporting and received no government dole, a subtle comment on Mexican policy as opposed to U.S. treaty obligations. Agriculture was seen as a sign of their advancement over Plains Indians; men were said to own considerable land and to cultivate it very well. Their industriousness was noted by the fact that they supplemented their food supplies by hunting and gathering and working as temporary laborers on Mexican plantations. The women were described as industrious and good housekeepers.[45]

The press was disappointed by Cocopa clothing. Both men and women dressed in their normal attire, not fancy outfits, such as those worn by the Dakotas in the Wild West show or by others on the Pike. Cocopa men wore dungarees and boots, long-sleeved, collarless cotton shirts, and neckerchiefs. Older men wore plain, dark vests and light-colored shirts, while young men and boys wore dark-colored cotton shirts without vests. The only items that distinguished Cocopa men from non-Cocopa residents of northern Mexico were their highly prized, T-shape bead necklaces and hairstyles, which according to one visitor had never seen the necessity of a hair cut. Another called them great hairdressers, although the use of mud as a cleansing agent was considered somewhat suspect. Barefoot Cocopa women wore pioneer-style, calico shirtwaist dresses and shawls. McGee often responded to visitors' disappointment by saying their attire might not be as exotic as other Natives, but that the Cocopas were still interesting because of their "copper-tinted" skin and the "luxuriance of [their] hair."[46]

Like other groups, the Cocopas lived as an extended family, ostensibly following their daily pursuits. Women cooked on an open fire pit outside the ramada. When not caring for their families, they produced baskets for sale. The men were to cultivate typical foods but no fields or gardens were planted. What the men were supposed to do instead is unknown. McGee did note that Colorado "much enjoyed the comparative leisure of life at the Exposition, and still more greatly the lengthy and ceremonious councils with the special agents and other officials" (McGee 1905d, 106).

There were generally harmonious relations within the Cocopa compound, but one of the group members, Shokee, caused problems and was sent home in July. McGee considered Shokee the most "picturesque member of the group," but was very upset with the young man's conduct. Several Cocopas complained to Cushman that on three different occasions, Shokee "had used violence in attaining his ends upon the person of one of the younger women of the tribe, and had even attempted assault upon the person of a young girl not more than ten years old." The Cocopas did not condone attempted rape or assault and wanted him sent home in disgrace for his family to punish. The Cocopas made this decision, under their own laws; Cushman and McGee respected their wishes and did not turn Shokee over to the police. On July 7, a "submissive but weeping" Shokee, who spoke no English, was placed on a train with two dollars to purchase coffee and food and a letter to the railroad conductors to help him change trains. He made it safely to Yuma and Somerton a few days later. Soon after his arrival, Cocopa leader Frank Tejano sent a letter to Moore and Colorado asking for clarification about the problem that had prompted Shokee's expulsion. They were skeptical about his rendition of the affair.[47]

The Cocopas earned money in several ways. Fair organizers felt that producing art in front of exotic dwellings and conversing through sign language or pidgin was a great attraction to visitors as well as economically beneficial for the participants. One of the main sources of income for women was the sale of bead jewelry, which McGee's sign near the entrance to their encampment said signified their manual dexterity and creativity. No Cocopas had a booth in the Indian School; they simply used a sales bench in front of their dwelling. All had received wages prior to their arrival, and several expense reports note that Cushman paid individuals substantial amounts during the exposition; unfortunately he never indicated how much or for what. The Cocopas also charged visitors and professional photographers twenty-five cents to take their pictures.[48]

McGee wanted the Cocopas to demonstrate their talents in face tattooing. Cushman had collected materials but had informed McGee in March that the Cocopas had discontinued the elaborate ceremonies he wanted performed. "They content themselves now with simply tattooing the chin, and having a festival of feasting and song."[49] While Annie Flynn was originally confident that she could convince them to perform entire ceremonies, she was unsuccessful. They absolutely refused to perform any funeral, wedding, or puberty ceremonies and in fact refused to perform any rituals at all. Nor do the Cocopas appear to have earned money from dances of any kind as did the Nootkas, Lakotas, and Kwakiutls. They met tourists' gazes and McGee's quest for performative primitivism on their own terms.

Marksmanship was the area where Cocopa men excelled as competitors and performers. Cocopas generally won either first or second place—with their one-dollar and two-dollar prizes—during the frequent archery contests held throughout out the summer. Boys shot at coins provided by visitors to demonstrate eyesight, dexterity, and hunting ability, according to McGee, but for the Cocopa youth, for fun and money—the archer, upon hitting the coins, kept the money. Indian School staff described a typical activity designed to amuse visitors. "Two little long-haired Cocopa boys got out in front of the Indian School yesterday, with their bows and arrows, and soon attracted quite a large number of people. Pennies and nickels were stuck in the ground and the boys shot at them from a distance of about ten yards. In less than ten minutes they had cleared something like forty cents and made for the Indian store, rattling their change in high glee."[50]

It was inevitable, given McGee's pre-exposition publicity campaign and his lectures, that the Cocopas would be compared to the Tehuelches. The press generally said that the two groups were rivals for the tallest Indians in the Americas. It was felt that the Patagonian Giants won this fictitious contest because the Cocopas, while just as tall, had a wider height range and more small people, in part because there were more individuals present. To further distinguish the two groups, the press picked up the idea that the Cocopas had aquatic tastes: "The men are great fishermen, swimmers and boatmen, and join with the Moro tribes in their sports about Arrow Head Lake."[51]

McGee spent as many hours as he could with the Cocopas, whom he considered his personal friends. There are more photographs of him with this group than with any other. He often lectured to visitors, interpreted, or simply sat and relaxed with his friends Pablo Colorado and Tom Moore. He often ate with them. And it was to these friends that McGee went whenever his typhoid fever acted up; Mrs. Colorado nursed him. It was also to them that he turned after the fair, exhausted and ill, to recover his health.

Fisher Folk from the Canadian North: The Kwakiutls and Nootkas

McGee wanted men and women from the Northwest Coast as representatives of matrilineal social organization and communal house living. He was especially pleased about Kwakiutl (Kwakwaka'wakw) participation because he felt that the tribe was unusually light-skinned, produced fantastic art (elaborate heraldic crests painted or carved in a variety of media), and posed another taxonomic puzzle on which no two scientists agreed. The men and women

Fig. 8.5. Bob Harris, Kweeka Kwakiutl from Fort Rupert, British Columbia. Photograph by Charles Carpenter, June 1904. © The Field Museum, negative no. CSA13581.

Fig. 8.6. Chief Atlieu, Nootka, holding fishing spear. Photograph by Charles Carpenter. © The Field Museum, negative no. CSA13568.

from the north came in two groups. The two Kweeka Kwakiutl men, Bob Harris (fig. 8.5) and Charles Nowell, went first to Chicago and worked for several days with Dorsey identifying artifacts and posing for museum dioramas. They agreed to stay until the end of September.[52]

The two Nootka (Nuu-chah-nulth) families were from Clayoquot, a village on the west coast of Vancouver Island. The first family included Dr. Atlieu, his wife, Annie Atlieu, and his half-brother Jasper Turner. Atlieu was generally translated as "canoe maker"; he wore a copper nose ring and carried a wooden war spear with a handle carved as a snake, a symbol of traditionalism that greatly pleased McGee as well as fascinated fairgoers (fig. 8.6). The second family was Jack Curley and his mother, Mrs. Ellen Curley. Mrs. Emma George, a noted basket maker also came from Gold River, Vancouver Island. The men's main tasks were to perform dances and secular rituals, while the women were to produce art.

The Kwakiutl (also spelled Klackwah or Klaokwaht in reports) encampment, as the compound for all the Canadian Natives was called, was sited south of the railway station, next to the Cocopas. Both groups were to occupy a Nootka clan house, which Dorsey had hoped to build before their arrival to coincide with the fair's opening. Unfortunately the building and artifacts went astray in transit and arrived very late. Also misplaced were their boxes of raw materials, tools, and containers of dried herring. It seems that Newcombe's son gave part of the material to the Fred Harvey Company to ship. After sitting several days in Seattle, the boat and housing materials were shipped to Holmes, care of the Smithsonian Institution, labeled for the government exhibit. Since Holmes was not in St. Louis, he received no notice and the materials sat in a side car, along with Holmes's requests for his exhibits. On June 8, Newcombe told reporters he had been waiting for the supplies for more than six weeks. The lack of food proved to be a real problem. "The Clayoquots are accustomed to fine fish and salmon, taken fresh from the water. They were taken to the market in St. Louis a few days ago [June 5], and looked with scorn on the fish displayed. They were astonished that the white people would eat it, and declined to accept it as a gift." As a result the groups lived in tents for the first few months and ate beef.[53]

Some of the material arrived on June 9 after a circuitous journey around the country. In the first consignment were beautiful baskets and cedar mats that were spread in the compound for people to admire. There was also a large cedar pole that Dr. Atlieu began immediately to carve as a totem pole and a house post. Building materials slowly arrived during the next several weeks. It was not until August that the Kwakiutls and Nootkas were able to move from temporary tents into their magnificent house and finally eat their preferred foods. The sixty-by-forty-foot house, made of hand-hewn native cedar, had heavy puncheons and squared logs and was decorated with carved and painted totemic designs, carved on site. Its style was similar to the houses used in the 1770s at the time of European contact so that people could compare it with the Haida house (fig. 11.4) erected next to the Alaska building. It was one of the most talked-about structures, called by some a clan house, and by others a "tribal temple." McGee told visitors the house reflected tribal society "for each consanguineal group or family and each person therein has a fixed place within the structure so that the habitation both expresses and perpetuates the social organization or law of the tribe."[54]

The Vancouver group had typical expenses. It only cost thirty-two dollars to install them in their house but fifteen hundred dollars to transport the building materials, their equipment, and supplies. Food ran from seventy-five to two hundred dollars per month; salaries were three hundred dollars per month. It took great persistence for Newcombe and finally Dorsey to obtain the necessary funds because McGee, when his budget deficit ballooned in mid-summer, insisted he had not agreed to pay demonstrators for the time spent in construction. Dorsey wrote his assistant, Stephen Simms, who was on site, to make sure that McGee fulfilled his obligations. "The Kwakiutl Indians should be paid at so much per diem for building their house. They have been put against a regular throw-down proposition ever since they left home, and it is nothing but fair and right that they be paid for building this house. The Pawnee were paid, and the Wichita were paid. Make life a burden to McGee until they get it."[55] Evidently Simms did. Fiscal records show that by September everyone had been paid.

Newcombe also had problems obtaining reimbursement and his salary from McGee. Serving as special agent in St. Louis, his salary and per diem expenses were paid by the Field Museum as a loan because McGee was, as usual, slow in paying his bills. By the end of July, Newcombe had still not been reimbursed for expenses incurred during negotiations with the Canadian Indians. Tired of the situation he complained to associates that McGee was running behind by several months because of his typhoid and purposely drawing out his bills so as not to alarm LPEC fiscal agents about his expenditures. Newcombe was also tired of fighting daily with McGee and McCowan over supplies for the Kwakiutls and Nootkas. He alleged that McGee owed him more than a thousand dollars and wrote Dorsey that he was very weary of St. Louis because he was penniless. Newcombe also suffered from the heat and crippling leg problems. He and his son slept on the floor of the Kwakiutls' house, even though only Native participants were supposed to live in the compounds, not their agents. No one seems to have evicted them. Newcombe longed to return to Chicago to work in the quiet of the museum.[56]

The Nootkas were fond of their privacy and did not like people coming uninvited into their houses. Even Newcombe stayed with them only at their invitation. They also did not like to participate in the impromptu activities that McGee, McCowan, and fair officials constantly thought up to entertain visitors, especially when they learned that demonstrators were expected to perform without extra compensation. A staff member of the Indian School offered another reason: "The Clayoquot [Nootka] people are very reserved and averse to any display. They took no part in the Indian sports on [opening] day and left for their tent before the sports were finished. They do not associate much with the peoples on the grounds. This is mainly because their spears, bows, and ceremonial clothing have not yet arrived and they recognize the superior spectacular appearance of the Indians of the Interior."[57]

This was evidently an important consideration during the early months since the men were extremely active later. However, all participated only in events for which they received financial remuneration or culturally appropriate gifts, as was required by the rules of their cultures, and they only performed rituals, dances, and told stories that were seasonally appropriate and for which they had hereditary rights. They wore elaborate masks and ceremonial attire in their staged demonstrations and pantomimes of important legends, and also gave speeches that Nowell interpreted. Unlike other performers, the Northwest Coast group charged people to see every performance, even those held in their compound.[58] McGee eventually paid them for special events. The only exceptions were the special performances the Kwakiutls and Nootkas designed specifically to honor other Native peoples.

Whenever Nowell began a formal lecture, he told people that his name was Klalish, "Whale on the Beach." Harris told people his name was Klakoglas, "Man Who Has Copper." The two men often told stories and explained the iconography and symbolism of their ceremonial attire, for which they had individual rights and family responsibility. Visitors found this particularly fascinating because of their striking character. Nowell also demonstrated a skin-piercing ritual that was part of a Kwakiutl war ritual. This was a highly theatrical production in which blood flowed from a kelp tube concealed in the hemlock headdress. He and Harris had brought a Hamatsa raven mask with twisted cedar-bark hair that opened and closed with a loud clap, a favorite with visitors.[59] The Nootka men performed part of a winter ceremony in which the participants wore magnificent eagle-and-wolf capes and wolf headdresses. Jack Curley, whose Nootka name meant "The Heir of a Chief," brought his Thunderbird headdress for a summer performance. The Nootka men also told the elaborate origin stories that were their right to relate, while Nowell or Newcombe translated.

Soon the press began to compare these complicated and breathtaking narratives and rituals with those of the Ainus. They also began to think of both groups as having similar origins. There was much speculation, which in some cases was transformed into certainty about racial affinity.

> There is no question that these Indians are an entirely different race from the Indians of the states. They are not like them in features, manners, or customs. There seems very little doubt that they are of comparatively recent Asiatic origin. They have the features and manners of the Japanese. In fact, they look so much like them that tourists are often guilty of mistaking them for the little people of Japan. Their own legends tell of a deluge and their people crossing a great sea and settling in Alaska, but these legends have been so imperfectly preserved and have become so much mixed up with the smattering of Christianity the Indians have received from the missionaries that it is hard to tell which is which.[60]

The most spectacular ceremony at the exposition, more compelling than the Ainu bear rituals or Igorot dog feasts, according to dozens of newspaper accounts, was the "cannibal dance performed repeatedly by the Kwakiutl priests." Francis wrote, "The Kwakiutl Indians have practiced human sacri-fice and anthropophagy until recently, and the members of the tribe on the grounds still bear scars of the symbolic cannibalism of their fiducial feasts." This ritual was a Hamatsa, their most prestigious performance (McGee 1905d, 108; Francis 1913, 528).

Peter Macnair (1982, 5) has described the Hamatsa ceremony. The dancer is "inspired by the spirit of a ferocious man-eating monster, who at the be-ginning of time stole humans from a village and took them to his mountain fastness at the north end of the world to eat. Inflamed by this awesome spirit power, the Hamatsa dancer circles the floor of the ceremonial house and ap-pears to bite the arms of certain members of the audience." The Hamatsa can also enter the ritual area holding a corpse in his arms and appear to eat it. The participants eventually subdue the spirit through their songs, prayers, and ac-tions, and he is returned to a state of normalcy.

Nowell recalled in his autobiography one especially memorable "cannibal dance." Harris and a Mbuti decided to play a joke on visitors and the "big people" they were supposed to impress.

> There was a little African pygmy that used to come and see us. He liked to come because we always had bananas, and this little fellow loved bananas. He didn't seem to want to eat anything else; as soon as he come in, he look at the bananas hanging up and say, "Huh—Ba-nana!" Bob Harris wanted to make a little man just like him, so I told him to come in every day, sit down and eat bananas while Bob Harris was making a little man with some bones and mutton flesh. He made it just like him and when it was finished it was put in an oven, and Bob Harris looked after that while it was baking. He take it out and hold it up alongside of the little man, and the little fellow would offer it a banana. (Ford 1949, 186–87)[61]

Harris's articulated model had a moving mouth and a wood whistle that imi-tated a man's squeal concealed under the clothing. The head was carved from wood and, like the body, smoked to obtain the right skin color, also had a "blood" bladder inside the torso.

It was time for a scheduled performance in the Government Building's main plaza. Nowell recounts: "We went to the place where all the people was;

they say there was about twenty thousand people that came that time. . . . We had a screen that was painted in a square—about eight feet square. We told the little fellow how it was going to be done, and not to tell his friends about it or we won't give him any more bananas." They hid the mutton model inside a screen.

The performance began with a Bella Bella Dance. The Nootkas next sang and drummed while Harris and Nowell danced. Then Harris, now attired in his breathtaking regalia and mask, began the Hamatsa songs. Nowell and the Nootkas intentionally made a mistake in beating the cadence during the final song, signaling the new additions to the dramatics. This "mistake" angered the Hamatsa who began to demonstrate his displeasure on stage, and Nowell announced the fact to the audience.

> *I got behind the screen and dressed as an Indian and came back and told the people in English that the Cannibal is mad now, because they made a mistake in beating the board, and we don't know what he is going to do, because he is so fierce. [Jasper Turner and Jack Curley] came and held him—trying to keep him from going toward the other people. Bob Harris was struggling to get free from their hold. Finally he got away from them, and he ran around. When he got to where this little fellow was sitting, he picked him up and ran behind the screen and left him there.*

The enraged Hamatsa captured and then "killed" the screaming Pygmy off-stage. He returned and stood in front of the screen, yelling loudly and carrying the dummy, handling it roughly while the real Pygmy continued to scream, squatting down behind the screen. The Hamatsa set the mutton Pygmy down and bit the neck until blood squirted all over his face. So realistic were the Hamatsa's actions that none of the audience realized that the dummy was being ritually sacrificed. "All the little pygmies got up with their spears and was coming to kill Bob, and all the people in the audience thought sure he had bitten his neck off, but the guards just pushed them back and told them to sit down." Then the Hamatsa proceeded to ritually eat the Pygmy, stripping flesh off the corpse, while blood squirted from the bladder. The other Africans were so upset that they left and refused to perform their dance set. Meanwhile, the Hamatsa continued to eat mutton strips cut from the dummy. As Nowell describes it, "When he got through eating—some of us helped him because we were hungry—I looked around and saw there was no Indians in that place; they had all got frightened and went home." Nowell then addressed the remaining mesmerized fairgoers.

> *I told the men in the hall that we have done a great thing that is only done in the wintertime, and that we are going home to our Indian house where we will try to bring [the pygmy] to life again. Dr. Newcombe never came near us, he was so scared at what Bob Harris had done. "That was a murder. That means he is going to be hanged." I told him to keep away from us. "You are a white man," I says, "and you better not come near us." I told the guards to put fire into our house. While he was gone, we kept on singing songs, turning around as we go. People come with the Kodaks taking our picture; the guards couldn't keep them away.*

The entire event ended on this dramatic note, since none of the other Native participants remained. The Kwakiutls and Nootkas returned to their encampment dance-house with the real Mbuti hidden in their dance screen. McGee was quickly called to investigate. Newcombe, constables, fair officials, and visitors accompanied him. Meanwhile Harris, still attired as the Hamatsa, ritually prepared to resurrect the real Mbuti, while the Nootkas and Nowell danced around them. Nowell recalled the scene.

> *It was evening when we get to our house and the house was already full of white people. The people that owned the Fair came and sat in the front end of the house. All the ladies and gentlemen were sitting right on the ground with their silk dresses on because they were told by the guards that is the way the Indians sit. Dr. Newcombe came over to us and wanted to have a talk. I look at him with a strong fierce look on my face and told him not to come near.*
>
> *After singing another song, Harris rose and walked around the fire singing to the accompaniment of his rattle. Then he went to the body he had eaten and said, "The bones are all stuck together now." Nowell interpreted for everyone. Then both sang another song, and Harris, still portraying the Hamatsa, moved to a table upon which the Mbuti was lying hidden under a mat.*

The Hamatsa [Harris] says, "He has flesh on his bones now; the whole body is in good order." Then we sang another song, and he went around again, lifted up the mat, and felt. "He is quite warm now," he says. He came back and we sang the last song. Then the West Coast men [Nootka] were dancing over the dead man with their hands shaking while we were singing. When we got through, Bob Harris went around the house, still using his rattle, singing, and went toward to where the little man was lying and lift up the mat. He took the mat off, and took the little man up and sit him up on the table, and he begin to look around stiff like as we told him to do. Bob Harris took him down from the table and took him around the house, holding him by the hand. And all he say is, "Banana. Banana."

The audience was astounded. Nowell addressed them. "I am very glad to learn that our friend here, Bob Harris, done this great thing. You all saw him when he ate the flesh of this little man that is standing by his side. This is the same man that was dead, and his flesh was all eaten up. Now he has his flesh and his life back, and now he is alive. And I am glad that there will be no law that will come against us." Everyone, including Newcombe and McGee, had been outwitted, but this did not stop Newcombe giving a speech about Kwakiutl customs, much to Nowell's amusement.

At the end of the evening Harris and Nowell walked the Mbuti back to his compound. "When he got near their hut, they all got up and ran away. They were scared, thinking he was only the dead that was eaten up, and he hollered out to them, telling them that he is alive and not a ghost." McGee tried to quickly downplay the trick and did not comment on it in his final report, probably tired of all the letters it had generated, but the newspapers extensively covered the event. Many Native people now avoided them, including individuals with whom they had become close. Harris and Nowell had frequently visited and slept with two Mexican women working on the Pike. The next evening, "when we got into their tent they just rushed out and ran away. They didn't want us to come near them—a man-eater. Bob was called 'man-eater' after that."

The Kwakiutl men were often seen walking around the exposition. One of their favorite activities was riding on the observation wheel. The concessionaire let them ride for free, as he did Geronimo, because it generated publicity. Harris and Nowell generally went on Saturday and Sunday afternoons but appear not to have been joined by the Nootkas, who tended to remain by themselves or walk in the nearby woods. The Northwest Coast demonstrators also conducted more mundane activities such as carving, painting, weaving, and making baskets for sale. There was a ready market for medicine beads, miniature totem poles, model houses, reproductions of weapons, masks, and "emblems." The totem poles ranged in size from one to three feet and were painted with appropriate totemic designs. The Nootka men had also brought slightly larger (three to four feet high) totem-pole-replica posts from their village, which sold quickly. The women made mats and small, lidded baskets of red cedar bark and grasses. According to Ira Jacknis, the Nootkas did not make as much money as had their compatriots at the 1893 Chicago Columbian Exposition, much to their displeasure. Nowell and Harris did not produce much art to sell to tourists, earning most of their money from performances. They concentrated on carving thirty-six commissioned pieces for the Field Museum: masks, ceremonial paraphernalia, and utilitarian objects.[62]

At the beginning of October, Nowell, Atlieu, Turner, and Harris traveled to Chicago for the first truly collaborative collections management and exhibit assessment project of Native peoples at the Field Museum. Dorsey stressed the importance of these collaborative efforts to McGee who was concerned that the men would be gone for so long. In another precedent, the men were paid well for their services. Harris and Atlieu received fifty dollars per month and Nowell received seventy-five dollars. The eloquent Nowell also developed a new exhibit technique. On his own initiative he decided to stand inside an exhibit case, "a big glass room," and answer visitors' questions. "Some of the people would come up and shake hands with me, having money in their hands which they gave to me, besides what I was paid" (Ford 1949, 191).[63] Enjoying the museum work immensely, Harris, Nowell, and Newcombe decided to go to New York City to look at the collections in the American Museum of Natural History, while Atlieu and Turner returned to St. Louis to be with their families and help them pack.

Understandably McGee was upset when the four men and Newcombe left. He complained to Dorsey that he had never been informed about their plans; Newcombe quickly countered that he had. With Harris and Nowell deciding not to return, the Nootka families wished to leave, because they could not interact well with visitors. They no longer had interpreters. Dorsey apologized but stated that he knew Simms had informed him that Nowell and Harris would be in Chicago for only a "few days." He admitted that McGee had not been informed of Atlieu's or Turner's plans. He also noted that both he and Newcombe had told McGee repeatedly that none of the Northwest Coast people had consented to stay beyond September. All had agreed to come only if they could return home in time for the fall fishing season, which supplied the bulk of their winter food. McGee had conveniently forgotten this agreement in his hopes of keeping the anthropology groups together.

Dorsey also reminded McGee that the LPEC had not really fulfilled its bargain with any Indian demonstrator. Staying in St. Louis had proven to be a hardship for all. "You will understand, of course, that all the Indians of this group are exceedingly thrifty, and are great money earners; and had it not been for the money which I have enabled them to earn here and the material I bought in St. Louis, amounting to nearly $400, the summer would have been a disastrous one for them from a financial point of view." Dorsey was upset with McGee over this incident and what he had finally come to consider mismanagement (see chapter 10) and because once again he had been unwillingly thrust into the middle of negotiations, placed in an untenable position. It was a crisis. Newcombe, still unpaid, was threatening not to escort the group home, telling both Dorsey and McGee that he had had enough. Newcombe had written Dorsey that McGee was desperate to have his prize attraction stay and now offered to "advance" them some of their money and speed up Newcombe's reimbursement but only if the entire group consented to remain. But McCowan had stopped supplying food and cut off their line of credit in the sutlery, forcing Newcombe to purchase food at higher prices. Dorsey suggested that Newcombe begin the return journey on faith that everything would work out. Newcombe refused, having learned from bitter experience not to trust McGee. He would go only if he were given travel funds and salary in advance. Dorsey consented to these terms and forcefully wrote McGee, telling him how the Kwakiutls and Nootkas were to spend their last days in St. Louis. Atlieu and Jasper would return on October 9 to pack. Newcombe, Nowell and Harris would return from New York and all would leave for Victoria on October 15. Train reservations were made. Dorsey instructed McGee to have prepaid tickets ready and sufficient funds for Newcombe to buy food and space in Pullman coaches.[64]

McGee had little choice but to agree, although he proceeded extremely slowly to keep the group in St. Louis as long as possible. He sent the promised money to Dorsey at the Field Museum rather than give it to Newcombe, a tactic that made Dorsey even angrier. Simms and Newcombe helped the group pack and sell the remaining art. Atlieu used the money to purchase his own souvenirs from the Ainus, Moros, and Maoris (New Zealand pavilion).[65]

The promised railway tickets and cash finally materialized on October 18, sent by Dorsey from Chicago. The group left the next day without fanfare—McGee did not see them off—and had an uneventful trip to Vancouver and from there to their homes. With their departure, McGee's grand plan to have races from the four corners of the world for the entire exposition came to a premature end. It was a remarkable feat to have assembled them, for all the transportation to work, for all the people to arrive safely and in good health, to overcome the inevitable freight problems, and to erect a truly remarkable architectural exhibit of Native houses, one that has never been duplicated. But without the Canadian matrilineal peoples, McGee's central exhibition message was harder for people to visualize.

Never one to be downcast for long, McGee placed new placards near the entrance to the Kwakiutl compound, where the houses had been left for visitors to inspect, and told people to go to the Pike and visit the Inuits—Eskimos from the far, far north—and the matrilineal Puebloans. His earlier clear distinctions about the differences between the authentic, educational Anthropology Department and the commercial, inauthentic midway were now blurred as he strove to keep his central evolutionary message seamless and extend anthropology's reach to the entire exposition. McGee had moved anthropology in with the world of hucksterism and entertainment.

9. The Polyglot Pike

Communities from all parts of the world had their abiding places.
William Curtis, reporter

The entertainment zone along the north side of the fair was a mile long, three-hundred-foot-wide avenue, billed as the "Street of All Nations," a place where races and cultures mingled as never before. It was often referred to as the "Ten Million Dollar Pike," ballyhoo to signify that it was bigger and better than Chicago's 1893 Midway Plaisance, but also to remind people that it was a place to spend money. The LPEC made more than three million dollars' profit from Pike concessions. Concessionaires bore the cost of erecting and maintaining the buildings and paid 25 percent of the gross receipts to the LPE corporation. More than five hundred separate businesses provided entertainment and food to visitors tired of the serious exhibits. There was amusement for everyone, restaurants, Coney-Island-style sideshows, jugglers, illusionists, and special novelty acts. Not all concessions were frivolous. The LPEC wanted the Pike to have some educational, cultural, and historical value, not simply be the site of humbug and illusion. Technological innovations, such as the Infant Incubator—a working hospital that cared for premature babies—were celebrated. But in general, the realm of the imagination, entrepreneurship, and diversion ruled the lively Pike as *spielers* (orators who had mastered the art of alliterative persuasion) grabbed people's attention with their slick talk, exaggerations, and tales of wonders that awaited everyone within for a dime or a quarter.[1]

While some visitors came to marvel and learn, most came to relax or be amazed. Children saw exotic animals or watched Igorots ride elephants in the two-thousand-seat arena of Hagenbeck's Zoo and Animal Show. Tired visitors quenched their thirst in the beer garden and watched American waitresses pretend to be German. More energetic visitors pretended to climb the Alps or rode the great Observation Wheel (recycled from the Chicago Fair). For many, the ride provided their most vivid memories of the LPE. Native participants and Indian School students rode it often, for free. Geronimo remembered his first ride.

The guards took me into a little house that [had] four windows. When we were seated, the little house started to move along the ground. Then the guards called my attention to some curious things they had in their pockets. Finally they told me to look high up in the air, and the people down in the Fair Grounds, looked no larger than ants. The men laughed at me for being scared. Then they gave me a glass to look through and I could see rivers, lakes, and mountains. But I had never been so high in the air, and I tried to look into the sky. There were no stars and I could not look at the sun through this glass because the brightness hurt my eyes. Finally I put the glass down and as they were all laughing at me, I, too, began to laugh. Then they said, "Get out" and when I looked we were on the street again. After we were safe on the land, I watched many of these little houses going up and coming down, but I cannot understand how they travel. They are very curious little houses.[2]

Elsewhere, American women and the Indian School senior girls watched fashion shows or gazed at costumed manikins in the Palais du Costume, while in Battle Alley American men and the Indian School senior boys reviewed dioramas of great battles that had influenced American history, including Custer's Last Stand. Visitors paid twenty-five cents to see tableaux of the biblical origin story at Six Days of Creation. A few hardy souls saw everything on the Pike—a feat which took several days and cost about twenty dollars.

The Pike as an institution amused many commentators who were amazed at concessionaires' abilities to hoodwink the so-called highly civilized American public. Mrs. Charles Lusk (1905, 53) was very skeptical that it actually demonstrated progress or was an indication that the fair was educational.

Ah, the Pike, the great, the only, the much-heralded Pike, the highway of high-priced restaurants, of crowded beer-gardens, of inharmonious bands, of spielers careless of the truth, of people careless of everything, good-natured American people from county and town, ready, willing, yea anxious, to be separated from their money, the dear old Pike of numberless "Shows" alluring from the outside and disillusioning from within. I would not call the Pike a fake. Its purpose, I take it, is to amuse, and it does so. To see the American people hum-bugged and

enjoying the [process] is alone worth the price of admission. To see fifty
thousand Americans "out for a good time" as the expression goes, and
getting it, is worth a long journey.

Many people were skeptical of, yet enamored with, the amusement zone. Despite the potential threat of being fooled, visitors found the Pike exciting. Something novel was always happening. On opening day, President Roosevelt was honored at a banquet for six hundred at the Tyrolean Alps and serenaded by the exposition orchestra. While special events attracted huge crowds, the thoroughfare was always crowded since most people simply came to stroll and gape. "Visitors pass from nation to nation, and speed from clime to clime. From the desert sands and tropical wilderness of Africa it was only a step to the perpetual icebound shores of Arctic regions; from the savagery of least-known lands one might pass into salons of European royalty, and greet the bedizened effigies of historically great men and women."[3]

The Pike truly was a Street of All Nations, a place where the world's exotic peoples served as colorful and intriguing contrasts to the abundant evidence of American triumphs in the Main Picture. It was where McGee's two halves of the world interacted. One visitor remembered seeing "wild nomads of the plains, painted and be-feathered" interacting with "low bodiced, high heeled, silk arrayed, representatives of fashion." An LPE historian wrote, "[T]he barbarous clans of many countries were there with their instruments, productive of wild, weird, tuneless sounds, mixing freely with the civilized tongues, contributing to the Babel of tongues and toward making the whole thing of vivid human interest." Such encounters were always educational, McGee claimed, pulling the Pike under the umbrella of the LPE's general theme—the Exposition as University—and extending anthropology's scientific authority to the realm of amusement as had been done in Chicago (Buel 1904, vol. 10, 3809–10).

In many ways, the Pike was the ideal research site for the anthropologist as McGee hoped the public would perceive him, a serious scientist who would take advantage of its unparalleled opportunity. Others picked up on McGee's contention:

The ethnologist reveled in the scenes. As he mingled with the crowds,
listened to the strange murmurings, and was jostled by the people of all

lands he absorbed information and experienced sensations that were
not to be secured from the libraries of the world. The mannerisms and
methods of living of the polyglot population scattered along the entire
mile of The Pike offered the student of sociology a variety of valuable
suggestions, and their industries furnished those interested in the ques-
tions of economic man instructive lessons. (Bennitt 1905, 713)[4]

But this union was problematic and forced. The Pike was the place where fantasy, illusion, and commerce held center stage and ambiguous inauthenticity was always present. Indeed, that was the point. Visitors went into Pike concessions knowing they would probably be hoodwinked and were generally happy to pay for the privilege. But they expected truth and enlightenment in the educationally based, and scientifically verified, LPE- and government-sponsored exhibits. Or at least that was the intent. As the rhetoric used by McCowan, McGee, and Jenks shows, intent and means were often indistinguishable to the average visitor. The spielers' claims of professional authority or academic credentials were sometimes confused with those claimed by the ethnologists.

McGee walked a fine line in his views about exhibits on the Pike and their applicability to the promotion of scientific anthropology. His views changed during preparations for the fair. At first McGee considered several of the concessions to be competitive with his exhibits, but later he attempted to extend the reach of his department to include some Pike concessions to meet his goal of exhibiting all the races of the world in one spectacle. By June, McGee was impressed with the anthropological quality of some, but not all, concessions. (He excluded from his list those that were obviously fakes or which he felt had no redeeming ethnological value.) He had several favorites to which he directed visitors: Cummins's Indian Congress (a part of his Wild West show), Tobin's Cliff Dwelling, Crane's Eskimo Village, Fair Japan, the Chinese Village, Mysterious Asia, the Irish Village, the Tyrolean Alps, and the Gates of Jerusalem. "The assemblage of ethnic types [in the official displays] was notable," he wrote, "with these [peoples on the Pike] it was unprecedented—approaching the ideal often expressed by the President of the National Commission, 'The world's first assemblage of the world's peoples'" (McGee 1905d, 115).[5] He omitted concessions that featured Native Africans, black Americans, and Southeast Asians, that is, groups he felt did not support his conceptual scheme.

McGee selectively used Native peoples on the Pike to trace the record of human progress and illustrate its stages of development. In the process he legitimized the concessions and their ethnographic claims as well as made it acceptable (in his eyes) for middle-class Americans to enjoy their public fascination with curiosities. If one was to truly understand human cultural evolution, one had to visit the Pike. McGee quickly became the expert authority the press consulted when they wanted to write human-interest stories on ethnological concessions. He gave them an enveloping interpretive framework and context for their stories. Savage and primitive peoples were to be seen in the Anthropology Villages and the Philippine Reservation, while representatives of barbarism and early civilization were on the Pike. For ten, fifteen, or twenty-five cents, Euro-Americans could see how the world's Middle Eastern, Indian, Asian, and Caucasian "races" had advanced. This remarkable variety was especially apparent on Pike Day, June 4, 1904, when people from all the concessions marched in a gigantic parade around the fairgrounds.

> *Down the Pike comes a babble of strange tongues, the sound of unfamiliar instruments, the noise of many bands, the roar of animals from many climes, the voice of "barkers" descanting upon the various entertainments along this great cosmopolitan thoroughfare, the tramp of countless feet and the indescribable din that only thousands hastily thrown together from all parts of the globe could make in the exultation of a play day, free from all restraint. (Hanson 1905, 105)*

Describing his meal at one of the Pike's restaurants, later the same day, the visitor also remembered:

> *At the next table sits a grim old Sioux warrior in all the glory of paint and feathers. Beside him is a Boer, resting after the performance at the South African Concession. A giant Negro in the habiliments of the African desert makes up the third member of this strange group. Near at hand are a dozen young women from the Russian village opposite, who have run in to rest a moment before their next show. Robust, swarthy of face and in the gay attire of peasants of the Crimea they form a strange contrast to the solemn visaged and ebony hued son of the desert who sits staring at them. Three Turks in fez and baggy gar-*

ments have stopped to chat with them and a couple of Filipinos are
drawing up chairs. Far Cathay is represented, for have we not a group
of Chinese in court costume drawing near? (Hanson 1905, 106)

As Burton Benedict has noted, exposition midways were ethnic worlds of the imagination as much as reflections of real people from real places that gave the public the exotic ethnology it wanted (Benedict 1983, 54).[6] The Pike was not so different from the Anthropology Villages when Natives demanded remuneration for performing. On the Pike, visitors were enticed to view foreign customs and ceremonies for a small fee and encouraged to buy souvenirs purportedly made by indigenous men and women. They could do the same in the Anthropology Villages. Part of McGee's problem had to do with location; one of the main ways visitors reached the anthropology exhibits was by walking through the Pike. McGee needed to co-opt some of its exhibits as extensions of his vision.

And much of the Pike did complement anthropology and McGee's messages in many ways. For the public, the distinctions between the various departments where Native peoples were exhibited quickly blurred as science justified showmanship and showmanship advanced science. But there was something different in St. Louis. Unlike previous fairs, the Pike was not the area to display the most exotic primitives—cannibals, headhunters, hairy men, or missing links. That honor was reserved for the Anthropology Villages and the Philippine Reservation, justified by their claims to advance scientific knowledge. The claims of the 1904 ethnological Pike concessions were reserved compared to previous expositions, even if they were still filled with a good deal of humbug and remarkable packaging. And they were certainly fun, and having fun was a new American middle-class preoccupation.

Cummins's Wild West Show

If visitors liked gazing at living curiosities gathered in one place, they appreciated them in action even more. This included Indians who had appeared in sideshows, dime museums, and carnivals since the early nineteenth century. The largest concession was located north of the Pike outside the fairgrounds, Cummins's Wild West Show, Indian Congress, and Rough Riders of the World. The concessionaire, "Colonel" Frederick T. Cummins, had considerable exposition experience. He had managed the Indian Congress at the 1898 Greater American Exposition in Omaha, and the Indian Congress and Village Company at the 1901 Pan-American Exposition in Buffalo, specializing in sham battles, which McCowan felt erroneously glorified the image of the wild Plains warrior. Born in Council Bluffs, Iowa, Cummins had been an Indian trader, prospector, cowboy, Indian Service agent, "gallant soldier of fortune," and bronco breaker in Deadwood and Helena. He had lived among the Coeur d'Alenes and the Standing Rock Sioux, or so he claimed. According to his highly romanticized biography, which reads like a dime novel, he mysteriously acquired a military title. He later toured as a promoter of productions that always included the words "Wild West Show." Prominent among his stars in 1901 had been Calamity Jane, Red Cloud, and Chief Joseph.[7]

According to Cummins, Francis and LPEC commissioners approached him in Buffalo and requested he restage his Indian Congress in St. Louis, pledging "him their best wishes and hearty support." Cummins replied he would "reproduce his Indian Congress in such a manner as would be a credit to, and one of the crowning features of the Great Missouri Exposition." Since Francis and the LPEC Board visited Buffalo there is no reason to doubt that they spoke to Cummins, although in all likelihood they simply suggested he apply for a concession. LPEC records show that the board was interested in obtaining a Wild West show primarily because Chicago had one, but they thought the Cody extravaganza too expensive. They wanted a Wild West show only if they could negotiate an advantageous deal. The result was a year of constant negotiation, due to objections from McCowan and the Indian Service, who claimed that an Indian Congress would undermine government educational programs and provide visitors with an erroneous view of Indians. As a result, Cummins's concession was one of the last awarded by the LPEC. Cummins agreed to pay a ten-thousand-dollar rental fee and 15 percent of the gross proceeds—a much worse deal than Cody had negotiated in Chicago. Finding the appropriate site also required extensive bargaining.[8]

Cummins had waited to obtain the LPEC concession before assembling a troupe so he had to scramble to find performers and financial backing at the last minute. Initially, he subcontracted with "Colonel" Zack Mulhall to produce a Wild West show that included a group known as the "Cummins Indians." Mulhall hired Will Rogers to do rope tricks, dressed in baggy pants, a derby hat, and a large fake clown's nose. He also hired Tom Mix, who had arrived in St. Louis in the "non-remunerative position as a drum major with the Oklahoma Cavalry Band, despite a lack of musical ability and no membership in the militia." Both appeared in the show for a few weeks. When Mulhall shot and killed his head stable man on the Pike, he was banned from the fairgrounds. Despite his arrest in June and the resultant scandal, he opened another "Indian show" at the Delmar Gardens in downtown St. Louis.[9]

Cummins's show was patterned after William Cody's Wild West Show, as were many similar troops that toured Europe and the United States until 1930. Cody's shows were popular entertainment programs designed to selectively replicate frontier experiences on the Great Plains and celebrate Western heroes, adventurous deeds, and Americans' belief in Manifest Destiny. This meant subjectively depicting the demise of the region's Native peoples who were viewed as obstacles to western expansion. Promoters had added "Indian Congresses," to celebrate Indians as natural warriors and add authenticity to their fictive scenarios. Wanted were men from multiple tribes to relive the old, pre-reservation ways before their cultures declined or, as newspaperman Edward Rosewater, the man who coined the phrase asserted, before "the bronze sons of the forests and the plains, who have resisted the encroachment of the white man, are gathered to the happy hunting ground."[10]

There was something for everyone in the action-packed Wild West shows: cowboys, settlers, Indian captives, soldiers, marksmen. The idea of the Rough Riders derived from the volunteer U.S. Army cavalry unit commanded by Leonard Wood and Teddy Roosevelt in Cuba during the Spanish-American War, and from Roosevelt's book, published in 1899, which glorified nationalistic imperialism.[11] Riders demonstrated trick riding, shooting, and roping. In St. Louis, participants from the Boer War concession and the Tehuelches regularly joined the Rough Rider performances to earn extra money. For the men from Patagonia, simply being able to ride horses made life more bearable. Cummins provided a great service to McGee for which McGee expressed his gratitude.

Cummins liked to call himself "Colonel" in his publicity, feeling that it provided him with status and credibility; he also called himself "Chief La Ko'Ta," which he felt demonstrated his first-hand knowledge of Indians. Cummins advertised that his "most interesting and educational" show included seven hundred and fifty "blanket Indians" from fifty-one different tribes, one hundred cowboys, one hundred and fifty Mexicans, soldiers, Cossacks, Zouaves, and more than three hundred wild horses. *The Piker*, a publication that promoted the Pike's amusements, put the number of participants at eight hundred and fifty, "including cowboys, those centaurs of the American Plains." How many performers actually participated depends on who got counted and when, for the numbers fluctuated. Historian L. G. Moses estimates that Cummins employed two hundred American Indian men plus an indeterminate number of women and children. Cummins's higher numbers are probably exaggerated since he tended to claim credit for any Indian residing in any part of the fairgrounds (including all the Lakotas demonstrating in the Anthropology Department) and for any celebrity who visited his show, including Geronimo and Chief Joseph. The latter may have stopped in St. Louis for one day on a trip from Washington DC but according to Cummins's publicity, spent five months. John Hanson listed the following tribes: Apaches, Arapahos, Assiniboines, Blackfeet, Cayugas, Cheyennes, Chippewas, Crows, Flatheads, Gros Ventres, Iowas, Jicarilla Apaches, Kiowas, Mescalero Apaches, Mohawks, Mojaves, Moquis [Hopi], Ojibways, Omahas, Oneidas, Onondagas, Osages, Otos, Pawnees, Peigans, Poncas, Pottawatomies, Pueblos, Sauk and Fox, San Carlos Apaches, Santee Sioux, Senecas, Shoshones, Sioux, Tuscaroras, Wichitas, and Winnebagos. While it included some peoples from the Anthropology Village, the list omitted the Cocopas, Navajos, Pimas, Pomos, Inuits, Kwakiutls, and Nootkas. The Canadian Ojibways, Oneidas, and Onondagas were Indian athletes who played lacrosse games every hour-and-a-half several days a week on the Plaza of St. Louis and gave demonstrations at special events. Although a separate concession, Cummins took care of their publicity.[12]

Apparently the majority of Cummins's Indian performers were Lakotas or Dakotas. The public expected to see these Sioux men with their long hair, dignified features, and superb equestrian skills. There were participants from at least ten bands: Brule, Crow Creek, Lower Brule, Oglala, Pipeclay, Porcupine, Rosebud, White Clay, White River, and Wounded Knee. The most famous Oglala Lakotas were Comes Out Holy, Spotted Horse, Mrs. Dreaming Bear, and the Leading Hawk family. Leading Hawk was regularly mentioned by the press since he had been a diplomatic delegate to Washington DC and wore beaded epaulets and a George Washington medal. Shooting Cat also wore a George Washington medal given for his diplomatic service. Most Lakotas, including several men in the Indian Village, had previously worked for Cody's Wild West Show.[13]

Unfortunately, one Lakota group never made it to St. Louis. On April 7, while traveling to Washington where they were to meet with President Roosevelt before proceeding to St. Louis, a mail train approaching Maywood, Illinois, hit their train during a heavy fog. Of the sixty-three travelers, three were killed and fifteen seriously injured. The *St. Louis Post-Dispatch* reported that "Chief White Horse" was fatally injured and died soon thereafter. Indian Service personnel reported the deaths of Phillip Iron Tail, Comes Last, and Kills Ahead. Chief High Bear and his wife were badly injured. Carlos Montezuma, a local independent physician and surgeon of Native American descent (Yavapai), who later became a noted reformer and activist, attended the injured Indians. In responding to Montezuma's written offer of assistance, Indian Service Commissioner Jones at first wrote to him that John Brennan, Indian agent at Pine Ridge, was "looking out for the interests of the Indians." Brennan negotiated a relatively low settlement for the railroad's negligence. The Indians found a local judge and Montezuma wrote letters of protest on their behalf to Commissioner Jones. Jones asked Montezuma for an assessment of injuries and "estimate of pecuniary damages." Montezuma, who had a "natural dislike of litigation," felt he was impartial and proposed much higher settlement rates. The Indian Service sided with Brennan and considered the matter closed.[14]

The core of the Sioux contingent in shambles, Cummins returned to South Dakota and hired new employees. He did this in a remarkably short period of time, probably because he treated Indians fairly, advertised them as the most outstanding equestrians in the world, and offered them an opportunity to provide for their families in ways that the repressive reservation system did not. Each man was a salaried employee, with an individual contract. Women were not always paid separately, but men received more money if their families came with them. Stars, such as the young Will Rogers (Cherokee), were given higher wages as were the most outstanding athletes, Leaping Panther (Comanche), Black White-bear (Crow), and DePoe (Rock River). Jim Walker, a Comanche, was singled out because he spoke English and was a boarding-school graduate.[15]

Cummins's publicity celebrated his performers in exaggerated hyperbole using photos of Chief Joseph, Peo-Peo-ta-likt, and Red Thunder at the 1901 Buffalo Exposition. Nevertheless, the press captured the excitement and imagination of the program.

> *Nebraska Bill and Bounding Fawn illustrate the border Bowie knife and impalement act; the Hoosier Zouave corps has been engaged to show their high scaling feats and kaleidoscopic displays of military tactics. The Pony Express is illustrated by Thomas Johnson with marvelous whiplash dexterity. Nanona, a champion rifle shot of the world; double six horse chariot races, and cowboy exhibitions of phenomenal skill with the lariat, picking small objects from the ground while riding at full speed, are marvelous exploits which precede the realistic hold-up of the overland stage coach by Indian raiders. And yet another is the running of the gauntlet and the burning of a white captive at the stake.*[16]

Other publicity blurbs combined images of the noble savage and the menacing warrior under a theatrical extravaganza the "Great Assembly of Savages." One reporter noted that this image drew crowds: "The Indian of ideally picturesque aspect, the one who realizes completely the noble savage of Fenimore Cooper and Ned Buntline, is the most effective poser on The Pike. . . . At the entrance of the Indian Congress he stands in a stately strut or stalks majestically to and fro, unresponsive to the most adulatory salutations of 'How?'" Simultaneously a most insistent barker claimed a pseudo-anthropological authority. One visitor remembered him crying, "Here we have the biggest aggregation of Indians ever consummated, the greatest of anthropological exhibitions to educate you, the grandest of savage spectacles to amaze you, and all for a half a dollar. It will be the memorable occasion of your whole lifetime: Nine hundred Indians, from forty-two different tribes, including famous chiefs, brawny braves, lovely squaws, and pretty papooses, shown in their pastime pleasures and wartime woes!"[17]

Doors to Cummins's Indian Village opened at 10:00 a.m. with a daily parade to exercise the horses and advertise the upcoming performance. Performances were held at 2:00, 4:00, 6:00, and 8:00 p.m., with a Congress of American Indian Nations at 3:00, 5:00, and 7:00 p.m. The arena covered more than eight acres and had a grand monumental entrance. It cost fifty cents to see each show or twenty-five cents just to walk around the encampment where the Indians resided when not performing. Here visitors could see the "real thing": "Native Indians displaying primitive habits and customs, Navajo blanket weavers, bead and basket workers, and silver artisans." As in the Anthropology Department, visitors could also purchase curios and see relics in a museum of antiquities.[18]

The Congress of American Indian Nations, with representatives from historic tribes attired in regalia and engaged in mimic warfare, was the climax of the program. There were "historical" tableaux (Indian attacks on wagon trains), feats of horsemanship, foot races, archery and rifle contests, tournaments of strength, and dance competitions. McCowan intensely disliked these activities and tried to distance the official anthropological display of Indian life and the Indian School from the concession: "The government is especially desirous of keeping out of the [anthropology] exhibit any suggestion of bloodthirstiness." Government policy was "to show the Indian exactly as he is, and not as fiction has painted him." The Wild West show challenged government authority in much the same way as ethnology did by displaying and celebrating traditions as if they were alive, creative, and timeless. The Indian Service had condemned Wild West shows since their inception in the 1880s, arguing that they undermined the image the government wanted to project—Indians embracing civilization and settling into a self-sufficient agrarian lifestyle. McCowan referred to Indians employed in these venues as "Show Indians," professional entertainers who still clung to the "blanket," that is tradition. And entertainers they were, as L. G. Moses has so insightfully shown.[19]

Cummins encountered many problems with his concession since he was not allowed to present shows on Sunday. One of the first LPEC Board of Directors' decisions was to close the LPE on Sunday so employees could rest, that is, to not offend powerful Protestant groups. While people could walk around the grounds, there would be no secular entertainment. Sometime in June, Cummins decided to ignore this regulation and give Sunday matinees. These were well-attended but brought down the LPEC's wrath. Francis told Cummins to stop but he refused, arguing he was not on the fairgrounds. Cummins and Francis took the matter before Judge Ferriss, who ruled that a Sunday show would violate municipal labor laws. Cummins next tried political pressure, asking Senator Thomas H. Carter to convince Francis to make an exception in his case. Francis did not, and Judge Ferriss supported him.[20]

Cummins was distraught; he needed the revenue generated from Sunday matinees. He was in dire financial straits by the beginning of August since housing a live production in St. Louis was extremely costly, and his expenses were higher than his income. Cummins complained to Francis that his LPEC contract called for him to give the company 35 percent of all merchandise and gate receipts. The standard contract for concessionaires gave 25 percent of gross income to the LPEC, and Cummins complained that fair officials were penalizing him with an extra 10 percent surcharge. After protracted negotiation, the board of directors agreed. The hope was that when the temperature fell in September attendance would improve. But by the close of the exposition Cummins was close to bankruptcy. His backers were called upon to ante up for back salaries and railroad tickets. In December, the LPEC brought suit against Cummins in civil court, alleging he owed them $4,531.38. The suit dragged on as Cummins dissolved his corporation. He did not come close to entertaining the four million people or netting the one million dollars Cody reputedly had in Chicago. The two Sunday performances each week that Chicago allowed made a great deal of difference.[21]

The Cliff Dwellers: Illusions of the Hopi

At each new exposition, concessionaires strove to convince the public that their displays were fresh and enriched. In 1893, Chicago had a Cliff Dwellers display that contained models of southwestern archaeological ruins set within a replica of Battle Mountain Rock in Colorado, but without living "cliff dwellers." At St. Louis, W. Maurice Tobin insisted that his larger, enhanced version was educational, historical, dramatic, and sensational, unparalleled in history: "An exhibition of intense realism, showing, in a manner never heretofore attempted, the ancient ARTS, CRAFTS, SCIENCES, HISTORY, ETHNOLOGY and Progress of the Inhabitants of Yesterday. THE CLIFF DWELLERS and their descendants—the Moki [Hopi] and Zuni Tribes—form a complete Exposition in itself."[22] Publicity stated that these real Indians had never appeared in any concession at any exposition. Furthermore, for an extra twenty-five cents, the lucky visitor could see remarkable rituals—Snake, Eagle, and Ghost Dances as a unique form of theater.

Originally McGee did not view this concession as truthful and was quite disturbed when it was proposed. When he learned the LPEC Board of Directors was going to vote on the concession, he warned Skiff that commercial Indian exhibits were becoming uncontrolled and would serve as competition to the LPEC's exhibits. He noted that Tobin's proposal to bring Hopi and Zuni artists to manufacture and sell pottery, textiles, and silver jewelry meant that McGee and McCowan would be unable to secure artists. Tobin would pay salaries and when word reached other Indians, McGee was sure no one would participate in the Department of Anthropology without compensation. He also argued there would be no educational value in Tobin's display, and it would be maintained solely for the purpose of making money without any regard for the ethnographic facts. McCowan was even more opposed. He feared the exhibit would be "nonrealistic and barbarous, devoid of educational or scientific value" and that any concession on the Pike would "destroy in large measure the value of the Government's true exhibit of the Indian and his life." Following Indian Service policy, he was particularly opposed to Hopi exotic, sensational, and pagan snake dances and maintained that Tobin was displaying Indian backwardness, not progress.[23]

LPEC directors disagreed; Indians would attract visitors. They were especially desirable on the Pike since they were "free." Ironically the Cliff Dweller concession was awarded to Tobin on October 3, 1903, at the same meeting that the Indian School and Department of Anthropology plans were approved. At McCowan's and McGee's insistence the directors agreed not to award any other Indian concessions that memorialized the violence of the Indian wars. (Unbeknownst to McCowan, Battle Alley had a tableau of the Battle of the Little Big Horn.) Nor did their protest stop the LPEC from awarding traders concessions in the Manufacturing Building.[24]

Tobin was considered one of the best spielers on the Pike, called "America's best-known exhibitor of strange people," and the "King of the Midway" because of his effective verbal promotions. He specialized in giving audiences what they wanted—exotic difference. As one would expect in a sideshow, the spiel was based on exaggerated illusions. The actual Cliff Dwellers concession was much smaller than Tobin described it, but visitors still had a commanding view of the Pike from its top level (fig. 9.1). A ticket entitled the visitor to an "adventure" starting in a tunnel that pierced cliffs containing "the

Fig. 9.1. On the Pike in front of Tobin's Cliff Dweller's exhibit. Missouri Historical Society, St. Louis, negative no. GPN WF 0585.

most famous caves of the stone age, as the remains exist today in the canons [*sic*] of Arizona, New Mexico and Colorado." In the interior of the cliff were more caves and crevices containing ancestral Puebloan relics and "treacherous" mountain trails rising one hundred feet. Visitors could walk up or ride a burro. Inside was a replica of a tiered, multistoried Zuni Pueblo, which Tobin claimed was home to the "Moki" [Hopi] Indians, "whom science classes as the descendants of the ancient race of this kind." Flanking three sides of a plaza, the building walls were covered in "strange hieroglyphics" and there were long ladders ascending to the roofs. In the central plaza or "Assembly Hall," visitors could see "Moki life" for an additional twenty-five cents. Here were "prehistoric people in all their industrial activity." Sitting in front was a reproduction of the famous church of San Miguel. To add interest there was a museum of curios and ancient relics; the "Moki" catacombs with a "burial of the ancient race"; and native goats, burros, and dogs wandering about the village, to give "a touch of realism to the exhibition."[25]

Even more enticing were performances of "Moki" dances in the freely adapted open-air kiva, Tobin's "temple to worship the sun." Here visitors saw fantasy. "In this theater, the Indians perform the dance of Kachina or masks, [and] the poetic flute dance. The Kachina is distinguished by the use of the heads of buffalo and bear which are worn by the warriors over their heads so as to conceal the features." Other supposedly accurate activities were also staged: "The lighter side of the life was shown; quaint bridal costumes, ancient chants, a native orchestra playing on stringed instruments made of dogs' ribs, sheep's toes, tortoise shell rattles and sun-baked squash."[26] For most people, however, the highlight was the Snake Dance.

Tobin advertised daily performances of "Moki Snake Dances." The American public had been both fascinated and repelled by the Hopi ritual since 1884, when John Gregory Bourke's description was published, followed by other reports. In 1899, the Santa Fe Railway published Walter Hough's *The Moki Snake Dance*, in part to encourage tourism to the Hopi Mesas and the Grand Canyon. Since Hough was a curator of the U.S. National Museum, his description carried great cachet and was the basis for Tobin's interpretive performances. Hough called the Snake Dance "an unparalleled dramatic pagan ceremony" (Hough 1899; Bourke 1884). Tourists flocked to the Hopi Mesas to witness the summer rituals despite Indian Service bans on the performances. Tobin was marketing what he knew the public wanted to see. But it was all fake.

Publicity photos for the Cliff Dwellers exhibit, generally labeled "Moki Snake Dance," show men with real and fake snakes in their mouths (fig. 9.2) and make some outlandish claims. Bennitt's history contains a similar photograph with the caption "Zuni and Moki Indians, whom ethnologists class

Fig. 9.2. "Cliff Dwellers—Snake Dance." Indian men with fake snakes in their mouths pretending to be Hopi in Tobin's Cliff Dweller's concession. Missouri Historical Society, St. Louis, negative no. LPE 1265, OWFN 4580.

as descendants of an ancient race of Kings." During the exposition, the authenticity of such claims was questioned and debated in the pages of *Scientific American* and with good reason. The participants were neither Hopis nor Zunis. According to McGee, "There were no Hopi Indians on the grounds either in connection with the Indian School or on The Pike; certainly there were none in the Ethnologic Section of this Department. I have been told that certain natives in [this exhibit] were habitually proclaimed in the ballyhoo as 'genuine Moki snake dancers.'"[27] The dancers were, in fact, from San Ildefonso, Laguna, San Juan, and Santa Clara pueblos and performed parodies of Hopi and Zuni dances and ceremonial performances based on Tobin's interpretations of Hough's accounts. The "traditional" attire worn by the men was a mixture of Northern Plains (Arapaho or Teton Sioux), Plateau (Nez Perce), and Prairie (Ioway or Santee Sioux) items. The men did dance some of their own social dances; the Kachina Dance was actually a Rio Grande Pueblo winter dance to attract the buffalo, not a Hopi plaza dance.

Tobin claimed to have recruited 150 Hopis and Zunis. This was an inflated figure because, like Cummins, he thought that lots and lots of Indians meant higher visitor receipts. A photograph reproduced by Eric Breitbart shows twenty-one men, twelve women, and twelve children in Indian attire, eight men in business suits, and seven men with American musical instruments, who look "phenotypically" Indian. San Juan governor Ramon Archuleta was their leader and proudly carried one of the canes of office that President Lincoln presented to Rio Grande Pueblo leaders in 1863, as well as an 1837 silver medal presented to his ancestors by President Van Buren.[28]

In addition to the staged performances of inappropriate, pseudo-rituals, the Cliff Dweller concession focused on culturally appropriate artistic accomplishments to demonstrate that Puebloans were not savages. Potters, weavers, silversmiths, and basket makers produced art, which visitors bought. Tobin considered art production to be the educational part of the concession. So did museums. Zella so impressed Dorsey that he purchased her baskets for the Field Museum, comparing them to the best pre-contact examples. Other artists included Maria and Julian Martinez, of San Ildefonso Pueblo on their honeymoon. For Maria, who would go on to become one of the most celebrated San Ildefonso potters, this was the first of many expositions she would attend. Her experiences mirrored those of the Pueblo artists in the Anthropology Department. She later told Alice Marriott that she, Julian, and the others only spoke Tewa. "The Indians pretended they did not understand what was said, and then they had something to laugh about when the white people had gone home and the Indians were alone on the fair grounds." Maria told Susan Peterson that she met Geronimo in San Diego in 1915, but it had to have been St. Louis since Geronimo died in 1909. She liked him; "We talked in Spanish because we didn't know each other's Indian."[29]

Although his ballyhoo may seem spurious to us today, for the public and exposition chroniclers, the Cliff Dweller's exhibit was what Tobin claimed, a study in authenticity. John Hanson thought the Cliff Dweller's one of the Pike's educational highlights since participants were "the True Americans."[30] For McGee the concession's cardinal sins were that Tobin intentionally misidentified participants and imbued them with ethnographic inaccuracies.

McGee was not upset that the exhibit's publicity presented the illusion of antiquity, of Indians living in a time warp, misused the concept of race, or that all evidence of modern American material culture was carefully hidden. Nor was McGee upset that Tobin created mystery, a technique McGee used to entice fairgoers, or that the spiel hinted at degeneration and diffusionism. "Did the Cliff-dwellers antedate the Pyramids of Egypt? Were they of blood relation to the early inhabitants of the land where the Nile is god?" Tobin, like McGee, made participants exotic proxies for the past. The pseudo-Hopi were reenactors of all Puebloan ancestors. What McGee disliked was that Tobin made them examples of the best modern Indians, a technique he used to distance his concession from the Anthropology Department and the Indian School. It could even be seen in their bodies: "The members of these tribes are of stronger build, handsomer, and of brighter color than the ordinary North American Indian, from whom they hold themselves aloof with dignity."[31] Mc-Cowan was particularly upset with this contention because it implied that hope for Indian peoples rested not on government assimilative policies but with civilized Indians adhering to their traditions. And, while they might have been aloof to Tobin, his participants spent most of their spare time with the Puebloans in the Indian Village.

The Esquimaux Village

New York to the North Pole was the last exhibit on the Pike, situated near the LPEC administration buildings, Cupples Hall, and the foreign pavilions. Here visitors could pretend to be explorers, following in Perry's footsteps. If they wanted to see Native life in the Far North, McGee suggested they go to the Esquimaux Village, located between Constantinople and the Magic Whirlpool (fig. 9.3). In fact, McGee considered it essential that fairgoers visit this exhibit to complete their survey of the world's races. Dick Crane and George Voris of the Alaska Esquimaux Company organized the concession, which offered seventeen tons of hunting tools and art for sale. The time period depicted was not a timeless past but 1865, when Secretary Seward bought Alaska. The concession featured an artificial Arctic landscape where Inuits resided in caribou-hide huts on the banks of a miniature lake named Lake Aleut. Alaskan dogs dragged a heavy sled along the top of papier-mâché icebergs where visitors pretended they were Alaskan gold prospectors meeting Inuit. It cost ten

Fig. 9.3. Inuit exhibit, Eskimaux Village concession on the Pike. Nancy Columbia stands at center. Photograph by the Gerhard sisters. Library of Congress, Prints and Photographs Division, 3796–42381.

cents to enter the exhibit, fifteen cents for activities, and twenty-five cents for a dog-sled ride.[32]

Reporters and visitors were disappointed that there were no Inuit in the Anthropology Villages. Since they had been participants in earlier fairs, their omission was considered a flaw. According to Francis, this was a conscious decision on McGee's part even though it would have made his exhibit more complete. "None of the short and well-rounded Eskimo . . . were represented in the department by reason of the risk to life of Arctic folk attending the average St. Louis summer."[33] McGee based his concern partly on the fact that several Inuit and their dogs had perished in the Chicago heat in 1893. It is more likely, however, that McGee did not have enough money to mount another expedition and used physical discomfort as a justification. The hot, humid climate likely bothered the Inuit, although most had been living in the lower United States as professional performers for several years.

Twenty-eight Inuit lived in the village. Eighteen came from the Bering Sea area and the rest from Labrador and eastern Hudson Bay. Those from the eastern Arctic were under the care of L. L. Bales, a guide who had taken President McKinley to Alaska. All were considered to be exceedingly friendly and clean: "The sociability of the Eskimos has won them many friends among fairgoers; their abodes are sweet and wholesome, and they may be seen continually washing their clothes, [and] in spite of their close quarters there is no offensive odor noticeable."[34]

The Inuit and Aleuts demonstrated customary pursuits of hunting and preparing food in their winter attire, although "[t]hey were always good humored, even in July and August when it made one feel uncomfortably warm even to look at the heavy fur clothing. The smiles were broader and the greetings were heartier when the cool nights came, and the reindeer coats and trousers were desirable." Periodically, men demonstrated spear and harpoon throwing and, in a rare instance of contemporaneity, how they now hunted with guns. They engaged in sports, sang hunting songs, and rode in kayaks in the lagoon. Daily reenactments of a Native wedding, a funeral, and dog-sled racing were treated as special events. In an attempt to portray the multicultural nature of the Far North, concessionaires staged life in a gold-mining camp and displayed Arctic animals and ice floes. There were also some questionable features (totem poles next to a caribou tent). The owner interpreted the Northwest Coast materials as a sign of the people's progress toward civilization and asserted that visitors expected them.[35]

Despite these supposedly evolutionary symbols, the children and dogs were the concession's real stars. "The Eskimo children are a merry lot, less stolid than their parents, and enter with zest into the play of their new and temporary home. Their massive dogs take kindly, too, to a less strenuous life than they have enjoyed in Labrador and British Colombia [sic], whence they come." There were at least six children, including Nancy Columbia. Born at the World's Columbian Exposition in 1893, she had been named by Mrs. Potter Palmer, the president of the Women's Commission in Chicago, and was affectionately called "Little Columbia." Now aged eleven, she was one of the most photographed individuals, as was her mother, an interpreter for Lieutenant Peary on his Polar expeditions, and "Hootch," the U.S. mail dog who had helped concessionaire Crane deliver the mail.[36]

The attire, rhetoric, dances, sports, singing, and wedding ceremonies, gave the illusion of authenticity to this concession. Except for the totem poles, it was quite ethnographically correct. "The whole exhibit is one of the most genuine of its kind, and the American citizen may see these strange people from the North housed in their summer tents of sealskin or their winter 'igloos' or snow houses, and engaged in their domestic duties."[37]

American Blacks and Africans: The Old Plantation
and the Boer War Spectacular

As at other expositions during this era, there were no pavilions devoted to the lives and accomplishments of African Americans, because dark skin was equated with mental inferiority and inherent savagery, and due to the rampant Jim Crow racism of the time. Most blacks at the LPE were employed as janitors, a few as Pike entertainers; for example, in the House of Mirrors they created illusions. Like many other visitors, Geronimo was very taken with the use of black faces in the Creation concession, where black actors were used as allegories for the world in darkness. John Walker described another formulaic illusion in which "the Coney Island Negro holds his head in a canvas slot for any savage to fire a ball at," while later "you find a veritable Coney Island Negro upon a pitchfork with two tines of the fork running right up into the neck and all the rest of his body missing."[38] These were standard freak show illusions. They were not on McGee's list of authentic concessions, nor was the Old Plantation.

If the Wild West show idealized the violence and adventure of the American imagination, the Old Plantation homogenized and sanitized the pre–Civil War years in the American South. The concession was recycled from the 1898 Omaha and 1901 Buffalo fairs and subsequently appeared at fairs through 1915. It was billed as having genuine scenes of cotton fields and music performed by "Negroes" (many in black face), as well as the nostalgic charm of a Southern plantation mansion. It was only nostalgic for white audiences, however, and showed nothing of the horrors of slavery. It portrayed blacks stereotypically, as creatures of low intelligence. This was nothing new. Since 1810, Africans had been portrayed as "sub-human freaks, missing links between man and animal and the epitome of primitiveness."[39]

The prospectus for the concession's 1915 version stated that the Old Plantation "housed an array of coal black mammies preparing real corn pone while a group of black boys in the corner [sang] Negro melodies to the accompaniment of the banjo and the lively capering of a few frizzle-headed pickaninnies." We assume that such derogatory but common rhetoric was used in 1904 as well. As a visitor remembered it, "We entered an open court where there were four or five typical log cabins in which the 'darkies' lived, then passed into a hall where there was a show of about a half hour's duration. It consisted of about twenty darkies singing, dancing, [and] cake walking. Some of them were very comical, and they put up a pretty good show."[40] The performances by the forty men and women were actually minstrel show performances emphasizing Negro spirituals and songs.

Many black pianists who played at restaurant concessions on the Pike played ragtime music, which was becoming all the rage across the nation. Scott Joplin, well along on his climb to music immortality, came to St. Louis for the opening of the fair in May. His "The Cascades," composed for the exposition, received much play, by both pianists and the bands on the fairgrounds. Unfortunately his music was not heard in the concert hall. The most famous black American to appear there was Booker T. Washington.

Old Plantation was the only concession dedicated to African Americans. Many people noticed the deliberate omission and that the concession was a portrayal of white imagination designed to make slavery appear desirable. A letter to the editor of the *St. Louis Globe-Democrat* by S. A. Duke on the day the fair closed asked, "Why, when the products of all nations and peoples were given a show at the Fair, was the American Negro not represented? The American Indians had an expensive inning to show their advancement, and while the remotest parts of the world were ransacked to find the original specimens of the Negro race, there was nothing to show the advance that race has made through its sojourn in enlightened America. Why this omission?" There was no answer from LPEC officials.[41] But every midway had Africans presented as evolutionary "missing links," "wild men," or recently tamed colonials. There had been about one hundred Dahomeans in Chicago, sometimes billed as "African cannibals and their Amazon wives." In St. Louis, "original specimens from Africa" were displayed in the "Boer War" extravaganza.

The second Anglo-Boer War (1899 to 1902) was a particularly vicious affair fought to control South Africa's immense gold and diamond fields. It cost tens of thousands of British, Afrikaner, and black African lives and untold suffering for hundreds of thousands more. The British ultimately fielded five hundred thousand troops, the Boers between sixty-five thousand and eighty thousand. The British lost approximately six thousand troops killed in action and another sixteen thousand to infectious diseases; the Afrikaners lost about fourteen thousand men killed in action and another twenty-six thousand (including thousands of women and children) in British concentration camps. It is not clear how many black Africans died (tens of thousands had died previously in the almost constant warfare attendant on the European settlement of the region since the seventeenth century), but estimates are that thirteen thousand died in concentration camps during the Boer War.[42]

The war had been officially over less than two years when forty to fifty black Africans, two hundred white Afrikaners, and one hundred and fifty British and Welsh troops (including many who had been actual combatants on both sides) signed on to be Boer War reenactors in St. Louis. Hostilities between these groups began even before the exhibit opened. A headline in the *St. Louis Post-Dispatch* proclaimed: "Boers Lose Skirmish with Britons for a World's Fair Kopje. Coveted Hill Taken by 'Tommy Atkins,' while Cronje's Men Stay in Cars Rather than Venture the Mud Below." The special eighteen-car train that transported the participants from Newport News, Virginia, had arrived late at night in an April sleet storm. When the Boers marched to the concession compound after waiting for the storm to abate, they found that the British group had taken the best tents. The Boers retreated to a hill near the Agricultural Pavilion and planted their national flag; their wives and children returned to the train. "The Boers exhibit much ill feeling toward the British in the party," according to a reporter. "They insist that they have traveled with the Britons enough and do not care to be quartered with them a day longer than necessary." The black Africans' plight was even worse: "These poor fellows were almost frozen" by the next morning. "Their clothing is not suitable for this climate and they suffered severely when they left their cars." Officials belatedly supplied wood to make tent platforms for them and erected three compounds for the groups. The men met at the concession only for performances.[43]

The Boer War concession opened in a fourteen-acre arena near the Palace of Horticulture beyond the Observation Wheel. Arthur W. Lewis, a Missourian by birth and British officer during the war, organized the event, which several

St. Louis businessmen underwrote. Battle reenactments were staged daily at 3:30 and 8:30 p.m. General admission was twenty-five cents, one dollar for a box seat. Actual generals were the stars and they put on a stunning show. John Walker was very impressed with what he saw: "The quick spat-spat-spat of a rapid fire machine gun . . . shells from the guns seemed to drop and burst" among the combatants, "horses fell to the earth and rolled over, seemingly in mortal agony . . . guns and wagons were covered with mud." He found the reenactment entirely believable. "It was real war; much more like the real thing than the majority of the war correspondents will see along the Liao Tung Peninsula [a reference to the 1904 Russian-Japanese battles]; as realistic as the greatest war enthusiast might desire."[44]

Significantly, Walker's description did not include any mention of black African participants because they did not play major roles in the battle reenactment. They were there for other purposes, to perform "war dances," engage in daily activities, and compete in athletic events, primarily foot races. In addition to adding authenticity to the concession, the Africans were expected to provide manual labor and take care of the livestock, just as they did in South Africa. Visitors could watch them perform daily activities (execute "war dances") or run away from Boers after a brief skirmish in the opening tableaux.

Tellingly, Lewis referred to the Africans as a homogenous group using a derogatory term derived from Arabic, *Kaffirs*, meaning "infidels." Chief Umkali, a Zulu, led the ethnically diverse contingent whose members were from at least six sociolinguistic groups: Zulus, Swahilis, Basutos, Matabeles, a Khoisan group, and Bushmen. There was at least one woman with a baby, most likely one of the men's wife. Unlike at other nineteenth-century fairs, circuses, and sideshows, the Bushmen were barely mentioned by the press, supplanted in the American imagination by the Anthropology Department's Pygmies and the Philippines' Negritos. The emphasis instead was on the "ferocious and haughty" Zulus.[45]

The group built a kraal (a circular, walled fence, six feet high) to enclose thatched huts, as soon as they arrived. Materials had been brought from South Africa, supplemented by mud and yellow clay from the Mississippi bottom lands. When their clothing proved inadequate for the late April storms, they used extra pieces of thatch to provide warmth, since the concession publicity stated they would wear only Native attire. While we have found no indications that the Africans produced art for sale, this does not mean that they did not have separate entrepreneurial activities.

St. Louis newspaper reporters saw the "Kaffirs" as private, dignified men and fierce warriors who had great pride. While they drew rations from the camp's quartermaster and performed their duties, they had their own community and followed their own rules. This was the only concession where the press mentioned black Americans as visitors—noteworthy because the press generally ignored non-middle-class, nonwhite visitors. Possibly the Africans saw a difference between themselves and American blacks. "Chief Umkalali [*sic*] expressed himself, through an interpreter, regarding his American negro visitors in the following language: 'In Africa the Kaffirs live as they please, have their own language, laws, and costume, but in America the Kaffir has no language of his own and disgraces himself by copying the white people in every manner possible.'"[46]

Despite their perceived differences, local blacks continued to court the South Africans. On May 6, a man identified in the press as "Kaffir Tom" exhorted the Africans to stop work. Many agreed. As the Africans "marched down the hill in solid phalanx," general manager Frank Fillis beseeched them to stay. When the men did not respond, Fillis called on the British and Boer soldiers to stop them but the soldiers apparently did nothing. Meanwhile "Kaffir Tom" rallied the Africans to fight for their liberty. According to a reporter the next day, "the half-clad blacks rushed to a lumber pile and seized sticks, which they brandished like their native war spears, at the same time hurling words of defiance at the British and the Boers." The soldiers "charged the blacks, disarmed them, hustled them about, and after a sound drubbing, sent them back to the camp."[47]

In early June, St. Louis black citizens, led by Mrs. Willeltha Smith, tried to liberate fifteen African laborers. This time Fillis asked for local police reinforcements to force the Africans back and stop the "riot." Once again the British and Boer actor-soldiers began to cane blacks, Americans and Africans alike, and injured Mrs. Smith. A LPEC police sergeant stopped them and told Fillis and his staff that they could not use physical force. According to a newspaper account the Africans claimed that they were leaving the concession because, instead of the four dollars per week they had been promised, they had received nothing. The sergeant concluded that any man was free to leave a job and that Fillis could not stop him. All fifteen left and became coal heavers for the Donk Brothers Coal Company. Another twenty quietly walked away from the concession and melded into the St. Louis community. Neither exposition records nor the press mention that anything was done to force them to remain with the concession or return to South Africa.[48]

While McGee had no comment on, or played any role in, political labor activism, he often saw the Zulus. The Boer War Africans interacted regularly with the Africans living in the Anthropology Villages. One reporter described a Sunday "ceremonial" visit he had witnessed. "Resemblances, physically, were striking. It was difficult to distinguish the Kaffirs from the Batwas. A relationship was evidently anticipated on both sides. Conversation began at once, without introduction; but after several minutes' effort it ceased. The Kaffirs were not able to understand one word said by the Batwa; the Batwa, quick witted as he is, could not comprehend anything the Kaffir tried to communicate. Both Kaffirs and Batwa laughed heartily at the confusion, esteeming the fruitless attempt to be sociable a good joke."[49]

It is noteworthy that McGee never referred to the Boer War concession or its African participants in his lectures, press releases, or final report, even though their presence filled holes in his evolutionary scheme. Given their interaction with the Batwas this must have been a purposeful decision. The groups that McGee lauded instead were the ancient civilizations of the Orient and Middle East, examples of his third culture-grade.

Ancient Civilizations: The Mysterious Orient

Mysterious Asia, Moorish Palace, the Streets of Cairo, the Streets of Constantinople, the Chinese Village, and A Trip through Siberia lured people into the Pike's Orient. Off the Pike, in the middle of the fairgrounds, were two exceptionally large concessions, the Gates of Jerusalem and Moorish Village (fig. 9.4). All contained Natives people as specialty entertainers, artisans, laborers, and retailers. While ethnographic appeal and even authenticity were strengths, these concessions' raison d'être was commerce. Street sellers were everywhere, their voices producing a cacophony along with the spielers: "From every niche and corner a merchant fresh from the bazaars of the Orient calls forth the quality of his strange wares." Others had regular booths or stores; Hadji

Fig. 9.4. Old Jerusalem concession looking south toward the Pike, the observation wheel, and the Machinery Building. The Fine Arts Building is on the right, the Moroccan and Japanese Pavilion on the left. Photograph by the Official Photographic Company. Missouri Historical Society, St. Louis, negative no. WF 0448.

Ephraim Benguiat, from San Francisco, ran the Benguiat Palace of Ancient Art, selling Oriental rugs, armor, and ceremonial and sacred relics. Every concession had ethnographic and often archaeological artifacts for sale. The Gates of Jerusalem featured a collection of ancient Egyptian glass jars (valued at nine hundred dollars) that were similar to those on display in the Anthropology Building. McGee directed visitors there to see the remnants of the remarkable civilization that had produced such rare and valuable antiquities.[50]

The Gates of Jerusalem exhibit opened on May 17. A wall enclosed eleven acres of winding streets, an open bazaar, houses, full-sized temples, and chapels. The "houses" lining the narrow streets were actually booths selling souvenirs. Despite this commercialism, the emphasis was on Jerusalem as a holy place; concessionaires reproduced the Wailing Wall, the Tower of David, and the Dome of the Rock. The Temple of Solomon was decorated with replicas of altars and sacred utensils the organizers believed would have been in the temple. In addition, the building contained a huge canvas depicting the Israelites' camp at the foot of Mount Sinai. While guides discussed the flight from Egypt and Moses obtaining the Ten Commandments, a light show made the scene change from dawn to midday, then dusk to the black of night.

The Gates of Jerusalem was a place of constant activity to give visitors the flavor of daily life. Visitors walked or rode camels and saw more than five hundred employees dressed in ethnic attire. There were beggars, philosophers who sat and talked to visitors, and fifteen fortunetellers operating in the bazaar. Daily religious processions wound through the streets and well-trained young men gave guided tours and lectures on the sacredness of the Holy Lands' places to the different religions. The Jewish and Muslim cultures portrayed were an interesting mixture of biblical times and Palestine under British rule. There was a foreign hotel (where visitors stayed) and even a U.S. consulate. Special events, including a wedding on June 25, were written up on the society pages of the St. Louis newspapers.[51]

Constantinople Village was free but visitors paid twenty-five cents to see the theater. And pay they did, for the highlight was famous dancing girls, "whose muscles obey every desire" and who perform "weird revolutions for the edification of the open-eyed and open-mouthed throng." Similar entertainments were staged at the Streets of Cairo concession, which provided men with an "opportunity to see strange sights" that had been seen at every exposition since 1889. Here visitors watched belly dancers with famous names—La Belle Fatima and La Belle Rose. At Chicago, the press had dubbed one particularly energetic dancer "Little Egypt." By 1894, there were four Little Egypts performing at Coney Island. Whether these women performed in St. Louis is unknown.

In addition to watching the dancing girls, visitors took camel or donkey rides along the narrow, twisting streets, heard men reciting the Koran, or became immersed in "typical scenes." They could also meet "Dahomey" men, veterans of earlier fairs. The Palace of Damascus, first seen at the 1877 Antwerp Exposition, and a Moroccan concession had similar types of entertainment. The latter presented historic, poetic, and scenic tableaux. All sold exotic items, pistols, swords, armor, and lamps. Since it was questionable whether participants were actually from their countries of origin, McGee did not suggest that visitors see them. Instead he suggested people see relics in the anthropology exhibits.

The Chinese Village opened June 16. While the Chinese government did not officially sponsor the attraction, Chinese workers helped build and decorate the building after finishing the official pavilion. A merchants' association from Philadelphia, the Yeo Ging Company, underwrote the concession, and for twenty-five cents visitors could see dramas enacted every half-hour by Chinese actors or hear a stringed instrument orchestra. Visitors sampled foods in the Chinese restaurant and drank tea in a special tea house. They walked around the roof garden, visited a "Joss House" (temple), or watched wandering performers. One visitor especially remembered the fire eater and slight-of-hand magician. In numerous curio booths visitors purchased souvenirs—silks, teas, and ivory carvings. About a dozen children were employed "to attract customers by wandering around in their native dress and attempting to converse" with them.[52] At night several thousand electrical Chinese lanterns drew people to the busy restaurant.

The Japanese Village, Gardens, and Theater had a tea house as its central feature where people partook of an authentic tea ceremony. The compound was entered through impressive gateways, including a replica of the gateway to Ieyasu's tomb at Nikko. An important draw was the fifty-four geisha girls who had been sent from Japan. Fair records indicate that the Japanese Village took in nearly three hundred thousand dollars and was the tenth most popular concession. At the end of a visit, fairgoers took a jin-ricksha ride for ten cents before entering Mysterious Asia (with a Polynesian Native theater McGee thought was ethnographically accurate), or Mysterious Siam, filled with Native peoples from Thailand. Siam had a theater performance every hour, a camel, elephant, and rides on sacred cattle for fifteen cents and a small museum.[53]

The Empire of India concession focused on India and Ceylon and it was here that visitors could see more performances of McGee's valued ethnographic rituals—at least theoretically. There were sixteen snake charmers who seemed to lull venomous reptiles to sleep with their music, Indian elephants that performed and could be ridden, and Singalese dances. Visitors were most impressed with the devil dancers who performed nightly to the chanting of their leader, Kattendija. The exoticism was heightened by torch light and the pleasant fumes of burning incense. Kattendija said prayers over the dancers and audience before and after each ritual because to dance invoked powerful spirits (devas), who had to be properly propitiated lest they do harm. "The dancing is done to strange toned instruments, which give forth music of better quality than that associated with the Oriental dances with which this country has hitherto been familiar," remembered one fairgoer. "At times, members of the orchestra break out into song, as the dancers sway with increasing rapidity."[54] Visitors were fascinated by juggling acts and rope tricks, illusions that led McGee to question the authenticity of this part of the concession.

Civilization's Peasants: European History and Folklore

Moving up McGee's evolutionary paradigm, fairgoers could visit European civilization as it was before its move into modernity. This was a bifurcated picture, however, for like American enlightened civilization, the present and the future were displayed in different parts of the fairgrounds. On the Pike, concessions presented European history and folk culture, epitomized by German beer gardens, theaters, vaudeville houses, vendors, and what has been called "dime museums" designed to appeal to urban immigrants.[55] All European-themed concessions were designed to encourage the American public to buy and buy and buy. The Royal Castle had a museum filled with ethnic curiosities that owners hoped to sell to American decorative art museums. While in each country's main pavilion, objects for sale and on exhibit were reserved for royal and elite culture, on the Pike, entrepreneurs stressed heritage to emphasize the nostalgic side of peasant life. Paris and French Village were essentially tourism advertisements with minimal folklore, the realm of pre-Disney portrayal rather than ethnology. McGee treated them as such with two exceptions he felt had educational artifact exhibits.

The first was the German Tyrolean Alps built and operated by a St. Louis brewer's association. It provided a restaurant and an Oberammergau panorama with scenic views of the Alps for twenty-five cents. Visitors rode past towering, snow-capped mountains and tumbling waterfalls that were described as "so good that it is difficult to tell where the rocks and soil end and the painted pasteboard begins." There were Tyrolean singers and souvenir booths attended by attractive young women. "The music of an excellent band diverts your attention from the [mountainous landscape], and a thousand people sitting at little tables around the stand form objects of immediate interest for wandering eyes." John Walker liked the ancient church and bell tower and the "pretty flower girls modestly offering boutonnières."[56]

The Irish Industrial Village, McGee's second selection, similarly emphasized trade and souvenirs in a bazaar and replica of Blarney Castle. An exhibit hall contained Celtic and historic objects and there was a chapel, theater, and model of President McKinley's ancestral home, a memorial to the president who had been assassinated at the 1901 Pan-American Exposition. Women wove carpets and made lace. Popular exhibits were gender specific, a display of whiskey distillation methods for men, and Irish laces, cordage, and wool cloth for women. McCowan was pleased with this concession and took senior students to see it. Of course, students had different ideas about the importance of these outings. Ida Starr, a Cherokee student, found the Ireland Village "one of the most interesting places to visit on The Pike. They certainly knew how to entertain, for when you enter Ireland, you never realize how quickly the time passes away."[57]

Historian Curtis Hinsley has called Chicago's Midway Plaisance a "bazaar of exotica" and the same can be said of the Street of All Nations and its plethora of national concessions.[58] It was a place where people mingled as never before and saw nostalgic entertainment from their homelands as well as peoples they had never even imagined.

All the foreign village concessions on the Pike, the government-sponsored Philippine Reservation and Indian School, and the LPEC-sponsored Anthropology Villages were part of an elaborate entertainment package, which McGee hoped was also edifying. When people finished walking through the Pike and came to the anthropology displays, many did not even notice the transition. And this lack of distinction was apparent to Native participants as well. All were on display. Public and private spaces were not distinguished, at least by fair promoters. The people in all the displays were constantly under the public gaze. It was not easy being an anthropology exhibit.

10. Being a Living Exhibit

Before the exposition opened, reporter W. C. M'Carty imagined what life would be like for Native participants. Relying heavily on McGee's rhetoric, he boldly asserted that the Native peoples "will live EXACTLY as they would were they at home on their reservation instead of being the center of the greatest exposition ever held" (M'Carty 1903, 6). M'Carty did not stop to think about what life would *really* be like, nor did McGee ever admit that living in a compound with strangers constantly peering through windows could never remotely be like life at home. To have done so would have undermined his promise of authenticity.

What was life like for the people who were on exhibit? Was it an adventure? Was it tedious? Was it enjoyable? Was it dangerous? Was it absurd? Did it resemble in any way what visitors would have seen and experienced if they had visited the people in their homelands? What was it like to have people constantly asking questions and peering in windows and doorways, and to have no privacy? What did the people think of the fairgoers? How did they deal with the tedium and repetition of their work? How did they feel about having their skin color equated with savage exoticism or as a symbol of racial inferiority? We will never know the answers to these questions for certain because we cannot interview the participants, but it is important to ask the questions nonetheless because, as indicated in earlier chapters, we cannot understand the meaning of exposition anthropology by looking only at McGee's intentions and practices. We must try to grasp the meaning of performance events for participants as well as organizers, visitors, reporters, and publicists.

Luckily some hints are available in documentary records. To say that life in St. Louis appears to have been memorable but difficult and sometimes intolerable may sum it up. We have more evidence of the negative than the positive aspects, because problems were related more frequently than successes in correspondence, newspapers, and LPEC files. From these documents, we get glimpses of areas of contention: living conditions, safety issues, boredom, health, and contact with peoples from other cultures (especially fair visitors),

Fig. 10.1. Stereocard of woman buying pottery from Acoma women in the ramada of their encampment in front of the Indian School. Photograph by William H. Rau. Library of Congress, Prints and Photographs Division, 2966-J696-58.

lack of money, bureaucratic impediments, and personal rivalries. Other issues (a desire for certain foods that were impossible to obtain) are mentioned less frequently. Food was most likely a bigger concern (we have not found the sutlery transaction records) and it is unlikely that most interpreters wrote formal complaints to McGee about Natives' wishes. Informal verbal requests were likely common, but these cannot be traced in the extant documentary record.

What is evident is that individuals and groups used different strategies to cope with the many problems of living constantly in the public gaze. Native people managed daily life by using role inversions, pranks, ironic language, poise, authority, educative speeches directed at officials and fairgoers, defiance, humor, and compassion. Often they ignored and actively defied rules. They staged passive protests, renegotiated extensively, and controlled economic transactions (fig. 10.1). When all else failed, Indians simply left; the foreign Natives did not have that option. In no case were the Native performers the compliant individuals of McGee's, McCowan's, Jenks's, or the concessionaires' dreams.

Other adaptive techniques must have been used behind the scenes. Life on stage made people circumspect. As one reporter noted, "During the day, when they know they are under inspection, the red people are very reserved; they are as careful regarding what they do and say as if life itself depended on their actions; but in the evening, when they are left to themselves they fully enjoy their freedom."[1]

Coping with "Rubbering" Fairgoers

One reason for this reserve was that demonstrators had to cope with visitors' insatiable curiosity and boorishness. This story is fairly typical: "An Indian woman came running toward her sod lodge, and behind her a white woman sped in pursuit. The Indian got there first, and entering, quickly closed the door behind her, or pulled down the curtain, or whatever they do in sod lodges. The white woman stood outside and cried to her, 'Can I look at your baby, can I look at your baby?' And when she received no response, she walked away in anger, saying, 'The savages.'"[2] Americans' reactions to not getting their way were to resort to stereotypes or label the intended victim discourteous. Offenders never saw themselves as rude or offensive.

McGee had tried to educate visitors, distributing courtesy lists to newspapers before the fair. On the May 1 opening of the exposition, a newspaper columnist published a multistanza poem about the indigenous peoples and instructed visitors how they should treat them. After describing the Patagonian Natives, Ainus, Filipinos, and other groups, he wrote:

There'll be others to amaze you—
Plenty of them, black and red;

Some will please you, some will faze you,
To such crazy customs bred,
And as on these freaks you gaze you
Will on wondrous thought be fed.

After several stanzas describing each group, he offered the following advice:

But remember, while you ramble
Rubbering, big-eyed, at these
Funny-looking guys that amble
Round with bracelets on their knees,
Something just as odd, I'll gamble,
Each of them about YOU *sees.*[3]

While most people heeded this advice, some did not or chose to think of the indigenous peoples as freaks in a carnival sideshow who existed only for their amusement and who presumably had no feelings. The *Indian School Journal* recorded many instances of rude or ignorant behavior: "An old Sioux was surprised out of his usual stoicism today when a mischievous girl tweaked the tail of his long coiled hair." Visitors asked demonstrators if they were "really" Indians or said they did not know that Indians were still alive. John Hanson took a photograph of another type of typical interaction. Nine Euro-American visitors are standing under the Cocopa ramada looking into the house. A Cocopa man sits "in silence, coolly surveying the throng of sight-seeing visitors." There is no interaction and visitors depart without greeting or asking his permission to enter the compound.[4] Similar behavior can be seen today at craft demonstrations. The lack of acknowledgment and the accompanying assumed invisibility were as rude in 1904 as they are today. Such uninvited voyeurism and assumption of free access at all times were discourteous and dehumanizing; in all cultures people must respect privacy, a feature conspicuously absent at fairs and one that required senior men to constantly assert their basic rights.

The heights of rudeness seem to have occurred when people were by themselves, away from the encampments. A fifty-four-year-old bookkeeper, Sam P. Hyde, was an avid fairgoer, amateur photographer, and collector of art and war relics. He kept a diary of his fair experiences, including stalking unsuspecting indigenous men. One entry reads:

I had carried the Kodak about all the morning and not done much business, when on descending the steps from the Government Building I spied an old savage in all his glory of bead and feather, striding along with the step of a king. "There's my game," said I, "I'll shoot him if I lose my scalp for it." I well knew the antipathy of the Indian to having his picture taken and that there was some danger attending the enterprise, but this was such a fine specimen I determined to take the chance.

Calculating quickly the distance I wanted, the direction of the light, and at what point I could catch him with a good background, I followed him a few paces and running quickly ahead, passed him, and touched the button at the supreme moment. My next thought was to get away, for the old fellow had seen my camera and heard the shutter snap. It was not a wholesome place for me to remain. As he stopped in his tracks with a savage grunt I shot across the lawn. He stood there for a moment glaring at me and uttering grunts like a hog. As I headed for the Liberal Arts Building where I could lose myself in the crowd and render pursuit difficult, I yelled back at him, "O you will die sure." But he resumed his path and I escaped with my prize. He had his feather headdress on when I spotted him and I did not know that he had taken it off till I developed the film, such was the excitement of the moment, and such the vicissitudes of Kodaking. However I doubt if he would have put it on again if I had asked him.[5]

This is a clear example of what anthropologist Julie Brown has termed "contested terrain," one that reveals the asymmetrical relationships embedded in photography when negotiations are absent (Brown 1994, xiii–xvi). The rudeness, sense of entitlement, disrespect for individual privacy, and then the photographer's rationalization of his paparazzilike behavior, are themes that echo today. The Native peoples' experiences must have been comparable to those of contemporary celebrities trying to avoid photographers. One difference, however, is that celebrities know they are famous for being famous and that their celebrity depends on being noted in the media. Another difference is that the Native participants had nowhere to flee, for their private sanctuaries were on display. Native expectations were also based on different cultural

Fig. 10.2. Cheyenne men standing next to the Indian School, including three identified as: Richard A. Harris (*second from left*), Bull Bear (*third from left*), and Bushy Head (*second from right*). Note fairgoers gazing out a window in the Indian Building. Photograph by Charles Carpenter. © The Field Museum, negative no. CSA15398.

ideals of privacy and propriety, hence the necessity for avoidance tactics and sharp language in the face of unremitting impoliteness. Many men spent their days policing their compounds, often confiscating cameras.

The press labeled this common phenomenon "intrusive rubbering," presumably from the term *rubbernecking* (gaping in every direction), and "the tortures of photography" (figs. 10.2, 10.3). "Rubbering" also referred to the assumption that everything at the exposition was public, available to anyone with a camera. And many people had cameras including the more than 750 professional photographers accredited by the Department of Exploitation.[6] Except for the Tehuelches, most men and women put up with being photographic subjects for a short time but all quickly grew tired of the interminable intrusions. It became the most discussed problem in LPEC records. Every two or three weeks there was a newspaper article in which McGee, Jenks, or Mc-

THE RUBBER NECK IS THE CURSE OF CIVILIZATION,
Says the Patagonian Giant

Fig. 10.3. "Rubbernecking" cartoon by Chopin for the *St. Louis Post-Dispatch*, September 1, 1904. McGee Papers, box 32, newspaper scrapbook, Library of Congress.

Cowan set forth proper rules for "politely inspecting" the human exhibitors so that their rights would not be violated. While a problem for everyone, the foreign participants were the most vocal in their complaints. The Ainus continuously protested that visitors were peering through their windows even though they had said that they had agreed to interact only with visitors outside their home. Their interpreter spent much of his time guarding the building and corralling insistent visitors who expected an exception to be made for them. Some compounds originally did not have gated fences but these soon were erected everywhere as a means of crowd control. But even fences were not enough. Destroying cameras thrust into their faces became one of the Tehuelche leader's main occupations. Geronimo's male relatives helped ensure that anyone who took a photograph paid for the privilege or their cameras were confiscated. Irate visitors called on the Jefferson Guard to arrest the Apaches and retrieve their cameras.

Signs went up all over the Department of Anthropology and the Philippine Reservation that the LPEC would not be responsible for broken cameras. These reminders seemed to have done little good, for Native peoples constantly had to assert their rights, as the following incident relates.

> *A visitor with a camera visited the Wichita grass lodge yesterday, and, by promise of a reward, succeeded in getting two little Wichita boys to pose for him. After taking the picture, the visitor started off without fulfilling his promises. The Wichita boys were plucky and made a grab for the man's coat tail. To this they valiantly clung in spite of all the visitor's efforts to get away and it finally became a matter of either paying up, or seeing the Fair with a fringe of Wichita boys attached to the rear of his coat. The boys' mother and a friend of the visitor finally came to the rescue, and the boys received damages.*[7]

On July 5, following a particularly obnoxious Fourth of July crowd, McGee forbade all cameras in the Anthropology Villages. People had to apply for permits, pay a small fee, ask permission of the participants, and pay them. If photographers refused to obey these rules, McGee said he would not issue any permits. Requests for permits began to arrive on July 6 and continued until December. One typical applicant wrote of his "desire to take some Kodak pictures of the Indians and other species of the Genus Homo, and I believe that a special permit is required to do this, that is, [in order] to avoid a fight." And fights there now were because photographers assumed that a permit gave them permission to do whatever they wanted, including taking souvenirs or photographs with no opposition.

After visiting the Pike, visitors expected Natives to respond to their stares with the blank, unseeing stare of the seasoned professional performers. Photographers were often disconcerted and offended when their activities were met with looks of resentment or hostility. Exposition security forces tended to accede to visitors' wishes since they had not been told formally of the policy changes. On July 7 a man took a picture of the Cocopas without paying them the fifty cents that a clearly posted sign requested. Interpreter Annie Flynn confiscated the camera and handed it to Thomas Moore. The irate individual went for help. A Jefferson Guard took the camera from Moore and said he would "arrest the whole of the Indians if [they] didn't look out, and said that visitors could take pictures any time they wanted to." The Cocopas stood their ground and turned their backs. McGee supported Flynn and Moore. Similar incidents occurred during the next two weeks until McGee and the Jefferson Guard commander worked out procedures.[8]

The Mbutis often complained about American presumptions. "Latuna said that the people did nothing but lean on the fence and ask questions, which they could not understand. 'When a white man comes to our country,' complained Latuna, 'we give them presents, sometimes of sheep, goats or birds, and divide our elephant meat with them. The Americans treat us as they do our pet monkey. They laugh at us and poke their umbrellas into our faces. They do the same to our monkey.'" The Mbutis may have been bothered more by the crowds than other groups. McGee relates a number of tales in his final report about overly attentive visitors.[9]

Earning Money from Visitors

There were probably times when the demonstrators never wanted to see another tourist again, but they had to interact with them if their sojourns were to be economically profitable. As noted previously, one of the ways that Native peoples earned money was by the sale of their arts and crafts, and certainly the opportunity to find a ready market was one of the motivations for attending for some people. But before the fair opened, selling art was problematic and McGee spent many hours arguing with LPEC officials on behalf of Native artisans so they could gain individual control over sales transactions. The problem seems to have been that this practice technically violated exposition rules—sales were only to occur on the Pike or the small industries or manufacturing departments through registered concessionaires, who paid an exhibition fee and a percentage of gross sales to the LPEC. Thus, Indian artists in Pike concessions and those in retailer booths had established outlets, but not the artists in the Anthropology Department. Concessionaires and retailers objected to McGee's plans, seeing individual artisans as direct competition. Since McGee had (theoretically) eliminated compensation in the form of wages or honoraria for participants in order to stretch his budget, he had to have the individualized sales to retain participants. Native men and women were not willing to stay if it meant additional economic hardship.

McGee argued strenuously that groups would not come if they could not sell their products and that this was a necessary exhibit component that showed levels of technological achievement, analogs for mental development.

In addition, "visitors will obtain as souvenirs or as specimens for scientific study objects of Indian handiwork produced by native methods under their own inspection." Natives controlling their own entrepreneurship should not be taxed. McGee's argument was eventually effective, and the LPEC Executive Committee approved their one exception to the rule, as long as the pieces were minor and the sales amounts small. Large purchases had to go through a retailer. McGee also had this rule extended to the Philippine Reservation.[10]

Native peoples produced and sold blankets and woven belts, pottery vases, cooking baskets, silver and copper jewelry, moccasins, medicine bags, and articles of dressed animal skin, feathered and beaded objects, bow, arrow, and quiver sets, stone arrowheads, and fire drills. People made money, even when McCowan kept a percentage from those working in the Indian School, actually in violation of McGee's rules. It was an area of constant contention between the two men. McCowan considered the one-, five-, and ten-cent "tax" as payment for maintenance of the Indian booths. McGee lost that round, since McCowan's staff controlled the money.

Being a successful artist and entrepreneur had invisible costs for which demonstrators were not paid. Visitors purchased interactions with the artists as much as the art itself. Indian Service agents tried instructing visitors to make these interactions "more meaningful," and in the process sometimes created negative stereotypes about "blanket" Indians to make the contrasts with students clearer. E. Mattox, who was assigned to facilitate the Lakotas' stay, explained to one reporter: "The Indian is vain. He likes attention. He delights in compliments like an actress. If you show him a little attention, you make a hit with him. The attention they attract at the fair pleases them clear down into their moccasins. The Indian weaver or pottery maker is proud of his art and you can't please him more than by praising it." Despite (or because of) such instructions, even the most respected Native demonstrators had to put up with inane comments. The *Indian School Journal* repeatedly asked visitors to treat artists with respect: "White people are often made to feel ashamed of their own race on observing the rudeness with which apparently sane and educated visitors sometimes treat the Indian, whom we are supposed to be trying to civilize, the absurd questions asked, the impolite remarks made, and the prying curiosity shown." McCowan remembered that one day a lady approached Mrs. Benson "saying, 'Would you like to feel my hair?' Mrs. Benson looked surprised and politely declined the honor. 'Well then,' said the visitor, 'Let me see your hair,' taking a lock of Mrs. Benson's hair and rubbing it up and down. 'Why, it isn't so very coarse, is it? Really not much coarser than mine!'"[11]

On other occasions visitors acted as if artists were invisible or stupid. In August the teachers watched as Ojibwa elder Ah-yah-sha-wah-she-quah was busily engaged in weaving delicately colored beads into a belt with her usual exquisite workmanship. Silently she worked while curious onlookers crowded around the booth, leaning over the rail to admire her belt.

> *A stylishly attired [but heavily made-up] young woman, remarked to her companion: "I wish she could talk English. I want to ask her why she paints her face." The consternation of this fair interlocutor is more easily imagined than described when Ah-yah-sha-wah-she-quah promptly replied: "Maybe for the same reason that you paint yours." The audience smiled.*[12]

Not all encounters were hostile, intentionally rude, or inconsiderate; many visitors were respectful and the interactions brought pleasure to everyone. One day three blind and deaf children visiting the Indian School tried to converse through sign language. One young man was so eager to meet an Indian "that his little hands fairly trembled as they fluttered rapidly over everything within his reach. Lone Star, the Sioux Indian, kindly stooped down and let him pass his quick fingers over his face and the feather in his hair, to the great delight of the child."[13] People wanted to talk with the indigenous demonstrators, and not just when they were on public display. Participants received numerous invitations to visit St. Louis residents in private settings and many did, but only after McCowan or McGee agreed to the visit and obtained reentry passes, of which they had only a limited number. These were often welcome events for they meant a change in routine and there are no reports of any negative consequences—only good will. Jenks allowed even fewer requests for the Negritos, Igorots or Moros but allowed the Visayans to visit often.

Relieving Boredom and Enjoying the Fair

Being a living exhibit on public display was routinized and unexpected, exciting and tedious. Boredom and monotony were major problems, although special agents and newspaper reporters liked to say that the Native demonstrators were happy and only occasionally homesick. McGee acknowledged, however, that one of his greatest difficulties was "keeping alive the spirit and interest of the primitives under (to them) the deadly dull monotony of Exposition existence" (McGee 1905d, 90).[14] To prevent apathy, staff was instructed to provide guided outings both within and outside the fairgrounds, several times a week. There are few records of official outings except for those reported by the press or mentioned in visitors' diaries.

Reporters often put fanciful interpretations on cross-cultural encounters, making Natives, generally the Filipinos, the butt of a cultural joke about "primitives." In other cases LPEC publicists used these opportunities to comment on how advanced America's indigenous peoples were compared to the Igorots or the Negritos. Typical commentaries included reference to dehumanizing ethnocentric stereotypes like male laziness, gender-specific work habits, nakedness, or eating preferences. Still, the outings provided Natives with opportunities to see how the other half of the world lived, to gaze at and scrutinize Americans.

Outings were somewhat varied. Indians often went to see movies, a new phenomenon in 1904, while others liked to go to the Delmar horse races. Some liked participating in special celebrations such as Transportation Day, Children's Day, and Manufacturing Day. Native children played "universal games" with other children in the model city exhibit's playground in the Education Department. Adults often accompanied Indian students on their educational outings and Indian Service personnel welcomed them because of their supposed acculturative value. Individuals had favorite pastimes; for example, Blue Horse regularly rode on the Ferris wheel. A few of these free-time activities are important because they highlight jurisdictional issues at the fair. One Saturday evening in August, Special Agent Cane took the Tehuelche men to experience St. Louis's nightlife. When a heavy rainstorm hit after several hours, they returned to the exposition to change their clothes and secure their tents. But Cane had forgotten their readmission passes and they were turned away, even though Cane insisted that the guard knew who they were since he had seen them leave. The guard was under orders not to let anyone without a pass enter. An argument and shoving match ensued and Cane and the Tehuelches were incarcerated at the police station. McGee was called from his bed, wrote new passes, and went to the jail to secure their release at 2:00 a.m. Mc-

Gee spent many days placating Cane (who filed an official protest with Skiff) and the Tehuelches while trying to keep the incident out of police reports and the newspapers.[15] He was apparently successful but upset about this and many other instances of guards humiliating Natives. It was not how he had envisioned cross-cultural encounters.

Most encounters were pleasant and even greatly anticipated as weekly events, especially the Sunday outings following Reverend Scott Charges Alone's church services. McGee noted that each group had its preferences. The Mbutis walked in a nearby forest; the Ainus went to church in town; the Tehuelches and most Indians visited Cummins's Wild West Show on Saturday afternoons. Natives working on the Pike visited other groups before and after their work day or joined them outside the exposition grounds. Everyone liked to stroll and watch Americans just as the latter liked to watch them. By mid-August these walkabouts were so common that the LPEC Executive Committee had grown weary of the publicity stemming from the off-site St. Louis excursions and questioned why local merchants should reap the benefit of the Natives' money. They felt that the profits should go to exposition merchants and the LPE corporation. Skiff ordered McGee to confine all Natives to the fairgrounds. McGee responded that allowing individuals and families to travel outside helped to "maintain their health and spirits" and that releasing them from the "confinement within the grounds on Sundays" provided an effective form of recreation. He went with different groups whenever possible and often took them to the race track and on boat rides on the Missouri River. He reminded Skiff repeatedly that Native peoples were "here not as prisoners but as participants in the Fair, either as citizens or subjects of foreign nations or wards of our own government." Finally he emphasized the trips' promotional value: "Even when they travel on streetcars, they may be used for purposes of publicity; this publicity is not only inevitable but is one of the most effective means of promoting the interests of the Exposition that has come to my knowledge." Skiff was never swayed by McGee's logic and repeatedly told him to confine the Native peoples to the grounds. McGee ignored him, earning reprimands. He never wavered in his belief that a change in scenery and amusement was beneficial. Skiff told McGee to obtain his permission before issuing exit permits. McGee again politely refused. To say that Skiff was displeased with McGee would be an understatement. McGee came perilously

Fig. 10.4. Navajos visit the Igorot Village on a Sunday outing. Photograph by the Gerhard sisters. Library of Congress, Prints and Photographs Division, LC-USZ62–80332.

close to losing his job in July over his determination to ensure that Natives not be treated as captive animals but as human beings who needed and deserved freedom and respect. McGee won that battle.[16]

Participants devised their own leisure activities. After work each evening there was much informal visiting (fig. 10.4). Wichita children commonly sat with their mothers while the men wandered around the Pike or visited acquaintances. The Pawnees gathered around their fire to tell stories; people from other compounds came to listen. The Pimas, Maricopas, and Cocopas visited each other. The Puebloans, Kwakiutls, and Nootkas formed strong friendships conversing "together in beautiful English," singing, and dancing.[17] Conversely, the Natives in the Philippine Reservation were restricted. The gates were locked each night and they were not allowed to visit people in the Anthropology Villages except on supervised outings.

Friendships were formed, often based on mutual humor. The Mbutis were said to keep the Dakotas regularly doubled up with laughter by parodying visitors and McGee. They were not the only group to satirize those with "strange" customs. Cocopa boys regularly attended practices to make fun of the Indian School band. "This morning, one of the boys, baton in hand, his long hair streaming out behind with every movement of his head and a broad grin on his face, accurately imitated every motion of Mr. Nelson, the band leader, to the great amusement of his companions."[18]

While women supposedly did less visiting and touring than the men, they also developed friendships that helped alleviate the isolation and loneliness. The Ainu and Tehuelche women often visited and conversed about their clothing and pet dogs, at least according to one reporter's view of what women would naturally discuss. "The tall woman sat down on a small bank so she might finger the embroidered short skirt of the Ainu woman and as she examined it with the air of a woman who had worn skirts all her life instead of scant girdles, she emitted grunts of satisfaction. From head to foot they looked each other over, the Ainu woman finding much of curiosity in the rough emergency clothing of the tall woman who had left her home ill prepared for the cold winds of a St. Louis April and the tastes of American people."[19]

Language barriers were no problems for the younger Cocopas and Tehuelches. They communicated in Spanish and spent a good deal of time teaching each other archery, bola throwing, and lassoing techniques. These informal lessons were held every few days in the morning, until the crowds became too large, forcing them to stop. Men often went to Benham's sutlery, which quickly became a gathering place for Indians, Mbutis, Tehuelches, and Euro-American visitors who wanted to see and interact with them or buy fine art. Under the direction of Benham and E. J. Bush, the sutlery had a highly attractive exhibit, since art works from their trading posts lined the walls. Brisk business was done daily.[20]

Demonstrators regularly exchanged gifts and traded art. Trade and gifting also occurred on official and semiofficial outings. Big Horn, a Crow leader with the Wild West show, attempted to trade some of his wife's beadwork for beads made by Sibucao, a Visayan, but the trade was apparently unsuccessful, an uncommon occurrence. In fact, Native demonstrators interacted so extensively that they created "unexpected problems" for McGee and his assistants, who were trying to maintain the illusion of timeless cultural distinctiveness. Native people began wearing each others' clothing, thereby rendering their cultural purity suspect, at least according to McGee. Even worse from his standpoint were the manufactured goods Natives purchased on their outings. "Professor McGee has made desperate efforts to protect them from the influences of each other and the civilized people by whom they are surrounded. . . . Some are gone all day" (Curtis 1904a). There were times when all encampments were empty. Often the Osages hired whites to watch their property so they could attend some event. They shrugged their shoulders when McGee complained. McCowan had no sympathy; he said he had warned McGee that the Osages were independent.

Inevitably, people returned with baby carriages, cigars, hats, reading glasses, and even new typewriters that a Choctaw entrepreneur was selling in the Manufacturing Building. To McGee such purchases were disastrous for the department's reputation since he had billed it as the last place to see *real* Indians and "primitive" peoples. American goods meant acculturation, indications that the LPE had served its purpose and had educated Natives or shown them the material advantages of American culture. But the symbolic markers of evolutionary progress were not welcome—they came too soon. McGee had reason to worry; reporters were noticing the changes. "The Indian is being civilized, or, at any rate, weaned from the wigwam, the 'blanket,' the war paint, the headgear, the moccasin and the bow and arrow of his ancestors. [At the LPE], he wears store shoes and cloths, lives in a house, and lives on 'canned goods.'" The fair, while celebrating old ways, was aiding in their inevitable demise. Some visitors told Natives to stop mimicking civilized peoples, while simultaneously giving them manufactured goods as gifts. McCowan refused to allow American goods in the artists' booths, confiscating hundreds of items. The dichotomy between adults and school children had to be maintained; alterations "would result in destroying the real sense and appearance of the exhibit."[21] McCowan and McGee's missions were paramount. The inevitability of real-life interaction and cultural borrowing were not part of their plans. The irony was that McGee missed an opportunity to study cross-cultural interaction and borrowing that would have advanced cultural anthropology theory.

Living in a restricted space with minimal privacy inescapably led to friction. The *World's Fair Bulletin* noted that the arrival of each new group created problems and rivalries, reporting that when the Mbutis arrived some Dakotas became "jealous."

Until the arrival of these little black men, the Indians were one of the chief attractions. Each tribe exerted every effort to make their camp the most attractive. The braves could be seen each morning comparing their records of attendance, which they keep by cutting notches in a stick, or depositing a bead in a bowl. Since the Pygmy camp has been established, the Indians have been somewhat neglected and the Pygmies are holding the center of the stage. This morning, Chief Yellow Hair, Hollow Horn Deer, Long Grand, and Cut Finger, arrayed in all their finery, stationed themselves near the Pygmy camp, and tried to induce visitors to ignore them. In conversation with some of the visitors, Yellow Hair made the statement that the intruders "were no good, hair too short, not much clothes." He would point with pride to himself and companions, then to their tepees, and beckon visitors to leave and visit them.[22]

According to another report, these initial concerns over visitor share (and resultant tips) lessened as people came to know each other. The Mbutis, to show their friendship for the Dakotas, "went over to the Sioux camp and gave a farewell concert and dance. Some of the Sioux braves were greatly pleased with the exhibition of friendship, and joined in the dance. Mrs. Yellow Hair was rather unappreciative, and demonstrated her disapproval by throwing a pail of water on one of the musicians, who interpreting the act as [a request for] an encore, renewed the concert with increased vigor."[23]

Administrative Quandaries, or Who's Really in Charge Here?

Simply living on the exposition grounds posed many problems for Native participants. For example, McCowan complained to Skiff when one of the Jefferson Guards (the LPE's police force) brutally assaulted a Mbuti in the Indian School in mid-July. McCowan insisted the man be fired in lieu of leveling criminal charges, and he was.[24] Anticipating such incidents McGee and McCowan had hired special agents and chaperones to assist Native people. On a less dramatic and dangerous scale, Natives' lives were constrained by the rhythms of the daily openings and closings. Except for the South Africans working in the Boer War concession, who quietly disappeared into the city, the majority of foreign Natives remained for the duration of their contracts.

Some individuals and Filipino groups were sent home and some Indian groups left when LPEC and Indian Service actions and policies made life unbearable.

While McGee expected that the Native groups would interact cordially with each other and cope with the visitors, there were still problems that the LPEC expected him to solve, including ensuring general welfare. McGee saw this as both a weighty moral and personal duty as well as a necessary policing function. He was more worried about visitors bothering Natives than ensuring that participants be passive. McGee also wanted LPEC policies and actions to be consistent with national, state, country, and municipal laws. He tried to respect foreign governmental statutes and also the laws, customs, and traditions of each culture. He insisted on each group's right of self-determination. McCowan, on the other hand, was more concerned with enforcing discipline using only Indian Service standards. Pomo artists William and Mary Benson left early "because of what they conceived as constant ill-treatment on the part of Superintendent McCowan, in which view I am compelled to coincide." McGee told Skiff that the Bensons were protected by rights accorded them under the Treaty of Guadalupe Hildago; this meant that they were not Indian wards under Indian Service control. But McCowan ignored this distinction and demanded they work only in a booth in the Indian School (where he could also impose his sales tax), an arrangement they had not agreed to and disliked because it was confining. McGee informed McCowan that the Bensons were under his direct charge and could work in their compound, but McCowan ignored him. After Benson's further complaints, McGee informed McCowan that the Jefferson Guards would protect them from any further contact with McCowan. McGee arranged for the two guards to stand on each side of the Bensons' booth. As the situation escalated, the Bensons decided it was better to leave.[25]

According to McGee, the premature departure of the Bensons was not the only negative effect of McCowan's authoritarianism. He complained to Skiff in July that, "[t]he Sioux chief, Yellow Hair, with his party are going tomorrow; the Arapaho group are already gone; the Kickapoo bark house is empty; the great Pawnee earth lodge is practically vacant; the Wichita grass house is empty; of all of the picturesque United States Indians on the Ethnologic Grounds six weeks ago hardly a quarter remain. . . . The chief cause of dissatisfaction and withdrawal in each case has been real or fancied ill-treatment by

Superintendent McCowan."[26] The departures of the Reverend Scott Charges Alone, Chief Yellow Hair, and the Lakotas was apparently the result of Mc-Cowan's refusal to allow them to institute what he called a "dancing school" or to use the parade ground for powwows with Wild West show friends.

Minimizing drinking was a major concern for both McGee and McCowan. In his final report McGee noted that the Tehuelches' special agent had overcome "grave difficulties" managing "the robust savages (arising especially when liquor was furnished them surreptitiously) through an admirable combination of tact and vigor." While occasional drunkenness and rowdiness arose on Saturday nights, only a few cases of alcoholism were reported. McCowan sent one Arapaho family and several unidentified single men home "because of repeated drunkenness. . . . They resisted my order for them to leave, and at first declared they would fight if not allowed to remain." But he hastened to assure Indian Commissioner Jones that this was an isolated incident. "Our Indians are more contented than I ever imagined they would be; they are in nearly every case, making money; there is no sickness in the camps and everything in connection with our exhibit is running as smoothly, as harmoniously and as successfully as I would wish."[27]

But not everything was running smoothly. There were problems compounded by McCowan and McGee passing the buck whenever they could and their constant fights for power and control. The situation derived from their ambitious personalities and from structural ambiguities and disputes over who was in charge of the Indian and Anthropology Villages. Each man wanted sole control. Theoretically McGee was to care for foreign groups, Mc-Cowan all Native Americans. There had been extensive discussion about these responsibilities starting with a September 1903 letter to Skiff in which McGee forcefully stated that McCowan, as his departmental assistant chief, had "definite and complete" authority only over Indians who were indisputably wards of the federal government.[28] In reality each stepped on the other's toes at every opportunity.

To ensure people's welfare, McGee and McCowan needed help, since participants spoke more than thirty mutually unintelligible languages and the scope of the entire undertaking was so ambitious. LPEC or Indian Service agents oversaw each group or compound, facilitating transportation to and from the fair, helping build the houses, seeing to daily needs and safety, and trying to ensure that people were not bothered by visitors. While this system worked fairly well for the foreign Natives, it was a failure for the American Indian parties. At times some contingents had no agents while others had three or four people, all claiming absolute authority. The situation resulted from McCowan's practice of assigning his Indian Service friends based on their vacation schedules. Each new agent had to learn the ropes. As a result there were constant disputes over responsibilities, with the Indians bearing the brunt of the confusion.[29]

Before the fair began, McGee and McCowan had decided to appoint one individual to oversee all agents and encampments. It was an important position with oversight for personnel, health, safety and discipline, crowd control, and food procurement and distribution in a timely manner. According to McCowan, the individual also had to make the fiscal allotment last as long as possible. Theoretically this individual would free McCowan to look after the Indian School and McGee to install some static, badly needed exhibits. But it never worked out. On April 19, McGee chose Charles Armstrong of Iowa as custodian and head of the guards detailed to protect Native peoples. Armstrong, a student at Iowa State College and a captain of his college's militia organization, was hired to please Senator William Allison, and at first McGee thought him capable. However, Armstrong had no prior experience or knowledge of people from other cultures. After only two weeks McGee reassigned him to protect static exhibits in Cupples Hall.[30]

McGee next chose W. H. O'Brien, Denver's former chief of police, and they developed a policing plan. McGee felt their goal was to maintain harmonious relations while respecting peoples' rights. To accomplish this he proposed a complicated scheme based on ward status, treaty, and legal considerations.[31] Native peoples were thus both constrained and protected by a complex set of regulations that were impossible to enforce.

Newspapers noticed the overly complex policing regulations and they became notorious. The *St. Louis Post-Dispatch* labeled McGee the "Overlord of the Savage World" since he brought so many exotic peoples to town and treated them like children. The *St. Louis Chronicle* made a similar point: "A feature at the Indian reservation is the fact that the lads and lassies are being forced to adopt the custom of their white brothers and sisters of having chaperones. To many who are familiar with the delightful Hiawatha, and the charming maid of Juanita fame, and other maids of Indian fiction, the idea of providing a chaperone for the supposed wild and free redskin youth seems incongruous."[32]

McGee, McCowan, and O'Brien quickly came to a parting of the ways over the chaperones' duties. O'Brien received contradictory orders from McCowan and McGee and was often in a quandary over whom to obey, although he generally heeded McCowan and tried to follow the restrictive Indian Service policies, feeling they were more appropriate for maintaining control. He basically ignored McGee's elaborate scheme and treated every Native the same, claiming authority over their every movement. Adults in every group complained. O'Brien and McGee disagreed vocally and in public. McGee insisted O'Brien's primary duty was to protect "the primitives against injudicious visitors" while O'Brien thought he should rigidly control the camps and ensure that "the primitives" were always on display. He tried to force Natives to comply with visitors' requests, regardless of their appropriateness. More complaints poured in: O'Brien was treating them poorly, refusing to give them enough food or types they had been promised. (O'Brien withheld food from "offenders.") McGee came to feel that O'Brien was incompetent and created more problems than he solved. O'Brien resigned at the end of May without giving notice. There was no supervision or crowd control for several weeks. The men in each encampment and the special agents took over.[33]

McGee and McCowan continued to fight about duties and appropriations and to disagree about new issues, such as McGee's impromptu plan to place Indian artists around the fairgrounds as walking advertisements for the archaeology exhibits, which had very low attendance. McCowan was interested only in the success of the Indian School and cared little for the Native peoples who were not directly involved, especially those he had not chosen. Late in June a brief detente was called after a series of articles in the *St. Louis-Globe Democrat* severely criticized the manner in which Indians were being treated. Francis and Skiff indicated their displeasure over the negative publicity. McCowan insisted that at least two members from each tribe work in the Indian School under his direct supervision but conceded that others could work in their encampments or other places unsupervised. McCowan insisted that Skiff reimburse the Indian Service for transportation and subsistence for anyone not working in the school. He agreed that the foreign Natives (including the

Cocopas, Kwakiutls, and Nootkas) would each have a special agent but that the care of the Indians would be assigned to one prominent man who would be called "ethnologist-in-charge" (McGee's term) and all would report to Mc-Cowan.[34] McGee agreed, until he discovered McCowan's choice.

McCowan reassigned Robert D. Shutt, who had overseen construction of the Indian School building and was McCowan's administrative assistant at Chilocco. He was transferred temporarily from the Indian School Corps to supervise both the foreign and Indian peoples. McGee was not pleased, feeling Shutt knew nothing about ethnology, was a manual laborer, and loyal only to McCowan. McGee felt his opinion was upheld when Shutt refused to acknowledge his directives. Shutt also insisted that rules laid down for Indian School students be followed without question by all adults, including curfews and regimented common meals. Shutt resigned after a week and was permanently transferred to a new position as industrial teacher at a school in Tulalip, Washington, but stayed on a few days to make repairs to the building. McCowan told McGee the problem was now his and refused to provide food or any services for the upkeep of any Native peoples. Again there was no one in charge. Several groups had insufficient food.

As the department opened, McGee turned to Dorsey who was completing his assignment to oversee construction of the Indian dwellings. But Dorsey did not trust McGee, and knew enough not to get caught between him and McCowan. He suggested James Mooney, of the Bureau of American Ethnology (BAE), who was highly respected in Indian country and whom Dorsey thought could soothe the frayed nerves. Mooney must have agreed to consider the idea, if for no other reason than to be nearer his cherished Kiowa field site or as a way to extend his Smithsonian duties in St. Louis, which involved erecting a static display on Kiowa heraldry.

Tough bargaining went on for a month with Dorsey caught in the middle because of what he called McGee's secretiveness and fundamental disagreements with McCowan. The main problem was salary. In late June, Dorsey wrote Holmes, now head of the BAE: "I finally got WJ to show his hand, and I think we know just how much money he has. . . . We prepared a document yesterday in McCowan's office, which was signed by McCowan, Mooney, McGee, and myself. This is specific and definite and will bear Mr. Skiff's signature and approval." Dorsey beseeched Holmes to give Mooney a leave of absence to help them. "In the name of Heaven, grant it, for the Indians are in a pitiable state, and without Mooney, it means an absolute wreck up there on the hill. I do not ask you to do this for McGee's sake or for the sake of the Exposition at large, but purely in the interests of humanity."[35]

Mooney had been involved in many expositions. He had helped organize the Indian Congress at the 1898 Omaha Exposition, so he was a logical choice for this assignment. When Mooney arrived in St. Louis on June 8 to install his Kiowa camp circle, he had been appalled at the living conditions and state of the grounds. The sewage system had never been properly installed nor the area graded so that after a rain it was a muddy swamp (more on that later). After touring the camp, Mooney recommended sending the Indians home as soon as possible. He wrote Holmes that the camps were "small, badly located, without trees, grass, running water, or any provisions for sanitation." Indians were leaving daily because they were dissatisfied. It was a "thoroughly bad business." Indians agreed; half left by June 20.[36]

Mooney decided he wanted no part of the mess and asked Holmes to refuse to grant him a leave of absence. Mooney did not trust McGee; they had clashed when McGee was running the BAE. Holmes replied he would leave the decision to Mooney. Mooney wrote back that he did not want to be stuck working for six months managing a "glorified medicine show." He feared that the poor reputation of the Indian exhibit would damage his reputation, and that of the BAE, in Indian country. He was also not sure that McGee or McCowan would really pay his salary once he was transferred. Mooney told McGee of his decision but agreed to help improve some of the camp conditions before he departed for Oklahoma. It seems that McGee misunderstood (accidentally or intentionally) for he took the offer of assistance as an agreement to manage both the Anthropology Villages and Indian Village. After Mooney fixed the drainage in some camps he returned to his exhibit. When McGee realized Mooney was going to do nothing else, he rehired Shutt, who agreed to stay for two weeks as a favor to McCowan while they sought a permanent administrator.[37]

Never one to give up, McGee tried to pressure Mooney. He met with Skiff and Mooney at the end of June and once again "invited" Mooney to be reassigned from July to November, offering to double his current salary. McGee wrote to Holmes on July 1 arguing that "it is essential to the prestige of American Ethnology that the best possible ethnologic play be made on the Exposition grounds, despite the numerous curtailments of appropriations below the original estimates which you helped to make. In the second place, the only feasible way of putting and keeping the best face on Ethnology here is through the help of Mr. Mooney."[38] Astonishingly, McGee further argued that Mooney would have better opportunities for ethnographic fieldwork in St. Louis than he would in Oklahoma. His arguments did not impress Mooney, who had little reason to save McGee's face. Holmes said Mooney could have a leave of absence if he wished; Mooney declined and left St. Louis on July 15 to resume his research in Oklahoma.

Dorsey was increasingly concerned about the Indian Village and disillusioned with McGee. He returned to St. Louis. As he later related to Holmes, he felt that McGee was unhappy with Mooney for even mentioning the encampment problems, "for I believe he realizes that he has made a miserable failure of the business and that any credit which might come out of it at this late day would accrue to Mooney."[39] Dorsey felt some responsibility but decided he would not shoulder the responsibilities himself. With the blessing (and probably orders) of his boss, Skiff, who was tired of the increasingly negative publicity, Dorsey detailed his assistant curator, Stephen Simms, to McGee on July 19.

Simms had been at the Field Museum since 1897 or 1898. He had worked in the northeast among the Iroquois and in 1901 undertaken a trip to the Southwest to collect materials among the Pima, Maricopa, and River Yuman communities. In 1902 he had visited the Crows in Montana and the Crees, Assiniboines, and Ojibwas in Canada. He had no formal anthropological training, which is one reason why he remained an assistant curator until 1912. But he was related to a Field Museum founder and he eventually became the institution's director. Now he was assigned duties that he did not want to perform in a place he did not want to be. The job was a special concession to McGee by Skiff; the Field Museum paid Simms's salary. Simms's title was ethnologist-in-charge; he remained with the exposition until it closed, much to his regret.[40]

Trying to Care for Participants

Simms's job was damage control. He had little say in planning and constantly wrote Dorsey or Skiff begging to let him return to Chicago. He was told to keep the Indians from leaving and to make their lives better. He found that McCowan refused to increase food supplies and that more Indians were refusing to work in the Indian School as a result. No food, no demonstrations. When Skiff convinced Simms that he would be in St. Louis until December (or he could look for another job), Simms actively tried to avert disasters and was called the "trouble man." At the end of July, McGee happily informed Dorsey, "Simms is doing admirably what Mooney at last thought it impracticable to do. The Indians are beginning to feel better; and while Simms is of the opinion that it may be better to let all those now on the grounds go home [and] begin again on a better basis, he may decide to keep several."[41]

There were still significant problems, however; participants continued to be more dissatisfied than McGee chose to acknowledge. Simms tried to address their needs and complaints, sometimes successfully, sometimes not. One area he worked on in vain was the road and pathway conditions from Arrowhead Lake to the Indian School. The slippery mud made ascending the hill treacherous. Indians complained daily about the deplorable conditions.

St. Louis had undertaken a massive program of upgrading its infrastructure for the exposition, and Forest Park required an infrastructure built from scratch, but work on the anthropology area was never completed. The general problems were addressed only after the other areas of the grounds were finished, which in many cases meant not at all or in a piecemeal manner. To make matters worse, the area west of Arrowhead Lake (classic Mississippi River bottomlands) had never been well drained when the River des Peres was rechanneled underground. As a result the area was unstable and visitors avoided it. In late June, an Indian Service staffer overheard visitors on a streetcar talking about going to the Indian School as soon as they arrived at the exposition. One fairgoer was heard to reply, "I'd like to, but we simply can't get to it for the mud." Dr. Edward Spitzka, a friend of McGee's, wrote in October: "My father and I were very much interested by our visit to the Hokkaido Ainus, despite the ankle-deep mud which surrounded their home on that rainy Saturday afternoon."[42] Many tourists recorded that mud was what they remembered most about their visits to the Anthropology Department. There were even theories that it was part of a grand LPEC conspiracy to force visitors to buy intramural railroad tickets.

Garbage and fecal waste made the situation even worse. The LPEC had a corps of janitors and scavengers whose duties were to care for and clean the roadways, paths, and aisles between the exhibit buildings, as well as the campgrounds. Exhibitors were responsible for the cleanliness of their own buildings and camps. While McCowan had a paid janitor for the Indian School and McGee one for Cupples Hall, there was no paid position for the indigenous camps, which meant some were cleaner than others. Native people were expected to remove their night slops and garbage to central collection locations. Several groups protested because to perform all these duties, as well as to pick up the significant amounts of litter produced by visitors, had not been part of their contracts. McGee and McCowan had clearly stipulated to everyone that these services would be provided, but they never were, in an attempt to cut costs. Nor did the promised separate toilet facilities and bathhouses ever materialize. Participants had to use the public toilets; fortunately these were well cared for but were not close by. Fair officials had granted a concession to a company to handle the toilets and had the Sanitary Department ensure that they remained in good condition; they were cleaned daily with fumigants and disinfectants. But it smelled. No covered sewage system was ever installed despite McGee's almost daily written protests. LPEC directors decided that to install one would disrupt the proceedings too much. Unfortunately some visitors interpreted this to mean that Native peoples were dirty and smelly.

Finally there was the lack of a water system. Fair visitors could purchase filtered water from machines for one cent per glass, while unfiltered water was free and much more accessible, although on opening day there was a "scarcity of drinking water which almost amounted to a famine."[43] The Native camps had only unfiltered water, and McCowan and McGee's budget did not include any funds for filtered water. The situation was ripe for the spread of disease.

Major Thomas Underwood Raymond, formerly chief surgeon for the U.S. Expeditionary Forces in the Philippines, directed the Sanitary Department. The department practiced what was essentially preventive medicine and public health initiatives. Raymond daily tested the water supply, reviewed the disposal of garbage, waste, and sewage, checked for contamination of food and drinks offered for sale (including the meat in the sutlery), tested the sanitary maintenance of toilets and lavatories and reported his findings to Francis. Raymond was also in charge of inspecting the military camps, Indian and foreign Native camps, Wild West show encampment, Indian School, and the Pike concessions. He tried to exercise "vigilance to prevent any contagious or infectious disease from gaining a foothold on the grounds." Thomas W.

Raynard, an Army physician, was responsible for Native encampments. He inspected the Indian Village on August 10 and reported to Francis that there was some improvement from his previous inspection but his picture of the mud and filth was still grim (Bennitt 1905, 737).

The weather did not help. The year 1904 was at first extremely cold and rainy, then hot and rainy. Newspapers frequently commented on how the Natives coped:

> If any one remembered about the tent dwellers out on the Indian reservation during the late windy rain, it was to feel sorry for them and to expect to hear they had been left shelterless or blown with their tepees off the hill, but Monday's sunlight found them unconcernedly going about their work. The little boys sailed bark boats in a puddle and made adobe bricks of the plentiful mud, while one, in the airy morning negligee of a green calico skirt, slid down a wet clay embankment on a barrel stave. It was washday, too, and some of the braves were doing the heavy work of minding the babies while the squaws chopped kindling or bent over the up-to-date washtubs and boards and scrubbed out the family wash.[44]

The Natives' resiliency and their ability to cope was not enough for other visitors who were vocal in their concerns and displeased with McGee. Natalie Curtis Burlin, a politically influential ethnomusicologist who lectured at the exposition, wrote to McGee after visiting the camps and reading articles in New York newspapers that discussed how the LPEC management was neglecting Native participants. She informed McGee that a number of prominent Boston citizens, including Charles Eliot Norton, Carl Schurz, Bishop Lawrence, Mrs. Charles Russell Lowell, and several medical doctors, had sent Francis a petition demanding that sanitation and other problems be addressed. She sent copies of Francis's inadequate response, as well as her own account of how the Ainu encampment turned into a swamp after even a gentle rainstorm, in order to call attention to the problems. McGee responded that weeds had been cleared, pits filled, rubbish collected, and some drains rerouted, in no small part because of her petition and the social status of the signatories.[45] Unhappily for the Native participants, Burlin took McGee's word that the most egregious problems had been rectified. They never were.

The overall health of the Native participants remained an important concern for McGee, McCowan, and Simms. Before the fair McGee had arranged with L. H. Laidley, the LPEC medical director, for maternity facilities for the inevitable births. Dr. Ehrenfest, who had evidently worked among indigenous peoples at some time in his career, was appointed to assist all indigenous women in their birthing. There were three or four births that apparently went well; no women are listed as having died in childbirth. But there were other major health issues stemming from contagious diseases, accidents, and the effects of inclement weather. At the end of the exposition, official LPEC publications blithely issued a piece of propaganda: "Not a case of contagious diseases of serious character was reported, not withstanding the residents came from the four quarters of the globe." This was clearly not true. There was smallpox, tuberculosis, cholera, and chicken pox. Several Natives died from illness and construction accidents; they were simply not put in the hospital and therefore there was no record. Official records for the hospital list twenty-three violent deaths, seventeen from disease, and twelve from natural causes among employees and visitors. In addition, fourteen thousand visitors were treated mainly for heat prostration, as were the parka-clad Inuit, during the summer.[46]

Sanitation problems, continued wetness, overcrowding, and so many people in close contact, could have and did foster disease. While LPEC records indicate that deaths from tuberculosis and smallpox on the grounds were low, reports for the City of St. Louis for 1904 and 1905 showed a significant increase in both diseases. In fact, smallpox almost closed the exposition when two construction workers and several Filipino workers became sick in May. A corps of physicians vaccinated everyone, including the Indian children and indigenous peoples and their escorts. Anyone who evidenced symptoms of disease was sent home or quarantined.

Some groups fared relatively well. The Philippine Scouts had a low daily sick call, despite an outbreak of chicken pox. Several students were sent home from the Indian School due to illness, following the LPE protocol to immediately isolate or eliminate infections. All recovered, except for the one young O'odham girl in the kindergarten class. By June, all the Ainus had contracted malaria and were placed in quarantine. Several Sioux adults did too, and they were immediately sent home, as were others as soon as any illness appeared. The most spectacular case was that of the Cocopas who were all immediately escorted back to Yuma in October when Mrs. Colorado became seriously ill (a tuberculosis relapse) so that one of their members would not perish on the fair grounds. She lived one month after reaching her home. McGee followed this protocol because he did not want to have to deal with State Department officials or accrue bad publicity.[47]

The individual who was sickest during the exposition ironically was McGee. He developed typhoid fever in the fall of 1903 and never completely recovered. Some of his administrative quandaries were as much a result of his recurring illness as his inability to solve problems in a timely manner and his scheming.[48] The departmental offerings that were most noticeably affected were the static exhibits, which were never as good as McGee wanted and never even remotely approached the quality of Putnam's department at the Chicago Exposition. But static exhibits there had to be, even though not memorable, for a holistic anthropology was not complete without archaeology and anthropometry.

11. In the Anthropology Building

*Impressions are so tabulated and arranged
as to afford a means of tracing with scientific accuracy the physical
as well as the intellectual development of mankind.*
William J McGee, 1904

After viewing the Anthropology Villages and the Indian School some visitors braved yet more mud and walked north past the Physical Education stadium and the Administration Building to Cupples Hall to see static displays "of the curious or more conventional products of [Native] peoples' hands and brains." There were over fifty thousand densely packed objects according to the official catalogue.[1] One of Skiff's LPE themes was that the past is the guide to the future. Major pavilions and subsidiary exhibit halls (like anthropology) were to demonstrate that civilization was advancing in a known, purposeful direction in their exhibits. Hundreds of thousands of objects, variously displayed, made the point. Skiff argued that the past as evidenced in archaeological remains provided the opportunity to teach visitors how to interpret the progress Americans had made, especially in technology. McGee illustrated this theme in the Anthropology Building but used recycled Smithsonian exhibits, called the synthetic series, as his corporation exhibits; he argued they were useful only to illustrate anthropological principles dealing with time, technological change, and how culture had developed in the prehistoric past. To McGee it was the living groups who brought the past into the living present.

McGee had originally wanted a holistic, seamless unity of message inside his Anthropology Building, one without categorical distinctions to "facilitate interpretation" and illustrate what he considered to be the most important generalization of the Science of Man: that "the various races and peoples advance along nearly parallel paths, so that the industries and ideas of living savages and barbarians represent fairly the industries and ideas prevailing among the prehistoric ancestors of more advanced peoples."[2] But the fair was not structured for intellectual authoritarianism and Skiff vetoed his fluidity and

Fig. 11.1a–b. *Destiny of the Red Man* by A. A. Weinman, front and side views. Photographs by D. W. C. Ward. Missouri Historical Society, St. Louis. Front view: Ward negative 523; WF 1078; side view: Ward negative 519; WF 0939.

the inclusion of a new category, the protohistoric. McGee had little control over most anthropology exhibits and the resulting rhetoric was confusing and contradictory, especially as it reflected on the role of Natives in the contemporary world—should they be celebrated for their heritage or denigrated as peoples who were to make way for civilization? This duality was especially reflected in evolutionary assumptions that it was imperative for Native people to progress toward civilization or perish. Traditional arts and lifeways were celebrated as "interesting, though primitive," or as "old ways" being shed for "new ways." If, however, Native people clung to the old ways, then tradition-

alism was denigrated as "holding them back" from the blessings of civilization. To nonanthropologists, Native peoples were making way for civilization around the world, and this assumption was reflected in the layout of the exposition grounds, where the glories of American and European technology and advancement centered on the Main Picture and the Native peoples and nature were pushed to the perimeter.

This conception as it applied to the Louisiana Purchase Territory was also made symbolically clear by major statues sited on the plazas in the Main Picture. *Sioux Chief* was Cyrus Dallin's "idealized chief . . . protesting against the advances of the Whites upon what he had considered his domain" (Bennitt 1905, 85, 171). The second was Adolph Weinman's powerful *Destiny of the Red Man*, with its robed and hooded Indian skeleton of death pointing Indian

Fig. 11.2. *A Step toward Civilization* by Solon Borglum. Missouri Historical Society, St. Louis, Negative 71, no. 31041.

people and the buffalo toward extinction. This message was heightened by a vulture perched menacingly on a totem pole (fig. 11.1). In contrast was Solon Borglum's *A Step toward Civilization* (fig. 11.2) with an Indian man clutching a book and pointing his son toward the "White man's way." On the ground were his stone tools, which he had cast away, and his wife, weeping for her son and her traditional lifeway. This duality was mirrored inside the Anthropology Building. The first floor contained celebratory archaeology and ethnology while the second contained history with an overall message of the vanished Red Man.

Busy elsewhere, lacking funds to purchase artifacts, uninterested, and unable to erect the exhibits until after the exposition opened because LPE administrators refused to vacate their offices, McGee paid little attention to the static exhibits. The synthetic series was actually installed by archaeologist Gerald Fowke. The series had four parts that illustrated humanity's progressive advancement by highlighting "the intimate connection between primitive artifacts and the highest products to which the Exposition was devoted." They showed a continuous, directional, evolutionary advancement in basic tools and argued that human thought evolved concurrently with manual dexterity, rational thought, and mental skills. The sections were Conquest of Fire, Development of the Knife, and the Evolution of the Wheel, supplemented by the Development of Smoking, the Indians' gift to humanity. The exhibits were densely packed and obtusely labeled with a heavy dose of McGee's anthropogenic rhetoric and convoluted theories. The moribund exhibits did not advance knowledge; at best they showed visitors some interesting artifacts. Even McGee thought them boring. He made no attempt to match Putnam's displays at the Chicago Exposition.[3]

The same can be said of most of the other exhibits in the Anthropology Building. As noted in chapter 3, McGee had little idea of what would be shown because of the frantic, often haphazard work of an ever changing mix of individuals and organizations, as well as the last minute addition of history, which required rearranging the entire building. Three late additions were to his liking: (1) the Fred Harvey Company's exhibits of Indian basketry arranged by Herman Schweitzer, John Huckel, and Dorsey, featuring Hupa and Pomo pieces and a Hopi collection arranged by Henry Voth, which made up in part for the lack of a Hopi presence; (2) the Wyman Brothers' display of pre-contact copper implements and historic materials from the Great Lakes region; and, (3) the Davenport Academy of Natural Science exhibit of purported tablets from the Old World, found in mounds in Iowa in the 1880s and declared fakes by Smithsonian scientists at the time. He was also saddled with two diplomatic and political exhibits for which he had to underwrite their enormous installation and armed guards costs, much to his displeasure. One was the Vatican's collection of mosaics that illustrated its patronage of the arts as well as illuminated manuscripts lent by Pope Pius XIII. The second was the Queen's Jubilee Collection, which contained thirty cases of King Edward VII's collection of the artistic spoils from Britain's colonial empire: carved ivory, wrought gold, unset gems, and set jewels. McGee assigned them to the history section as examples of the upward course of human achievement. Both were the most popular of the anthropology exhibits.[4]

Many individuals and organizations erected displays in the Anthropology Building. Three states within the Louisiana Purchase Territory (Louisiana, Missouri, and Ohio) submitted extensive archaeological exhibits. Both Starr and McGee felt that the Ohio exhibit (four rooms of models, maps, and artifacts on the region's mound-building peoples), designed by William C. Mills, curator of the Ohio State Archaeological Society, illustrated the most advanced pre-contact cultures in the region. They were less impressed with the Louisiana exhibits, which consisted of rows of unidentified pre-contact objects without any organizing theory. McGee felt that the Missouri Historical Society exhibits only celebrated American expansion and Euro-American heroes, even though he tried to make history into an extension of archaeology to pull the building's disparate contents together. His feelings about the other historical exhibits were the same.[5]

These were not the only archaeological (or ethnographic) artifacts in museum display cases around the fair. Thousands of pieces were in more central buildings, labeled as treasures, relics, heirlooms, scientific specimens, commodities, potential commodities, souvenirs, curiosities, and wonders. Many were isolated artifacts tucked into larger tableaux designed to convey the exhibitor's wealth and nationalistic progress. Rickshaws could be seen in the Transportation Building, native Egyptian looms in the Forestry, Fish, and Game Palace, rare four-thousand-year-old Chinese coins in the Commerce Building, while indigenous art was for sale in the Small Industries and Manufacturing buildings. It was here that several prominent Indian art retailers fought for souvenir dollars. Benham's Indian Hill concession in the Manufacturing Building stressed Indian art in the modern American home. There too was the Wetherill Brothers' Mercantile Company, Benham's chief rival, who employed a dozen Navajo demonstrators from Chaco Canyon to try to improve their business. There was also Mrs. Ella Ongman, a gold miner who had traveled to the Arctic Circle and returned with Inuit, Aleut, Haida and Northern Athabascan art for sale and compelling life-and-death adventure tales to entertain visitors.[6]

At least sixteen foreign governments displayed indigenous artifacts. McGee was especially impressed with Siam, Belgium's Natural History Museum, China, New Zealand National Museum's Maori exhibit, the East Indian Pavilion, and the Ceylon Tea House. In the Palace of Agriculture he found the German East-African, Siamese, and Japan's Formosa displays very educational. Some countries, such as Brazil, Argentina, and Egypt, placed their treasures (thousands of objects usually presented without label copy) in the Anthropology Building. For McGee these scattered displays demonstrated the transition from barbarian to civilization and from civilization to enlightened civilization. For collectors and American museums they provided opportunities to acquire specimens that resulted in a feeding frenzy and intense competition from July until the end of the fair.

The largest and most popular static anthropological displays were in the Government Building, designed to illustrate the federal government's work with Indians. The Indian Service's display in the Department of the Interior section conveyed a message consistent with that in the Indian School. The Commissioner wanted a strong contrast to the Smithsonian Institution exhibit, which he felt presented an unrealistic picture glorifying traditional ways and undermining government policies. The Indian Service exhibit contained the standard materials and exercises designed to illustrate progress. Its most noteworthy features were four oil paintings by Angel de Cora (Hinook-Mahiwi-Kilinaka), a Ho-Chunk woman who became one of the foremost artists of her time, and a moving picture and stereopticon program of Navajo and Hopi Indians shot in 1903.[7]

The Smithsonian Institution's two anthropology exhibits from the U.S. National Museum and Bureau of American Ethnology, designed by Holmes, were impressive, despite the problems that went with their erection. They

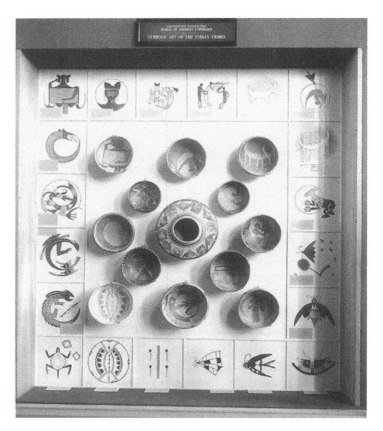

Fig. 11.3. Comparative ceramic design exhibit. Zuni and Hopi pottery exhibit designed by Jesse Walter Fewkes and Matilda Coxe Stevenson, Bureau of American Ethnology. Photograph by Walter Hough. Courtesy of the Smithsonian Institution Archives, RU 95, box 62B, f. 13, image no. 2005-34774.

were intended to demonstrate that anthropologists were "saving" traditional Indian heritage by collecting and displaying valuable objects, keeping them from being taken to foreign lands. The exhibits focused on Mesoamerican and North American Indian art united by an overarching theme of mythological symbolism. Unlike McGee's exhibits they were not sweepingly evolutionary although there were "comparisons" between developments in Europe and the Americas. Holmes wanted to show how artistic the American Indians were, "filled with the impulse to model, to carve, to paint, to weave, and

Fig. 11.4. Gov. John G. Brady stands in front of Haida totem poles, mortuary columns from Kaigani, and Haida house with Haida house panels at Alaska exhibit. Tongass Tlingit house in background on right. Photographer unknown. Library of Congress, Prints and Photographs Division, LC-USZ62-10548, HCP 3C05486.

to construct works of taste and beauty" (fig. 11.3).[8] His centerpiece consisted of several large, meticulously researched and ornately decorated scale models illustrating what Holmes considered the American Indian's highest artistic achievement—Mesoamerican monumental architecture. These were supplemented by long, instructive labels that provided visitors with information on cultural and historic contexts. Interspersed were casts of colossal, freestanding sculpture (stelae) and statues from Mexican and Central American museums (fig. 11.5). Holmes also showed smaller masterpieces of pottery, carving, baskets and sculpture in the BAE exhibits stressing regional and cultural variability, especially the stylistic climaxes in each region.

Fig. 11.5. Models of Mesoamerican temple and stelae, U.S. National Museum exhibit designed by William H. Holmes. Photograph by Walter Hough. Courtesy of the Smithsonian Institution Archives, RU 95, box 62B, f. 12, image no. 2005-34773.

There was little ethnographic material in the state pavilions—a few "Indian" symbols (Missouri had a giant statue depicting an Indian woman made of corn shucks), Euro-American sculpture depicting the vanishing (or vanished) Indian, and an occasional projectile point. However, there were some exceptions. New Mexico had an Indian beadwork display, and Geronimo's daughter Lena, who was employed by the El Paso and Northeastern Railroad to distribute literature for a resort; Idaho exhibited a private collection of Southwestern baskets, textiles, and pottery; Indian Territory featured art produced by "honest, industrious and thriving people" to show that Indians were ready for statehood; and, Alaska, which had two Haida houses and fifteen Tongass Tlingit totem poles, as well as Haida mortuary columns (fig. 11.4), and an entire floor of Governor John Brady's Inuit, Athabascan, and Aleut art collection.[9] McGee found this exhibit impressive, probably because he had been consulted during the planning stages and it conformed to his overall scheme.

He conceptualized it as an extension of the Indian Village and it was located nearby rather than on the distant Plateau of States.

There were, in short, tens of thousands of objects from around the world shown in what Starr called "collections of dead material" and over which McGee had no control for their didactic content.[10] However, unlike earlier fairs where Native villages from colonies supplemented displays, in St. Louis McGee felt that museum-case exhibits complemented the exhibits of living peoples. This was a major conceptual shift in museological emphasis and marked an advance in anthropological techniques to disseminate knowledge. But it meant that the LPE displays in the Anthropology Building were decidedly boring to almost everyone. The vitality of the Philippine Reservation, Native Villages, and the Pike had much greater appeal. With the exception of Queen Victoria's jewelry, most people ignored McGee's exhibits and their messages. For anthropology, the action was in the basement, and it was the scientific experiments people remembered.

In the Basement: Actively Measuring Racial Difference

McGee asserted that fairgoers were part of his grand anthropological experiment. The millions of men, women, and children supplemented the racial groups on display and provided raw observational and comparative data for scientists. McGee thought visitors would like to actively participate in anthropological activities after they had viewed the static models and relics. In short, visitors could be research subjects in the anthropometry and psychometry laboratories housed in the Cupples Hall basement. In addition to having a memorable experience and helping advance scientific knowledge, they would understand better how pure and applied science operated. They would see how individuals functioned as organisms and how the physiology, minds, and anatomies of white people had advanced over other races. Scientifically obtained information about themselves would help visitors understand anthropogeny and the course of human development—as McGee conceived of them.

To McGee the laboratories, built in cooperation with universities and manufacturers of scientific equipment, were focal points for basic scientific research. "It was there that the original or investigative work of the Exposition culminated and the conduct of the work . . . forms a substantial contribution to knowledge." The contribution was to "determine and decode the physical and intellectual characteristics of the assembled race-types and culture-types assembled on the Exposition grounds."[11]

A key aspect of science in the eighteenth and nineteenth centuries was increasingly precise measurements and the use of mathematics to describe data and formulate hypotheses. The more specific the measures and the more mathematical formulae used, the more "exact" or "scientific" the field of inquiry. As modern scientific disciplines emerged after 1850, they came to be ranked according to their degree of "exactness." In the twentieth century this ranking was expressed in degrees of "hardness" or "softness." No one doubted that astronomy, physics, chemistry, biology, and geology were exact, or hard, sciences. All other fields of inquiry, economics, political science, sociology, psychology, ethnology, and later anthropology, became "soft" sciences.

Hopes for a "Science of Man" began in the 1720s. From the outset, the key issue was the measurement of human differences and the meanings assigned to them. "Race" was the central factor in an age of imperialism, colonialism, and slavery. The questions were: (1) Are "races" physically, psychologically, socially, and culturally commensurable? and (2) How might likeness or variations be measured scientifically? The real issues dealt with apologies for, and campaigns against, slavery, the subjugation of colonial and indigenous populations, and the socio-political structures of the recently freed Spanish colonies in the Americas.[12]

In the 1770s, German anatomist Johann Friedrich Blumenbach developed the science of craniometry, the idea that a metrically defined skull form was a certain indicator of race. His "racial" classifications of humanity greatly influenced the development of both ethnology and physical anthropology during the nineteenth century. Philadelphia physician George Morton in the 1840s popularized craniometry in the United States. He argued that cranial capacity (the total number of cubic centimeters of brain volume) was a "true index" of relative intelligence; the higher the capacity, the higher the intelligence. This contention became a research issue throughout the nineteenth century.

Soon measurements were being extended to the rest of the human body. Measuring the heads and bodies of living people was collectively called anthropometry. The Belgian astronomer and mathematician Adolphe Quetelet (1796–1874), in his 1835 *Treatise on Man and the Development of His Faculties*, advanced the concept of the statistically defined "average man." In later works he argued that certain statistically defined "types" of humans had a propensity for crime or other anti-social behaviors or attributes. As it developed in Europe and America after about 1848, a central supposition of ethnology was that each human "race" had an *innate* set of physical, psychological, and possibly social and moral characteristics. Anthropometric data, manipulated by Quetelet's and others' statistical tools, seemed to be the perfect means to "scientifically" define races, if the data sets demonstrated that races could be placed in rank order. For example, if "whites" on average, had more cranial capacity than "blacks" on average, the assumption was that whites were higher on the evolutionary scale than blacks. By the 1850s whole armies were being measured to test the idea; hundreds of thousands of Union soldiers were subjected to anthropometric measurements during the Civil War. Sheaves of data were accumulated throughout the nineteenth century when whole populations of indigenous peoples were measured and statistically categorized. But despite the mathematical tools, anthropometry was never an exact science. At best it was a pseudo-science masquerading as the real thing. Anthropometry came to be used to define "races," criminality, and personality types (e.g., a woman with certain average anthropometric measurements would be a "good wife"), and to predict that certain individuals would be great artists or geniuses. Statistical tools became the methodological cornerstones of criminology, psychology, sociology, anatomy, physiology, and anthropology.

By the 1870s it was evident to some that all the measuring was spurious. Many anthropologists noted the methodological problems, especially the fact that the strict racial evolutionary typologies obscured cultural differences. There was also the age-old question of nature versus nurture: How much of human form, psychology, and behavior is innate and how much is environmentally determined or conditioned? The question would increasingly become central to American anthropology in the twentieth century. The societal issues, of course, still had to do with justifications for, and campaigns against, the subjugation of colonial populations, questions as to whether indigenous peoples were ready for self-government, and issues of social class. Anthropometrics came to be used to "scientifically" validate, or occasionally invalidate, these moral and political issues cast in racialist terms.

In 1904 McGee, mired in the assumptions of the older "scientific" anthropology, still regarded anthropometric data as valid, as true scientific indicators of race, although he recognized several problems. He felt that experiments, guided by superior research designs and undertaken in his laboratories at the exposition, would eliminate past methodological errors. The racial comparisons between Natives and Euro-Americans would be valid because, he argued, all the individuals tested would be "average" representatives of their groups, thereby ensuring consistency, and the numbers would be large, thereby lending reliability to the conclusions.[13] The argument was, of course, spurious, but no one seems to have noticed, least of all McGee.

And the public loved it, even in its less credible forms, such as the "sciences" of phrenology (determining personality by reading bumps on the head) and physiognomy (determining personality from facial features). The popular press was enamored of both. In the *Woman's Magazine* section of the *St. Louis Post-Dispatch* in January 1904 a special article described how a man could recognize the personality of his potential wife by the shape of her nose: "A single glance at the bridge of a dainty aquiline or the tip of a tiny pug nose [can] warn a man against a lifetime of domestic squabbles."[14] McGee hoped the anthropometry and psychometry labs would help the public distinguish real science from such chicanery as nose analysis.

Designing the Laboratories

If McGee cared little for the static archaeology and ethnology exhibits, he had very strong ideas about what he wanted the laboratories to do: first, make customary anthropometric measurements; second, develop new tests for strength, delicacy of touch, intelligence, coordination, and endurance to assess "the relative physical value of the different races of people." To develop the anthropometry and psychometry laboratories, McGee conferred with three prominent individuals. The first was Franz Boas. Boas, who had organized an anthropometry department at the 1893 Chicago World's Fair, taught courses in statistics, general physical anthropology, and morphology at Columbia University. The second was James McKeen Cattell, head of the Department of Psychology at Columbia University. The third was Aleš Hrdlička, a dogmatic MD and young physical anthropologist recently hired by the U.S. National Museum (USNM) who felt that American society did not understand or appreciate the "public utility" of physical anthropology and that an exposition was an excellent venue to make his case.[15]

McGee initially hoped that Boas and Cattell would supervise the two labs and worked hard for several months to convince them. Boas did submit a plan in September 1903 and recounted his positive experiences in Chicago, especially what visitors liked. He provided McGee with a list of scientific apparatus manufacturers to contact and identified the most productive experiments. When McGee admitted to Boas and Cattell that he could only allot $1,250 for each section, not enough to cover their salaries for eight months, both declined.

McGee next turned to Hrdlička, who developed a plan by which the U.S. National Museum would utilize the proposed laboratory space for several months. Hrdlička's plans were based on his desire for a new physical anthropology exhibit at the USNM, a laboratory to demonstrate the newest techniques, and a formal exhibit to display the brain's evolution and racial variation in bodily features. The LPEC anthropometric labs would have three research rooms, one each for measuring, photography, and casting. Another would be outfitted for "popular anthropometry." The USNM would be responsible for furnishing and operating the research spaces, while the LPEC would support the popular anthropometry section. Hrdlička would conduct experiments on Natives in April, May, and September; an assistant would measure visitors at other times, while a second produced casts continuously. The LPEC and the Smithsonian would jointly bear the expenses.[16]

Hrdlička wanted this public venue because physical anthropology had no place in the Holmes-designed Smithsonian exhibits at the LPE. Hrdlička had hoped for a paid LPE position, but by late February his prospects had dimmed. Otis T. Mason, the head of the USNM Anthropology Department, told McGee that he had attempted to convince Smithsonian Assistant Secretary Richard Rathbun to detail Hrdlička to St. Louis, but there was no congressional authority to establish laboratories outside the U.S. Government Building. Nor were there sufficient government funds for an independent laboratory, research expenses, or Hrdlička's salary. Holmes declined to use his money for the project, since it was extremely limited and already over obligated. Mason had no extra departmental funds either. To bring the futility of the matter home to McGee, Mason informed him that McGee's final government paycheck for his 1903 salary would not be forthcoming, due to lack of funds. Hrdlička and McGee then tried a new approach, making an end run around

Holmes. On March 1 they met with Boas, Cattell, and Robert Woodworth at Columbia University to discuss the situation. As a result of this meeting, Hrdlička asked Mason to write to Frederick True, who was in charge of the Smithsonian LPE appropriation, for permission to conduct experiments in the Department of Anthropology laboratory. Mason did so. After consulting the government board, True set aside fifteen hundred dollars from the anthropology allotment without informing Holmes.[17]

Hrdlička set to work and announced his plans at a meeting of the American Association for the Advancement of Science (AAAS), without telling Holmes. He related his priorities for the scientific experiments to first test specific ethnic groups: (1) American Indians (adults and children); (2) Negritos, Ainus, and Filipinos; (3) Caucasians, including athletes, scientists, and intellectuals visiting the fair; and, (4) general visitors. Hrdlička also developed a scheme for the Native peoples to become scientific specimens in death as well. As he suggested to McGee,

> [i]t must be expected that some individuals of the assembled ethnic material will succumb to the climate and from other causes. These bodies will be a precious material for both anatomy and anthropology. If a physician can be employed for assistance in the laboratory, he could also be charged with looking after such subjects. . . . As to the bodies that may be obtained, the soft parts, except the brain, will be utilized by the Medical Department of the Columbia University, New York, while the brain and skeleton will be deposited in the U.S. National Museum.[18]

Like the skeletons, other data would become a permanent scientific record in the USNM. Copies would be placed in other museums upon request. Hrdlička would publish the results of all investigations.

Holmes was furious and refused to authorize Hrdlička's reassignment. He also had a showdown with True and stopped work on the Smithsonian exhibits until True rescinded his order. True finally did so, although the work stoppage resulted in the government anthropology exhibits being late and ultimately never finished. Holmes had fifteen hundred dollars back in his budget. The LPEC anthropometry lab reverted to its small appropriation, although McGee transferred some funds from the ethnology static exhibits, effectively eliminating those exhibits. McGee informed Hrdlička that he was returning to Boas's original plan, and he blamed Holmes.

As Hrdlička was unable to run the laboratory, McGee searched for young scientists who would see the fair as a career opportunity, as Boas had in 1893. On Boas and Cattell's advice, he hired Robert Sessions Woodworth of Columbia University as the superintendent of psychometry and anthropometry. Woodworth had received his doctorate under Cattell in 1899 and studied with Boas, from whom he learned anthropometry and statistical methods; he was convinced that anthropology was important to any psychologist. He had just become an assistant professor in Columbia University's Psychology Laboratory after finishing postdoctoral studies in England. While officially on the fair payroll on April 1, 1904, because McGee was yet again trying to save money, Woodworth had actually begun making preparations in January. He was paid an honorarium of twelve hundred dollars to cover his salary, living, and incidental expenses while in St. Louis.

Woodworth, an expert in psychometry with some experience in anthropometry, was interested in muscular motor control, mind-body relationships, physiology, and quantitative experiments. He consulted Boas, Cattell, and Joseph Jastrow, a prominent University of Wisconsin psychologist, who had conducted psychological tests at the 1893 Chicago exposition, about the proper tests to be used. After corresponding with W. H. R. Rivers of Cambridge University, he decided to use the same measures Rivers was using on Torres Strait Native peoples. Woodworth spent several weeks measuring New York City immigrants to ensure that the procedures would work, for the key to this type of experimentation was proper and consistent measurements.[19]

Woodworth was assisted by Frank G. Bruner, his doctoral student who hoped to use the psychometry data for a dissertation. Bruner ran the anthropometry lab while Woodworth supervised psychometry, although both worked together and often exchanged places. The work required a great deal of specialized equipment for which the department had no funds. They contacted American and foreign manufacturers of testing apparatus and obtained equipment loans, with the condition that the manufacturers' names be prominently displayed. Anthropologists and psychologists at Clark and Columbia universities also lent devices designed specifically to test nonliterate peoples. In less than three weeks, Bruner brought the equipment from New York, installed electrical lines, got the laboratories set up and ready, and installed several static displays. He had everything ready when Woodworth arrived on opening day.[20]

The basement laboratories were quiet and conducive to serious research without crowds bustling past. The locale was not easy to reach, so McGee did not anticipate that casual visitors would be attracted to them. But the labs were well covered by the press and McGee noted in his final report that they were visited "by the intelligent public in considerable numbers, the actually-interested visitors averaging 1,000 or more daily" (McGee 1905d, 79).[21]

The two scientists began to administer their first tests on May 6 and opened the rooms to the public on May 16. In the first month, visitors watched as they took a complete series of measurements on one hundred individuals to test the equipment. From then until the closing of the fair, people were measured and tested daily. Each subject was given a copy of the results as a souvenir of the experience and shown how to compare them to a preconceived racial chart. Volunteers were always plentiful and Woodworth and Bruner quickly accumulated data on the two hundred middle-class white adults they wanted as a baseline for comparisons to other races and ethnic groups. After this they intended to measure Native demonstrators but word had spread about the labs and they had to concentrate on visitors. In order to free up time as well as provide an entertaining and informative visitor experience, Woodworth made available simple and unbreakable instruments (scales, spirometers, and height measurers) for visitors to use themselves. They also devised instruction sheets and coding forms so visitors could measure each other. They did not, of course, include such information in their data bases to ensure that inconsistencies did not creep into their measurements. But it did provide them with time to begin to measure the Natives.

Visitors interested in Native peoples came to watch the experiments. Woodworth and Bruner began with those Native people directly under the McGee's control. The first two groups, the Cocopas and the Kwakiutls, were completed by July 20. The press reported, "After a series of mysterious experiments it was found that the Cocopa exceeds in strength and the Alaskan in intelligence." Next nearly all the students in the Indian School were measured, followed by the adult Indians. Many individuals refused to be measured; very few Cheyennes or Chippewas agreed. But coercion helped raise the final tally. Woodworth and Bruner reported that, "[o]ur success in obtaining good sets of measurements from these peoples was largely due to the co-operation of the gentlemen who had them in charge" (Woodworth 1905, 195).

After completing their work with Indians, Woodworth and Bruner turned to the Philippine Reservation. They consulted with the headmen in each village; only the Visayan villagers refused. People were tested in their villages rather than in the laboratory, which necessitated using special equipment. To weigh individuals, Woodworth brought a Tiermann dynamometer and people swung from the spring scale attached to a tree branch. This attracted quite large crowds. In addition, Majors Haskell and Johnson gave permission for the two Filipino military groups, the Constabulary and the Scouts, to be tested and nearly every man was measured. In November the scientists turned their attention to the Pike but had time to test only the Inuits, Puebloans, Singhalese, and the few black Africans left in the Boer War concession. Overall Woodworth and Bruner measured eleven hundred individuals and placed them in twenty-two ethnic groups and eight races (Woodworth 1932, 373).[22]

The Laboratory Tests

People were measured each day between 10:00 a.m. and 4:00 p.m. To begin, Bruner obtained basic data: name, sex, age, skin color, weight, hair (color, quality, abundance), height (standing and sitting), and eye color. Next came the anthropometry measurements: arm spread, stature, girth, head form (length, breadth, height, distance between the inner eye angles), facial angles (width and length), nasal angles (width and length), eye attitude (placement and shape), chest (expansion, breadth, depth), body and limb girth, and relative lengths of limbs to the body. They also included measures of how "well" the body worked: pulse and respiration rates, lung capacity, strength tests, and digital and joint movements (rapid hand movements, motor control).

Some techniques were fairly simple. To measure height the subject stood on the floor barefoot, heels together, and a vertical measuring rod touched heels and the head. Other tests required more specialized equipment. To measure chest breadth a Narragansett shoulder caliper was used to record the distance between the nipples during extremes of exhaling and inhaling, the two numbers averaged to form a mean. Most of the tests were fairly benign but some people refused to be poked or prodded or slightly shocked to see how much pain they could withstand.

All these tests, especially those for racial comparisons, purportedly required the elimination of researcher subjectivity and observational bias. To this end, Woodworth and Bruner frequently asked visitors to return a second day or measured the same individual again, to ensure consistency. As an additional check, they had Hrdlička and a member of the Sectional Award Jury (see chapter 13) repeat some of their measurements. As a third precaution they photographed many individuals and used a standardized racial chart for typologies.[23]

After being photographed, the subjects proceeded to the psychometry lab where intelligence and the senses were tested. By 1904 experimental psychology was well established in American universities and was concerned with how culture affected the physical and mental system, especially in body movement, agility, and coordination. All tests were proxies for mental power, sensitivity, and intelligence because the body was viewed as being under the control of the brain and nervous system. The leaders in the field had all studied in Germany with the founder of experimental psychology, Wilhelm Wundt (1832–1920), also a major German anthropologist. His students included G. Stanley Hall, president of Clark University, who theorized that societies recapitulated evolutionary stages in their play, Cattell, and Edward Titchener, of Cornell University. These individuals, their peers, and students were busily devising and trying out dozens of tests for intelligence, motor reactions, and acuity of the senses. The LPE labs added a few more to the list (McGee 1904a, 8).

Measurements included hearing (high decibels, acuity-loudness, pitch discrimination), sight (acuity, refraction, defects, astigmatism, color blindness, color matching, faint color recognition), touch or sense reaction (sensitivity, pain recognition), and sensorimotor reactions (the form and expression of features). Intelligence was measured through reactions to optical illusions. In addition, body movements and actions were tested to determine individual and collective agility and coordination. The goal was to ascertain quantitatively "the effects of civilized and enlightened life on the physical system."[24]

Special attention was given to color recognition because it was thought possible to "determine the relative prevalence of sense defects in the different races and culture stages, and thus to ascertain the effects of civilized and enlightened life on the physical system" (Bruner 1908, 1). The invalid reasoning behind the test is obvious, but was thought to be valid at the time, for psychologists had not yet realized that variation within groups was greater than variation between groups. Woodworth also wanted to answer the question whether dark-skinned or primitive races are different from white or advanced races in their recognition of the color blue. He devised elaborate tests, but they all failed to reveal racial differences. The problem, of course, was not physical, but linguistic. Later color-term research clearly demonstrated that all humans with normal vision recognize the full visible spectrum of colors. What differ are the specific color terms, which vary from one language to another. The problem was not "racial" differences in color recognition, but linguistic labeling of segments of the visible light spectrum. When his test failed to provide consistent results, Woodworth devised another to detect noticeable racial differences in which subjects were asked which colors they liked or disliked. Each was asked to select what he or she liked best from 125 pieces of colored Holmgren wool (used for the color blindness test). It is unclear what results were achieved or how they might have been interpreted, because Woodworth never published them.

Hearing acuity tests were designed to determine both individual and racial variations by measuring the ability to discriminate sounds. The hearing tests were the special interest of Bruner, who later (1908) published a monograph on his experiments, concluding that racial differences existed, with whites possessing a heightened sense of hearing. Other tests included the optical illusions and geometric blocks so beloved of experimental psychologists, then as now, and measurements by devices designed to record sensitivity to temperature and delicacy of touch and taste. There were also tests to assess reaction time to stimuli, sensorimotor reactions, and hand-eye coordination. Some of these tests seem bizarre today; for example, accuracy of movement was ascertained by a blindfolded subject trying to point a stick at a target. To measure rapidity of hand movement, Bruner had participants hold a stylus connected to an Edison battery and a brass plate. Each time the research subject touched the brass plate a bell rang. Bruner recorded how long it took the individual to ring the bell one hundred times. Such tests were thought to measure the power of coordination as expressed in the rapidity and accuracy of forming judgments.

The final tests measured intelligence and memory, at least in theory. Woodworth found that the most useful of these were "form tests"—early versions of the timed placing-pegs-in-holes tests inflicted on children and college freshmen for decades. Subjects were given the test three times to see if their speed improved; this was considered a test for whether people had the ability to learn. There was also a test involving a door with a concealed combination lock, which the subject had to figure out how to open. The test was obviously (in hindsight) culturally specific, and so it is not surprising to learn that Native peoples, who had no experience with combination locks and spoke no English, did more poorly than middle-class whites. The last intelligence test involved a marble maze, a device similar to popular puzzles of the day. A marble was inserted in one end of a maze and the subject was timed as he or she worked the marble through the maze by moving the board without touching the marble. The maze was covered for a second trial so that Bruner and Woodworth could see how insightful a subject was. Again, it was no surprise that Natives did less well on these tests than English-speaking Caucasians, especially when there were no interpreters to instruct them in how to proceed.[25]

Other Scientists Using the Laboratory

In keeping with the theme of the exposition as a research university, McGee opened the laboratories to physicians and scientists, but they had to prove their professional legitimacy first. A local podiatrist from St. Louis, Dr. Philip Hofmann, and his wife, investigated the shape and activity characteristics of feet, comparing people who wore shoes with those who wore sandals or went barefoot. While there was a racial component, the focus was on what shoes did to feet and what natural feet (that is, feet that had never been shod) were like. The objectives of the study were to: (1) gather general observations on the shape, functions, range of motion, and relative length of the foot; (2) study the height and shape of the longitudinal arch; and, (3) determine if a relationship existed between the arch height and a person's gait, reflecting straightness or eversion.

The Hofmanns measured 186 individuals, including the Mbutis and many Filipinos. They also made prints on smoked paper as a record of the weight-bearing areas of the foot, and two plaster of Paris casts, one in repose and the other bearing the body's weight. People were also photographed climbing and grasping with the feet, standing, and walking. Their report resonates with everyone who finds fashionable shoes constricting or painful.

The lasts over which the footwear of civilization is shaped are rarely modeled in that spirit of truth, which would make them conform to the contour of a normal foot. The whim of society and the manufacturers' enterprise alone regulate their shape. Society, apparently, agrees that the human foot as formed by Nature is coarse, vulgar and unsightly, and that its width, especially at the toes, is entirely too great. It regards the small, and especially the narrow foot, as the beautiful one, and the dictum of fashion has greater influence than reason. Perhaps, the statement that society admires the small foot is not exactly true; for society, as such, never sees the naked foot, but what it so commonly does admire is the dainty little show that hides its own handiwork—the distorted, cramped, calloused and repulsive foot. Here beauty is less than skin deep. The manufacturer finding it to his financial interest to fit the desires of his patrons rather than their feet, places upon the market footwear that more or less crowds the front of the foot.[26]

The Hofmanns noted that deformity was greater for women than men. Such abuse was evident in all shoe wearers, but most pronounced with the Chinese and their practice of foot-binding elite women. Hofmann used his study to demonstrate civilization's problems and the plasticity of the human body in all races. Race was irrelevant and not a causal variable.

Several other scientists were interested in anatomy. Dr. E. H. Bradford of Boston made casts of the Ainus' feet for his orthopedic surgery training program. Like the Hofmanns, Bradford was particularly interested in having casts of the feet of people who did not wear shoes, to determine natural shapes. Dr. Robert J. Terry investigated racial variations of the papillary markings of hands and feet, while Dr. Hugo Ehrenfest researched pelvic and parturitional characteristics. Dr. Edward A. Spitzka measured the Ainus as part of a long-term study of Japanese crania.[27]

Art also met science in the labs; sculpture and photography provided critical supplementary data to the experiments. Caspar Mayer, of the American Museum of Natural History, made an extensive series of ethnic life casts at the suggestion of Franz Boas. Mayer was quite adept at cast making and was willing to make casts of Natives at ten dollars apiece (which included making the mold, preparing it for shipment, and three photographs of each research subject). His laboratory was quite popular with visitors who stood and watched the delicate processes for hours; many paid his fifty-dollar fee to have their own hand-painted busts made. More than fifty busts and several complete life casts of Native peoples were produced and exhibited during the exposition, then sent for display to the American Museum of Natural History and the Field Columbian Museum. Copies of the busts from individuals in the Philippine Village also went to the national museum in Manila and the Commercial Museum in Philadelphia at the request of the Bureau of Insular Affairs. Mayer spent two weeks camping with the Wild West show and making plaster casts of famous Indians, which he sold for fifty dollars each. After the exposition, his museum sold the molds to Ward's Scientific Establishment, the major American supplier of specimens and furniture for museum exhibits.[28]

Photographic head portraits, from the front and side, and full body shots were considered critical physical anthropological data that could tell much about racial body types. Dorsey had the Field Museum's photographer, Charles Carpenter, take more than three thousand ethnological photographs and portraits of American Indians, including students at the Indian School, people from the Philippines, and many from Asia and Africa. Carpenter also took photographs of habitations and people producing art to document these activities. But there had been so many requests from so many people, as noted in the last chapter, that many participants refused to let Carpenter take pictures when they learned others had not received the prints they had been promised. Some were very vocal about their refusal, saying that all white men were liars. McGee was upset about this and insisted that Dorsey fulfill his obligations. In September Dorsey sent Simms and Newcombe two copies of each photograph taken by Carpenter. One was given to the subject and the other to Samuel McCowan for a documentary record. In exchange for the photograph Newcombe was to obtain information on the person, the name of the tribe, the mixture of blood, and age.[29]

Other individuals interested in race wanted to use the labs or the Natives for their own projects but McGee turned them down. J. H. Stover, a lawyer from Milwaukee, suggested to McGee that a registry book be placed in the Indian School and the laboratories so that visitors could write down their names, tribal ancestry, and the number of generations they were removed from their "pure" Indian heritage. Stover, who said he had ⅟₃₂ Delaware blood, had found tracing his Indian heritage a fascinating pastime and felt that the visitors would find it interesting to record their heritage as well. He argued that the record would provide interesting "statistics" for scientists. McGee disagreed, stating that the information would be too haphazard to be of use and would provide no training for people on how to trace their ancestry. Samuel Cherry, who was developing a new science of "otyognomy" or the language of the ear, thought he could determine personality and character based on the size, shape, texture, convolutions, and position of the external ear. He proposed to test fair visitors and Natives, for a small fee. His normal fee was five dollars per person, but for a place in the anthropometry lab he offered a discount. McGee and Woodworth declined the offer.[30]

Finally, institutions whose faculties were interested in somatology sent static displays to adorn the laboratory walls. Bryn Mawr College apparently produced a noteworthy exhibit that awards judge Alice Fletcher said "showed so marked a comprehension of the value of this line of study and its observations, and the results in this branch of science were so clearly and well presented, as to receive a special award" (Fletcher 1906). Unfortunately, we have not discovered what the exhibit documented.

Hrdlička: Collecting Skulls, Brains, and Cadavers

Given the number of people living on the fairgrounds and the state of medicine in 1904 it was inevitable that several Natives died in St. Louis, as noted in the last chapter. While American Natives could be readily sent home when disease struck, for foreign participants, being whisked away was not an option. The scanty information shows that several Filipinos had smallpox when they arrived and were quarantined in San Francisco or upon reaching St. Louis; several also died on board ship. As a precaution, anyone from the Philippines was immediately vaccinated by the LPE medical staff. During the fair there were forty-five officially recorded cases of beriberi in the Igorot group, resulting in three deaths. Medical personnel were not familiar with the disease and did not know how to treat it; they suggested that the entire Igorot contingent be sent back to Manila without delay. Dr. Hunt, who oversaw the Igorot encampment, concluded that the problem was due to dietary deficiencies rather than a communicable bacterium. Their diet was changed and everyone improved. Pneumonia killed several people in May and July. There were eight other deaths, but since the individuals died in the Filipino rather than the LPE hospital, they were not counted in official LPEC statistics. In general, the spotty records list different names and numbers of deceased individuals.[31]

In 1904 there were no repatriation or burial laws to protect Native peoples and human remains. Whenever a death occurred, Hrdlička saw an opportunity to increase the physical anthropology and anatomical reference collections of the Smithsonian Institution. He especially wanted brains, which he hoped to study to understand ontogeny, morphology, and phylogeny of this "most vital organ." By July he had over two hundred specimens. He was particularly interested in the relative effect of preservation of brains to prevent shrinkage and distortion and found St. Louis an excellent location to try out techniques that included measuring the skull cavity. As he wrote to Mason, "At St. Louis I was able to make two autopsies on deceased Igorrotes, and secured the brains. One of these is perfect and very valuable. At the same time, with the aid of Doctor Horwitz, of the Filipino hospital, I secured the brain of a female Moro. Both the physicians of the Filipinos, as well as their other superiors, have given their promise to secure for us brains of any of the natives who may die in the future." In most cases the brains were cremated before the remains were shipped to the Philippines for burial.[32]

Hrdlička also secured other specimens. He had learned that colored indigent men and women who died in St. Louis were interred at public expense. The city hospital's director and the city pathologist gave him brains and skeletons. Hrdlička also made replicas of exhibited prehistoric materials as well as casts of African natives in the German East African exhibits. The Belgian exhibit contained Professor Houzé's private collection of skulls, which Hrdlička worked diligently to have donated to the Smithsonian. He was especially impressed with the Philippine exhibits and obtained a series of facial casts and several hundred photographs that showed body types.[33]

The Value of the Laboratories

The anthropometry-psychometry section was an example of what McGee and his colleagues considered the principal methods used in research relating to the physical and mental characters of mankind. They hoped that the experiments would "lead to results of such permanent value as to form one of the lasting monuments to the world's greatest exposition."[34] To McGee this meant that they would support his ideas about the capacities of races to transcend blind natural forces through purposeful action and their ability to progress toward American democracy. He wanted to ensure that his visualized cultural and physical taxonomy was supported by systematically obtained research results that neatly reflected his racial and cultural types. He also wanted to guarantee that methodological advances had been made and statistical errors avoided by the use of standard tests on large numbers of research subjects, both primitive and civilized.

Visitors considered the laboratories successful in part because the experiments were foregone conclusions and simply reinforced the celebration of human progress seen throughout the fair. John Hanson wrote that only in anthropology "were records made of such comparative examinations of the different human races as would furnish a knowledge of their present condition, physical and mental, with their advancement through the past." And comparison was the key, for the entire exercise was to understand individuals and population differences. Visitors saw difference being scientifically proven and took home tangible souvenirs, that their bodies and minds were advanced. As Robert Rydell has noted, most fairgoers left the laboratories with their own racial superiority "firmly ingrained in their minds."[35]

One of the great anthropological debates of the nineteenth and twentieth centuries dealt with the nature of race, as social and historical concepts and as possible biological realities. These all centered on scientific rationalizations of difference and how difference may be constructed and measured. Today, most people realize that little useful knowledge was gained from all the anthropometric and psychometric data collected when conclusions and generalizations based thereon were used to hierarchically categorize human groups in terms of cultural progress. And much harm was done. Pseudo-scientists used the questionable assumptions and results to justify and rationalize stereotypes and eugenic and misogynist policies about which immigrants were desirable or why segregated schools were needed to ensure that whiteness remained supreme. As Woodworth stated in 1909 in his vice-presidential address to Section H (Anthropology and Psychology) of the American Association for the Advancement of Science, "Our inveterate love for types and sharp distinctions is apt to stay with us even after we vitiate our use of statistics to such an extent that the average becomes a stumbling-block rather than an aid to knowledge. . . .

When our measurements are all obtained and spread before us, they convey to the unaided eye no clear idea of a racial difference, so much do they overlap." Unfortunately people then make a transformation based on some average that differs slightly. "Such transforming of differences of degree into differences of kind, and making antitheses between overlapping groups, partakes not a little of the ludicrous."[36]

Thus five years later, Woodworth began to question the entire enterprise. Even if it was done using sophisticated statistics and showed trait frequency and distribution, the best one could hope for were tendencies, since all groups have the same mental and sensory capabilities. "Statements to the contrary, denying to the savage powers of reasoning, of abstraction, or inhibition, or foresight, can be dismissed at once. If the savage differed in these respects from the civilized man, the difference is one of degree, and consistent with considerable overlapping of savage and civilized individuals." It is noteworthy that the "exhaustive" racial comparisons produced so little scholarship and had so little impact on the development of physical anthropology over the next twenty years. It had more impact on evolutionary psychology and was used as a cautionary tale and one that debunked myths about extraordinary powers of "savages" in vision, hearing, and smell. Woodworth concluded that Native races tended to be better than Caucasians in vision and pain thresholds, slightly worse in hearing, and about the same in smell, color vision and matching, mental speed, right-handedness, intelligence, concentration, memory, and touch. There were no strong correlations between the supposed degree of primitiveness and people's abilities. His conclusion was that evolutionary paradigms were incorrect and that inferring mental endowments of a group from their supposed cultural stage and then applying this method to the comparison of different epochs in the history of a nation was false. "The more settled condition of society does not imply greater native capacity for industry or government. Only the patient and prolonged labors of the ethnologist can inform us as to what a tribe does and thinks." Like his colleague Franz Boas, Woodworth called for a change in research paradigms. Psychologists were asking the wrong questions. It was a powerful message.[37]

With the exception of Bruner's dissertation on hearing acuity, few research findings from the exposition were reported in the scientific literature. Woodworth published nothing except his influential AAAS address. The labs never lived up to McGee's hopes that research would reveal "so far as measurements may—the relative physical value of the different races of people," because as Woodworth demonstrated, they never could. Value and worth were the wrong questions. Woodworth essentially said McGee's theory was wrong. What they should have been testing was human inventiveness in all areas of culture, not simply technology, in humanity as a whole. One should look at group size, group isolation and migration patterns, mating customs, chance, group preferences about what is important, and how people feel about change; and the definition of what constitutes progress must be broadened. Woodworth concluded that great racial differences in mental and moral traits were illusions. Anthropometry was being questioned and would slowly fall into disfavor, although Hrdlička and a few others continued to measure people for four more decades and make irrelevant statements about race and evolutionary potential.

But that was in the future. Anthropometry and racial measurements had another large role to play in St. Louis, one that was immediately infamous. For they were part of a special event, the "Special Olympics," a research program that tested racial strength and endurance as part of the third modern Olympiad. It was here that anthropology as science was performed for the public to help another emerging discipline, sports science, in what became a comedy of errors, "a spectacle indeed extraordinary and rare in the records of human experience."[38] It is to anthropology as public performance we now turn, as we review the Olympics and other special programs that McGee and others developed to demonstrate the utility of anthropological knowledge and to extend the Native presence at the exposition beyond the confines of the Indian Village and the Anthropology Village.

12. Anthropological Performances

The people are in a holiday, communicative, inquisitive mood;
but it is not an idle mood.
They are very much in earnest. . . . Everything is a passing show.
Walter Page, 1904

The Louisiana Purchase Exposition was a place of constant movement, of spectacle and performance. And this melding of performance and national celebration, entertainment and education, was continuously renewed and reinvigorated. Skiff and his department heads tried to ensure that people would come more than once. This meant new activities to entice repeat visitors, so that each day spent at the exposition would be memorable. Pavilion openings and dedications, foreign dignitary visits, and the wining and dining of politicians filled the fair's official calendar. Military events proliferated; West Point cadets gave dress parades while units of the armed forces, state guards, and military schools executed precision troop drills. Music filled the air. There were six daily organ recitals in the Iowa Building; marching bands paraded continuously. Peoples thronged John Philip Sousa's concert band as they did the Garde Republicaine Band of Paris and the Philharonische Blas Orcherster from Berlin. On the Pike there were ethnic orchestras at the Russian, Burmese, Japanese, Irish and Tyrolean concessions. The LPE's official band, under the direction of William Weil, gave two daily concerts. There were private receptions and reunions for hundreds of groups, from college alumni associations and fraternal organizations to veterans who had served in the Civil and Spanish-American wars. There were special days, state days, patriotic days, and days to honor individuals, countries, and business corporations: Cincinnati Day, Eclectic Day, Mark Twain Day, National Hay Making Day, Children's Day, Philippine Day, Railroad Day, National Cash Register Day, Improved Order of the Red Men Day, and the Pike Day, complete with a parade of all nations. Other days commemorated the annexation of land by the United States; New Mexico Day was August 19, the anniversary of General Kearney's taking formal possession of the Province of Nuevo Mexico in Santa Fe. Many programs of national celebration used Native peoples as metaphors.[1]

Dozens of theatrical events were staged after the exhibit halls closed at 6:00 p.m. Several plays commemorated the Louisiana Territory with themes of patriotism and the cant of conquest. "Indians" were used as figurative stock characters who represented virtues to emulate or obstacles to overcome. One of the most popular was an allegorical pageant, Bolossy Kiralfy's *Louisiana Purchase Spectacle Libretto* that had Indian characters but used Euro-American actors for the major symbolic roles. It opened on May 28 with a cast of more than six hundred. "Indians" symbolized the wilderness in the prologue and the first scenes, during which Hernando de Soto's explorations were honored, followed by a battle between explorers, settlers, and Indians in which the latter lost control of their lands. In the final scene, the character of "Civilization" triumphed over the chained Indians, "Spirit of Mississippi" and "Columbia," who then paid homage to the Caucasian "New Louisiana." An equally popular play at the Delmar Garden Theater was Hiram W. Hayes's *Louisiana, A Spectacular Extravaganza in a Prologue and Two Scenes*. This musical used two hundred Indian characters (including several genuine Indian performers) in the prologue as allegorical characters to represent the wilderness before European pathfinders and settlers arrived. The Indian characters paddled canoes in a one-hundred-foot long canal built around the front and sides of the stage. As in Kiralfy's play, the central figures, played by Euro-American actors, included Miss Columbia, Miss Dixie, the American Eagle, Louisiana, and the Grotesque Traveler. Vaudeville acts were interspersed and Indians received enthusiastic press reviews for their special ballet, *My Sweet Dakota Maid*.[2] The dramas' messages were reassuring to the audience for the use of Indians as metaphors reinforced existing notions of racial hierarchies and the right of Euro-Americans to inhabit indigenous lands.

Special programs, designed to both educate and entertain visitors about indigenous peoples, augmented the Anthropology Department's daily activities. McGee spent hundreds of hours planning spectacular events and regular performances that would demonstrate central disciplinary concepts of cultural differentiation overlying basic human similarity. His goal was to show that anthropology could entertain as well as disseminate knowledge to people eager to learn. Both professional anthropologists and Native participants performed. Anthropologists lectured; educated Indians held congresses. Indian students staged band concerts, dance exhibitions, dramatic presentations, and marched in parades. Indigenous people attempted to educate the public about who they were and their right to exist.

Representatives from ethnic groups gave impassioned speeches about their rights and cultural values in impromptu public programs that quickly became bi-weekly events because of audience interest. Often the speeches were interspersed with performances that earned Native participants much-needed money. On Saturday afternoons small groups of Native performers gave short programs arranged and introduced by McGee. Like any good showman, McGee knew that in order to draw crowds to his peripherally placed department he had to take anthropology where the crowds were—the plazas and streets of the Main Picture. The audiences were usually sizeable. On July 15 and 16, Native peoples staged a program on Plaza Saint Louis watched by fifteen thousand people; it "proved a satisfactory feature—except that on completion of the program most of the gathering ushered in for closer inspection of the aliens [i.e., Native peoples], who were extricated only with difficulty." Even more elaborate programs were staged in front of the Government Building for over twenty thousand people. They were repeated the next week and seen by twenty-five thousand spectators. These short programs consisted of four segments: an Ainu bear feast dance; a Mbuti social dance (fig. 8.2); a Kwakiutl winter ceremonial song and dance; and a "Red African" cannibal song and dance.[3]

Several LPE department heads requested large-scale Native performances for their special days, paying performers from their departmental funds. On Manufacturing Day, people on Plaza St. Louis witnessed an Ainu bear feast dance, a Santa Clara and Acoma Pueblo moon dance, a Mbuti social dance and music, a Kwakiutl winter ceremony, an African "cannibal dance" and songs, and Cheyenne ceremonial dances and songs. National holidays were similarly celebrated, financed by the LPEC Executive Committee. On July 4th, a morning event included a tipi-raising contest by the Cheyennes, Apaches, and Rosebud Lakota women, followed by an archery contest, and Omaha, Dakota, and Cheyenne (including—theoretically—Ghost Dance) songs. The afternoon event included a concert and exercises by the Indian School children and closed with a basketball game by the Fort Shaw Blues. Even impromptu and informal gatherings (like archery practices and anything that included children) quickly turned into publicized special events. Native children played in the Education Department's Model City Playground almost daily. Organizer Ruth Ashley Hirshfield wanted to show that all children could play together and learn from her innovative program. It was part of a national education urban-reform movement, which held that physical education had the same "uplifting" relation to the body as religious education did to the soul and that proper training in play helped immigrants assimilate to American urban culture (Cavallo 1981).

Parades were always extremely popular. On Children's Day children dressed in Native attire rode on conveyances decorated with flowers and bunting. Most parades were less elaborate, but no less exciting. A children's parade was described as follows:

> As it proceeded through the exposition avenues preceded by mounted police, Jefferson Guards, and H. Wylie's Indian boy band, it was composed of Pawnee, Sioux, and Chippewa boys mounted on burros. Japanese children in jin-ricksha, five Boer boys on ponies escorting five little girls in General Joubert's South African spider, Eskimo children in Eskimo sleds drawn by Eskimo dogs, Chinese children in pony carriages drawn by ponies, four Irish children in Irish jaunting cars, accompanied by an Irish boy piper; six travois carrying Indian children drawn by Indian ponies, Indian squaws leading ponies ridden by Indian boys, a Tyrolean boy mounted on a pony, Persian and other Asiatic children on camels, four little Pueblo children on burros, four Syrian children in a children's carriage, pick-aninnies on burros, Russian children in native costumes, boys and girls from Jerusalem in costume, Philippine oxcarts carrying children of Igorrotes, Malays, Moros, and others; twelve Navajo, Osage, and Creek boys on burros; baby fire engine and cart drawn by Shetland ponies and manned by fifteen boy firemen from Hale's fire fighters. (Bennitt 1905, 156–57)

In July the Kwakiutl and Nootka men paddled Dr. Atlieu's gigantic sea canoe and the Inuits demonstrated kayak techniques in several water processions on Arrowhead Lake. During one water parade, a float carried ten geisha girls from the Fair Japan concession, a second carried Indians with a tipi, and a third, shaped like a Philippine banana tree, had several Moros. On Transportation

Day, fifty thousand visitors watched Native men use travois and wagons in the Olympic Stadium. Even more saw the LPE's largest theme parade designed to illustrate transportation methods used throughout the world with Native peoples representing primitive foils for modern advances. Native peoples were also very visible in division 2, "automobiles," which gave many Native people their first automobile ride.[4]

McGee hoped that these parades would draw visitors to the Anthropology Villages, not just to the Pike. He had to compete with the Pike's barkers, who enticed visitors to their concessions using techniques McGee felt were undignified. Instead he publicized events at Native encampments. Soon, however, he had to stop because they became too popular. "These events . . . were found to involve serious risk to the people and their custodians by reason of the overwhelming crowds brought together and crushes sometimes developed" (McGee 1905d, 89–90; Rydell 1984, 155). Plaza St. Louis, the Olympic Stadium, the Government Building's plazas, and the Indian School lawn were larger and safer spaces. They became the preferred venues for those ethnographic performances that McGee held to be highly educational in keeping with the LPE's University of the Future theme. The villages remained sites of more controlled and sedate educational lectures and demonstrations.

Congresses and Conventions: Celebrating the "Sovereignty of the Mind in Human Progress"

Conventions and international congresses had gradually become part of all the great expositions, and St. Louis was no exception. Educational programs were critical if the LPE was to succeed as the envisioned place of universal education. Organizers also wanted to host more conventions and congresses than had been held at previous fairs, 140 in all. The first convened on May 16, when reporters from around the world attended the World's Press Parliament and wrote about their experiences. Others followed—dentists, publishers, lawyers, firemen, and the Women's Christian Temperance Union, among many. Hundreds of fraternal organizations gathered, including the Improved Order of the Red Men, a Masonic-like organization whose members dressed up as "Indians." This latter group even had their own day when as "Indians" they paraded throughout the fairgrounds, including stops in the official Indian Villages, much to the amusement of the authentic Indians (Davis 1904, 5, 7).

Scientific societies came to St. Louis, combining annual professional meetings with family vacations. The National Geographic Society sponsored the Eighth International Geographical Congress; as the society's vice president, McGee chaired the organizing committee and made local arrangements. New ideas were floated and critical policy initiatives formulated at these meetings. One was particularly important for anthropology. The Archaeological Institute of America met on September 22, 1904, and discussed antiquities preservation in the Americas. Delegates appointed a special subcommittee (Charles Bowditch, John W. Foster, Holmes, and Putnam) that drafted antiquities legislation presented to the U.S. Congress in January 1905. A revised version ultimately became the federal Antiquities Act of 1906.[5]

Fair organizers considered these congresses to be academic accompaniments to pavilion exhibits and a celebration of the pure knowledge behind the technological products. Lehmann, the chair of the anthropology committee, spent most of his time organizing and directing these programs, which meant he had little time to promote the Anthropology Department. Lectures were given in the Hall of Congresses, situated next to Cupples Hall, or in Festival Hall. Each congress was required to give free public lectures and professional presentations. Anthropology was well represented.

The most famous gathering was the International Congress of Art and Science, held the week of September 19–25. It was organized and presided over by Simon Newcomb, McGee's father-in-law. As we noted in chapter 2, Newcomb detested McGee but agreed to participate because of the event's importance. With its more than one hundred sections, Skiff considered the congress the LPE's crowning achievement. "In it the great minds of all nations will unite in fixing the thought of this epoch. . . . While the exhibit of material things will establish the condition of our productiveness, these congresses will traverse the intellectual courses through which this yield has come, and from these reflections will point the way to achievements yet to be recorded." Featured speakers included German sociologists Max Weber, who discussed rural communities, and Frederick Toennies, who spoke on social structure. Other noted speakers included Henri Poincaré, the great French mathematician; William Rainy Harper, University of Chicago president; Hugo Münsterberg, a pioneer psychologist; and Woodrow Wilson, Princeton University president. Topics ranged from urban sanitary conditions to educational reforms, from mathematical theory to international peace. The congress was designed to visualize science and humanistic knowledge as an integrated whole, "to exhibit the totality of intellectual achievement, to formulate the interrelations of the several branches of knowledge, and . . . [to harmonize] the confused mass of knowledge scattered through a bewildering multiplicity of specialties."[6] And it did.

The congress was organized into grand divisions that met simultaneously. Each was further split into departmental sections: (1) normative science (philosophy, mathematics); (2) physical sciences (physics, chemistry, astronomy, anthropology, geology, biology); (3) historical sciences (political history, economic history, the histories of law, language, literature, art, religion); (4) mental science (psychology, sociology); (5) utilitarian science (medicine, technology, economics); and, (6) social regulation and social culture (politics, jurisprudence, religion, education). An authoritative American scholar was chosen as the key speaker for each section and asked to discuss the field's internal unity, its fundamental concepts and methods, and reflect on how the field had progressed during the nineteenth century. Following this address, another scholar, hopefully *the* outstanding man in the field, discussed the current research problems and his vision of its future. More than two thousand individuals registered to hear the approximately five hundred speakers. The LPEC underwrote ninety foreign scholars who were asked to discuss how their specialty fit within the scheme of science as seen from Europe.[7]

Anthropology staged a small program. McGee had it placed in physical sciences because he considered it "pure" science, that is, it had laboratories as part of its main exhibit. Three sections of papers—representing somatology, archaeology, and ethnology—were held, as well as a plenary session. Speakers included individuals such as Holmes, Mills, Starr, and Jenks, who were actively involved in the exposition, as well as senior European scholars, including ethnographer Alfred C. Haddon, of Cambridge University, and Mesoamerican archaeologist Edward Seler, from the University of Berlin. Younger, up-and-coming scholars, such as Alfred Kroeber, of the University of California, presented ten-minute papers on their research but were not given honoraria.

McGee became the main speaker for the anthropology section despite his objections. He had originally wanted Boas to take this position and had suggested to Newcomb that Boas would be the appropriate speaker. Newcomb, however, wanted an established member of the old guard who was affiliated with a university and asked Putnam to be the chair and deliver the keynote address. Putnam thought McGee, as president of the American Anthropological Association, was the more appropriate person to be the main speaker. After several months of negotiation with McGee, he finally agreed that Boas was the best choice. Boas wrote McGee, stating he had heard from Newcomb who felt they should distribute the speaking duties as they saw fit. "It would be better for you to adopt the first-named subject, i.e., progress of anthropology during the past century, partly because this would enable you to review the work of the American ethnologic bureau. . . . It may be added that quite apart from this consideration, my personal preference would be for the other subject, fundamental conceptions and methods of anthropology."[8] McGee responded that he would rather talk about concepts and methods, but eventually agreed to let Boas outline the twentieth century's key concepts. The two men met in New York City and outlined their papers to prevent redundancy.

McGee gave a historical summary of nineteenth-century anthropology and Boas presented a paper on methodological advances and the pressing problems the field would address in the future. McGee's presentation was his typical sweeping summary of the abstract work of evolutionary thinkers, and anthropology's importance in human intellectual development, sprinkled heavily with his own unique jargon. It would be considered racist by today's standards, for he suggested that the mental development of races was the equivalent of physical and cultural development, with Caucasians at the top. He predicted that the enlightened Caucasians, as evidenced by their accomplishments in St. Louis, would spread over the world. Anthropology's job was to document this new era of human history as the world became more unified under the "white man's burden." For McGee human advancement was commensurate with industry and American cultural and political expansion. It was basically a restatement of his earlier work and his proposal for the exposition and its congress of races.[9]

Boas's address, "The History of Anthropology," was very different, indeed revolutionary. He began by refuting McGee's conclusions and then went on to undermine the premises of nineteenth-century, unilinear evolutionary anthropology. In essence, he gave a revisionist historical summary that emphasized European intellectual contributions. He also discussed the methodological and statistical problems with anthropometric and psychometric studies, beginning what was to become a long debate with scholars such as Hrdlička over their ability to generalize about race and intellectual abilities. Boas's lecture contradicted and undermined all that McGee was trying to prove at the LPE. He demonstrated that McGee's grand scheme was ethnocentric and that it fell into the trap of doing nothing more than validating "preexisting popular prejudices" and preconceptions.[10] In the history of American anthropology, the McGee and Boas papers mark a major turning point from the evolution and racism of the nineteenth century to the historical particularism and cultural relativism of the twentieth century (chapter 14).

Other association meetings and conferences were of interest for anthropology including, the Eighth International Geographic Congress presided over by Captain Robert Peary, the famous Arctic explorer. In addition to attending lectures, delegates "devoted a day to a study of the Philippine Reservation, the Indian School, and of the various savage tribes at the Exposition, and to a reception held on board the 'Discoverer,' at the New York to the North Pole concession." One of the most important conferences was the week-long National Education Association. It was the largest congress, with more than fifteen thousand educators. Sessions were devoted to Indian education—as a subgroup of the national organization.

A Congress of Indian Educators convened from June 28 to July 1 and highlighted issues pertinent to anthropology and the Indian Service. McCowan and Rosa Bourassa, the Chippewa secretary of the Anthropology Department, spent a great deal of time planning the professional convention and a display of Native peoples to show what they could do with proper training and motivation. McCowan claimed that it was the first national convention of educated Indian men and women ever held in the United States. He invited the most famous Indians to give inspirational speeches. "It is our intention to have only prominent Indian speakers address the Congress, such well-known men as Congressman Curtis of Kansas, Pleasant Porter, chief of the Cherokee [*sic*, actually Osage] Nation, and others equally well known." And they did. At the opening ceremonies, A. M. Dockery, Governor of Missouri, commended the Indian Service on its efforts to train the nation's wards. The *Indian School Journal* reported that McGee spoke of the lessons that whites may learn from the Indians. He said he had been in many Indian homes and had "never seen one brother strike another or a child disrespectful or disobedient to its parents.

He said that we have nothing more artistic than some of the Indian rugs, pottery and silver work, and that we owe much that is beautiful in our literature and music to Indian legends and songs."[11]

The key speakers were Emily S. Cook and Estelle Reel of the Indian Service, Natalie Curtis, and Alice C. Fletcher. Cook described her static exhibit, the art forms produced by Indian students in government schools, and the importance of domestic science. It was a standard statement of official Indian Service policy that emphasized the importance of teacher training. Reel gave a similar talk, touting the importance of her *Uniform Course of Study*, the preservation of Indian art, especially that produced by women for home use, and how Indian Service educators had made Indians economically self-sufficient citizens. Fletcher, a past Anthropological Society of Washington president, spoke on Indian names. A noted ethnologist who had worked with the Omahas, Lakotas, Ho-Chunks (Winnebagos), Hunkpapas, Pawnees, Santee Sioux, and Poncas, she was also infamous for her role in implementing the Dawes Act and working extensively with Native anthropologists Francis La Flesche and James Murie. Curtis was a noted professional pianist, ethnomusicologist, activist, and reformer. In the years to come she would work to help restore religious freedom to Indians and persuade President Roosevelt to remove the assimilationist ban on the singing of Native songs. At the conference Curtis challenged existing Indian Service policy, probably one of the few speakers who did. She called for a reversal of government policies that banned the speaking of Native languages in schools. "She made a strong appeal for the preservation of the best characteristics of the race, and begged the teachers assist not only in preventing the loss of the primitive Indian melodies, but in developing still further their harmonies." Other speakers lauded the Indian Service educational program and called for more federal support for assimilative and educational efforts.[12]

Indian students worked to make the Education Congress a success. The Congress of Indian Educators began with a special concert in Festival Hall on June 27, which drew a good-sized crowd despite torrential rain. While most performers were from the Indian School, the Ainus sang a folk song and the Pawnees sang "When the Night Dreams Come." The highlight was a solo by Pima vocalist Katherine Valenzuela. There was a special reception and dinner at the Indian School on the evening of June 28. On June 29, the domestic-science class designed, cooked, and served a special dinner to honor Reel. On

June 30, the girls' quartet, the umbrella drill team, Grace Miller, and Walter Rhodes entertained a group of educators from Oklahoma in the Oklahoma Building. By all accounts the entertainment and dinners were the most memorable parts of the conference.[13]

Many LPE conference speakers presented public lectures, although for fiscal reasons anthropology had fewer than other disciplines. McGee and McCowan arranged for Frances Densmore, a noted ethnomusicologist, to give public lectures on June 29 and July 1. She discussed how Indian life was expressed in songs, playing and singing a number of love songs. On June 30, she gave a lecture-recital on Indian music as America's first music in the Festival Hall. According to the program announcement, "The lecture depicts the Indians' natural sense of harmony and Indian life expressed in music. Songs of the warpath and battle, love songs, a description of tom-tom, medicine rattles and the numerous musical instruments, their manufactures and uses will be given." She also gave a second lecture in the recital hall accompanied by the school's musical-literary exercises. "After a few introductory songs, she gave the songs of battle, love, and the Haethuska society. The teachers were delighted with Miss Densmore's beautiful tribute to the songs of the Indians."[14]

McCowan had discouraged Indians he did not consider educated from speaking at or even attending the Congress of Indian Educators and tried to distance himself from them and anyone who worked in Wild West shows. However, he made exceptions for the best-known orators. Chief Blue Horse, of the Oglala Lakota, and Red Cloud, both eighty-three years old, agreed to speak. Their interpreter was Henry Standing Soldier, an educated man who had been a participant in the 1901 Pan American Exposition Wild West Show. McCowan, however, refused to let Standing Soldier speak and said that he should participate in one of McGee's congresses of primitive peoples. These summer "congresses" were actually a series of performances with speeches held in the Plaza St. Louis, as alluded to in earlier chapters. A typical program consisted of a Mbuti ceremonial dance, an Ainu bear feast dance, a Tehuelche song, and Chief Bull Bear leading a Cheyenne war dance after speaking, followed by Cocopa, Kwakiutl-Nootka, and Filipino performances. The announcer, Jenks on this occasion, discussed peoples' attire and the instruments they played. The largest of these "primitive congresses" was called the "Pan-Savage Conclave." Held on July 16, it was described in the *St. Louis Republic* using typical stereotypes, focusing on the participation of the stars, Geronimo, Yellow Hair, and the Mbutis.[15]

Another type of popular anthropological program included the Competitive War Dances, held on the Aeronautic Concourse. Like modern powwows, individuals from seven or eight tribes competed for prize money, judged by elders such as Yellow Hair. The events began with grand processions from Cupples Hall to the arena. Men and women from each tribe danced at the beginning of the parade, walked, and periodically stopped to dance along the way in the hopes of gathering a large crowd. Admission was fifteen cents, and the receipts were generally good, but on July 14 it was so hot, more than one hundred degrees Fahrenheit, that the anticipated crowd did not come. Ainus, Mbutis, and Tehuelches sat in prominent places in the bleachers, but there were few fairgoers. With a disappointing gate receipt, participants realized there would be little prize money and "danced without much enthusiasm, and only a few tribes took part, although all were present in full dress."[16]

Special Classes: The Fair as University Classroom

The main forms of anthropological performance were classroom teaching and formal lectures or having people watch while research was conducted in the laboratories. Watching ethnographers was a difficult task because it required extensive travel and a long time commitment; the researcher went to the research subjects in their communities. It also presented difficulties, since the presence of outsiders affects the research endeavor, and was somewhat boring. It looked like hanging around, sitting, talking, doing daily tasks, not very spectacular or engaging. By 1900 long-term "participant-observation" field study was the common rite of passage for would-be anthropologists. One of the difficulties anthropology encountered in its quest for scientific status was that its methodologies were difficult to teach; each field site was held to be so unique that data collection techniques could not be replicated. This drew into question ethnology as a comparative endeavor. How could comparable data be obtained? One possibility was a field school where students could hone their observational and interviewing skills and learn to take field notes before being sent out on their own in "real" field situations.

McGee felt that the assemblage of Native peoples provided a rare opportunity for comparative training in systematic data-collection techniques, and student research could go beyond the questions casual visitors posed to demonstrators. To McGee, the fair was a great place for professors and students to conduct summer research or teach. It was cost effective since a condensed course on racial comparisons could be given in a single place using live subjects. Students could obtain anthropological experience for themselves; the fair could become a living laboratory and provide an unparalleled educational experience. Potential research subjects were segregated from the rest of the fair but were close enough to the "impressive display of the achievements of modern man in the large exhibit palaces" so that students would not miss the other attractions. Fun and teaching could be easily combined as it never had been before.[17]

McGee's ideas on educational experiences are extremely modern; he sounds like contemporary educators who want students to learn by doing, to encounter the job of discovery, rather than simply sit passively in a classroom memorizing a professor's words. McGee promoted engaged pedagogy. In a letter to about fifty university and museum officials he trumpeted "opportunities for original and instructional work such as could not be enjoyed otherwise except at the cost in time and money of extensive journeys with attendant hardships." These opportunities included: Record Work, Somatology, Psychology, Arts and Industries, Law and Socialtry, Faiths and Philosophies, General Anthropology, Languages, and General Ethnology. McGee would ensure that teachers would receive all possible assistance in terms of facilities and access because "the sole purpose of the department [is] to educate." Students could compare physical types, see actual behavior, conduct experiments in psychic character, document how tools are made, compare how artists in different cultures use their hands, record languages, study how different culture-grades define laws, compare primitive and advanced peoples, help with the anthropometry experiments, or make life casts. As far as we can tell no one took him up on the offer. No master's theses or dissertations were written by students attending the fair; nor does it appear any university or even high school expeditions came to see the indigenous people. Densmore was the only anthropologist to use the LPE as a research site. She studied Filipino music and concluded that it belonged to a developmental period preceding that of American Indians.[18]

McGee wanted a university to conduct a field school concentrating on race at the fair. The only individual to respond to the offer was Frederick Starr.

He organized a Louisiana Purchase Exposition class in ethnology, the first ethnographic field school in the United States, although it came perilously close to never happening. Starr called it a systematic class in Practical Ethnology. McGee promised to help with planning and to send out announcements, but did little. After numerous procedural and scheduling problems, Starr held the class in the lecture hall in the Alaska Building, an ideal site because of the extensive ethnographic collections lining the walls of the room.[19]

Starr had two men and twenty-seven women students from the universities of Wisconsin and Chicago as well as several St. Louis school teachers. Students all enrolled at the University of Chicago and received three credit hours in ethnology; nonstudents were given certificates upon completion of a term paper and review of field notes. Tuition was twelve dollars for the full course or five dollars for one week; living expenses were underwritten by an anonymous gift of five thousand dollars. There were fewer students than Starr had anticipated and he was upset because his salary was based on class size. To make more money, he developed a new category of "student." For people wanting to attend only a one-hour lecture, he charged thirty-five cents; a one-hour demonstration cost fifty cents. Students paid Starr directly and he gave the University of Chicago its cut as an official, university-extension-service laboratory class, rather than an LPEC event. Starr regularly taught anthropology lab courses at the University of Chicago and he was excited about this one. "Live Igorrotes and Patagonian giants are better than textbooks and pictures in teaching anthropology classes," he told one reporter. It was a class where students would actually see Native peoples with "their dances and other antics, their habitat, their modes of life, their idiosyncrasies, and other matters of interest concerning them."[20]

The class ran from September 1 to 21, and consisted of lectures, practical talks, directed independent research, and tutorials, daily except Sunday. At 9:00 a.m. Starr gave a general lecture about one or two of the groups. At 10:00 a.m. he lectured on a synthetic subject or special problem—industry, art, customs, practices or beliefs—accompanied by a demonstration of a manufacturing process. Thus, the Ainus were the subject of Starr's lecture on September 12, followed by a lecture entitled "The Physical Characteristics of Race." At 11:00 a.m. the class visited the group being discussed to inspect their homes, and then students worked individually in the afternoon.

By all accounts, the first class was quite spectacular. The Kwakiutls performed a Hamatsa initiation ceremony while Starr explained the cultural significance interspersed with his thoughts on cultural evolution. According to one reporter, the class found the performance very realistic. "No human flesh was actually eaten, but the dancers went through the motions so vividly that several of the ladies in the class were obliged to turn their heads away. Savage and blood curdling yells, horrible expressions of fear on the faces of the dancers, fastening of the teeth in the flesh and smacking of lips, were the climax of the wild dance. When they finished, the dancers, worn out by the tremendous emotional strain, sank to the floor. A burst of applause from the cultured audience of well-dressed women greeted the thespians of primitive origin at the conclusion of the dance."[21]

On another occasion, Starr lectured about the development of manners and politeness, the effects of civilization, clothing, art, and the nature of women's work. On September 7, the group saw the Snake Dance in the Cliff Dweller concession while Starr lectured on Hopi culture (he never acknowledged this was a fake performance). The press attended almost every day, fascinated with the idea of young women watching semi-naked men "with broad bronzed shoulders". Most demonstrations were realistic and graphic. A Negrito woman carved tattoos on her husband's back while Starr lectured. He also held a fire-making competition in which the Negritos beat the Ainus and Mbutis.[22]

Of course, no one had asked the Native peoples if they would like to be the subject of a university class. McGee neglected to inform most special agents that there would be daily lectures and a set of special Saturday afternoon lectures for high school teachers, which meant that Native participants would lose one of their free periods. When the students descended on their homes, unannounced, some Natives responded to the intrusion more courteously than others.[23] Starr stayed in St. Louis for the month, often giving impromptu and free lectures at the Ainu village, which were technically part of the college series but open to everyone. When the class ended on September 21, however, he read term papers, turned in his grades and left for Mexico. He did not return and never taught another field school.

Special Competitions: Formal and Informal Athletic Events

Sport was serious business at the exposition. The human body was on display as much as the human mind, and both were measured to document advancement. Sport was also considered a way to advance the republic and meld immigrant peoples into a single body politic. As historian Mark Dyreson has noted, "Many Americans came to see sport as a powerful reform instrument that could revitalize their rapidly modernizing nation. Intellectuals espoused ideas that mixed sport into the struggles between classes, races, ethnic groups, and genders."[24] The development of the human body was also an important component of social Darwinian theories reflected in public opinion and policies. Ideas about team and individual sports, the human body, and their places in evolutionary theory and modern educational programs were played out daily. It was inevitable that ideas about progress and evolution would be expressed through athletic competition.

Demonstrations of physical fitness were advertised as special events in the daily programs describing Native peoples' activities. Educators at the Indian School assumed that compulsory physical training was morally uplifting. According to Reel, "In order to get the best out of life, it is necessary to look into the physical condition of pupils and give them the training that will counteract the influences of unfortunate heredity and strengthen the physique, in order that they may be able to bear the strain that competition in business and earning a living will impose." Visitors watched such training exercises at the Indian School. Every morning the Pima kindergarten class performed calisthenics; every afternoon older students executed marching drills or competed on the parade ground. The women's basketball team from Fort Shaw, which performed numerous competitions and exhibitions of skill, was of special interest to visitors, as noted in chapter 6. Sport was thus an important part of an educational assimilationist curriculum but quickly became a symbol of Indian pride as well. Indians excelled in football, baseball, track, lacrosse, and boxing. In the mid-1890s, Carlisle Indian School began a successful football program and was soon joined by Haskell Institute, the latter coached by H. B. Peairs, who was on the model Indian School staff. In 1899, Carlisle hired legendary coach Glen S. "Pop" Warner, who led the school's team to victories over university teams such as Harvard, Syracuse, Yale, Villanova, and Chicago for the next four years. Both Haskell and Carlisle beat all their opponents in 1904. On November 26, 1904, they played each other at the LPE for the NCAA championship in what was billed as the first "Olympic College Football" tournament. Carlisle won 38 to 4. Each team received fifteen thousand dollars.[25]

Fig. 12.1. Anthropology Days competition. Frank Moore (Pawnee) shooting an arrow in the preliminary heat of the distance competition. Photographer unknown. Published in the LPE official scrapbook. St. Louis Public Library, image no. LPE00365.

In addition to championships there were abundant informal displays of athletic prowess, such as Arapaho and Pawnee shinny contests or Tehuelche bolo-throwing from horseback. Visitors' demands for novelty and demonstrators' need to earn money sparked many of these impromptu events. Marksmanship was one area where Native American men and boys excelled as spontaneous competitors and performers. McGee encouraged these popular events where visitors supplied nickels and quarters as targets for archers. But in the name of "authenticity," let alone safety, he did not allow competitions with firearms even though most Indian participants were used to shooting with rifles. Such athletic competitions and displays of physical dexterity were definitely entertaining. Whether they were also educational is open to question. McGee hoped they would be events where new scientific knowledge was generated. The results of Native athletic activities could be compiled systematically and then compared to American athletes to understand the "mental characteristics of mankind." He classified them as anthropometry and psychometry experiments that supposedly tested physical strength, endurance, and motor skills.

Fig. 12.2. Igorot man throws a javelin in the Anthropology Days competition, August 12, 1904. Stephen Simms (*right*) and other Filipino participants look on. Chief Antonio, the leader of the Bontoc Igorots, squats on the ground. Timon, a Lanal Moro, is in the white shirt standing behind the thrower. Photographer unknown. St. Louis Public Library, image no. LPE00226.

The most popular were athletic contests in which Natives competed for prize money. On June 2 field sports were held in front of the Indian School in which more than one hundred dollars was distributed to indigenous athletes.[26] There were also intertribal archery and javelin-hurling contests (see figs. 12.1, 12.2), foot races, tugs-of-war, lacrosse games, and a tipi-raising contest. The Indians often wagered with fairgoers on the outcomes as well as impromptu horse races or modified "chicken pulls" with men from the Wild West show. It was one of their favorite forms of entertainment.

One of the prime areas of "scientific" comparison, where McGee hoped that "scientific laws" about race could be generated, were Western-style competitions between Native peoples and Caucasian athletes, that is, "primitive" versus "civilized" races. Woodworth was initially skeptical about such comparisons because they required one to assume that the athletes were representative of all Caucasians and that the small number of Natives could stand for entire racial populations. McGee held that these comparisons—which he saw as basically comparing the results of independently run foot races, would be valid because all individuals tested would involve "average" representatives of their racial groups, thereby ensuring valid comparisons. Moreover, he held that the research populations would be large, lending reliability to any conclusions reached (McGee 1905d, 191). For James E. Sullivan, head of the Department of Physical Culture, who had a vested interest in insuring that trained Caucasian Americans won athletic contests, such experiments were very important. He suggested something even more spectacular, a "Special Olympics," which historians of sports science and popular writers have for too long blamed on McGee.

Athletic events were major features of the entire LPE, not only the Anthropology Department. The LPEC Board thought that athletic events would be inexpensive attractions and generate free publicity. If progress meant obtaining better health through a fit body, LPE organizers wanted to demonstrate that Americans were the world's fittest people. By extending this logic, they could then claim that Americans were the most progressive people, naturally selected and poised for future greatness. It was almost inevitable that ideas about primitive peoples, assimilation, the value of modern education, and notions of physical progress would be expressed through a Department of Physical Culture.

The department was under the direction of James E. Sullivan, a dominant figure in athletics. Sullivan was an active athlete who had won many trophies for running and was also a professional sports writer, editor, and publisher. A self-taught Irish immigrant who was working his way up the social ladder, he had been instrumental in the formal organization of sports since the 1880s. He had served as president of the Pastime Athletic Club in New York City, vice president of the National Association of Amateur Athletics of America and a founder of the Amateur Athletic Union (AAU). He was extremely ambitious, powerful, arrogant, influential and a superb self-promoter and meticulous organizer. By 1900, as editor of the official *Athletic Almanac* and chair of the AAU Records Committee, he virtually controlled championship competition. LPE publicists stated, without exaggeration, that "he [has] managed more athletic meetings than any other man in America today. . . . He is the acknowledged authority on athletics, the preferred referee at nearly all the important athletic meets in this country."[27] He was also experienced in international competition, having overseen the American delegation at the second Olympics held at the 1900 Paris Exposition and serving as director of athletics at the 1901 Pan-

American Exposition. Sullivan's goal was to establish that American methods of scientific training produced the best athletes.

Sullivan was very proud that the LPE had a separate Department of Physical Culture; previously exposition athletic events had been subsumed under liberal arts or social departments. His department emphasized scientific physical training and the progress Americans had made in attaining better health through sport. Sullivan convened a committee of scholars to oversee his exhibits in a three-story building next to Cupples Hall and provide the scholarly basis for competitions. In addition to the usual charts, photographs, diagrams, catalogues, circulars, and programs from schools, athletic unions, YMCAS and YWCAS, there was anthropometric equipment to assess athletic ability. Scientists measured visitors' physical fitness while children played in a model playground. The physical training section revolved around a complex demonstration program with school gymnastics classes for various ages using American, German, and Swedish techniques. There was also a thirty-five-thousand-seat stadium for track and field events, equestrian polo, football, and baseball games. The department sponsored authoritative addresses on physical training and the human body as part of a World's Olympic Lecture Course that carried college credit. Several speakers lectured on anthropological topics: Paul C. Philips, of Amherst College, spoke on "Anthropometric Methods"; G. Stanley Hall, president of Clark University, discussed "Health as Related to Civilization"; Luther Gulick, director of New York City's public school educational program, theorized about "Athletics and Social Evolution"; and McGee presented "The Influence of Play in Racial Development, with Special Reference to Muscular Movement." Skiff talked on "The General Advantage of Athletic Exercises to the Individual."[28]

To the general public, however, the department's raison d'être was to host professional and amateur athletic competitions. More than ninety-five hundred athletes competed in four hundred separate events between May 14 and November 19, as Sullivan strove to present all known sports and offer more prize money than ever before. There were high school and college meets, competitions for seniors and disabled individuals, an amateur baseball tournament, the world fencing championship, a golf tournament, lacrosse, and bicycling. There were also Gaelic football, quoits, skittles, and lawn tennis. The most popular were gymnastics competitions, drawing hundreds of contestants and thousands of spectators. The least popular was roque (croquet), with three contestants and a mere hundred viewers.[29] While these competitions were critically important, Sullivan's quest to glorify the fit male body was ultimately accomplished by "holding the greatest athletic tournament known to history and the most extended exposition of the science of physical culture that has ever been made" — the Olympic Games.

The Third Olympiad of the modern era, the first held in the Western Hemisphere, lasted one week, from August 29 to September 3. Events were open to all amateur athletes who could pay the two-dollar general entrance fee and fifty cents per event. The program was expanded from the previous venues in Athens and Paris. In addition to official events (running, jumping, weightlifting, steeplechase, pole vaulting, wrestling, swimming, shot put, hurdles, gymnastics, and the marathon) there were myriad demonstrations, an international tug-of-war, lacrosse, baseball, and plunge-for-distance in the swimming pool. Women had one official event, archery, and several demonstrations. To be designated as an Olympic event, the contest had to be open only to amateurs and include foreign participants. Despite these restrictions Sullivan referred to almost every athletic meet or demonstration as an Olympic event, creating great confusion. While many of his competitions were never officially approved, he did convince the International Olympic Committee to designate eighty events as official Olympic trials. Several served also as U.S. championships.

More than four thousand individuals, whom exposition officials modestly declared were the "greatest athletes in the world," came to compete in the Olympics. Of the 687 competitors in the official events, 525 were Americans and 41 Canadians; it was a decidedly North American, Caucasian, and male affair. Most European countries did not send delegations, nor did foreign athletic clubs. France pretended the games were not being held; Russia and Japan were at war and Great Britain was involved in the conflict. A few countries sent small delegations whose athletes paid their own way. As one participant remembered, "The Olympics didn't amount to much then. They were only a little tiny part of the big show in St. Louis. There was not a lot of international flavor to the Games. It was largely a rivalry between Eastern and Western American athletic clubs according to the press. Nevertheless, athletes set numerous world records. Winners were given gold medals and souvenir cups; Americans won eighty gold medals."[30]

The St. Louis Olympics were not without memorable moments from the standpoint of racial participation. Black and Native American men officially competed for the first time in Olympic events. Two Zulu members of the Boer War concession, Lehouw and Yamasani, ran in the marathon. They did well—Lehouw finished ninth and Yamasani twelfth—after a series of minor incidents including being chased off the course by two dogs. George Poage of Milwaukee placed third in the four-hundred-meter hurdles, the first black to win an individual Olympic medal. The first American Indian, Frank Pierce, whose tribal affiliation is not recorded but who was probably Comanche, is pictured in *Spaulding's Official Almanac* wearing number nine in the marathon, a first unfortunately unnoticed in any Olympic official history. Pierce was employed by the Wild West show (Becht 2004; Sullivan 1905b, 186).

The International Olympic Committee (IOC) basically washed its hands of the entire affair. The Olympic president, Pierre de Coubertin, refused to attend because he felt politics had tainted the entire affair; the Olympics would be a financial disaster and little more than a LPE sideshow. He had wanted the Games to be held in Chicago under the auspices of the University of Chicago but when Sullivan, Francis, and other LPEC officials threatened to stage competing games if they were not allowed to host the Olympics, President Roosevelt changed the game's venue to St. Louis. The IOC bowed to political pressure and awarded the games to St. Louis in December 1903. De Coubertin officially asked Sullivan to take charge in early 1904 but, unbeknownst to Sullivan, he and other IOC members decided to distance themselves and hold organizational meetings elsewhere for the 1908 competition during the St. Louis events. Sullivan and his Amateur Athletic Union oversaw the contests rather than the IOC.[31]

Like McGee, Sullivan hoped the LPE would be the site to generate new knowledge—particularly insights that would support his theories on physical training—as well as the locale where he could generate the interest needed to promote his new professional field. The early twentieth century was a period of experimentation in sports science, just as it was in anthropology. In their quest to discover who was a natural athlete, researchers sought to learn how biological traits and physical morphology could be influenced by physical education. Sullivan saw the athletic competitions as an excellent venue in which to test his theories about fitness, the benefit of physical training, drug enhancement, and stimulants to enhance performance. All athletes were apparently asked to undergo anthropometric testing, and extensive records were taken on performance. To test Sullivan's most radical ideas, he and several personal trainers chose the grueling marathon. Instead, the race served as an excellent example of flawed science, dubious comparisons, and rigged athletic events.

The marathon was run on a hot, humid August day, in mid-afternoon. Thirty-one men began the race; fourteen finished the twenty-four-mile course in oppressive ninety-degree heat and humidity over dusty, uneven roads across seven hills. There was one official water stop to minimize fluid intake to test how far purposeful dehydration could be taken. The track conditions were challenging as well. At the start of the race a dozen men on horseback raced over the course to clear spectators, raising a cloud of dust. Next came a dozen official automobiles directly in front of the runners, while personal trainers, physicians, nurses, and scientists rode in more cars, essentially surrounding each runner. There were actually more cars producing noxious fumes on the course than runners and one man almost died of asphyxiation. Another was rushed to the hospital halfway through the race; he had ingested so much dust that it had ripped his stomach lining. Emergency surgery saved his life. The streets and roads were also busy with cross-town traffic, delivery wagons, men walking their dogs, railroad trains, and trolley cars. It was as much a steeplechase as a marathon.

Research subject Thomas Hicks ran a good race, leading for the first fifteen miles. When he showed signs of collapse his personal trainer, Hugh McGarth, gave him "assistance" that almost killed him. Like Sullivan, McGarth believed that drinking water hindered performance. He denied Hicks water but at milepost seventeen gave him a grain of sulphate strychnine and an egg white. At milepost twenty he gave Hicks another dose of strychnine, two egg whites, and a sip of French brandy. McGarth administered another shot of brandy and two more egg whites when Hicks entered the stadium after three and a half hours. Denied water for the sake of the "scientific" experiment, except for being sponged in hot water heated by the car radiator, Hicks was so dehydrated he lost eight pounds. He was so weak and dazed that he had to be held up by two people in order to cross the finish line. He "won" the marathon but was so exhausted he wandered around the stadium in a stupor; he was rushed off to bed without receiving his trophy. Sullivan wisely concluded that strychnine did not enhance performance. The marathon was actually the last and most controversial in a series of bizarre "scientific" experiments undertaken by the Department of Physical Culture. Most were harmless and involved measuring athletic endurance under varying conditions or testing the effectiveness of equipment through observation. As dubious as was the marathon, the series of experiments called "the Special Olympics" was more infamous.

The "Special Olympics"

Sullivan held that Caucasians were the best natural as well as the best-trained athletes in the world. Whites (especially those of Northern European heritage) were superior to all other races, and if they followed his training program would be unbeatable. But since the early days of European exploration there had been accounts of the remarkable physical abilities of indigenous peoples. Sullivan had noticed "disturbing" statements and "startling rumors" made in the press about the assumed speed, stamina, and strength of the Native peoples participating in the exposition. One reporter stated that the Cocopas were superb swimmers, while another held that "Patagonian horsemen" were "nearer living Centaurs than any other riders on the earth." Sullivan wanted to know if the heralded presumptions of the Indians' "marvelous endurance" as long-distance runners, the stamina of black South Africans, the Filipinos' remarkable climbing and diving feats, the agility and muscular strength of the "giant Patagonians," and the natural all-around abilities of "savage" peoples in athletic feats—as asserted in McGee's and the LPEC's extensive publicity—was true. If they were proven valid, it could undermine his entire philosophy and social agenda as well as make his department suspect. These assertions, which fundamentally challenged all he was doing, should be tested. Since McGee had claimed to have gathered all the races of the world, he suggested a Special Olympics be held in the track stadium in July or August, to accompany the regular Olympic competition so that "many physical directors and gentlemen interested in scientific work could be present and benefit by the demonstrations." In addition, Sullivan saw the research competition as a way to increase lagging ticket sales for the real Olympic Games. To Sullivan, a Special Olympics for Native peoples would be good publicity.[32]

Sullivan wrote McGee, suggesting a jointly sponsored event. They could combine the agendas of anthropology and physical culture under the rubric "the exposition university" and conduct entertainment as pseudo-experiments to demonstrate the natural athletic ability of the different races. Sullivan imagined that evolution, heritage, and athleticism could be tested without the contestants even realizing they were being used. Sullivan's hypothesis was that primitive people have certain physical abilities only because they lead lives that demand a high level of physical performance; they were not natural athletes as were more advanced Caucasians. McGee liked the idea that environment affected physical development; it fit in well with his evolutionary theories.[33] Also he and Woodward had been searching for more effective ways to test several hypotheses about the comparative strength and endurance of different races. Sampling was now an issue, because many Native peoples refused to be measured, photographed, or climb trees in their bare feet simply to see how long it would take them. Several experiments were bogging down and Woodworth had informed McGee he did not think he could finish by November, potentially negating all their efforts. Instead of continuing at the same pace, McGee and Woodworth decided to concentrate on testing strength, speed, and stamina during the proposed athletic competition.

McGee readily agreed to Sullivan's proposition and the latter named the event "Anthropology Days" in his honor; Sullivan later recalled that McGee "used his influence toward making the days the brilliant success which they terminated in" (Sullivan 1905a, 249). McGee began to search for participants by informing McCowan, Jenks, and concessionaires that "the object of the contests will be to obtain for the first time what may be called interracial athletic records." Scientific "evidence" would test "common beliefs" about "primitive" man's athleticism. His letter to W. P. Wilson, chair of the Philippine Exposition Board, is typical.

> Doctor J. E. Sullivan suggests a general Anthropology Day in his stadium on July 8 for athletic contests open to the world, barring Americans and Europeans, with the understanding that the events will be determined by the customs of the respective peoples participating, and the further understanding that so many winners in these events as may desire may participate in finals open to all the world on the day following. . . . I am proposing to cooperate through my peoples from outside the United States; yet the program cannot be made a success

without your support and that of Mr. McCowan and the entry of our
Filipinos and Indians.[34]

McGee never directly asked any Native men if they wanted to participate; he worked exclusively through agents. While expedient from a hierarchical organizational standpoint, it was not very courteous when viewed from Native standards of etiquette. McGee assumed that if the Caucasians in charge of a group told Native men to participate, they would. He was wrong. Arranging for Native athletes proved to be laborious and ineffective and at first yielded meager results; it took many hours of McGee's time before he felt safe to announce in the *World's Fair Bulletin* that the landmark competition would actually take place.

Ascertaining how many people actually competed in "pretests," "trials," and the actual events is difficult because no contestant lists have survived and no LPEC reports provide any numerical figures. Native people working in the anthropology exhibits, several foreign pavilions, the Philippine Reservation, and the Pike concessions took part in the trials and the winners were asked to participate in the "real" competition, during which the official comparisons to white athletes would be made. But many Natives who were asked refused because they were not to be paid, as they had been for other athletic competitions and entertainment events, including the trials. Others refused because they did not understand what was expected of them. To help convince more men, Natives were "allowed" to watch Olympic trials not held in the stadium. They saw athletes jump, race, lift weights, and swim. After watching swimming trials, everyone except the Moros refused to consider a swimming competition, and aquatic events were discarded. As a result of these excursions and McGee's persuasive abilities, Native men assembled at the stadium on August 12 for the heats of the Special Olympics (see fig. 12.1 and 12.2). Other people staged dance competitions, dramatic reenactments, or sang. McGee wrote that most Native people participated freely, but this statement is highly suspect. He never provided exact figures or stated how these men were either coerced or convinced to become athletes and research subjects.[35]

No Native men had any experience in Olympic-style field sports. Many did not understand what was expected of them, nor apparently did most of the "officials." McGee assigned Simms to organize, decide on appropriate events, and run the program with two days warning, leaving him so upset that he threatened to go back to Chicago. Simms eliminated events such as tennis, water polo, most forms of weightlifting, and relay races, often over Sullivan's objections. He did, however, retain the tug-of-war and focus on the running events, since he thought there was a good chance that all Natives knew how to run; it was a universal human activity. Dr. Luther H. Gulick, Sullivan's departmental assistant, served as referee, and Dr. Martin Delaney of St. Louis University demonstrated the basics once before the start of each event, unfortunately without interpreters. Simms later told McGee that many participants wanted to rerun heats because the rules were unclear; for others the goals of the competitions and what was expected of them remained elusive. Gulick did not allow reruns because it would have "violated" the established rules for track meets and invalidated the racial comparisons. Since whites only had one chance to perform, so should Natives. In addition, the stadium was booked for only two days. There was no time.[36]

According to Simms, while the competition's goals remained elusive for almost everyone, different tribes and ethnic groups (or "races") competed only against each other on the first day and the winners of these heats met on the second day in the interracial finals. There were several field events (16-pound shot put, 15-meter tree climbing, throwing the fifty-six-pound weight, running high and broad jumps, throwing stones and baseballs for accuracy, throwing baseballs for distance, a 220-yard race in which the runner carried 25 percent of his weight in a bag), and demonstrations of manual dexterity and physical fitness. The latter included the Mbutis playing shinny, a game they had learned from the Indians, archery, speed pole climbing, a Mohawk versus Seneca lacrosse game, blow guns, fighting methods, bola throwing, and Haskell scrimmaging with Carlisle in football. Most contests involved running because running was considered the ideal event to test claims that "savages" were athletes and fleet of foot. Sullivan noted that no one had ever tried sprint racing before. "With eight or ten men on the mark it was a pretty hard thing to explain to them to run when the pistol was fired. In running their heats, when coming to the finish tape, instead of breasting it or running through it, many would stop [wait for friends] and others run under it." Anyone who disregarded such rules was eliminated. Winners were those who actually crossed the finish line by themselves.[37]

While there are no records that provide direct evidence of how Native athletes felt about Anthropology Days, there are some hints that particular events were more interesting to them than others. According to Sullivan, the distance baseball-throwing competition was met with enthusiasm by many Native men who seemed to have "a weird fascination about the ball that appealed to them. No less than two dozen took part in throwing the baseball." Conversely, almost no one agreed to participate in throwing the fifty-six-pound weight, which was a bizarre idea for everyone. Three Patagonians and three Ainus tried; all refused second attempts when they were offered the opportunity to see if their performance could be improved. Simms reported that all the Indians thought the event was silly and not worth the effort. Sullivan later refused to consider this a valid motive to explain the results and concluded that "it can probably be said, without fear of contradiction, that never before in the history of sport in the world were such poor performances recorded for weight throwing." Sullivan was similarly disappointed in the javelin throwing competition. He assumed (incorrectly) that javelins could be thrown exactly as a spear and therefore Native peoples would excel in the contest for they were "natural" hunters. To him a javelin was simply an enlarged spear. While more than twenty-four men participated in the contest and each made three attempts, only three individuals hit a twenty-five-foot post. Sullivan concluded that "savages" had poor upper body strength, never questioning that practice was required to effectively use any tool.

While Sullivan was extremely disappointed in his Special Olympics, Simms was thoroughly embarrassed and insisted that no conclusions could be drawn from any test nor any overarching racial dyadic comparison reached. He told McGee and Dorsey that the whole experiment was a farce and at best all that was being tested was how modern training could make one run faster and throw farther. The performances had nothing to do with race or evolution. He felt that the Native people had been misused. If they ever did the events again, and he hoped they would not, the Native contestants needed to practice as much as the Caucasian athletes and have events explained to them in their Native languages. He advised McGee and Woodworth not to use the data they had collected because they were hopelessly flawed.[38]

It is telling that the Anthropology Days results were described and analyzed in Department of Physical Culture reports, rather than Anthropology reports. Sullivan ignored Simms and used selective data to "prove" his theories of Caucasian superiority. His conclusions were clearly designed to support his evolutionist and reformist suppositions: White Americans were the best athletes in the world; unorganized and uncontrolled sport was inferior; and team sports and training would solve social ills and promote political socialization in a rapidly changing world. To Sullivan the Special Olympics proved that his opinions about sport as a medium for shaping the moral and cognitive development of young people were correct but that Native peoples were intellectually, socially, and morally inferior by nature. They were not good prospects for assimilation. Rhetorically he ridiculed every event, disparaging and marginalizing Native performances when they were as good as or excelled Caucasian results, equating adult men with giggling twelve-year-old girls, extrapolating from individual performance to entire "races," and disparaging individuals' capabilities in manual dexterity, coordination, and physical fitness. He used the dubious data to conclude that primitive peoples were not intelligent enough for team sports.[39]

In concluding his report, Sullivan stated that unidentified scientists and physical education directors found "the only disappointing feature of the season" to be Anthropology Days. He was equally disappointed in anthropology as a science and thought the discipline hoodwinked people with "statements made by those who should know about the innate abilities of Native peoples." Anthropology, McGee, and primitive peoples in general could be dismissed because the performances were so poor. "The Anthropology Days were only successful in that they were destructive of the common belief that the greatest natural athletes were to be found among the uncivilized tribes in various parts of the world." To Sullivan the results of his experiment demonstrated that adult "savages" had abilities that were the equivalent of civilized children, a common idea of evolutionary rhetoric. Without supervision they expressed unhindered "anarchy." Team sports required obedience to the game's rules and attitudes of obedience, loyalty, willingness to sacrifice glory for a common cause, and the glorification of victory. As adults, "primitives" had not developed the group consciousness and cooperation that were seen to be cornerstones of team sports. Sullivan no longer thought there was hope for their evolutionary advancement or assimilation. Like many other Americans he concluded that Native peoples were destined to disappear or remain wards of the state.[40]

The Native participants did not realize that they had disappointed anyone. Nor did they know that their performances were being used to generalize about the athletic abilities of all "primitive" peoples or that their location in an evolutionary hierarchy would be reaffirmed by the rigged competition, faulty logic, or Sullivan's overgeneralizations. From Simms's letters to McGee, it appears that most of the Natives saw no purpose in the events, thinking they were not harmful but simply ridiculous.[41]

McGee, Woodworth, and Sullivan had planned to conduct anthropometric and psychometric tests on European and American athletes who participated in the regular Olympics. The idea was to establish norms of physical fitness for this special group of Caucasians to see how they varied from average visitors and Natives. Sullivan, however, was so dismissive of the Native results he became lukewarm about continuing the research project. There was no longer any need to conduct the experiments, he informed McGee, since the Native results only reinforced what everyone already knew—that trained Americans were the best natural athletes. He would continue independent anthropometric tests on outstanding athletes but not make further racial comparisons. As a consequence, planned tests of visitors' athletic abilities were never done. In the end, there were no "scientific" data on which to base comparisons of Caucasian and others, although this did not stop Sullivan from reaching sweeping conclusions. The grand comparison of "racial" athletic abilities was a bust but McGee was not ready to give up, nor could he. He had to salvage the money spent and save face—the reputation of anthropology was now an issue because Sullivan had written disparaging letters to Skiff, Francis, and the LPEC Board, apparently in an attempt to distance himself from what he considered a public relations humiliation. McGee decided to try again, this time with interpreters.

For McGee, the real disappointments of the Special Olympics were that he had been unable to educate people, including Sullivan, about the scientific value of anthropology and that he had not filled his departmental coffers. He had counted on ticket sales to help finance the event and pay the department's large grocery bills. He was also disappointed with the paltry advance publicity and the resulting poor attendance. He decided to organize a second competition in September to "give the audience a chance to see the pick of the primitive tribes contesting in modern and native games of strength, endurance, and agility."[42] While Anthropology Days had convinced Sullivan that "savages" were hopeless, lacking any natural athletic abilities, McGee felt they simply demonstrated that participants had not been properly shown how to perform. Natives needed to practice, just as American athletes did. McGee suggested to Sullivan that if they could find a professional trainer, practice, and restage the event after the regular Olympics, he predicted that the Natives would be as proficient as many Caucasian Americans and a valid comparison made.

Sullivan was not convinced and refused to approve the projected expenditure or plan for additional competitions; he felt there was simply no need. McGee proceeded on his own in order to "give the audience a chance to see the pick of the primitive tribes contesting in modern and native games of strength, endurance, and agility."[43] He convened an Emergency Exploitation Committee to organize the event and generate publicity. He also attempted to raise prize money but was unsuccessful and had to use his contingency fund. Jenks donated a set of American flags for the winners of each event; every entrant was given twenty-five cents for participating in any event. Groups began to practice under Simms's direction and "training meets" were held. The groups competed against each other, race by race, using the same model as before.

The September event was relatively successful, attracting thirty thousand viewers, according to McGee, of whom three thousand paid ten to twenty-five cents to sit on bleachers erected in front of the Indian School. He labeled the event an anthropological meet because Sullivan did not want "Special Olympics" used. As a reporter for the *St. Louis Globe-Democrat* remarked, "The meeting was a grand success from every point of view, and served as a good example of what the brown men are capable of doing with training."[44] Simms and his assistants kept records of the participants and their times. Unfortunately, these have not been located so we cannot identify the participants or compare their times to the August competition to see what training could do. McGee stated in a special report to Skiff when he repaid a loan that the results were better, but he also provided no records with his statement. Francis attended and noted in a *World's Fair Bulletin* that it was these races rather than the August events that had the greatest scientific value and that they were much more colorful and visually interesting than the regular Olympic Games because the participants wore their Native attire.

The "scientific" outcome of the events was almost a foregone conclusion, even if McGee was ambivalent about them. While McGee kept hundreds of newspaper articles on indigenous participation and departmental activities in his personal scrapbooks, he kept none on Anthropology Days or the September Races, even though many were written. After assessing the two sets of results, McGee concluded that "[o]n the whole [the results] are in harmony with the view of the course of human development by which the plans of the Department were shaped; making every allowance for the lack of training on the part of the primitives, the tests nevertheless established in quantitative measure the inferiority of primitive peoples, in physical faculty if not in intellectual grasp" (McGee 1905d, 99–100).

The Games really demonstrated nothing of the sort but McGee had too much at stake to acknowledge this, although his final LPEC report alludes to just that. McGee alerted readers to several caveats, as well as actual flaws in the research design. He concluded that: (1) the comparisons were one-sided since American athletes did not have to compete in Native events; (2) results differed "significantly" from August to September; (3) important anomalies had to be explained, not simply shoved aside as Sullivan had done; (4) there were sampling problems; and (5), the Natives were simply not interested, although some had fun. People do not put time and effort into things they find boring or silly.

What Anthropology Days ultimately showed was that competitions were culturally meaningful, but meaningful in different ways to organizers, viewers, and participants. It also showed that practice could affect performance and that people who had been sedentary for four or five months would not perform well in a series of athletic events that had never been explained to them and were not part of their cultural or performance repertoire. There were no valid measures of "natural ability." The Games really demonstrated that most Natives were simply not interested in Olympic-style athletic events (except for the marathon) or performing for visitors' amusement without compensation. In fact, many participants, especially the Mbutis, thought it fun to satirically mimic the events, pantomime the athletes and referees, disrupt the proceedings, and conduct the races their way. The games clearly demonstrated cultural preferences and cultural knowledge. To McGee, such cultural understandings were important, but not as important as bio-cultural evolution. While noting the flaws from both a performance and scientific standpoint, McGee never really came to grips with this special event. In the end he could not bring himself to reject completely the flawed experiment because it would have brought his assessment of anthropometry and anthropogeny into question and made his position at the LPE and in anthropology even more marginal than it was. Like Sullivan, McGee still believed as he had before the start of the exposition.

Sports science had no such qualms. Anthropology Days from Sullivan's standpoint and the racism inherent in his assessment went unchallenged until recently; similar tests comparing Native demonstrators with Olympic athletes were never held again in any venue. The Special Olympics of the 1904 St. Louis Exposition became synonymous with Coney Island and sideshows. IOC president Pierre de Coubertin noted in his memoirs that in no other place but America would anyone have dared to place such events on the Olympic program. He wrote an assessment in his 1979 book *Olympic Memoirs* of the St. Louis Olympics in general, and Anthropology Days in particular, even though he had not attended.

> *So the St. Louis Games were completely lacking in attraction. Personally, I had no wish to attend them. I harboured great resentment against the town for the disillusionment caused by my first sight of the junction of the Missouri and the Mississippi rivers. After reading [James] Fenimore Cooper, what had I not been led to expect of the setting where these rivers with their strange resounding names actually met! But there was no beauty, no originality. I had a sort of presentiment that the Olympiad would match the mediocrity of the town. As far as originality was concerned, the only original feature offered by the programme was a particularly embarrassing one. I mean the "Anthropological Days," whose events were reserved for Negroes, Indians, Filipinos, and Ainus, with the Turks and Syrians thrown in for good measure! That was twenty-six years ago! As for that outrageous charade, it will of course lose its appeal when black men, red men, and yellow men learn to run, jump, and throw and leave the white man far behind them. Then we will have progress.*

While the games were lauded in 1904 newspapers for their novelty and because they showed that Native peoples had great skill and agility, Anthropology Days became infamous in the literature on sports and Olympic history, with scholars relying solely on the scathing assessments of both Sullivan and de Coubertin. They have used words such as *colonialist, insulting, bizarre, infamous, disreputable, embarrassing, farce, foolish, shameful,* and *vulgar* for the event that "will long live in infamy as the most ridiculous event at any Olympics."[45] Anthropology Days also became a symbolic scapegoat, the epitome of bad taste and folly, one reason why St. Louis came to be considered the low point in the history of organized sport.

An alternative approach, and one taken by anthropology, was to pretend it never happened, until recently. McGee and others wanted it quickly forgotten and it was, even at the time. Anthropology Days was given no awards or official recognition at the close of the fair. It quickly became a non-event.[46]

13. Celebrating the Fair and Going Home

It was [the anthropology] department which not only
bound together the Louisiana Purchase Exposition as a whole,
but gave to it its broadest, highest and grandest significance.
John W. Hanson, 1905

As the oppressive summer heat passed into the cooler weather of autumn, fewer visitors came to the exposition, since children were back in school. After September 1, the remaining American Indian demonstrators began to go home in small groups. Their houses remained standing but were less enticing without inhabitants. There were vacant artisan booths, but still many activities at the Indian School. Sale of doughnuts and coffee remained brisk and football and basketball games were enjoyed. With the onset of frigid November winds, Geronimo decided he had had enough; all the Chiricahuas and Western Apaches returned to their homes. There were now few Indians except in the Wild West show.[1] McGee's foreign natives held center stage, but all wanted to go home, barely waiting for December 1. The Negritos, Mbutis, and Igorots suffered greatly in their scanty tropical attire, but for the sake of "authenticity" Jenks and McGee insisted they not wear overcoats during visitor hours.

Operations ran as smoothly as they were ever going to do, but the ephemeral nature of the buildings became all too apparent when the Missouri Pavilion burned to the ground. LPEC officials began to concentrate on post-fair activities and dismantling the exhibits. Museums and collectors began a feeding frenzy to purchase the over fifty thousand ethnographic and archaeological artifacts. Skiff and McGee in early June had hosted a dinner for foreign exhibitors to encourage them to sell or donate their objects to American institutions. By early July, Walter Hough, who was systematically canvassing exhibitors, noted that few people were willing to donate to the Smithsonian: "This scarcity is perhaps due to the zeal of individual collectors and dealers who have funds to purchase, thus creating a market and rendering it difficult for governmental or municipal organizations to secure them." And one major competitor was Skiff himself who, even before the exposition opened, had "his men on the ground listing everything they felt would be desirable, and [writing] letters asking leading exhibitors to donate these materials [to them] at the close of the exposition."[2] Stephen Simms's official job was to purchase objects for the Field Museum, while he was "unofficially" assisting McGee with the Indian Village. Dorsey traveled to St. Louis repeatedly during the fall to identify items to enhance the museum collections. Simms and Dorsey successfully negotiated at least twelve major acquisitions, transforming the Field Museum's Anthropology Department from a focus on the Americas to the entire world. Among others, they acquired all of Verner's African collections.

While not everything was for sale—several exhibitors took their objects to a special exhibition sponsored by the New York Art Exposition Company in Madison Square Garden after the fair—by early October the raids on all expositions exhibits, not only anthropology's, were so extensive that Skiff issued an ineffective proclamation that exhibits were not to be dismantled until December 2. By early November a third of the anthropology exhibits were gone and everything of value in the German East African display had been removed except for some zoological materials and a few busts, which the commissioner, D. von Luschan, gave to Hrdlička for the U.S. National Museum when no one purchased them.[3]

Belatedly, the LPEC Board and St. Louis citizens realized they were missing an opportunity to show how advanced their city was. They considered founding museums as a permanent monument to the exposition, just as Chicago had. A committee was formed in late October to explore the possibility of a history and anthropology museum and an art museum, in the hopes of obtaining collections cheaply. It was rather late in the game, however, for an undeveloped plan to work but this did not stop national newspapers reporting on Skiff's conflict of interest. Skiff quickly offered to split any collections slated to go to the Field Museum with the City of St. Louis if a city museum was established. A subcommittee began to think about raising funds and began to talk to McGee about being its first director.[4]

All of these activities and behind-the-scene negotiations created a problem. How could they honor the individuals and organizations responsible for the outstanding and highly professional LPE exhibits if the exhibits were now full of holes and many Native peoples had left? September was the month to adjudicate the exhibits and present awards; October through the next year was the time when awards and omissions would be contested.

Judging Merit

Public recognition and assessments of quality were important features of all international expositions and generated much controversy, for medals and certificates of merit were highly esteemed tokens. They carried great advertising cachet. Many manufacturers trumpeted the gold medals they received at international expositions. Thus those who controlled the judging process wielded considerable economic and social power. Influence peddling began early. Skiff developed a thick book of rules, definitions, and regulations on how to nominate and judge exhibits, based on previous expositions. Thousands of awards were given under the supervision of a LPEC commission on juries and awards. Each department organized a separate award committee to oversee actual adjudication of the myriad exhibits eligible for recognition. The LPEC commission had to approve these awards and reserved the right to award grand prizes based on departmental jury recommendations. Awards for anthropological displays were available using Skiff's elaborate classificatory scheme and what the jurors felt were exceptional efforts. Required LPEC categories included ethnology (living groups and collections), the Indian School, archaeology, history, anthropometry, and psychometry. These awards could be made for any exhibit, anywhere in the fair.

McGee spent July and August locating anthropologists for a departmental superior jury that would work with the top-level International Jury of Awards, a department-level jury, and several sectional juries. He wanted only professionals so that the research content of exhibits would be the focus of competition rather than the aesthetics of display techniques. In this way he hoped to institute the equivalent of the peer-review process used for professional journals and monographs. McGee invited many well-known and promising anthropologists, but most turned him down. Alfred Kroeber agreed when the judging was scheduled for the summer, but was unable to participate in September due to his teaching duties at the University of California. Others McGee nominated declined due to lack of interest, the prohibitive amount of time involved (six weeks), and scheduling conflicts. The final anthropology juries contained an impressive group of individuals from both the United States and abroad. Several foreign jurors also spoke at the congresses.[5]

McGee was unable to limit his judges to professionals because several appointments were political. Francis named Lehmann as co-chair, over McGee's objections. McGee was somewhat mollified when jurors elected Putnam cochair, deciding he would be in control with Dorsey serving as secretary. Francis appointed McGee, Putnam, and archaeologist J. C. Alves de Lima (University of New Orleans) as departmental representatives to the LPEC superior jury. Zelia Nuttall (a famous archaeologist and ethnohistorian who worked in Mexico) was designated the Board of Lady Managers' representative. Women jurors also included Alice Fletcher, Alice Palmer Henderson, and Cora Peters, a teacher in the Indian School. McGee had recommended these women because of their "eminent fitness, their experience at Chicago, and the endorsement of colleagues."[6] Senator George McBride of Oregon also recommended the wealthy Mrs. Henderson, an added incentive for McGee to suggest she be part of the general anthropology jury. The women judges reported that the most impressive work in the Department of Anthropology created by women was found in the history exhibits. Anthropology was a decidedly male affair.

Judging was intensive and drawn out over several weeks. Only those exhibits still in St. Louis were considered for awards; this eliminated demonstrators (like the Pawnees) or exhibitors who had left during the summer or whose collections had been sold and removed. Although groups of jurors were responsible for separate sections and met twice a day in joint sessions, it took almost three weeks of negotiation for them to agree on adjudication procedures and quality criteria and to decide which exhibits fit each category. The problem was that they were constrained by Skiff's classification, McGee's installation flexibility, last-minute additions, and the multidimensionality of exhibits that fell into more than one category. McGee presided at the early sessions and kept a general record that has not survived. Dorsey kept a log of the decisions, but this too has not survived. A final list of criteria was presented in McGee's final report.

Jurors split the ethnology category into outdoor and indoor exhibits. Criterion number four for the outdoor exhibits stated that all other criteria were "largely dependent on the completeness of control by the attendant in charge of the group." Other criteria reflected the amount of "danger, time, labor, effort and difficulty" that had gone into bringing the group to St. Louis, as well as the "previous inaccessibility of the tribe." The "presence of culturally appropriate or authentic implements, weapons, tools, gaming and amusement appliances, musical instruments, ceremonial paraphernalia," and racial purity, age, and gender representation were also considered, reflecting McGee's desire for completeness. The final criterion was the willingness of Native participants to perform "acts and feats to adequately represent the complete culture" of the group. This meant that several Indian groups were penalized for their unwillingness to perform ceremonies they felt were inappropriate for public settings.[7] Awards for outdoor exhibits basically assessed how well McGee and McCowan's special agents had done their work rather than the quality of the house construction, authenticity or appropriateness of the portrayal, or the amount of effort on the part of individual demonstrators. No one considered what conditions they had to put up with.

The indoor ethnology category included all static exhibits, books, and photographs as well as objects. Not surprisingly, the *American Anthropologist* was given a grand prize, with a special award going to its editor, Frederick Webb Hodge. The archaeology and ethnology categories were blurry. The Fred Harvey Company was given an award in archaeology, even though their exhibit contained primarily contemporary Indian blankets and baskets and featured the work of Mary Benson and an exhibit of Hopi art designed by missionary and Field Museum collaborator Henry Voth for the Hopi House at the Grand Canyon. In this case, the room in which the exhibit had been placed became the determinant for the award category, a compromise solution that reflected a last-minute rearrangement during exhibit installation. Since the Harvey Company exhibit was in a room designated archeology, it received an archaeology award. This did not diminish its importance to the exhibitors. John Huckel and Herman Schweitzer were immensely proud of the award and used it in promotional brochures for years.[8]

The LPEC International Jury gave most awards to organizers and sponsoring organizations. The Ohio Historical Society received a grand prize for its archaeological exhibit, while William C. Mills was given a gold medal for his conceptualization and installation work. Most individuals and participants had to be content with silver and bronze medals. The Indian Service and Superintendent McCowan were awarded grand prizes while teachers and department heads were given commemorative awards. Mrs. McCowan was given a special award in recognition of her services to the school and camps of foreign natives, although McGee never stated what these special services were. One can speculate they included ministering to the sick, since she nursed students, as well as reflected her position as McCowan's wife. We have no doubt that she worked hard to earn the acclamation. This was actually the highest award given to a woman, for men rather than women generally were awardees. Other women awardees worked in the Department of History or the Indian School.

The anthropology committee also presented special commemorative awards to those whom the committee, after consulting McGee, felt had been helpful. Some commendations were political and included individuals whom McGee wanted to thank for their LPE assistance or for their devotion to the professionalization of anthropology. Even though Boas actually did little with the anthropometry display (he spent more time on the Northwest Coast display in the Bureau of American Ethnology exhibit), McGee wanted to thank him for his support and friendship. Similarly, a gold medal went to Kroeber for his help with establishing anthropology as an outstanding scientific discipline rather than for anything he did in St. Louis. Conspicuously absent were Holmes and McGee's Smithsonian ex-colleagues, except Mooney, which is ironic since Mooney was such a vocal critic of the LPE and McGee. The committee also awarded McGee a special gold medal for the collective exhibits and awarded themselves awards for their efforts. All of these commemorative awards went to professional anthropologists.[9]

In contrast, the awards sent forward to the LPEC International Jury reflected both living and static exhibits. Starr earned two grand prizes, one for the Ainu encampment and another for the field school (which technically did not meet any adjudication criteria). Verner and Cane were awarded grand prizes because of their expeditions' distance and danger. Other special agents who had traveled shorter distances received gold medals, as did Mrs. McCowan for bringing together the "general assemblage." Interpreters received silver medals and the male leaders of compliant Native groups received either silver or bronze. The same scheme was used for indoor exhibits; effort, assistance to McGee, and distance traveled earned men gold medals. Benham was awarded a grand prize for "cultural artifacts," as well as a gold medal for his exhibit of exquisite Pomo baskets.[10] Starr also won another award for his display of Mexican ethnic photographs.

The anthropology committee also judged anthropological exhibits around the fairgrounds, including in their purview anything that could remotely be placed under Department N of Skiff's classification. Kroeber and Pliny Earl Goddard received a gold medal for their small ethnic and linguistic map of California in the Education Building; Governor Brady and the state of Alaska received a gold medal for the Haida totem pole display. Awards for ethnographic exhibits in the foreign category were given for the Palace of Ancient Art, the Jain Temple, Siam, and the German East-African display, while Argentina, Brazil, and Mexico took home top awards for foreign archaeological displays. To ensure that there were no diplomatic incidents, every government which sent any sort of archaeological display, even if it was only one or two artifacts, was presented with an award. Even with this breadth of coverage several individuals complained when they were awarded bronze rather than gold medals.

The main area of contention and fundamental disagreement among jurors was how properly to recognize Native participants. As McGee wrote in his final report: "Prolonged consideration was given the suggestion emanating from the Section Jury in Ethnology, that each primitive (man, woman, and child) connected with the Department be given a special medal or other token provided the Exposition Management approved; the suggestion was adopted by a small majority, on reconsideration the vote was at first a tie and later, after a change of one vote, the negative prevailed" (McGee 1905d, 374). The result was negative; the debate shows that judging was highly political and discriminatory. Professional concerns overruled humanist considerations for the Native participants' feelings. Diplomacy was not a consideration with regard to colonized, indigenous men and women. McGee was very disappointed with this decision because he wanted Native participants to be individually recognized and take home with them a souvenir to remind them of the wonders they had seen in America. Instead, Caucasian special agents received gold medals and grand prizes while only a select few Native leaders, interpreters, or assistants (called collaborators) received a silver or gold medal in recognition of their helpfulness. No Native women were given awards with the exception of Mary Benson, who was noted for being extremely courteous to tourists; she received a bronze medal while her husband was given silver. Special awards were also made to Chief Antonio (Igorot), Datto Facundi (Samal Moro), and several other unnamed Native leaders in the Philippine Exhibit (even though it was not technically part of the Department of Anthropology and had its own competition). These awards were made on the basis of the faithfulness in the building of huts and portrayal of daily life, but also mirrored the elements of control, good behavior, and gender exclusion seen in other anthropology awards.[11]

St. Louis newspapers commented on the discrepancy between the approved methods for considering recognition and the anthropology committee's politicized and ethnocentric awards. Some felt the anthropology jury was unfair, although they noted progress was being made; according to one reporter this was the first time *any* Indian had received official recognition at *any* exposition.

> *Contrary to the method of awarding medals, which in every case is made direct to the manufacturer or exhibitor, the subservient squaw, who weaves her bright-colored blanket, who makes the much-admired baskets, and who molds her exclusive designs of pottery, will not share some of the honors of the exhibitor and manufacturer in receiving the medals for excellent workmanship and industry. The chief of her tribe will be entitled to the prize as the representative head of her particular group. But as the question of "woman's rights" does not enter the life of the squaw, she has expressed herself as being perfectly satisfied with the proposed method of awarding the emblematic prizes for her work, and she is working faithfully and diligently to obtain the prize for her chief and the glory of her tribe.[12]*

As with the Olympics, we doubt that anyone actually asked the Native people how they felt about the awards. There is no evidence in the LPEC files that any Native person "officially" protested. In contrast, there were hundreds of protests from American exhibitors and foreign dignitaries who felt slighted.

Anthropology bestowed 243 awards, not counting honorable mentions. This seems like a large number, until one considers that the jury for the Philippine Reservation awarded 6,775 medals: 136 grand prizes, 552 gold medals, 785 silver medals, 1,226 bronze medals, and 4,076 honorable mentions. But the Filipino adjudication criteria effectively eliminated Native participants. Medals did go to the titular heads of three indigenous groups: Datto Facundi (Samal Moro) and Chief Antonio (Igorot) received gold medals, while the

Sultans (Lanao Moro) received silver. "One or two [leaders] who had behaved badly" were disqualified; they received "lesser recognition." LPE historian Mark Bennitt does not say what the bad behavior was or why most Native groups were not given any commemorative recognition. A few Natives received honorable mentions, which meant a diploma. Conversely every one of the fifty Westernized Filipino honorable residents was given a medal in recognition of their participation (men received gold or silver while women received bronze). Assimilation was clearly rewarded.[13]

While the Department of Anthropology was technically in charge of adjudicating any anthropology or history exhibit, McGee refused to include government displays. The Smithsonian Institution received fifty-six awards, including one for its collective exhibit, one for the U.S. National Museum collective exhibits, and three for the ethnology section, the Mexican temple models, and the Bureau of American Ethnology exhibit. Frederick W. Hodge also received a gold medal for his bibliographic display, and Holmes, Cyrus Abbott, O. T. Mason, Walter Hough, Paul Beckwith, DeLancey Gill, Mary Gill, Matilda Coxe Stevenson, Jesse W. Fewkes, John Swanton, James Mooney, and Aleš Hrdlička received commemorative awards. Conspicuously absent from the list was Boas, whose contribution was effectively ignored.[14]

With the awards distributed it was time to think about dismantling the fair and sending the Native participants home safely. McGee also had to think about how he could keep the exhibits open until December 1, since he was essentially out of money by October. He and McCowan considered closing on November 1 and McCowan did close the school mid-month. McGee decided to continue as long as he could even though he had many expenses yet to come. He needed help and some came from museums that paid for dismantling the static exhibits. But this solution came at a cost, especially for any visitors who came to the Anthropology Building after November 1. There was not much to see except for the labs and the synthetic archaeological series.

Closing Down

Edward Schneiderhahn attended the Louisiana Purchase Exposition's closing ceremony. "At promptly [midnight] President Francis turned the switch that controlled the power and the light. The flood of light grew fainter and fainter and of a sudden all was darkness. The Cascades were silent. The scene was dead. The World's Fair was no more. It passed into history forever." It had been the largest exposition in terms of space; the over fifteen hundred separate buildings exceeded all previous expositions combined. As one visitor reflected, "I have not been able to inspect all the exhibits very well. It is unthinkable that all may be seen. The mind reels at the mass of various and wonderful exhibits."[15]

It had cost the LPEC twenty-two million dollars to stage the event and the expenditures of states and foreign governments had been more than nine million. It would cost one million dollars to restore Forest Park and dismantle the buildings over a three-year period. In his closing speech, Francis said that stockholders would see a small profit. Individual exhibitors had worked hard and most had also made a profit. Over nineteen million visitors from every state and several foreign countries had paid admission.[16] But despite all the attractions and special events, the total attendance was below the 1893 Chicago Exposition. Francis and the Board of Trustees were disappointed. They had not outdone Chicago despite their best efforts, at least not in total attendance.

McGee estimated the number of visitors who actually ventured inside the remote Anthropology Building to be 1.5 million. Most had come to see the Victorian Jubilee Tributes rather than the synthetic archaeology exhibits; McGee estimated that the "unbroken tally of visitors to the [Tributes] room" exceeded a million. Over three million visitors watched the demonstrations and programs in the Indian School while over four million people were thought to have visited the Indian Village and the Anthropology Villages, although no official numbers were kept. McGee was sure people had learned a great deal from their visits. James Buel thought the archaeology exhibits had shown him everything there was to learn from a "museum of human relics," which had made it "comparatively easy to trace man's progress from his earliest manifestations through all the pauses, periods, and epochs of his advancement, even to the heights of his accomplishments in the dawn of the twentieth century." How much most visitors actually learned about anthropology is open to question. One conversation overheard in the Indian School summarized the problem: "Let's go over to the Anthropology Building." "Oh no, I don't know anything about bugs. Why should I go over there?" Whether they understood the intricacies of McGee's theories of cultural and biological evolution and human progress is hard to assess. But they did remember the Native peoples. The living displays were very impressive.[17]

The LPE had been a meeting ground for the world's people and it had lived up to the expectations of at least one *Washington Post* reporter who had predicted in 1901 that it would "cover all the world." As he told readers in mid-December 1904, "[T]here is nothing which aroused so tremendous a curiosity in the world's mind. The one feature talked about while the world's fair was in progress, and as it passed into history, was its splendid and unique exhibit of the earth's living tribes of primal humanity." It was a remarkable achievement, never to be repeated. While it fell short of McGee's lofty (and impossible) goals, it was the largest and most complex gathering of Native peoples ever seen at an international exposition. McGee had wanted to conduct a census of all the fair's Native peoples but never completed it, due to the pressures and chaos normal to exposition administration and his recurring illnesses. He did estimate there had been more than three thousand indigenous peoples in attendance: about 50 foreign people in the Department of Anthropology display; over 325 "old Indians" encamped around the Indian School under the Indian Service's appropriation; and 175 Indian students and teachers. McGee also estimated there were over 200 Indians, 150 "Kaffirs," Hindus, and Singhalese, 600 Japanese, and 250 Chinese on the Pike and approximately 1,200 Filipino Natives in the Philippine Reservation.[18] These estimates did not include many others we have located in our documentary searches who worked in state pavilions or in the Manufacturing Building. There were also Native peoples who were visitors or attended conferences. We will never know the real figures, in part because they were always fluctuating.

Upon reflection as the LPE closed, McGee did not feel he had achieved his grand vision of displaying anthropology's knowledge or proving his synthetic theory. He did not feel that he had really been able to show his half of the world how the other half of the world lived and that the course of human progress was marked by stages in an inevitable progression. He felt that the fault was not with his vision, theories, assumptions, or methods of presentation. He had failed because the LPEC had not given him enough money to bring representatives of all the world's peoples to St. Louis. At best, he argued, the people who participated only whetted anthropology's appetite for more study. McGee felt he should try again at the next fair. But all was not a loss, for the LPE demonstrated the centrality of anthropology to any future advances in Western knowledge. To McGee the St. Louis Exposition ultimately "gave renewed and fuller meaning to the opinion of Pope that 'the proper study of mankind is man'" (McGee 1905d, 26).

While disappointed, McGee was still proud of his results. He thought anthropology's press coverage exceeded that of any other exposition department and reflected his goal of extending the field's evolutionary message to the general public. He had succeeded there, he thought, although we may question how good some of the publicity was because so many newspaper reports were satirical or simply reinforced preexisting stereotypes. He considered Starr's formal university-level field school a major pedagogical breakthrough in terms of institutional cooperation, fulfilling the LPEC's mission to be the "University of All Expositions." He also felt the college course was critical in establishing the research experiments' credibility, legitimizing his goals, and moving anthropology forward as a valid science. McGee had been concerned that research conducted at an ephemeral institution would not be given the professional status of university-centered research, and he was correct. The fair-generated research was never recognized.

McGee convinced himself that his assemblage of human types was more than simply a source of curiosity and attraction. He thought it had served several professional and policy ends. But he would have to prove that to the anthropological and scientific communities in the future. First he had to see that the Natives arrived home safely. And this was hard work, undertaken with a diminished staff, racing against time. The LPEC wanted to dismantle the buildings and eliminate services and Washington University wanted its building back for classes in January. For McGee there was an additional problem. He had no money.

How Are the Natives Going to Get Home?

McGee had badly overspent his allocation by the end of November. Most funds had gone toward the initial expeditions to bring Native peoples to St. Louis, a cost of over fifteen thousand dollars between August 1903 and June 1, 1904. Another major expense was salaries and agent fees. The monthly salary for each special agent was three hundred dollars for the Ainu, Cocopa, and Kwakiutl groups, three hundred and fifty for the Mbutis, and five hundred dollars for the Patagonians and the U.S. Indians. Then there had been installation costs, McGee's travel expenses, and food and supplies for the participants. The anthropometry and psychometry laboratories required two hundred and fifty dollars in salaries and fifty dollars for materials every month. McGee was several thousand dollars in debt.[19]

In mid-July McGee had sent Skiff the first of many requests for more money. His estimates for dismantling the exhibits (which he calculated would take two months) were several thousand dollars. He predicted it would cost eight thousand dollars to return all the Native groups to their homelands (including salaries for the special agents), McCowan's one thousand dollars' special honorarium for administering the Indian School (in addition to his salary), one hundred dollars to return laboratory equipment, and three thousand dollars in salaries. McGee needed an additional twelve thousand dollars. Skiff and the LPEC executive committee were not pleased and, as a penalty for fiscal mismanagement, reduced McGee's salary from $416 to $364 per month. Similarly, salaries for his assistants were cut; several quit and were not replaced, which meant more work for McGee and Simms. The LPEC found the additional money but only after McGee admitted he had completely depleted his contingency funds by mid-August.[20]

In his final report, McGee wrote that the total cost for the ethnology section was $48,042, not counting the $40,000 Indian Service allocation for the Indian School expenses. The most expensive group was the Mbutis ($12,400) followed by the Tehuelches ($11,600). Ainu expenses amounted to $6,300 and the Cocopas $4,700. The combined total for Indians was $13,000. Total expenses for the static anthropology and history exhibits combined with the laboratories were $5,000. The estimate for these sections had been $16,000, but McGee had repeatedly transferred monies to the Native village accounts. His figures were actually low because he hid expenses and never included others in his final report. The most glaring was the $4,400 that it took to have the Kwakiutls and Nootkas perform in St. Louis and the expenses for sending them home. McGee never stopped hoping that the Field Museum would pick up more of these expenses, but it never did.[21]

By September, every special agent had become concerned about the lack of funds, the repeated requests they had to make for supplies, and the fact that their monthly allocations and salaries were not forthcoming. The most vocal agent and the one who created his own fiscal headaches for McGee was Verner, who had contracted to stay with the Mbutis for the entire exposition and take them back to the Belgian Congo. Instead he left them under the care of John Kondola in July and went to Africa on his own without informing McGee. He now claimed he was stranded in the Upper Kasai Valley of the Congo Free State. When McGee informed him that his appropriation for the rest of the exposition and the trip home would have to be cut and that he could not cover all his expenses (especially those of his present trip), Verner began writing Francis and the LPEC Executive Board. He wrote President Roosevelt, asking for money so he could return to St. Louis, a round trip back to Africa at government expense. He also requested that Roosevelt receive the Mbutis at the White House on their way home. Roosevelt refused all requests (Bradford and Blume 1992).

Francis told McGee to take care of the matter. After a series of wires and letters involving long, complex negotiations with Verner and his wife, Francis told McGee to use the money in his contingency fund. McGee had been hiding the fact that he had no money from Skiff and Francis and there followed a humiliating request to the LPEC Board in which McGee noted that Verner had already exceeded his agreed-upon contract with the LPEC by more than 50 percent, but that he needed him or they would have to figure out some other way to get the Mbutis back to Africa. The board authorized an additional five hundred dollars with a formal reprimand.[22]

Verner returned just in time to escort the Mbutis back to Africa. They were more than ready to leave, for November had been a month of cold, icy rain and they had been forced to live in the Anthropology Building's basement, taking over the anthropometry laboratory, which closed early. It was very depressing. On December 4, the Mbutis said good-bye to Francis, wearing new suits the LPEC had given them as departing gifts. Francis personally gave them a cask of salt and a necklace for King Ndombe and his wife, watch fobs (but no watches), and $1.35 in spending money for the journey home. The next morning Verner and Ota Benga took a train to Washington DC so Verner could collect a "reward" (a land concession near the Ndombe) from the Belgian ambassador, Baron Moncheur, for not reporting atrocities he had seen in Africa. Meanwhile, Kondola took the other eight men to New Orleans, having agreed to take care of them until Verner arrived. There they waited while

Verner and Ota Benga stopped in North Carolina to see Verner's family. Unfortunately, all contracted chicken pox and were quarantined for two months. After reaching New Orleans, Ota Benga told his compatriots through a closed door about the wonders he had seen. Near the end of their quarantine, the Mbutis decided they could stand the confinement no longer and took part in a Mardi Gras parade. Finally they were allowed to leave and sailed to Havana, where it took them two weeks to recover from grippe and took Verner two more weeks to secure passage on a ship. The men did not arrive home until May 3, 1905. When Verner wrote about the journey it became an adventure featuring wild animals and hostile tribes, rather than a heart-wrenching tale of illness and boredom.[23]

None of the American Indians' return trips were as problem-ridden as the voyage to Africa, primarily because of good luck. They were certainly no better planned or executed. It was Simms's job to ensure that people made it off the fairgrounds and onto trains. Then they were on their own, accompanied only by an interpreter. To the best of our knowledge all Indians arrived safely to their homes.[24] But Simms found the duties onerous; he was busy securing collections and assuming Skiff's duties, Skiff having contracted malaria, as well as battling customs agents. By late November, Newcombe described Simms as fighting bouts of fever, often in a stew, wanting nothing more than to leave St. Louis and the LPE far behind.

The younger children left the Indian School when classes resumed at their individual schools. Several older students remained to help dismantle the building and ship equipment to Chilocco. It fell to Mrs. McCowan to run the Indian School for the last two months and oversee the dismantling because McCowan had contracted malaria and spent most of November and December in Hot Springs, Arkansas, recuperating. There was no evidence of any problems and the school was completely closed by December 2 when the fair closed; the building was razed the next week. Nothing remained on the top of the hill.

The remaining foreign Natives went home at the same time as the Mbutis. The Tehuelches left on December 2 after visiting Francis, who presented them with silver jewelry, gold stick pins, and emerald and garnet rings. They traveled to New York and from there sailed to South America. Apparently they arrived home without incident or after only minor delays.

The same cannot be said for the Ainus. They left for Chicago on December 3, accompanied by Charles Hulbert, McGee's assistant, and the Haidas, who had worked in the Alaska territorial exhibit. There they were to rendezvous with Starr before continuing by train to Vancouver. Starr, however, had apparently made no plans to accompany them back to Japan, having so informed McGee and thinking other arrangements had been made. Starr was surprised to see the group on his doorstep and angry with McGee, for whom he no longer had any respect. He had written McGee from Mexico in November relating concerns he had received from Simms, Inagaki, and even Batchelor in Japan that there was apparently no money to pay the Ainus or funds for their fares back home. "I feel sure you are doing all that any man can do in the matter. I assured Mr. Batchelor that the money is likely to be paid in full, and I sent word to the Ainu that I believe they will be started home very soon after December 1 and that they will surely be paid all."[25] McGee eventually sent the money, but not until the last possible minute, and he even paid the Ainus "overtime." He also gave Sangea Hiramura a special present, as was appropriate for an elder, and a personal gift to Kutoroge Himaruma, the bear hunter who felt the compensation for the work they had done was inadequate and that he had been bewitched and made ill because of the trip to America.

Hulbert accompanied the Ainus. On December 11, Inagaki wrote that the Ainus and Haidas had encountered no problems, had been well cared for, and the railway company very courteous. The Haidas had left for their homes and the Ainus were sailing the next day. "It is raining here today but not stormy. I hope for a calm voyage though they say this is the worst time to cross the Pacific. Kutoroge to whom your great case was given is in good spirits. There was no trouble about him on the way coming down here. I hope he will remain so until he gets back to his home."[26]

McGee waited anxiously to hear that the Ainus had arrived safely in Japan but no letter came. On December 20, Hulbert wrote Inagaki asking him to send a one word telegram with a code. "Let 'perfect' mean that you have arrived with the people in the best of shape; let 'good' mean that you have arrived but have encountered difficulties on the way; let 'fair' mean that you have arrived in only fair condition and with many difficulties; let 'poor' mean that some of the people have not survived; and let 'bad' mean that Kutoroge has died on the way."[27] We located no cable in McGee's papers but there was a letter indicating they were in Japan by early January and safe. Apparently Kutoroge was still alive and well despite his misgivings.

How the Ainus were reincorporated into their villages was discussed in a short, undated article from the *St. Louis Post-Dispatch* found in Starr's scrapbook, probably written in August 1905. It noted that a St. Louis woman who had befriended Santukno Hiramura had received a letter from her. She reported that the money Santukno and Sangyea had earned in St. Louis enabled them to buy a house and purchase a horse and pig. In 1909 Starr and his traveling companion, Manuel Gonzales, journeyed to Japan and made a brief trip to Hokkaido to visit the Ainus. When they arrived in Piratori, Kutoroge, Shutratek, and their children were well and received Starr in ceremonial attire as befitted an honored guest. With money earned in America they had added two new rooms to their house and were considered quite wealthy. Yazo and Shirake were living with Batchelor in Sapporo where they had chosen to remain.[28]

One of the most hair-raising trips was experienced by the Cocopas who braved a blizzard, stranded for several days in Colorado. In early September, Mrs. Colorado had grown seriously ill, suffering from a relapse of tuberculosis contracted earlier. McGee decided to rush her home and Pablo Colorado decided to accompany her, as did Pahup and Ilpuk. To speed them back to Yuma, McGee had Hulbert (who left with "an exceeding great relief" to escape "from the dull, almost ambitionless slavery of St. Louis") accompany them. Expenses for the journey to Arizona were probably around $250 although Hulbert had to wire McGee for a return fare. McGee had given him only enough money for the group's journey to Yuma, barring any delays or mishaps.[29]

Unfortunately, the group encountered "trouble on top of trouble." Hulbert reported to McGee on October 12 that they had reached Trinidad, Colorado, by easy stages, with the assistance of the Fred Harvey Company and railroad personnel. They slept on the train and ate their own food, apparently mingling little with other travelers. Then they were stranded for three days due to a washed-out train bed, next a flood cut a railway station in half (luckily they were on high ground when this happened), and then there was an unexpected blizzard. The Harvey Company gave them hotel rooms for free. When they could finally leave, Hulbert settled them on a train, returned to the station to make final arrangements for food, and the train left without him. The Cocopas had no interpreter and no food. Hulbert reached Albuquerque the next day, where the Cocopas were supposed to be waiting for him, but found that they had been put on another train for Lamy Junction. When he reached them, they had not eaten for two days. Hulbert wired McGee on October 19 from Deming, New Mexico, that they were finally headed for Yuma. Reaching there without further incidents, the Indians started downriver and made it home safely.[30]

Mrs. Colorado, of course, had a more difficult journey than anyone else. Hulbert later acknowledged he had not realized how sick she was and how ill-prepared he was to care for her. She grew steadily weaker, but the unexpected troubles in Colorado probably helped her survive the journey. She "was in pretty good shape at La Junta so long as she was lying still, but the motion of the train doesn't seem to agree with her very well, though she appears to pick up immediately when we stop." Hulbert speculated about the benefits of the Fred Harvey Company restaurants. "Perhaps, too, the good food has helped, for I am quite sure the group never had such good fare as they are getting here." Hulbert had originally thought being stranded at a high altitude would have made her plight especially difficult, but Mrs. Colorado improved during the trip, in part due to a doctor's ministrations, but she relapsed and died a month after returning home.[31]

With little money to spare for any return trips, agents had to fight for every penny. In late October, McGee finally gave Newcombe five hundred dollars to take the Kwakiutls and Nootkas home. As Newcombe wrote Dorsey, "[T]his sum does not cover my own time and expenses but I thought it best to speed away and not wait for the full amount." It was also not enough for the trip itself. The Native participants had over one ton of baggage, including the large canoe, which they wanted to take with them, but Newcombe felt he had to ship some pieces by freight and discard others. This led to a serious cultural misunderstanding. "Atlieu and some of the others got very excited and said it was a robbery. He also jumped on a lot of things, broke all he could and drowned his sorrows in the evening so that he was quiet and depressed during the journey. Annie joined him in his libations and both have renewed the revel since their arrival here in Victoria." Dorsey was upset about the incident, feeling Newcombe had dealt with the situation inadequately and was omitting something in his description. Dorsey investigated further and learned that Atlieu had tried to tell Newcombe the materials were to go to the Field

Museum. The items Newcombe had thrown away because they were too expensive to ship included roof boards and long rafters Dorsey wanted to repair the museum's Haida houses. The trunk Newcombe sent by freight to Seattle contained items hand-carved by Atlieu and Jasper Turner, designed to be sold to the Field Museum, and for which the artists felt they would now never receive compensation. They were correct, for the trunk was lost and never found. Despite Newcombe's disastrous decisions, the groups made it home. Soon thereafter Atlieu contracted pneumonia but recovered. By mid-December the men and women requested that Newcombe and Dorsey send their awards, certificates of merit, and photographs. Dorsey did so.[32]

As Jenks dismantled displays, the Philippine Reservation residents began the long journey home. Many younger Filipinos wanted to extend their stay in the United States, while "homesick" older members left for Manila on November 15 in several groups going by different routes. A few young Igorots, Bagobos, Moros, and Visayans remained until mid-December before embarking on a government-sponsored tour of the country. The popular Constabulary Band and Visayan entertainers had received numerous offers from entertainment promoters to tour in the United States during 1905. Visayan musicians went to New York City for a two-week engagement (December 17 to 30, 1904) in a miniature world's fair held at Madison Square Garden. McGee tried to help them book other venues through his connections. Ever the promoter, he received a multiweek offer for them and had Benham, the sutlery trader who had returned to New York, track them down. They declined, however, and went home on January 13, 1905, after deciding that they had spent enough time in America. For them the trip went well. For one group of Igorots who were to have gone home via Chicago it was a nightmare. They were abandoned there by their guide who stole all their money and clothes. They were outside in the snow when people found them. It was a national scandal.[33]

Scouts with expired enlistments were sent to San Francisco and discharged from the U.S. Army upon landing in Manila. Those who had reenlisted were sent to Fort Thomas, Kentucky, where they spent the winter. The band and one unit performed in President Roosevelt's inauguration parade after which they went to San Francisco, arriving in Manila on May 2, 1905. Upon reaching home the unit disbanded; the men returned to their original companies (Laurie 1994–95, 53).

14. The Experiences of an Exposition

The Anthropology exhibit has the interest of strangeness,
for it is an exhibit of races of men whose lives and whose crafts
have no counterpoint in our lives and crafts.
WJ McGee

Although tired and ill as the fair wound to a close, McGee wanted to try again to assemble the world's peoples but he was not given the opportunity and his overtures to the organizers of the next exposition—the Lewis and Clark Centennial and American Pacific Exposition and Oriental Fair, in Portland—were respectfully declined. He had learned much from St. Louis and had definite ideas about how anthropological displays could be done right the next time. On November 15, 1904, he presented a paper to the Anthropological Society of Washington entitled "Anthropology at the Louisiana Purchase Exposition." A note in the *American Anthropologist* states it dealt with race and how the exposition's activities had helped to clarify the concept. Joining McGee were Alice Fletcher, who talked about the Indian School and the history of Indian Service participation in expositions, and William Henry Holmes, who discussed how he had illustrated the aesthetic achievements of Indians in the Smithsonian displays.[1] Each spoke only about the successes of their endeavors.

McGee was more forthcoming in his final report to the LPEC, which he submitted on May 10, 1905. He began by noting his successes, despite the lack of financial support, and the difficulties he had encountered, getting in one more dig at the LPEC officials for the lack of foresight and not agreeing with his grandiose plans. The exposition had not been personally rewarding. "The experiences of an exposition" had included many mistakes, much "arduous labor, [and] innumerable disappointments," and only a few "fortunate accidents, rare recreations, [and] infrequent gratifications." But he had a wealth of suggestions for the next corporation that attempted exposition anthropology displays. All were subsumed under a single general recommendation.

A conscientious review of Anthropology at the Universal Exposition of 1904, and a careful weighing of methods and results: of the expressions of thousands of visitors and of the vague ideas hardly expressed by all; of the fact that a third of the paying attendants took the long journey from the Main Picture to the meagerly supplied Anthropology Grounds; of the fact that despite tardy beginning and relatively minute results, Anthropology at the Fair inspired a full third of the spontaneous press publicity given the Exposition; of the fact that despite strong prejudice the Philippine Exposition proved the most attractive exhibit at St. Louis—the weighing of these and other considerations warrant the judgment that if another million dollars had been added to the Department of Anthropology there would have been three million additional admissions, and if two million dollars had been added, the take at the gates would have been five and ten million greater—and the permanent benefit of the Exposition to the public mind would have been many times multiplied. (McGee 1905d, 413)

To McGee, St. Louis would remain his, and anthropology's, missed opportunity, stymied by short-sighted others who lacked his vision. He never lost his belief that if only he had been given ample funds he could have fulfilled his life-long dream. Unfortunately for him, no one else shared his vision of a complete assemblage of the world's peoples, and no future expositions ever attempted it on any scale.

McGee concluded by conveying his contemporary-sounding views on education, showmanship, and exhibits, views that speak to all educators and museologists today. He knew Americans' short attention spans necessitated novelty. One had to capture their attention and imaginations to encourage learning. This was the duty of anthropologists. "It is the chief lesson of this Exposition that the public must be attracted by the prospect of seeing that which it has not seen before—and so long as human nature remains as it is, the human mind can conceive of no more novel and attractive spectacle than an assemblage of all the world's peoples living in their accustomed ways" (McGee 1905d, 413).

Anthropology Moves On

In 1904 anthropology was just becoming established in American universities. It was in transition from a "field of study" pursued by self-taught individuals to a "scientific discipline" practiced by those properly credentialed through postgraduate training and the possession of advanced degrees awarded by universities organized on the German model (Darnell 2001). This volume has focused on one self-taught individual, WJ McGee, and his quest for professional authority and recognition as he envisioned them and the consequences of this quest for anthropology and the peoples who formed the discipline's subject matter. When he took the job at the LPE, McGee was president of the newly created American Anthropological Association. He saw himself as the discipline's leader, with a unique opportunity to present anthropology to the world as well as advance his political, social, and cultural agendas on the grand stage of an international exposition. Others connected with the LPE used anthropological concepts, as well as Native peoples, to present different messages and further their own sociopolitical schemes. We have attempted to depict how anthropological concepts were variously presented to the public, and how the personal, theoretical, and political agendas of both presenters and those being presented, affected this undertaking.

As sites of intense, confined interaction, world's fairs provide unique opportunities to trace the interplay of important ideas and values of both the host and guest cultures and attempts by various parties to introduce new ideas—technological, social, and political—to the public. The great world's fairs were nationalistic celebratory mega-events of their age. They generated huge amounts of publicity, and newspapers and magazines wrote volumes about the exhibits and the people associated with them. The fairs were sites of ritual and spontaneity, spectacle and festival, as well as marketplaces of things and ideas. They were sites of anticipation, awe, novelty, reflection, and hope. They were also, as McGee so insightfully put it, sites "with the interest of strangeness," where one half of the world could meet and interact with the other half (McGee 1904a). McGee saw this interaction as a two-way didactic process. White Americans would meet and learn about Native peoples, particularly how those peoples represented presumed earlier stages of human development. The Native peoples would learn about the progressive civilization of the whites, a civilization to which they might aspire, with proper training. The Model Indian School was an example of how that process was supposed to work. The Native peoples apparently did learn useful things, although not necessarily that they should strive to become culturally pseudo-whites. The whole undertaking was suffused for McGee with an aura of essentialist scientific respectability and justification for why anthropology was needed in a colonial world, which ipso facto validated anthropology itself.

At the end of the exposition, officials expressed their feelings about the fair and the role of anthropology and Native peoples in its success. Speaking to the Commercial Clubs of Chicago and Cincinnati visiting St. Louis, Skiff reiterated the same themes that he had espoused while planning the exposition.

> *A modern universal exposition is a collection of the wisdom and achievements of the world, for the inspection of the world—for the study of its experts, by which they may make comparisons and deductions and develop plans for future improvements and progress. . . . It constitutes a classified, compact, indexed compendium (available for ready reference) of the achievements and ideas of society, in all phases and its activity, extending to the most material as well as the most refined. It offers illustrations covering the full field of social performance from the production of the shoes on our feet and the pavement beneath them to the presentation of the rarest and most delicate creation of the hands and brains of men in what are classified as the fine arts of civilization.*

He also felt the world benefited because the LPE was an exposition of processes as much as things. "The yield to the world is in the universalizing of things, in the realizing of interdependence, in the growing brotherhood of man and fatherhood of God" (Skiff 1904b, 3).

But some "advanced" elements, such as the sideshows and the belief in racialized classifications, are questionable. The simplification and overgeneralization of very complex issues raised by the LPE did not go unnoticed even at the time. What roles did indigenous peoples have in the American vision of itself poised to be an imperial global power? What role did anthropology really play in the developing ideology? Was it the young intellectual discipline that would draw together all forms of knowledge, as McGee claimed? Or was it a set of ideas that simply legitimized bringing the "odd" Other to a Midwestern town? Was McGee just the "Overlord of the Savage World," as the *St. Louis Republic* claimed? LPE historian James Buel thought the balance of the primitive "before" with the technological "after" advancements was appropriate, educational, and should be repeated.

Expositions are not designed to be merely an entertainment, an amusement for the multitude; for in the highest sense they fulfill two distinct purposes, viz.: as object lessons they stimulate patriotic impulse, and thereby encourage better citizenship; and as competitive exhibitions they powerfully incite more strenuous efforts to excel in all pursuits, intellectual and manual. But the greatest benefit is not gained by viewing the sights and enjoying the beautiful and wonderful things exposed to view. . . . To obtain the largest benefit from an exposition the visitor must examine with a critical understanding and with a mind intent upon study by comparison. Our surest enjoyment will be found in comparing the perfect product with preceding attempts to accomplish the same result, thereby bringing ourselves to know the successive stages of development, from initial efforts to final achievement. To see so much accomplished through perseverance on special lines makes us not only appreciative of what is being done to advance civilization and bring the world to its own, but it stimulates every individual with an ambition to exert his own talents and to encourage the belief that he too may be able to contribute something to the general betterment of the nation as well as to himself.[2]

St. Louis boosters felt good about their international showcase. Improvement, process, comparison, patriotism, nationalism, accomplishment, exclusivity, and the advancement of knowledge were lofty goals. They felt they had achieved these and moved America forward. They had lived up to President William McKinley's notion that "[e]xpositions are the time-keepers of progress. They record the world's advancement. They stimulate the energy, enterprise and intellect of the people and quicken human genius. They broaden and brighten the daily life of the people. . . . Every exposition, great or small, has helped to some onward step."[3]

But it was all ephemeral and it was time to move on to other places, other regions, other fairs. As Robert Rydell has noted, America was still "gripped by world's fair fever," and exposition organizers saw their task as "keeping visions of empire before the American people" (Rydell 1984, 188). But rarely did anthropology serve as a centerpiece. While no subsequent exposition ever tried to match the LPE's scope, most used the same universalizing comparisons of the "before" and "after" pictures. Exposition organizers wanted the subjects of anthropological research to highlight technological advancement, or to serve as justification for colonialism or evolutionary superiority, or simply to attract people thirsty for exotic novelties. Exposition organizers who had worked at Chicago, Omaha, or St. Louis later wanted to include some Native peoples and their "primitive" technology as the foil for American success in new expositions, but they wanted it to be like Portland turned out to be—cheap.

The Decline of Exposition Anthropology

Skiff had declared before the fair that "a universal exposition is a vast museum of anthropology and ethnology, of man and his works."[4] But after St. Louis, this idea faded. Anthropological participation in expositions decreased rather than expanded. Portland marked the beginning of a new trend.

The Lewis and Clark Centennial ran from June 1 to October 15, 1905. Like the LPE, its overarching themes were the territorial expansion of the United States, the conquest of the wilderness, and the expansion of international commerce, especially in the Orient. Imperialism and America as a world power were stressed. But unlike the LPE, Portland's fair was regional in scope, focusing on the Northwest and its hopes for American expansion as shores of influence along the Pacific Rim. Intentionally smaller in scope, it had fewer pretensions than St. Louis, and emphasized "beauty and entertainment." Portland's civic leaders had learned from St. Louis the need to select that which was most attractive and discard the unimportant and uninteresting. Portland was meant to be fun, not educational. The fair corporation only authorized expenditures that enhanced economic development and resource exploitation in the Orient. There was no need for a corporate-funded anthropology department.[5]

Portland organizers wanted to save money (spending one or two million) and decided to reuse any parts of the Louisiana Purchase Exposition they could. Many of the LPE static exhibits were crated up and sent directly to Portland, essentially extending the LPE for another six months, but in a new venue. McGee's synthetic archaeology series was shown one last time before being returned to the Smithsonian and placed on permanent display. They were placed in the Forestry Building, called the Timber Temple, to illustrate the development of wood-working tools. Parts of the Smithsonian exhibit—five of the Mexican temple models, two screens, and architectural photographs—went to Portland, along with Mooney's Kiowa heraldry collection. Alaska, Arizona, New Mexico and twelve other states sent their pavilions intact. The Indian School sent their static displays of objects from the boarding schools, reinstalled under the direction of Edwin Calcraft, superintendent of the Chemawa School, when McCowan declined the honor. He added a new display of historic tribal heirlooms of the Native nations met by Lewis and Clark but had no student demonstrators. While Turkey, Austria-Hungary, Canada, and Russia accepted invitations, most foreign countries declined because of the poor treatment they had received in St. Louis. Most historical societies declined but regional merchants and national labor organizations, like the AF of L, recycled their LPE displays. Concessionaires from the Pike reassembled their buildings on Portland's midway, the Trail. Fair Japan, the Streets of Cairo, the Esquimaux Village, Trip to Siberia, Oriental Bazaar, and Old Plantation were ready to be seen by a new group of fairgoers.[6]

No LPE division head was asked to lend his expertise nor was there any pretense to showcase groundbreaking innovations or theoretical knowledge. There were no congresses, lecture series, or scientific experiments. McGee was not consulted although he offered his services. The Portland Exposition made no attempt to include anthropological perspectives or portray the discipline's theories, evolutionary or otherwise. While progress and empire building were themes, there was no attempt to show one half of the world how the other half lived, and no interest in racial differences studied as a scholarly pursuit.

Nor was there much interest in American Indians, an unexpected omission given the thematic celebration of the Lewis and Clark Expedition. Except for rows of totem poles mingled with more than four hundred large sculptures, Indians were conspicuously absent from the Portland fair. The only ethnographic artifacts were relics and heirlooms in a small history exhibit. There were no demonstrators and no Wild West show. The only concession to feature Indians was the Esquimaux Village.

Emphasis was on the Philippines, America's economic and political target in the Pacific. People who had heard about the Igorot Dog Eaters wanted to see them. Henry Dosch, a member of Oregon's LPE commission, noted that Filipinos would be needed to draw crowds. The Philippine Reservation "is of so much interest . . . that I do not see how we can get along without it."[7] Secretary of War Taft wanted the colonies represented but decided to concentrate on resource potential, not Natives or material culture. The Insular Bureau erected a scaled-down version of the LPE's static exhibits, without Jenks's assistance or the collections that had gone to the Field Museum and the Philadelphia Commercial Museum.

A few Native Filipinos did go to Portland but not at government expense. Truman K. Hunt, who had managed the LPE Igorot Village, founded the Igorot Exhibit Company, while three other LPE officials, Edmond Felder (a midway showman), Richard Schneidewind (an exhibit cataloguer who ran an LPE cigar concession), and Samuel McCowan (the head of the Indian School) founded the International Anthropological Exhibit Company. The latter was short-lived, however, and was soon reincorporated as the Filipino Exhibition Company, without McCowan. Both companies sponsored entertainment troupes from the Bontoc region who toured Europe and America at country fairs and amusement parks. Both groups came to Portland with approximately one third of the Igorot who had been in St. Louis. By all accounts they were very popular. Portland organizers considered these troops "meritorious anthropology and educational exhibits," and awarded them gold medals.[8]

Native peoples returned to the midway as Filipinos became professional showmen. As Rachael Adams has noted:

> *During the period of their greatest productivity, freak shows consistently trafficked in representations of non-Western races that combined pedagogy and entertainment, pseudoscientific jargon and fantastic hyperbole. In doing so, they offered simplified answers to the pressing concerns about race that would have provoked their predominantly white audiences, already anxious about the consequences of slavery and its aftermath, great waves of seemingly inassimilable immigrants and imperial expansion. (Adams 2001, 164)*[9]

Race, especially black bodies and "primitive peoples" in general, remained deviant. They were placed in the land of humbug away from the exposition's center of white excellence. Their "strangeness" played into public policy discussions about immigration, eugenics, self-government, and assimilation for the next thirty years. Certain peoples, because of their racial heritage, were always seen as different, and the midways magnified and reified those differences. Attempts to control messages about "primitive" peoples never again came under anthropological purview to the extent it had in St. Louis. The businessmen, promoters, and hucksters who ran sideshow concessions used anthropologists' words, convoluted their theories to support the popular views of the day, and played on the fears and desires of their audiences. Popular rather than scientific evolutionism held sway and the fabrication of ethnographic "Others" continued unabated, despite the occasional protests of anthropologists.

Seen in this light, McGee's attempt to make race the centerpiece of a fair, to confront it directly, and to ensure that "primitive" peoples were highly visible and treated with respect, not seen as simply sideshow freaks, was a remarkable achievement. It was also a highly ethical one. Despite his theoretical jargon, which from our standpoint downgraded Natives, his evolutionary assumptions, and his insistence on total authority and his right to speak for and about others, McGee had great respect for the men and women who worked at the fair. He actually had more respect for them than for most Anglo-Americans he knew. He felt Native peoples should not simply be seen as curiosities, but as authentic wonders who would enlighten and educate people.

While McGee did not realize it, the St. Louis and Chicago fairs were exposition anthropology's peaks. Size and completeness of cultural or racial coverage were no longer among later organizers' goals, because those who staged and controlled expositions had other agendas. Nor was the idea that an exposition should be a universal educational experience analogous to a university ever repeated. Expositions were never again conceived of as sites for original scientific research. Uniqueness, aesthetic concerns, regional promotion, nationalism, and targeted economic development were more the order of the day than the advancement of scientific theories or disciplinary agendas. This meant that there was no need systematically to assemble all the peoples of the world to create a complete racial typology. A few well-chosen peoples were all that were needed to illustrate a fair's theme, and it was generally assumed that assistance by federal anthropologists legitimized the fair corporation's endeavors. Organizers wanted the government to supply the education, science, and Native peoples, thereby reinforcing pervasive Social Darwinian theory and utopian notions of America's future without an expenditure of funds. As a result there was no need for extensive anthropology departments to illustrate the primitive beginnings from which America had supposedly advanced and that cost exposition corporations large sums of money and considerable trouble.

Anthropology was simply not profitable. Never again would a newspaper label an anthropologist the "Overlord of the Savage World." Well-financed entrepreneurs would be given such titles in the twentieth century.

There were two exceptions to this trend. Anthropological displays were featured at two subsequent expositions where the discipline's ideas were used in the service of tourism and economic development and in one case to further pure science. In only this latter case was there one last attempt to make race scientifically based and therefore socially comprehensible and acceptable.

The first was the San Diego Panama-California Exposition of 1915–16. There anthropologists helped display the romanticism of the Native American Southwest and simultaneously took concepts of racialized, universal evolution to their ultimate and essentially illogical end. The San Diego exposition was a regionally oriented event that attracted about three-and-one-half million visitors. Ostensibly it celebrated the opening of the Panama Canal, but really focused on California's history and promoted the agricultural and industrial development of the greater American Southwest. Organizers chose as their central themes the more ambitious topics of the "science of man" and the "humanization of science." These themes made anthropology a focus of the fair that organizers hoped would create a lasting impression on visitors. The themes also distinguished the San Diego from the competing 1915 San Francisco Panama-Pacific International Exposition, which Congress had designated as the official exposition celebrating the opening of the canal. The San Francisco organizers decided not to have corporate-sponsored anthropology displays because of their expense. There anthropology was left to the concessionaires and to dioramas supplied by the Smithsonian Institution for free.[10]

The San Diego Exposition Corporation hired Edgar Lee Hewett (1865–1946), a key figure in Southwestern archaeology, and at the time director of both the School of American Archaeology and the Museum of New Mexico in Santa Fe, to oversee the anthropology displays. Hewett was to develop "a synopsis of man's evolution through a demonstration of the myriad processes which mark the present acme of civilization, and embody the history of man." Exposition president Collier wanted the fair to have an anthropology exhibit that would surpass St. Louis and contain an abundance of archaeological exhibits to illustrate "the progress and possibilities of the human race." He was willing to back this up with a pledge of one hundred thousand dollars and the promise of a permanent anthropology museum in San Diego, with Hewett as its director.[11]

Hewett quickly brought in Smithsonian anthropologists to help develop the exhibits as a joint federal-corporation endeavor. The idea was that the government would help sponsor (but not pay for) collecting expeditions in archaeology and physical anthropology for exhibits in three broad areas: the "Physical Evolution of Man," the "Evolution of Culture," and the "Native Races of America." Noticeably absent from the initial plan was ethnography, which was later added but only on a regional scale. Linguist-ethnographer John P. Harrington, then in Hewett's employ, constructed an exhibit on California Natives, which focused on the peoples living in the southern half of the state. There were also ample Indian crafts in the Indian Art Building, including five thousand pieces of ancient and historic Puebloan pottery, and house models designed to show cultural distinctions. California and New Mexico Natives demonstrated and sold pottery and baskets.[12]

While the corporation exhibits contained no extensive anthropology colonies, the Santa Fe Railway and the Fred Harvey Company financed the equivalent of the St. Louis Indian Village to promote Southwest tourism. Called the "Painted Desert," it was located beyond the midway (the Isthmus) on an area now occupied by the main parking lot of the San Diego Zoo. It was designed by Kenneth Chapman, Hewett's Museum of New Mexico associate, and built by San Ildefonso Pueblo workers under archaeologist Jesse Nusbaum's direction. It contained replicas of Taos Pueblo, the main kiva at San Ildefonso Pueblo, as well as Navajo hogans, Apache wickiups, and a two-story set of Cliff Dweller caves. Some of the same individuals who had been employed by the Tobin's Cliff Dwellers exhibit in St. Louis, including Julian and Maria Martinez, served as artists, singers, and dancers. There were Hopi, San Ildefonso, Acoma, Laguna, and Zuni participants, as well as Navajos, Western Apaches, and Havasupai. They produced textiles, pottery, baskets, jewelry, and bow-and-arrow sets for sale (Fowler 2000, 273–74).

Archaeological exhibits concentrated on the Maya of Central America. Hewett, Nusbaum, and Sylvanus Griswold Morley used corporation funds to finance archaeological research in Guatemala, excavating and recording glyphs on monuments at Quiriguá. Hewett made casts of the Maya stelae and had murals of Maya cities painted by Carlos Vierra. Both the stelae and the murals became part of the San Diego Museum of Man and can still be seen today.

Meanwhile, Aleš Hrdlička spent nearly one hundred thousand dollars on field research, finally realizing the plan that he had originally suggested for the Louisiana Purchase Exposition. He and his assistants traveled to Europe, Siberia, Mongolia, Alaska, Africa, North America, and the Philippines to collect skulls, cast hominid fossils, and make measurements and life masks for the human evolution exhibit. The resulting display of models of "well-chosen racial types" was shown in five rooms in the Science and Education Building. It included thirty busts modeled from men and women of what he termed the three main races (black, yellow-brown, and white) arranged in the usual evolutionary sequence with the darkest races at the lowest "scale of evolution" and the whites at the highest. The highest of the high race he called "Old Americans" and included busts of eminent personages of Northern European descent. The display ended with busts of those hardy souls who would make California the place of the future. These fantasies left little doubt about Hrdlička's vision of evolutionary racism. It is noteworthy that Hrdlička was himself born in southeastern Europe, but in some of his publications he stated that people of his ethnic background were, in the United States, becoming morphologically more like the "Old Americans" he placed at the top of his evolutionary scheme.[13]

The second and last fair to prominently display anthropology and its research subjects, Native peoples, was the 1939 Golden Gate International Exposition on Treasure Island in San Francisco Bay. There, however, the fair corporation itself did not sponsor a major anthropological display. A new federal agency, the Indian Arts and Crafts Board (IACB), built an impressive exhibit to educate citizens about Native American art and culture and to encourage the purchase of Indian art for their homes. As a result there was no physical anthropology, and the archaeology displayed was a direct descendent of Holmes's 1904 LPE exhibits that theorized aesthetics.

René d'Harnoncourt (director of the IACB) and Frederic Douglas (curator of Indian art at the Denver Art Museum) designed the display. The exhibit was groundbreaking because it showed Indian material culture as fine art rather than as ethnographic specimens or curios. At the end of its tour in San Francisco, the exhibit was taken to the Museum of Modern Art in

New York to demonstrate how Indian art was one inspiration for European and American abstract artists. The value of this move was also that it marked the development of applied anthropology in support of the goal of economic development for American Indians. But in general the exhibit had a greater impact on art, art history, and exhibition techniques in art museums than it did on anthropology.[14]

EPILOGUE

Passing into History and Moving On

It was 1905 and the anthropologists had returned to their former lives; Gerald Fowke and William Mills went back to their museums and students found new jobs not in anthropology. Native anthropologists continued to work, write, and lobby for sovereign rights. Some anthropologists left the busy world of the fair behind to pursue new professional interests. Albert Jenks returned to the Philippines to complete his studies of Native culture in the Luzon region. In 1906 he began teaching sociology at the University of Minnesota, soon becoming a full professor. He created an anthropology department in 1918, which he chaired until his retirement in 1938. Leaving ethnology he later pursued archaeological studies in the northern Plains. He never returned to the Philippines or worked in exposition anthropology again.[1]

Frederick Starr taught at the University of Chicago until his forced retirement in 1923; he was increasingly marginal and remained a dogmatic evolutionist to the end. He was frequently in trouble with University of Chicago administrators because of his outspoken opinions. He continued to travel as often as he could, but never took students with him. He did not build a strong reputation within the field but continued to entertain large audiences on the Chautauqua and other lecture circuits. The Department of Anthropology at Chicago did not expand or become distinguished until after he left.[2]

James Mooney returned to his fieldwork and a distinguished career as an ethnographer, writing several classic ethnographies and ethnohistories. He remained with the BAE for his entire career but also worked with Dorsey under the auspices of the Field Museum. He championed activist causes, such as having children educated on reservations rather than in boarding schools, and also became embroiled in what became known as the peyote controversy, fighting for religious freedom and basic human rights, earning sanctions from the Indian Service. His books on the Ghost Dance, demography, and Kiowa culture remain classics. He tried hard not to be involved in exposition activities again but without success (Moses 1984).

William Henry Holmes was exceedingly busy after his return from Europe and his grand tour. But he was also tired and dispirited because of changes occurring within the Smithsonian Institution. He undertook little new research, consumed with administrative duties and museum matters. He was a member of Roosevelt's inauguration committee and served as chief of the Bureau of American Ethnology until 1909. As a distinguished anthropological statesman he traveled frequently to conferences, giving papers defending his past positions. After years helping design and erect exposition exhibits he had three more yet to come—Portland, the 1907 Jamestown Tri-Centennial Exposition, and the Alaska-Yukon-Pacific Exposition in Seattle in 1909. He served for many more years in the National Museum of Natural History, classifying and installing the archaeological collections, and became the first director of the National Gallery of Art in 1920 until he retired in 1932. He remained an important figure in anthropological organizations, serving as president of the American Anthropological Association in 1909-10, fighting to make archaeology the center of the field, and won many awards, including election to the National Academy of Sciences in 1905.[3]

Aleš Hrdlička stayed at the Smithsonian Institution and basically defined physical anthropology as a separate field of inquiry. He established the *American Journal of Physical Anthropology* in 1918 and edited it until his death in 1943. A founder of the American Association of Physical Anthropologists, he was also president of the American Anthropological Association in 1926–27. He remained interested in the peopling of the Americas and dedicated to anthropometric research as long as it remained descriptive. He continued to be involved in exposition anthropology, especially the 1915 San Diego Exposition (Marks 2002).

George Dorsey and Stephen Simms returned to the Field Museum with their thousands of new acquisitions from the LPE. Simms remained his entire career at the museum, working in several departments, eventually becoming director from 1928 to 1937. He was a champion of public education, his heart never really in anthropology. He produced no publications or made any lasting impression on the field. Dorsey continued to work with the Fred Harvey Company but broadened his scope to South America and the Pacific with a multiyear grant from Chicago businessman R. F. Cummings. Now fascinated with the Philippines based on what he had seen at the LPE, he sent departmental collectors to the islands on five expeditions by 1910, including William Jones, the first Native American ethnologist and curator in the United States. Dorsey became interested in Melanesia and in 1908 visited German New Guinea. Around 1910, however, he lost interest in anthropology, tired of the low pay, and began writing for the popular audience. As part of a midlife crisis, he left the museum in 1915 after marrying a wealthy heiress. Settling in New York City he became a journalist and a filmmaker, interacting little with the anthropological community. He never worked at an exposition again.[4]

McGee: Life after the Fair

The biggest changes of all came for McGee. He worked for the Louisiana Purchase Exposition Company for one year and eight months, from August 1, 1903, to March 15, 1905, staying longer than his original contract. By March 1905 he was a very sick man; he had contracted typhoid fever in 1902 and had never really recovered. Needing to recuperate, he went to Yuma, Arizona, to live with his Cocopa friends. He stayed at Tinajas Altas in the Gila Mountains, about seventy-five miles southeast of Yuma, from May 20 to September 1, camping rough, sleeping on the ground under the stars, eating bacon, navy beans, rice, and tea, accompanied by José, a Cocopa youth.[5] McGee later stated that the effect of desert life on his health was all he had anticipated and that when he returned to civilization he was well rested. He also had a store of new adventures with which to regale *National Geographic* readers—including his dramatic rescue of two Mexican prospectors in July. However, McGee was putting a good public face on his life. He ended his desert sojourn knowing his prostate cancer (which had been diagnosed in 1895) had returned and that his marriage was irrevocably broken, but that he had a new job and big plans for furthering anthropology and his own career.

McGee was appointed the first director of the St. Louis Public Museum, a general municipal museum built around the remnants of the LPE collections. David Bushnell, the Peabody Museum archaeologist in charge of excavating the Forest Park fair site, was hired as his assistant. McGee spent the summer organizing the new institution and trying to raise money. Opening in the fall of 1905, it was housed in the LPE Fine Arts Building as a temporary measure, since none of the remaining LPE pavilions were structurally sound; they had been meant to last only a year. Like the Field Columbian Museum, an outgrowth of the 1893 Chicago Exposition, the St. Louis Museum was to have four departments: geography, anthropology, geology, and biology. There were tremendous problems, however. The Missouri Historical Society decided to remain a separate history museum and the City of St. Louis elected to fund a separate art museum. This did not stop McGee. He had big plans, as always; he wanted the St. Louis Public Museum to be better and more innovative than the Field Museum. He planned to have divisions of ethnology, archaeology, and technology and envisioned special exhibits devoted to primitive arts and crafts, which would have live demonstrators to stimulate interest, arguing that museums had to be places of activity. He also planned to have static evolutionary exhibits on the development of implements and tools, clothing, houses, utensils (baskets and pottery containers), and spinning and weaving decorative devices.

The first exhibit McGee and Bushnell erected was on Indian basketry, the only collection complete enough for a retrospective. But for the other object types, McGee needed more artifacts and that required collecting expeditions to the far corners of the world. McGee made another million-dollar request to his board, updating his original LPEC plan. And that was just for ethnology. His plans for other departments were equally expensive. McGee again had grandiose plans that would make him as famous as Putnam and put him on as permanent a professional footing as Skiff and Dorsey.[6]

It was little surprise when the museum's board of trustees did not approve McGee's plans and asked for more modest goals. The response he received to all his proposals was similar to those he had received from the LPEC Board. The museum quickly atrophied, becoming moribund due to St. Louis politics and the Forest Park restoration. Costs were higher than expected and there was little money left to build permanent monuments to the exposition. Nor was there much interest in new organizations that were not going to make a profit. The citizens simply did not want to spend money for a permanent building or purchase ethnographic objects. In September 1906, the St. Louis Public Museum board informed McGee that his building would be destroyed and that he would have to move the collections. The move from the condemned building depleted the museum's meager treasury. The St. Louis Museum folded and the anthropology, biology, and geology collections were transferred to the Field Museum, the art museum, the historical society, or placed in storage. A few pieces were unearthed years later when a fledgling science museum, the Academy of Science, was opened. It later was transformed into the St. Louis Science Center but by then the history of the original undertaking and its anthropological foundation had been lost.[7]

McGee was again unemployed and there were few jobs in anthropology. Times had changed since the 1880s when he had worked his way into the field and risen in stature. No new professorships at universities opened in 1905 or 1906. The few positions in historical societies and museums were filled and the individuals whom McGee asked for help, like Mills, had nothing to offer. McGee did not have a patron he could convince to underwrite expeditions—there were no Phoebe Hearsts or Mary Hemenways as there had been for Frank Hamilton Cushing. McGee did not have the training or experience to direct an archaeological expedition either. There were also no jobs for McGee personally; no one wanted to hire him. Even his friend Boas was unsuccessful, although he recognized that he owed McGee much for having helped him in his time of need after he was not given an expected position at the new Field Museum in 1894. A major problem was that McGee did not have the credentials now required of professionals nor did he have any teaching experience. Without a doctorate, master's, or bachelor's degree, he could not become a professor. Kroeber turned him down when he began to talk about coming to teach at the University of California, as did Starr at Chicago. Similarly, schools in Iowa declined his offers. Boas could think of nowhere he could teach; he was having trouble finding sufficient university or museum posts for his own students. In their quest to raise the status of anthropology within the academy, professionals with doctorates did not want to hire non-degree-holding "pre-professionals," men who had earned their stature through years of experience rather than by attending a suite of specialized courses, passing a comprehensive examination, and writing a dissertation that led to a degree. Anthropology and its concept of itself as a professional discipline had changed. As historian L. G. Moses has insightfully noted, anthropologists were no longer professionals by nature of their employment but because they possessed degrees. Anthropology was becoming more exclusive in its attempt to appear rigorous and theoretical to the university world that was increasingly being built on the German model and a nation in search of professional knowledge. In addition, McGee appeared "old fashioned" by 1906. He was hampered by his staunch evolutionary views. Kroeber, when looking at his Seri material, concluded that McGee's assumptions about Native peoples and his obsessive drive to ensure they fit his developmental models skewed his observations and interpretation.[8]

McGee's old tried-and-true routes were also closed. Federal anthropological employment was out of the question; there were no bridges to mend for him in Washington while Holmes and Langley were in control of anthropology at the Smithsonian Institution. As Boas had warned McGee in 1902, "I believe that after you once begin to attack the Secretary, it will be practically impossible to undo the action that has been taken." And it was. The wounds were still too deep and the acrimony too great. When Langley died in 1906, his successor, Charles D. Walcott, continued to insist on direct oversight of all bureau correspondence and plans. McGee's position had been abolished in 1903 and it stayed abolished. Approved work was more restrictive and less activist in keeping with the 1879 mandate to be a research tool for Congress. Holmes was not an assertive leader and while current ethnography projects continued, only John Swanton, a student of Putnam and Boas, and Mooney undertook creative research. Other initiatives were archaeological in nature, for Holmes wanted to centralize archaeology and combine the efforts of the USNM with the BAE whenever he could. According to Walcott, however, the BAE was to focus *all* its efforts on completing *The Handbook of North American Indians*, a thankless undertaking that required teamwork, not McGee's conception of government science as an individualistic undertaking that supported, but did not direct, researchers loyal to science in general and the pure pursuit of knowledge for its own sake.[9] Nor was there any hope of employment with the Indian Service. Commissioners Jones and Leupp felt McGee had been critical of Indian Service policy and McCowan did not trust him. There was also nothing for him to do there, since the Indian Service was not interested in anthropological research, and if there was any, Alice Fletcher was their anthropologist of choice.

McGee tried the exposition circuit again. The corporation for the next major exposition after Portland, the Alaska-Yukon-Pacific Exposition being planned for Seattle in 1908 or 1909, declined his offer to organize and run an anthropology department. He was finished in exposition anthropology, museums, and public education initiatives. Next he turned his pragmatic skills to a project with his friend and long-time supporter Alexander Graham Bell. They formed a corporation to manufacture a "Gasimotor" that would convert low-grade coal into gas. Always a visionary, McGee thought that gas was the fuel of the future. But the corporation was unsuccessful, in part because Bell had turned his attention to the airplane and McGee could not find enough backers on his own. Discouraged, McGee returned to the Papagueria Desert to visit Cocopa friends and recuperate from another bout of typhoid fever.[10]

It was sad. In 1902, Holmes had written of McGee in his diary, "He is the strongest man in Anthropology today in America if not in the world and is energetic and resourceful." In 1906 McGee's life was in shambles and he had lost much of his social and political capital. He was close to being an anthropological outcast, humiliated and deeply disappointed. He never regained his prominent position in the field although he regained some of his influence. He served on the executive council of the American Anthropological Association in 1909 but he never again tried to conduct fieldwork, nor did he try to publish anything relating to American Indians or evolutionary theory.[11]

But McGee was an incredibly strong individual who was never down for long. He now, finally, faced reality and let go of his dogged persistence and obstinacy. He decided to leave anthropology behind, just as anthropology had moved beyond his and John Wesley Powell's brand of unilinear evolutionary theory. McGee reinvented himself, leading to a lasting legacy of immense importance to America.

McGee still had powerful friends in Washington, in geology. He firmly believed that science without reform was useless and that scientists had responsibilities to work for the betterment of society by discovering truths and then using these understandings to address issues and concerns. Since the 1880s, McGee and Powell had been deeply concerned about the haphazard development of the American West and the way water was being misused. In 1907 McGee decided to do something about it. He was ready for another fight. So he called on his friend Gifford Pinchot and was hired by the Department of Agriculture. That summer he and Pinchot camped in the California Sierras and laid the plans for what became a major focus of the conservationist movement of the early twentieth century.[12]

McGee's new career utilized his anthropological perspectives. He essentially founded a new field, applied environmental anthropology, in water and land conservation and public policy development, probably the most important and fulfilling work of his entire life. McGee worked with a group of businessmen developing waterways as transportation routes. He generated the theoretical basis for comprehensive water management, which he then developed into national policy, working closely with President Roosevelt. He was very successful. Gifford Pinchot, the man who officially is credited with establishing the Inland Waterways Commission, in his autobiography *Breaking New Ground* called McGee "the scientific brains of the conservation movement." Historian Whitney Cross agreed and stated that McGee, more than any other scientist of his day, developed the explicit theoretical framework that set the stage for the conservation movement and transmitted his beliefs and those of like-minded men to the general public.[13]

McGee devoted the remaining years of his life to the conservation movement, serving as secretary for the Inland Waterways Commission and its successor, the National Conservation Commission. He also worked for the Bureau of Soils (Department of Agriculture) as a specialist in subsoil and water erosion. He presented several seminal papers on water erosion in arid environments, water pollution, the relationship between geology and soils, and how eroded land could be reclaimed for agricultural development. He wrote extensively about the need for comprehensive management of the earth's resources and for an advanced, civilized, and democratic government to manage resources in the promotion of human happiness. He used Cocopa models of resource conservation, and land and water use, condemning wasteful American capitalism.

McGee died in his room at the Cosmos Club in Washington on September 8, 1912, estranged from his wife, children, and most of his fellow anthropologists but aided by his geological colleagues. Ever the scientist, he wrote a description of the course of his prostate cancer a few days before his death, which was published in *Science*. He left more than three hundred publications and the basis for a conservation program that continues a century later. As Cross has observed, McGee helped make anthropology socially useful. In his last few years his personal and professional problems drove him to elevate "his lifelong devotion to the general welfare for a final decisive stroke of public service."

McGee felt he had helped Americans move on to more enlightened civilization through his insistence on the ideas that all government policy should
work through "essential principles of natural equity" and that he had made
anthropology relevant and critical to American society (Cross 1953, 156; Mc-
Gee 1912a, 1912b). And he had.

Professional Anthropology after the Louisiana Purchase Exposition

Just as McGee moved away from expositions and museums, so did anthropology. The lessons McGee articulated about his experiences in St. Louis no
longer coincided with how international fairs were evolving (with the exception of San Diego), and they no longer coincided with developments in the
discipline. Anthropologists needed more permanent institutions in which to
base their discipline rather than with the transient, impermanent, and ephemeral, if grandiose, expositions. Expositions also presented a dilemma for anthropologists as they professionalized. Fairs were illusionary and ultimately
unscientific, with an inherent tension: Did the field's subject matter belong in
the grand pavilions that represented progress, or on midways, where it represented the exotic and the huckster? Fairs came to be viewed as unprofessional,
as did most attempts to popularize the discipline. Museums came to be seen
as old-fashioned, atheoretical, and mundane as universal evolution and mate-
rial-culture studies became indefensible as their intellectual base (Parezo and
Hardin 1992; Thompson and Parezo 1989; Collier and Tschopik 1954). Universities became the discipline's internally accepted permanent home as the site
for intellectual endeavors requiring specialized knowledge.

The Louisiana Purchase Exposition was the most extensive, but also the
last, major public celebration by anthropologists of nineteenth-century
unilineal, cultural evolution and anthropometry (except for Hrdlička's 1915
physical anthropology exhibit). Cultural anthropology moved in the new direction articulated by Boas in his address to the LPE congress, although the
intellectual advancement of the field was not without its share of conflict for
the next twenty years.[14] As Boas noted in his speech, evolutionary anthropology was the result of Darwin's overpowering influence on Western European
and American thought, as well as the untrained men who studied the world's
peoples, and the eclecticism of their methods and goals. Boas thought new
perspectives were required.

The grand system of the evolution of culture, that is valid for all hu-
manity, is losing much of its plausibility. In place of a simple line of
evolution there appears a multiplicity of converging and diverging
lines which it is difficult to bring under one system of control. Instead
of uniformity, the striking feature seems to be diversity. . . . Later
than the older sciences, [anthropology] has outgrown the systematiz-
ing period, and is just now entering upon the empirical revision of its
theories. (Boas 1904, 480)

It was now time to understand cultural distinctiveness and conduct empirical studies of entire societies to understand them as unique wholes with unique histories. The speech was, in essence, a devastating critique of the outdated anthropology that was the foundation for McGee's LPE department, as we have noted.

Boas concluded his speech by stating that anthropology's great importance in the twentieth century would be "its power to make us understand the roots from which our civilization has sprung, to impress us with the relative value of all forms of culture, and thus serve as a check to an exaggerated valuation of the standpoint of our own period, which we are only too liable to consider the ultimate goal of human evolution, thus depriving ourselves of the benefits to be obtained from the teachings of other cultures, and hindering an objective criticism of our own work" (Boas 1904, 482; 1906). As George Stocking has noted, evolutionism became the old school against which Boas's students fought in their attempt to establish their own paradigms, to create a critical skepticism toward all generalization, and to bring to the surface the methodological problems and racist biases of studies such as those undertaken at the Louisiana Purchase Exposition. Boas's revisionist anthropology had a sense of humility that was lacking in McGee's encompassing scheme in which race integrated the physical, the cultural, the linguistic, and the mental in a totality that had never actually existed. While anthropology moved on, the ideas displayed in St. Louis remain with some segments of the American public to this day, as the late Stephen J. Gould so eloquently noted in his extensive writings on the misuse of science to support racism and the quest for social distinctiveness (Stocking 1974a; Gould 1977).

The racialist ideas promulgated at the LPE were prominent in the rhetoric of supporters of the eugenics movement, which had begun to gather steam in the United States in the 1890s. Francis Galton, a cousin of Charles Darwin, had coined the term *eugenics* in 1883. The movement, to increase the population of genetically "superior" humans (usually whites of Western European descent), and decrease the populations of genetically "inferior" humans (usually every one else) became increasingly popular in the decades after the LPE. Federal legislation restricted emigration. Boas and others conducted many studies to disprove the rhetoric of the eugenicists, but little heed was paid to them. The movement peaked in the United States in the 1930s, then receded in the face of the horrors of the Nazi eugenics programs of the 1930s and 1940s, but is still active. Racialist rhetoric was also used to support the triumph of Jim Crow laws in the American South and elsewhere, restricting or abolishing those civil rights and liberties that African Americans had gained after the Civil War. Certainly the rhetoric of McGee's exhibits fed into both eugenics and Jim Crow.

Taken at face value, McGee's anthropology justified these views since it espoused an essentialist "force" somehow at work that would result in the triumph of Progress and the emergence of white Americans as naturally superior world leaders. Although Boas and McGee were friends at some levels and had worked together for years to establish anthropology as a respected scientific discipline, their views on race and sociocultural evolution were diametrically opposed. The speeches they gave at the exposition's anthropology congress (chapter 12) make that quite clear. By 1925 the Boasian vision of anthropology had prevailed within American universities and continued to be the dominant paradigm until the 1960s. But that is another story, artfully chronicled by several histories of science and anthropology.[15]

In 1904 anthropology went to the fair. Anthropologists and others used then-current anthropological concepts to interpret the exhibits, both static displays and groups of living peoples, at the Louisiana Purchase Exposition. For one individual, WJ McGee, it was an opportunity to showcase his discipline as the premier science that could contribute to the ongoing progressive perfection of American civilization. But few saw the displays and exotic peoples from McGee's perspective. Each visitor took away her or his own impressions of the nearly overwhelming grand spectacle and its multitudes of constituent displays and people that was the Louisiana Purchase Exposition. McGee's ideas and perspective did not prevail, either in academic anthropology or in American popular culture. Even if McGee's experiment failed, it was, nonetheless, a grandiose attempt, a unique moment in American popular and intellectual history.

Appendix 1.
McGee's Racial Classification Schemes

Table 1.1 McGee's Culture-Grade Classification Scheme

Activities	First	Developmental Stages		
		Second	Third	Fourth
Arts	Mimetic	Symbolic	Conventionalistic	Idealistic
Industries	Imitative	Divinitive	Constructive	Inventive
Laws	Maternal	Patriarchal	Royal	Social
Languages	Demonstrative	Descriptive	Associative	Reflective
Philosophies	Zooic	Theurgic	Metaphysic	Scientific

Table 1.2 McGee's Rationales for Including Ethnic Groups

Ethnic Group	Physical Types and Characteristics	Cultural Characteristics to Be Illustrated
Pygmies (Belgian Congo)	Least removed from the subhuman or quadrumane form: small stature, small proportions, dark color, small cranium.	Maternal family, avuncular council for tribal control.
Ainu (Hokkaido, Japan)	Fairly well developed with tree-climbing ancestry approximated to quadrumanes: small stature, centripetal movements, use of feet as manual adjuncts, elongated arms, incurved hands, facility in climbing.	Industries connected with bodyward movements; a primitive agriculture with a distinctive form of millet; specialized architecture appropriate to difficult climate; primitive musical system; bear cult.
Tehuelche (Patagonia)	Gigantic. Stature exceeds the average of most advanced peoples; their bodily proportions and physical strength are heroic.	Use of bolas; maternal or clan organization; religious feeling and philosophy.
Cocopa, Sonora (Mexico)	Extremely tall men and extremely short women.	Native American agriculture pursued continuously and unchangingly since pre-Columbian times; native lore and legend; extravagant mortuary customs with destruction of house and goods and cremation; elaborate marriage and puberty rites; transition of tribal law from maternal to paternal principles.

Table 1.2 (*cont.*)

Ethnic Group	Physical Types and Characteristics	Cultural Characteristics to be Illustrated
Kickapoo		Industries; special house type
Pawnee	Extremely tall.	Animal skin tanning and dressing; organization of paternal family or gens; special house type.
Dakota Sioux	Powerful and agile.	Animal skin tanning and dressing; organization of paternal family or gens; tipis and fabrics showing sacred insignia; barbaric philosophies; musical instruments.
Wichita		Industries; special house type.
Navajo		Blanket weaving; special house type.
Pima-Maricopa	Dark skinned with notable agility and endurance.	Pottery making; special house type.
Pomo	Short handed, squat, flat-faced.	Basket making.
Pueblo	Short stature.	Pottery making and blanket weaving. Agriculture.
Kwakiutl (Vancouver, Canada)	Singularly light-colored.	Special type of housing designed to fix social organization and facilitate maintenance of law; elaborate totems and animal tutelaries.

Appendix 2. Native Participants

Table 2.1 American Indian Participants in the Indian Village

Cultural Group	Number in Department	Participants
Acoma Pueblo	20	*Family 1:* Juan Antonio Sarrascino (age 35), Santa Garcia (age 28), Lupe Sarrascino (daughter age 5), Lorenzo Sarrascino (son), Marie Garcia (sister-in-law, age 21); *Family 2:* Vincente Chavez (age 30), Lupe Chavez (age 25), Santa Ana (daughter, age 2), Dolores San Juan (sister-in-law, age 30); *Family 3:* Marie Antonio (age 24), Lorenzo Antonio (son, age 2); *Family 4:* Juan Ray (age 40), Juan Marie Ray (age 40), Juana Ray (daughter, age 22), Charles Garcia Ray (son, age 4), Ascension Garcia Ray (daughter, age 2), Juanita Ray (daughter, age 17); *Individuals:* Lenta, Simon Marks (possibly Isleta), Richard Codah (age 26)
"Apache" from White River AZ	15	*Family 1:* Martine, Alice Martine, Mary Martine, James Sago (adopted); *Family 2:* Ya-no-zah, Rachel Ya-no-zah, Kate Ya-no-zah, Charles Karne, Bou-ge-gum
Chiricahua or San Carlos Apache, Fort Sills, and Mescalero Apache	9 or 10	Geronimo, Elaya, Bah-dah-go-gilth-ilth (Charles Martine, cousin of Kayihtah), Lena (Mescalero Apache, daughter of Geronimo), Natchez (Naiche, son of Cochise), Pedro, Yanozah, Julia, Thomas (son of Geronimo), Crisbin Pisenta, later joined by daughter Eva, (Mescalero Apache)
Arapaho	13, then 24 possibly 45	*Family 1:* Cut Nose, Mrs. Cut Nose; *Family 2:* Earl White Shirt, Mrs. Alice White Shirt, Francis Nelson White Shirt (baby); *Family 3:* Cleaver Warden (interpreter), Mrs. Eva Warden, George Warden (child); *Family 4:* Chief Black Coyote (Watanga), Mrs. Black Coyote; *Family 5:* Black Lodge, Mrs. Black Lodge; *Family 6:* Ben Franklin, Mrs. Ben Franklin, Asy Franklin (child), unnamed child; *Family 7:* Black White-man, Mrs. Black White-man, Mary Black White-man (daughter); *Family 8:* Cut Finger, Mrs. Cut Finger, Harry Cut Finger (son); *Family 9:* Yellow Hair, Mrs. Yellow Hair; *Family 10:* Big Heart; *Family 11:* John Stanton, Mrs. John Stanton; *Individuals:* Short Man, Lone Bear, Henry Blind, Bichea, Creeping Bear, Jack Bull Bear, Jesse Bent, Mrs. Buffalo; *Child:* Goes Up Hill

Table 2.1 (*cont.*)

Cultural Group	Number in Department	Participants
Cheyenne	12, then joined by 35	*Family 1:* Bushy Head, Mrs. Bushy Head; *Family 2:* Jack Bull Bear, Florence Bull Bear; *Family 3:* Richard Davis, Mrs. Richard Davis, children are Lulu Davis, Nannie A. Davis, Richenda Davis, Mary A. Davis, Esther Davis, Edna Davis, Roy Davis, Henry Davis (baby); *Family 4:* White Buffalo, Mrs. White Buffalo, Amy White Buffalo (daughter); *Family 5:* Charles Wicks, Jesse Wicks, Nellie Wicks (baby); *Individuals:* Blue Bear, Rich A. Harris, Little Raven, Poor Elk, Emma Red Hair, Red (Painted) Woman, George Rye, Wolf Robe, Herbert Walker
Comanche	15	Per-da-sof-py, At-dtah-vich, Phil Per-da-sof-py, Maggie Per-da-sof-py, Ya-po-cha (mother-in-law), Chief To-pa-no, Naomi Tenequah (and two children)
Jicarilla Apache	12	*Family1:* Chief Diloya Tagoya, Raman Tafoya, Darcia Tafoya, Lena Smith, Deloya Tafoya (son); *Family 2:* Truata Tovlezeter, Christian Vasalta, Lamonta Trovezeter, Mrs. Truata Trovlezeter, *Individuals:* Christine Pisente, Lena Smith, Lassar
Kickapoo	7	D. H. Roubedoux
Laguna Pueblo	1	Ridget
Maricopa	5	*Family 1:* James Bluebird, Gaudalupe Bluebird; *Family 2:* Mrs. Mollie Boatman, Henry Boatman, Sally Boatman (daughter)
Navajo	23	*Family 1:* Vincente/Becinta Begay, Mrs. Vincente Begay, Ah-Zhe-Ne (daughter), Es-kee (baqby); *Family 2:* Good Luck, Mrs. Good Luck, three children (daughter Eh-sah-to); *Family 3:* Etcitty Jose, Mrs. Etcitty Jose, daughter Yah Tso (also in Indian School); *Family 4:* Peshlakai, Mrs. Skyblue Peshlakai, Chi-'e (baby); *Family 5:* Taos, Mrs. Taos; *Individuals:* Frank Smith, Hotine Tsosi
Nez Perce	3	Flying Hawk, David Williams, John Williams
Ojibwa/ Chippewa	20 or 25	Poitre, Nah-ee-gance (Wolf), Little Wolf, Etta Loafman, Mary Nuennell, Da-Kim-ee-gee-shig, Nay-Tah-Wash, E-Ne-Ne-Zaw (or In-ne-ne-si), Mrs. Lederboer, White Eagle, Jane Me-Gay-Zeuce Walters (or Eagle), Mon-e-do-wats (Mrs. Spirit Seeker), Mahshahkegesyhig (Lowering Feather), "High-Up-in-the-Sky," "Crossing-the-Wind"

Cultural Group	Number in Department	Participants
Osage	29	*Family 1:* Chief Olohowallah and wife; *Family 2:* Fred Lookout, Mrs. Fred Lookout, with children Nora Lookout, Gus Lookout; *Family 3:* John Straight, Mrs. John Straight; *Family 4:* Chief Che-Ke-Kuh or (Che-sho-hun-kah), Mrs. Che-Ke-Kuh; *Family 5:* Foster Strike Axe, Mrs. Foster Strike Axe, with children Minnie Strike Axe, Annie Strike Axe; *Family 6:* Henry Red Eagle, Rosa Red Eagle; *Family 7:* Charles Michelle, Mrs. Charley Michelle, Ida Michelle (daughter); *Family 8:* Pet-tsa-maoie, Mrs. Pet-tsa-maoie; *Individuals:* Harry Big Eagle, Frank Coondropper, Richard Fine Walker, Ray James, Bryant, William Pryor, Robert Warrior, Wilson Wink
Pawnee	27, possibly 40 or 50	*Family 1:* Alfred Murie, Annie Murie, Henry Murie, Julie Murie: *Family 2:* Roan Chief (Roaming Chief), Eva Roan Chief, Ethel Roan Chief, Charley Richards (stepson), Henry Richards (stepson); *Family 3:* William Sutton, Annie Sutton, Pollie Sutton: *Family 4:* Jonathan Eustis, Annie Eustis, Raymond Adams (adopted); *Family 5:* Alfred Boy Chief, Mrs. Bertha Boy Chief; *Family 6:* James Murie, Mrs. Mary Esau Murie, with children Wallace Murie, Nora Murie, Lawrence Murie; *Individuals:* Jennie Brave Chief, Pitahauerat, Roaming Scout, Frank Moore, Tom Moore
Pima (Akimel O'odham)	9	*Family 1:* Henry Adams, Mrs. Martha Adams, daughters Eliza Adams, Elizabeth Adams, son Henry Adams; *Family 2:* Alice Peters; Effa Rhodes; Amy Enos; Kista Jackson
Pomo	2	James Benson; Mrs. Mary Benson
Santa Clara Pueblo	15	*Family 1:* Aniseto Suaz or Suasa, Mrs. Aniseto Suasa, Hessosita (daughter), sons Vincent Suasa, Pietro Suasa; *Family 2:* Pedro Cajite, Mrs. Pedro Cajite, Genevieve Cajite (daughter); "Pueblo": Helaris Sierra or Hessoseta
Sauk and Fox	5	Unknown
"Sioux" Lakota from Rosebud Agency	43	*Family 1:* Chief Yellow Hair, Mrs. Yellow Hair, Julia Yellow Hair (granddaughter, age 15); *Family 2:* Afraid of Eagle, Mrs. Afraid of Eagle; *Family 3:* Black Tail Deer, Mrs. Lottie Blacktail Deer, daughter; *Family 4:* Buffalo Hide, Mrs. Buffalo Hide; *Family 5:* He Dog, Mrs. He Dog; *Family 6:* Keeps-the-Mountain, Mrs. Keeps-the-Mountain, small child; *Family 7:* Light, Mrs. Light; *Family 8:* Belle Little Horse, Mrs. Little Horse; *Family 9:* One Star, Mrs. Lucy One Star, child; *Family 10:* Scott Charging Alone, Mrs. Scott Charging Alone, two small children; *Family 11:* Tall Crane, Mrs. Tall Crane, daughter (age 3), baby; *Family 12:* Foster Thunder Hawk, Mrs. Foster Thunder Hawk; *Family 13:* Two Charges, Mrs. Two Charges, infant; *Family 14:* Good Bird, Mrs. Good Bird; *Family 15:* Singing Goose, wife, and baby; *Individuals:* Little Horse, Little Black Tail Deer (age 18), Mrs. Bull Head

Table 2.1 (*cont.*)

Cultural Group	Number in Department	Participants
"Sioux" Dakota, Brule, or Oglala from Pine Ridge Agency	42 or 45	*Family 1:* Eagle Louse, Mrs. Eagle Louse, Vicky Eagle Louse, Esther Eagle Louse; *Family 2:* Hollow Horn Bear, Mrs. Hollow Horn Bear; *Family 3:* Leading Hawk, Mrs. Leading Hawk; *Family 4:* Mrs. Lost Horse (Delphine High Hawk), Lost Horse, child; *Family 5:* Painted Horse, Mrs. Painted Horse; *Family 6:* Point At Us Bow, Mrs. Point At Us Bow, daughter; *Family 7:* Left Hand, Mrs. Left Hand, child; *Family 8:* Little Elk, Frank Little Elk, Lucy Little Elk; *Family 9:* Adolph Knock, wife and child; *Family 10:* Left Hand Bull, Mrs. Left Hand Bull, son: *Family 11:* Dreaming Bear, Mrs. Dreaming Bear, and children; *Family 12:* Chief Lone Wolf, Nathan Lone Wolf; *Family 13:* Titus Scout, Mrs. Titus Scout. *Individuals:* Amos Conquering Bear, Edward Bad Hair, John Bear Robe, Big Turkey, Daniel Black Horn, Comes Out Holy, Thomas Crow, Cut Finger, William Dietz, Phillip Dripper, Mrs. Eagle Horse, Elbow Shield, Chief Flat Iron, Flying Hawk, Good Eagle, Hard Heart, Hollow Horn Deer, Eddie Iron Cloud, Bert Janice, Nellie Jumping Eagle and children, Rosa Leaving Bear, Little Hawk, Frank Little, Little Soldier, Living Bear, Long Bull, Long Grand, Simon Max, John Milk, Pick's His Arrow, Jim Red Cloud, Red Hawk, John Returns From Scout, Short Man, Shooting Cat, Sleeping Bear, Spotted Elk, Spotted Horse, Edward Star, Ivan Star Comes Out, Susie Thunder Hawk, Troubling Hawk, Two Lance, Mrs. Herbert Walker, John White Thunder
Wichita	25 possibly 30 or 35	*Family 1:* Chief Towakani Jim, Mrs. Towakani Jim, Grover Towakani (son); *Family 2:* John Tatem, Julia Tatem; *Family 3:* Ah-ka-hi-dick, Na-sho-ho-iash (wife), Ferdinand Fifer (grandson); *Family 4:* Walter Ross, Anna Ross; *Family 5:* Isaac Luther, Jacob Johnson; *Family 6:* Ge-chas, Ne-ah-chas, Oscar Stevens (grandson); *Family 7:* Burgress Hunt, Josephine Hunt, Daniel Hunt, Henry Hunt, Louisiana Francis Hunt (baby); *Individuals:* Henry Adams, Amos Black Hawk, Burgress Wheeler, Grundy Wheeler

Table 2.2 Anthropology Village Participants: Ainus

Name	Relationship	Age (in years)	Home Village	Occupation
Sangyea Hiramura	Man	57	Piratori	Farmer
Santukno	Wife	54	Piratori	
Kehttle	Daughter	6	Piratori	
Kutoroge Hiramura	Man	39	Piraotri	Bear hunter
Shutratek	Wife	37	Piratori	
Kiku	Daughter	2	Piratori	
Yazo Osawa	Man	23	Niikap (Nibutani)	Farmer
Shirake	Wife	18	Niikap (Nibutani)	
Goro Bete	Man	26	Sapporo	Servant

Table 2.3 Anthropology Village Participants: Batwa Pygmies and "Red Africans"

Name	Age (in years)	Tribe	Reason for Participation	Physical Characteristics
Kondola (John)	19 or 22	Batetele	Warrior in powerful and warlike tribe, Verner's assistant, educated.	Has a small hole in one ear; 5′6″ tall, 150 pounds
Lumbango	15 or 16	Bakuba	Nephew of King Ndombe, prince of important tribe.	Youngest; short.
Latuna	18	Bakuba	Lumbango's servant required by King Ndombe to accompany him. Family of premier, Joka.	Very black skin; 5′6″ tall; very slender.
Kalamma	23	Bakuba	Source of American slaves; incidental attaché to the party.	Has an elaborate tattoo on chest; tallest in group, 5′9″; 160 pounds.
Shamba	28	Batwa	Pygmy	Oldest; 5′ tall; 103 pounds; wears a tuft of hair on top of his head; very black skin.
Malengu	20	Batwa	Pygmy	Copper skin color; wears a hair tuft; 5′ tall.
Lumo	20	Batwa	Pygmy	
Bomushubba	20	Batwa	Pygmy	Smallest; brown hued skin; has a bad scar on his face.
Ota Benga	18 or 20	Badinga	Pygmy, "Ideal representative," filed teeth, cannibal.	Incised teeth; characteristic chuckle; taller than Batwa; 4′10″ tall.

Table 2.4 Anthropology Village Participants: Cocopas

Family	Name	Relationship	Age (in years)
1	Pablo Colorado	Chief/husband	50
	Quischur	Wife	45
	Artuckero	Son	30
	Kushmush	Artuckero's wife	14
2	Chinyum Sacup	Husband	40
	Hureux	Wife	33
	Cheouch	Son	8
	Catchwall	Daughter	4
	Killwhorewhoy	Son	2
3	Tom Moore	Elder/leader	70
	Oui	Wife	50
	Shur	Grandson	12
	Nirsa	Granddaughter	9
4	Cherry	Husband	38
	Hushputt	Wife	30
	Caush	Son	7
	Chuchquoi	Son	7 months
5	Ecusheputt	Unmarried woman	17
	Unnamed girl	Daughter	?
Single	Annie Flynn	Interpreter	?
	Pahupp	Nephew of Colorado	13
	Ilpuck	Teenage boy	15
	Skick	Tennage boy	14
	Shokee	Man	"in prime"

Table 2.5 Anthropology Village Participants: Kwakiutls and Nootkas

Name	Group	Specialty
Charles James Nowell	Kweeka Kwakiutl, Fort Rupert	Religous specialist, dancer
Bob Harris (Xa'Niyus)	Kweeka Kwakiutl, Denatkot	Religious specialist, dancer
Mrs. Emma George	Nootka, Gold River	Basket maker
Dr. Atlieu (Atliu)	Nootka, Clayoquot	Carver, dancer, singer
Annie Atlieu	Nootka, Clayoquot	Mat maker, dancer
Jasper Turner	Nootka, Clayoquot	Carver, dancer, singer
Jack Curley (Salitzin)	Nootka, Clayoquot	Carver, singer
Mrs. Ellen Curley	Nootka, Clayoquot	Unknown

Table 2.6 Anthropology Village Participants: Tehuelches

Name	Age (in years)
Chief Guechico	71
Lorenza (wife)	45
Giga (daughter)	8
Sinshel (a subchief)	45
Colojo	30 to 35
Casimiro	28
Bonifacio	25

Table 2.7 Indian School Student Participants

Student	Tribe	School	Fair Department
Eliza Adams	Pima	Sacaton	Kindergarten
Lizzie Aiken			(paid)
Michael Alve	Yaqui		Music
Paul American Horse	Cheyenne	Chilocco	Printing
Lulu Anderson	Kickapoo	Chilocco	Domestic science
Alfred Andrews	Lakota	Chamberlain	Sick (leaves early)
Francis Andrews	Puyallup	Haskel	Manual training
Sivileana Anton	Pima	Sacaton	Kindergarten
Mamie Antone	Oneida	Chilocco	Domestic science
Irene Archiquette	Oneida	Haskel	Domestic arts
Tulie Arispie	Wichita	Chilocco	Domestic science
Nellie Arthur	Pima	Sacaton	Kindergarten
Amy Bagnelle	Siletz	Haskell	Domestic arts, recitation, oration, drama
Fred Bean	Chippewa	Chilocco (transfer from White Earth)	Printing
James Bennett	Chippewa	Chilocco	Printing
Hamilton Big Leg	Cheyenne	Haskell	Blacksmithing, wheelwright
Lulu Bigwater	Sauk and Fox		
Joseph Blackwater	Pima	Sacaton	Kindergarten
Amos Blaker	Chippewa	Michigan	
Joshua Blaker	Chippewa	Michigan	
Rene Boisvert	Chippewa	Haskell	Manual training
Alice Boone		Seneca MT	
Gus Brenninger	Cherokee		Music
Ada Breuninger	Menominee		Music, vocalist
Gertrude Brewer	Puyallup	Graduated	Music, piano
Joe Buffalo Hide	Osage	Chilocco	Printing
Mary Burnett	Chippewa	Chilocco (transfer from Chamberlain)	Seventh grade
Blanche Burson	Comanche	Haskell	Domestic arts (age 10), lacework

Table 2.7 (*cont.*)

Student	Tribe	School	Fair Department
Minnie Burton	Shoshone	Fort Shaw	Basketball, music, drama
Genevieve Butch	Yankton Sioux	Fort Shaw	Basketball, music, drama
Mary Cadreau	Chippewa	Chilocco	Domestic science, music
Lena Cayuga	Seneca	Chilocco	Domestic science
Joseph Chapman	Umatilla	Haskell	Manual training
Lonson Cholla	Pima	Sacaton	Kindergarten
Edward Crawford	Dakota Sioux	Genoa	Harness making
Harrison Diaz	Paiute/Hopi (Oraibi)	Chilocco	Printing
Thomas Dahkeya	Chiricahua Apache	Chilocco	To accompany Geronimo
Magdalene Dubray	Sioux	Chilocco	Music
Nannie Ellis			Bow-and-arrow drill
Andrew Elm	Oneida	Chilocco	Music, vocalist
Amy Enos	Pima	Phoenix	
Mabel Enos	Pima	Sacaton	Kindergarten
Frank Fish	Peoria	Chilocco	Seventh grade, recitation
Thomas Flood	Pine Ridge Sioux	Chilocco	Seventh grade, recitation, oration
Joseph Flores	Tohono O'odham	Haskell	Blacksmithing, wheelwright
Pablo Flores	Tohono O'odham	Haskell	Blacksmithing, wheelwright
Bessie Gayton	Ponca	Chilocco	Music
Lottie George	Banco	Haskell	Domestic arts
Genevieve Goose	Ponca	Chilocco	Domestic science, Seventh grade
Leona Gray Eyes	Sauk and Fox	Chilocco	Domestic science
Anna Hale	Potawatomi	Haskell	Domestic arts
Stella Hall	Cherokee		Music
Elwood Harlan		Genoa	
Pearl Hartley			(paid)
Edward Hatchet	Winnebago	Genoa	Harnessmaking (paid)
Anna Hauser	Cheyenne	Haskell	Domestic arts
Louise Hauser	Cheyenne	Haskell	Domestic arts
Annie Havier	Pima	Sacaton	Kindergarten
Genevieve Healy	Gros Ventre	Fort Shaw	Basketball, music, drama
Homer Hill	Cherokee	Chilocco	Printing (paid)
Kista Jackson	Pima	Phoenix	
Ida James	Sauk and Fox	Chilocco	Domestic science
Roy James	Osage	Chilocco	Printing
Belle Johnson	Blackfoot	Fort Shaw	Basketball, music, drama
Bertha Johnson	Wyandotte/ Potawatomi	Chilocco	Domestic science, music, vocalist
Philip Johnson	Pima	Sacaton	Kindergarten
Susette Jones	Oto		
Alice B. Juan	Pima	Sacaton	Kindergarten
Clayton Kirk		Alger, California	
Harry Lama	Navajo		Writing, recitation, and poetry

Student	Tribe	School	Fair Department
Mary Leeds	Pueblo		Music
Richard Lewis	Pima		Music
Lizzie Little Cook	Ponca	Chilocco	Seventh grade
Mary Lockley	Pawnee	Haskell	Domestic arts
Flora Luciro	Chippewa	Fort Shaw	Basketball, music, drama
Miguel Maquinna	Chippewa	Chilocco	Music, vocalist
Felix Nanuel	Pima	Sacaton	Kindergarten
Dan McGlaslin	Oto	Chilocco	Printing
Joseph McGinnes		Albuquerque	
George B. Menz	Lakota Sioux, Standing Rock	Genoa	Harness making
Grace Miller	Shawnee		Music, drama, dining room
Iva Miller	Shawnee		Music, recitation
Joan Minesinger	Snake	Fort Shaw	Basketball, music, drama
Sarah Mitchell	Sioux	Fort Shaw	Basketball, music, drama
Lloyd Montclaire		Underwood ND	Possibly band
Frank Moore	Pawnee	Haskell	Blacksmithing, wheelwright
Miguel Morallis	Pueblo	Chilocco	Music, vocalist
James Morris	Warm Springs	Haskell	Manual training
William Moses	Chippewa	Michigan	
Mary Munel	Chippewa	Chilocco	Domestic science
Frank Munidue	Chippewa	Genoa	Harness making
Caroline Murie	Pawnee	Haskell	Music, daughter of James Murie
Peter Navarre	Potawatomi	Chilocco	Printing
Frank Nelson	Pima	Sacaton	Kindergarten, music
Mary Nuennell	Chippewa	Chilocco	Domestic science (age 18)
Oscar Norton	Hupa		Music, vocal soloist
Agnes Oliver	Chippewa	Chilocco	Domestic science
Frank Oliver	Chippewa	Chilocco	Music, vocal
Esther Parker	Comanche	Chilocco	Domestic science, music, Seventh grade, daughter of Quanah Parker
Jesse Parker	Banco	Haskell	Domestic arts
Alice Peters	Pima	Phoenix	
Leon Poitra		Genoa	
Ida Prophet	Shawnee	Haskell	Domestic arts, music
Ellen Prue	Sioux	Chilocco	Seventh grade
Francisco Ramon	Tohono O'odham	Haskell	Blacksmithing, wheelwright
Louis Ray	Lakota Sioux	Genoa	Harness making
John Red Owl	Sioux	Genoa	Harness making
Mae Regineer	Potawatomi	Haskell	Domestic arts
Effie Rhodes	Pima	Phoenix	
Mary Rhodes	Pima	Chilocco	Domestic science
Walter Rhodes	Pima	Chilocco	Printing, recitation
Joie Roberts	Pima	Sacaton	Kindergarten

Table 2.7 (cont.)

Student	Tribe	School	Fair Department
Jessie Rodgers		Underwood ND	Possibly band
Francisco Roman	Tohono O'odham	Sacaton	
James Ryan		Genoa	
George Rye	Cherokee		Music, recitation
Emma Sansaver	Chippewa	Fort Shaw	Basketball, music, drama
Mary Selby	Cherokee	Chilocco	Seventh grade, domestic science
George Selkirk	Chippewa	Chilocco	Seventh grade
Bert Short Bear		Underwood ND	Possibly band
Helerio Sierra	Pueblo		Music
Anna Sitting Eagle	Pawnee	Haskell	Domestic arts
Ida Skenadore	Oneida	Haskell	Domestic arts
Frank Smith		Phoenix	Possibly band
Katie Snell	Gros Ventre	Fort Shaw	Basketball, music, drama
Lucy Snyder	Chemehuevi	Chilocco	Domestic science
Peter Somers	Oneida	Haskell	Manual training
Ida Starr	Cherokee	Chilocco	Seventh grade
Harry Stevens	Chippewa	Michigan	Possibly band
Pat Stevens	Chippewa	Michigan	Possibly band
Mary Suds			Music
John Swan	Oneida		
Naomi Tanequa	Comanche	Haskell	Domestic science (age 11), lacework
Mary Thomas	Pima	Sacaton	Kindergarten
William Toombs	Sioux	Chilocco	Seventh grade
Jesse Tooms	Oglala Sioux	Chilocco	Seventh grade
Zah Tso	Navajo	Santa Fe	Weaving (mother is demonstrator)
Katherine Valenzuela	Tohono O'odham Pima	Graduated Phoenix	Music, assisted in dining room
Belle Tenis Venus	Blanco	Haskell	Domestic arts
Addison Walker	Miami	Chilocco	Seventh grade
Lela B. Walker	Sauk and Fox	Haskell	Domestic arts
Russell Warrior	Osage	Chilocco	Seventh grade
Daisy Washington	Washoe	Haskell	Domestic arts
Mayte Wasson	Washoe	Haskell	Domestic arts
Grace Waukon	Winnebago	Haskell	Domestic arts
Blake White Bear	Crow		
Julia White Feather	Chippewa	Haskell	Domestic arts
Grace White Spider	Chippewa	Chilocco (transfer from Chamberlain)	Seventh grade
Addie Williams	Cherokee		Music, recitation
Lizzie Wirth	Assiniboine	Fort Shaw	Basketball, music, drama
Nettie Wirth	Assiniboine	Fort Shaw	Basketball, music, drama
Hugo Woodall	Cherokee		
Annie Xavier	Pima	Sacaton	Kindergarten
Louis Youpee	Chippewa	Genoa	Recitations and printing

NOTE: Empty cells indicate no information was available.

Table 2.8 Philippine Reservation Participants

Igorot

Alab: Domingo and wife Coaoy

Bontoc: **Men:** Aggos (age 18), Alonney, Angay, Angpeo (age 19), Chief Antonio (Tetep-an, elder and leader, age 27), Aongay, Apaggnet (age 20), Apoguet (father of child born in St. Louis), Asil (age 11), Aspil (age 20), Attao, Ayhawan (age 25), Baliscao (age 17), Ballicas, Balison (age 22), Balonglong (Antero Cabera, age 15), Bayungorin (age 45), Benigna, Lazardo Bibit (assistant), Bocasen (age 26), Bomatang (age 18), Pedro Bonito, Bugti, Cbayao (age 32), Calutin (age 20), Caplaan, Caplis, Chainen, Chonegma, Congo (age 26), Cortapia, Coyoyas, Dagumay, Dasinan (age 49), Domegma (age 45), Domingo (age 48), Ducyon (age 20), Faclamgan, Falagsay, Fangrove (age 30), Fattane (age 40), Fngging, Ititan (age 20), Kiney, Ladoy, Langilang (age 22), Lape, Leeafun (age 15), Lepanto, Limanan (age 22), Liney, Locogan (age 25), Lodindot (age 18), Loiod (age 18), Lomioes (age 34), Losnoy, Loyan (age 25), Maiyoc (age 20), Maklan, Mangenteo, Mariano, Moling, Ngole (age 18), Ogoy, Ossey, Otinguey (age 35), Padagueg (age 22), Pangamy, Paolo (age 13), Pelo, Pig (age 22), Pinmaing (age 18), Pinns (age 14), Ponchad (age 22), Puiasen, Rsacla, Rufina, Sadoy (age 14), Saperono (age 27), Semey, Sdoecag, Soyam, Soyan, Tidioy, Todiog (age 15), Tongay (age 14), Isidoro Tuason (age 27), Ynis; **Women:** Francisca Alejio (age 36), Maria Alegio (age 18), Petra Antonio (age 26), Petra Arranz (age 50), Atlas (age 30), Beninga (age 20), Caploan (age 50), Cartapia (age 17), Lepo (age 22), Liney (age 20), Elizabeth and Sarah Metcalf, Oassay (age 45), Sabia and son Emilio, Saleyam (age 29), Semey (age 19), Yinis (age 29). Three members of Jenks' household in Luzon: Bugti, Falikao and Maklan.

Lepanto Cartapia (female, age 17).

Suyoc: **Family 1:** Boyongasan (Lepdagen), wife Kinay; **Family 2:** Pettit and wife, Dang-usan (age 17); **Family 3:** Pepe Betuagan, his wife Tugmina (age 17) and their two daughters; **Family 4:** Singwa Tangpap (age 5, nephew of Buli-e and Oning. **Men:** Billy Coytop, Demeya, Buliq (age 11), Bolia Caligtan, Pig, Lebanay Cosme, Oulacan, Paquin (age 40), Pakeyan, Pngcoy Bugtong (aged 8), Polocon (age 21), Quilton (age 1), Sadipan (age 29), Saqued (age 12), Sedro (age 23), Sudong (age 22). **Women:** Babgnuid (age 18), Doniena (age 19), Lagniy (age 38), Lubug (age 17), Oblika (age 19).

Tagolog and Ilocano Julio and Maria Balinag (interpreter).

Tucucan Anawasel and Peher Felingai.

Tinguian Isiguan (leader, age 18), Aonen, Apaling, Blanay, balog, Beitado, Bungay, Cadalig, Catilano, Danangan, Lagban, Latacan, Paloay, Pangao, Taguiay, Ulasim, Valen, Yblogan, Ysiguan.

Moro

Bagobo Men: A-be (age 21), Akil (age 20), Bulon (age 19), Dansa (age 15), Modesto Barrera (age 21), Ubal (age 30), Ramon Untas (age 20).

Lake Lanal Men: Datta, Ambulong, Demasanky, Pitulian, Sungud, Asume, Marabui; Rajah Muda Sumbayangui was the highest-ranking, Sultan Demasanky; Mandae (interpreter).

Samal Men: Acong (age 24), Amil (age 20), Arsenio (age 26), Badin (age 57), Baja (age 21), Buleng (age 25), Dabat (age 36), Danani (age 12), Danga (age 32), Datto Facundi (age 36), Galo (age 22), Gonan-Glali, priest of Pandita, (age 48), Lapucni (age 27), Leone (age 9), Maldani (age 44), Mandan (age 50),

Melasee (age 11), Monona (age 31), Ormo (age 6) Rajah Muda Mand, Sala (age 22), Tasn (age 28), Tingi (age 8), Tuda (age 28), Ucat (age 42); *Women*: Anis (age 12), Arum (age 32), Balila (age 25), Ebidi (age 15), Juli (age 20), Kiedahom (age 22), Manjane (age 40), Sadini (age 12), Salalio (age 29), Sampili (age 28), Sarangbam (age 18), Sumsia (age 32), Tubac (age 15), Tundua (age 13), Uby (age 30).

Negrito

Men: Andang (age 45), Bandong (age 1), Basilio (age 25), El Captain Gamot (age 55, leader), Clario (age 25), Gbag (age 50), Humalin (age 35), Jorge (age 12), Jose (age 21), Juan (age 15), Julian (age 2), Kalmen (age 18), Kamahalin (age 40), Kario (age 25), Marsia (age 24), Millong (age 8), Pedro (age 2), Rupino (age 42), Sayas (age 23), Tiberio (age 30), Tili (age 6), Toyang (age 12), Unda (age 22), Luis Francis Wilson (born in St. Louis July 19, 1904). *Women*: Andia (age 21), Bihinang (age 22), Biria (age 1), Filomena (age 40), Kika (age 2), Luisa (age 22), Polonia (age 22), Sebia (age 45), Teresa (age 37).

Visayan

Juan de la Cruz and his sister Mirtina.

Notes

Abbreviations

BIA	Bureau of Indian Affairs/Indian Service
CHS	Colorado Historical Society Archives
CP-fairs	Chilocco Indian School Papers–fairs
FM	Field Museum of Natural History, Department of Anthropology
FSP	Frederick Skiff Papers, Colorado Historical Society Archives
LC	Library of Congress
LCCC	Lewis and Clark Centennial Corporation
LPEC	Louisiana Purchase Exposition Company as publisher
LPEC-CF	Louisiana Purchase Exposition Company corporate files
LPEC-DRPC	Louisiana Purchase Exposition Company, Departmental Reports, Publicity, and Catalogues
LPEC-ODP	Louisiana Purchase Exposition Company, *Official Daily Program*
LPEC-OPA	Louisiana Purchase Exposition Company, Official Photograph Albums
LPEC-WFB	Louisiana Purchase Exposition Company, *World's Fair Bulletin*
MHS	Missouri Historical Society
MP	WJ McGee Papers, Library of Congress
NA	National Archives, Washington DC
NA–Fort Worth	National Archives, Southwest Regional Branch, Fort Worth, Texas
NAA	National Anthropological Archives, Smithsonian Institution
OHS	Oklahoma Historical Society
OrHS	Oregon Historical Society
RG	Record Group
RU	Record Unit
SIA	Smithsonian Institution Archives
SP	Frederick Starr Papers, University of Chicago
UC	University of Chicago Library, Special Collections

Note on Archival Sources

Louisiana Purchase Exposition organizers left a plethora of operational records, now housed in the Missouri Historical Society as the Louisiana Purchase Exposition Corporation Records: personal correspondence and newspaper scrapbooks, daily records, official publications, monthly departmental reports, rosters of daily activities, visitors' comments, oral histories, and final reports submitted at the close of the fair by each department head. Of special interest are the files of the publicity department, McGee's incomplete report, exhibit catalogues, and the official photographic albums. Unfortunately the files of nations, states, and individual businesses are exceedingly incomplete. More comprehensive in this regard are the LPEC's published volumes and daily programs. These include information from the standpoint of the LPEC. Other information on the exposition is scattered around the country and is cited herein based on archival location and author.

McGee kept most of the Department of Anthropology's files and correspondence after the LPE closed. He considered these materials his personal papers, which means that the materials in the MHS are sketchy. Much of the departmental material is now in McGee's papers at the Library of Congress. Of special use have been McGee's scrapbooks of newspaper clippings, (boxes 16 and 32, labeled LPE scrapbooks). Frederick Skiff, William H. Holmes, and Frederick Starr compiled similar scrapbooks. We have utilized these materials extensively. If incomplete information is found in an endnote reference it is because citation information was missing from these scrapbooks. In many cases we have been able to locate the original publication either online or through interlibrary loan. Other newspapers have been accessed online.

Materials for the Bureau of Indian Affairs and the Indian School are found in three primary locations: the National Archives in Washington, the Southwest regional branch of the National Archives in Fort Worth, and the Oklahoma Historical Society. The most complete run of the *Indian School Journal* was found at the Fort Worth branch of the National Archives. Like McGee, Samuel McCowan took all the Indian School records with him; they are today found in the papers of the Chilocco Indian School in seventeen boxes identified as "fairs," arranged consecutively by date from June 1895 to December 1904. We refer to these as Chilocco Papers. A special word should be said about the *Indian School Journal.* While most issues are sequentially numbered by volume and date, a special October issue is not in numerical sequence with other issue numbers. In addition, the title of many articles is the same in multiple issues. In order to identify the source of particular information we have referred to the article title and then given the month and day of publication. Finally, since author attribution is not given here or in many of the official LPE publications, we have chosen not to use "Anonymous" but to cite as author the publisher in order to avoid untold confusion.

Prologue

1. Slocum (1904) quoted in Moses (1996, 151) and Rydell (1984, 155).
2. Francis quoted in McGee (1905d, 115). While earlier fairs had utilized Native dem-

onstrators, the LPE's size and complexity went beyond anything that had occurred previously.

3. Findling and Pelle (1990, 63–107); Rydell, Findling, and Pelle (2000); Rydell (1984); Curti (1950). The English poet Alfred, Lord Tennyson is said to have declared it "the world's great fair." Official names of these extravaganzas were usually *exhibitions* or *expositions* (the term used first by the French in 1855). The French used the term *exposition universelles*, the British and the Americans *international*, with either *exhibition* or *exposition*, with the latter winning out after 1876. The popular term, however, became *world's fair*. Several excellent books have addressed issues of nineteenth- and early-twentieth-century racism, evolution, imperialism, commercialism, nationalism, identity, and progress and we will not reinvent those wheels here. See Rydell, Findling, and Pelle (2000) for an excellent review and bibliography of this literature.

4. In 1852, the British set the precedent by using the 186,000 pounds in profits from the Great Exhibition to buy eighty-seven acres of land in South Kensington to finance new cultural institutions: the Natural History, Geology, Science, and Victoria and Albert museums, components of the Imperial College and the Royal College, and the Royal Albert Hall (Findling and Pelle 1990, 8; Williams 1985).

5. These materials were deposited in the Smithsonian Institution. See Parezo (1987); Fogelson (1991); and Findling and Pelle (1990, 55).

6. The "Wild Men of Borneo" subsequently joined P. T. Barnum's circus and the term became an American catch phrase. The original Philadelphia "wild men" were "[African American] gentlemen [in fright wigs and Minstrel-show makeup] who had grown up on Long Island" (Findling and Pelle 1990, xv, 60).

7. Findling and Pelle (1990, 19); Read (1964, 48) cited by Williams (1985, 156). See also Greenhalgh (1988, 82–111); Bennett (1995, 27); Mathieu (1989, 109–117); Mason (1890, 32); and Tenorio-Trillo (1996). Diorama-style natural history exhibits with mannequins were developed to replace the mind-numbing rows of repetitive artifacts in glass cases.

8. Skiff quoted in Rydell (1984, 160).

9. Milton (1981); Stocking (1968, 1974b). Bruce Trigger (1989, 110) calls this the "Imperial Synthesis," an essentialist justification for progress defined by policymakers as the expansion of Western capitalism and industry through the exploitation of natural resources and cheap labor in colonies.

10. Patricia Afable (1997) has been the only person to our knowledge to obtain exposition stories from descendents of participants. Some researchers have obtained celebrities' stories, e.g. Robinson (1995). Our work should be seen as a first attempt to uncover the LPE's historic actors; more work must be done to obtain oral histories with exposition participants' descendents.

11. Trying to uncover how Native participants felt about the LPE was a daunting task, since few left any written records and LPE agents partially edited those that exist. Such sources must be read with a filter that assumes preconceptions and prejudices.

12. Pierre Chouteau and William J. Seever (1898), quoted in Bennitt (1905, 81). The

original organization was formalized in 1899. At first Indians were conceptualized as part of the wilderness: "We have had to deal with a territory that a hundred years ago was, throughout almost its entire extent, a wilderness or desert" (original organizing committee statement quoted in Bennitt 1905, 87).

1. Organizing the Louisiana Purchase Exposition

1. Francis quoted in LPEC-DRPC (1904b, 4–5).

2. Skiff (1904b, 4), reprinted in Clevenger (1996, 4); see also Greenhalgh (1988, 12–24); Findling and Pelle (1996, 178); and Rydell (1984, 157). Congress later gave the LPEC a second five-million-dollar loan to cover construction costs.

3. Buel (1904, 1292–98); LPEC-DRPC (1903); *Columbia Encyclopedia* (2001); *Terry's 1904 World's Fair Page* (1997).

4. Fox and Sneddeker (1997, 6); Raiche (1972); S. Williams (1904). Francis needed one thousand acres for exhibits (*St. Louis Republic* 1901).

5. Rogers (1904, 5) reprinted in Francis (1913, 55); Provenzo (1976); Stevens (1909).

6. Walter Hough quoted in Mason (1895, 90).

7. Rydell (1984, 157); Board of Directors' Minutes, May 14, 1901, LPEC, MHS.

8. LPEC-WFB (1901). This is an early instance of salvage archaeology (Bushnell 1904a, 1904b). Inexplicably, McGee did not ask Bushnell to help with the archaeology exhibits (Swanton 1942, 104; Demb 1998).

9. A lawyer, Lehmann chaired the International Congress section; King, vice chair of the manufacturing and liberal arts division, owned a jewelry company; Hill, a banker from a wealthy Virginia family helped the hospital and humane society; Blanke, a businessman specializing in coffee and banking, served on the committee on concessions. LPEC-DRPC (1904b); Reedy (1906); Stevens (1909, 276–77, 1029–30).

10. Frederick Starr to McGee, Aug. 2, 1903, MP, box 14, LC. The committee hired as their secretary Charles E. Hulbert, son of the University of Chicago's theological school dean and Jane Addams's nephew, who had studied anthropology.

11. "Cardinal principles" followed from Goode's maxim: Each object must illustrate an idea, clearly explained on its label, and be placed so that "their relations to each other may be recognized by the visitor, so that, taken together, they suggest certain general conclusions" (Goode 1883, 82–86).

12. Boas (1887a, 587; 1887b). This began a great debate with Mason (1887) and Powell (1887).

13. Executive Committee Minutes, Aug. 23, 1901. This and subsequent minutes, reports, and letters are found in series 11, subseries 3, folders 2, 4, or 5, LPEC files, MHS.

14. Holmes and McGee (1901); Holmes to Lehmann, no date, LPEC files, MHS.

15. Executive Committee Minutes, Sept. 12, 1901.

16. Executive Committee Minutes, Oct. 1 and Nov. 1, 1901; Skiff to Francis, Nov. 1, 1901, LPEC files, MHS. Skiff had been a journalist in Kansas and Colorado, served a term in the Colorado legislature (1885–86), and held several government jobs. He prepared Colorado's

exhibits for the 1893 Chicago Exposition and served as chief of the division of mines. On September 16, 1901, he was hired by the LPEC as director of exhibits (scrapbooks, FSP, CHS). Rydell (1984, 69) notes that by 1915 Skiff "was considered the world's foremost authority on expositions."

17. Executive Committee Minutes, Mar. 11 and Apr. 8, 1902. The fair committee partly reorganized due to rampant corruption in St. Louis (see Steffen 1902, 1903).

18. Skiff (1904b, 3; 1902, 2; 1903); Skiff quoted in Rydell (1984, 159), and from the *Atlanta Journal* (1904); Walker (1904e). The idea of a fair as a mass educational venue was most highly articulated at the 1900 Paris Exposition where organizers stressed education as the source of future progress. Skiff devised a complex scheme for the LPE that illustrated "a sequential synopsis of man's development" and progress: 16 departments, 148 groups, and 807 classes. Education was given central place, followed by art, liberal arts, and applied sciences, which "indicate the result of education and culture, illustrate his tastes and demonstrate his inventive genius, scientific attainment and artistic expression." These three divisions equipped man "for the battle" of life and "prepared him for its enjoyments." Next came departments representing the raw materials that humanity uses, followed by manufacturing, machinery, and transportation. Finally, there was electricity, which "indicates the great forces man has discovered and utilized to convey power and intelligence." At the end of the sequence were the newest problem-solving sciences, Anthropology and Social Economy. Skiff assigned Anthropology four groups, replicating the Field Museum's format. The final department was Physical Culture in which "man is able to treat himself as an animal, realizing that his intellectual and moral constitutions require a sound physical body to prompt them to the proper performance of their function" (Skiff 1904b, 4, 3).

19. The LPEC paid the university $650,000 in rent. Since Cupples Hall was already finished, the exposition administrators moved in. One reason the anthropology displays were so late was because many officials only moved out just before opening day (Executive Committee Minutes, Dec. 2, 1902).

20. Fox and Sneddeker (1997, 24–26); LPEC-WFB (1902b). The other board action was to vote against having a Negro building to highlight black accomplishments.

21. Skiff to Francis, Dec. 2, 1902, Executive Committee Minutes, Dec. 2, 1902.

22. Skiff to Board, Mar. 4, 1903, Executive Committee Minutes, Mar. 16 and Apr. 2, 1903.

23. Executive Committee Minutes, July 14 and Sept. 13, 1903.

2. WJ McGee and the Science of Man

1. Personal data on McGee from Cross (1953); Darnell (2002); Darton (1912); Hinsley (1981); Hodge (1912); Keyes (1913); Knowlton (1913); McGee (1905b); and LPEC-WFB (1904l).

2. Hinsley (1981, 233). McGee's often untenable views, while characteristic of the period, helped articulate the research agenda of the 1880s and 1890s (Hodge 1912, 684; McGee 1888b, 1889a, 1889b, 1890b, 1893). McGee published important geological publications on a number of topics, especially water (McGee 1888a, 1890a, 1891, 1894c).

3. Powell, a geologist noted for his expeditions on the Colorado River, was director of the U.S. Geographical and Geological Survey of the Rocky Mountain Region, one of four federal "Great Surveys" exploring and mapping the West in the 1870s. In 1879 he became director of the Bureau of Ethnology, later the Bureau of American Ethnology [BAE] and in 1881, director of the U.S. Geological Survey while continuing to hold the Bureau of Ethnology directorship. McGee quickly rose in the USGS, becoming head of the Potomac Division. He mapped more than thirty thousand square miles in the Southeast, improved cartographic methods, compiled a thesaurus of American geological formations, and completed several geological maps.

4. Dearing (1971, 464). She had attended Newham College of Cambridge University and the University of Geneva in her teens.

5. McGee wrote the section of the Army Reorganization Act dealing with nurses. With the rank of an army officer, she spent a year reorganizing the Japanese nursing corps during the Russo-Japanese War (1904–5). McGee was the first woman officially designated a U.S. military veteran (Dearing 1971, 465; Darrah 1951, 279; Fowler 2000, 144–45; Lamphere 2004; E. McGee 1905, 61–62).

6. Powell to Langley, Aug. 9, 1894, Outgoing Correspondence, BAE files, NAA; B. Fontana (1971, 2000); H. Fontana (2000); McGee (1895c; 1896b; 1898b, 55–94; 1901b; 1902; 1905b); Powell (1904, xxxiv). McGee produced several geological theses and adventure tales on the expeditions (McGee 1896b, 1896c). Hinsley (1981, 240) has said of his fieldwork: "[D]espite McGee's attempts to picture a dangerous, heroic adventure among bloodthirsty savages, the hunt for the Seri emerges as a series of blundering, foolish decisions by an ignorant and glory-hungry greenhorn."

7. McGee (1895a, 1896a, 1896b, 1897a, 1897b, 1898a). McGee romanticized his own bravery by portraying the Seri as wary, hostile, and warlike.

8. Hinsley (1981, 234); Stocking (1973); Watters and Fowler (2002); Darnell (2001).

9. McGee to Emma Dean Powell, Nov. 19, 1902, Langley notes, Oct. 15, 1902, Records of the 1903 BAE Investigation, NAA; Hinsley (1981, 236); Cross (1953, 154). Langley, who came to the Smithsonian in 1886, was "reserved, shy, socially inept, belonging to an older generation" (Hinsley (1981, 237). He was also described as cold and aloof, living a lonely life (Adler 1907; Cross 1953).

10. Langley to Holmes, Nov. 19, 1902, BAE Investigation 1903; Langley, Feb. 19, 1902, Incoming Correspondence, BAE files, NAA. Hinsley (1981, 236, 248–49); Fernlund (2000); Fowler (2000); Moses (1984); Parezo (1993). Langley had been under considerable political pressure from Congress to have the BAE produce only work needed for the development of Indian policy. In Langley's opinion, this meant impartial descriptions without the interpretations, visionary philosophical statements, synthetic paradigms, or unpopular policy suggestions that Powell and McGee promulgated. Langley also resented McGee's challenges to his authority over annual appropriations. But Powell was powerful and had many friends in Congress, and Langley could not openly challenge him. In addition, Langley was Powell's intimate friend and he tolerated much of the BAE's independence in deference to him.

11. Langley to McGee, Jan. 29, Feb. 3, 1894, MP, box 7, LC.

12. Langley's personal notes and testimony, Langley to McGee Oct. 9, 1902. Untitled articles, *Washington Times*, Oct. 15, and the *Pittsburgh Press*, Oct. 2, 1902, press attachments, BAE Investigation 1903, NAA; Langley to Holmes, Oct. 11, 1902, Incoming Correspondence, BAE files, NAA. Holmes accepted the position on Oct. 15. McGee felt he remained on good terms with Holmes but Holmes was deeply hurt by McGee's public betrayal.

13. McGee to David Henderson, Oct. 30, 1902, BAE Investigation 1903, NAA.

14. Boas (1902, 829); *Popular Science* (1904); *Science* (1902a, 1902b). Boas stated he was paid $4,527 for his manuscripts (Boas testimony, BAE Investigation 1903, NAA).

15. J. C. Barnes to A. D. White, Dec. 15, 1902, BAE Investigation 1903, NAA.

16. Additional administrative files, McGee testimony, BAE Investigation 1903, NAA.

17. McGee to Holmes, July 8, 22, 1903, BAE Incoming Correspondence, NAA.

18. McGee to Holmes, July 31, 1903, Holmes to Rathbun, July 31, 1903, Rathbun to McGee, Aug. 1, 1903, Langley to Holmes Sept. 1903, BAE Investigation, NAA. The results of the investigation were devastating to the bureau, although some individuals felt vindicated (Parezo 1993). Langley essentially placed the unit in receivership, which made producing the Smithsonian's LPE exhibits problematic.

19. Anita kept custody of the children with whom McGee had little interaction after leaving Washington.

20. *St. Louis Globe-Democrat* (1903b, 1903c).

21. M. Harris (1968, 255). Harris further states that McGee was blatantly wrong about almost everything and that he confused the concepts of race, language, and culture. See also Boas (1916).

22. Gould (1981). The blood complexity argument was used by British biologists in the 1930s to counter the "pure Aryan blood" racial superiority arguments of the Nazis. British history was, of course, an ongoing mixture of peoples of many "bloods," Celts, Angles, Saxons, Danes, Norsemen, Normans. It is thus not surprising that American WASPs would opt for "complexity" rather than "purity" of blood as an indicator of "vigor."

23. McGee (1905d, 8, 9, 14–15, 17). See also L. H. Morgan (1877); Powell (1878, 1885, 1896, 1898); McGee (1895b, 1896a, 1897a, 1897b). McGee saw laws, i.e., human force and judgment directed to human ends, as particularly important. At each higher stage, laws become more inclusive in terms of their social control.

3. Planning the Anthropology Department and Model Indian School

Epigraph. McGee (1905d, 115).

1. McGee (1905d, 15–16, 26). In other publications McGee stated that gratifying visitors' instinctive curiosity was important. He knew he had to draw crowds to justify his budget.

2. McGee (1905d, 2, 4–5, 19); *St. Louis Republic* (1903b); McGee to Skiff, July 6, 1903, LPEC files, MHS.

3. McGee (1905d, 21; 1901a, 1901b); Letter to the Editor, unnamed St. Louis newspaper, Aug. 19, n.d.; LPEC Executive Committee Minutes, MHS; McGee (1904a, 5; 1898a, 294).

4. McGee to Skiff, July 6, 1903, LPEC files, MHS.

5. McGee (1904a, 5); *St. Louis Republic* (1903b). McGee insisted that all archaeological materials exhibited by individuals, museums, states, or foreign governments in the Department of Anthropology illustrate his theoretical paradigm.

6. Memo, no author, July 12, 1904, MP, box 28, LC.

7. McGee to Skiff, Sept. 18, 1903, LPEC Board of Director Minutes for Sept. 24, 1903, LPEC files, MHS. McGee's salary was $416.67 per month for sixteen months.

8. *St. Louis Republic* (1903a); *St. Louis Globe-Democrat* (1903a).

9. M'Carty (1903); McGee quoted in *Chicago Inter-Ocean* (1903); Jacobs (1903). McGee also stressed that Indian celebrities were well known to dime-novel readers. His descriptions are reminiscent of how he described his own ethnographic adventures.

10. *New York Times* (1903).

11. Morgan quoted in F. W. Clarke, Department of the Interior to the Secretary of the Interior, Nov. 8, 1893, World's Columbian Exposition Correspondence, 1891–94, box 1, Records of the Office of the Secretary of the Interior, RG 48, NA; T. Morgan (1894).

12. Commissioner of Indian Affairs (1905, 53) reprinted in McGee (1905d, 33); *Washington Times* (1902); Jones (1904, 53–54); W. A. Jones to McCowan, Oct. 22, 1903, CP-Fairs, box 1, OHS. Jones, commissioner from 1897 to 1904, was a transitional figure (Prucha 1984, 686). Exhibits were to include people of different tribes as well as artifacts "to illustrate the past and present conditions of the Indian tribes" and their advancement to civilization. Jones felt congresses "retard Indian civilization generally, are inconsistent with the announced policy of the Department, and chiefly gratify an idle curiosity or pander to a desire for sensationalism." Chilocco Indian Agricultural School was a federal off-reservation boarding school in north central Oklahoma with enrolled students from more than forty tribes between its inauguration in 1882 and 1904 (Lomawaima 1994; Trennert 1988, 60).

13. LPEC-WFB (1903, 30, 82); McCowan (1899); Trennert (1993).

14. James Fanceen to McCowan, Dec. 16, 1903, Haddon to McCowan, Dec. 16, 1903, McCowan to Haddon, Dec. 18, 1903, Charles Peirce to McCowan, Dec. 24, 1903, CP-fairs, box 1, OHS.

15. McGee to Skiff, Aug. 1, 1904, MP, box 14, LC; Hanson (1905, 265–72); Moses (1984, 156); E. A. Hitchcock to McCowan, May 22, 1903, reprinted in McGee (1905d, 17). McGee (1905d) inconsistently gives the amount of additional funds McCowan received (fifteen thousand or twenty-five thousand dollars). McGee later convinced the LPEC to give him twenty-five hundred dollars for the Cocopa exhibit. Trennert (1988, 145) states that McCowan obtained primarily Indians from the Southwest because he was familiar with the region but most were from the Louisiana Territories.

16. McCowan to Widmann, Walsh, and Boiesselier, Feb. 5, 1904, McCowan to Henry W. Schlueter, Dec. 17, 1903, McCowan to Taylor, Dec. 17, 1903, CP-fairs, box 1, OHS.

17. McCowan to Fink and Schuster Plumbing Co., Dec. 21, 1903, Otto Kuhn to McCowan, Dec. 30, 1903, J. Crandall to McCowan, Dec. 18, 1903, CP-fairs, box 1, OHS; McGee (1904a, 6). Funds for interior work were not included in the congressional appropriation.

18. Committee on Grounds and Buildings Minutes, Jan. 2, 1902, LPEC files, MHS; McCowan to Taylor, LPE staff, Dec. 17, 1903, McCowan to H. B. Peairs, Feb. 11, 1904, CP-fairs, box 1, OHS.

19. C. B. Jackson to McCowan, Dec. 30, 1903, and Feb. 10, 1904, A. B. Iliff to C. E. Birch, Dec. 29, 1903, Theodore Lemmon to McCowan, Feb. 1, 1904, McCowan to Joseph Hart, Dec. 28, 1903, Hart to McCowan, Jan. 21, 1904, McCowan to Jones, Dec. 28, 1903, and Jan. 2, 1904, CP-fairs, boxes 1, 2, and 3, OHS. McCowan complained to many friends in hundreds of letters that McGee forgot he had another job, running the Chilocco School.

20. Benham to McCowan, Dec. 24, 1903, Benham to Jones, Dec. 15, 1903, Jones to McCowan, Dec. 26, 1903, CP-fairs, box 1, OHS. Benham, a former Arizona cattleman, operated a large Indian curio store in Phoenix, Arizona, between 1885 and 1895, specializing in Pima basketry and Maricopa pottery.

21. Benham to McCowan, Dec. 14 and 18, 1903, and Feb. 27, 1904, McCowan to Benham, Dec. 17, 1903, and Feb. 27, 1904, McCowan to Morris Gregg, Dec. 17, 1903, CP-fairs, boxes 1 and 3, OHS; McGee (1905d, 112). The sutlery freed space in the Indian School. Benham did not pay the LPEC their 25 percent commission on his sales. The Wetherill brothers were famous early explorers and excavators of the Mesa Verde, Colorado, and Grand Gulch, Utah, cliff dwellings who had exhibited archeological artifacts at several fairs. McNitt (1957, 202–13) discusses the animosity between Richard Wetherill and Benham and their battle for control of the Hyde Exploration Company.

22. McCowan to Hygienic Food Co., Jan. 8, 1904, Figprune Co. to McCowan, Jan. 20, 1904, Charles H. Mundy to McCowan, Jan. 13, 1904, CP-fairs, box 2, OHS. Food included apples, beans, butter, cheese, cinnamon, eggs, ice, lard, condensed and fresh milk, rolled oats, onions, peaches, dried fruit, pepper, potatoes, prunes, pumpkin, raisins, rice, and tomatoes.

23. Frederick Freeman was transferred to Chilocco as head tailor to oversee making uniforms for the boy's drill team. This was no small undertaking. McCowan had ordered two hundred yards of dark green and cadet-gray cloth—enough for forty uniforms (Freeman to McCowan, Dec. 24, 1903, McCowan to Freeman, Jan. 5, 1904, McCowan to Woolley and Co., Jan. 16, 1904, McCowan to Cook, Dec. 5, 1903, McCowan to Jones, Jan. 7, 1904, CP-fair, boxes 1 and 3, OHS).

24. McCowan to Jones, Feb. 5, 1904, Goodman to McCowan, May 7, 1904, McCowan to Valenzuela, May 11, 1904, CP-fair, boxes 3 and 4, OHS.

25. McCowan had to obtain BIA approval before contacting impresarios (Harry Wilson to McCowan, Feb. 5, 1904, A. E. Palmer to McCowan, Jan. 22, 1904, McCowan to Palmer, Jan. 12, 1904, McCowan to Fred Pelham, Jan. 12, 1904, McCowan to Southern Lyceum, Jan. 12, 1904, Pelham to McCowan, Feb. 5, 1904, L. W. Potter to McCowan, Jan. 13, 1904, CP-fairs, boxes 2 and 3, OHS). The Chicago Lyceum booked the band for fourteen weekly concerts for eight weeks.

26. McCowan to J. B. Alexander, Feb. 5, 1904, McCowan to Charles E. Peirce, Dec. 24, 1903, CP-fairs, boxes 1 and 3, OHS; Commissioner of Indian Affairs (1905, 55–56).

27. John Seger to McCowan, June 22, 1903, Sayre to McCowan, June 21, 1903, Seger to McCowan, June 22, 1903, CP-fairs, boxes 1 and 7, OHS.

28. McCowan to O. A. Mitscher, June 12, 1903, and Feb. 2, 1904, Mitscher to McCowan, June 24, 1903, and Feb. 2, 9, 1904, CP-fairs, boxes 1 and 3, OHS.

29. L. Potter to McCowan, Jan. 13, 1904, McCowan to Potter, Jan. 25, 1904, CP-fairs, box 2, OHS.

30. McCowan to Hugh Nobel, Feb. 2, 1904, Alexander to McCowan, Aug. 13, 1903, Nobel to McCowan, Feb. 14, 1904, J. Crandall to McCowan, Feb. 4, 1904, L. Wright to McCowan, Feb. 4 and Apr. 12, 1904, McCowan to Charles S. Bush, Dec. 28, 1903, CP-fairs, box 1, OHS. Many agents did not like the fact that demonstrators would not be paid for their labor because of the expense involved in art production and the need to make a living. McCowan basically ignored them; he did not have funds for consignments or stockpiling.

31. George Gibbs to McCowan, July 21, 1903, McCowan to McGee, July 31, 1903, MP, box 14, LC; Gibbs to McCowan, Dec. 28, 1903, CP-fairs, box 1, OHS.

32. Pratt remarks quoted in Moses (1984, 151); McGee to Pratt, Feb. 27, 1904, CP-fairs, box 8, OHS.

33. McGee (1904a, 5); N. Shabert to McCowan, Apr. 23, 1903, McCowan to Shabert, Apr. 30, 1903, CP-fairs, box 7, OHS. Others offered to bring descendants of the ancient Greeks and Romans for adequate compensation. McGee turned down these offers as he did Carl Hagenbeck of Hamburg, Germany, who suggested his nephew be hired for fifty thousand dollars to make life-size papier-mâché racial figures and dress them in national costumes, which would be cheaper than caring for demonstrators in St. Louis (Carl Hagenbeck to Mr. Tate, Sept. 22, 1903, MP, box 14, LC). Hagenbeck had a zoological concession on the Pike that proved to be a favorite with Native participants. McGee also received myriad requests to purchase collections for display. With few exceptions he turned these down since he had no collections budget.

34. Cora Eddleman to McCowan, Dec. 17, 1903, McCowan to Eddleman, Dec. 28, 1903, CP-fairs, box 1, OHS.

35. *Weekly Review* (1903); Unattributed newspaper clipping of 1904, "Woman on Committee," MP, box 32, LC. Individuals asked to be hired to conduct research. One physician requested a salary higher than McGee's to do an urban anthropological study (Willis Everette to McGee, Sept. 28, 1903, MP, box 14, LC).

36. McCowan to McGee, July 14, 1904, MP, box 19, LC.

37. Holmes, no date; Charles Hubert to Holmes, Aug. 1, 1901, and Jan. 10, 1904, McGee to Holmes, Dec. 29, 1903, McGee to Langley, Jan. 5, 1904, SIA. It is evident from diary entries that Holmes felt betrayed by McGee whom he earlier referred to as his fast friend and best advisor.

4. Assembling the "Races of Mankind"

1. McGee quoted in Francis (1913, 523); McGee to Lehmann, Feb. 20, 1904, MP, box 19, LC; LPEC-WFB (1904a).

2. McGee to Japanese ambassador, Nov. 12, 1903, MP, box 14, LC.

3. McGee (1905d, 6). Verner collected for the U.S. National Museum and was a founding member of the AAA. See Bradford and Blume (1992) for additional information on the expedition.

4. Verner claimed the Tuekis were a foot shorter than other Pygmies and completely covered with hairy fur. He sometimes referred to the Batwa as Tueki, however (Verner 1903 notes, LPE files, box 30, series 3, sub II, folder 6a, MHS). McGee sent a contract for fifty-five hundred dollars and insisted Verner never sue the LPEC for any accidents. (Verner to McGee, Oct. 20, 1903, and Feb. 2, 1904, MP, box 16, LC).

5. Verner to McGee, Mar. 20, 1904, MP, box 14, LC; McGee to Verner, Oct. 21, 1903, S. P. Verner Collection, Carolina Library, Univ. of South Carolina; *New York Times* (1903); Bradford and Blume (1992, 98–99); Verner (1904b, 76; 1904c).

6. Verner (1904b, 80); Bradford and Blume (1992, 103–5). See Verner (1904a, 1904c, 1907) for fictionalized and romanticized accounts of Ota Benga's rescue, which are remarkably similar to the "true life" pamphlets written about individuals in freak shows which were "filled with exaggeration, fabrication, and out-and-out lies" (Bogdan 1988, 19).

7. *St. Louis Post-Dispatch* (1904l).

8. Verner (1904a, 80); Verner to McGee, Feb. 2, 1904, Verner Collection, Carolina Library, USC; McGee (1905d, 101).

9. Verner sold seventy-eight items to the Field Museum for two hundred dollars (Accession 892, catalogue numbers 88161–88265, FM).

10. In retrospect Hatcher's refusal was propitious because he died on the voyage to Antarctica (Bennitt 1905, 767; McGee 1905d, 63).

11. McGee (1905d, 63); *St. Louis Republic* (1904n); Vicente Cane to McGee, Mar. 25, 1904, MP, box 15, LC.

12. McGee to Barlow, Chavero, Clayton, Corral, and Leon, Nov. 23, 1903, Cushman to McGee, July 31, Aug. 9, 18, Oct. 1, Nov. 15, 1903; McGee to Cushman, Nov. 12, 1903, MP, box 14, LC.

13. Cushman to McGee, Nov. 15, 22, Dec. 1, 1903; Corral to McGee, Dec. 1, 1903, MP, box 14, LC.

14. McGee to Cushman, Jan. 11, 1904, MP, box 20, LC. The Cocopa were not federally recognized until 1917 (Kroeber 1920; Tisdale 1997, 121–22; Williams 1983).

15. McGee to Pablo Colorado, Jan. 5, 1904, MP, box 20, LC.

16. McGee "Expense Account," Jan., Feb., and Mar. 1904, MP, box 19, LC. The trip cost $205. The Cocopas lived on the Andrade Grant. Colorado stated he found Cushman an honorable man (Colorado to McGee, Jan. 20 and 26, 1904, Cushman to McGee, Mar. 3 and 28, 1904, McGee to Cushman, Apr. 16, 1904, MP, boxes 19 and 20, LC).

17. Cushman to McGee, March 28, 1904, MP, box 19, LC; McGee (1905d, 65). Cushman remained until the end of July when either typhoid fever or a respiratory disease forced him to resign.

18. *St. Louis Post-Dispatch* (1904c). Field agents were expected to obtain supplies and buy coffee at stations en route. McGee tried to placate Cushman by rationalizing that it was

all for the best: "Weather here too cold and wet for Indians if they can be held a few days without demoralization" (McGee to Cushman, Apr. 26, 13, and 16, 1904, MP, box 19, LC).

19. F. Cole (1935, 532–33); Miller (1978, 52); biographical sketch, finding aid, Frederick Starr Papers, UC Library; Starr to McGee, Aug. 2 and 28, 1903, Starr to Charles Hulbert, Feb. 4, 1903, MP, box 14, LC. Starr stated repeatedly that Japan would win the war with Russia (*Rochester Chronicle* 1904).

20. Miller (1978, 51); Rydell (1984, 166); Starr (1895, 283). Stocking (1979, 12) has characterized Starr as a person "rooted permanently in late nineteenth-century evolutionism." The Ainu taxonomic problem is today considered a non-issue (Omoto and Saitou 1997, 445). Starr planned to display his Mexican photographs and as early as July 1903 had reserved a place when he brought McGee to Chicago to give lectures on the LPE (Starr to McGee, Aug. 2, 28, 1903; Starr to Charles Hulbert, Feb. 4, 1903. MP, Box 14, LC).

21. Starr (1904a, 3); McGee to Starr, Oct. 13, 1903, Starr to McGee, Oct. 12, 1903, MP, box 14, LC.

22. McGee (1905d, 65); Starr (1904a, 16). Starr's final report to McGee states he left on Jan. 20 but his notes state the 26th.

23. Starr (1904a); Van Stone (1993). Starr sold his collection to the Brooklyn Museum of Art (Kotani 1999, 136; Lotani 1999).

24. Contracts, Mar. 1, 2, 1904, MP, box 28, LC; Starr to McGee, Mar. 13, 1904, McGee to Starr, March 24, 1904, MP, box 20, LC; Starr field notebooks, SP, box 15, UC; Starr (1904a, 76).

25. Starr (1904a, 75); field notebooks, 1904, SP, box 15, UC.

26. Starr (1904a, 97); Starr to McGee, Apr. 11, 1904, MP, box 19, LC; Starr to his mother, March 19, 1904, SP, box 6, folder 5, UC.

27. Starr (1904a, 98); Starr to his mother, Apr. 8, 1904, SP, box 6, folder 5, UC.

28. Starr to his mother, Apr. 9, 1904, SP, box 6, UC; Starr (1904a, 104); Van Stone (1993, 85).

29. McGee to Starr, May 11, 1904, MP, box 19, LC; Starr (1904a, 105).

30. Dorsey to McGee, Aug. 3, 1903, MP, box 14, LC.

31. Dorsey took a partial unpaid leave of absence from the Field Museum between January 1903 and April 1904 to work for the Harvey Company (Harvey 1996, 7; Howard and Pardue 1996, 26). His publications dealt with archaeology and Hopi and Arapaho ethnography. He had tried to obtain a position at the University of Chicago, which Starr vetoed (Miller 1978, 55).

32. Welsch (2003, 101); Eggan (1979, 3–4). Information on Murie is from Parks (1978) and Coleman and Almazan (2003). It was unfortunately the standard practice not to have data gatherers (Native or non-Native) as coauthors on monographs. Murie was an author in his own right (Murie 1914). Murie married Mary Esau and had eight children, three of whom came to St. Louis. His daughter, Caroline, was an Indian School student who sang in several quartets (George W. Nellis to McCowan and Lipps, Apr. 24, 1904, CP-fairs, box 4, OHS). Dorsey had a similar relationship with Cleaver Warden, an Arapaho (Almazan and Coleman 2003b).

33. Dorsey to McGee, Feb. 24, 1904, MP, box 19, LC; Dorsey to Skiff, Jan. 1, 1904, FM; McGee (1905a).

34. Dorsey to Voth, June 6, 1904, FM.

35. McGee (1905d, 107; 1904b, 823); L. H. Morgan (1954). McCowan had extensive correspondence with individuals who had sponsored Iroquois artists at Buffalo and desired to do so again. None came.

36. Information on Newcombe from D. Cole (1985), Macnair (1982), and Jacknis (2002); information on Nowell from Ford (1949) and D. Cole (1985). Newcombe and Nowell continued to work together until 1924.

37. McGee (1905d, 68, 107); Dorsey to McGee, Mar. 25, 1903, MP, box 19, LC. For his services Newcombe would receive an honorarium (out of which he would pay Nowell) and travel expenses. "The great trouble," he wrote Dorsey, "has been in getting them to believe that they can make enough from their basketry and woodwork to [equal] what they would get from fishing and hop-picking" (Newcombe to Dorsey, Apr. 13, 1904, FM).

38. Dorsey to McGee, no month, 16, 1904, MP, box 19, LC; Newcombe to Dorsey, Apr. 13, 1904, FM.

39. Dr. Atlieu to Newcombe, Apr. 4, 1904, FM; also printed in Cole (1985, 201). Newcombe obtained objects to fill the longhouse at Koskimo Sound using Field Museum funds.

40. Jacknis (2002, 90); Anonymous, 1904, Vancouver Indian Group Statement of Cost, MP, box 28, LC; Accessions 901, 910, and 912. The six-hundred-dollar freight bill put an unexpected dent in McGee's budget.

41. McCowan to McGee, May 31, 1904, CP-fairs, box 3, OHS; Fiscal Records, LPEC files, MHS; McGee (1905d, 110).

42. Parezo (1993); Fiscal Records, LPEC files, MHS.

43. C. Burton to McCowan, Apr. 13, 1904, CP-fairs, box 3, OHS; Breitbart (1997, 78); Whiteley (1988, 93–94); James (1974, 123–29).

44. Henry Voth to McGee, Mar. 2, 1904, P. Staufer to McGee, March 7, 1904, MP, box 17, LC; McCowan to Burton, Apr. 23, 1904, CP-fairs, box 5, OHS.

45. McGee (1905d, 109–10); McCowan to McGee, June 2, 1904, MP, box 19, LC.

46. Boas to McGee, Mar. 5, 1904, MP, box 19, LC.

47. Dorsey to McGee, Mar. 4, 1904, MP, box 19, LC; McCowan (1905b); McGee (1904f). Other noted artists were Joseppa and Jeff Dick and Clara and Tom Mitchell.

48. McGee to William Benson, Apr. 6, 1904, Dorsey to Benson, Apr. 6, 1904, MP, box 19, LC. McGee paid for their train tickets from Albuquerque ($37.80) and food; *St. Louis Republic* (1904i).

49. *Chicago Inter-Ocean* (1903).

50. Haddon to McCowan, Feb. 2, 1904, CP-fairs, box 3, OHS. Esther Parker espoused standard policy: "When visiting our school, visit the homes of the old Indians, and after you have carefully studied each, draw your own conclusion as to whether the Indian is making any progress or not" (Parker 1904, 74).

51. McCowan first tried to find Chief Joseph in Spokane, saying he was wanted as an intelligent and progressive man who could earn a considerable amount of money. Nez Perce leader Luke A. Wilson informed McCowan that Chief Joseph had just left for a trip to Washington DC. Agents in Idaho, Montana, Oregon, and Washington responded to McCowan saying Chief Joseph had gone to the Flathead Reservation to visit friends or they had seen him a week before but he had left to visit relatives. Many said that they were sure he would like to come since he had been a member of Cummins's 1901 Wild West Show in Buffalo and had a good time. All agents offered to escort him themselves, in exchange for a free train ticket. E. T. McArthur informed McCowan that Chief Joseph's relatives were ready to go too but McCowan only wanted them if Chief Joseph came (M'Carty (1903); McCowan to Chief Joseph, Dec. 16, 1903, McCowan to Albert Anderson, Jan. 29, 1904, Luke Wilson to McCowan, Jan. 13, 1904, Anderson to McCowan, Feb. 4, 1904, E. T. McArthur to McCowan, Dec. 22, 1903, CP-fairs, boxes 1 and 5, OHS; *New York Times* (1904a).

52. Francis (1913, 529); F. Sayre to McCowan, Apr. 21, 1904, CP-fairs, box 4, OHS; M'Carty (1903); Burbank and Royce (1946); *St. Louis Republic* (1904f).

53. A. Tanner to McCowan, Dec. 19, 1903, H. Young to McCowan, Jan. 6, 1904, Sayre to McCowan, Jan. 8, 1904, CP-fairs, box 2, OHS. Their rail tickets cost $37.80.

54. Geronimo, quoted in Barrett (1970, 160).

55. Clum (1928, 249, italics in original). Clum was an Apache agent who considered Geronimo a criminal. See Barrett (1970, 161); Burbank and Royce 1946, 23); Debo (1976, 251, 410); Santee (1947, 174–76); Turner (1996, 33).

56. O. Lipps to McCowan, Apr. 21, 1904, CP-fairs, box 4, OHS. Some students waited until their June graduations before coming.

57. McGee to J. McCormick, Dec. 1, 1903, June 6, 1904, MP, box 14, LC.

58. McGee to Skiff, Sept. 28, 1903, LPEC files, MHS. McGee tried to convince the Pike concessionaires to make their pavilions more educational by writing a guidebook for visitors describing each group and what physical and cultural features visitors might observe.

5. Presenting Worthy Indians

Epigraph. Indian School Journal (1904f).

1. Francis (1913, 522–23); McGee (1905d, 18); M'Carty (1903), quoted in Hanson (1905, 337). See also Nicks (1999); MacCanell (1973); and MacAloon (1984) for discussions of Native villages designed as spectacles in modern societies. These allowed Native peoples to claim public space and affirm their cultural integrity.

2. McGee (1904g, 5187). Arrowhead Lake was designed to look natural and the Cascades to illuminate how humans controlled nature. The villages around the lake were intended to demonstrate evolutionary mastery of water. See Fox and Sneddeker (1997) and Magnaghi (1983–84).

3. McGee worried there were not enough Indians after the July mass exodus (Foster Thunderhawk to McGee Aug. 14, 1904, and Sept. 9, 1904, McGee to Thunderhawk, Sept. 17, 1904, MP, boxes 6 and 19, LC).

4. McCowan (1905b); McGee (1904f); "Family Register" published in McGee (1905d, 118); McGee to Skiff, Jan. 12, 1904, MP, box 19, LC; *Indian School Journal* (1904aa, June 16; 1904bb, June 16). Each source lists different numbers for every tribe. The final government count of 310 adults in the Indian Village excluded people in state pavilions, Pike concessions, private exhibits, or people who came at their own expense.

5. McGee (1904e); Monthly Fiscal Report: McGee to Skiff, May 1904, MP, box 16, LC.

6. McGee (1905d, 108; 1904c, 16; 1904e); LPEC-ODP (1904r, 28); Hanson (1905, 348); *St. Louis Republic* (1904r).

7. *St. Louis Post-Dispatch* (1904kk); Hanson (1905, 340).

8. *Indian School Journal* (1904bb, July 6).

9. Dorsey quoted in Hanson (1905, 339).

10. McGee (1904e); John Buntin to McCowan, Jan. 26, 1904, McCowan to Buntin, Feb. 2, 1904, CP-fairs, box 2, OHS. The group was actually larger than McCowan had wanted or had budgeted for.

11. McCowan to Buntin, Jan. 4, Feb. 2, and Apr. 18, 23, 1904, Buntin to McCowan, Jan. 26, and Apr. 12, 19, 1904, CP-fairs, boxes 2 and 4, OHS; *Scientific American* (1904d, 218).

12. *Indian School Journal* (1904f, June 9); *St. Louis Post-Dispatch* (1904dd).

13. Dorsey to McCowan, Apr. 19, 1904, CP-fairs, box 5, OHS; Simms to McGee, Feb. 14, 1905, MP, box 14, LC; Dorsey to James Mooney, March 22, 1902, Incoming Correspondence, BAE, NAA; LPEC-OPA (1905, 225). See Bol (1996) and Almazan and Coleman (2003b) for more on Warden and his work with Dorsey.

14. McGee (1905d, 109); *Indian School Journal* (1904b).

15. *St. Louis Post-Dispatch* (1904e); *St. Louis Republic* (1904d).

16. McCowan to Commissioner Jones, June 14, 1904, RG 75, BIA Incoming Correspondence, NA-Fort Worth.

17. Hanson (1905, 337, 338); *St. Louis Republic* (1904d); Dorsey to McGee, summer, 1904, MP, box 14, LC; *Indian School Journal* (1904f, June 20). Hanson's statement is an unattributed reuse of a Dorsey quote (*St. Louis Post-Dispatch* 1904mm).

18. McCowan to H. Johnson, Apr. 18, 1904, Johnson to McCowan, Apr. 14 and 26, 1904, H. Dawson to McCowan, Apr. 14, 1904, CP-fairs, boxes 1 and 4, OHS; Simms to McGee, Feb. 14, 1905, MP, box 4, LC; *Indian School Journal* (1904f, June 3); Hanson (1905, illustration caption: "Tepee of the Apache Indians").

19. McCowan to C. Crouse, March 9 and 29, 1904, CP-fairs, box 4, OHS; Anonymous, 1904, World's Fair Ground, no attribution, LPE notebook, MP, box 19, LC.

20. LPEC-ODP (1904aa, 12). The canvas for each tepee cost fifteen dollars (Sayre to McCowan, Apr. 2, 1904, McCowan to Sayre, Apr. 18 and 23, 1904, Haddon to McCowan, Apr. 13, 1904, McCowan to Haddon, Apr. 18, 1904, CP-fairs, boxes 4 and 6, OHS).

21. Hanson (1905, 340); Debo (1976, 400); Francis (1913, 529); A. Brown to James Carroll, July 1; Carroll to Sayre, July 11; Carroll to McCowan, July 23 and Aug. 6, Irving McNeil to McCowan, Aug. 24, McCowan to W. Sickels, Aug. 27, Sayre to McCowan, Apr. 21, 1904, CP-fairs, boxes 4, 10, 11, and 12, OHS.

22. Everett (1904, 337–38); LPEC-WFB (1904a, 71).

23. M'Carty (1903); McGee (1904c, 7); (Barrett 1970, 145–49). For information on earlier expositions see Burbank and Royce (1946); Debo (1976); Reddin (1999); Santee (1947); and Turner (1996).

24. Geronimo quoted in Barrett (1970, 160); LPEC-WFB (1904i, 4).

25. Geronimo quoted in Barrett (1970, 160); *Indian School Journal* (1904v); LPEC-WFB (1904a, 71). Geronimo remembered that many people invited him to their homes but his "keepers" always refused. He received money and goods in exchange for the use of his visage (Burbank and Royce 1946). Indian School staff helped fill orders. Responding to one potential customer McCowan stated, "The old gentleman is pretty high priced, but then he is the only Geronimo" (McCowan to G. E. Follansbee, Oct. 4, 1904, CP-fairs, box 15, OHS). Geronimo made more money than any demonstrator although he may not have kept it all since he and his male relatives played poker and monte (Debo 1976, 383, 399).

26. *Indian School Journal* (1904aa, Oct., p. 68; 1904f, June 10).

27. *St. Louis Globe-Democrat* (1904e); *St. Louis Post-Dispatch* (1904p; 1904q; 1904v); Anonymous, 1904, Geronimo as Exhibit, no source, MP, box 16, LC; Hinckley (1967, 299); *St. Louis Republic* (1904g).

28. *Indian School Journal* (1904f, June 18, 30, July 27; 1904aa, Oct., p. 68); *New York Times* (1904b).

29. Geronimo quoted in Barrett (1970, 169).

30. Geronimo quoted in Barrett (1970, 129).

31. McCowan to Richard Davis, Dec. 28, 1903, CP-fairs, box 2, OHS; Davis to McGee, March 19, 1902, BAE Incoming Correspondence, 1888–1906, NAA. Davis later served as head of the combined Cheyenne tribes in the 1920s to 1930s and was associated with an Indian theater and culture center (Thunderbird 1976a; 1976b).

32. Davis to McCowan, Feb. 5, 24, 1904, McCowan to Davis, Mar. 2, Feb. 9, 1904, CP-fairs, boxes 1 and 2, OHS. This was a strategy used by Indians at other expositions (Gleach 2003).

33. Davis to McCowan, Apr. 18, 19, 1904, McCowan to Davis, March 2, Apr. 22, 1904, CP-fairs, box 4, OHS.

34. Davis to McCowan, Apr. 30, 1904, McCowan to Davis, May 4, 1904, CP-fairs, box 3, OHS.

35. *Indian School Journal* (1904f, June 21, Aug. 17, 19, 22). Davis bought art for the Field Museum and collected ethnographic data (Dorsey to Stephen Simms, Nov. 1, 1904, FM).

36. McCowan to Haddon, Apr. 18, 1904, Haddon to McCowan, Apr. 13, 20, 22, 1904, McCowan to "Herbie," Apr. 16, 1904, travel vouchers, CP-fairs, boxes 3, 4, and 6, OHS. McCowan was not pleased when Haddon could not find tipi poles and suggested the Comanche stay in army-style tents, like the Apache.

37. Hanson (1905, illustration caption: "Comanche Indian Tepee and Good Indians").

38. *St. Louis Republic* (1904l).

39. *Scientific American* (1904d, 218); LPEC-ODP (1904u, 1904s). The two men left as soon as the house was completed.

40. Mitchner to McCowan, Feb. 9, 1904, cp-fairs, box 2, ohs; lpec-opa (1905, 23).

41. Information on Lookout from Wilson (1984); lpec-opa (1905, 212); *Indian School Journal* (1904aa, Sept. 17).

42. McGee (1905d, 111); lpec-odp (1904b).

43. *Indian School Journal* (1904f, Sept. 15; 1904aa, Sept. 17); lpec-opa (1905, 23). Another celebrity was General Pleasant Porter, Creek Nation leader, whose wedding to a socially prominent St. Louis woman was commented on extensively. Porter, one of the wealthiest men in the United States and a graduate of Forest Park University in St. Louis, was a fifty-five-year-old lawyer and politician, "gentleman of education, refinement and attributes which have won him the respect of all the people of Indian Territory, red and white alike" (*St. Louis Post-Dispatch* 1904o).

44. James K. Allen confirmed a Navajo family but trader Lorenzo Hubbell objected because he wanted them to produce goods for his store. Because of Hubbell's political influence, McCowan rescinded the invitation. In late March, James Crandall, superintendent of the Santa Fe school, located two single women but McCowan declined; he only wanted families with babies (Allen to McCowan, Jan. 3, 1904, McCowan to Allen, Feb. 3, 1904, Hubbell to Commissioner Jones, Jan. 20, 1904, McCowan to Hubbell, Feb. 12, 1904, Crandall to McCowan, Apr. 2, 1904, McCowan to Crandall, Apr. 6, 1904, cp-fairs, boxes 2, 3, and 4, ohs; *Scientific American* (1904d, 218).

45. *Indian School Journal* (1904aa, Oct., p. 80). Cullom (1829–1914) was on the Senate committees for expenditures of public monies and foreign affairs (*Biographical Directory of the United States Congress, 1774–Present*, http://bioguide.congress.gov).

46. *Indian School Journal* (1904f, June 9, July 13; 1904u); *St. Louis Post-Dispatch* (1904ll). Many comments recorded in the *Indian School Journal* were printed to show that visitors, especially blacks, were ignorant.

47. One man remembered, "It will be observed in watching the Navajo Indians making blankets that it is as easy as weeding strawberries. . . . I feel confident I could sit down and do the same thing with my eyes shut. Navajo blanket making taught in twenty easy lessons should be a tuition taken up by any one who wishes to earn money without leaving home; no outfit required; send for circular" (*St. Louis Globe-Democrat* 1904i).

48. *St. Louis Republic* (1904p). McCowan daily tried to forbid the donning of "inappropriate" clothing or the use of "inappropriate" tools without much success.

49. McCowan to Simon Michelet, May 10, 1904, cp-fairs, box 1, ohs; lpec-opa (1905, 19); McGee (1904c, 16). Michelet asked whether the Ojibwa should reenact the play *Hiawatha* but McCowan declined.

50. J. B. Alexander to McCowan, Apr. 14, 1904, McCowan to Alexander, Feb. 5, 1904, cp-fairs, boxes 1 and 4, ohs; lpec-odp (1904b). McCowan wanted archers but none were willing to come.

51. *Scientific American* (1904d, 218); *Indian School Journal* (1904x). Adams's daughter Eliza was a member of the Sacaton kindergarten class and the Adamses served as parental chaperones.

52. *St. Louis Republic* (1904x, June 13).

53. W. Hudson to McGee, Apr. 12, 1904, MP, box 19, LC; *Indian School Journal* (1904f, June 3). Marvin Cohodas (1997) gives birth and death dates: Mary (1876–1930) and William (1862–1937). See also McLendon and Holland (1979) and McLendon (1990).

54. McGee (1905d, III). Quote originally from *Indian School Journal* (1904f, June 8); *St Louis Republic* (1904e).

55. Hudson to McGee, Apr. 12, 1904, Dorsey to McGee, Mar. 4, 1904, MP, box 19, LC; *St. Louis Republic* (1904e); *Indian School Journal* (1904i). Later William worked with Stewart Culin, Alfred Kroeber, and William Barrett (Smith-Ferri 1996, 131).

56. McCowan (1906). Crandall estimated he would have to ship over two thousand adobe bricks. One Santa Clara man was an excellent belt weaver; Crandall was unable to locate enough wool for him, and McGee had to buy it in St. Louis. Other Acoma artists had originally been slated to go but Josephine Foard talked them out of it (Crandall to McCowan, Nov. 29, 1903, McCowan to Crandall, Dec. 10, 1903, Crandall to McGee, Apr. 3, 14, 15, 1904, Allen to McCowan, Apr. 2, 24, 1904, McCowan to Allen, Apr. 6, 1904, CP-fairs, boxes 1 and 4, OHS and MP, box 18, LC). The Acoma women tried to use the Indian School ovens but decided the loaves did not taste right. There were always ready customers for the fresh loaves. So much corn and cooking supplies were bought that the food bill for their stay totaled over $1,025.

57. *Indian School Journal* (1904f, June 10).

58. LPEC-OPA (1905, 43).

59. *Indian School Journal* (1904f, June 6); originally published in *St. Louis Republic* (1904l). McGee and McCowan were somewhat mollified that the Hopi had not come when they saw how well the Acoma women made piki bread.

60. LPEC-ODP (1904aa, 1904s); *Indian School Journal* (1904f, June 3); *St. Louis Republic* (1904e).

61. LPEC-ODP (1904o). The LPE catalogue says twenty-eight men and women were at the fair but the number varied each month. Rosebud Agency day-school inspector A. E. McFatridge and his wife escorted them and were given free room and board in the Indian School for thirty days (McFatridge to McCowan, Apr. 2, 5, 12, 1904, McCowan to Jones, Apr. 5, 1904, CP-fairs, box 4, OHS).

62. *Indian School Journal* (1904f, June 18); *St. Louis Republic* (1904b).

63. H. Kinner to McGee, July 26, 28, 1904, McGee to Kinner, July 27, 1904, MP, box 16, LC.

64. *St. Louis Post-Dispatch* (1904nn).

65. LPEC-WFB (1904i).

66. *Indian School Journal* (1904aa, June 6; 1904ff, June 30); *(Brocton MA) Times* (1904); Bennitt (1905, 678); LPEC-OPA (1905, 130).

67. *St. Louis Post-Dispatch* (1904s); Hanson (1905, 341); *St. Louis Republic* (1904t).

68. According to the *Indian School Journal* (1904f, Aug. 6), "They left with kind farewells to the Indian school. Chief Yellow Hair bade good-bye to Superintendent McCowan, say-

ing: 'My heart is full of kindness to you all,' and Mrs. Yellow Hair wept on the shoulders of one of the young Indian girls." *Indian School Journal* (1904f, July 1); *St. Louis Republic* (1904h).

69. *Scientific American* (1904e, 414); McGee (1904g, 5188).

6. The Model Indian School

1. Francis (1913, 524); McGee (1905d, 26); *Indian School Journal* (1904c, 1904h, 1904bb).

2. Lomawaima (1996, 13). By 1898 there were over two hundred and fifty federal boarding schools with two thousand teachers and twenty thousand students. The Indian Service needed to convince the American public that its policies justified the expense, see "Exit the Traditional Indian," *Troy Times* (1904); Adams (1995); and Coleman (1993).

3. Francis (1913, 529) summarizes McGee's position.

4. This had evolutionary implications because the public was debating whether indigenous peoples had to do a step-wise evolution, going through every stage, or could advance directly to civilization. McGee felt that at the LPE, "the actual transformation from comfortless camp life into comfortable householdry was illustrated not only by every intermediate step but by the actual passage of individuals and families from the one stage to the other during the exposition period."

5. McCowan (1905a, 54); LPEC-WFB (1904j, 71); Hoxie (1984). McCowan was very aggressive in ensuring that all his undertakings were successful; "He often resorted to questionable methods, running roughshod over anyone white or Indian—who opposed him" (Trennert 1988, 57). Trennert considers him a gradualist who thought Indians required a slow, steady road to assimilation and training in occupations where they would not directly compete with whites.

6. *Indian School Journal* (1904f, Sept. 6, June 9).

7. LPEC-DRPC (1905b, 344–45); LPEC-WFB (1904k, 40); McCowan (1905b, 119; 1904b, 85); *Indian School Journal* (1904bb, June 14; 1904bb).

8. Student work included compositions, penmanship, arithmetic exercises, drawings, sewing, lace, beadwork, china painting, and photographs. Cook's exhibits in the government building contained the same types of materials (*Indian School Journal* 1904f, June 27).

9. The head of the farm was C. A. Peairs from Chilocco (*Indian School Journal* 1904f, June 3); McGee (1904g, 5187).

10. *Indian School Journal* (1904f, Sept. 6, June 14). An intense storm on Aug. 18 blew down all the tents and tepees. No one was hurt but it took several days to repair the damage.

11. *St. Louis Republic* (1904s); *Indian School Journal* (1904f, June 16; 1904p, 1). Most articles in the *Indian School Journal* are anonymous but we assume McCowan or his staff wrote them. McCowan printed positive remarks and written visitors' comments almost daily. They provide a skewed view of reactions to the pavilion.

12. McCowan to Jones, June 2, 1904, RG 75, BIA files, NA, Fort Worth; LPEC-ODP (1904l, 15); *St. Louis Globe-Democrat* (1904f). We have been unable to identify Chief Good Water. The titles of the different compositions cited by the reporter should be taken with a grain of salt, as should musical assessments.

13. LPEC-ODP (1904h, 5; 1904j, 71); *St. Louis Republic* (1904n).

14. LPEC-ODP (1904aa, 12; 1904o, 13; 1904r, 27); *Indian School Journal* (1904x; 1904bb, June 10). More expensive pieces were displayed and sold in the sutlery. After hours, visitors acquired artifacts directly from the makers.

15. *Indian School Journal* (1904p).

16. *Indian School Journal* (1904f, June 28).

17. McGee (1904a, 6); *St. Louis Republic* (1904m).

18. There was much personnel trading between McCowan and other superintendents, similar to the shifting of personnel among professional sports teams (Nellie Barada to Mc-Cowan, Jan. 19, 1904, McCowan to Barada, Jan. 27, 1904, CP-fairs, box 1, OHS).

19. LPEC-WFB (1904j, 71); *Indian School Journal* (1904f, July 26, Sept. 13; 1904bb, July 21). Daily religious, military tactical instruction, and sports were abbreviated. S. Toledo Sherry also had the class demonstrate grammatical work in the education pavilion.

20. *Indian School Journal* (1904bb, June 14).

21. *Indian School Journal* (1904f, Aug. 16, June 20, Oct., p. 81); Peters (1904, 1). Pies were especially popular.

22. *Indian School Journal* (1904f, June 26).

23. *Indian School Journal* (1904n; 1904bb, July 26, 28; 1904f, Aug. 24).

24. LPEC-ODP (1904s, 8); *Indian School Journal* (1904bb, June 7).

25. *Indian School Journal* (1904f, June 7; 1904bb, June 14, 15); Peters (1904, 81). The *Indian School Journal* (1904f, June 3) recorded that one visitor remarked, "I thought the Indian girls were not taught to wash by hand. From speeches made in Congress I supposed Indians were all supplied with machinery for washing and that the children were taught nothing but painting, higher mathematics and astronomy." Most were more interested in the new electric irons and the young women's beauty than their skills.

26. *Indian School Journal* (1904f, June 7; 1904aa, June 17).

27. *Indian School Journal* (1904bb, July 6).

28. LPEC-ODP (1904s, 10); *Indian School Journal* (1904f, July 22, 30). McCowan decided to use only trades that furthered Indian Service policy (McCowan to W. M. Peterson, Feb. 24, 1904, McCowan to Dr. Winslow, Feb. 24 and 27, 1904, CP-fairs, box 3, OHS).

29. The photograph sold well (*Indian School Journal* 1904bb, June 30; 1904f, June 8 and 22, Sept. 15). The department also produced two thousand copies of Chilocco's annual catalogue. Scrapbooks were given to the Congressional House Appropriation Committee.

30. Emma Johnson to McCowan, Dec. 14, 1903, Apr. 2, 1904, McCowan to Johnson, Dec. 28, 1903, Jan. 26, 1904, CP-fairs, boxes 1, 2, and 4, OHS. Preparations for their trip were complicated since McCowan instructed them to bring everything the children needed. Second-grade teacher Addie Beaver, Tecumseh's granddaughter, served as McCowan's special assistant.

31. *Indian School Journal* (1904f, June 16).

32. *Indian School Journal* (1904k; 1904f, July 7).

33. *Indian School Journal* (1904bb, June 30; 1904f, June 14). One woman was heard to say, "Dear me! I have a little girl about the age of the older child and she can't get along without a nurse maid." By mid-June students participated in the model playground and Education Department programs as well as at local schools.

34. *Indian School Journal* (1904bb, Oct., p. 46, July 25, June 9; 1904f, June 28).

35. McCowan (1904f, 4). McCowan worked vigorously to entice the best elocutionists from other schools (McCowan to Lemmon, Apr. 1 and 4, 1904, CP-fairs, box 4, OHS).

36. In the pole drill women maneuvered pieces of cloth in crisscross patterns like a May pole dance (*Indian School Journal* 1904bb, July 25; 1904l, Oct., p. 30; 1904f, July 28).

37. *Indian School Journal* (photo caption: Sept. 17, 1904f, July 25; 1904c, Oct., p. 50).

38. Periodically the Ainus, Tehuelches, Mbutis, or Chippewas were honored special guests. On June 28, the Pawnees closed a special evening program in Festival Hall with a song listed as "When the Night Dreams Come." The inclusion of traditional music drew larger crowds (*Indian School Journal* 1904f, July 23; LPEC-ODP 1904k, 7).

39. McCowan (1904c, 47); *Indian School Journal* (1904d). George Rye (Cherokee) and Grace Miller (Shawnee) performed a special skit called "Darky Dialogue" in which they donned black face and plantation slaves' attire. Their dialogue was supposed to mimic the minstrel show in the Old Plantation, a Pike concession.

40. *Farmer and Stock Grower* (1904). Mary Van Buel accompanied students on the piano during May and June. In early July she was replaced by Pearl McArthur.

41. LPEC-ODP (1904q, 7); *The Chronicle* (1904a, 5); *Indian School Journal* (1904bb, Oct., p. 55; 1904f, Sept. 13, 14). "I never heard 'The Lost Chord' sound sweeter. Isn't it remarkable what the Indians can do under proper training?" (Chapple to McCowan, July 12, 1904, CP-fairs, box 14, OHS.)

42. *Indian School Journal* (1904bb, June 10). See Ellis (1996) and Green and Troutman (2000).

43. Untitled press release May 1904, CP-fairs, box 3, OHS. McCowan signed with Pelham after ensuring that all the players were real Indians and that the soloists had performed in St. Louis. Another Lyceum Bureau sponsored the Haskell band for a four-week engagement (McCowan to Palmer, Jan. 12, 1904, Pelham to McCowan, Feb. 22, 1904, CP-fairs, box 1, OHS).

44. John Flinn to McCowan, July 11, 1904, CP-fairs, box 1, OHS; *Indian School Journal* (1904f, Aug. 16). Salaries ranged from incidental spending money to $125 per month.

45. What the "weird" compositions were is unknown because the band specialized in patriotic, religious, and American popular music. Tunes ("In Kansas," "First Cavalry," "Peoria Star," "Mississippi Rose," and "Officer of the Day,") were chosen to please audiences. "Weird" might have referred to their signature encore, "Indian War Dance," by Herman Bellstedt, who wrote "Turkey in the Straw" (*Indian School Journal* [1904f, July 26, 29, 22, Aug. 17, 24, Sept. 14, 15]; LPEC-ODP [1904p, 13; 1904m, 13; 1904o, 13]). July 26 was one of the band's most strenuous days: six concerts and a parade.

46. The repertoire reflected successful requests for donations (LPEC-ODP 1904k, 7; *Indian School Journal* 1904f, June 29, July 25; Lem Wiley to McCowan, Feb. 2, 1904, McCowan to J. W. Jenkins Music Co., Feb. 4, 1904, CP-fairs, boxes 2 and 3, OHS). McCowan's son, Roy, served as assistant director. McCowan considered having dancers for the Indian War Dance but decided it might evoke criticism from Indian Service administrators.

47. LPEC-ODP (1904m, 13).

48. McCowan to N. Bartlett, Feb. 12, 1904, CP-fairs, box 3, OHS. Dozens of schools offered their bands but McCowan declined all, including the Wyandotte Band, which came anyway.

49. McCowan (1905b, 126–27); McCowan to O. Lipps, Apr. 18, 1904, CP-fairs, box 5, OHS; *Indian School Journal* (1904f, Aug. 12).

50. McCowan (1904g); *Indian School Journal* (1904r, 1904f, June 10). McCowan considered drilling important. He wrote Captain Farrand Sayre, the commandant of Fort Sills, asking him to find a competent drillmaster for the Indian student companies, so they could compete in contests with other military units (McCowan to Sayre, Dec. 28, 1903, CP-fairs, box 1, OHS).

51. Students who fell ill were Alice Boone, Alfred Andrews, James and William Arquette, James Ryan, Louis Youpee, James Bennett, and Blake White Bear. The most common affliction was tuberculosis.

52. *Indian School Journal* (1904bb, July 22; 1904f, July 12).

53. McCowan to James E. Sullivan, Jan. 12, 1904, CP-fairs, box 2, OHS; *St. Louis Republic* (1904l); *Indian School Journal* (1904j). See Peavy and Smith (2001) for a history of the team. Some of the greatest American athletes trained at boarding schools (Bloom 1996).

54. *Indian School Journal* (1904f, July 6); *St. Louis Republic* (1904j, 1904k); press quotes from Peavy and Smith (2001).

55. *Indian School Journal* (1904z; 1904f, July 29). Peavy and Smith (2001, 20–21) note that the game was actually played on July 27 although some newspapers reported it as July 28.

56. Peavy and Smith (2001, 21); *Indian School Journal* (1904o); *St. Louis Post-Dispatch*, untitled article, Sept. 4, 1904, MP, box 16, LC. The St. Louis team forfeited the third game.

57. Visitor comments reported in McGee (1905d, 127–28); *Indian School Journal* (1904o; 1904f, June 20, Aug. 23, Sept. 6).

58. *Indian School Journal* (1904f, June 18; 1904bb, Oct., p. 56).

59. Many remarks were racist. McCowan viewed changes in appearance as a sign of successful assimilation. He recalled with pleasure that "Two gentlemen were watching the girls in the Domestic Arts Department. 'Why,' said one of them, 'those girls are as white as we are. It only goes to show that these people can be developed.'" Another man remarked after watching the Cocopa boys then seeing the school boys march in their evening drill, "Well, there's one thing sure. Civilization improves the looks of the Indian" (*Indian School Journal* 1904bb, June 14, Aug. 12; 1904f, Sept. 8, 14). A few visitors thought white students were not treated as well as Indians and as a result the white race was falling behind (*Indian School Journal* 1904w, July 25).

60. McCowan (1904b, 58); McCowan quoted in McGee (1905d, 116). See Hoxie (1984) for more on changes in Indian Service policy in light of evolving discussions of race in American society.

7. The Philippine Reservation

Epigraph. Lusk (1905, 54).

1. Historical information based on Agoncillo (1975) and Karnow (1989). As an aftermath of the Spanish-American War, the United States annexed the Hawaiian Islands, American Samoa, Guam, Wake Island, Puerto Rico, and Cuba. See Dawley (2003).

2. Bennitt (1905, 465); Clevenger (1996, 13); Taft quoted in LPEC-WFB (1902, 20). Reporters selectively used the Natives to argue for or against self-government. William E. Curtis commented that to base the assessment on what one saw at the fair was silly. The exhibit "represents the best, the most advanced, the most progressive, the most highly civilized portions of the population and gives the visitor an intelligent idea of what about 3 percent or perhaps 5 percent, of our 'little brown brothers' are doing" (Curtis 1904b). Others thought it a good idea that Native peoples were in St. Louis so Americans could see Filipino character.

3. Most funds came from the federal government although the LPEC underwrote one hundred thousand dollars. W. P. Wilson, chairman of the Philippine Exposition Board, coined the phrase "exposition within an exposition" (quoted in Rydell 1984, 167). Wilson started the Commercial Museum as a clearinghouse for international trade with exhibits he purchased at the 1893 Chicago exposition. Also on the steering committee was Dr. Gustavo Niederlein, a self-trained ethnologist, who had helped with colonial exhibits at the Pan-American Exposition and the Latin American exhibits at Chicago.

4. LPEC-WFB (1904b, 28); Swarthout (1904, 48); Laurie (1994–95, 47); Chitty and Hall (1904, 143); *Scientific American* (1904b); Parezo (2004a).

5. Newell (1904, 5129). The cathedral housed an exhibit promoting the value of English, with a section devoted to the Moro Industrial School. Each pavilion thematically mirrored their counterparts in main exposition and expressed a regional housing style (Bennitt (1905, 467–68); Rydell (1984, 171).

6. Swarthout (1904, 52, 49); A. Jenks (1904, 262); Newell (1904, 5133); LPEC-ODP (1904y); Bennitt (1905, 468); Buel (1904, vol. 10, 3758, 3761). Albert Jenks displayed representative items used in daily and ritual life and Spanish-influenced technological changes (M. Jenks 1951, 123, 133, 138).

7. *New York Times* (1903). The first American scientist to study Filipino natives was University of Michigan zoology professor Dean Worcester, in the 1890s. Based on anthropometric measures, he labeled them half-naked savages and headhunters. His views became policy and were the foundation for how the Native groups were categorized in St. Louis and how McGee referred to them (Gems 2004; Worcester 1913).

8. Jenks had Bachelor of Science degrees from Kalamazoo College (1896) and the University of Chicago (1897) and a master's (1899) and doctorate (1900) in economics from the

University of Wisconsin. Taft appointed him to head the Ethnological Survey and design the LPE exhibits. His wife, Maude, helped collect, catalogue, and ship the ethnological materials and locate demonstrators (Richards 1951, 155). Jenks served as overall director of the ethnology section and as its medical director. Each village had its own supervisor (Bennitt 1905, 466; see also Afable 1997).

9. Swarthout (1904, 53); LPEC-OPA (1905, 79); Worcester (1913, 1157–58); Fossett and Tucker (1997, 237–41).

10. Buel (1904, vol. 5, 1724). Affiliations are from official catalogues, LPEC-OPA (1905, 153), Bennitt (1905, 184, 470), and Field Museum records. No two sources agree on the exact number of Native participants. Our numbers should be considered estimates.

11. Rydell (1984, 171); Bennitt (1905, 184); Johnston (1905, 30–31); Woolard (1975, 132–35); Laurie (1994–95, 50, 47); Chitty and Hall (1904, 142–43); LPEC-ODP (1904y). The Scouts constituted a corps of 431 men and the Constabulary 300.

12. Chitty and Hall (1904, 141–42); LPEC-OPA (1905, 140).

13. Curtis (1904b) commented favorably on the neat khaki uniforms and how the troops were distinguished from "our little brown brethren who wander naked about the grounds."

14. Woolard (1975, 132–53) concludes that officers supervised troops closely during their stay and gave them little free time or opportunities for mischief.

15. Afable (1997:19, 1995:15); LPEC-OPA (1905:82); Jenks (1905: 15), Curtis (1904b). The group's name, *Igorot*, was spelled in a variety of ways: Igorrote, Igorot, Ygorotte, Ygorot. Unless used in a quotation, we use Igorot, following Afable (1997).

16. *Indian School Journal* (1904f, July 20, 7); Roosevelt quoted in *St. Louis Globe-Democrat* (1904d); Rydell (1984, 176). Maps were prominently displayed, especially one of North America and the Philippine Islands with a special line between Manila and St. Louis as a symbol of modern global involvement.

17. LPEC-OPA (1905, 439).

18. We would like to thank Dr. Afable for help with this section.

19. *St. Louis Post-Dispatch* (1904r). The inclement spring weather forced them to live in the Cuartel (barracks), which they disliked; they were only seen outside working on their compound.

20. Each group policed itself and dealt with internal infractions. Antonio required officials in Government House to telephone him at regular intervals. It was not uncommon for him to stop in the middle of a performance to take a telephone call (LPEC-OPA 1905, 48, 144; Newell 1904, 5138).

21. Bennitt (1905, 471); Newell (1904, 5134, 5138); LPEC-OPA (1905, 140); LPEC-ODP (1904t).

22. LPEC-OPA (1905, 140).

23. Taft to Edwards, June 4, 1904, Edwards to Taft, June 23, 1904, Edwards to Niederlein, June 27, 1904, RG 350, Records of the Bureau of Insular Affairs, NA; McGee to Jenks, June 25, 1904, MP, box 16, LC; Rydell (1984, 172).

24. Starr (1904a); *(Peoria IL) Star* (1904); *St. Louis Post-Dispatch* (1904w). Visitors were

fascinated with their small rimless fezzes, where men carried pipes and money, tattoos and their meanings, men's large wooden earplugs, the women's brightly colored clothing and everyone smoking cigars. "The best way to study these peoples is to take a number of cigars to the village. They carry cigars in their hair or over their ears" (*St. Louis Globe-Democrat* 1904g; *Chicago Tribune* 1904; *Sterling Gazette* 1904; Newell 1904, 5138, 5140; LPEC-OPA 1905, 48, 69).

25. Newell (1904, 5140); LPEC-OPA (1905, 44). See Afable (1997, 2000) for a list of participants. After the exposition the group traveled to Tampa, Florida, before returning to the Philippines.

26. LPEC-OPA (1905, 44); Bennitt (1905, 476).

27. *St. Louis Post-Dispatch* (1904v).

28. LPEC-OPA (1905, 48); Newell (1904, 5138).

29. LPEC-OPA (1905, 153); Curtis (1904b); Jenks (1951, 123, 139, 197); LPEC-OPA (1905, 66, 144, 146, 439); Laurie (1994–95, 51). The *St. Louis Post-Dispatch* (1904r) commented on the treatment of Natives considered U.S. military allies versus insurgents.

30. Three other members of Jenks's household staff came to St. Louis: Bugti, Falikao, and Maklan (Afable 1997, 21–22).

31. *St. Louis Post-Dispatch* (1904z); Rydell (1984, 172); *Indian School Journal* (1904f, July 16).

32. *St. Louis Post-Dispatch* (1904k); Newell (1904, 5140).

33. *St. Louis Post-Dispatch* (1904d, 1904cc); Pilapil (1994); Birk (1979, 64).

34. *St. Louis Post-Dispatch* (1904t, 1904u); Afable (1997:20); LPEC-OPA (1905:44). Educated Filipinos took umbrage that the Igorots represented their country (Kramer 1998:235).

35. Afable (1995:16); Bennitt (1905:472); LPEC-OPA (1905:23, 72). A Moro battalion was also part of the Constabulary, distinguished from other troops by their fez hats (Newell 1904:5136).

36. LPEC-OPA (1905, 71).

37. LPEC-OPA (1905, 72).

38. LPEC-OPA (1905, 71).

39. Bennitt (1905, 472). Men wore turbans as a symbol of their faith (LPEC-OPA 1905, 74, 82). Facundi visited President Roosevelt on a diplomatic mission during the fall (Newell 1904, 5136).

40. LPEC-OPA (1905, 76, 77); M. Jenks (1951, 169).

41. LPEC-OPA (1905, 67).

42. Newell (1904, 5134); LPEC-OPA (1905, 67). Frederick Lewis, a man who knew "the natives as well as any American and understands how to get along with them," assisted the Samal Moros (M. Jenks 1951, 169).

43. Bennitt (1905, 471); *Indian School Journal* (1904f, Aug. 18); LPEC-OPA (1905, 73). There is another group of Bagobos who were Ifugaos from the northern Luzon region and this probably is what confused the press who mistook them for Igorots (Curtis 1904b).

44. LPEC-OPA (1905, 73, 78).

45. LPEC-OPA (1905, 70, 78).

46. Curtis (1904b); Bennitt (1905, 471); Newell (1904, 5133).

47. Newell (1904, 5138); LPEC-OPA (1905, 68). The small population figures were used as a sign of their impending demise and a reason why visitors should interact with them now.

48. LPEC-ODP (1904w); Curtis (1904b).

49. LPEC-OPA (1905, 80, 250). Their last name is also given as de la Croix. Advertisements noted they were smaller than Tom Thumb.

50. LPEC-OPA (1905, 78); *St. Louis Globe-Democrat* (1904k).

51. LPEC-OPA (1905, 78).

52. Buel (1904, vol. 5, 1724). It cost a thousand dollars a day to feed the 1,257 individuals (Curtis 1904b; Newell 1904, 5128).

53. Anonymous, 1904, untitled clipping on p. 86 of LPE scrapbook, *St. Louis Republic*, n.d., n.p.

8. The Anthropology Villages

Epigraph. Francis (1913, 526).

1. Francis (1913, 522); *St. Louis Globe-Democrat* (1903a).

2. *St. Louis Post-Dispatch* (1904n).

3. *St. Louis Republic* (1904p); *Indian School Journal* (1904a, 69); Bennitt (1905, 678).

4. McGee (1905d, 98; 1904c, 6); Francis (1913, 526); *Indian School Journal* (1904a, 69).

5. Anonymous, 1904, "Patagonian Giants Here: Ask for Diet of Horse Meat," no source, Apr. 15, n.p., MP, box 16, LC. Lorenza's authority impressed visitors who interpreted it as a sign of matriarchy.

6. *St. Louis Republic* (1904m, 1904o).

7. *Scientific American* (1904e, 414).

8. Hanson (1905, 393); *St. Louis Republic* (1904v).

9. W. Williams (1904, 796); *St. Louis Republic* (1904p).

10. Salaries were $1,640 in July (McGee 1904d). Fiscal accounts sent to LPE financial officers, MP, box 16, LC).

11. McGee (1905d, 191); Lusk (1905, 54). A photograph of three young men in European suits is in Bennitt (1905, 678).

12. Bennitt (1905, 677); *Indian School Journal* (1904f, June 7).

13. *St. Louis Republic* (1904g). A satirical poem of the time reads:

> *You must seek the savage giant*
> *From his Patagonian beat*
> *Very strong and self-reliant;*
> *Strangely ample as to feet*
> *Who declares, in tones defiant*
> *Horse-flesh only will he eat. (St. Louis Post-Dispatch 1904ff)*

14. *Indian School Journal* (1904u); McGee (1905d, 100). Giga befriended the young Ainu girl and they often played together. Giga spoke Japanese by December. Reporters noted the four young men quickly spoke fairly good English (*St. Louis Republic* 1904q).

15. McGee (1904c, 16; 1904d, 1; 1904a, 5–6).

16. *Indian School Journal* (1904f, Aug. 25).

17. Newspaper article quoted in Bradford and Blume (1992, appendix 1); LPEC-OPA (1905, 439); Verner (1904c). If Geronimo was considered silent, Ota Benga was too vocal and ridiculed for his pronunciation and verbal miscues. Of course, those criticizing him never attempted to learn his language. Ota Benga learned enough Bakuba to converse with his compatriots (Francis 1913, 527).

18. *St. Louis Post-Dispatch* (1904gg).

19. LPEC-OPA (1905, 438); Verner (1904c; 1904a, 76); Francis (1913, 526); *Indian School Journal* (1904y; 1904f, Aug. 16, 17, 20).

20. McCowan to Joseph H. Dortch, July 4, 1904, CP, NA-Fort Worth; Troutman (1997, 18).

21. Newspaper reports reprinted in Bradford and Blume (1992, 252–55). Controversy about the Pygmies' nakedness periodically erupted since the men disrobed to perform certain tasks like tree or greased pole climbing (Stanaland 1981, 104).

22. Bennitt (1905, 676); LPEC-OPA (1905, 439).

23. Curtis (1904a); Verner (1904a, 1904b, 1907). Adams (2001, 35) notes that Verner used the same rhetoric as the sideshow spielers.

24. The monkeys and the Pygmies became associated: "The pygmies live in rather intimate association with parrots and monkeys which seem to be regarded as tutelaries, and their inconsequent habits of thought are curiously akin to those of the lower creatures" (Bennitt 1905, 676).

25. *St. Louis Post-Dispatch*, "Pygmy Dance Starts Panic in Fair Plaza," printed in Bradford and Blume (1992, 250–51).

26. *Indian School Journal* (1904aa, Aug. 20).

27. According to Francis (1913, 526) the Batwas were the instigators of the humorous pranks at the expense of Lumbango and Latuna as well as other ethnic groups.

28. Bennitt (1905, 676); *Indian School Journal* (1904f, Aug. 22).

29. LPEC-WFB (1904g, 40); Verner to Dorsey, Oct. 11, 1904, Accession 892, FM; *St. Louis Republic* article, "Trying Ordeal for Savages," Aug. 16, printed in Bradford and Blume (1992, 254).

30. *Indian School Journal* (1904f, Sept. 8).

31. *Indian School Journal* (1904f, Aug. 16). Ota Benga chose to remain in the United States with Verner because he had no home. They traveled together until Verner went bankrupt and left him in the care of William Hornaday, director of the Bronx Zoo, where he was displayed in a cage in the Monkey House as an evolutionary missing link. See Bradford and Blume (1992) and Adams (2001) for extensive accounts of this infamous adventure.

32. Bennitt (1905, 674); Hanson (1905, 386). McGee thought the Ainu showed few phenotypical features associated with Mongolians but were a remnant population being pushed north by the Japanese. The Ainu are thought today to be the descendants of early Jomon people from Asia (Van Stone 1993, 78; Hanihara 1991; Watanabe 1973).

33. *St. Louis Republic* (1904a); Hanson (1905, 394); McGee to Rev. D. S. Tuttle, Apr. 7, 1904, MP, box 19, LC. Starr had little to do with their daily life while he was teaching in Chicago. McGee and Starr convinced the Department of Concessions not to assess a percentage against book sales (Starr to McGee, Aug. 10, 1904, Starr to Hulbert, Aug. 15, 1904, MP, box 19, LC).

34. *St. Louis Post-Dispatch* (1904a). McGee was ill and unable to push his assistants to search for the packages, which had been sent to Korea rather than San Francisco. Starr left instructions with McGee on how the encampment should be arranged, the buildings oriented, and the house-blessing procedures conducted. This ceremony was followed by a Christian blessing service conducted by Inagaki (*St. Louis Post-Dispatch* 1904x).

35. LPEC-ODP (1904x).

36. McGee (1905d, 97); *Indian School Journal* (1904f, June 3). Mustache sticks were used to lift facial hair while drinking.

37. *Scientific American* (1904d, 218). Starr gave lectures in April and May and said the Japanese-Russian War was a war for racial supremacy: "Upon its outcome depends the question of whether the yellow race will rule supreme over the white race and nations of the earth. England and the European nations are on the decline. They are exhausted. They are unnatural and their end is near. As every dog has his day, I believe the day of the white race is about over" ([*Chicago*] *Olympia* 1904).

38. *Indian School Journal* (1904t; 1904f, June 8); *Scientific American* (1904e, 414); Bennitt (1905, 544–57, 675); McGee (1905d, 97–98); *Chicago Inter-Ocean* (1904); *The Chronicle* (1904b); *St. Louis Post-Dispatch* (1904ii). According to Hanson (1905, 385) visitors were disappointed that the Ainus were not more savage.

39. McGee (1905d, 97); *St. Louis American* (1904). A poem in the *St. Louis Dispatch*'s (1904y) *Rhymes and Jokes* column commented on the relation between physical appearance and capitalistic success:

> *Now if knowledge you would gain, you*
> *During Exposition Times,*
> *Must seek out the hairy Ainu*
> *Who has come from distant climes*
> *For to please and entertain you*
> *For a trinity of dimes.*

40. Francis (1913, 526); McGee (1905d, 96–97); *St. Louis American* (1904); Lusk (1905, 54). Curtis (1904a) felt their hair made them look like poodle dogs. Clothing had elaborately embroidered geometric designs reflecting gender and village affiliation. Women wore a band of velvet around the neck and tied their hair back; men wore earrings (Starr 1904a, 34–37).

41. McGee (1904f, 5187; 1905d, 22) also in Francis (1913, 525). The seeds were still in their sack in December, much to McGee's dismay. Cushman states that the reason the crops were not sown was his ill-health. For an in-depth discussion of the Cocopas' experiences at the exposition, see Parezo and Troutman (2001).

42. *St. Louis Post Dispatch* (1904c).

43. McGee (1904c, 16, 1904e); LPEC-OPA (1905, 89); Anonymous, 1904, "Foreign Indians Arrive at Exposition Grounds," no source, MP, box 16, LPE scrapbook, LC). The Cocopas built another next to the Kwakiutls and the Tehuelches. Typical monthly bills were twenty-four dollars for meat and seventy dollars for groceries.

44. Bennitt (1905, 680); McGee (1905d, 63, 105, 188); Breitbart (1997); Sullivan (1905b, 259); Kelly (1977, 13); Cushman list, Cushman to McGee Apr. 13, 1904, MP, box 20, LC; Skiff to Francis, Sept. 28, 1903, LPEC Executive Committee Minutes.

45. LPEC-OPA (1905, 89).

46. Lusk (1905, 55); Hanson (1905, 347). Women's hair was cut like men's; only one woman wore a bead necklace (McGee 1905d, 109).

47. The girl was most likely Nirsa, Tom Moore's daughter (McGee 1905d, 106; Cushman to McGee, July 7, 1904, MP, box 20, LC). Cushman deputized two of the largest male Lakotas to stand guard over Shokee and ensure the peace in the Cocopa encampment. McGee wrote Territorial Judge Herbert Brown explaining the situation (McGee to Brown, July 7, 8, 1904, Frank Tehano to Captain Tomas and Pablo Colorado, July 29, 1904, MP, boxes 19 and 20, LC; McGee 1905d, 106. He was happy the press never mentioned the incident.

48. Cushman to McGee, Feb. 27, March 3, 1904, MP, box 20, LC).

49. Cushman to McGee, March 28, 1904, MP, box 20, LC.

50. *Indian School Journal* (1904f, Aug. 25), LPEC-OPA (1905, 89); McGee (1905d, 106). As foreigners Cocopa children did not have to attend the Indian School.

51. *Indian School Journal* (1904s). Reporters compared the Cocopas unfavorably to other Indians. Placing mud on the hair was viewed as "dangerously near to primitive man" (*St. Louis Republic* 1904g).

52. Grumet and Weber (1982, 67) refer to Nowell and Harris as Southern Kwakiutls; Macnair (1982, 5); Jacknis (2002, 78); *American Anthropologist* (1906a, 477); Cole (1985, 201). Jacknis (2002, 403n30) notes there is some confusion about Harris's identity.

53. Newcombe quoted in *Indian School Journal* (1904f, June 8).

54. *Indian School Journal* (1904f, June 9); Francis (1913, 528). Atlieu placed his thirty-eight-foot whaling canoe, his whaling outfit, and harpoons next to the house.

55. McGee (1904e); Dorsey to Simms, Aug. 11, 1904, FM.

56. McGee was not as fiscally irresponsible as Newcombe makes it appear. Newcombe was caught in the middle of a misunderstanding; Skiff thought McGee would pay part of his salary and expenses and McGee kept insisting that the Field Museum bear the entire burden (Newcombe to Dorsey, July 30, Aug. 3, 1904, Simms to Dorsey, Aug. 8, 1904, Dorsey to Simms, Aug. 11, 1904, FM).

57. *Indian School Journal* (1904f, June 8).

58. Nowell quoted in Ford (1949, 186).

59. Nowell had a thunderbird headdress and Harris a killer whale. Luckily they brought their irreplaceable ritual paraphernalia with them (LPEC-OPA 1905, 56).

60. *Indian School Journal* (1904q).

61. Other quotes in this section are from Nowell in Ford (1949, 187–90).

62. Newcombe to Dorsey, Oct. 3, 1904, Dorsey to Skiff, Oct. 5, 1904, Accession 883, FM; LPEC-OPA (1905, 42); *Philadelphia Ledger* (1904); Jacknis (2002).

63. They posed in ritual attire for museum photographer Charles Carpenter and documented Newcombe's collections. Atlieu worked on masks while Harris made objects and recorded ethnographic explanations for dance ensembles. They critiqued the permanent exhibits, assessed their accuracy, dressed mannequins appropriately, and painted the faces of mannequins. Harris and Nowell also worked on the Field Museum's Hagenbeck collection of Northwest Coast artifacts obtained during the 1893 World's Columbian Exposition, but never adequately catalogued (Grumet and Weber 1982, 68); Dorsey to McGee, Oct. 5, 1904, MP, box 19, LC. See Jacknis (1991; 2002, 53–54) for a fuller account of Newcombe, Harris, and Nowell working for the Field Museum. The amount of money they earned was in line with regular museum wages. All four men preferred museum work to being on display.

64. Dorsey to McGee, Oct. 5, 1904, MP, box 19, LC; Newcombe to Dorsey, Oct., 9, 16, 24, 1904, Dorsey to McGee, Oct. 12, 1904, FM.

65. Ford (1949, 190–92). Newcombe and his son eventually received $150 per month from McGee. In all it cost $4,366 to have the Kwakiutls perform at the fair (Anonymous, 1904, Vancouver Indian Group, Statement of Cost, MP, box 28, LC).

9. The Polyglot Pike

Epigraph. Curtis (1904a).

1. Bennitt (1905, xii); Hanson (1905, 106); Sprague (1975). In comparison, Chicago's Midway grossed more than four million dollars. Many LPE concessions had been at Chicago: Streets of Cairo with Little Egypt, Hagenbeck's Zoo and Animal Show, Japanese Tea House and Bazaar, and Old Vienna (N. Harris 1975; Fogelson 1991, 75; Rydell 1984). Concessions of more questionable character and raunchy entertainment were located outside the fairgrounds (Bogdan 1988).

2. Barnett (1970, 163). At the 1893 Chicago fair, Indian demonstrators spent leisure time on the merry-go-round and riding in boats on Lake Michigan (Fogelson 1991, 77–78).

3. Buel (1904, vol. 10, 3809); Bennitt (1905, 171); LPEC-*The Piker* (1904b, 41–45). The LPEC authorized over eight hundred concessions (Hinckley 1967). Some (such as the Colorado Gold Mine, Coal Breakers, Glass Weaving and Spinning, Grant's Log Cabin, and Hunting in the Ozarks) were attached to pavilions. All exotic concessions were supposed to be based on ethnological fact, but most were embellished with prevalent cultural stereotypes (see Hirschfelder, Molin, and Wakim 1999).

4. Many newspapers picked up McGee's view. Bogdan (1988, 7, 8) defines a freak show as a formally organized exhibition of human and animal physical anomalies and novelty acts exhibited for amusement and profit He categorizes the sideshow acts into born freaks (real physical anomalies), made freaks (e.g. tattooed people), and novelty acts (unusual performative abilities, such as sword swallowers).

5. McCowan and McGee were originally in accord on the Pike's deviousness and agreed that ethnological concessions would undermine their authority and messages. McCowan always saw concessionaires' claims as threats. He began to complain officially to Skiff as early as October 1903. The exhibit techniques were so similar that Native participants saw little difference, except for the lack of wages in nonconcession exhibits.

6. There is an extensive literature on midways, amusement parks, and carnivals that utilized Native peoples as attractions: Adams (2001); Burton Benedict (1991); Bennett (1995); Bronner (1989); Greenhalgh (1988); Hinsley (1991); Kasson (2000); Kirshenblatt-Gimblett (1998); Moses (1991, 1996); and Rydell (1984). For illustrations of the Pike, see Breitbart (1997). The "Shantyville" outside the 1876 fair in Philadelphia had sideshows such as the "Wild Men of Borneo," the "Wild Australian Children," and the "Man-Eating Feejees" (McCabe 1876).

7. At Buffalo, Cummins's show included free static displays, and for ten cents one could see Indians "dance, sing, and shout war whoops." For more on Cummins in Buffalo see Moses (1996, 145–47) and Amon Carter Museum (1970). At the entrance to the St. Louis show stood Remington's full-sized statue of mounted cowboys engaged in the recreational activity of *Shooting Up a Town*, (Bennitt 1905, 713). Cummins toured in 1905–6, without the Indians, and added a circus (*Bandwagon* 1962; Hill 1912).

8. Cummins wanted to place his concession between the Transportation Building and Skinker Road but the executive committee refused (Hill 1912, 15; Cummins to Francis, July 18, 1904, Executive Committee Minutes, March 15, 1904, pp. 2298, 2277, Feb. 13, 1904, p. 2197, lpec files, lpec series II, subseries 2, folders 5 and 6, mhs).

9. On Mulhall, Rogers, and Mix in St. Louis see Robinson (1996, 66–67) and Reddin (1999, 189).

10. Rosewater (1897, 3); Moses (1996). These extravaganzas employed Sioux as their principal actors, characterized as heroic warriors. Cummins felt his show had educational value for it showed the "real" West and what Indians "were really like." It was, of course, the West of his imagination.

11. Roosevelt (1899). Cody extended the name Rough Rider to include equestrian performers from Europe, South America, Africa, and Central Asia, and Cummins followed suit.

12. lpec-*The Piker* (1904a, 16); Moses (1991, 227; 1984, 157); Hanson (1905); *St. Louis Globe-Democrat* (1904i).

13. Hanson (1905, 341); lpec-opa (1905, 138); Bennitt (1905, 683). At Chicago, Cody had employed 175 people from Pine Ridge, Standing Rock, and Rosebud.

14. *St. Louis Post Dispatch* (1904r); Montezuma to Jones, Apr. 21 and May 20, 1904, Jones to Montezuma, Apr. 30, 1904, John A. Brennan to Jones, May 2, 1904, Judge Edward F. Dunne, G. Frank Lydston, MD, Carlos Montezuma, MD, and the Honorable J. Jaxon to Jones, May 6, 1904, Correspondence Files, Commissioner of Indian Affairs, RG 75, NA; Memorandum of Agreement, Chicago and Northwestern Railway Company and the Indians injured in the wreck on Apr. 7, 1904. There was no Chief White Horse; the reporter had the name wrong. The injured Lakotas returned to their reservation.

15. *Indian School Journal* (1904f, July 25); Deloria (1981, 54). Fogelson (1991, 78) has made this same observation for the Chicago exposition in which Lakotas participated so freely.

16. LPEC-*The Piker* (1904a).

17. *San Francisco Chronicle* (1904); Everett (1904, 341). Note the similarity to McGee's flowery rhetoric.

18. Hanson (1905, caption for "Daily Scene on the Pike"); LPEC-ODP (1904e).

19. LPEC-ODP (1904f); Moses (1991, 208; 1996). Indians also performed in LPEC parades (*St. Louis Globe-Democrat* 1903b).

20. Cummins to Francis, July 18, 1904, and LPEC Executive Committee Minutes for July 20, 1904, p. 2898, LPEC files, LPEC series II, subseries 2, folder 5, MHS.

21. Cummins to Francis, Aug. 1, 1904, and Executive Committee Minutes, Aug. 15, 1904, pp. 2948–49, 3410, LPEC files, LPEC series II, subseries 2, folder 5, MHS; Yost (1979); Moses (1991, 218).

22. LPEC-WFB (1904d, 4), emphasis in original; *Scientific American* (1904a). The Chicago Cliff Dweller exhibit by the H. Jay Smith Exploring Company displayed archaeological materials excavated by the Wetherill family in the Mancos, Colorado, region (Blackburn and Williamson 1997; H. Jay Smith Exploring Company 1893; Starr 1893; Putnam 1895).

23. McGee to McCowan, Oct. 6, 1903, McCowan to Skiff, Oct. 26, 1903, CP-fairs, box I, OHS; McGee to Skiff, Oct. 6, 1903, MP, box 16, LC. McGee was more opposed to this exhibit than Cummins's because it was partly responsible for Stevenson's unsuccessful Southwest expedition (see chapter 4).

24. Board of Directors Minutes, Oct. 3, Oct. 15, Nov. 3, 1903, LPEC files, LPEC series II, subseries 2, folder 5, MHS; W. A. Jones to Secretary of the Interior to Francis, Oct. 22, 1903, Secretary of the Interior Hitchcock to Francis, Oct. 23, 1903, RG 75, BIA Records, NA.

25. LPEC-WFB (1904d) also published in LPEC-*The Piker* (1904c); Hanson (1905, 112); Bennitt (1905, 724); LPEC-OPA (1905, 200); *St. Louis Globe-Democrat* (1904b). In the plaza was a reproduction of the famous Rock at Walpi. "Moki" is a derogatory term. While researchers used it initially, by 1920 everyone was using Hopi, which means the Peaceful People.

26. LPEC-WFB (1904d, 5); Hanson (1905, 112, 121).

27. The attire was definitely not that of the Hopi Snake Society, Zuni, or Eastern Puebloan men. The props (including rubber snakes) were never used by the Hopi (McGee to J. Bernard Walker, Dec. 16, 1904, Walker to Mark Bennitt, Dec. 1, 1904, MP, box 18, LC; Bennitt 1905, 17). When informed of the error Bennitt did not fix it in LPEC publicity or in his own publications. This misinformation has found its way into the scholarly literature.

28. Trennert (1987a); Breitbart (1997, 75); Dilworth (1996). There is no extant list of participants. A photograph in an LPE album shows at least forty-five men, women, and children (LPEC-OPA 1905, 189). A report on a June 4 parade lists Tobin's division as one hundred and fifty Indians on foot, fifteen carriages containing Native women, eight men on horseback and a thirty-piece Indian marching band (*St. Louis Globe-Democrat* 1904i). Trennert (1987a, 149) appears to base his figures on LPEC publicity, which simply repeated Tobin's inflated figures (Hanson 1905, 345). Members included Ramon Archuleta, governor of San Juan, and his wife and children.

29. Dorsey to Simms, Oct. 5, 1904, FM; Marriott (1948, 119–20); Peterson (1981, 109). At the fair, Julian Martinez danced as an eagle dancer and painted Maria's pottery.

30. Hanson (1905, 112, 121).

31. Tobin quoted in W. Williams (1904, 800). Some probably misinterpreted the Fred Harvey Company's brochures distributed in the Anthropology Building. Hoxie (1984, 88); MacMechen (1904, 22); LPEC-WFB (1904e).

32. Francis (1913, 524). Inuits had been performers in expositions since 1501 and were featured at the Chicago Exposition, where they lived in moss-covered log cabins rather than igloos (Burton Benedict 1979, 43). The most extensive Inuit display was erected at the 1909 Alaska-Yukon-Pacific Exposition in Seattle.

33. Quoted in *Scientific American* (1904b, 302).

34. LPEC-OPA (1905:192); LPEC-ODP (1904g). An 1893 description of the Inuit stands for St. Louis: "dressed in their furs these people looked truly polar, but we are assured that as spring came on they rebelled against wearing these heavy garments, which were unlike anything they ever wore before" (Starr 1893, 619–20).

35. LPEC-ODP (1904g).

36. W. Williams (1904, 800–801); LPEC-OPA (1905, 193); Hanson (1905, 122). There were twenty-five dogs, a reindeer, and a polar bear. The LPE was Nancy's fourth fair.

37. *Scientific American* (1904b).

38. Walker (1904b:553–54). See Rydell (1999) for a discussion of Black exclusion at American expositions and Adams (2001) and Lindfors (1983) for sideshow portrayals. Unlike earlier fairs, American Blacks were not hired as missing links or savages at the LPE, in part because of McGee's protests over inaccuracies.

39. Burton Benedict (1979, 36, 37).

40. Panama-Pacific Exposition Company (1914, 267); Edmund Philbert quoted in Clevenger (1996, 99).

41. Duke (1904, 2). See Liebenguth (1979), Shattinger International Music Corp. (1975), or Lerner (1988–89) for a complete list of LPE ragtime musicians.

42. *Encyclopedia Britannica* (2004).

43. *St. Louis Post-Dispatch* (1904h); Gillis (1904). The Boers included fifty women and children, the British only men. Apparently Boer leader General Cronje went to Mexico to arrange for the Boers to homestead. They did not intend to return to South Africa.

44. Walker (1904b, 553); Bennitt (1905, 714).

45. LPEC-OPA (1905, 54, 55). Burton Benedict (1979, 4) and Bogdan (1988, 106) note that actual and phony Xhosas and Zulus had been exhibited at expositions since 1851. The Boer War and "Savage South Africa" had been shown at the 1899 Greater Britain Exhibition in London. Bushmen were referred to as Earthmen and Troglodytes (*St. Louis Post-Dispatch* 1904f; W. Williams 1904, 801).

46. "Many American negroes have visited the Kaffir kraal and have attempted to establish relationship, at least to satisfy curiosity" (LPEC-OPA 1905, 53). The Curio Shop sold "Kaffir" souvenirs, animal skulls and pelts, butterflies, insects, horns, coins, and historical miscellanea from Africa.

47. *St. Louis Republic* (1904y). These incidents deserve research by labor historians. Given the exhibit backers' political power, the adverse publicity was very powerful. McGee made no comment on these incidents and there is no evidence that American blacks tried to organize the Batwa Mbutis.

48. Hinckley (1967); untitled newspaper accounts: *St. Louis Republic*, May 7, Nov. 29 and *St. Louis Globe-Democrat*, June 2, 1904.

49. LPEC-OPA (1905, 53).

50. Paul Beckwith to Richard Rathbun, June 14, June 21, 1904, RU 70, boxes 68 and 69, SIA. Walker (1904d) noted that the employees were required to tell visitors they were from the Holy Land; several were New York City or Hoboken residents.

51. Hanson (1905, 121).

52. Edmund Philbert quoted in Clevenger (1996, 14); Cortinovis (1977, 66).

53. Immigration officials held up the Japanese and Thai women in San Francisco for over a month. They arrived in time to participate in the colossal June 4 Pike Day Parade (Harris 1975, 49; *St. Louis Globe-Democrat* 1904j).

54. LPEC-OPA (1905, 196).

55. Bogdan (1988, 35).

56. Hanson (1905, 106). There was also a chapel, schoolhouse, small castle, shops, and Tyrolean singers.

57. Ida Starr (1904, 75).

58. Hinsley (1991, 353); see also Burton Benedict (1983, 3, 5, 34).

10. Being a Living Exhibit

1. *St. Louis Westliche Post* (1904).

2. *Indian School Journal* (1904f, Aug. 24).

3. *St. Louis Post-Dispatch* (1904bb).

4. *Indian School Journal* (1904f, June 16); Hanson (1905, caption: "Commanche [sic] Indian Shack"). Hanson mistook the Cocopas for Comanches.

5. Quoted in Clevenger (1996, 132). The photograph is also published. The reference to dying is based on the stereotype that all Indians were superstitious and believed photo-

graphs robbed them of their souls. Troutman (1997) has interpreted Hyde's bellicose actions and aggrandizement as an indication that he understood he had acted inappropriately.

6. *St. Louis Republic* (1904p); Breitbart (1997, 11). Several articles criticized the practice and reminded people how it would feel to have people sticking cameras in their faces.

7. *Indian School Journal* (1904f, June 20).

8. William Hencke to McGee, July 6, 1904, McGee to J. England, July 20, 1904, Flynn to Cushman, July 21, 1904, McGee to H. Kingsbury, July 21, 1904, MP, box 20, LC; *St. Louis Republic* notice July 7, 1904; Troutman (1997, 43–44); Parezo and Troutman (2001). Jefferson Guards were later ordered to check permits and confiscate cameras.

9. Blume and Bradford (1992, 252, reprint of *St. Louis Republic* article, Aug. 6, "Say It's Cold in St. Louis"); McGee (1905d, l04).

10. McGee (1904a, 6); McGee to Skiff, Sept. 23, 1903, LPEC files, MHS. McGee argued that a 25 percent sales tax would simply transfer funds from one department to another.

11. Anonymous, 1904, "Indians Fond of Compliments," no source, MP, box 16, scrapbook, p. 86, LC. Note gender misrepresentations in the quote by E. Mattox. *Indian School Journal* (1904aa, July 7).

12. *Indian School Journal* (1904f, Aug. 22). A similar incident happened to Yellow Hair and his wife. The Lakotas decided most tourists simply talked too much (*St. Louis Post-Dispatch* 1904kk, May 22). See Troutman and Parezo (1998) for similar ethnocentric encounters.

13. *Indian School Journal* (1904f, June 20).

14. Interpretations of cross-cultural encounters tell us more about the reporters' preconceptions and prejudices than they do about the people involved. See Hanson (1905, 394) for a description of Yellow Hair's visits to the Bontoc Igorots.

15. The LPEC never gave Cane an official apology and he prepared to leave, feeling that America was a savage nation (Vincent Cane to McGee, Aug. 20, 1904, McGee to Cane, Aug. 21, 1904, Col. Dick Plunkett to "My Dear Boys," July 31, 1904, McGee to Skiff, Aug. 21, 1904, MP, boxes 16, 19, and 20, LC; McGee, Monthly Report for Aug., MP, box 16, LC; *Indian School Journal* (1904f, June 13, July 2, 8). McCowan battled with North White, chief of the Department of Admissions, for several weeks attempting to work out a system for demonstrators to leave and return to the fairgrounds. White treated Natives like prisoners, greatly angering McCowan on several occasions (McCowan to White, June 25, 1904, CP-fairs, box 10, OHS; Troutman 1997, 53). Since White never made a plan, McCowan and McGee had Skiff's office issue extra passes.

16. McGee to Skiff, Aug. 21, 1904, MP, box 20, LC; Troutman (1997, 50–52).

17. *St. Louis Westliche* (1904); LPEC-ODP, Aug. 2, 1904; *Indian School Journal* (1904f, June 13).

18. *Indian School Journal* (1904f, June 17, July 14); Bradford and Blume (1992, 6).

19. *St. Louis Post-Dispatch* (1904b). The press assumed the gendered stereotype of mutual interest in clothing and fashion was universal. Some referred to women's interactions as forever feminine with no need for an interpreter.

20. The Natives also came weekly to obtain their food rations under McCowan's supervision (LPEC-WFB 1904h; Hanson 1905, 342–47); Francis 1913, 520; *St. Louis Republic* 1904c).

21. *Pennsylvania Ledger* (1904); *St. Louis Republic* (1904r); see Trennert (1993).

22. LPEC-WFB (1904f). Tempers were also short when tired travelers learned how inadequate their living arrangements were upon arrival and there was always friction over food rationing.

23. LPEC-WFB (1904g).

24. McCowan to "dear sir," July 23, 1904, MP, box 19, LC. McGee was worried about the diplomatic consequences of the assault and responded to an inquiry by C. Spruyt, Belgium's exhibition secretary. He downplayed the incident, calling it a slight infraction (McGee to Spruyt, July 23, 1904, MP, box 19, LC).

25. McGee to Skiff, July 31, 1904, McGee to McCowan, July 30, 1904, McCowan to McGee, July 30, 1904, MP, boxes 16 and 19, LC; see also Troutman (1997, 41).

26. McGee to Skiff, July 31, 1904, MP, box 19, LC; Moses (1995, 160); *St. Louis Republic* (1904g). This is a good example of McGee not taking responsibility for his actions or inactions.

27. McGee (1905, 67); McCowan to Jones, June 14, 1904, RG 75, BIA Incoming Correspondence, NA-Fort Worth. McGee concluded that the Tehuelches were the most difficult to control, with the capricious and impulsive Mbutis a close second. Only the Ainus were described as compliant. McCowan felt he had serious problems with Indians that Dorsey had chosen but not with those he vetted.

28. McGee to Skiff, Sept. 28, 1903, LPEC Executive Committee files, MHS.

29. McCowan to Ted Lemmon, Feb. 24, 1904, CP-fairs, box 3, OHS.

30. In his final report McGee spoke very highly of Armstrong, stating he worked with discretion in performing administrative duties. Armstrong was in charge of protecting indoor exhibits (McGee 1905d, 69).

31. McGee to Skiff, May 2, 1904, LPEC files, Executive Committee files, MHS; McGee (1905d, 69). McGee also noted that the Indian ward category was not technically more complex. While it covered a number of statuses based on treaties he argued that "while the status of the U.S. Indians varies in the original territory and some of the later accessions, the variable conditions have not been maintained administratively by the Indian office for some years past, and may comfortably be neglected in the administration of the Exposition." McGee manipulated these distinctions to ensure that the Cocopas were under his direct supervision.

32. *Indian School Journal* (1904aa, Aug. 6); *St. Louis Post-Dispatch* (1904bb); *St. Louis Chronicle* (1904).

33. McGee (1905d, 69). Food was a continuous topic for newspaper reporters. It "does not suit the Indian Exhibit colony," wrote one (*Indian School Journal* 1904f, July 14).

34. Moses (1984, 156); McCowan to McGee, June 30, 1904, BAE Records, Incoming Correspondence, box 14, NAA.

35. Dorsey to Holmes, June 30, 1904, BAE Records, Incoming Correspondence, box 14, NAA.

36. Quoted in Moses (1984, 156); Mooney to Holmes, July 3, 1904, BAE Records, Incoming Correspondence, box 14, NAA. McGee had wanted Mooney to run the Indian encampments to make sure they did not turn into a Wild West show (Moses 1984, 156).

37. Dorsey to Mooney, June 6, 1902, Dorsey to McGee June 13, 1902, Mooney to Holmes, July 3, 12, 14, 1904, BAE Records, Incoming Correspondence, box 14, NAA; McGee to Dorsey June 23, 1904, MP, box 19, LC. Shutt remained until July 20.

38. McGee to Holmes, July 1, 1904, BAE Records, Incoming Correspondence, box 14, NAA. Mooney did not trust McGee because in 1902 McGee had tried to curtail his ethnographic research and ordered him to work on the *Handbook of North American Indians*. Dorsey had intervened and Mooney now called on him again.

39. Dorsey to Holmes, July 12, 1904, BAE Records, Incoming Correspondence, Box 14, NAA.

40. Information on Simms is very sketchy and contradictory. Our thanks to James Van Stone and Stephen Nash of the Field Museum, Chicago, for locating what we have. Simms was born in Georgetown, Washington DC, in 1863 and worked as a reporter and assistant managing editor of newspapers from 1884 to 1890. In 1891, he worked for the Department of Foreign Affairs at the Chicago World Columbian Exposition. He was hired as a Field Museum preparator, then assistant curator in the Department of Industrial Arts, before moving to Anthropology. After the St. Louis Fair, Simms was sent to the Philippines to study the Igorots. In 1912, he was appointed curator of the Harris Public School Extension and in 1928 director, a position he held until his death in 1937 (Almazan and Coleman 2003a; *American Anthropologist* 1906a, 474; Dorsey 1909b; Marquis 1936).

41. McGee to Dorsey, July 25, 1904, MP, box 19, LC; Newcombe to Dorsey, Aug. 3, 1904, FM. One of his first crises dealt with the photographs Charles Carpenter took for Dorsey and Woodward to record racial types (see chapter 11). McGee later said of Simms, "His services proved invaluable, and a large share of the success of the Section is to be credited to him" (McGee 1905d, 70).

42. Taylor (1905); *Indian School Journal* (1904f, June 28); Edward Anthony Spitzka to McGee, Oct. 6, 1904, MP, box 20, LC; Lusk (1905, 51, 52).

43. *St. Louis Post-Dispatch* (1904y). A new plant sand-filtered the water before pumping it into Forest Park.

44. *Indian School Journal* (1904aa, July 8).

45. Natalie C. Burlin to McGee, Sept. 8, 1904, McGee to Burlin, Sept. 17, 1904, MP, box 18, LC.

46. McGee to Dr. Laidley, Apr. 18, 1904, MP, box 19, LC; Bennett (1905, xii); *The Medical Brief* (1903); Francis (1913, 630–32); *Medical Record* (1903); *Medical Fortnightly* (1905). Anonymous, 1909, *First Report and Recommendations of the Municipal Commission on Tuberculosis to the Municipal Assembly of the City of St. Louis*, pp. 9 and 26, cited in Keefer (1988, 37); Laurie (1994–95, 53); McCowan to Isaac S. Taylor, June 10, 1904, CP, NA-Fort

Worth; Moses (1984, 155–57). There were eighteen gunshot wounds treated and seven babies delivered to visitors.

47. See Parezo and Troutman (2001) for a description of their journey home and how McGee dealt with this situation.

48. Given the weather and living conditions it is surprising that more people did not become ill. According to McGee's sister, Emma, McGee went back to Cocopa country after the fair closed and he had finished his paperwork. McGee felt that the arid desert was the only place to cure his illness (E. McGee 1905d, 84).

11. In the Anthropology Building

Epigraph. McGee (1904c, 2); opening quote is headline from *St. Louis Republic* (1904v).

1. W. Williams (1904, 794); McGee (1904c); Skiff (1903, 203; 1904a); *St. Louis Republic* (1904u).

2. McGee (1904c, 23), also published in Francis (1913).

3. McGee (1905d, 26, 70, 75; 1904a, 7, 8, 23; 1904c, 22–23); label copy; Starr (1905, 41); Walker (1904a). McGee said this series combined "the earliest human motives and the highest human interpretations," in "the simple activities of the lowly primitives with the sublime accomplishments of the higher parts of mankind as shown in the Exposition picture and exhibit palaces" (McGee 1905d, 138–39). Mason and Hough had used the exhibits at previous expositions but Fowke gave them new labels reflecting McGee's theories.

4. Dorsey (1900, 250); McKusick (1991); Starr (1897); McGee (1904a, 6). The Vatican had a display of Bibles in Native languages. Wyman Brothers contributed life casts of Andrew Jackson in the general history exhibits.

5. Starr (1905, 41); McGee (1904a, 7; 1904c, 7l; 1905d, 24, 133; 1905c, 24–26); Buel (1904, vol. 5, 1585); McGee to Mills, Nov. 15, 1904, reprinted in McGee (1905d, 7). McGee and Chouteau fought continually over the space that history would have. One reason the archaeology exhibits were so dismal was that history was a last minute addition and Chouteau was only interested in celebrating his ancestors and conquest, not being part of a process by which barbarism makes way for civilization.

6. The fairs proved very unprofitable for all Indian traders except Ongman. See Hanson (1905, 362, 366); McNitt (1957, 216); Benham to Holmes, Sept. 9, Oct. 7, Nov. 10, 1904, BAE Incoming Correspondence, 1888–1906, NAA.

7. Archuleta (2000); J. C. Boykin to Edward Dawson, June 27, 29, July 8, 1903, MP, box 21, folder 6, LC; *Biograph Daily* (1904); LPEC-ODP (1904z, 11).

8. Holmes (1905, 2, 26, 28, 33; 1907a; 1903a; 1904); James C. Hornblower to F. W. True, July 6, 1903, with note entitled "Booths for the Exhibit," RU 70, box 62, folder 18, SIA; Holmes to True, Sept. 3, 1903, RU 70, box 62, folder 16, SIA; *Washington Post* (1903). See Ewers (1978) for Mooney's Kiowa shield exhibit.

9. *Indian Territory Bulletin* (1904); Obear (1904, 9); Bennitt (1905, 405, 443, 456–57); Trennert (1987a, 149–50); Debo (1976, 142); Edmund Philbert, diary, quoted in Clevenger

(1996, 111); Holmes to Hough, Nov. 25, 1904, RU 70, box 62, folder 16, SIA); *New York Times* (1904c); Cole (1985, 202–5); Hinckley (1982); Hanson (1905, 361); John Brady to McGee, May 2, 1904, McGee to Brady, May 2, 1904, MP, box 20, LC; *The World's Work* (1904). Near the Oklahoma Territory Building's entrance were five hundred large photographs to show how civilized and commercially advanced Indians were. Mirroring Indian School activities, the Presbyterian Mission Training School of Sitka installed an exhibit in the Alaskan building.

10. Starr (1905, 41); Francis (1913, 530). We found no newspapers that mentioned the static anthropology exhibits, nor any photographs.

11. McGee (1904c, 88). McGee noted these were the LPE's only research undertakings.

12. Shipman (1994); Haller (1975). See also Baker (1998), Forbes (1990), Horsman (1981), or Tucker (1994) for a discussion of the science and politics of racial research.

13. Montague (1960, 3); McGee (1905d, 191); Blumenbach (1865); Boas (1899); Garson (1887). See Gould (1977 and 1981). Haller (1975, 98) has labeled both Powell and McGee neo-Lamarckians who saw each generation of humans as more developed than the last and this development could be seen in the human body. The language McGee used was common in the late nineteenth century.

14. *St. Louis Post-Dispatch* (1904i).

15. Boas to McGee, Sept. 18, 1903, McGee to Boas, Sept. 31, 1903, McGee to J. McKeen Cattell, Sept. 15, 1903, Feb. 20, 1904, MP, boxes 7, 14, and 20, LC; Rydell (1984, 164); McGee, 1904 Monthly Report for June, MP, box 16, LC; *American Anthropologist* (1906a, 466–67); Hrdlička (1908); Spencer (1979, 267). Hrdlička was named assistant curator of physical anthropology at the United States National Museum on May 1, 1903. McGee had at first regarded his appointment as an attempt by Holmes to undermine the BAE's role as the Smithsonian's active research arm. Holmes (1903c) noted that McGee and Powell had shown little interest in physical anthropology.

16. Hrdlička to Holmes, Aug. 27, 1903, Holmes Papers, NAA; Hrdlička to McGee, March 14, Apr. 12, 1904, MP, box 20, LC. The laboratory would cost three hundred dollars to outfit.

17. McGee to Boas, Feb. 27, 1904, Mason to McGee, March 17, 1904, MP, boxes 1 and 20, LC; Mason to True, March 9, 1904, True to Mason, March 12, 1904, RU 70, box 63, folder 1, SIA. McGee was leery of working with Hrdlička because of his dogmatic convictions.

18. Hrdlička (1903); McGee to Lehman, Feb. 20, 1904, MP, box 19, LC.

19. Woodworth (1905; 1910; 1932, 36); *New York Times* (1904d). McGee tried several strategies to have Columbia University pay part of Woodworth's expenses, including having him take an honorarium rather than a salary, use his vacation time, or serve as a juror so the awards committee would pick up his expenses and salary. Woodworth did not agree to these schemes but the university did release him from his summer school courses (McGee to Woodworth, Jan. 8, 15, Feb. 17, March 24, Apr. 14, 1904, Woodworth to McGee, Jan. 12, Feb. 19, March 16, Apr. 19, 1904, McGee to Lehmann, Feb. 20, 1904, MP, boxes 19 and 20, LC).

20. Rydell (1984, 164). Bruner transformed classrooms into labs in what is now the Mathematics Library in Cupples Hall. He used a large room for the anthropometric lab, two smaller rooms for psychometry and a fourth for an office. He cleaned the areas himself because there were no janitors (Woodworth 1905, 195).

21. Starr considered both labs excellently equipped (1905, 42).

22. Woodworth (1932, 373). Woodworth later remembered that the number was almost nine hundred.

23. Woodworth (1905, 197). The chart used listed twenty-four racial and ethnic types.

24. Woodworth (1905, 22); *New York Times* (1904d). Woodworth obtained equipment provided that the manufacturer's name was prominently displayed. He also designed several instruments for mental tests of nonliterate Natives. Woodworth's color test consisted of arranging strips of colored paper from light to dark. Dark blue shades were handed to the subject who matched them to corresponding light shades. This exercise turned out to be very difficult and Woodworth called it a failure.

25. Woodworth (1910) later demonstrated that these tests were spurious. What Bruner was measuring was not racial but linguistic and cultural factors.

26. Hofmann (1904). We have been unable to discover whether this study was ever published. We thank Mary Ellen Morbeck for reviewing the anthropometric data.

27. E. H. Bradford to McGee, Sept. 6, 1904, Edward A. Spitzka to McGee, Apr. 20, 1904, MP, box, 16, LC.

28. Boas to McGee, Feb. 5, March 5, 1904, MP, box 19, LC; Hill (1912, 17). Boas suggested a more elaborate scheme but McGee did not have fourteen hundred dollars to implement it. He distributed flyers to museums but received no takers. Dorsey said they were leery that Boas would keep the best busts for his museum and only sell rejects. Other sculptors used the Native peoples as models for their work. Sometimes they took measurements from the subjects themselves, at other times relied on photographs. McGee supported Allen Hutchinson who wanted to make ethnic and racial diorama models for museums, but the project never materialized (McGee to Chouteau, Dec. 13, 1904; Leon M. Guerrero to McGee, Aug. 20, 1904. MP, Boxes 15 and Box 20, LC).

29. Dorsey to Simms, Sept. 3, 1904, FM. The paperwork on the Carpenter photographs and Newcombe's field notes is miniscule. Dorsey purchased 350 photographs from the Philippine Photograph Company for forty-four dollars (Accession 891, FM; Moenster (1987). Beal's photographs adorn many LPE official publications. Moenster estimates she took over 5,000 negatives, many of the Native peoples and their encampments. Some are now housed in the Missouri Historical Society and the St. Louis Public Library. What happened to McCowan's photographs is unknown.

30. J. H. Stover to McGee, May 31, 1904; McGee to W. J. Hencke, July 8, 1904; Samuel T. Cherry (1904) Promotional fliers and excerpts from press clippings. MP, Boxes 16 and 19, LC.

31. There were also 7 births and 1,315 accidents that required an ambulance. Some 13,800 cases required surgery. The medical department was under the direction of Leonidas Laid-

ley with a staff of eight physicians and a dozen nurses. They vaccinated all the Igorots for smallpox when they arrived, since several had died on board ship (Laidley 1905). The Filipinos' bodies were autopsied. Peplon, a Moro, died on July 28, two other unnamed Igorots on August 27, and another in November. People who died in other facilities were not counted in official fair statistics (Buel 1904, vol. 10, 3767); Afable (2000); see Buel (1904, vol. 10, 3765–3769) for a copy of Peplon's autopsy report. Several Chinese participants were stopped in San Francisco by the immigration service as well (Coolidge 1968).

32. Hrdlicˇ ka (1904, 14; 1906, 245–320; 1907, 177–232); Hrdlicˇ ka to Mason, July 23, 1904, RU 70, box 68, folder 3, SIA; Afable (2000). See Rydell (1984, 165) for background on collecting racial cadavers and body parts. Under Hrdlicˇ ka's plan Columbia University and the American Museum of Natural History were to receive the soft body parts and the Smithsonian the brains. The other institutions declined; all the remains went to the Smithsonian.

33. Hrdlička to Rathbun, Aug. 8, 1904, RU 70, box 68, SIA.

34. Hanson (1905, 277); McGee (1904a, 8; 1905d, 191, 373). Many of McGee's ideas about racial progression and cranial size were obtained from Frank Baker (1890) and were an attempt to synthesize ideas from Darwin, Spencer, and Lamarck.

35. Hanson (1905, 278); Rydell (1984, 166); Woodworth (1910, 172; 1904a; 1904b; 1905; 1932; 1939). Woodworth states they spent 1905 working up the data and presenting it at scientific meetings but published little. Woodworth never liked publishing his results and was noted for producing little record of his activities. He never did finish the analysis.

36. Woodworth (1910, 174, 175, 182, 181). Woodworth found that simply measuring the cranium was an unfair measure of mental ability, since it only correlated with body size.

37. Woodworth (1910, 174); McGee (1904a, 7; 1904c, 45).

38. Francis (1913, 530).

12. Anthropological Performances

Epigraph. Page (1904, 5110–11).

1. LPEC-DRPC (1904a, 1905a, 1905b); Bennitt (1905, 706); LPEC-WFB (1904c, 54). Other bands engaged by the LPEC Bureau of Music included: Frederick Neil Innes's Band, Grenadier Guards Band, Haskell Indian Band, Conterno's Band, Ellery's Band, Fanciulli's Band, Boston Band, Banda Rossa, the Kilties Band, Weber's Band, and Phinney's Band (Liebenguth 1979, 1). The Philippine Band and the U.S. Marine Band performed twice daily. Some special events we find questionable today—on May 23, Dr. George Kuntz gave a radium demonstration using people from the audience as guinea pigs!

2. Clevenger (1996, 124); Liebenguth (1979, 32); Reedy (1904, 15). Indian performers were used to entertain between the historic scenes and sang "Good Old Mountain Dew," "The Spear and the Bow," and "When the Eagle Screams." The metaphorical character of Mississippi, the Indian leader, was portrayed as an evil spirit. The script of Hayes's *Louisiana* is available in the Missouri Historical Society.

3. Programs for Anthropology Groups, July 15, 16, 23, and 30, Aug. 6 and 8, 1904, MP,

box 19, LC; McGee (1905d, 89); LPEC-ODP (1904x, 3). It was at one of these regular Saturday performances that the Kwakiutls, Nootkas, and Mbutis performed their infamous Hamatsa ritual. Francis deemed these events satisfactory because they generated large attendance and were very entertaining (Francis 1913, 530). See Henry (2000), Radforth (2003), and Raibmon (2000) for excellent discussions of this kind of theater.

4. McGee to McCowan, June 11, 1904, MP box 19, LC; LPEC-ODP (1904c, 1; 1904aa, 1; 1904v, 4–5).

5. *American Anthropologist* (1906b, 504); *National Geographic Magazine* (1903); Fowler (2000, 263–64); Densmore (1906).

6. Davis (1904, 8); Skiff (1904b, 4); Coats (1961); Butler (1904). Newcomb, the retired director of the Nautical Almanac Office at the U.S. Naval Observatory and a professor of astronomy and mathematics at Johns Hopkins University, was the country's foremost astronomer and mathematician. The other organizers were University of Chicago pragmatic philosopher Albion Small, William Rainey Harper, and social psychologist Hugo Münsterberg.

7. The congresses were held to establish a "unity of knowledge" in three branches and brought an estimated one hundred and twenty thousand delegates and two hundred separate organizations to St. Louis. The Congress of Arts and Sciences was to be a forum to structure the world's knowledge under one universalizing framework. Of course no one agreed on what this was and the organizers fought constantly and publicly (Dewey 1903; Münsterberg 1903, 1904). The LPEC spent $200,000 on foreign scholars (including a $150 honorarium) (*Popular Science Monthly* 1904, 101). Many prominent speakers withdrew before the congress and the LPEC ran out of food and meeting space during the congress, which did little to enhance St. Louis's reputation. The seven-day congress still attracted over ten thousand attendees (Rogers 1905). No women were asked to speak. It was hoped that informal interactions over the two-week period would lead to new syntheses.

8. Boas to McGee, Feb. 17, Feb. 20, 1904, MP, box 19, LC. Stocking (1974b, 21) states that McGee usurped the theoretical paper despite other peoples' objections, but it was Putnam's decision. Boas never wanted to write the history paper.

9. McGee (1906). McGee basically expanded on his earlier ideas on human progress (McGee 1892, 1896d, 1897a, 1897b, 1901a, 1899). See also Rydell (1984, 160–61).

10. Boas (1906, 482); Clevenger (1996, 10). The editor of *Popular Science Monthly* (1904, 102–3) felt that overall the congress was disappointing and too ambitious. Most speakers dealt with esoteric topics and keynote speakers were superfluous and divisive. Since there were overlapping sessions, only about fifty people attended departmental meetings. People seldom listened to talks in other fields. Instead they enjoyed the fair.

11. Bennitt (1905, 694); *Indian School Journal* (1904f, June 28, June 30, July 8).

12. *Indian School Journal* (1904l); LPEC-ODP (1904n, 10). For Reel's biography and her importance in the development of Indian Service educational policy see Lomawaima (1996); for Curtis, see Babcock and Parezo (1988); for Fletcher, see Mark (1980) and Hough (1923).

13. *Indian School Journal* (1904l). The menu was consommé, crackers, cream of corn, croutons, olives, celery, sweet pickles, roast turkey, currant jelly, peas, creamed potatoes, sliced tomatoes, lemon sherbet, fruit salad, hot biscuits, coffee, cherry pie, cake, cheese, nuts, and raisins.

14. LPEC-ODP (1904v, 16); *Indian School Journal* (1904e, 1904o).

15. Anonymous, 1904, "World's Fair Is to Have First Congress of Educated Indians," no source, MP, box 32, LPE scrapbook, LC; Chief Blue Horse to McCowan, Jan. 28, 1904, CP-fairs, box 2, OHS; LPEC-ODP (1904d; 1904z, 3); *St. Louis Republic* (1904s); *Indian School Journal* (1904f, July 1). See Rydell (1984, 111–18) and Moses (1996) for good summaries of the Omaha Indian Congress.

16. *Indian School Journal* (1904f, July 15); LPEC-WFB (1904i, 4); Francis (1913, 530).

17. McGee (1904e, 253–54; 1904a, 5–6). McGee considered adding two sections, Research and Conservation and University Instruction, to be run by educational institutions (McGee, no date, untitled page, MP, box 20, LC).

18. McGee to Dear Sir, June 1, 1904, recorded in McGee (1905d, 83–84); McGee to Gus Mechin, Sept. 11, 1904, MP, box 19, LC; Densmore (1906). By general anthropology, McGee meant the study of man and his creations, exemplified in stages of psychic development. Record work included making lists and tables of measurements, sketches and diagrams, photographs, life casts, life models, paintings, and sculptures. McGee basically followed Daniel Brinton's and Dorsey's teaching categories (Brinton 1892; Dorsey 1894).

19. Starr to McGee, June 14, 1904, MP, box 20, LC; Starr to My Dear Mother, Aug. 16, 1904, SP, box 6, folder 5, UC; McGee to Joseph B. Marvin, Alaska Building, Aug. 26, 1904, McGee to Starr, Aug. 26, 1904, SP, box 5, LC. Starr had little respect for McGee's leadership. See Parezo and Fowler (2006) for an extended discussion of anthropology's first field school.

20. Starr (1905, 40–42, 1904b); McGee (1904a, 4); Rydell (1984, 273–74); *Chicago Recorder* (1904). Starr's scrapbooks contained an announcement stating the class would be on the Pike and students would see odd people (Starr quoted in *Chicago News* 1904). The *Chicago Journal* (1904) said Starr would conduct a class on psychology so "seekers after knowledge" could analyze the "wicked" place. The reporter was concerned that the topic was improper for women but Starr reassured him. "When the professor reduces the strange customs to an ethnological, historical and psychological basis, he believes the co-eds who are going with him will not have to blush or the others students to grin at what they see and hear." Starr taught because he had missed the spring semester and had to take an unpaid leave of absence. Working for McGee turned out to be expensive (Starr to McGee, Jan. 22, 1904, MP, box 19, LC).

21. *St. Louis Examiner* (1904a).

22. *American Anthropologist* (1904); *St. Louis Examiner* (1904b); unattributed newspaper articles (1904), "Chicago Co-Eds See Woman Carve Husband" and "Negritos Defeat Other Tribes in Fire-Making Competition," SP, scrapbook 8; Richard Spamer to Starr, Sept. 12, 1904, SP, box 5, UC; McGee to A. J. Smith, Sept. 2, 1904, MP, box 19, LC; LPEC-OPA (1905,

66). While Starr defended the women's presence he believed in a strict sexual division of labor; unattributed newspaper article (1904), "What Prof Starr, Expert on Savages, Thinks of Effects on Civilization," SP, scrapbook 8, UC).

23. Starr charged two dollars for a tour, generating a good deal of cash and press coverage (*St. Louis Post-Dispatch* (1904j, 1904m); *St. Louis Globe-Democrat* (1904b); Rydell (1984, 166); Marion (1904, 1); Starr (1904b).

24. Dyreson (1998, 3). See also Carnes and Griffen (1990), Dyreson (1993) and Hoganson (1998).

25. Reel (1901); *Indian School Journal* (1904f, June 22); Peavy and Smith (2001). For analyses of Indian sport see Churchill, Hill, and Barlow (1979), Littlefield (1989), and Oxendine (1988).

26. *Indian School Journal* (1904g); *St. Louis Republic* (1904l); Parezo and Troutman (2001). McGee (1904a, 8; 1905d, 106, 89) reported that Cocopa boys won these opportunistic competitions.

27. McGee (1905d, 191); Findling and Pelle (1996, 18); LPEC-DRPC (1904c, 57). Physical education was seen as a prime mechanism to improve moral and mental conditions. A trim body was the enemy of illness and laziness, in "the national culture of strenuous living" (Rydell 1984, 155).

28. Sullivan (1905b, 185–86; 1904, 58); Bennitt (1905, 565). The static exhibits told how man as an athlete could be trained; women were not included (LPEC-DRPC (1904c, 1904d). Mark Dyreson (1998, 2004) has noted that Skiff and Boas were interested in physical education and were both members of the American Association of Physical Education. Skiff was also Spaulding's friend, an official in the Amateur Athletic Union, and on the American Olympic Committee.

29. Bennitt (1905, 565); Sullivan (1904, 8). The Olympic water polo, soccer, and lacrosse tournaments were also unsuccessful.

30. Emil Breitkreutz quoted in Johnson (1972, 120). Some sources say the number was eighty-one out of a possible ninety-four gold medals (Findling and Pelle 1996, 22). Athletes from Germany, Cuba, Canada, and Hungary won several medals.

31. United States Olympic Committee (1993, 37). It is evident from de Coubertin's memoirs that he intensely disliked Sullivan and did not want him associated with the IOC. The kindest thing he had to say about Sullivan is that he was a man often "carried away by enthusiasm" (de Coubertin 1979, 41). The fight to have the Olympics in St. Louis is a fascinating example of politics in sports (Dyreson 1998; Kieran and Daley 1965; and Loland 1994). The St. Louis Games were poorly organized; people ran in the wrong events because Olympic and non-Olympic competitions were held simultaneously (Johnson 1972, 121; Wallechinsky 1988).

32. *St. Louis Post-Dispatch* (1904f, 1904ee, 1904m, 1904gg); Sullivan (1905a, 250; 1904b; 1904c); Rydell (1984, 166); Hobermann (1977); *St. Louis Republic* (1904q).

33. McGee to Sullivan, July 13, 1904, MP, box 19, LC.

34. McGee to William P. Wilson, June 28, July 13, 1904, MP, box 19, LC. Existing records show that informal Native athletic events were used as pretests (Woodworth 1904a, 1904b).

Corresponding measurements were made of "typical" Euro-American athletes participating in athletic contests. The goal was to "cover the widest possible range in physical development as well as in ethnic affinity" (McGee (1904a, 8–9).

35. McGee (1905d, 89). For photographs of these events and snide comments about the participants' performances using prejudiced standards see Bennett (1905).

36. True to Lyon, June 18, 1904, RU 70, box 64, folder 12, SIA. Sullivan confessed later it had been a mistake to not have another day when interpreters for each group could have explained what was expected of them. See Parezo (2004b) for an in-depth analysis and how the competition constituted badly designed and rigged pseudo-science.

37. LPEC-ODP (1904i, 2); Sullivan (1905a, 253). Sullivan never understood that such cooperative behavior was a sign of graciousness and a symbol of respect.

38. Simms to Dorsey, Aug. 15, MF; Simms to McGee, Aug. 14, 16, 17, MP, box 16, LC; Sullivan (1905a, 255–59).

39. Sullivan (1905a, 259, 256, 258, 263). Like other evolutionists, Sullivan had counterarguments to support his preconceptions about Caucasian superiority.

40. Sullivan (1905a, 251–54, 260); Gulick (1899).

41. Simms to McGee, Aug. 14, 16, 17, 1904, MP, box 16, LC; Simms to Dorsey, Aug. 11, 15, 1904, FM.

42. McGee to Sullivan, Aug. 18, 1904, Sullivan to McGee, Aug. 19, 1904, MP, box 19, LC; Sullivan (1905a, 260).

43. McGee (1905d, 99–100). Winners received five dollars for first place, one dollar for second, and fifty cents each for third and fourth.

44. *St. Louis Globe-Democrat* (1904a, 1904g, 1904h); McGee monthly reports to Skiff, MHS; Francis (1904, 50; 1913, 530).

45. De Coubertin (1979, 43). De Coubertin made sure that future Olympic Games were independent competitions. See also Parezo (2004b) and Roche (2000).

46. Johnson (1972, 124); Findling and Pelle (1996, 22); Stanaland (1981); Toohey and Veal (2000).

13. Celebrating the Fair and Going Home

Epigraph. Hanson (1905, 278); *St. Louis Republic* (1904x).

1. Geronimo traveled to Washington in March 1905 and rode in President Roosevelt's inauguration parade along with Quanah Parker and American Horse, an Oglala Lakota leader. In 1909, he died of pneumonia, still a prisoner of war (Turner 1996, 33; Reddin 1999, 161).

2. McGee (1904c); Walter Hough to Richard Rathbun, July 8, 1904, RU 70, box 68, folders 1 and 7, SIA; Paul Beckwith to Rathbun, July 2, June 4, 1904, George P. Merrill to Rathbun, Sept. 20, 1904, RU 70, box 68, folder 1, SIA; Merrill to Rathbun, Sept. 20, 1904, RU 70, box 68, folder 7, SIA; *Atlanta Journal* (1904); *American Anthropologist* (1906a, 476); Accessions 891 892, 914, and 919; Verner to Dorsey, Oct. 11, 1904, FM. The selling price was two hundred dollars. The estimate of fifty thousand artifacts did not include collections

in the Philippine Reservation, state buildings or major pavilions. The major institutions involved were the Smithsonian Institution, the American Museum of Natural History, the Philadelphia Commercial Museum and the Field Museum; most outstanding pieces had been promised by July. Other institutions and individual collectors were more selective. Department store owner John Wanamaker brought the Egyptian tomb and all its contents from the anthropology exhibits. He paid for dismantling and shipping costs, saving McGee a good deal of money.

3. Von Luschan decided it was cheaper to give them away than to ship them back to Africa. Foreign exhibitors often gave unsold items to the Smithsonian, which was cheaper than transporting the items home. Holmes needed thirty railroad cars to transport the ethnographic materials from St. Louis back to Washington (Ravenel to Rathbun, Oct. 31, Nov. 5, Nov. 8, Nov. 9, Nov. 2, 1904, RU 70, box 68, folder 8, SIA; Rathbun (1906b, 9).

4. Hough to Rathbun, Oct. 4, 1904, William Ravenel to Cyrus Adler, Nov. 22, 1904, Rathbun to J. Howard Gore, Aug. 11, 1904, Mason to Rathbun, Nov. 3, 1904, RU 70, box 68, folders 6 and 13, SIA; *New York Evening Post* (1904). A museum was founded but folded after a few years due to lack of community support and patronage.

5. Kroeber's LPE participation is not documented in McGee's papers nor is there much mention in Kroeber's papers (Bancroft Library, University of California, Berkeley) with the exception of letters from McGee asking for assistance or discussing American Anthropological Association activities. Individuals who declined included: Mooney, Livingston Farrand, Francis W. Kelsey, Volney Foster, Boas, George Grant MacCurdy, Rueben Thwaites, Guy Carleton Lee, Grace King, Joseph Jastrow, and G. Stanley Hall.

6. McGee to Skiff, July 31, 1904, printed in McGee (1905d, 368); Fowler and Parezo (2003). The Board of Lady Managers had their own award competition for women exhibitors and women's work, mirroring procedures initiated at earlier fairs.

7. McGee (1905d, 370–73). McGee took no part in the deliberations and was not present during the final vote.

8. McGee (1905d, 371); *American Anthropologist* (1906d, 442). Another categorical distinction was whether an exhibitor was American or foreign. The Fred Harvey Company had produced the last-minute exhibit when L. Bradford Prince's prehistoric art collection from the Northern Rio Grande region failed to arrive in mid-May. Schweizer and Huckel (a founding member of the AAA) saw the exhibit as an opportunity to advertise their Indian Department, expand their retail concession in the Manufacturing Building, and further legitimize their efforts in the eyes of museum anthropologists (Harvey 1996, 72; Huckel 1905; Howard and Pardue 1996).

9. See list published in *World's Fair Bulletin* (1904b).

10. Putnam (1905). Some sources say Mary Benson was given a silver medal. Since there was little anthropometry or psychometry research the awards went to companies who had supplied equipment or to universities for their publications.

11. LPEC-WFB (1904b, 28); McGee (1905d, 379–93).

12. *Indian School Journal* (1904m).

13. Many awards were politically based. Mrs. William H. Taft, wife of Governor Taft, received a gold medal for her small exhibit of a wooden chest and chiffonier (Bennitt 1905, 477).

14. List of awards and medals, June 20, 1904, RU 70, box 65, folder 4, SIA; Henderson (1906). Judging was expensive; the LPEC spent $2,383.65 on anthropology jurors. Luckily the cost was not subtracted from McGee's budget but paid by the Foreign Commission and the International Congress accounts (McGee 1905d, 377–78).

15. Schneiderhahn quoted in Clevenger (1996, 50). Sadness and loneliness became prevalent themes in journalists' reports by October. William Curtis said, "[I]t makes me sad to be reminded that all this beauty, glory and majesty will be torn away. It is a pity that it cannot be preserved in marble" (Curtis 1904c).

16. *New York Times* (1904e). Bennitt (1905, xii) gives the final figure as 19,694,855, excluding the thousands of employees, their families, demonstrators, militia, police, concessionaries, and entertainers. Fair officials estimated that twenty thousand people lived permanently on the fairgrounds.

17. Buel (1904, vol. 5, 1571–72); McGee (1905d, 26). Exact figures would have been impossible given the layout of the department and the fact that people took the path without visiting compounds.

18. *Washington Post* (1901, 1903); BAE, folder 2214, James Mooney, miscellaneous clippings, NAA; McGee (1905d, 115).

19. McGee (1905d, 53–56). Salaries included: McGee ($416.67) and secretary ($150); stenography ($75); custodian ($65), superintendent ($100); McCowan as special commissioner ($150); custodian for the history division ($50), office boy ($20), and janitors ($130). Other costs were $100 per month for McGee's travel and $200 for supplies. The total was over $2,250 per month.

20. McGee to Skiff, McGee to Francis, July 20, 1904, MP, box 16, LC; Executive Committee Minutes, July 23, 1904, LPEC files, series II, subseries 2, folder 5, MHS. When McGee made additional monetary requests, he became something of a persona non grata.

21. McGee (1905d); Anonymous, 1904, "Vancouver Indian Group, Statement of Cost," MP, box 28, LC. For his services, Newcombe was compensated $150 per month, from which he paid his son. Travel for Newcombe and the Kwakiutl and Nootka demonstrators was $2,451.08 and living expenses en route totaled $393.34.

22. McGee to Francis, Sept. 5, 1904, Executive Committee Minutes, Sept. 11, 1904, 6313–14, LPEC files, series II, subseries 2, folder 5, MHS.

23. Bradford and Blume (1992); Verner (1907); Crawford (1982). Kondola remained in the United States to continue his education. Verner tried to extort money at least three times from the LPEC but was unsuccessful. In February 1906, in the *Washington Post*, he alleged the LPEC caused him difficulties in Africa and America because it would not supply him with agreed-upon funds. The figures he used were McGee's original LPEC estimate, not those in his contract or original offer. The reporter noted that Verner had taken an additional five hundred dollars and used it for purposes other than transportation. McGee was

incensed and wrote a scathing letter to Francis. The affair dragged on for two years, causing McGee many headaches. The LPEC lawyer told him to simply stop answering Verner's requests (McGee to Francis, Sept. 5, 1904, Executive Committee Minutes, Sept. 11, 1904, 6314, LPEC files, MHS; McGee to Francis, Dec. 12, 1904, Jan. 15, Feb. 20, March 18, June 5, 1905, McGee to Counsel, March 5, 1906, MP, box 18, LC).

24. Newcombe to Dorsey, Nov. 30, 1904, FM.

25. Starr to McGee, Nov. 16, 1904, MP, box 19, LC.

26. Inagaki to McGee, Dec. 11, 1904, MP, box 19, LC; Newcombe to Dorsey, Nov. 30, 1904, FM.

27. Hulbert to Inagaki, Dec. 20, 1904, MP, box 19, LC. In April 1905, Starr sent McGee a final fiscal accounting and noted he was still owed $5.06 for railroad expenses in March. McGee paid him from his personal funds.

28. Reported in Van Stone (1993, 89); also in SP, scrapbook 9, UC.

29. Troutman (1997); see Parezo and Troutman (2001) for a fuller account. Hulbert was ill-prepared for the task (McGee 1905d, 54; Hulbert to McGee, Oct. 8, 12, 19, 1904, MP, box 20, LC). McGee took the second group back to Yuma on Oct. 31. An assistant named Bush took the final group home on Nov. 4.

30. Hulbert to McGee, Oct. 11, 1904, MP, box 20, LC; Esther Hulbert to Oral Etter, Aug. 28, 1952, LPE files, Correspondence of C. E. Hulbert, 1904–7, appendix series 3, subseries 11, box 30, folder 1, MHS. Hulbert told McGee he had "enjoyed every minute" of the trip for it was "a rare pleasure to meet real difficulties and over come[sic] them." Without knowing more about Hulbert it is impossible to conclude whether he was being ironic.

31. Hulbert to McGee, Oct. 11, 12, 1904, MP, box 20, LC.

32. Turner (1996, 33); Reddin (1999, 161); Newcombe to Dorsey, Nov. 1, Dec. 10, 1904, Dorsey to Simms, Dec. 15, Oct. 5, Nov. 1, 8, 1904, FM. Dorsey was also upset with McCowan who kept funds Dorsey sent for the Kwakiutls and Nootkas to visit the Field Museum in October, undermining his research plans.

33. *American Anthropologist* (1906c, 522); *St. Louis Republic* (1904y, 1904o); Benham to McGee, Dec. 17, 20, 1904, MP, box 15, LC; Anonymous, 1904, "Younger Igorrotes[sic] Want to Stay Here," newspaper article, no attribution, RU 70, box 68, folder 2, SIA.

14. The Experiences of an Exposition

Epigraph. McGee (1904g, 5185).

1. *American Anthropologist* (1905, 754); see also Wolf (1994) and Takaki (1992) on early-twentieth-century race concepts.

2. Buel (1904, vol. 10, 2–3); *Scientific American* (1904f).

3. New York Times (1901), cited by Rydell (1984, 4).

4. Skiff quoted in Rydell (1984, 155); *St. Louis Republic* (1903b). Rydell (1984, 235) has called anthropologists who helped exposition organizers "high priests" because they "produced an intellectual scaffolding for the cumulative symbolic universe under construction at the fairs." But, we would add, only so long as the federal government paid for the

exhibits and research. An excellent literature exists in cultural and American studies on the role fairs played in developing American ideology, empire, industrialism, urbanization, architecture, and identity, and the construction of concepts about gender, the human body, performance and art, society, race, and progress, as well as cultural evolution and technological advancement. See Anderson (1979, 1983); Burton Benedict (1991); Celik (1992); Celik and Kinney (1990); Crane (2000); Gillis (1994); Handelman (1990); N. Harris (1990); Hobsbawm (1989); J. F. Kasson (1978); Kirshenblatt-Gimblett (1998); Lears (1981); Mattie (1998); Moore (2000); Rydell (1993); Rydell and Gwinn (1994).

5. *Literary Digest* (1905); Piper (1905); Bauer (1905) in Records of the Lewis and Clark Centennial, box 1, ORHS; Abbott (1981). Portland's profit was a mere $84,462 (http://www. PdxHistory.com.tripod.com, accessed Feb. 2004). Rydell (1984, 188–91) also notes that the idea of an extensive exposition was not as popular in Portland as it had been in St. Louis because of class antagonisms and labor disputes. Community leaders eventually decided on the exposition as a way to overcome a pronounced economic depression. There was also less money to work with; the Oregon state legislature provided only five hundred thousand dollars in 1903.

6. Holmes (1908, x); Holmes to True, Nov. 15, 1904, RU 70, box 65, folder 10, SIA; *American Anthropologist* (1905, 754); Rathbun (1906a, 74; 1906b, 35); Chalcraft (1905, 56–57); Leupp (1905). American, German, French, English, Dutch, Japanese, Chinese, and Austrian exhibitors participated (Van Stone 1993; Poster 1999; Carl 1904; Skiff 1905; LPEC-ODP 1904a; Pieris 1904; McGee 1905d, 410; Hutchin 1905). The Chinese had born the bunt of discriminatory behavior in St. Louis (Cortinovis 1977).

7. Henry Dosch to Henry W. Goode, Oct. 5, 7, 1904, LCCC, boxes 7 and 21, ORHS. The War Department had exceeded its appropriation in St. Louis and wanted to minimize its Portland expenses.

8. Records of the Bureau of Insular Affairs, General Classified Files, nos. 9640–43, RG 350, NA; Afable (1997, 21). One troop went to fairs in Jamestown (1907) and Seattle (1909) as well as performed in San Francisco, Chicago, Los Angeles, and England. While in England they served as consultants for Carl Seidanell's linguistic study. Most people saw these trips as adventures, not as turning points in Igorot history (Afable 1995, 16).

9. As Adams (2001), Bogdan (1988), and Rydell (1999) have all noted, most Zulu warriors, Wild Men from Borneo, Negritos, and Dahomeans in sideshows were usually black American actors.

10. The Panama-Pacific Corporation hired Skiff as director-in-chief and he tried to resurrect the same inclusive themes used in St. Louis as well as celebrate the canal's completion. Skiff decided not to have an anthropology department because of the prohibitive cost. Instead he used Smithsonian lay-figure dioramas, midway concessions, and art to make his points about progress and evolutionary developments (Rydell 1984, 219). See also Panama-Pacific Exposition (1915); Howard and Pardue (1996).

11. Charles F. Lummis to D. C. Collier, Dec. 3, 1911, Lummis Papers, SWM. For more on Hewett see Chauvenet (1983); Fowler (2000, 261–74); and Stocking (1982). Hewett worked

on the San Diego exposition from 1911 to 1915 and then served as director of the San Diego Museum of Man from 1915 to 1928.

12. Hewett (1915), "Prospectus of the 1915 Exposition," Hrdlička Papers, box 17, NAA; Rydell (1984, 220).

13. Hrdlička (1917a, 1917b, 1925, "Scientific Features at the San Diego Exposition," and "The Division of Physical Anthropology at the Panama California Exposition San Diego," Hrdlička Papers, box 11, NAA). See Rydell (1984, 220–23) for a full description of the physical anthropology exhibit and its racialized eugenic elements.

14. A second, more traditional, exhibit was later built by Barrett and Kroeber from materials in the anthropology museums at the University of California–Berkeley and the Milwaukee Public Museum to replace the IACB exhibit.

Epilogue

1. Anonymous, 2002, Albert Ernest Jenks, 1869–1953, http://emuseum.mnsu.edu/information/biography/fghij/jenks_albert.html.

2. Stocking (1968); Miller (1978, 55–56).

3. Hough (1933). See also Hinsley (1981); Fernlund (2000).

4. Dorsey wanted to expand and reorganize Chicago anthropology but met opposition at the Field Museum and the University of Chicago because of his constant disagreements with Starr and Skiff, which had begun with Dorsey's refusal to do more in St. Louis. He left the Field Museum ostensibly to join the war effort. Dorsey wrote many magazine articles and in 1925 published *Why We Behave Like Human Beings*, one of the most popular books of his times (Calhoun 1991, 153–54; Cole 1931, 413–14; Dorsey 1909a, 1925).

5. McGee to Skiff, Sept. 18, 1903, attached to Board of Directors' Minutes, LPEC for Sept. 24, 1903, LPEC files series 11, subseries 2, folder 5, MHS; McGee (1905b), also reprinted in E. McGee (1905d, 83–88). McGee's salary was $416.67 per month, considerably less than he had earned in Washington.

6. *American Anthropologist* (1906e).

7. Board of Directors' Minutes, Sept. 11, 1906, LPEC series 11, subseries 2, folder 6, MHS. The current collections manager of the St. Louis Science Center had never heard of McGee or the collections' history (personal communication, 2005).

8. Moses (1984, 210–11). Kroeber noted later that McGee was an excellent field observer but "slender in range," his work permeated with conjectures and doubtful assumptions. Kroeber and others in his era thought one needed to be more than a good field observer to be a professor (quoted in Hinsley 1981, 243).

9. Boas to McGee, Oct. 29, 1902, MP, box 4, LC; Hinsley (1981, 254).

10. Letters between McGee and Bell in Alexander Graham Bell papers, 1904–7, LC.

11. Holmes (no date) "1902." Holmes earned a series of prizes, including election to the National Academy of Sciences.

12. Hinsley (1981, 255); see West (1992), for an extensive analysis of McGee's work as

applied anthropology, and Hays (1959) and Lacey (1979), for his critical role in the conservation movement.

13. Pinchot (1947, 359–60). Cross (1953, 159) states that it is very probable that McGee wrote Roosevelt's 1902 message first advocating an Appalachian National Forest.

14. Darnell (1971, 1998, 2001); Stocking (1968, 217–19; 1973; 1974a).

15. See, for example, Darnell (1998, 2001); Stocking (1974a).

References

Abbott, Carl. 1981. *The Great Extravaganza: Portland and the Lewis and Clark Exposition*. Portland: Oregon Historical Society.

Adams, D. W. 1995. *Educating for Extinction: American Indians and the Boarding School Experience, 1875–1928*. Lawrence: Univ. Press of Kansas.

Adams, Rachel. 2001. *Sideshow U.S.A.: Freaks and the American Cultural Imagination*. Chicago: Univ. of Chicago Press.

Adler, Cyrus. 1907. Samuel Pierpont Langley. *Annual Report of the Smithsonian Institution for 1906*. Washington DC: Government Printing Office.

Afable, Patricia O. 1995. The Peoples of Eduardo Masferré's Photographs. *Discovery: The Magazine of the Yale Peabody Museum of Natural History* 25(2):10–19.

————. 1997. The Exhibition of Cordillerans in the United States during the Early 1900s. *The Igorot Quarterly* 6(2):19–22.

————. 2000. Nikmalika, the "Igorrotes" of the Early-Twentieth-Century Fairs: A Chronology and Name Lists. *The Igorot Quarterly* 9(4):18–31.

Agonocillo, Theodoro. 1975. *A Short History of the Philippines*. New York: New American Library.

Allwood, John. 1977. *The Great Exhibitions*. London: Studio Vista.

Almazan, Tristan T., and Sarah Coleman. 2003a. George Amos Dorsey: A Curator and His Comrades. In *Curators, Collections, and Contexts: Anthropology at the Field Museum, 1893–2002*, ed. Stephen E. Nash and Gary Feinman. Chicago: *Fieldiana*, Anthropology, n.s., 36:87–98.

————. 2003b. Cleaver Warden and George A. Dorsey: Notes and Manuscript on Arapaho Religion and Material Culture, 1903, 1905, 1906, and n.d. Archival Finding Aide. Chicago: Field Museum, Department of Anthropology.

American Anthropologist. 1904. Professor Frederick Starr. *American Anthropologist* 6:582.

————. 1905. Anthropological Society of Washington Meeting. *American Anthropologist* 7(4):754.

———. 1906a. Recent Progress in American Anthropology. *American Anthropologist* 8(3):466–67.

———. 1906b. Recent Progress in Anthropology. *American Anthropologist* 8(3):504.

———. 1906c. Recent Progress in American Anthropology. *American Anthropologist* 8(3):522.

———. 1906d. Recent Progress in American Anthropology. *American Anthropologist* 8(3):451–55, 528.

———. 1906e. St. Louis Public Museum. *American Anthropologist* 8(1):197–99.

Amon Carter Museum. 1970. *The Wild West: Exhibit Catalogue.* Fort Worth: Amon Carter Museum of Western Art.

Anderson, Benedict. 1979. Rituals of Representation: Ethnic Stereotypes and Colonized Peoples at World's Fairs. *European Contributions to American Studies* 27:1–28.

———. 1983. *Imagined Communities: Reflections on the Origin and Spread of Nationalism.* London: Verso.

Archuleta, Margaret L. 2000. The Indian Is an Artist: Art Education. In *Away from Home: American Indian Boarding School Experiences, 1879–2000*, ed. Margaret Archuleta, Brenda Child, and K. Tsianina Lomawaima, 84–97. Phoenix: Heard Museum.

Atlanta Journal. 1904. Director F. J. W. Skiff Tells of Great Work. *Atlanta Journal*, Apr. 30.

Babcock, Barbara A., and Nancy J. Parezo. 1988. *Daughters of the Desert: Women Anthropologists and the Native American Southwest, 1880–1980.* Albuquerque: Univ. of New Mexico Press.

Baker, Frank. 1890. The Ascent of Man. *American Anthropologist* o.s. 3(4):297–319.

Baker, Lee. 1998. *From Savage to Negro: Anthropology and the Construction of Race, 1896–1954.* Berkeley: Univ. of California Press.

Bandwagon. 1962. Cummins' Wild West Show. *Bandwagon* 6(July):4.

Barrett, Samuel M., ed. 1970. *Geronimo: His Own Story.* New York: E. P. Dutton. (Orig. pub. 1906.)

Bauer, E. Francis. 1905. The Development of an Empire. *Music Trade Review* 41(Sept. 30):7.

Becht, June W. 2004. George Poage: Clearing Hurdles at the 1904 Olympics. *Gateway Heritage* 24(4):56–58.

Benedict, Barbara M. 1990. The "Curious Attitude" in Eighteenth-Century Britain: Observing and Owning. *Eighteenth Century* 14:70–80.

Benedict, Burton. 1979. Rituals of Representation: Ethnic Stereotypes and Colonized Peoples at World's Fairs. *European Contributions to American Studies* 27:28–1.

———. 1983. *The Anthropology of World's Fairs: San Francisco's Panama-Pacific International Exposition of 1915.* London: Scolar Press for the Lowie Museum of Anthropology.

———. 1991. International Exhibitions and National Identity. *Anthropology Today* 7(3):5–9.

Bennett, Tony. 1995. *The Birth of the Museum: History, Theory, Politics.* London: Routledge.

Bennitt, Mark. 1905. *History of the Louisiana Purchase Exposition.* Ed. Frank P. Stockbridge. St. Louis: Universal Exposition Publishing Co. Repr., New York: Arno Press, 1976.

Biograph Daily. 1904. U.S. Government Building. *Biograph Daily.* Daily Official Program for May 19.

Biographical Directory of the United States Congress, 1774–Present. http://www.bioguide.congress.gov.

Birk, Dorothy Daniels. 1979. *The World Came to St. Louis: A Visit to the 1904 World's Fair.* St. Louis: Bethany Press.

Blackburn, Fred M., and Ray A. Williamson. 1997. *Cowboys and Cave Dwellers: Basketmaker Archaeology in Utah's Grand Gulch.* Santa Fe: School of American Research Press.

Bloom, John. 1996. "Show What the Indian Can Do": Sports, Memory, and Ethnic Identity at Federal Indian Boarding Schools. *Journal of American Indian Education* 35(3):33–48.

Blumenbach, Johann F. 1865. *The Anthropological Treatises of Johann Friedrich Blumenbach,* translated from the 1840 German edition by T. Bendyshe. Published for the Anthropological Society of London by Longman, Green.

Boas, Franz. 1887a. Museums of Ethnology and Their Classification. *Science* 9:587–89, 614.

———. 1887b. The Occurrence of Similar Inventions in Areas Widely Apart. *Science* 9:485–86.

———. 1899. The Cephalic Index. *American Anthropologist* 11:448–61.

———. 1902. Letter. *Science* 16:828–29.

———. 1904. The History of Anthropology. *Science* 20:513–24.

———. 1906. The History of Anthropology. Vol. 5 of *Congress of Arts and Sciences: Universal Exposition, St. Louis, 1904*. Ed. Howard J. Rogers, 468–82. Boston: Houghton, Mifflin.

———. 1916. *McGee Memorial Meeting of the Washington Academy of Sciences*. Washington DC: privately published.

Bogdan, Robert. 1988. *Freak Show: Presenting Human Oddities for Amusement and Profit*. Chicago: Univ. of Chicago Press.

Bol, Marsha C. 1996. Collecting Symbolism among the Arapaho: George A. Dorsey and C. Warden, Indian. In *The Great Southwest of the Fred Harvey Company and the Santa Fe Railway*, ed. Marta Weigle and Barbara Babcock, 110–24. Phoenix: Heard Museum.

Bourke, John G. 1884. *The Snake Dance of the Moquis of Arizona*. New York: Charles Scribner's Sons.

Bradford, Phillips Verner, and Harvey Blume. 1992. *Ota Benga: The Pygmy in the Zoo*. New York: St. Martin's.

Breitbart, Eric. 1997. *A World on Display: Photographs from the St. Louis World's Fair, 1904*. Albuquerque: Univ. of New Mexico Press.

Brinton, Daniel G. 1892. The Nomenclature and Teaching of Anthropology. *American Anthropologist* 5:263–71.

Bronner, Simon, ed. 1989. *Consuming Visions: Accumulation and Display of Goods in America, 1880–1920*. New York: W. W. Norton.

Brown, Julie K. 1994. *Contesting Images: Photography and the World's Columbian Exposition*. Tucson: Univ. of Arizona Press.

Bruner, Frank. 1908. The Hearing of Primitive Peoples. *Archives of Anthropology*, July. Repr. as *The Hearing of Primitive Peoples*. New York: Science Press, 1908.

Buel, J. W., ed. 1904. *Louisiana and the Fair: An Exposition of the World, Its People, and Their Achievements*. 10 vols. St. Louis: World's Progress Publishing Co.

Burbank, Elbridge A., and Ernest Royce. 1946. *Burbank among the Indians*. Caldwell ID: Caxton Printers.

Bushnell, David I. 1904a. The Cahokia and Surrounding Mound Groups. *Memoirs of the Peabody Museum* 3(1).

———. 1904b. The Cahokia and Surrounding Mound Groups. *Science* 19:450–51.

Butler, Nicholas Murray. 1904. Educational Worth of the St. Louis Exposition. *American Monthly Review of Reviews* 30(Sept.):323–26.

Calhoun, Michele. 1991. George A. Dorsey. *International Dictionary of Anthropologists*, ed. C. Winters, 153–54. New York: Garland.

Carl, Francis A. 1904. China at the Fair. *World's Fair Bulletin* 5:56.

Carnes, Mark C., and Clyde Griffen, eds. 1990. *Meanings for Manhood: Construction of Masculinity in Victorian America*. Chicago: Univ. of Chicago Press.

Cavallo, Dominick. 1981. *Muscles and Morals: Organized Playgrounds and Urban Reform, 1880–1920*. Philadelphia: Univ. of Pennsylvania Press.

Celik, Zeynep. 1992. *Displaying the Orient: Architecture of Islam at Nineteenth-Century World's Fairs*. Berkeley: Univ. of California Press.

Celik, Zeynep, and Leila Kinney. 1990. Ethnography and Exhibitionism at the Expositions Universelles. *Assemblage* (Oct.):3–27.

Chalcraft, Edwin L. 1905. Report: The Indian Exhibits at the St. Louis Exposition. *Annual Report of the Commissioner of Indian Affairs for the Fiscal Year Ending June 30, 1904*, 51–54. Washington DC: Government Printing Office.

Chauvenet, Bernice. 1983. *Hewett and Friends: A Biography of Santa Fe's Vibrant Era*. Santa Fe: Museum of New Mexico Press.

Cherry, Samuel T. 1904. Promotional fliers and excerpts from press clippings. WJ McGee Papers, box 16, Library of Congress.

Chicago Inter-Ocean. 1903. Gone to Seek Pygmies. *Chicago Inter-Ocean*, Nov. 8.

———. 1904 Will Eat Insects While in Search of Lost White Race. *Chicago Inter-Ocean*, Aug. 3.

Chicago Journal. 1904. The Psychology of the Pike. *Chicago Journal*, June 6.

Chicago News. 1904. Starr to Have "Pike" Class. *Chicago News*, June 30.

Chicago Recorder. 1904. The Pike as an Educator. *Chicago Recorder*, June 28.

Chicago Tribune. 1904. Igorottes Clad in Modesty. *Chicago Tribune*, July 19.

Chitty, Arthur B., and James O. Hall. 1904. *World's Fair Authentic Guide*. St. Louis: Louisiana Purchase Exposition Co.

The Chronicle. 1904a. The Chilocco Quartet. *The (Chicago) Chronicle*, Dec. 10.

————. 1904b. Writes History of Ainus. *The (Chicago) Chronicle*, Aug. 16.

Churchill, Ward, N. S. Hill, and M. J. Barlow. 1979. An Historical Overview of Twentieth-Century Native American Athletics. *The Indian Historian* 12(4):2–32.

Clevenger, Martha R., ed. 1996. *"Indescribably Grand" Diaries and Letters from the 1904 World's Fair.* St. Louis: Missouri Historical Society Press.

Clum, John P. 1928. Geronimo. *New Mexico Historical Review* 3(1):1–40; 3(2):121–44; 3(3):217–45.

Coats A. W. 1961. American Scholarship Comes of Age: The Louisiana Purchase Exposition 1904. *Journal of the History of Ideas* 22(July):404–24.

Cohodas, Marvin. 1997. *Basket Weavers for the California Curio Trade: Elizabeth and Louise Hickox.* Tucson and Los Angeles: Univ. of Arizona Press and the Southwest Museum.

Cole, Douglas. 1985. *Captured Heritage: The Scramble for Northwest Coast Artifacts.* Vancouver and Seattle: Univ. of British Columbia Press and Univ. of Washington Press.

Cole, Fay-Cooper. 1931. George A. Dorsey. *American Anthropologist* 33(4):413–14.

————. 1935. Frederick Starr. *Dictionary of Biography* 17:532–33.

Coleman, M. C. 1993. *American Indian Children at School, 1850–1930.* Jackson: Univ. Press of Mississippi.

Coleman, Sarah, and Tristan T. Almazan. 2003. George A. Dorsey and James R. Murie: Notes and Manuscripts on Pawnee and Arikara Society and Religion, 1902–7. Archival Finding Aide. Chicago: Field Museum.

Collier, Donald, and Harry Tschopik Jr. 1954. The Role of Museums in American Anthropology. *American Anthropologist* 56(4):768–79.

Columbia Encyclopedia. 2001. Francis, David Rowland. *The Columbia Encyclopedia.* 6th ed. New York: Columbia Univ. Press.

Commissioner of Indian Affairs. 1905. The Indian Exhibits at the St. Louis Exposition. *Annual Report of the Commissioner of Indian Affairs for the Fiscal Year Ending June 30, 1904,* 51–57. Washington DC: Government Printing Office.

Coolidge, Mary Roberts. 1968. *Chinese Immigration.* Taipei, Taiwan: privately printed.

Cortinovis, Irene. 1977. China at the St. Louis World's Fair. *Missouri Historical Review* 72(1):59–66.

Crane, Susan M. 2000. *Museums and Memory.* Palo Alto CA: Stanford Univ. Press.

Crawford, Jack. 1982. Pioneer African Missionary: Samuel Phillips Verner. *Journal of Presbyterian History* 60(Spring):42–57.

Cross, Whitney R. 1953. WJ McGee and the Idea of Conservation. *Historian* 15(1):148–62.

Curti, Merle. 1950. America at the World's Fairs, 1851–1893. *The American Historical Review* 55(4):833–56.

Curtis, William E. 1904a. Pike Is a Novel Sight. *Chicago Record-Herald,* Oct. 14.

———. 1904b. Huge Exhibits by Isles. *Chicago Record-Herald,* Oct. 13.

———. 1904c. Many Improvements. A Decade's Progress. St. Louis Fair Compared with Chicago. *Washington Star* Sept. 29.

Darnell, Regna. 1971. The Professionalization of American Anthropology. *Social Science Information* 10:83–103.

———. 1998. *And Along Came Boas: Continuities and Revolution in Americanist Anthropology.* Amsterdam and Philadelphia: J. Benjamin Publishing Co.

———. 2001. *Invisible Genealogies: A History of Americanist Anthropology.* Lincoln: Univ. of Nebraska Press.

———. 2002. WJ McGee. In *Celebrating a Century of the American Anthropological Association: Presidential Portraits,* ed. Regna Darnell and Frederic W. Gleach, 1–4. Lincoln: Univ. of Nebraska Press.

Darrah, William C. 1951. *Powell of the Colorado.* Princeton: Princeton Univ. Press.

Darton, N. H. 1912. Memoir of WJ McGee. *Annals of the Association of American Geographers* 3:103–10.

Davis, William Harper. 1904. The International Congress of Arts and Sciences. *The Popular Science Monthly* 66(Nov.):5–32.

Dawley, Alan. 2003. *Changing the World: American Progressives in War and Revolution.* Princeton: Princeton Univ. Press.

Dearing, Mary R. 1971. Anita Newcomb McGee. In *Notable American Women, 1607–1950: A Biographical Dictionary,* ed. Edward T. James, 464–66. Cambridge: Harvard Univ. Press.

Debo, Angie. 1976. *Geronimo: The Man, His Time, His Place*. Norman: Univ. of Oklahoma Press.

de Coubertin, Pierre. 1979. *Olympic Memoirs*. Lausanne: International Olympic Committee.

Deloria, Vine Jr. 1981. The Indians. In *Buffalo Bill and the Wild West*, ed. George Weisman, 83–94. Pittsburgh: Univ. of Pittsburgh Press.

Demb, Sarah. 1998. David Ives Bushnell, Jr. (1875–1941). Collection Records, 1845–1942: A Finding Aid. Cambridge: Harvard Peabody Museum. http://www.oasis.harvard.edu/html/pea00006.html.

Densmore, Frances. 1906. The Music of the Filipinos. *American Anthropologist* 8(4):611–32.

Dewey, John. 1903. The St. Louis Congress of the Arts and Sciences. *Science* 18(452): 665.

Dilworth, Leah. 1996. *Imagining Indians in the Southwest: Persistent Visions of a Primitive Past*. Washington DC: Smithsonian Institution Press.

Dorsey, George A. 1894. The Study of Anthropology in American Colleges. *The Archaeologist* 2:368–73.

———. 1900. The Department of Anthropology of the Field Columbian Museum. *American Anthropologist* 2:247–65.

———. 1909a. One Hundred Installments of a Diary of a 47,000 Mile Journey. *Chicago Daily Tribune*, Aug. 16 to Nov. 23.

———. 1909b. Recent Progress in Anthropology at the Field Columbian Museum. *American Anthropologist*, n.s., 3:737–47.

———. 1925. *Why We Behave Like Human Beings*. New York: Harper and Brothers.

Duke, S. A. 1904. The Negro and the Fair. *St. Louis Daily Globe-Democrat*, Dec. 1.

Dyreson, Mark. 1993. The Playing Fields of Progress: American Athletic Nationalism and the 1904 St. Louis Olympics. *Gateway Heritage* (Fall):4–23.

———. 1998. *Making the American Team: Sport, Culture, and the Olympic Experience*. Urbana: Univ. of Illinois Press.

———. 2004. The "Physical Value" of Races: Anthropology and Athletics at the Louisiana Purchase Exposition. Paper presented at the International Congress of Olympics, St. Louis.

Eggan, Fred. 1979. H. R. Voth, Ethnologist. In *Hopi Material Culture: Artifacts Gathered by H. R. Voth in the Fred Harvey Collection*, ed. Barton Wright. Flagstaff and Phoenix: Northland Press and the Heard Museum.

Ellis, Clyde. 1996. Boarding School Life at the Kiowa-Comanche Agency, 1893–1920. *Historian* 58(4):777–93.

Encyclopedia Britannica. 2004. Kaffir. *Encyclopedia Britannica* CD-ROM. Chicago: Encyclopedia Britannica Co.

Everett, Marshal. 1904. *The Book of the Fair: The Greatest Exposition the World Has Ever Seen*. St. Louis: Louisiana Purchase Exposition Co.

Ewers, John C. 1978. *Murals in the Round: Painted Tipis of the Kiowa and Kiowa-Apache Indians*. Washington DC: Smithsonian Institution Press.

Farmer and Stock Grower. 1904. World's Fair Indian Exhibit News. *Farmer and Stock Grower* (Apr.) Chilocco, Oklahoma.

Fernlund, Kevin J. 2000. *William Henry Holmes and the Rediscovery of the American West*. Albuquerque: Univ. of New Mexico Press.

Findling, John E., and Kimberly D. Pelle. 1990. *Historical Dictionary of World's Fairs and Expositions, 1851–1998*. Westport CT: Greenwood Press.

———. 1996. *Historical Dictionary of the Modern Olympic Movement*. Westport CT: Greenwood Press.

Fletcher, Alice. 1906. Jury Report. In *Report of the Board of Lady Managers Final Report of the Louisiana Purchase Exposition Commission*. 59th Cong., 1st sess., S. Doc. 202, 480–481. Washington DC: Government Printing Office.

Fogelson, Raymond D. 1991. The Red Man in the White City. Vol. 3 of *Columbian Consequences: The Spanish Borderlands in Pan-American Perspective*, ed. David H. Thomas, 73–90. Washington DC: Smithsonian Institution Press.

Fontana, Bernard L. 1971. The Seri Indians in Perspective. In *The Seri Indians of Bahia Kino and Sonora, Mexico*, ed. WJ McGee. Glorieta NM: Rio Grande Press.

———. 2000. Introduction. In *Trails to Tiburon: The 1894 and 1895 Field Diaries of WJ McGee*, ed. Hazel McFeely Fontana. Tucson: Univ. of Arizona Press.

Fontana, Hazel McFeely, ed. 2000. *Trails to Tiburon: The 1894 and 1895 Field Diaries of WJ McGee*. Tucson: Univ. of Arizona Press.

Forbes, Jack D. 1990. The Manipulation of Race, Caste, and Identity: Classifying Afro-Americans, Native-Americans, and Red-Black People. *Journal
of Ethnic Studies* 17(4):1–51.

Ford, Clellan S. 1949. *Smoke from Their Fires: The Life of a Kwakiutl Chief.*
New Haven: Yale Univ. Press.

Fossett, Judith Jackson, and Jeffrey A. Tuckers, eds. 1997. *Race Consciousness:
African American Studies for the New Century.* New York: New York Univ.
Press.

Fowler, Don D. 2000. *A Laboratory of Anthropology: Science and Romanticism
in the American Southwest, 1846–1930.* Albuquerque: Univ. of New Mexico
Press.

Fox, Timothy J., and Duane R. Sneddeker. 1997. *From the Palaces to the Pike:
Visions of the 1904 World's Fair.* St. Louis: Missouri Historical Society
Press.

Francis, David R. 1913. *The Universal Exposition of 1904.* St. Louis: Louisiana
Purchase Exposition Co.

Garson, J. G. 1887. The International Agreement on the Classification and
Nomenclature of the Cephalic Index. *Journal of the Anthropological Institute of Great Britain and Ireland* 16(1):17–20.

Gems, Gerald R. 2004. The 1904 Anthropology Days and the Construction
of Whiteness. Paper presented at International Congress on the 1904 St.
Louis Olympic Games and Anthropology Days: A Centennial Retrospective. Univ. of Missouri-St. Louis.

Gillis, Frank E. 1904. *The South African Boer War Exhibition: The Greatest
and Most Realistic Military Spectacle Known in the History of the World.* St.
Louis: Louisiana Purchase Exposition Co.

Gillis, John R., ed. 1994. *Commemorations: The Politics of National Identity.*
Princeton: Princeton Univ. Press.

Gleach, Frederic W. 2003. Pocahontas at the Fair: Crafting Identities at the
1907 Jamestown Exposition. *Ethnohistory* 50(3):419–45.

Goode, George Brown. 1883. Report of the Assistant Director of the United
States National Museum for the Year 1881. *Annual Report of the Smithsonian
Institution for 1881,* 81–159. Washington DC: Government Printing Office.

———. 1895. *Annual Report of the United States National Museum for 1893.*
Washington DC: Government Printing Office.

Gould, Stephen J. 1977. *Ever Since Darwin*. New York: W. W. Norton.

———. 1981. *The Mismeasure of Man*. New York: W. W. Norton.

Green, Rayna, and John Troutman. 2000. "By the Waters of the Minnehaha": Music and Dance, Pageants and Princesses. In *Away from Home: American Indian Boarding School Experiences*, ed. Margaret Archuleta, Brenda Child, and K. Tsianina Lomawaima, 60–83. Phoenix: Heard Museum.

Greenhalgh, Paul. 1988. *Ephemeral Vistas: The Expositions Universelles, Great Exhibitions, and World's Fairs, 1851–1939*. Manchester: Manchester Univ. Press.

Grumet, Robert S., and Ronald L. Weber. 1982. Maritime Peoples of the Arctic and Northwest Coast at the Field Museum. *American Indian Art Magazine* 8(1):66–71.

Gulick, Luther H. 1899. Psychological, Pedagogical, and Religious Aspects of Group Games. *Pedagogical Seminary* 6(Mar.):135–51.

Haller, John S. 1975. *Outcasts from Evolution: Scientific Attitudes of Racial Inferiority, 1859–1900*. New York: McGraw-Hill.

Handelman, Don. 1990. *Models and Mirrors: Towards an Anthropology of Public Events*. Cambridge: Cambridge Univ. Press.

Hanihara, K. 1991. Dual Structure Model for the Population History of the Japanese. *Japanese Review* 2:1–3.

Hanson, John W. 1905. *The Official History of the St. Louis World's Fair*. St. Louis: The Louisiana Purchase Exposition Co.

Harris, Marvin. 1968. *The Rise of Anthropological Theory: A History of Theories of Culture*. New York: Thomas Y. Crowell.

Harris, Neil. 1975. All the World's a Melting Pot? Japan at American Fairs, 1876–1904. In *Mutual Images: American and Japanese Relations*, ed. Akira Iriye, 2–54. Cambridge: Harvard Univ. Press.

———. 1990. *Cultural Excursions: Marketing Appetites and Cultural Tastes in Modern America*. Chicago: Univ. of Chicago Press.

Harvey, Byron III. 1996. The Fred Harvey Company Collects Indian Art: Selected Remarks. In *The Great Southwest of the Fred Harvey Company and the Santa Fe Railway*, ed. Marta Weigle and Barbara A. Babcock, 69–85. Phoenix: Heard Museum.

Hays, Samuel P. 1959. *Conservation and the Gospel of Efficiency: The Progressive Conservation Movement, 1890–1920*. Cambridge: Cambridge Univ. Press.

Henderson, Alice Palmer. 1906. Jury Report. *Report of the Board of Lady Managers.* In *Final Report of the Louisiana Purchase Exposition Commission.* 59th Cong., 1st sess., S. Doc. 202, 481–82. Washington DC: Government Printing Office.

Henry, Wade A. 2000. Imagining the Great White Mother and the Great King: Aboriginal Tradition and Royal Representation in the "Great Powwow" of 1901. *Journal of the Canadian Historical Association* 11:87–108.

Hewett, Edgar L. 1915. Ancient American at the Panama-California Exposition. *The Theosophical Path*, no pages.

Higginbotham, Harlow. 1898. *Report of the President to the Board of Directors of the World's Columbian Exposition.* Chicago: Rand, McNally and Co.

Hill, Richmond C. 1912. *A Great White Indian Chief: Col. Fred Cummins.* Privately printed, n.p.

Hinckley, Ted C. 1967. When the Boer War Came to St. Louis. *Missouri Historical Review* 11(3):285–303.

———. 1982. *Alaskan John G. Brady: Missionary, Businessman, Judge, and Governor, 1878–1918.* Columbus: Ohio State Univ. Press for Miami Univ.

Hinsley, Curtis M. Jr. 1981. *Savages and Scientists: The Smithsonian Institution and the Development of American Anthropology, 1846–1906.* Washington DC: Smithsonian Institution Press.

Hirschfelder, Arlene, Paulette Fairbanks Molin, and Yvonne Wakim. 1999. *American Indian Stereotypes in the World of Children.* 2nd edition. Lanham: Scarecrow Press.

H. Jay Smith Exploring Company. 1893. *The Cliff-Dwellers.* Chicago: Privately printed for the H. Jay Smith Exploring Company.

Hobsbawm, Eric. 1989. *The Age of Empire: 1875–1914.* New York: Vintage Books.

Hodge, Frederick W. 1912. WJ McGee. *American Anthropologist* 14(4):683–87.

Hofmann, Phil. 1904. A Study of the Feet of Barefooted Peoples in the Purpose of Comparison with Those of Shoe-wearers. Unpublished manuscript, WJ McGee Papers, box 16, Library of Congress.

Hoganson, Kristin L. 1998. *Fighting for American Manhood: How Gender Politics Provoked the Spanish-American and Philippine-American Wars.* New Haven: Yale Univ. Press.

Holmes, William Henry. 1898. Anthropological Exhibit of the U.S. National Museum at the Omaha Exposition. *Science*, n.s., 8(184):37–40.

————. 1900. Ancient Monuments of Yucatan. *Monumental Record* 1:140–42.

————. 1902. Classification and Arrangement of the Exhibits of an Anthropological Museum. *Science* 16:487–504.

————. 1903a. The Exhibit of the Department of Anthropology. *Annual Report of the United States National Museum for 1901*, 200–18. Washington DC: Government Printing Office.

————. 1903b. Report of the Anthropology Department. *Annual Report of the United States National Museum for 1901*, 21–29. Washington DC: Government Printing Office.

————. 1904. The Exhibits of the Smithsonian Institution in the Government Building at the St. Louis Exposition. *American Anthropologist* 6(4):754.

————. 1905. Report on the Exhibit of the Department of Anthropology at the Louisiana Purchase Exposition. Folder 1 and List of Objects, folder 7, record group 70, box 7, Smithsonian Institution Archives.

————. 1907a. Report of the Chief. *Twenty-fourth Annual Report of the Bureau of American Ethnology for 1902–1903*, vii–xl. Washington DC: Government Printing Office.

————. 1907b. Report of the Chief. *Twenty-fifth Annual Report of the Bureau of American Ethnology to the Secretary of the Smithsonian, for 1903–1904*, iv–xxix. Washington DC: Government Printing Office.

————. 1908. Report of the Chief. *Twenty-sixth Annual Report of the Bureau of American Ethnology for 1904–1905*, vii–xxxi. Washington DC: Government Printing Office.

Holmes, William H., and William J McGee. 1901. Plan for the Anthropology Department of the Louisiana Purchase Exposition. LPEC files, Missouri Historical Society.

Honour, Hugh. 1975. *The New Golden Land: European Images of America from the Discovery to the Present Time*. Englewood Cliffs NJ: Prentice Hall.

Horsman, Reginald. 1981. *Race and Manifest Destiny: The Origins of American Racial Anglo-Saxonism*. Cambridge: Harvard Univ. Press.

Hough, Walter. 1899. *The Moki Snake Dance*. Chicago: Passenger Department, Atchison, Topeka, and Santa Fe Railway System.

————. 1923. Alice Cunningham Fletcher. *American Anthropologist* 25:254–58.

————. 1933. William Henry Holmes. *American Anthropologist* 35:752–64.

Howard, Kathleen L., and Diana F. Pardue. 1996. *Inventing the Southwest: The Fred Harvey Company and Native American Art.* Flagstaff: Northland Press.

Hoxie, Frederick E. 1984. *A Final Promise: The Campaign to Assimilate the Indians, 1880–1920.* Cambridge: Cambridge Univ. Press.

Hrdlička, Aleš. 1903. Proposed Plan of a Joint U.S. National Museum and World's Fair Anthropometric Laboratory, St. Louis, Missouri. WJ McGee Papers, item 651, box 19, Library of Congress.

————. 1904. Directions for Collecting Information and Specimens for Physical Anthropology. *Bulletin: United States National Museum* 39(Part R):14–15.

————. 1906. Brains and Brain Preservatives. *Proceedings of the United States National Museum* 30:245–320.

————. 1907. Measurements of the Cranial Fossae. *Proceedings of the United States National Museum* 32:177–232.

————. 1908. Physical Anthropology and Its Aims. *Science*, n.s., 38:33–43.

————. 1917a. The Genesis of the American Indian. *Proceedings of the Nineteenth International Congress of Americanists*, 559–68. Washington DC: Government Printing Office.

————. 1917b. The Most Ancient Skeletal Remains of Man. *Smithsonian Institution Annual Report for 1916*, 49–52. Washington DC: Government Printing Office.

————. 1925. *The Old Americans.* Baltimore: Williams and Wilkins.

Huckel, John. 1905. *American Indians: First Families of the Southwest.* Chicago: Passenger Department, Atchison, Topeka, and Santa Fe Railway System.

Hutchin, George L. 1905. Hit the Trail Is the Favorite Diversion at the Lewis and Clark Exposition. *Lewis and Clark Journal* 3(June):48–58.

Indian School Journal, Bureau of Indian Affairs. 1904a. Among the Patagonians. *Indian School Journal* 4(Oct.):69. Repr. from *Chicago Record-Herald.*

————. 1904b. Black Coyote, Chief of the Arapaho (Illustration). *Indian School Journal* 4(Oct.):15.

————. 1904c. Can See and Judge. *Indian School Journal* 4(Oct.):21.

————. 1904d. The Champion Team. *Indian School Journal* 4(21):1.

————. 1904e. Densmore Lecture. *Indian School Journal* 2(23):2.

————. 1904f. Exhibit News Notes. *Indian School Journal* 4(10–79):1; (Oct.):46, 81.

————. 1904g. Field Sports and Winner. *Indian School Journal* 4(9):4.

————. 1904h. From the Reporters' Notebook. *Indian School Journal* 4(9):4.

————. 1904i. "Good" Indians. *Indian School Journal* 4(36):2. Repr. from *St. Louis Post-Dispatch*, July 6.

————. 1904j. Heard after the Concert. *Indian School Journal* 4(46):1.

————. 1904k. How Indians Learn. *Indian School Journal* 4(23):1. Repr. from *St. Louis Star*.

————. 1904l. In Honor of Miss Reel. *Indian School Journal* 4(29):1.

————. 1904m. Indian Art Rewarded. *Indian School Journal* 4(Oct.):67–68. Repr. from *St. Louis Republic*.

————. 1904n. Indian Exhibit Opening: A Good Day and a Very Large Crowd in Attendance. *Indian School Journal* 4(9):1.

————. 1904o. The Indian School at the Fair. *Indian School Journal* 5(1):14.

————. 1904p. Indian Wafer Bread. *Indian School Journal* 4(26):2. Repr. satirical column from the *St. Louis Globe-Democrat*.

————. 1904q. Look Like Japanese. *Indian School Journal* 4(40):1. Repr. from *The Exchange*.

————. 1904r. Most Interesting Exhibit. *Indian School Journal* 4(79):3. Repr. from *The Jefferson*.

————. 1904s. Patagonian Rivals. *Indian School Journal* 4(52):1. Repr. from *Pittsburgh Dispatch*.

————. 1904t. Patagonians and Ainus. *Indian School Journal* 4(52):1. Repr. from *Pittsburgh Dispatch*.

————. 1904u. Patagonians Like Us. *Indian School Journal* 4(8):1.

————. 1904v. The Right Kind of a School. *Indian School Journal* 4(1):14. Repr. from *Los Angeles Times*.

————. 1904w. Said of the Indian's Way. *Indian School Journal* 4(19):3.

————. 1904x. Something of the Pygmies. *Indian School Journal* 4(35):2. Repr. from *St. Louis Republic*, July 6.

————. 1904y. A Trip to Bellville. *Indian School Journal* 4(54):1.

————. 1904aa. Untitled Articles. *Indian School Journal* 4(12):4; (21):2; (29):1; (65):1; (79):4; (Oct.):68, 80.

————. 1904bb. Visitors' Remarks. *Indian School Journal* 4(13–65):1; (Oct.):54–56.

Indian Territory Bulletin. 1904. No title. *Indian Territory Bulletin* no. 12. Oklahoma City: no publisher.

Jacknis, Ira. 1991. *Northwest Coast Indian Culture and the World's Columbian Exposition.* Vol. 3 of *Columbian Consequences: The Spanish Borderlands in Pan-American Perspective*, ed. David H. Thomas, 91–118. Washington DC: Smithsonian Institution Press.

————. 2002. *The Storage Box of Tradition: Kwakiutl Art, Anthropologists, and Museums, 1881–1981.* Washington DC: Smithsonian Institution Press.

Jacobs, Alexander Eli. 1903. *World's Fair Manual with Maps of Grounds and Description of Buildings.* St. Louis: Ivory City Publishing and Novelty Co.

James, Harry C. 1974. *Pages from Hopi History.* Tucson: Univ. of Arizona Press.

Jenks, Albert E. 1904. Anthropology. In *Official Handbook of the Philippines and Catalogue of the Philippine Exhibit*, 261–62. Manila: Bureau of Public Printing.

————. 1905. *The Bontoc Igorot.* Department of the Interior Ethnological Survey, Publication 1. Manila: Bureau of Printing.

Jenks, Maud. 1951. *Death Stalks the Philippine Wilds: Letters of Maud Huntley Jenks*, ed. Carmen Nelson Richards. Minneapolis: Lund Press.

Johnson, William O. Jr. 1972. *All That Glitters Is Not Gold: The Olympic Games.* New York: G. P. Putnam's Sons.

Johnston, William H. 1905. First Battalion Philippine Scouts. *Infantry Journal* 1:30–31.

Jones, William T. 1904. *Annual Report of the Commissioner of Indian Affairs for the Fiscal Year Ending June 30, 1904.* Washington DC: Government Printing Office.

Karnow, Stanley. 1989. *In Our Image: America's Empire in the Philippines.* New York: Foreign Policy Association.

Kasson, John F. 1978. *Amusing the Million: Coney Island at the Turn of the Century.* New York: Hill and Wang.

Kasson, Joy S. 2000. *Buffalo Bill's Wild West: Celebrity, Memory, and Popular History.* New York: Hill and Wang.

Keefer, Karen M. 1988. Dirty Water and Clean Toilets: Medical Aspects of the 1904 Louisiana Purchase Exposition. *Gateway Heritage* 9(1):32–37.

Kelly, William H. 1977. *Cocopa Ethnography*. Anthropological Papers of the University of Arizona 29. Tucson: Univ. of Arizona Press.

Keyes, Charles. 1913. WJ McGee, Geologist, Anthropologist, Hydrologist. *Annals of Iowa* 2(3):6–10.

Kieran, John, and Arthur Daley. 1965. *The Story of the Olympic Games: 776 BC to 1964*. Philadelphia: J. B. Lippincott.

Kirshenblatt-Gimblett, Barbara. 1998. *Destination Culture: Tourism, Museums, and Heritage*. Berkeley: Univ. of California Press.

Knowlton, F. H. 1913. Memoir of WJ McGee. *Geological Society of America: Bulletin* 24:18–29.

Kramer, Paul. 1998. The Pragmatic Empire: U.S. Anthropology and Colonial Politics in the Occupied Philippines, 1898–1916. PhD diss., Princeton Univ.

Kroeber, Alfred L. 1920. Yumans of the Lower Colorado. *University of California Publications in American Archaeology and Ethnology* 16(8):475–85.

Lacey, Michael. 1979. The Mysteries of Earth-Making Dissolve: A Study of Washington's Intellectual Community and the Origins of American Environmentalism in the Late Nineteenth Century. PhD diss., George Washington Univ.

Laidley, Leonidas. 1905. Report on the Department of Medicine to Frederick Skiff, March 1, 1905. LPE files, Missouri Historical Society.

Lamphere, Louise. 2004. Unofficial Histories: A Vision of Anthropology from the Margins. *American Anthropologist* 106(1): 126–39.

Laurie, Clayton. 1994–95. An Oddity of Empire: The Philippine Scouts and the 1904 World's Fair. *Gateway Heritage* 15(3):44–55.

Lears, T. J. Jackson. 1981. *No Place of Grace: Antimodernism and the Transformation of American Culture, 1880–1920*. New York: Pantheon.

Lehmann, F. W. 1901. Anthropology Committee Report to David Francis, August 31. LPEC files, Missouri Historical Society.

Lerner, Michael. 1988–89. "Hoping for a Splendid Summer": African American St. Louis, Ragtime, and the Louisiana Purchase Exposition. *Gateway Heritage* 19(3):28–41.

Leupp, Francis E. 1905. The Indian Exhibit at the Portland Exhibition. *An-*

nual Report of the Department of the Interior for the Fiscal Year Ending June 30, 1905. Indian Affairs, pt. 1, 56–57. Washington DC: Government Printing Office.

Liebenguth, Jane Anne. 1979. Music at the Louisiana Purchase Exposition. *Bulletin of the Missouri Historical Society* 36(1):27–34.

Lindfors, Bernth. 1983. Circus Africans. *Journal of American Culture* 6(2):9–14.

Literary Digest. 1905. Portland's Successful Exposition. *Literary Digest* 31 (Oct. 28):3.

Littlefield, Alice. 1989. The BIA Boarding School: Theories of Resistance and Social Reproduction. *Humanity and Society* 13(4):428–41.

Loland, Sigmund. 1994. Pierre de Coubertin's Ideology of Olympism from the Perspective of the History of Ideas. In *Critical Reflections on Olympic Ideology*, ed. Robert Barney and Klaus Meier, 26–45. London, Ontario: Univ. of Western Ontario.

Lomawaima, K. Tsianina. 1994. *They Called It Prairie Light: The Story of Chilocco Indian School*. Lincoln: Univ. of Nebraska Press.

———. 1996. Estelle Reel, Superintendent of Indian Schools, 1898–1910: Politics, Curriculum, and Land. *Journal of American Indian Education* 4:5–31.

Lotani, Yoshinobu. 1999. Ainu Collections in North America: Documentation Projects and the Frederick Starr Collections. In *Ainu: Spirit of a Northern People*, ed. William W. Fitzhugh and Chisato O. Dubreuil, 136–47. Washington DC and Seattle: Smithsonian Institution Press and Univ. of Washington Press.

Louisiana Purchase Exposition Company—Departmental Reports, Publicity, and Catalogues. 1903. *Chronology of the Louisiana Purchase Exposition*. St. Louis: Louisiana Purchase Exposition Co.

———. 1904a. *Military Camps and Special Days and Events: A Program*. St. Louis: Louisiana Purchase Exposition Co.

———. 1904b. *Official Directory of the Louisiana Purchase Corporation*. St. Louis: Louisiana Purchase Exposition Co.

———. 1904c. *Physical Culture: Division of Exhibits*. St. Louis: Louisiana Purchase Exposition Co.

———. 1904d. Promotional Literature. *Universal Exposition, Magnitude and Scope*. St. Louis: Louisiana Purchase Exposition Co.

————. 1905a. Report of the Bureau of Music. St. Louis: Louisiana Purchase Exposition Co.

————. 1905b. *Final Report of the Louisiana Purchase Exposition Company, 1906.* U.S. 59th Cong., 1st Sess., Doc. 202, XIV, entire volume.

Louisiana Purchase Exposition Company—Official Daily Program. 1904a. Ceylon's Quaint Pavilion. *Official Daily Program* May 7:14.

————. 1904b. Chippewas Arrive. *Official Daily Program* May 16:14.

————. 1904c. Children's Day. *Official Daily Program* Aug. 8:1.

————. 1904d. Congress of Primitive Peoples. *Official Daily Program* Aug. 8:5.

————. 1904e. Cummins' Wild West Show. *Official Daily Program* June 10:5.

————. 1904f. Cummins' Wild West Show. *Official Daily Program* July 22:3.

————. 1904g. Esquimaux Village. *Official Daily Program* June 27:7.

————. 1904h. Ethnology Building Opening. *Official Daily Program* May 31:5.

————. 1904i. Field Day for Primitive Peoples. *Official Daily Program* Aug. 11:2.

————. 1904j. Geronimo. *Official Daily Program* May 19:13.

————. 1904k. The Government Indian Band. *Official Daily Program* July 4:7.

————. 1904l. Government Indian School Opening Day. *Official Daily Program* June 1:15.

————. 1904m. Haskell Indian Band. *Official Daily Program* June 17:13.

————. 1904n. Indian Congress. *Official Daily Program* July 1:5.

————. 1904o. Indians at Work. *Official Daily Program* May 6:13.

————. 1904p. Indian School Band. *Official Daily Program* May 3:13.

————. 1904q. Indian School Entertainment. *Official Daily Program* Sept. 14:7.

————. 1904r. Indian School Exhibit. *Official Daily Program* May 31:27.

————. 1904s. Indian School Items. *Official Daily Program* June 16:8.

————. 1904t. Igorotte Village. *Official Daily Program* May 19:11.

————. 1904u. Kickapoos Arrive. *Official Daily Program* June 11:11.

————. 1904v. Lecture. *Official Daily Program* June 21:16.

————. 1904w. Philippine Daily Program. *Official Daily Program* June 24:5.

———. 1904x. Teepee Raising. *Official Daily Program* July 4:3.

———. 1904y. Tree Dwelling Moros. *Official Daily Program* June 3:23.

———. 1904z. U.S. Government Building. *Official Daily Program* May 19:9.

———. 1904aa. U.S. Government Indian School Exhibits. *Official Daily Program* May 30:12.

Louisiana Purchase Exposition Company—Official Photograph Album. 1905. *Official Photograph Album.* Reprinted and reedited as an eight-volume series entitled *The Greatest of Expositions.* St. Louis: Louisiana Purchase Exposition Co.

Louisiana Purchase Exposition Corporation—The Piker. 1904a. Advertisement *The Piker* 1(2):16.

———. 1904b. The Official List of Concessionaires. *The Piker* 1(2):41–44.

———. 1904c. The Pike. *The Piker* 1(2):20.

Louisiana Purchase Exposition Corporation—World's Fair Bulletin. 1901. Indian Mounds in Forest Park. *World's Fair Bulletin* 3(2):9.

———. 1902. The Philippines Display. *World's Fair Bulletin* 3(May):20.

———. 1903. Samuel M. McCowan. *World's Fair Bulletin* 5(1):30, 82.

———. 1904a. Geronimo: Famous Apache Chief Now at the World's Fair. *World's Fair Bulletin* 5(9):71.

———. 1904b. The Jurors of Awards: Philippine Section. *World's Fair Bulletin* 5(12):28.

———. 1904c. Official List of Special Days and Events. *World's Fair Bulletin* 5(May):54.

———. 1904d. The Pike. *World's Fair Bulletin* 5(7):4–5.

———. 1904e. Popular Prices of Admission Will Prevail to Shows on the Ten Million Dollar Pike. *World's Fair Bulletin* 5(8):6.

———. 1904f. The Pygmies Now on World's Fair Grounds. *World's Fair Bulletin* 5(10):44.

———. 1904g. Pygmy Orchestra. *World's Fair Bulletin* 5(11):40.

———. 1904h. Savage Classes. *World's Fair Bulletin* 5(10):9.

———. 1904i. A Unique War Dance. *World's Fair Bulletin* 5(9):4.

———. 1904j. United States Indian Exhibit at World's Fair Shows Marked Progress Made by the Savages. *World's Fair Bulletin* 5(9):71.

———. 1904k. Untitled Notes. *World's Fair Bulletin* 5(3):40.

———. 1904l. WJ McGee. *World's Fair Bulletin* 5(5):4.

Lusk, Mrs. Charles. 1905. My Impression of the Fair. *Indian School Journal* 5(2):51–54.

MacAloon, John, ed. 1984. *Rite, Drama, Festival, Spectacle: Rehearsals Toward a Theory of Cultural Performance*. Philadelphia: Institute for the Study of Human Issues Press.

MacCanell, Dean. 1973. Staged Authenticity: Arrangements of Social Space in Tourist Settings. *American Journal of Sociology* 79(3):589–603.

MacMechen, John. 1904. The Pike and Its Attractions. *The Cosmopolitan* 37(5):622.

Macnair, Peter L. 1982. The Northwest Coast Collections: Legacy of a Living Culture. *Field Museum of Natural History Bulletin* 53(4):3–12.

Magnaghi, Russell M. 1983–84. America Views Her Indians at the 1904 World's Fair. *Gateway Heritage* 4(3):20–29.

Marion, Rose. 1904. Chicago Co-Eds Who Hitched Their Wagon to Prof. Starr Are Finding Anthropology a Live Study at World's Fair. *St. Louis Post-Dispatch*, Aug. 31.

Mark, Joan. 1980. *Four Anthropologists: An American Science in its Early Years*. New York: Science History Publications.

Marks, Jonathan. 2002. Aleš Hrdlička. In *Celebrating a Century of the American Anthropological Association: Presidential Portraits*, ed. Regna Darnell and Frederic W. Gleach, 45–48. Lincoln: Univ. of Nebraska Press.

Marquis, Albert Nelson, ed. 1936. *Who's Who in America: A Biographical Dictionary of Notable Living Men and Women in the United States*. Chicago: A. N. Marquis Co.

Marriott, Alice. 1948. *Maria: The Potter of San Ildefonso*. Norman: Univ. of Oklahoma Press.

Mason, Otis T. 1887. The Occurrence of Similar Inventions in Areas Widely Apart. *Science* 9:534–35.

———. 1890. Anthropology in Paris during the Exposition of 1889. *American Anthropologist*, o.s., 3(1):27–34.

———. 1892. Report of the Anthropology Department. *Annual Report of the United States National Museum for 1891*, 135–43. Washington DC: Government Printing Office.

———. 1894a. Ethnological Exhibit. *Annual Report of the United States National Museum for 1892*, 211. Washington DC: Government Printing Office.

————. 1894b. Summary of Progress in Anthropology for 1893. *Smithsonian Institution Annual Report for 1893*, 601–17. Washington DC: Government Printing Office.

————. 1895. Report of the Anthropology Department. *Annual Report of the United States National Museum for 1893*, 58–90. Washington DC: Government Printing Office.

Mathieu, Caroline. 1989. Invitation au Voyage. In *1889: La Tour Eiffel et l'Exposition Universelle*. ed. C. Mathieu, 102–42. Paris: Éditions de la Réunion des Musées Nationaux.

Mattie, Erik. 1998. *World's Fairs*. New York: Princeton Architectural Press.

McCabe, James D. 1876. *The Illustrated History of the Centennial Exhibition*. Philadelphia: National Publishers.

M'Carty, W. C. 1903. The Tribes Last Stand. *Bridgeport (Conn.) Herald*, Dec. 6.

McCowan, Samuel M. 1899. Omaha Exhibition. *Annual Report to the Commissioner of Indian Affairs for the Fiscal Year Ending June 30, 1899*, 384–85. Washington DC: Government Printing Office.

————. 1904a. Awards. *Indian School Journal* 4(Oct.):50.

————. 1904b. The Lessons of the Indian School. *Indian School Journal* 4(Oct.):58.

————. 1904c. Résumé of Government's Indian Exhibit, L.P.E. *Indian School Journal* 4(Oct.):47.

————. 1904d. School Activities. *Indian School Journal* 4(Oct.):46.

————. 1904e. Untitled article. *Indian School Journal* 4(55):1.

————. 1904f. Untitled quote as a newspaper article "From the Reporters' Notebook." Repr. in *Indian School Journal* 4(9):4.

————. 1904g. Untitled comments. *Indian School Journal* 4(Oct.):51.

————. 1905a. Report to the Commissioner of Indian Affairs on the Louisiana Purchase Exposition. In *Commissioner of Indian Affairs: Annual Report of the Department of the Interior, Indian Affairs, part 1, for the Fiscal Year Ending June 30, 1904*, 51–57. Washington DC: Government Printing Office.

————. 1905b. Résumé of Government's Indian Exhibit. Included in McGee (1905b, 117–31).

————. 1906. United States Government Indian Exhibit. *Final Report of the Louisiana Purchase Exposition Commission*. 59th Cong., 1st Sess., Senate

Document 202, 343–47. Washington DC: Government Printing Office.

McCusick, Marshall. 1991. *The Davenport Conspiracy Revisited*. Ames: Iowa State Univ. Press.

McGee, Emma R. 1905. *Life of WJ McGee*. Farley IA: Privately printed.

McGee, WJ. 1888a. The Geology of the Head of Chesapeake Bay. *Annual Report of the United States Geological Survey*, vol. 7, 537–646. Washington DC: Government Printing Office.

———. 1888b. Paleolithic Man in America: His Antiquity and Environment. *Popular Science Monthly* 34 (Nov.):20–36.

———. 1889a. The Geological Antecedents of Man in the Potomac Valley. *American Anthropologist*, o.s., 2(3):227–34.

———. 1889b. An Obsidian Implement from Pleistocene Deposits in Nevada. *American Anthropologist*, o.s., 2(4):301–12.

———. 1890a. Remarks on Certain Peculiarities of Drainage in the Southeastern United States. *Bulletin of the Geological Society of America* 1:448–49.

———. 1890b. Some Principles of Evidence Relating to the Antiquity of Man. *Proceedings of the American Association for the Advancement of Science* 38:333.

———. 1891. The Pleistocene History of Northeastern Iowa. *Annual Report of the United States Geological Survey for 1890*, pt. 1, 189–577. Washington DC: Government Printing Office.

———. 1892. Comparative Chronology. *American Anthropologist*, o.s., 5(4):327–44.

———. 1893. Man and the Glacial Period. *American Anthropologist*, o.s., 6(1):85–95.

———. 1894a. The Citizen. *American Anthropologist*, o.s., 7:352–57.

———. 1894b. *The Earth, the Home of Man*. Anthropological Society of Washington, Special Papers no. 2. Washington DC.

———. 1894c. The Potable Waters of the Eastern United States. *Annual Report of the United States Geological Survey* 14(2):1–47. Washington DC: Government Printing Office.

———. 1895a. The Beginning of Agriculture. *American Anthropologist*, o.s., 8(3):350–75.

———. 1895b. Some Principles of Nomenclature. *American Anthropologist*, o.s., 8(3):279–86.

———. 1895c. Seri Notebooks and Journals for 1895 and 1896 field trips. WJ McGee Papers, Library of Congress.

———. 1896a. The Beginning of Marriage. *American Anthropologist,* o.s., 9:371–83.

———. 1896b. Expedition to Papagueria and Seriland. *American Anthropologist,* o.s., 9(3):383–91.

———. 1896c. Expedition to Seriland. *Science* 3(66):493–505.

———. 1896d. The Relation of Institutions to Environment. *Annual Report of the Smithsonian Institution for 1895,* 701–11. Washington DC: Government Printing Office.

———. 1897a. The Beginning of Zooculture. *American Anthropologist,* o.s., 10(2):215–30.

———. 1897b. The Science of Humanity. *Science* 6(142):413–33; *American Anthropologist,* o.s., 10(2):241–72.

———. 1898a. Piratical Acculturation. *American Anthropologist,* o.s., 11(2):243–60.

———. 1898b. The Seri Indians. *Seventeenth Annual Report of the Bureau of American Ethnology for 1896,* pt. 1, 1–298. Washington DC: Government Printing Office.

———. 1899. The Trend of Human Progress. *American Anthropologist* 1(4):401–47.

———. 1901a. Man's Place in Nature. *American Anthropologist* 3(1):1–13.

———. 1901b. The Old Yuma Trail. *National Geographic Magazine* 12(3):103–7; (4):129–43.

———. 1902. Mortuary Ceremonies of the Cocopa Indians. *American Anthropologist* 4(4):480.

———. 1904a. Anthropology. *World's Fair Bulletin* 5(5):4–10.

———. 1904b. Anthropology at the Louisiana Purchase Exposition. *Science* 22:823.

———. 1904c. Department N—Anthropology. *Official Exhibit Catalogue.* St. Louis: Louisiana Purchase Exposition Co.

———. 1904d. Lecture on the Pygmies. *Indian School Journal* 4(40):1.

———. 1904e. Monthly Reports and Fiscal Reports to Skiff. WJ McGee Papers, boxes 16 and 28, Library of Congress.

————. 1904f. Opportunities in Anthropology at the World's Fair. *Science* 20(503):253–55.

————. 1904g. Strange Races of Men. *World's Work* (Aug.):5185–88.

————. 1905a. *Annual Report for 1904*. Pittsburgh: Carnegie Museum of Natural History.

————. 1905b. In the Desert. *San Francisco Independent*, n.d., n.p.

————. 1905c. *Official Catalogue, Department—Anthropology*. Rev. ed. St. Louis: Louisiana Purchase Exposition Co.

————. 1905d. Report of the Department of Anthropology to Frederick J. V. Skiff, director, Universal Exposition of 1904. Division of Exhibits, May 10. LPE files, file series 3, subseries 11, Missouri Historical Society.

————. 1906. Anthropology and Its Larger Problems. Vol. 5 of *Congress of Arts and Science: Universal Exposition, St. Louis, 1904*, ed. H. J. Rogers, 449–67. Boston: Houghton Mifflin.

————. 1912a. Symptomatic Development of Cancer. *Science* 36 (Sept. 13):348–50.

————. 1912b. Principles Underlying Water Rights. *Official Proceedings of the Nineteenth International Irrigation Congress, 7 December 1911*, 309–20.

McLendon, Sally. 1990. Pomo Baskets: The Legacy of William and Mary Benson. *Native Peoples* 4(1):26–33.

McLendon, Sally, and Brenda Shears Holland. 1979. The Basketmakers: The Pomoans in California. In *The Ancestors: Native Artisans of the Americas*, ed. Anna C. Roosevelt and James G. E. Smith, 103–29. New York: Museum of the American Indian.

McNitt, Frank. 1957. *Richard Wetherill, Anasazi: Pioneer Explorer of Southwestern Ruins*. Albuquerque: Univ. of New Mexico Press.

The Medical Brief. 1903. Emergency Hospital, Louisiana Purchase Exposition. *The Medical Brief* 31(Feb.):296–99.

Medical Fortnightly. 1905. Emergency Hospital at the Fair. *Medical Fortnightly* 28(July 10):326.

Medical Record. 1903. Medical Aspects of the World's Fair. *Medical Record* 44(July 22):124–26.

Meltzer, David J., and Robert C. Dunnell. 1992. Introduction. *The Archaeology of William Henry Holmes*, ed. David J. Meltzer and Robert C. Dunnell, vii–i. Washington DC: Smithsonian Institution Press.

Miller, R. B. 1978. Anthropology and Institutionalization: Frederick Starr at the University of Chicago, 1892–1893. *Kroeber Anthropological Society* 51:49–60.

Milton, John R. 1981. The Origin and Development of the Concept of the Laws of Nature. *Archives of European Sociology* 22:173–95.

Moenster, Kathleen. 1987. Jessie Beals: Official Photographer of the 1904 World's Fair. *Gateway Heritage* 3(2):22–29.

Montague, M. F. Ashley. 1960. *A Handbook of Anthropometry.* Springfield IL: Charles C. Thomas.

Moore, Susan J. 2000. Mapping Empire in Omaha and Buffalo: World's Fairs and the Spanish-American War. In *The Legacy of the Mexican and Spanish-American Wars: Legal, Literary, and Historical Perspectives,* ed. Cornelia Candelaria and Gary K. Keller, 111–26. Temie: Bilingual Press.

Morgan, Lewis Henry. 1877. *Ancient Society, or Researches in the Lines of Human Progress from Savagery through Barbarism to Civilization.* New York: Henry Holt.

————. 1954. *League of the Ho-De-No Sau-Nee, or Iroquois.* New Haven CT: Human Relations Area Files. (Orig. pub. 1851.)

Morgan, Thomas. 1894. *Annual Report of the Commissioner of Indian Affairs for the Fiscal year Ending June 30, 1893.* Washington DC: Government Printing Office.

Moses, Lester G. 1984. *The Indian Man: A Biography of James Mooney.* Urbana: Univ. of Illinois Press.

————. 1991. Indians on the Midway: Wild West Shows and the Indian Bureau at World's Fairs, 1893–1904. *South Dakota History* 21(2):205–22.

————. 1996. *Wild West Shows and the Images of American Indians, 1883–1933.* Albuquerque: Univ. of New Mexico Press.

Muccigrosso, Robert. 1993. *Celebrating the New World: Chicago's Columbian Exposition of 1893.* Chicago: I. R. Dee.

Münsterberg, Hugo. 1903. The St. Louis Congress of Arts and Science. *Science* 18(451):1–8.

————. 1904. The International Congress of Arts and Sciences. *The Journal of Philosophy, Psychology, and Scientific Methods* 1(1): entire issue.

Murie, James. 1914. Pawnee Indian Societies. *Anthropological Papers* 11:543–644. New York: American Museum of Natural History.

National Geographic Magazine. 1903. Geographic Notes. *The National Geographic Magazine* 14(June):254–55.

Newell, Alfred C. 1904. The Philippine Peoples. *World's Work* 8:5128–45.

New York Evening Post. 1904. An Exposition Museum. *New York Evening Post*, Oct. 26.

New York Times. 1901. President McKinley Favors Reciprocity. *New York Times*, Sept. 6.

———. 1903. To Exhibit Man at the St. Louis Fair. *New York Times*, Nov. 1.

———. 1904a. Chief Joseph Dead. "The Napoleon of Indians," Whom Gen. Miles Finally Subdued. *New York Times*, Sept. 24.

———. 1904b. Letter to the editor, signed Impressed. St. Louis World's Fair. *New York Times*, Aug. 5, 9.

———. 1904c. Totem Poles Upside Down. *New York Times*, May 5.

———. 1904d. Woodworth of Columbia University Has Been Appointed to Go to St. Louis. *New York Times*, Apr. 30.

———. 1904e. World's Fair Closed; Over 18,000,000 Saw It. *New York Times*, Dec. 2.

Nicks, Trudy. 1999. Indian Villages and Entertainments: Setting the Stage for Tourist Souvenir Sales. In *Unpacking Culture: Art and Commodity in Colonial and Postcolonial Worlds*, ed. Ruth Phillips and Christopher Steiner, 301–15. Berkeley: Univ. of California Press.

Obear, Howard. 1904. *A Trip around the Main Picture and through the Plateau of States: Louisiana Purchase Exposition*. Chicago: Cable Company.

Olympia. 1904. Time to Quit. *Olympia*, June 10.

Omoto, Keiichi, and Naruya Saitou. 1997. Genetic Origins of the Japanese. *American Journal of Physical Anthropology* 102(4):437–46.

Oxendine, Joseph B. 1988. *American Indian Sports Heritage*. Lincoln: Univ. of Nebraska Press.

Page, Walter. 1904. The People as an Exhibit. *World's Work* 8(Aug.):5110–13.

Panama-Pacific Exposition Co. 1914. *Prospectus of the 1915 San Diego Exposition*. San Diego: Panama-California Exposition Co.

———. 1915. *Official Guidebook to the Exposition*. San Diego: Panama-Pacific Exposition Co.

Parezo, Nancy J. 1987. The Formation of Ethnographic Collections: The Smithsonian Institution in the American Southwest. Vol. 10 of *Advances in Archaeological Method and Theory*, ed. Michael B. Schiffer, 1–49. San Diego: Academic Press.

———. 1993. Matilda Coxe Stevenson: Pioneer Ethnologist. In *Hidden Scholars: Women Anthropologists and the Native American Southwest*, ed. Nancy J. Parezo, 38–67. Albuquerque: Univ. of New Mexico Press.

———. 2004a. The Exposition within the Exposition: The Philippine Reservation. *Gateway Heritage* 24(4):30–39.

———. 2004b. A "Special Olympics": Testing Racial Strength and Endurance at the 1904 Louisiana Purchase Exposition. Paper presented at the International Congress on the 1904 St. Louis Olympic Games and Anthropology Days: A Centennial Retrospective. St. Louis: Univ. of Missouri.

Parezo, Nancy J., and Don D. Fowler. 2003. Recognizing Women's Anthropology at the 1904 World's Fair. *Anthropology Newsletter* 42(2):12–13.

———. 2006. Taking Ethnological Training Outside the Classroom: The 1904 Louisiana Purchase Exposition as Field School. Vol. 2 of *Annual of History of Anthropology*, ed. Regna Darnell and Fred Gleach 69–102. Lincoln: Univ. of Nebraska Press.

Parezo, Nancy J., and Margaret A. Hardin. 1993. In the Realm of the Museums. In *Hidden Scholars: Women Anthropologists and the Native American Southwest*, ed. Nancy J. Parezo, 270–93. Albuquerque: Univ. of New Mexico Press.

Parezo, Nancy J., and John W. Troutman. 2001. The "Shy" Cocopa Go to the Fair. In *Selling the Indian: Commercializing and Appropriating American Indian Cultures*, ed. Carter Jones Meyer and Diana Royer, 3–43. Tucson: Univ. of Arizona Press.

Parker, Esther. 1904. The United States Indian School. *Indian School Journal* 4(Oct.):74.

Parks, Douglas R. 1978. James R. Murie: Pawnee Ethnographer. In *American Indian Intellectuals*, ed. Margot Liberty, 74–89. 1976 Proceedings of the American Ethnological Society. St. Paul: West Publishing.

Peavy, Linda, and Ursula Smith. 2001. World's Champions: The 1904 Girl's Basketball Team from Fort Shaw Indian Boarding School. *Montana: The Magazine of Western History* 51(4):2–25.

Pepper, George H. 1904. Section H—Anthropology. *Science* 19(481):449–53.

Peters, Cora. 1904. Domestic Science Notes. *Indian School Journal* 5(Oct.):85.

Peterson, Susan. 1981. *The Living Tradition of Maria Martinez.* Tokyo: Kodan-sha International.

Philadelphia Ledger. 1904. Kwagiutl [sic] Arts. *Philadelphia Ledger,* Aug. 13.

Pieris, Paul. 1904. The Ceylon Exhibit at the World's Fair. In *Ceylon Hand-book,* 158–75. St. Louis: Louisiana Purchase Exposition Publishing Co.

Pilapil, Virgilio R. 1994. Dogtown, U.S.A.: An Igorot Legacy in the Midwest. *Heritage: Magazine of Filipino Culture, Arts, and Letters and the Filipino American Experience* 8(2):15–18.

Pinchot, Gifford. 1947. *Breaking New Ground.* New York: Island Press.

Piper, Edgar B. 1905. Portland and the Lewis and Clark Centennial Exposition. *American Review of Reviews* 31(Apr.):1–13.

Popular Science Monthly. 1904. The International Congress of Arts and Sciences. *Popular Science Monthly* 66(67):97–103.

Poster, Amy. 1999. Batchelor, Starr, and Culin: The Brooklyn Museum of Art Collection. In *Ainu: Spirit of a Northern People,* ed. William W. Fitzhugh and Chisato O. Dubreuil, 155–61. Washington DC and Seattle: National Museum of Natural History and the Univ. of Washington Press.

Powell, John Wesley. 1878. A Discourse on the Philosophy of the North American Indians. *Journal of the American Geographical Society of New York* 8:251–68.

————. 1881. Report of the Director. *First Annual Report of the Bureau of Ethnology, 1879–80,* xi–xxxiii.

————. 1885. From Savagery to Barbarism. *Anthropological Society of Washington Transactions* 3:173–96.

————. 1887. Museums of Ethnology and Their Classification. *Science,* o.s., 9:612–14.

————. 1896. Relations of Primitive Peoples to Environment, Illustrated by American Examples. *Annual Report of the Board of Regents of the Smithsonian Institution for 1894–1895,* 625–37. Washington DC: Government Printing Office.

————. 1898. *Truth and Error, or, the Science of Intellection.* Chicago: Open Court Publishing Co.

————. 1904. Report of the Director. *Twenty-second Annual Report of the Bureau of American Ethnology for 1900–1901,* vii–xxxix. Washington DC: Government Printing Office.

Provenzo, Eugene R. Jr. 1976. Education and the Louisiana Purchase Exposition. *Bulletin of the Missouri Historical Society* 32(2):99–109.

Prucha, Francis P. 1984. *The Great Father: The United States Government and the American Indians*. Lincoln: Univ. of Nebraska Press.

Putnam, Frederic W. 1895. *Final Report on the Anthropology Department to the Board of Trustees, World's Columbian Exposition Company, January 7, 1895*. Putnam Papers, Harvard University Archives.

————. 1905. Anthropological Miscellanea: Louisiana Purchase Exposition Awards. *American Anthropologist* 7(1):157–64.

Radforth, Ian. 2003. Performance, Politics, and Representation: Aboriginal People and the 1860 Royal Tour of Canada. *The Canadian Historical Review* 84(1):1–32.

Raibmon, Paige. 2000. Theatres of Contact: The Kwakwaka'wakw Meet Colonialism in British Columbia and at the Chicago World's Fair. *Canadian Historical Review* 81(June):157–90.

Raiche, Stephen J. 1972. The World's Fair and the New St. Louis. *Missouri Historical Review* 67(1):99–121.

Rathbun, Richard. 1906a. *Annual Report of the United States National Museum for 1904*. Washington DC: Government Printing Office.

————. 1906b. *Annual Report of the United States National Museum for 1905*. Washington DC: Government Printing Office.

Reddin, Paul. 1999. *Wild West Shows*. Urbana: Univ. of Illinois Press.

Reedy, William. 1904. Review of "Louisiana." *The Mirror* 14(29):15.

————. 1906. *The Makers of St. Louis*. St. Louis: Mirror Publishing Company.

Reel, Estelle. 1901. *Uniform Course of Study for the Indian Schools of the United States*. Washington DC: Government Printing Office.

Robinson, Cedric J. 1995. Ota Benga's Flight through Geronimo's Eyes: Takes of Science and Multiculturalism. In *Multiculturalism: A Critical Reader*, ed. David T. Goldberg, 388–405. Oxford: Blackwell.

Robinson, Ray. 1996. *American Original: A Life of Will Rogers*. New York: Oxford Univ. Press.

Roche, Maurice. 2000. *Mega-Events and Modernity: Olympics and Expos and the Growth of Global Culture*. New York: Routledge.

Rochester Chronicle. 1904. A Yellow Atmosphere. *Rochester Chronicle*, May 21.

Rogers, Howard J. 1904. *Educational Exhibits*. Final Report of the Education Department, Universal Exposition of 1904. Division of Exhibits, LPEC files, file series 3, subseries 11, Missouri Historical Society.

———. 1905–7. *Congress of Arts and Sciences: Universal Exposition of St. Louis, 1904*. 8 vols. New York: Houghton Mifflin.

Roosevelt, Theodore. 1899. *The Rough Riders*. New York: Scribner's and Sons.

Rosewater, Edward. 1897. History of the Indian. *Omaha Daily Bee*, Aug. 16.

Russell, Frank. 1902. Know, Then, Thyself. *Journal of American Folklore* 15(56):1–13.

Rydell, Robert W. 1984. *All the World's a Fair: Visions of Empire at American International Expositions, 1876–1916*. Chicago: Univ. of Chicago Press.

———. 1993. *Worlds of Fairs: The Century of Progress Expositions*. Chicago: Univ. of Chicago Press.

———., ed. 1999. *The Reason Why the Colored American Is Not in the World's Columbian Exposition*. Urbana: Univ. of Illinois Press.

Rydell, Robert W., John E. Findling, and Kimberly D. Pelle. 2000. *Fair America: World's Fairs in the United States*. Washington DC: Smithsonian Institution Press.

Rydell, Robert W., and Nancy E. Gwinn. 1994. *Fair Representations: World's Fairs and the Modern World*. European Contributions to American Studies 27. Amsterdam: VU Univ. Press.

San Francisco Chronicle. 1904. The Pike Indian. *San Francisco Chronicle*, Sept. 14.

Santee, Ross. 1947. *Apache Land*. New York: Charles Scribner's Sons.

Science. 1902a. The Bureau of Ethnology. *Science* 16(408):676–77.

———. 1902b. Editorial: The Smithsonian Institution and Its Affiliated Bureaus. *Science* 16(412):1–2.

Scientific American. 1904a. The Cliff Dwellers at the St. Louis Exposition. *Scientific American* 91(Nov. 12):339.

———. 1904b. Eskimo Village at the World's Fair. *Scientific American* 91(Oct. 29):301–2.

———. 1904c. Government Philippine Exhibit. *Scientific American* 91(Nov. 19):64–66.

———. 1904d. Native Dwellings at the St. Louis Exposition. *Scientific American* 91(Sept. 24):218.

————. 1904e. The Racial Exhibit at the St. Louis Fair. *Scientific American* 91(Dec. 10):414.

————. 1904f. The Vast Palaces of the World's Fair. *Scientific American Supplement* 58(1498):24004–5.

Shattinger International Music Corp. 1975. *A Tribute to Scott Joplin and the Giants of Ragtime*. New York: Shattinger International Music Corp.

Shipman, Pat. 1994. *The Evolution of Racism: Human Differences and the Use and Abuse of Science*. New York: Simon and Schuster.

Skiff, Frederick J. V. 1902. Introduction. *Official Classification of Exhibit Departments*. St. Louis: Louisiana Purchase Exposition Co.

————. 1903. The Universal Exposition: An Encyclopedia of Society. *World's Fair Bulletin* (Dec.):2–3.

————. 1904a. Preface. *Official Catalogue, Department N—Anthropology*. St. Louis: Louisiana Purchase Exposition Co.

————. 1904b. The Universal Exposition: An Encyclopedia of Society. *World's Fair Bulletin* 6(1):2–4.

————. 1905. *Official Catalogue of Exhibits*. Rev. ed. St. Louis: Louisiana Purchase Exposition Co.

Slocum, William F. 1904. The World's Fair as an Educative Force. *Outlook* 77(Aug. 16):793–805.

Smith-Ferri, Sherrie. 1996. "Hidden at the Heard": The Harvey Company Pomo Collection. *The Great Southwest of the Fred Harvey Company and the Santa Fe Railway*, ed. Marta Weigle And Barbara Babcock, 130–40. Phoenix: Heard Museum.

Spencer, Frank. 1979. Aleš Hrdlička, M.D., 1869–1943: A Chronicle of the Life and Work of an American Physical Anthropologist. PhD diss., Univ. of Michigan.

Sprague, Stuart S. 1975. Meet Me in St. Louis on the Ten-Million-Dollar Pike. *Missouri Historical Society Bulletin* 32:26–31.

Stanaland, Peggy. 1981. Pre-Olympic "Anthropology Days," 1904: An Aborted Effort to Bridge Some Cultural Gaps. In *Play and Its Cultural Context*, ed. P. Stanaland, 101–6. West Point NY: Leisure Press.

The Star. 1904. It's an Outrage, Says Prof. Starr, to Make Igorottes Wear Pants. *The (Peoria IL) Star*, July 19.

Starr, Frederick. 1893. Anthropology at the Fair. *Popular Science Monthly* 43: 610–21.

———. 1895. *Some First Steps in Human Progress*. Meadville: Flood and Vincent.

———. 1897. The Davenport Academy of Natural Sciences. *Appleton's Popular Science Monthly* 51(May-Oct.):83–98.

———. 1904a. *The Ainu Group at the Saint Louis Exposition*. Chicago: Open Court Publishing.

———. 1904b. Draft Plans for Field School. WJ McGee Papers, box 20, Library of Congress.

———. 1905. Anthropology at the St. Louis Exposition. *American Antiquarian* 27(1):40–42.

Starr, Ida. 1904. Irish Village. *Indian School Journal* 4(Oct.):75.

Steffen, Lincoln, with Claude Wetmore. 1902. Tweed Days in St Louis: Joseph W. Folk's Single-handed Exposure of Corruption, High and Low. *McClure's Magazine* (Oct.):577–86.

———. 1903. The Shamelessness of St. Louis: Something New in the History of American Municipal Democracy. *McClure's Magazine* (Mar.):546–60.

Sterling Gazette. 1904. Are Americans Immodest? *Sterling Gazette*, July 25.

Stevens, Walter S. 1909. *St. Louis: History of the Fourth City*. Chicago: S. J. Clarke.

St. Louis American. 1904. Untitled article. *St. Louis American*, May 28.

St. Louis Chronicle. 1904. The Indian Reservation. *St. Louis Chronicle*, Aug. 12.

St. Louis Examiner. 1904a. Cannibal Dance to Please Girl Students. *St. Louis Examiner*, Sept. 2.

———. 1904b. Co-Eds See Indians in Unexpurgated Snake Dance. *St. Louis Examiner*, Sept. 7.

St. Louis Globe-Democrat. 1903a. Giant Patagonians Preparing to Visit World's Fair City. *St. Louis Globe-Democrat*, Oct. 7.

———. 1903b. Indian Display at World's Fair Is to Be the Most Elaborate Ever Made. *St. Louis Globe-Democrat*, Nov. 21.

———. 1903c. McGee to Head Department. *St. Louis Globe-Democrat*, Aug. 14.

———. 1904a. American Indians Capture Anthropology Athletic Meet. *St. Louis Globe-Democrat*, Aug. 13.

—————. 1904b. Celebration of Pike Day June 4 at World's Fair. *St. Louis Globe-Democrat*, June 5.

—————. 1904c. Chicago Co-Eds Will Study Pike People. *St. Louis Globe-Democrat*, Aug. 28.

—————. 1904d. Filipinos Excite President's Praise. *St Louis Globe-Democrat*, Nov. 26.

—————. 1904e. Geronimo Is Feeble and Quite Religious. *St. Louis Globe-Democrat*, Jan. 21.

—————. 1904f. Indians Give Big Reception in School. *St. Louis Globe-Democrat*, June 1.

—————. 1904g. Igorrotes Not to Wear Breeches. *St. Louis Globe-Democrat*, July 15.

—————. 1904h. Moros Win Championship of Philippine Natives on Track. *St. Louis Globe-Democrat*, Sept. 16.

—————. 1904i. No Mystery about Navaho Blankets. *St. Louis Globe-Democrat*, June 8.

—————. 1904j. Pike Parade Is Grand Spectacle. *St. Louis Globe-Democrat*, June 4.

—————. 1904k. Sights and Echoes of the Expositions: Opening the Philippines. *St. Louis Globe-Democrat*, Sunday, June 19.

St. Louis Post-Dispatch. 1904a. Ainus at World's Fair Build Prayer Stick Fence. *St. Louis Post-Dispatch*, Apr. 19.

—————. 1904b. Ainu Woman and Member of Giant South American Tribe Make Friends. *St. Louis Post-Dispatch*, Apr. 15.

—————. 1904c. Antique Indian Tribe Leave Monday for Fair. *St. Louis Post-Dispatch*, Apr. 24.

—————. 1904d. At Last Igorrotes Have Dog Banquet. *St. Louis Post-Dispatch*, Apr. 17.

—————. 1904e. Baby Whiteshirt, Red Papoose, Is Favorite with Women Visitors. *St. Louis Post-Dispatch*, May 2.

—————. 1904f. Barbarians Meet in Athletic Games. *St. Louis Post-Dispatch*, Aug. 13.

—————. 1904g. Boers Lose Skirmish with Britons for a World's Fair Kopje. *St. Louis Post-Dispatch*, Apr. 9.

—————. 1904h. Choosing a Wife by the Shape of Her Nose. *St. Louis Post-Dispatch*, Jan. 3.

———. 1904i. Cliff Dwellers in First Snow Storm. *St. Louis Post-Dispatch*, Apr. 20.

———. 1904j. Co-Eds Know All about Poor Lo. *St. Louis Post-Dispatch*, Sept. 1.

———. 1904k. Dog-Gone-Happy Are Igorrotes. *St. Louis Post-Dispatch*, Apr. 11.

———. 1904l. Exposition Envoy Pygmies' Victim? *St. Louis Post-Dispatch*, Apr.

———. 1904m. Fair as Textbook for Fair Co-Eds. *St. Louis Post-Dispatch*, Aug. 30.

———. 1904n. Famous Giants at the Fair. *St. Louis Post-Dispatch*, Apr. 24.

———. 1904o. Gen. Porter, Indian Chief, to Marry a St. Louis Girl. *St. Louis Post-Dispatch*, Apr. 13.

———. 1904p. Geronimo Only a Pill Mixer! *St. Louis Post-Dispatch*, June 8.

———. 1904q. "Good" Indians. *St. Louis Post-Dispatch*, July 6.

———. 1904r. Human Skulls to Adorn Fence. *St. Louis Post-Dispatch*, Apr. 24.

———. 1904s. Indian Chief Faces Death Like Stoic. *St. Louis Post-Dispatch*, Apr. 7.

———. 1904t. Igorottes Eat Dog Meat. *St. Louis Post-Dispatch*, Apr. 6.

———. 1904u. "Is It Beef Trust, Speaking through Humane Society, that Would Rob Igorrote of His Cherished Dog Meat?" *St. Louis Post-Dispatch*, Apr. 6.

———. 1904v. Just a Minute with the Post-Dispatch: Rhymers and Jokes. *St. Louis Post-Dispatch*, Apr. 16.

———. 1904w. Negritos and Igorrotes Build Their Bamboo Fence. *St. Louis Post-Dispatch*, Apr. 8.

———. 1904x. Odd Ceremony at Ainu Dedication. *St. Louis Post-Dispatch*, June 2.

———. 1904y. Opening Day. *St. Louis Post-Dispatch*, May 1.

———. 1904z. The Other Side of It. Just a Minute with the Post-Dispatch. *St. Louis Post-Dispatch*, Apr. 16.

———. 1904aa. The Other Side of It. Rhymes and Jokes. *St. Louis Post-Dispatch*, Apr. 16.

———. 1904bb. The Overlord of the Savage World. Cartoon. *St. Louis Post-Dispatch*, July 14.

———. 1904cc. Paducah Dogs for Igorrotes. *St. Louis Post-Dispatch*, Apr. 24.

———. 1904dd. Papoose Only a Girl. *St. Louis Post-Dispatch*, May 2.

———. 1904ee. Patagonian Giants to Have Rivals. *St. Louis Post-Dispatch*, Apr. 24.

———. 1904ff. Patagonians Pitch New Camp and Ainus Rejoice. *St. Louis Post-Dispatch*, June 2.

———. 1904gg. Pygmies Outdo Savage Athletes Risking Life and Limb to Make a World's Fair Holiday. *St. Louis Post-Dispatch*, Aug. 14.

———. 1904hh. Sweat Bath and Earth Lodge for Pawnee. *St. Louis Post-Dispatch*, May 3.

———. 1904ii. The Teachings of the Chinese Sages, Confucius and Mencius. *St. Louis Post-Dispatch*, Dec. 5.

———. 1904jj. This Indian Baby Bunting Sees Fair from an Envied Pinnacle. *St. Louis Post-Dispatch*, May 26.

———. 1904kk. Untitled news clips in McGee scrapbook. *St. Louis Post-Dispatch*, Apr. 16, Apr. 24, May 2, May 8, May 22.

———. 1904ll. Will Burrow i' th' Earth. *St. Louis Post-Dispatch*, May 8.

———. 1904mm. World's Fair Earth Lodge Built by Pawnee. *St. Louis Post-Dispatch*, June 19.

———. 1904nn. Yellow Hair, Chief of the Rosebud Sioux. *St. Louis Post-Dispatch*, May 22.

St. Louis Republic. 1901. Site Can Expand to More than 1,000 Acres. *St. Louis Republic*, June 26.

———. 1903a. Addresses Men's Club. *St. Louis Republic*, Sept. 19.

———. 1903b. Prof. H. J. McGee [*sic*] Tells of Anthropology Display. *St. Louis Sunday Republic*, Sept. 6.

———. 1904a. The Ainus. *St. Louis Republic*, Apr. 18.

———. 1904b. Chief Yellow Hair. *St. Louis Republic*, May 28.

———. 1904c. Crow Indian Unable to Trade with Filipino. *St. Louis Republic*, May 2.

———. 1904d. Cut Nose's Wife Calls Him Home. *St. Louis Republic*, June 29.

———. 1904e. Features of the World's Fair: Studying the Indians. *St. Louis Republic*, May 14.

———. 1904f. Geronimo. *St. Louis Republic*, May 28.

———. 1904g. Geronimo Serenades Squaws. *St. Louis Republic*, June 15.

————. 1904h. Inactivity Palls on Indian Chief. *St. Louis Republic*, June 21.

————. 1904i. Indian Art Rewarded. *St. Louis Republic*, Sept. n.d.

————. 1904j. Indian Basket-ball Team. *St. Louis Republic*, June 15.

————. 1904k. An Indian Beauty at the World's Fair. *St. Louis Republic*, June 20.

————. 1904l. Indian Exhibit Formally Opens. *St. Louis Republic*, June 2.

————. 1904m. Patagonian Death Watch Was Held in Vain. *St. Louis Republic*, May 8.

————. 1904n. Patagonian Giants Object to Camera. *St. Louis Republic*, Apr. 15.

————. 1904o. Patagonians Bid Francis Good Bye. *St. Louis Republic*, Dec. 2.

————. 1904p. Proud Navajo Mother Desires to Have Go-Cart for Her Papoose. *St Louis Republic*, June 18.

————. 1904q. Pygmies Indulge in Mud Fight. *St. Louis Republic*, Aug. 13.

————. 1904r. Real Indians Erect Their Own Building at the Fair. *St. Louis Republic*, Apr. 14.

————. 1904s. The Savage Conclave. *St. Louis Republic*, July 17.

————. 1904t. Scott Charging Alone. *St. Louis Republic*, May 11.

————. 1904u. Show No Novelty. *St. Louis Republic*, Apr. 21.

————. 1904v. To Measure Men of All Nations. *St. Louis Republic*, May 1.

————. 1904w. Total Admissions to Fair Nearly Twenty Millions. *St. Louis Republic*, Dec. 22.

————. 1904x. Untitled articles. *St. Louis Republic*, May 1, May 7, June 13, Sept. 6.

————. 1904y. Visayans to Go to Metropolis. *St. Louis Republic*, Dec. 2.

St. Louis Star. 1904a. At the Intertribal Games in the World's Fair Stadium. *St. Louis Star*, Aug. 12.

————. 1904b. Indians First; Filipinos, Second; Patagonians, Third. *St. Louis Star*, Aug. 13.

St. Louis Westliche Post. 1904. The Indian Reservation. *St. Louis Westliche Post*, July 26.

Stocking, George W. Jr. 1968. *Race, Culture, and Evolution: Essays in the History of Anthropology*. New York: Free Press.

————. 1973. Franz Boas and the Founding of the American Anthropological Association. *American Anthropologist* 62(1):1–17.

————. 1974a. Introduction. The Basic Assumptions of Boasian Anthropology. In *The Shaping of American Anthropology 1883–1911: A Franz Boas Reader*, ed. George W. Stocking Jr., 1–20. New York: Basic Books.

————. 1974b. Some Problems in the Understanding of Nineteenth-Century Cultural Evolutionism. In *Readings in the History of Anthropology*, ed. Regna Darnell, 407–25. New York: Harper and Row.

————. 1979. *Anthropology at Chicago: Tradition, Discipline, Department.* Manuscript on file at the Joseph Regenstein Library, Univ. of Chicago.

————. 1982. The Santa Fe Style in American Archaeology: Regional Interest, Academic Initiative, and Philanthropic Policy in the First Two Decades of the Laboratory of Anthropology. *Journal of the History of the Behavioral Sciences* 18:3–19.

Sullivan, James E. 1904. Physical Culture. *Division of Exhibits.* St. Louis: Louisiana Purchase Exposition Co.

————. 1905a. Anthropology Days at the Stadium. *Spalding's Official Athletic Almanac for 1905*, 249–63. New York: Spalding Athletic Co.

————. 1905b. Physical Training Programme. *Spalding's Official Athletic Almanac for 1905*, 185–86. New York: Spalding Athletic Co.

Swanton, John R. 1942. David I. Bushnell Jr. *American Anthropologist* 44(1): 104–10.

Swarthout, William N. 1904. A Descriptive Story of the Philippine Exhibit. *World's Fair Bulletin* 5(8):49.

Takaki, Ronald. 1992. The Tempest in the Wilderness: The Racialization of Savagery. *Journal of American History* 79(Dec.):892–912.

Taylor, Isaac. 1905. Final Report, Division of Works. LPEC Collection, box 2, series 2, folder 1, Missouri Historical Society.

Tenorio-Trillo, Mauricio. 1996. *Mexico at the World's Fairs: Crafting a Modern Nation.* Berkeley: Univ. of California Press.

Terry's 1904 World's Fair Page. 1997. David Rowland Francis. Terry's 1904 World's Fair Page. http://www.tlaupp.com/drfrancis.

Thompson, Raymond S., and Nancy J. Parezo. 1989. A Historical Survey of Material Culture Studies in Anthropology. In *Perspectives on Anthropological Collections from the American Southwest*, ed. Ann Hedlund, 3–5. Anthropological Research Papers no. 40. Tempe: Arizona State Univ.

Thunderbird, Chief. 1976a. Two boys from El Llano Estacado. *The Masterkey* 50(1):68–72.

———. 1976b. Two Fighting Ermine Pets. *The Masterkey* 59(2):109–11.

Times. 1904. Untitled article, *Brocton MA Times* May 5.

Tisdale, Shelby. 1997. Cocopa Identity, Indian Gaming, and Cultural Survival in the Lower Colorado River Delta, 1850–1966. PhD diss., Univ. of Arizona.

Toohey, Kristine, and A. J. Veal. 2000. *The Olympic Games: A Social Science Perspective.* New York: VABI Publishing.

Trennert, Robert A. 1974. A Grand Failure: The Centennial Indian Exposition of 1876. *Prologue: The Journal of the National Archives* 6(2):118–29.

———. 1987a. Fairs, Expositions, and the Changing Image of Southwestern Indians, 1876–1904. *New Mexico Historical Review* 62(2):127–50.

———. 1987b. Selling Indian Education at World's Fairs and Exposition, 1893–1904. *American Indian Quarterly* 11(3):203–20.

———. 1988. *The Phoenix Indian School: Forced Assimilation in Arizona, 1891–1935.* Norman: Univ. of Oklahoma Press.

———. 1993. A Resurrection of Native Arts and Crafts: The St. Louis World's Fair, 1904. *Missouri Historical Review* 87(3):274–92.

Trigger, Bruce B. 1989. *A History of Archaeology.* Cambridge: Cambridge Univ. Press.

Troutman, John W. 1997. "The Overlord of the Savage World": Anthropology, the Media, and the American Indian Experience at the 1904 Louisiana Purchase Exposition. Master's thesis, American Indian Studies Program, Univ. of Arizona.

Troutman, John W., and Nancy J. Parezo. 1998. "The Overlord of the Savage World": Anthropology and the Press at the 1904 Louisiana Purchase Exposition. *Museum Anthropology* 22(2):17–34.

Troy Times. 1904. Exit the Traditional Indian. *Troy (NY) Times* Jan. 21.

Tucker, William H. 1994. *The Science and Politics of Racial Research.* Urbana: Univ. of Illinois Press.

Turner, Frederick 1996. Introduction. *Geronimo, His Own Story: The Autobiography of a Great Patriot Warrior, as told to Samuel M. Barrett.* New York: Meridian Press.

United States Olympic Committee. 1993. *Athens to Atlanta: 100 Years of Glory.* United States Olympic Committee.

Van Stone, James. 1993. The Ainu Group at the Louisiana Purchase Exposition, 1904. *Arctic Anthropology* 30(2):77–91.

Verner, Samuel P. 1904a. The Adventures of an Explorer in Africa: How the Batwa Pygmies Were Brought to the St. Louis Fair. *Harper's Weekly* Oct. 22:1618–20.

———. 1904b. The Central African Group. *Indian School Journal* 4(Oct.):76–80.

———. 1904c. An Untold Chapter of My Adventures While Hunting Pygmies in Africa. *St. Louis Post-Dispatch*, Dec. 4.

———. 1907. The White Man's Zone in Africa. *World's Work* (Jan.):8227–36.

Walker, John B. 1904a. Anthropological: Concerning the Early Beginnings of Men and Women. *The Cosmopolitan* 37(5):609–14.

———. 1904b. The Boer War. *The Cosmopolitan* 37(5):553–54.

———. 1904c. The Pike. *The Cosmopolitan* 37(5):615–20.

———. 1904d. The Walled City of Jerusalem—in St. Louis. *The Cosmopolitan* 37(5):575–76.

———. 1904e. What the Louisiana Purchase Exposition Is. *The Cosmopolitan* 37(5):485–92.

Wallechinsky, David. 1988. *The Complete Book of the Olympics*. New York: Viking.

Washington Post. 1901. To Cover All the World. *Washington Post*, Aug. 30.

———. 1903. Exhibit of Ethnology Models of Yucatan Palaces for St. Louis Exposition. *Washington Post*, Aug. 31.

Washington Times. 1902. Object to Display Indians in Wild Dress. Character of Exhibit at St. Louis Causes Dispute. *Washington Times*, Nov. 2.

Watanabe, H. 1973. *The Ainu Ecosystem: Environment and Group Structure*. American Ethnological Society Monograph no. 54. Seattle: Univ. of Washington Press.

Watters, David R., and Don D. Fowler. 2002. The AAA's Place(s) of Emergence. *Anthropology Newsletter* 43(5):13–14.

Weekly Review. 1903. Miss Rosa Bourassa. St. Louis. *Weekly Review*, Sept. 19.

Welsch, Robert L. 2003. Albert Buell Lewis: Realizing George Dorsey's Vision. In *Curators, Collections, and Contexts: Anthropology at the Field Museum,*

1893–2002, ed. Stephen E. Nash and Gary Feinman. *Fieldiana*. Anthropology, n.s., 36:99–116.

West, Terry. 1992. *WJ McGee and Conservation as Applied Anthropology*. Washington DC: USDA Forest Service.

Whiteley, Peter. 1988. *Deliberate Acts: Changing Hopi Culture through the Oraibi Split*. Tucson: Univ. of Arizona Press.

Williams, Anita Alvarez de. 1983. Cocopa. Vol. 10 of *Handbook of North American Indians, Southwest*, 99–112. Washington DC: Government Printing Office.

Williams, Samuel. 1904. The Louisiana Purchase Exposition, Its Scope and Purpose. *Scientific American* 90(May 7):364–65.

Williams, Walter. 1904. Round the World at the World's Fair. *The Century* 46:794–803.

Wilson, Terry P. 1984. Chief Fred Lookout and the Politics of Osage Oil, 1906–1949. *Journal of the West* 23(3):46–53.

Wolf, Eric R. 1994. Perilous Ideas: Race, Culture, People. *Current Anthropology* 35(1):1–12.

Wonder, Karen. 1990. The Illusionary Art of Background Paintings in Habitat Dioramas. *Curator* 33(2):90–118.

Woodworth, Robert W. 1904a. Field Notes. Woodworth Personal Papers, Columbia Univ. Archives, New York.

———. 1904b. Monthly Reports to McGee. WJ McGee Papers, box 16, Library of Congress.

———. 1905. Final Report of the Anthropometry and Psychology Section to William J McGee. Contained in McGee (1905d).

———. 1910. Racial Differences in Mental Traits. *Science*, n.s., 31(788):171–86.

———. 1932. A History of Psychology in Autobiography. Vol. 2 of *The International University Series in Psychology*, ed. Carl Murchison, 359–80. Worcester MA: Clark Univ. Press.

———. 1939. Autobiography. In *Selected Papers of R. W. Woodworth*. New York: Henry Holt.

Woolard, James R. 1975. The Philippine Scouts: The Development of America's Colonial Army. PhD diss., Ohio State Univ.

Worcester, Dean C. 1913. The Non-Christian Peoples of the Philippine Islands. *National Geographic* 24(11):1157–256.

World's Work. 1904. The Inspiring Display of the States. *World's Work* 8(4):5164–78.

Yost, Nellie Snyder. 1979. *Buffalo Bill: His Family, Friends, Fame, Failures, and Fortunes.* Chicago: Swallow Press.

Index

Abbott, Cyrus, 366

Academy of Science (St. Louis), 395

accidents, 243, 448n14, 456n31

Acoma Indians: activities, 128–30; artists, 434n56; baking, 127–29, 138, 142, 434n56, 434n59; housing, 103; participants, 104; performances, 326; sales, 97, 267; at San Diego exposition, 387; selection for LPE, 91

Adams, Eliza, 433n51

Adams, Henry (Chief Blue Wing), 125–26, 433n51

Adams, Rachel, 384

adobe bricks, 128, 434n56

Aeronautic Concourse, 335

Afable, Patricia, 181, 183, 419n10

AF of L, 383

Afraid of Eagle (Lakota), 132–33

Africa, 74–77, 371–72

Africans. See black Americans; Boer War concession; Mbuti (Batwa) Pygmies; "Red Africans"

Age of Power stage, 51

Agricultural Room (Indian School), 146

Aguinaldo, Emilio, 164, 165

Ah-yah-sha-wah-she-quah (Ojibwa), 276

The Ainu Group at the Saint Louis Exposition (Starr), 84, 210, 444n33

Ainus: athletic competition, 351; awards, 363; baby, 108; behavior, 452n27; budget, 71, 369; ceremonies, 210–11, 444n34; at church services, 210; comparison to Canadian natives, 226; compensation, 84; and Congress of Indian Educators, 333; description, 210–14; free time, 278, 280; illness, 293; at Indian School programs, 437n38; location of encampment, 103; participants, 73, 81–86, 409; and Patagonian Tehuelches, 200, 443n14; performances, 326, 334, 335; physical appearance, 210, 212–14, 444n32, 444nn39–40; privacy, 272; public opinion of, 444n38; research on, 310, 317; return home, 373–74; sales, 97, 212; selection for LPE, 53; subject of Starr's field

school course, 337, 338; taxonomic problem, 82, 428n20; at war dances, 132

Alaska Building, 337

Alaska Esquimaux Company, 252

Alaska state exhibit, *303*, 304, 364, 383, 455n9

Alaska Territory, 72

Alaska-Yukon-Pacific Exposition (1909), 392, 396–97, 449n32

Albuquerque Indian School, 59, 97

alcoholic beverages, 198, 284

Alexander, J. B., 67

Allen, James, 126, 433n44

Allison, William, 285

Aluets. *See* Eskimos

Amateur Athletic Union (AAU), 342, 345

"America" (Fish), 152

American Anthropological Association (AAA), 9, 38, 40, 379, 392, 397

American Anthropologist, 38, 40, 45, 362

American Association for the Advancement of Science (AAAS), 9, 36, 38, 57, 310, 321

American Association of Museums, 38

American Association of Physical Anthropologists, 392

American Horse (Oglala Lakota), 461n1

American Journal of Physical Anthropology, 392

American Museum of Natural History, 8, 89, 231, 318, 457n32, 462n2

Americans, 3–4, 10–11, 55, 342–42, 388

Amsterdam International Colonial Exposition (1883), 6

Andrews, Alfred, 438n51

andrology, 48

Anishinabe Indians, 124–25

Antero (Filipino student), 169, 174, 180

Anthropological Exhibit Company, 384

Anthropological Society of Washington (ASW), 38, 40, 377

anthropologists, 22–23, 399, 464n4

anthropology: Boas's theory of, 47; in Bureau of American Ethnology, 40; development of discipline, 395–96, 399–402; employment

Boas, Franz (*cont.*)
  Congress of Art and Science, 330–32, 458n8; and McGee, 43–45, 48, 395, 396; on organization of exhibits, 24, 25; and planning of LPE, 29
Boer War concession: and anthropometry research, 313; description, 256–60; and Filipinos, 173; Great Britain Exhibition (1899), 450n45; and Mbutis, 208–9; Olympic participants from, 345; participants, 257, 282, 449n43; and Rough Riders performances, 241
bola, 199–200, 340
Bomushubba (Pygmy), 76, *202*
Bontoc Igorots, *176*; activities, 175; dances, *177*; dog feasts, 176, 179, 181–84; ethnology, 168–69; physical appearance, 177–78; village, 176–77
Boone, Alice, 438n51
Borglum, Solon, *298*, 299
Boston Band, 457n1
Bounding Fawn, 244
Bourassa, Rosa, 70, 332
Bourke, John Gregory, 249
"Bow and Arrow" Drill, 152
Bowditch, Charles, 329
Bowie knife demonstration, 244
Boyongasan (Suyoc Igorot), 179
Bradford, E. H., 317
Bradford, Samuel, 203
Brady, John G., 72, *303*, 304–5, 364
brains, 320
Brazil exhibit, 301, 364
Breaking New Ground (Pinchot), 398
Breitbart, Eric, 251
Brennan, John, 243
Brewer, Gertrude, 67, 153
Brinton, Daniel, 459n18
Bronson, 138
Brookhaven (MS) *Leader*, 149
Brooklyn Museum of Art, 428n23
Brown, Herbert, 445n47
Brown, Julie, 270
Brule Indian Indian band, 242
Bruner, Frank G., 311–16, 322, 456n20
Bryn Mawr College, 319
Buel, James, 367, 380
Buffalo (NY) Pan-American Exposition (1901): athletics at, 342–43; Chief Joseph at, 244, 430n51; Cocopa Indian materials, 39; Geron-

imo at, 96; Henry Standing Soldier at, 334; Indian Congress, 7, 240, 447n6; Iroquois artists at, 429n35; living exhibits, 11, 25–26; McKinley at, 265; Old Plantation concession, 255; and Starr, 82
Bugti (Filipino), 441n30
Bull Bear (Cheyenne), 116, 117, *271*, 334
Bulon (Bagobo Moro), 188
"A Bunch of American Beauties" (photograph), 149, 436n29
Buntin, John, 106
Bureau of American Ethnology (BAE): archaeology at, 396; awards, 366; control of, 39–47; Holmes at, 24, 392; McGee's resignation from, 45–46; McGee with, 38–47, 288; Mooney at, 391; scope of work, 422n10; static exhibits, 301–4. *See also* Bureau of Ethnology
Bureau of Ethnology, 8, 422n3. *See also* Bureau of American Ethnology (BAE)
Bureau of Insular Affairs, 165, 168, 318, 384
Bureau of Soils (Department of Agriculture), 398
Burlin, Natalie Curtis, 292
Burton, Charles V., 92
Burton, Minnie (Shoshone), 159
Bush, E. J., 280
Bushmen, 258, 450n45
Bushnell, David I., Jr., 21, 393, 394, 420n8
Bushy Head (Cheyenne), 117, *271*
Butch, Genevieve (Yankton Sioux), 159

Cadreau, Mary, 153
Cajiti, Genevieve "Belle of the Pueblos," 128–29
Calamity Jane, 240
Calcraft, Edwin, 383
California history, 386–88
Campbell, Mrs. (LPE planner), 29
Canada, 73, 88–91, 383
Canadian Geological Survey, 89
Canadian Indian tribes, 242
Canadian natives. *See* Kwakiutls; Nootkas
Cane, Vicente, 77–78, 277–78, 363, 451n15
cannibalism, 204, 226–30. *See also* Hamatsa ritual
Carlisle Indian School, 107, 156, 339, 350
Carnegie Museum, 88
Carpenter, Charles, 318, 446n63, 453n41, 456n29
carpentry and manual training, 149
Carter, Thomas H., 246

"The Cascades" (musical piece), 17, 256
Cascades (the), 430n2
cast making, 317–18, 388, 456n28
Catlin, Mrs. George, 139
Cattell, James McKeen, 308–11, 314
Caucasoid ethnic group, 82, 84, 214
Cayuga Indians, 242
celebrities, 93–96
Ceylon, 263, 301
Chapman, Kenneth, 387
Charges Alone, Rev. Scott, 133, 137, 154, 210, 278, 284
Chemawa Boarding School, 137, 383
Cherokee Indians, 70
Cherry, Samuel, 319
Che-sho-hum-kah (Claremore) (Osage), 119–20
Cheyenne Indians, *271*; activities, 115–18, 142; dances, 132, 326, 334; encampment, 103, 117; participants, 104; research on, 312; selection for LPE, 55, 56; and Wild West Show, 242
Chicago IL, 2, 8, 15
Chicago Lyceum Bureau, 66, 425n25
Chicago World's Fair (1893): Africans at, 256; anthropology exhibits, 25, 87, 385; anthropometry and psychometry at, 308, 309, 311; Antonio Apache at, 111; architecture, 4; attendance, 367; Canadian natives at, 90; classification of exhibits, 23; Cliff Dweller exhibit, 246; entertainment, 5–6, 262, 446n2; Eskimos at, 253, 254, 449n32; and Field Museum, 394; income, 446n1; Indian School, 57–58; international congress, 5; kindergarten, 150; midway, 5–6, 234, 265; Nootkas at, 231; Northwest Coast artifacts from, 446n63; planning, 29; site, 15; and Starr, 82; static exhibits, 299; Wild West Show, 246, 447n13, 448n15
chicken pox, 293, 372
Chief Antonio (Bontoc Igorot), 176, *341*, 364, 365, 440n20
Chief Guechico, 196–98
Chief Joseph (Nez Perce), 55, 94, 95, 240, 242, 244, 430n51
children: Ainu, 213; Cocopa, 220, 445n50; Eskimo, 254; Filipino, 174; free time, 277; Native American, 134, 150–51; performances, 326–27. *See also* babies
Children's Day, 277, 327
Children's Garden, 138

Chilocco Indian Agricultural School: annual catalogue, 436n29; band, 140, 154, 156–57; basketball team, 159; description, 424n12; Freeman at, 425n23; Indian School participants, 143–44, 148, 149, 152, 157; McCowan at, 425n19; participants from, 66, 67, 97; student labor, 63
China: and anthropometry research, 317; at Lewis and Clark Centennial, 465n6; LPE concession, 237, 260, 263; participants from, 368, 457n31; static exhibit, 301
Chippewa Indians: activities, 124–25; encampment, 103; at Indian School programs, 437n38; participants, 104; research on, 312; selection for LPE, 56; and Wild West Show, 242
Chiricahua Apache Indians, 96, 104, 107, 358. *See also* Geronimo
Chiri-chiri, 203, 204
Chizi (Cocopa), 216
Chouteau, Pierre, 15, 62, 454n5
Cincinnati exposition (1888), 25
clan house, 88–89, 103, 224. *See also* housing
Clark, George S., 193
Clark University, 8, 311, 314
classes, 335–38, 343, 369, 459nn17–18
Clayoquot. *See* Nootkas
Cleveland, Grover, 17
Cliff Dweller exhibit, *248*; attraction of, 91; Chicago World's Fair (1893), 448n22; claim of Hopis at, 92–93; description, 246–52; field school class at, 338; McGee on, 237, 448n23; participants, 449n28; at San Diego exposition, 387
Clum, John, 96, 430n55
Cocopa Indians: archery, 215, 216, 219–20; athletic ability, 340–41, 347, 460n26; children, 220, 445n50; classification, 452n31; compensation, 80; description, 215–20; encampment, 103, 216–17, *217*; expenses, 71, 80, 216, 369, 370, 424n15, 427n16, 445n43; farming, 215, 217–18, 445n41; free time, 279; illness, 293–94; interactions with other participants, 280; and McGee, 39, *217*, 220, 393, 397; participants, 78–81, 104, 410; performances, 219–20, 334; photography of, 219, 273; physical appearance, 215, 218–20, 445n46, 445n51; recognition, 427n14; research on, 312; resource conservation, 398; return home,

Cocopa Indians (*cont.*)
374–75, 464n29; sales, 97, 219–20; selection for LPE, 53; supervision of, 70, 216; and visitor behavior, 269
Cody, Buffalo Bill, 6, 240, 241, 243, 246, 447n13
Coldwater (Cocopa), 216
Collier, John, 386–87
Colojo (Tehuelche), *60*
colonial exhibits, static, 6–7
Colony Indian Training School, 67
Colorado, Chief Pablo, 79, *217*, 218, 220, 374, 427n16
Colorado, Mrs., 293–94, 374, 375
Colorado River expeditions, 39, 422n3
color-term research, 314–15, 456n24
Columbia, Nancy "Little Columbia," 254, 449n36
Columbia Historical Society, 38
Columbia University, 9, 308, 310, 311, 455n19, 457n32
Comanche Indians, 56, 104, 118, 142, 432n36
Comes Last (Lakota), 243
Comes Out Holy (Oglala Lakota), 242
commerce: deemphasis of, 98; European concession, 264; in Pike's Orient, 260–61; and special programs, 326; and visitor behavior, 274–76. *See also* sales *under specific groups*
Commerce Building, 300
Commercial Clubs (Chicago and Cincinnati), 380
Commercial Museum, 439n3
Committee of Fifty. *See* anthropology committee
competitive war dances, 132, 335
congresses, academic, 328–35
congresses, Indian, 7, 59, 237, 239–46, 447n6
Congress of Indian Educators, 332–34, 459n13
conservation movement, 397–98
Conterno's Band, 457n1
"contested terrain," 270
conventions, 328–35
Cook, Emily S., 333
Cook, Miss (director of Native American exhibit), 65
cooking and baking: Acoma, 127–29, 138, 142, 434n56, 434n59; Igorot, 179; Indian School students, 144–47
Cora, Angel de (Hinook-Mahiwi-Kilinaka), 301
Cornell University, 314

corn-grinding, 129
Corral, Ramon, 78–79
Cosmos Club (Washington), 398
Crandall, C. J., 128, 434n56
Crane, Dick, 252
craniometry, 306, 317, 457n34
Crawford, Lillie B., 159
Crawford, Miss (teacher), 151
Cronje, General, 257, 449n43
Cross, Whitney, 41, 398–99, 467n13
Crouse, Cornelius M., 111
Crow Creek Indian band, 242
Crow Indians, 56, 104, 242
Cruz, Juan de la, 191, 442n49
Cruz, Mirtina de la, 191, 442n49
Culin, Stewart, 40, 434n55
Cullom, Shelby M., 122, 433n45
cultural anthropology, 399–401
cultural preference and knowledge, 355
Cultural Product Classification matrix, 50–51, 403–4
cultural relativism, 332
Cummings, R. F., 393
Cummins, Frederick, 96, 241–42, 430n51. *See also* Cummins's Wild West Show
Cummins, Frederick T., 239–40
Cummins's Indian Congress, 237, 239–46, 447n6
Cummins's Wild West Show: casts of participants, 318; Cheyennes in, 117; Dakota welcoming ceremony at, 132; description, 239–46; at end of fair, 358; Geronimo at, 113; location, 240, 447n8; Olympic participants from, 345; participants, 104, 242; participants' attendance, 278; and Patagonian Tehuelches, 199; performance schedule, 244–46; publicity, 242–44; Sioux in, 130. *See also* Cummins's Indian Congress
Cupples Hall: attendance, 367–68, 463n17; condition of building, 291; fire exhibit, 212; laboratories, 99, 305–8; and planning of LPE, 32, 421n19; static exhibit content and quality, 295–305
Curley, Ellen, 91, 223
Curley, Jack, 90, 223, 226, 228
Curtis, Charles (Kansas congressman), 332
Curtis, Natalie, 333
Curtis, William, 189, 439n2, 440n13, 463n15
Cushing, Frank Hamilton, 23, 25, 395

Cushman, Edwin C., Jr., 78–81, 216, *217*, 218, 219, 427nn16–18, 445n41, 445n47
Custer's Last Stand diorama, 235
Cut Finger (Lakota), 282

Dahomeans, 256, 262, 465n9
Dakota Indians: activities, 130–34; and Mbutis, 279–82; participants, 104; selection for LPE, 53; special programs, 326; and Wild West Show, 242
Dallin, Cyrus, 297
dances: Ainu, 211; at Boer War concession, 258; at Cliff Dweller exhibit, 246, 249, 251; Cocopa, 219; competitive war, 132, 335; Ghost, 246, 326; Igorot, 172, 173, 179; Kwakiutl, 226–30; Negrito, 189–90; at Pike concessions, 262–64; programs, 326, 334–35; Samal Moro, 187; Snake, 91, 249–50, *250*, 338, 448n27; Visayan, 191. *See also* Hamatsa ritual
Darcia (Apache weaver), 111
"Darky Dialogue" (skit), 437n39
Darwin, Charles, 47, 339, 385, 401, 457n34
Daugherty, Miss (teacher), 147
Davenport Academy of Sciences, 97, 300
Davis, Henry, 117
Davis, Jefferson, 1
Davis, Lulu, 117
Davis, Richard, 115–17, 432n31, 432n35
Dawes Act, 333
Dawson, H. H., 110–11
deaths, 293, 310, 319–20, 456n31. *See also* illness
de Coubertin, Pierre, 345, 356–57, 460n31, 461n45
Delaney, Martin, 350
Delmar Gardens, 241, 277, 325
Delsarte poses, 151, 153
Demasanky, Sultan, 185
demology, 48
Densmore, Frances, 334, 336
Department of Exploitation, 73, 107, 177, 182, 271
Department of Physical Culture, 342–56; experiments by, 345–47; reporting of Anthropology Days results, 351–52
DePoe (Rock-River), 243
de Soto, Hernando, 325
Destiny of the Red Man (Weinman), *296*, *297*, 297–99
d'Harnoncourt, René, 388
Dick, Joseppa and Jeff, 429n47

Digger Indians, 56
"dime museums," 264
"Dixie," 153
Dockery, A. M., 332
dogs: Eskimos', 252–54; and Igorots, 176, 179, 181–84
Dog Soldiers, 116
Dome of the Rock reproduction, 261
domestic science area (Indian School), 138, 147–48, 333
Donk Brothers Coal Company, 260
Dorsey, George, *60*; acquisitions from exhibitors, 359; and American Anthropological Association, 40; and anthropology committee, 22; and anthropometry research, 318, 456nn28–29; on awards, 361; and Bensons, 126, 127; and Canadian expedition, 89, 90; on Cheyennes, 116; collaborations with Native Americans, 428n32; employment, 428n31; at Field Museum, 231–33, 391–93, 466n4; funding requests, 224; and Indian School participants, 61; and Kwakiutl, 223; and management of participants, 287–89; on Mbutis, 206; and Mooney, 453n38; and Native American complaints, 109; and Native American participants, 86–88, 91–94, 107, 452n27; on Pawnee housing, 105–6; planning of LPE, 29; Pratt on, 69; on Pueblo baskets, 251; on return of Canadian natives, 375–76, 464n32; settling-in period, 103; and static exhibits, 299; teaching categories, 459n18
Dosch, Henry, 383
Douglas, Frederic, 388
Dreaming Bear, Mrs. (Oglala Lakota), 242
drills, 150–52, 157, 208–9, 339, 438n50
Duke, S. A., 256
Dyreson, Mark, 339

Eagle-That-Dreams (Osage), 119
ears, 319
earth lodges, *102*, 103, 105–6, 121
"The Earth, the Home of Man" (McGee), 42
Eddleman, Cora V., 70
education: as assimilation strategy, 327, 342; in ethnography field school, 99, 335–38, 363, 369, 459–60nn20–23; and evolution, 339; goal of exposition, 19, 421n18; McGee on, 162, 378. *See also* Indian School; physical education

fire-making competition, 338
Fish, Frank (Peoria), 152
Fitzgerald, C. F., 149
flat bread, 142
Flathead Indians, 56, 242
Fletcher, Alice, 65, 88, 319, 333, 361, 377, 396
Flynn, Annie, 80, 219, 273–74
Foard, Josephine, 434n56
food: Canadian natives', 223–24; at Congress
    of Indian Educators, 334, 459n13; disputes
    over, 286, 289–90, 452n20, 452n22, 452n33;
    at Indian School, 65, 144–47, 425n22; partici-
    pants' requests for, 267
football, 339, 350
Forest Park: accommodation of pavilions,
    32–33; condition, 290; expenses, 367; Indian
    mounds, 21; restoration post-fair, 394; selec-
    tion as site, 17
Forestry, Fish, and Game Palace, 300
Fort Apache Reservation participants, 111
Fort Defiance participants, 121
Fort Mohave Indian school, 59
Fort Rupert, 90
Fort Shaw Blues, 68, 159–60, 326, 339
Fort Shaw (Montana) Indian school, 143, 152–53.
    See also Fort Shaw Blues
Fort Sheridan WY, 86
Fort Sill OK, 107, 112
Fort Thomas KY, 376
Foster, John W., 329
Foster, Volney, 462n5
Fowke, Gerald, 391, 454n3
France, 4, 6, 264, 465n6
Francis, David, 16; on Anthropology and In-
    dian villages, 100, 194; on Anthropology
    Days, 354; on awards, 361; background,
    17; closing of LPE, 366, 367; on education,
    19; on Eskimos, 253; Forest Park Indian
    mounds, 21; and Indian School, 135, 139;
    and Japanese expedition, 83; on manage-
    ment of participants, 286; and Mbutis, 204,
    207, 208, 443n27; McGee's correspondence
    with, 46; on McGee's funding requests,
    56, 73; objectives of LPE, 2–3; on Olympic
    Games, 345; organization of exposition,
    15; and Patagonian Tehuelches, 196, 372;
    Philippine Reservation attendance, 164; and
    physical condition of exhibits, 292; plan-
    ning of LPE, 28–31; on special programs,

458n3; and Verner's requests, 371; on Wild
    West Show, 240, 245–46
Frederick Neil Innes's Band, 457n1
Fred Harvey Company: award, 362, 462n8; Ben-
    sons with, 94; Canadian native exhibit, 89,
    91; and Cliff Dweller exhibit, 252, 449n29;
    and Cocopas, 374–75; and Dorsey, 87, 88,
    392–93, 428n31; and Hopis, 92; Kwakiutl
    supplies, 223; and Navajos, 120, 122; at San
    Diego exposition, 387; static exhibits, 299;
    Warden with, 107
Freeman, Frederick, 425n23
fry bread, 121–22, 129

Galton, Francis, 401
gardening. See farming
Garde Republicaine Band, 324
"Gasimotor," 397
Gates of Jerusalem concession, 237, 260, 261,
    450n50
Gayton, Bessie, 153
geisha girls, 263
Genoa (Nebraska) Indian school, 143
Geological Society of America, 38
George, Emma, 91, 223
German East-African exhibit, 301, 320, 359, 364
Germany, 465n6
Geronimo, 110; accommodations, 112; associates
    of, 111; and blacks, 255; Clum on, 430n55;
    expenses, 430n53; on Ferris wheel, 158–59,
    234–35; in inauguration parade, 461n1; Maria
    Martinez on, 251; at "Pan-Savage Conclave,"
    335; photography of, 272; popularity, 109–15,
    432n25; return home, 358; sales, 97, 113; se-
    lection for LPE, 55, 70, 94, 95–96; and Wild
    West Show, 242
Ghost Dances, 246, 326
giants. See Patagonian Tehuelches
Gibbs, Rev. Henry, 69
Giga (Patagonian Tehuelche), 195, 443n14
Gill, DeLancey, 366
Gill, Mary, 366
Gliddon, George, 49
Goddard, Pliny Earl, 364
Golden Gate International Exposition (1939),
    388
Gonzales, Manuel, 83, 85, 374
Good Bird (Lakota), 132–33
Goode, George Brown, 23–24, 420n11

Holmes, William Henry, *41*; acquisitions from exhibitors, 462n3; Anthropological Society of Washington presentation, 377; and anthropology committee, 23; and anthropometry and psychometry labs, 309–10, 455n15; at Archaeological Institute of America congress, 329; and awards, 363, 366, 466n11; and Bureau of American Ethnology, 42–45; credentials, 24–25; at Field Museum, 44; and Golden Gate exposition, 388; at International Congress of Art and Science, 330; and Kwakiutl supplies, 223; on management of participants, 287–89; and Newcombe, 89; planning of LPE, 26–31; post-fair activities, 392; relationship with McGee, 71, 397, 423n12, 426n37; at Smithsonian, 396; static exhibits, 301–4; and Stevenson, 91–92

Hoosler Zouave corps, 244

"Hootch" (U.S. mail dog), 254

Hopi Indians: award, 362; and Cliff Dweller exhibit, 246–52; and Cushman, 78; pottery, *302*; at San Diego exposition, 387; selection for LPE, 57, 92–93; static exhibits, 299, 301; subject of Starr's field school course, 338; and Wild West Show, 242

Hornaday, William T., 25

Horse Hair (Lakota), 131

horses: and Mbutis, 203, 208; and Patagonian Tehuelches, 199–200, 241, 347, 442n13

Horwitz, Dr., 320

Hough, Walter, 24, 25, 249, 358, 366, 454n3

housing: Ainu, 210–13, 444n34; Canadian native, 88–90, 224, 225; Cocopa, 216–17; Filipino, 167, 439n5; Haida and Tongass Tlingit, *303*, 304–5; Mbuti, 205–6; Native American, 55, 87, 88, 91–92, 105–9, 117–19, *121*, 124, 126, 138; Patagonian Tehuelche, 197; selection of Native peoples based on, 27; styles, 103, 104. *See also* architecture; tipis

Houzé, Professor, 320

Hrdlička, Aleš: acquisitions from exhibitors, 359; award, 366; background, 455n15; Boas's debate with, 332; collection of body parts, 319–20; lab design, 308–11; post-fair activities, 392; at San Diego exposition, 388; tests done by, 314

Hubbell, Lorenzo, 433n44

Huckel, John, 89, 299, 362, 462n8

Hudson, John H., 94, 126, 127

Hudson, J. W., 87

Hulbert, Charles E., 70, 216, 373–75, 420n10, 464nn29–30

human paleontology, 48

human sacrifices, 188

Hunt, Burgess, 106–7

Hunt, Dr., 319

Hunt, George, 90

Hunt, Josephine, 106–7

Hunt, Louisiana Francis, 106–7

Hunt, Truman, 175–76, 181–82, 384

Hupa Indians, 299

Huso dance, 189

Hutchinson, Allen, 456n28

Huxley, Thomas Henry, 47

Hwanyak Indians, 79, 216

Hyde Exploration Company, 425n21

Hyde, Sam P., 269–70, 450n5

Hygienic Food Company, 65

Idaho state exhibit, 304

Ieyasu's tomb, 263

Ifugaos, 441n43

Igorot Exhibit Company, 384

Igorots: assimilation, 165, 188; athletic competition, *341*; at Bagnelle's performance, 152; complaints about, 109; dancing, 172, 173; description, 170; encampment, 167–68, 176, 440n19; at end of fair, 358; free time, *279*; Geronimo on, 115; illness and death, 319, 320, 457n31; at Lewis and Clark Centennial, 383–84; participants, 171, 415, 441n34; perceptions about, 177–81; photography of, 175; physical appearance, 177–79, 441n24; on Pike, 234; popularity, 175–81, 384, 465n8; return home, 376; sales, 180; students, 174; tour of United States, 376; travel to St. Louis, 169; visits with St. Louis residents, 276. *See also* Bontoc Igorots

illness: Filipinos, 170, 319–20, 457n31; at Indian School, 438n51; McGee's, 45, 46, 90, 220, 294, 393, 397, 454n48; Patagonian Tehuelches, 197; types, 293–94, 319–20, 456n31. *See also* deaths

Ilpuk (Cocopa), 374

Imperial College and the Royal College (England), 419n4

"Imperial Synthesis," 11–12, 419n9

Improved Order of the Red Men, 328

Laidley, Leonidas H., 293, 456n31
Lake Mohonk Conference of Friends of the Indian, 162
Lakota Indians: activities, 130–34; departure, 284; participants, 434n61; performances, 326; physical appearance, 130; tipi-raising contests, 140; train accident, 243, 448n14; and visitor behavior, 275; volunteer participants, 104; and Wild West shows, 6, 242, 448n15
Lamarck, Jean-Baptiste, 455n13, 457n34
Lanao Moros, 169, 170, 185–87, 366
Langley, Samuel: and Bureau of American Ethnology investigation, 44–46, 423n18; description of, 422n9; and McGee, 41–45, 71, 396; scope of Bureau of American Ethnology work, 422n10
Last Great Congresses of the Red Man, 7, 59
Latuna (Bakuba), 76, 77, *201*, 207, 208, 274, 443n27
laundry (Indian School), 147, 436n25
Laurie, Clayton, 180
Lawrence, Bishop, 292
Leach Lake Reservation, 124
Leading Hawk family (Oglala Lakota), 242
Leaping Panther (Comanche), 243
Lee, Guy Carleton, 462n5
Lehmann, Frederick W., 22; and academic congresses, 329; on awards, 361; background, 420n9; chair of anthropology committee, 22; McGee's correspondence with, 46; on McGee's funding requests, 56; planning of LPE, 28–29, 31, 33
Lehouw (Zulu), 345
Lena (Apache weaver), 111
Lena (Lina) (daughter of Geronimo), 112, 304
Leopold III, King of Belgium, 75, 203
Leupp, Francis, 396
Lewis, Arthur W., 257–58
Lewis, Frederick, 441n42
Lewis and Clark Centennial (1905), 382–85; cost, 465n5, 465n7; exhibitors, 465n6; Holmes's exhibits at, 392
Liberal Arts Building, *20*
Lima, J. C. Alves de, 361
Limo (Pygmy), *201*
Lincoln, Abraham, 1, 251
"Little Anise" (Samal Moro), 187
"Little Egypt" (dancer), 5–6, 262, 446n1
Little White Day School, 133

living exhibits: awards, 360, 362, 363; coping with visitors, 266; cost, 11, 54–57; features at World's Fairs, 6; first use in United States, 25–26; popularity, 21, 99, 368; purpose, 9–14, 52, 99, 423n1. *See also* Native peoples
Lomawaima, Tsianina, 135
London, 3, 4, 419n4, 450n45
Lone Star (Sioux), 276
Long Grand (Lakota), 282
long houses, 89, 90, 429n39
Lookout, Fred, 119
Lorenza (Patagonian Tehuelche), 195, 197, 198, 442n5
"The Lost Chord," 153, 437n41
Louisiana, A Spectacular Extravaganza in a Prologue and Two Scenes (Hayes), 325, 457n2
Louisiana Purchase, 1, 59
Louisiana Purchase Exposition (LPE): attendance, 367, 463n16; awards, 360–66; classification of exhibits, 23–26, 32; closing, 366–69; concessions, 64–65; and development of anthropology field, 399–402; on Last Great Congress of the Red Man, 7; McGee's goals for, 12, 39, 46–47, 368–69; objectives, 1–2, 9–11, 13, 19–20, 328, 379–81, 385; organization, 13, 420n12; participants' experiences, 12, 419nn10–11; performances and special days, 324–28; public experience, 401–2; publicists on Filipinos, 165; reuse of exhibits in Portland, 382; significance, 14–17; site, 17–19, *18*
Louisiana Purchase Exposition Board of Lady Managers, 178, 361, 462n6
Louisiana Purchase Exposition Company (LPEC): and anthropometry and psychometry labs, 309; on athletic competition, 342, 347; awards, 127–28, 360–66, 463n14; Canadian native exhibit, 89; and Cliff Dweller exhibit, 247; dismantling of exhibits, 369; ethnology corps agents, 73–74, 362, 369–71; expenses, 11, 29, 54–57, 62, 73, 367–69, 463n23; incorporation, 15; and International Congress of Art and Science, 330, 458n7; McGee's contract with, 393; McGee's final report to, 377–78; museum, 359, 462n4; number of concessions, 446n3; objectives, 1–2, 369; on Olympic Games, 345; organization of Anthropology Department, 13, 45; and participants' health and well-being, 284–85, 291, 293; on participants' outings, 278; and

McCowan, Samuel (*cont.*)
332, 334; construction and budget of Indian School, 62–72, 97; dismantling of exhibits, 366; exhibit company, 384; on food service at Indian School, 146; on food supplies, 289–90, 452n20; on Fort Shaw Blues, 160; and Geronimo, 95–96, 432n25; illness, 372; and Indian School Band, 437n43; *Indian School Journal*, 435n11; on Indian Service, 122, 136–37, 142; on Irish concession, 265; on kindergarten, 150–51, 436n30; landscaping at Indian School, 139; on laundry at Indian School, 147; and Lewis and Clark Centennial, 383; on maintenance of Indian School building, 291; and management of participants, 283–89, 291, 293, 451n15, 452n27; and Mbutis, 205–7, 282, 452n24; and McGee, 396; Native American participants, 86, 91–96, 104, 140, 424n15, 429n35, 430n51, 434n59; and Navajos, 121, 433n44; opening day at Indian School, 139–40; organization of Indian School, 55, 57–61; on Osages, 119, 281; on Patagonian Tehuelches, 200; and performances and programs at Indian School, 151–57; on Pike concessions, 447n5; and Pimas, 125, 433n50; planning of LPE, 33; purpose of Indian School, 135–37, 142–43, 161–63; on sales at Indian School, 275; and school uniforms, 425n23; on student earnings at Indian School, 148, 149; on student free time, 158–59; on visitor behavior, 271–72, 276; on Wichitas, 431n10; on Wild West Show, 240, 245; working methods, 435n5; and Yellow Hair, 434n68

McFatridge, A. E., 434n61

McGarth, Hugh, 346

McGee, Anita (Newcomb): career, 37, 422n5; and Langley, 41; marriage, 37; separation from McGee, 46, 423n19

McGee, Emma, 454n48

McGee, Eric, 37

McGee, James, 35

McGee, Klotho, 37

McGee, Martha (Anderson), 35

McGee, WJ (William John), *36*; on adventure, 57, 424n9; and Ainu taxonomy, 82, 428n20; anthropological theory, 11–14, 47–51, 99, 102, 136, 162–63, 233, 331–32, 368–69, 379–80; and anthropology committee, 23; archaeologi-

cal paradigm, 55, 424n5; assessment of LPE, 368–69, 377; on authenticity, 100, 122–24, 171, 174–75, 199, 205–8, 280–81, 358; background, 35; budget, 54–57, 61–62, 71–72, 224–25, 369–71, 424n15, 463nn19–20; and Cocopas, 39, *217*, 220, 393, 397; death, 398; as geologist, 35–38, 421n2, 422n3, 422n6; as government anthropologist, 38–39; and Holmes, 24; illness, 45, 46, 90, 220, 294, 393, 397, 454n48; on laws, 50, 423n23; and Lewis and Clark Centennial, 383; and Native American participants, 69–71; and Native peoples, 385; "natural history" implements exhibit, 25; on participants' well-being, 277–79; planning of LPE, 26–34, 52–57; post-fair activities, 393–99; relationship with LPEC, 73; and requests for employment, 426n33, 426n35; resignation from Bureau of American Ethology, 45–46; salary, 370, 424n7, 463n19, 466n5; on visitor behavior, 268–69, 271–74, 276

McGuire (Oklahoma congressman), 161

McGuire, Joseph D., 40

McKinley, William, 164, 265, 381

"Meet Me in St. Louis, Louis," 2

Melanesia, 393

Memorial Hall (Philadelphia), 4

memory tests, 315–16, 456n25

Mescalero Apache Indians, 242

Mexico, 23, 44, 73, 78–79, 364, 366

Michelet, Simon, 433n49

Midway Plaisance (Chicago World's Fair), 5–6, 234, 265

Miles, General, 111

Miller, E. K., 149

Miller, Grace (Shawnee), 152, 334, 437n39

Miller, Iva, 152

Mills, William C., 300, 330, 362, 391, 395

Milwaukee Public Museum, 465n14

Mindanao tribes. *See* Moros

Mines and Metallurgy Building, *20*

Minesinger, Joan (Snake), 159

Minnesota, 44

"missing links," *54*, 189, 256, 449n38

Mission Indians, 56, 69

Missouri Historical Society, 62, 394

Missouri state exhibit, 300, 304, 358

Mitchell, Clara and Tom, 429n47

Mitchell, Sarah (Sioux), 159

Mitscher, O. A., 68

Mix, Tom, 241
Mohawk Indians, 242, 350
Mojave Indians, 242
Moki. *See* Hopi Indians
The Moki Snake Dance (Hough), 249
Moncheur, Baron, 371
Mon-e-do-wats ("Mrs. Spirit Seeker") (Anishi-nabe), *123*, 124
Monte (game), 187
Montezuma, Carlos, 243
Mooney, James: and awards, 363, 366, 462n5; at Bureau of American Ethnology, 44; at Lewis and Clark Centennial, 383; and management of participants, 287–89, 453n36; and McGee, 453n38; post-fair activities, 391–92; and Warden, 107
Moore, Frank, 106, *340*
Moore, Nirsa, 445n47
Moore, Tom, 80, *217*, 220, 273–74
Moorish Palace concession, 260
Moorish Village, 260–66, *261*
Morgan, Lewis Henry, 8, 47, 50, 88–89
Morley, Sylvanus Griswold, 387
Moroccan concession, 262
Moro Industrial School, 439n5
Moro-Moro (dance), 187
Moros: assimilation, 165, 188; and athletic competition, 349; awards, 365–66; deaths, 320, 457n31; description, 170–71; encampments, 168, 185–88; ethnology, 169; hostilities among, 169–70; participants, 171, 415–16; in Philippine Constabulary, 441n35; photography of, 175, 185; sales, 185; students, 174; U.S. relationship with, 185–87; visits with St. Louis residents, 276. *See also* Bagobo Moros; Lanao Moros; Samal Moros
Morris, Sam, 68
Morton, George, 306
Moses, L. G., 242, 245, 395
Mulhall, Zack, 240–41
Münsterberg, Hugo, 329, 458n6
Murie, Caroline, 153, 428n32
Murie, James (Young Eagle [Ri-tahkachiari']), 87–88, 105, 152, 333, 428n32
Murie, Mary (Esau), 428n32
Museum of Man, 4
Museum of Modern Art (New York), 388–89
music: black American, 256; Filipino, 336; Igorot, 179; Mbuti, 205, 208; Native American,

151–57, 334; Negrito, 189–90; popularity, 324, 457n1; Samal Moro, 187; Visayan, 191. *See also* Indian School Band; musicians; singing
musicians: at Indian School, 140; salaries, 155, 437n44; securing Native American participants, 66–67, 425n25. *See also* Indian School Band; music; singing
Muskwaki Indians. *See* Sac and Fox Indians
Muslims. *See* Moros
mustache sticks, 212, 444n36
Mysterious Asia concession, 237, 260, 263
My Sweet Dakota Maid (ballet), 325

Nah-ee-Gance (Anishinabe), 124, 125
Nanona, 244
Nashville exposition (1897), 25, 82
Natchez (Naiche) (Apache), 112
National Academy of Sciences, 392, 466n11
National Association of Amateur Athletics in America, 342
National Conservation Commission, 398
National Education Association, 332
National Gallery of Art, 392
National Geographic Magazine, 38, 393
National Geographic Society, 38, 329
National Museum of Natural History, 392
Native Americans: assimilation, 116, 281, 432n32, 438n59; athletic ability, 339–41, 347–49, 351; and Bureau of American Ethnology, 422n10; at California expositions, 386–89; at Chicago World's Fair, 446n2; congresses, 7, 59, 237, 239–46, 288, 424n12, 447n10; education, 332–34; expenses, 370; free time, 277, 278, 280; health and well-being, 290–94; lack of compensation, 68–69, 426n30; at Lewis and Clark Centennial, 383; as living exhibits, 7, 25, 267; management of, 283–94; and Mbutis, 205; misbehavior, 452n27; in Olympic Games, 345; participants, 65–69, 73, 86–88, 91–93, 100, 103–5, 368, 405–9, 411–14, 424n15, 431n4; photography of, 269–70, 318, 450n5; on Pike, 158–59, 234–35; research on, 310, 312–13, 318–19; return home, 358, 372; sales, 122, 142, 144–49, 300–301, 436n14; selection for LPE, 26, 53, 54–57; special programs, 325–27, 334–35, 457n2; static exhibits, 295–99, 301–4, 455n9; St. Louis Public Museum exhibit on, 394; ward category, 285, 452n31; Wild West shows, 6. *See also* Indian School; Indian Village; *specific tribes*

Native peoples: athletic ability, 347–57; attraction of, 99, 194, 447n6; awards, 362–66; categorization, 439n7; celebrities and artists, 93–96; congresses, 334–35; contracts, 282–83; cross-cultural encounters, 277, 279–81, 451n14; at end of fair, 358; expeditions to secure participants, 73–74; experiences at LPE, 12–13, 419nn10–11; as features at World's Fairs, 3, 6–7; free time, 276–82; health and well-being, 290–94; illness and death, 319–20; invasion of privacy, 268–74; management of, 283–89; McGee's attitude toward, 385; McGee's presentation of, 52–53; participants, 100, 103–4, 368; performances, 325–28; planning of LPE, 26–27, 32–33; public perceptions of, 35; research on, 309, 312; return home, 369–76; subject of Starr's field school course, 338; trade and gifting among, 280. *See also* Native Americans; *specific groups*

Navajo Indians: and Cushman, 78; free time, *279*; housing, 103, *121*, 121; participants, 104, 433n44; sales, 301; at San Diego exposition, 387; selection for LPE, 56; static exhibit, 301; weaving skills, 120–24, 433n47

Ndombe, King, 75, 76, 204, 371

Nebraska Bill, 244

Negritos, *54*; assimilation, 165; description, 170, 171; encampment, 167–68, 188–90; at end of fair, 358; participants, 171, 416; performances, 465n9; photography of, 175; physical appearance, 178; research on, 310; rumored extinction, 189, 442n47; students, 174; subject of Starr's field school course, 338, 460n22; visits with St. Louis residents, 276

Nelson, N. S., 154, 280

neo-Lamarckians, 455n13

Newark Call, 122

Newcomb, Anita. *See* McGee, Anita (Newcomb)

Newcomb, Mary (Hassler), 37

Newcomb, Simon, 37, 329–31, 458n6

Newcombe, Charles: as agent for Canadian expedition, 89–91; and anthropometry research, 318, 456n29; compensation, 224–25, 429n37, 445n56, 446n65, 463n21; at Field Museum, 87, 231–33, 446n63; funding requests, 224; and Hamatsa ritual, 229, 230; return of Canadian natives, 375–76; on Simms, 372

Newcombe (son of Charles), 223, 225, 463n21

Newell, Alfred, 177

New Mexico Building, 89, 112

New Mexico Day, 324–25

New Mexico state exhibits, 304, 383, 387

New Orleans LA, 25, 82, 371–72

New York Art Exposition Company, 359

New York Times, 57, 115

New Zealand National Museum exhibit, 301

Nez Perce Indians, 56, 104

Nichols, 138

nickel hunts, 133

Nootkas: classification, 216; compensation, 225; diet, 223–24; encampment, 103; expenses, 91, 224–25, 232, 370, 429n40, 463n21, 464n32; free time, 279; and Hamatsa ritual, 228; housing, 103, 224; participants, 73, 88–91, 104, 223, 410; performances, 226, 327, 334, 458n3; privacy, 225; return home, 375–76; sales, 231

Norton, Charles Eliot, 292

Nott, Josiah, 49

Nova Scotia, 44

Nowell, Charles: activities, 223, 225–30; compensation, 429n37; expedition, 89–91; free time, 230–31; headdress, 446n59; at museums, 231–32, 446n63

Nusbaum, Jesse, 387

Nuttall, Zelia, 361

O'Brien, W. H. O., 285–86

observation wheel. *See* Ferris wheel

O'Fallon High School, 159–60

Official Daily Program, 105, 144, 148, 211

Oglala Indian band, 242

Ohio Historical Society, 362

Ohio state exhibit, 300

Ohlo-ho-wallah (Osage), 119, 120

Ojibwa Indians, 104, 124–25, 242

Oklahoma, 73, 87–88. *See also* Fort Sill OK

Oklahoma Cavalry Band, 241

Oklahoma Territorial Building, 70

Old Plantation concession, 255–56, 383

Old Vienna concession, 446n1

Olympic Games (Third), 343–47; de Coubertin on, 356; events, 343–44, 460n29; organization, 345, 460n31; participants, 344, 460n30; and testing of athletes, 353

Olympic Memoirs (de Coubertin), 356

Philippine Constabulary (*cont.*)
  ticipants, 168, 172–73, 440n11, 440nn13–14;
  research on, 313; school, 173
Philippine Day, 173, 324
Philippine Ethnology Division, 168–70
Philippine Islands: Dorsey's interest in, 393; U.S.
  foreign policy, 2, 21, 164–67, 192
Philippine Photograph Company, 456n29
Philippine Reservation: activities, 172–75; attendance, 164, 192; award, 365–66; boycotts,
  178; design, 166–68; dignitaries at, 175; and
  Eighth International Geographic Congress,
  332; expenses, 71, 165, 439n3, 442n52; free
  time at, 279; at Lewis and Clark Centennial,
  383–84; Native American complaints about,
  109; participants, 368, 415–16; photography
  at, 272–73; planning, 32; purpose, 163,
  165–66, 168, 239, 439n2; sales, 275. *See also*
  Filipinos
Philippine Scouts: control of hostilities, 180;
  freedom at LPE, 180; health, 293; participants,
  168, 172–73, 440n11, 440nn13–14; and photography of participants, 175; research on,
  313; return home, 376; school, 173; travel to
  St. Louis, 169
Philips, Paul C., 343
Phillip Iron Tail (Lakota), 243
Phinney's Band, 457n1
Phoenix Indian School, 59
photography: anthropometric, 318, 456n29;
  award for Mexican, 363; of participants,
  149, 175, 185, 196–98, 219, 269–73, 436n29,
  446n63, 450–51nn5–6, 451n8
phrenology, 308
physical anthropology, 392, 399
physical education: effects of, 342, 460n27;
  Indian School, 151–52; performances, 327;
  research in, 345. *See also* athletes; sports
physical types, 99
Pierce, Frank, 345
Pike (the): concerts, 132–33; concessions at Lewis
  and Clark Centennial, 383; distinction from
  Anthropology Villages, 233, 239, 252; entertainment, 21; Eskimos on, 93; Geronimo on,
  113, 115, 234–35; Igorots on, 234; international
  features, 234, 236–39; McGee's attitude
  toward, 98, 236–39, 261–65, 430n58, 447n4,
  447n5; Native American retailers on, 274;
  Native American visitors on, 158–59, 234–35;

Orient concessions, 260–64; participant
  statistics, 368; planning, 32; public attitudes
  toward, 235–39; Samal Moros on, 187; site,
  19; spielers, 234, 237; types of concessions,
  234–35
Pike Day, 238–39, 324
The Piker, 242
piki bread, 129, 434n59
Pilapil, Virgilio, 182
Pima Bajo Indians, 39
Pima Indians: activities, 125–28; basket makers,
  141; encampment, 103; free time, 279; hous-
  ing, 126; kindergarten students, 150, 339;
  participants, 104; physical appearance, 125,
  126; selection for LPE, 56, 93
Pima Training School, 125
Pinchot, Gifford, 397, 398
Pine Ridge Reservation, 130, 447n13
Pipeclay Indian band, 242
Piratori, Japan, 374
Pisente, Christine, 111
Pittsburgh Press, 43
Pius XIII, Pope, 300
plays, 325
Plaza Saint Louis, 326, 328, 334
pneumonia, 319–20
Poage, George, 345
Poincaré, Henri, 329
Pomo Indians, 104, 125–28, 299, 363
Ponca Indians, 242
Pony Express, 244
Porcupine Indian band, 242
Porter, Pleasant (Osage), 332, 433n43
Portland exposition. *See* Lewis and Clark Cen-
  tennial (1905)
Pottawatomie Indians, 242
pottery, 128, 142, 251, *302*, 387
Powell, John Wesley: anthropological theory, 47,
  50; and Bureau of American Ethnology inde-
  pendence, 422n10; career, 422n3; Colorado
  River expeditions, 39; death, 40; on develop-
  ment of American West, 397; evolutionary
  theory, 39, 455n13; and McGee, 36–37, 45;
  professionalization of anthropology, 8
powwows, 132, 335
Prado (Apache), 112
Pratt, Richard Henry, 69
Presbyterian Mission Training School of Sitka,
  455n9

Uniform Course of Study (UCS), 135, 333

United States Congress: and Bureau of American Ethnology, 42, 422n10; financing of World's Fairs, 4, 6, 15, 56, 59, 420n2; and San Francisco exposition, 386; on Smithsonian Institution, 396

United States government, 50–51

universities, 399, 401

University of California, 9

University of California–Berkeley, 465n14

University of Chicago, 337, 391, 466n4

University of Minnesota, 391

"University of the Future" theme: adoption, 19; fulfillment of, 369; McGee's support of, 46–47; and performances, 328. *See also* classes

University of Wisconsin students, 337

U.S. Army, 37, 173, 376, 422n5. *See also* Rough Riders of the World

U.S. Army Nursing Corps, 37, 422n5

U.S. Department of the Interior: funding of Indian School, 55, 61, 63, 64; funding of McGee's plan, 57, 71; static exhibit, 301

U.S. Department of War, 166, 167

U.S. foreign policies, 2, 21, 164–67, 192

U.S. Geological Survey, 37, 38, 422n3

U.S. Marine Band, 457n1

U.S. National Museum: acquisitions from exhibitors, 359; and anthropometry and psychometry labs, 308–10; archaeology at, 396; awards, 366; and Bureau of American Ethnology, 42, 43; Hrdlička at, 455n15; organization of exhibits, 24; origin, 4; at Philadelphia World's Fair (1876), 23; static exhibits, 301–4

Valenzuela, Katherine (Pima-Tohono O'odham), 66, 153, 333

"The Value of Trade to a Reservation Indian" speech (Murie), 152

Van Buel, Mary, 437n40

Van Buren, Martin, 251

Vancouver, Canada, 85

"Vanishing Savage," 10–11

Vassar Preparatory School, 160

Vatican static display, 300, 454n4

Verner, Rev. Samuel Phillips: African collection, 359; award, 363; credentials, 427n3; expedition, 74–77, 206; identification of Pygmies, 202–3; on Mbuti housing, 206; and Ota Benga, 204, 443n31; and return of Pygmies,

207, 371–72, 463n23; sale of items, 77, 427n9

Victoria and Albert Museum, 419n4

Victorian Jubilee Tributes, 300, 305, 367

Vierra, Carlos, 388

Visayans: assimilation, 165; description, 170–71; encampment, 168, *190*, 190–92; and Igorots, 180; midgets, 171, 191, 442n49; participants, 171, 416; photography of, 175; physical appearance, 191; research on, 313; students, 174; tour of United States, 376; visits with St. Louis residents, 276

visitors: in anthropometry and psychometry labs, 305–8, 310, 312, 314, 321; behavior toward living exhibits, 268–74; earning money from, 274–76; experiences at LPE, 401–2; medical attention, 293, 454n46

Vlacks, 57

Voris, George, 252

Voth, Henry, 87, 92, 299, 362

Wailing Wall reproduction, 261

Walbridge, Doctor, 197

Walcott, Charles D., 396

Walker, Jim (Comanche), 243

Walker, John, 255, 257–58, 264, 450n50

Walters, Jane, 125

Wanamaker, John, 462n2

Ward, Lester F., 37, 42, 47

Warden, Cleveland, 105, 107, 428n32

Ward's Scientific Establishment, 318

Warner, Glen S. "Pop," 339

Washington, Booker T., 256

Washington, George, 1

Washington Academy of Sciences, 38

Washington Post, 368, 463n23

Washington Times, 43

Washington University, 32, 102, 369, 421n19

Washo Indians, 56

water carnivals and processions, 187, 327

water craft, 197

water management, 398

water system, 291, 453n43

weavers: Ainu, 212; Igorot, 179; Navajo, 120–24, 433n47; Visayan, 192

Weber, Max, 329

Weber's Band, 457n1

Webster, Daniel, 1

weddings, 192, 262

weight throwing, 351

In the Critical Studies in the History of Anthropology series

www.ingramcontent.com/pod-product-compliance
Ingram Content Group UK Ltd.
Pitfield, Milton Keynes, MK11 3LW, UK
UKHW041906060225
454777UK00001B/85